# The Mammoth Book of
# HOW IT HAPPENED
# WORLD WAR II

# The Mammoth Book of
# HOW IT HAPPENED
# WORLD WAR II

### Edited by
## JON E. LEWIS

ROBINSON
London

Constable & Robinson Ltd
3 The Lanchesters
162 Fulham Palace Road
London W6 9ER
www.constablerobinson.com

First published in the UK by Robinson,
an imprint of Constable & Robinson Ltd 2002

A copy of the British Library Cataloguing in
Publication Data is available from the British Library.

ISBN 1–84119–303–8

Printed and bound in the EU

1 2 3 4 5 6 7 8 9 10

*We may be destroyed, but if we are, we shall drag a world with us – a world in flames.*

Adolf Hitler, 23 November 1939

For those in my family who fought the good fight:
E.J. Lewis, R.J.J. Stempel, G. Charles, F. Williams, H. Knowles,
J. Stempel, M.P. Clary, S. Parry, H.A.G. Stempel.

# CONTENTS

## Part II   The Battle of the Atlantic: 1939–43   105

## Part III   The War in the Desert: North Africa, 1940–43   149

## Part IV  Barbarossa: The German Invasion of Russia, June 1941–February 1943     209

# PART V  Banzai: The War in the Pacific, December 1941–June 1942                                           257

# Part VI Resistance & Reconquest – The War in Western and Southern Europe, November 1940–May 1945 307

## Part VII   The Road to Berlin: The Eastern Front, February 1943–May 1945                    463

# Part VIII   Setting Sun:
# The War in the Pacific, July 1942–September 1945    493

# INTRODUCTION

World War II was the most destructive conflict in history. More than 50 million people were killed. The conflagration touched six continents and all the globe's oceans. It was the *Second* World War only in chronology; in everything else, the war of 1939–45 outdid that of 1914–18.

The pages following bear witness to that war. They are not a shot-by-shot history of the 1939–45 conflict, but the communication of what it felt like to live and fight in that time – be it as a Spitfire pilot in the Battle of Britain, a GI in a foxhole on Okinawa, a *Frontsoldaten* in the inferno of Stalingrad, a woman worker at an aircraft plant, a tank gunner at Sidi Rezegh, or a US Marine in boot camp. Some of the witnesses are leaders of men (and women), but in general I have selected the ground-eye view of events.

I have also consciously chosen words of testimony; that is, accounts of the holocaust against the Jews. The holocaust is the cruellest proof of the barbarity of Nazism. It reminds us that World War II was not a mere military happenstance, but a struggle for the soul of civilization. In the words of Herbert Mitang, for the Allies at least, World War II was "the good war". An Axis victory would have turned the world's clock to a moral Middle Ages.

This is not to say that the Allies were saints (think of the RAF's fire-bombing of Dresden; racial segregation in the US's armed forces), nor all the Axis forces sinners. It is just their masters were. What follows is the war of 1939–45 in all its brutality, glory, cock up, inspiration and destruction.

Originally I had intended to include eyewitness accounts of the rise of Adolf Hitler and the slide of the world into war, but even a book this size struggles to contain the main events, campaigns and theatres of war itself. (Some omissions are inevitable, but I hope few.) A little context is therefore in order.

Musing on the 1919 Treaty of Versailles which concluded World War I, Marshal Foch of France remarked, "It is not peace, it is an armistice for twenty years." The Marshal was right to the year. The terms of Versailles were punitive, demeaning, and left Germany shorn of considerable amounts of territory, money, the right to bear arms and, in the war-guilt clause, national honour. The new Germany was rackety and ashamed, thus wide open to a demagogue who promised economic stability, the restoration of German pride and geo-political position. A more enlightened Treaty might have left Adolf Hitler as a small-time beerhall orator in Munich.

In the event, Hitler assumed power in January 1933, and wasted little time in installing dictatorship and racial "purification" at home, and land-grabs abroad. This should not have surprised anyone, for he was as bad as his word, as given in his 1925 manifesto, *Mein Kampf*. Unfortunately, Hitler's territorial acquisitions – the demilitarized Rhineland, Austria, Czechoslovakia – tended to be encouraged by the democratic powers of Europe under the naive policy of "appease-ment". The reasons for appeasement were various: some in Europe saw Hitler as a useful bulwark against Stalin's Russia, some hoped that by sacrificing Czechoslovakia, Hitler's territorial appetite would be sated.

After so many green lights, it was with some surprise that, in September 1939, Hitler found France and Britain determined to defend the territorial integrity of Poland. Because, as even the most gullible Anglo-French politician was finally forced to concede, there was no limit to Hitler's demands. He had to be stopped sometime. Poland wasn't the issue; it was the pretext.

The Nazi invasion of Poland allowed the German Army to hone its theory and practice of "blitzkrieg" (lightning war) and the connected use of air and armour in decentralized offensives, to a high degree. Indeed, the *Wehrmacht* of early World War II was arguably the most accomplished professional army of all time, not least in the calibre and training of its officers and NCOs. Moreover, behind the *Wehrmarcht*, the armed SS, the *Kriegsmarine* and *Luftwaffe* (which in combined strength numbered 2.75 million at the outset of war, rising to 6 million at peak) stood an economy geared to military endeavour: in 1939 Germany poured an extraordinary 20 per cent of its gross national product into armaments. Small wonder, perhaps, that when the *Wehrmacht* turned west and north in May 1940 it bested France, Belgium, Holland, Norway and Denmark, plus the British expeditionary forces sent to aid them, in such dramatic fashion. The *Wehrmacht* of 1940 accomplished the invasion of France in six weeks; the army of the Kaiser hadn't managed it in four years. By the end of June 1940 Britain was the only force in the world still standing against Hitler and Mussolini. A prospective invasion of the UK was rebuffed in the air "Battle of Britain", but that country was powerless to lift the Nazi occupation of mainland western Europe and was hard pressed in the theatres where they did conflict with the Axis, North Africa and Greece. Conversely, the *Kriegsmarine* was unable to break the power of the Royal Navy in the sea lanes around Europe.

If the war had continued with these combatants only, it might have lasted indefinitely. As it was, 1941 brought more nations to the fray. On 22 June Hitler launched Operation Barbarossa, the invasion of the Soviet Union. The attack was largely compelled by ideology – Hitler wanted *lebensraum* (living space) for Germans in the east – although the Russian oil reserves in the Caucasus tantalized. Despite the *Wehrmacht*'s great victories, reaching to the very suburbs of Moscow in late 1941, the Russian campaign never boded well. Hitler expected the Soviet Union to collapse like a rotten shack ("You have only to kick the door in", he informed one field marshal), whereas even the considerable military ineptitude of Stalin was unable to undo the Soviet Union's natural strengths: almost unimaginable manpower and limitless space. The Red Army lost some 1.75 million men in the first two months of fighting, but kept finding more reserves. *Wehrmacht* General Halder lamented in the War Staff diary in August 1941: "We reckoned with about 200 enemy divisions. Now we have already counted 360." Even the Red Army's retreats caused the *Ostheer*, as the *Wehrmacht* in the East was termed, severe problems, since they over-extended its lines of communication and supply. Moreover, Nazi brutality rebounded spectacularly in Russia. Hitler urged his generals to promulgate the war in Russia "with unprecedented, unmerciful and unrelenting harshness". In practice, this meant that Russian prisoners of war were routinely massacred. The effect on the Red Army was to make it fight harder. For what had it to lose?

Then, of course, there was the Russian winter. Like Napoleon, another adventurer in Russia, Hitler was unable to comprehend the Russian winter, with temperatures touching minus 40 degrees. The *Ostheer* was unequipped for winter fighting and troops resorted to stuffing newspaper in their uniforms. By early December 1941 the German Army had ground to a halt. Then the Russians counter-attacked. In summer 1942, the Germans would again go on the offensive but any real chance of delivering a KO blow to Russia had long since disappeared.

This was not only due to the Soviet Union's tenacity, demography and geography. Its factories were beginning to outproduce Germany in war *materiel*. Moreover, Russia was also being supplied with armaments by Britain and, from December 1941, the new Allies' new partner, the United States.

The United States entered World War II on 7 December, when its naval base at Pearl Harbor, Hawaii, was attacked by Japanese fighter-bombers. The attack wasn't quite out of the blue, for the USA and Japan had often rattled sabres following Japan's invasion of Manchuria in 1931 and China in 1937. Determined to stop further Japanese expansion in the Pacific – which it saw as its sphere of interest – America imposed a trade embargo on Japan in July 1941. This embargo cut off nine-tenths of Japan's oil supply. Although the Japanese Prime Minister Tojo would later be hanged by the victorious Allies as a war criminal, there was nothing fascistic about the Japanese war party. Certainly, like their Axis partners, they were anti-Communist, but they were not genocidal racists. The Japanese, at base, went to war because honour and the economy seemed to demand it.

Japan's attack on Pearl Harbor was not its only assault of 7 December. There were attacks too on Wake, Midway and Guam islands, Hong Kong, Malaya and the Philippines. Within three months the Japanese had conquered all these places (with the exception of Midway), plus the Dutch East Indies and were well on their way to subduing Burma. Yet Japan's victories were flashy rather than substantial. Four US aircraft carriers escaped the "day of infamy" at Pearl Harbor. Japanese garrisoning of the new possessions was woefully thin.

In truth there was little or no prospect of Japan winning a war against the US, let alone the US and the British Empire. Wars, at base, are won by those with the big pockets. The US was the richest and most dynamic power in the world; ergo, it was likely to win any conflict in which it participated. In 1943, for example, the US produced 37.5 billion dollars worth of armaments. Japan produced 4.5 billion.

Japan was not the only country to feel the powerful effects of the US war economy, for in a fit of rash madness Hitler declared war on the US on 11 December 1941. By this act, what were essentially two wars – Hitler's in Europe, Tojo's in the Far East – became joined as one. With the Axis on the losing side. The intervention of the US in the conflict meant, in Churchill's words, that the rest of the war was "merely the proper application of overwhelming force". Unfortunately, the Axis powers, with the exception of Italy (which changed sides in 1943) either did not realize this or did not care. Indeed, all the war's most ferocious battles came after December 1941: Stalingrad,

Kursk, D-Day, Okinawa, Iwo Jima, Cassino. Despite being massively outnumbered, fighting on three fronts, the *Wehrmacht* of 1944 was still inflicting a superior casualty rate on its enemies; on the eastern Front it was killing five Russian soldiers for every one of its own lost. Japanese resistance was fanatical, buoyed by the belief that capitulation and defeat were slanders on a man's character.

But Churchill was right. After December 1941 the end of the war was never seriously in doubt. American productive capabilities were simply overwhelming. In 1943 alone, the US produced 85,898 aircraft; Germany and Japan produced 42,300. And, of course, to the US side of the balance sheet was to be added the 65,863 produced by the the USSR and Britain.

The only possible salvation for the Axis side would have been the deployment of atomic weapons. That Germany in particular failed to develop atomic weaponry, given its general technological wizardry in World War II (Me 262 jets, V-1 and V-2 rockets, for instance), is notable. And even ironic. For prominent among the brains behind the Manhattan project, the US's atomic programme, were German Jewish scientists who had fled Hitler's racial purging.

It hardly needs to be added that the Nazis' failure to build the A-bomb was freedom's salvation.

# CHRONOLOGY

| 1939 | EUROPE & RUSSIA | ATLANTIC | AFRICA | FAR EAST, PACIFIC & USA |
|------|------|------|------|------|
| 15 Mar | Germans enter Czech capital | | | |
| 7 Apr | Germany, Italy, Japan & Spain sign anti-Comintern pact; Italy invades Albania | | | see Europe |
| 23 Aug | Germany signs secret pact with USSR, containing agreement for division of Poland | | | |
| 25 Aug | Anglo-Polish mutual assistance treaty | | | |
| 1 Sept | Germans invade Poland | | | |
| 3 Sept | Britain, France, Australia and NZ declare war on Germany | | | |
| 17 Sept | USSR occupies Eastern Poland | | | |

| 1939 | EUROPE & RUSSIA | ATLANTIC | AFRICA | FAR EAST, PACIFIC & USA |
|---|---|---|---|---|
| 12 Oct | Stalin presents territorial ultimatum to Finns | | | |
| 13 Oct | | U-47 sinks *Royal Oak*, Scapa Flow | | |
| 27 Oct | | | | US Senate passes Neutrality Bill |
| 30 Nov | Russia invade Finland | | | |
| 13 Dec | | Battle of River Plate in S. Atlantic results in scuttling of *Admiral Graf Spee* on 17 Dec | | |

| 1940 | EUROPE & RUSSIA | ATLANTIC | AFRICA | FAR EAST, PACIFIC & USA |
|---|---|---|---|---|
| 12 Mar | Russo-Finnish treaty ends "Winter War" | | | |
| 9 Apr | Germany invades Norway and Denmark | | | |
| 10 Apr | First battle of Narvik | | | |
| 27 Apr | Himmler orders construction of Auschwitz concentration camp | | | |
| 10 May | Germany attacks Belgium, Holland, Luxembourg. Winston S. Churchill becomes British PM | | | |
| 13 May | Churchill makes "blood, sweat, toil" speech | | | |

| 1940 | EUROPE & RUSSIA | ATLANTIC | AFRICA | FAR EAST, PACIFIC & USA |
|---|---|---|---|---|
| 14 May | Dutch cease fighting | | | |
| 15 May | German breakthrough at Sedan; Dutch surrender | | | |
| 20 May | Kleist's panzers reach Channel at Abbeville | | | |
| 26 May–3 June | British Expeditionary Force evacuated from Dunkirk | | | |
| 3 June | British evacuation from Narvik, Norway | | | |
| 10 June | Italy declares war on France & Britain; Norway capitualates | | | |
| 14 June | Fall of Paris | | | |
| 22 June | France signs surrender at Compiègne | | | |
| 4 July | | | Italian troops occupy parts of British Sudan | |
| Aug 5–19 | | | Italians occupy British Somaliland | |
| 12 Aug–6 Sept | Main phase of the Battle of Britain | | | |
| 23 Aug | *Luftwaffe* raid on London begins "the Blitz" | | | |
| 25 Aug | RAF bombs Berlin | | | |
| 13 Sept | | | Italy invades Egypt | |
| 22 Sept | Japanese enter Indo-China | | | |

| 1940 | EUROPE & RUSSIA | ATLANTIC | AFRICA | FAR EAST, PACIFIC & USA |
|---|---|---|---|---|
| 27 Sept | Germany, Italy & Japan sign Tripartite Pact | | | Japan signs Tripartite Pact |
| 28 Oct | Italy attacks Greece (from Albania) | | | |
| 11 Nov | Italian fleet attacked by RN at Taranto | | | |
| 11 Dec | | | British capture Sidi Barrani | |
| 17 Dec | | | British recapture Sollum, Egypt | |

| 1941 | EUROPE & RUSSIA | ATLANTIC | AFRICA & MIDDLE EAST | FAR EAST, PACIFIC & USA |
|---|---|---|---|---|
| 22 Jan | | | British & allies take Tobruk | |
| 7 Feb | | | Italian surrender at Beda Fomm | |
| 8 Feb | | | | US House of Reps passes Lend-Lease Bill |
| 12 Feb | | | Rommel arrives in Libya | |
| 1 Mar | Bulgaria joins Axis | | | |
| 7 Mar | Allied troops land in Greece | | | |
| 8 Mar | | | | Lend-Lease Bill passed by US Senate |
| 16 Mar | | | British retake Somaliland | |
| 28 Mar | Night battle of Cape Matapan (Tainaron) | | | |
| 30 Mar | | RAF attacks *Scharnhorst*, *Gneisenau* at Brest | | |

| 1941 | EUROPE & RUSSIA | ATLANTIC | AFRICA | FAR EAST, PACIFIC & USA |
|---|---|---|---|---|
| 6 Apr | Germany invades Greece and Yugoslavia | | | |
| 9 Apr | | | Addis Abba falls to British | |
| 27 Apr | German troops enter Athens | | | |
| 28 Apr | British troops withdraw from mainland Greece | | | |
| 2 May | | | Iraq uprising against British | |
| 3 May | Bombing of Hamburg | | | |
| 10 May | Hess flies to Scotland | | | |
| 20 May | German paratroop landings on Crete | | | |
| 24 May | | HMS *Hood* sunk | | |
| 27 May | | *Bismarck* sunk | | |
| 30 May | | | Iraqi revolt collapses | |
| 8 June | | | British invade Syria | |
| 22 June | Germany invades Russia | | | |
| 26 June | Finland renews war with Russia | | | |
| 8 July | Germany and Italy partition Yugoslavia | | | |
| 12 July | USSR and Britain sign mutual assistance treaty | | | |
| 28 July | | | | Japan invades Indo-China |
| 5 Aug | | | | UK & US impose raw material embargo on Japan |
| 7 Aug | Stalin becomes Supreme Commander of Red armed forces | | | |

| 1941 | EUROPE & RUSSIA | ATLANTIC | AFRICA | FAR EAST, PACIFIC & USA |
|---|---|---|---|---|
| 3 Sept | Gas chamber at Auschwitz first used | | | |
| 5 Sept | Germans occupy Estonia | | | |
| 8 Sept | Siege of Leningrad begins (until Jan 1944) | | | |
| 26 Sept | 665,000 Russian soldiers taken prisoner in Kiev battle | | | |
| 28 Sept | | First Arctic convoy to Russia | | |
| 29 Sept | Germans reach Crimea; Jews massacred in Kiev | | | |
| 30 Sept | German "Typhoon" offensive against Moscow (until Dec 6, when Red Army counter-attacks) | | | |
| 17 Oct | | | | Tojo PM of Japan |
| 24 Oct | Germans take Kharkov | | | |
| 9 Nov | Germans capture Yalta | | | |
| 14 Nov | HMS *Ark Royal* sunk off Gibraltar | | | |
| 15 Nov | Arrival of winter, Russia; temp down to minus 20 | | | |
| 18 Nov | | | Eighth Army launches Operation Crusader counter-offensive | |
| 20 Nov | | | Tank battle at Sidi Rezegh | |
| 26 Nov | | | | US forces put on war alert |

| 1941 | EUROPE & RUSSIA | ATLANTIC | AFRICA | FAR EAST, PACIFIC & USA |
|------|-----------------|----------|--------|-------------------------|
| 28 Nov | Russian counter-attack pushes Germans out of Rostov | | | |
| 7 Dec | | | | Japan attacks Pearl Harbor, Hong Kong, Philippines & Malaya |
| 8 Dec | | | | US and Britain declare war on Japan. Russia neutral. |
| 10 Dec | | | | Guam captured by Japanese. HMS *Prince of Wales* and *Repulse* sunk |
| 11 Dec | | | | Japanese attack Burma; Germany and Italy declare war on US. |
| 23 Dec | | | | US garrison on Wake surrenders to siege (begun Dec 8) |
| 24 Dec | | | British retake Benghazi | |
| 25 Dec | | | | Fall of Hong Kong to Japanese |

| 1942 | EUROPE & RUSSIA | ATLANTIC | AFRICA & MIDDLE EAST | FAR EAST, PACIFIC & USA |
|------|-----------------|----------|----------------------|-------------------------|
| 2 Jan | | | | Japanese attack Manila |
| 7 Jan | | | | Slim's defences broken, c. Malaya |
| 16 Jan | | | | Japan invades Burma |

| 1942 | EUROPE & RUSSIA | ATLANTIC | AFRICA | FAR EAST, PACIFIC & USA |
|------|-----------------|----------|--------|--------------------------|
| 18 Jan | "Wannsee Conference" (Berlin) agrees "Final Solution of the Jewish Problem" | | | |
| 15 Feb | | | | Singapore surrenders |
| 19 Feb | | | | Darwin bombed by Japanese air force |
| 26–28 Feb | | | | Battle of Java Sea; Japanese enter Java |
| 8 Mar | | | | Japanese enter Rangoon (Burma) |
| 9 Apr | | | | Japanese take Bataan peninsula |
| 16 Apr | George Cross awarded to Malta | | | |
| 18 Apr | | | | USAAF raid Tokyo |
| 1 May | | | | Mandalay falls to Japanese |
| 6 May | | | | Japanese take Dutch E. Indies |
| 7–8 May | Germans open summer offensive, Crimea | | | Battle of Coral Sea |
| 26 May | | | Rommel attacks Gazala line | |
| 27 May | Germans take 250,000 prisoners in Kharkov battle; Heydrich assassinated in Prague | | | |
| 30 May | 1,000 bomber raid on Cologne | | | |
| 3–4 June | | | | Battle of Midway |

| 1942 | EUROPE & RUSSIA | ATLANTIC | AFRICA | FAR EAST, PACIFIC & USA |
|---|---|---|---|---|
| 21 June | | | Allies surrender Tobruk | |
| 24 June | | | Rommel reaches Sidi Barrani | |
| 27 June | | | German advance to Mersa Matruh | |
| 3 July | Germans take Sebastopol | | | |
| 4 July | | PQ-17 convoy to Russia attacked by German aircraft | | |
| 23 July | Rostov falls to Germans | | | |
| 12 Aug | First Moscow Conference | | | |
| 15 Aug | | | Montgomery appointed commander Eighth Army | |
| 17 Aug | Raid on Dieppe | | | US landings Solomon Islands |
| 26 Aug | | | | Japanese land at Milne Bay |
| 5 Sept | | | | Australians force Jap. evacuation, Milne Bay |
| 31 Aug | | | Alam El-Halfa Battle | |
| 23 Oct | | | Battle of El Alamein (until 5 Nov) | |
| 8 Nov | | | Allied landings in French North Africa (Operation Torch) | |
| 11 Nov | Germans occupy Vichy France | | | |
| 12 Nov | | | | Night naval battle at Guadalcanal |
| 13 Nov | | | Allies retake Tobruk | |

| 1942 | EUROPE & RUSSIA | ATLANTIC | AFRICA | FAR EAST, PACIFIC & USA |
|------|-----------------|----------|--------|-------------------------|
| 19 Nov | Russian counter-attack n. Stalingrad | | | |
| 20 Nov | | | Benghazi falls to Allies | |
| 9 Dec | | | | US & Aus troops retake Goa |

| 1943 | EUROPE & RUSSIA | ATLANTIC | AFRICA & MIDDLE EAST | FAR EAST, PACIFIC & USA |
|------|-----------------|----------|---------------------|-------------------------|
| 3 Jan | Germans begin withdrawal from Caucasus | | | |
| 14 Jan | Casablanca conference | | | |
| 23 Jan | | | Eighth Army advance to Tripoli | |
| 2 Feb | German capitulation at Stalingrad | | | |
| 8 Feb | Kursk retaken by Russians | | | First Chindit expedition into Burma |
| 14 Feb | | | German counter-offensive, Tunisia | |
| 25–25 Feb | | | Battle of Kasserine Pass | |
| Feb/March | | U-boat campaign at peak | | |
| 29 Mar | | | Battle of Mareth Line | |
| 7 May | | | Bizerta and Tunis fall to Allies | |
| 11 May | | | | US landings in occupied Aleutian Islands |
| 12 May | | | Surrender of Axis forces in N. Africa | |
| 17 May | RAF "Dambusters" raid on Ruhr valley | | | |

| 1943 | EUROPE & RUSSIA | ATLANTIC | AFRICA | FAR EAST, PACIFIC & USA |
|------|-----------------|----------|--------|-------------------------|
| 29 June | | | | US troops land in New Guinea |
| 5 July | German offensive ("Citadel") at Kursk | | | |
| 9–10 July | Allied landings in Sicily | | | |
| 25 July | Mussolini imprisoned by pro-armistice fascists | | | |
| 1 Aug | USAAF bomb Ploesti oil refineries, Rumania | | | |
| 17 Aug | USAAF raids on Regensburg and Schweinfurt; German resistance ends in Sicily | | | |
| 23 Aug | Kharkov falls to Russians | | | |
| 3 Sept | Allied invasion of Italian mainland | | | |
| 8 Sept | Italy surrenders; Germans occupy north and central Italy | | | |
| 12 Sept | Mussolini rescued by SS | | | |
| 25 Sept | Russians retake Smolensk | | | |
| 1 Oct | Naples caputured by Allies | | | |
| 1 Nov | | | | US troops land on Bougainville |
| 6 Nov | Russians recover Kiev | | | |
| 28 Nov | Teheran Conference | | | |
| 14 Dec | Russians open winter offensive | | | |
| 25 Dec | | | | Allies land on New Britain |

| 1943 | EUROPE & RUSSIA | ATLANTIC | AFRICA | FAR EAST, PACIFIC & USA |
|------|-----------------|----------|--------|--------------------------|
| 26 Dec | | RN sinks the *Scharnhorst* | | |

| 1944 | EUROPE & RUSSIA | ATLANTIC | AFRICA & MIDDLE EAST | FAR EAST, PACIFIC & USA |
|------|-----------------|----------|---------------------|--------------------------|
| 6 Jan | Russian advance into Poland | | | |
| 22 Jan | Allied landings at Anzio | | | |
| 25 Jan | Relief of Leningrad | | | |
| 30 Jan | Allies break into Gustav defensive line (Italy) | | | |
| 4 Feb | | | | Japanese offensive, Arakan |
| 8 Feb | | | | Battle of Admin Box, Arakan (until Feb 25) |
| 15 Feb | Monastery at Cassino destroyed by Allied bombardments | | | |
| 16 Mar | | | | Jap forces cut Kohima–Imphal road |
| 29 Mar | | | | Siege of Imphal (until Jul 4) |
| 9 May | Sebastopol recovered by Russians | | | |
| 16 May | Allies overrun Gustav Line | | | |
| 18 May | Allies capture Monte Cassino | | | |
| 3 June | | | | Japanese defeated at Kohima |
| 4 June | Fall of Rome to Allies | | | |

| 1944 | EUROPE & RUSSIA | ATLANTIC | AFRICA | FAR EAST, PACIFIC & USA |
|---|---|---|---|---|
| 6 June | Allied D-Day landings, Normandy | | | |
| 13 June | First V-1 flying bombs land on England | | | |
| 15 June | | | | US Marines land on Saipan |
| 19 June | | | | Naval air battle, Marianas; Philippine Sea Battle |
| 4 July | Russians recover Minsk | | | |
| 9 July | | | | Saipan falls |
| 20 July | Assassination attempt on Hitler | | | |
| 21 July | | | | US landings on Guam |
| 24–7 July | US forces break out of Normandy | | | |
| 1 Aug | Warsaw patriots uprising (until Oct 2) | | | |
| 15 Aug | Allied landings in S. France | | | |
| 22 Aug | | Fleet Air Arm attacks *Tirpitz*, Altenfjord | | |
| 24 Aug | Liberation of Paris | | | |
| 31 Aug | Russians take Bucharest | | | |
| 3 Sept | Brussels liberated | | | |
| 8 Sept | V-2 rockets begin landing on England | | | |
| 12 Sept | US 1st Army crosses German border at Aachen | | | |
| 17 Sept | Arnhem airborne landings | | | |
| 14 Oct | Athens liberated; Hitler forces suicide of Erwin Rommel | | | |

| 1944 | EUROPE & RUSSIA | ATLANTIC | AFRICA | FAR EAST, PACIFIC & USA |
|---|---|---|---|---|
| 20 Oct | Tito enters Belgrade US landings in Philippines | | | |
| 23 Oct | Russians invade East Prussia | | | Battle of Leyte Gulf |
| 16 Dec | Beginning of German counter-offensive in Ardennes | | | |
| 26 Dec | Bastogne relieved | | | |
| 27 Dec | Budapest encircled | | | |

| 1945 | EUROPE & RUSSIA | ATLANTIC | AFRICA & MIDDLE EAST | FAR EAST, PACIFIC & USA |
|---|---|---|---|---|
| 1 Jan | Last *Luftwaffe* offensive of war; 800 aircraft raid Allied airfields in France, Belgium and Holland | | | |
| 9 Jan | | | | US landings, Luzon |
| 11 Jan | | | | Allies establish bridgeheads over Irrawaddy |
| 17 Jan | Russians capture Warsaw | | | |
| 4 Feb | Yalta Conference | | | |
| 9 Feb | Allies reach Rhine | | | |
| 13 Feb | RAF fire-bomb Dresden; Budapest falls to Russians | | | |
| 6 Mar | German counter-offensive towards Budapest | | | |
| 7 Mar | US 1st Army crosses Rhine at Remagen | | | |

| 1945 | EUROPE & RUSSIA | ATLANTIC | AFRICA | FAR EAST, PACIFIC & USA |
|---|---|---|---|---|
| 16 Mar | Cologne falls to Allies | | | |
| 16 Mar | | | | Japanese resistance ends on Iwo Jima |
| 1 Apr | Allies encircle "Ruhr | | | Landing of US troops Pocket" on Okinawa |
| 7 Apr | Russians enter Vienna | | | |
| 12 Apr | | | | Roosevelt dies; Truman becomes President |
| 13 Apr | Liberation of Belsen death camp | | | |
| 21 Apr | Russians break into outer suburbs of Berlin | | | |
| 25 Apr | US and Soviet forces link up at Torgau | | | |
| 28 Apr | Mussolini killed by Italian partisans; 5th Army takes Venice | | | |
| 29 Apr | Capitulation of German troops in Italy; Dachau liberated | | | |
| 30 Apr | Hitler commits suicide in Berlin | | | |
| 2 May | Berlin captured by Russians | | | |
| 3 May | | | | Allies enter Rangoon |
| 8 May VE day | | | | |
| 13 May | Russian occupation of Czechoslovakia | | | |
| 10 June | | | | Aus 9th Division lands on Borneo |

| 1945 | EUROPE & RUSSIA | ATLANTIC | AFRICA | FAR EAST, PACIFIC & USA |
|---|---|---|---|---|
| 21 June | | | | Okinawa falls to US |
| 27 July | Attlee becomes British PM | | | |
| 6 Aug | | | | Atomic bomb dropped on Hiroshima |
| 8 Aug | | | | Russia declares war on Japan |
| 9 Aug | | | | Atomic bomb dropped on Nagasaki |
| 14 Aug | | | | Japan surrenders |
| 15 Aug | VJ Day | | | VJ Day |
| 13 Sept | | | | Japanese forces in Burma sign surrender |

# Part One

*Blitzkrieg*

*The War in Europe,
September 1939–October 1940*

# INTRODUCTION

World War II opened at 04.45 hours on 1 September 1939, when German tanks rolled into Poland. Hitler's previous territorial annexations had met only appeasement by the democracies of Europe (not a few of which saw the German Chancellor as a useful bulwark against Stalin's Soviet Union) but Polish territorial integrity had been explicitly guaranteed by Britain. This time there was no climbdown and generalized hostilities began on 3 September.

Although units of the Polish army fought determinedly, they had little chance against a German army superior in numbers, and *materiel*. The campaign in Poland was the Germans' first demonstration of "Blitzkrieg" (lightning war), spearheaded by air and armoured attacks. As if this was not enough, Poland found itself stabbed in the back, or at least on its eastern frontier: the Soviet Union, by the terms of a secret treaty with Germany, invaded Poland from the east on 17 September. By 6 October Polish resistance was finished. Unsated, the Soviet Union determined upon invasion of Finland, sending a million men into the "The Winter War". For three months 170,000 Finnish soldiers resisted, before Finland sued for peace. Their losses were 25,000 dead; the Soviet Union's 200,000.

Aside from some skirmishing on the Franco-German border, elsewhere in Europe the war slipped into quiescence. People talked of the "Phoney War" and more propaganda leaflets were dropped than bombs. British troops sang a hit song, "We're gonna hang out the washing on the Siegfried line". Yet, behind front lines the war was ticking away. In April 1940 it exploded. Deciding, after a spate of naval embarrassments, that the territorial waters of Norway should be denied to the Allies, Hitler invaded Norway and Denmark. The Norwegians, aided by British and French forces, resisted bitterly until late May 1940, when the Allies withdrew their troops through Narvik. By then the main show had started and these troops were needed at home: Germany had invaded Holland, Belgium and Luxembourg. To the horror and dismay of the French, the *Wehrmacht* inconsiderately ignored their magnificent concrete Maginot Line and tanked into Gaul via Belgium and the supposedly "impenetrable" Ardennes, and then sped towards the Channel ports. The British Expeditionary Force (BEF) and the French First Army became isolated in the north of France, and were evacuated in "the miracle of Dunkirk" between 29 May and 4 June. By 21 June France had fallen to the Stuka, the panzer and the *soldat* of Germany. The humbling of France had taken a mere ten weeks.

Under Operation Sealion, Germany then embarked on the defeat of her last standing enemy: Britain. On 10 July, recognizing that invasion of Britain could not begin until the air over the Channel was under Nazi control, the *Luftwaffe* of Herman Goring began its campaign to crush Fighter Command. The ensuing Battle of Britain lasted until 30 October 1940, by when the *Luftwaffe* had been decisively beaten by "The Few", the Spitfire and Hurricane pilots of the RAF.

It was Hitler's first check.

# HITLER ORDERS WAR, 31 AUGUST 1939

## *Adolf Hitler*

Most Secret
Directive No. 1 for the Conduct of War: 31 August

1. Now that all the political possibilities of disposing by peaceful means of a situation on the Eastern Frontier which is intolerable for Germany are exhausted, I have determined on a solution by force.
2. The attack on Poland is to be carried out in accordance with the preparations made for "Fall Weiss", with the alterations which result, where the Army is concerned, from the fact that it has, in the meantime, almost completed its dispositions.

    Allotment of tasks and the operational target remain unchanged.

    The date of attack – 1 September, 1939.

    Time of attack – 04.45 [inserted in red pencil].

    This time also applies to the operation at Gdynia, Bay of Danzig, and the Dirschau Bridge.

3. In the West it is important that the responsibility for the opening of hostilities should rest unequivocally with England and France. At first, purely local action should be taken against insignificant frontier violations.

Adolf Hitler

# GERMAN PANZERS INVADE POLAND, 1 SEPTEMBER 1939

## General Heinz Guderian

*A leading tank expert and exponent of the Blitzkrieg theory, Guderian created the Panzer armies which overran Poland in 1939. The invader numbered sixty-two divisions (six of them armoured); the Poles had forty divisions (none of them armoured).*

On the 1 September at 04.45 hours the whole corps moved simultaneously over the frontier. There was a thick ground mist at first which prevented the air force from giving us any support. I accompanied the 3rd Panzer Brigade, in the first wave, as far as the area north of Zempelburg where the preliminary fighting took place. Unfortunately the heavy artillery of the 3rd Panzer Division felt itself compelled to fire into the mist, despite having received precise orders not to do so. The first shell landed fifty yards ahead of my command vehicle, the second fifty yards behind it. I reckoned that the next one was bound to be a direct hit and ordered my driver to turn about and drive off. The unaccustomed noise had made him nervous, however, and he drove straight into a ditch at full speed. The front axle of the half-tracked vehicle was bent so that the steering mechanism was put out of action. This marked the end of my drive. I made my way to my corps command post, procured myself a fresh vehicle and had a word with the over-eager artillerymen. Incidentally it may be noted that I was the first corps commander ever to use armoured command vehicles in order to accompany tanks on to the battlefield. They were equipped with radio, so that I was able to keep in constant touch with my corps headquarters and with the divisions under my command.

The first serious fighting took place north of Zempelburg in and around Gross-Klonia, where the mist suddenly lifted and the leading tanks found themselves face to face with Polish defensive positions. The Polish anti-tank gunners scored many direct hits. One officer, one officer cadet and eight other ranks were killed.

Gross-Klonia had once belonged to my great-grandfather, Freiherr Hiller von Gärtringen. Here, too, was buried my grandfather Guderian. My father had been born in this place. This was the first time I had ever set eyes on the estate, once so beloved by my family.

After successfully changing vehicles, I rejoined the 3rd Panzer Division whose most forward troops had now reached the Brahe. The bulk of the division was between Pruszcz and Klein-Klonia and was about to settle down for a rest. The divisional commander had been sent for by the Commander-in-Chief of the Army Group, Colonel-General von Bock, and was therefore absent. I asked the officers of the 6th Panzer Regiment who were there to tell me about the situation on the Brahe.

The regimental commander did not believe that a passage of the river could be forced on that day, and he was eager to carry out the welcome orders for a rest. The corps order – that the Brahe should be crossed during the first day of the attack – had been forgotten. I walked angrily away and tried to decide what measure I should take to improve this unhappy state of affairs. A young Lieutenant Felix came over to where I was standing. He had taken off his tunic, his shirt sleeves were rolled up, and his arms were black with powder. "Herr General," he said, "I've just come from the Brahe. The enemy forces on the far bank are weak. The Poles set fire to the bridge at Hummermühle, but I put the fire out from my tank. The bridge is crossable. The advance has only stopped because there's no one to lead it. You must go there yourself, sir." I looked at the young man in amazement. He made a very good impression and his eyes inspired confidence. Why should not this young lieutenant have done the trick of Columbus and the egg? I followed his advice and drove through a confusion of German and Polish vehicles along the narrow sandy track that led through the woods to Hummermühle, where I arrived between 16.00 and 17.00 hours. A group of staff officers were standing behind a stout oak tree about 100 yards from the water's edge. They greeted me with the cry: "Herr General, they're shooting here!" They were indeed, both the tank guns of the 6th Panzer Regiment and the rifles of the 3rd Rifle Regiment blazing away. The enemy on the far bank sat in his trenches and was invisible. First of all I put a stop to the idiotic firing, in which I was ably assisted by the newly arrived commander of the 3rd Rifle Brigade, Colonel Angern. Then I ordered that the extent of the enemy's defensive positions be established. Motor-cycle Battalion 3, which had not yet been in action, was sent across the river in rubber boats at a point that was not under enemy fire. When they had crossed successfully, I ordered the tanks over the bridge. They took the Polish bicycle company, which was defending this sector of the stream, prisoner. Casualties were negligible.

# EVACUATION OF CHILDREN, LONDON, 1 SEPTEMBER 1939

## *Hilde Marchant*

The office had told me to cover the evacuation of some of London's schoolchildren. There had been great preparations for the scheme – preparations that raised strong criticism. Evacuation would split the British home, divide child and parent, break that domestic background that was our strength.

I went to a block of working-class flats at the back of Gray's Inn Road and in the early morning saw a tiny, frail, Cockney child walking across to school. The child had a big, brown-paper parcel in her hand and was dragging it along. But as she turned I saw a brown box banging against her thin legs. It bumped up and down at every step, slung by a thin string over her shoulder.

It was Florence Morecambe, an English schoolchild, with a gas mask instead of a satchel over her shoulder.

I went along with Florence to her school. It was a big Council school and the classrooms were filled with children, parcels, gas masks. The desks and blackboards were piled up in a heap in one corridor. They were not going to school for lessons. They were going on a holiday. The children were excited and happy because their parents had told them they were going away to the country. Many of them, like my little Florence, had never seen green fields. Their playground was the tarmac or a sandpit in the concrete square at the back.

I watched the schoolteachers calling out their names and tying luggage labels in their coats, checking their parcels to see there were warm and clean clothes. On the gates of the school were two fat policemen. They were letting the children through but gently asking the parents not to come farther. They might disturb the children. So mothers and fathers were saying goodbye, straightening the girls' hair, getting the boys to blow their noses, and lightly and quickly kissing them. The parents stood outside while the children went to be registered in their classrooms. There was quite a long wait before this small army got its orders through from the LCC [London County Council] to move off. In the meantime I sat in the school playground, watching these thin, wiry little Cockneys playing their rough-and-push games on the faded netball pitch. It was disturbing, for through the high grille their mothers pressed their faces, trying to see the one child that resembled them. Every now and then the policeman would call out a child's name and a mother who had forgotten a bar of chocolate or a toothbrush had a last chance to tell a child to be good, to write and to straighten her hat.

Labelled and lined up, the children began to move out of the school. I followed Florence, her live tiny face bobbing about, white among so many navy-blue school caps. She was chattering away to an older schoolgirl, wanting to know what the country was like, where they were going, what games they would play on the grass.

On one side of Gray's Inn Road this ragged crocodile moved towards the tube station. On the other, were mothers who were waving and running along to see the last of their children. The police had asked them not to follow, but they could not resist.

The children scrambled down into the tube.

## THE HOUSE OF COMMONS DISCUSSES WAR AND PEACE, LONDON, 2 SEPTEMBER 1939

### *Ralph Glyn, MP*

#### Diary: September 3

Last night in London was one of the great times in modern history. The half-hour in the Commons – 7.30 to 8 – was perhaps the most decisive half-hour that we have known.

All through the day the House had been in a schoolboyish, almost hysterical mood; they were laughing and shuffling. There was a feeling that something fishy was happening in Downing Street. The Cabinet was still sitting. Ministers were telephoning Paris – and the Germans were bombing Poland. *Why* were we not at war?

At half-past seven we met again, this time subdued and tense. Chamberlain we knew would declare war. The Ambassadors were looking down; Count Edward Raczijnsky pale and worn Chamberlain came in looking grey – a kind of whitish-grey – and glum, dour. Captain Margesson, the Secretary to the Treasury, came behind him, purple with anxiety. Chamberlain's statement! . . . In the house we thought he was only half-way through when – he sat down. There was a gasp, first of horror, then anger. His own back-benchers leaned forward to cry, "Munich, Munich!" The House seemed to rise to its feet with Mr Arthur Greenwood, the Labour leader.

Mr L.S. Amery, sitting very small near Anthony Eden, jumped up to shout at Greenwood – "Speak for England." Others took up the cry. Chamberlain white and hunched. Margesson with sweat pouring down his face, Sir John Simon, the Foreign Secretary, punctiliously looking holy.

Greenwood spoke slowly and very simply. He spoke for England and what is more he saved Chamberlain by most skilfully suggesting that it was the French who were delaying. Then one or two back-benchers, Chamberlain's own supporters, got up. It was not a joint Anglo-French pledge to Poland, they said, it was a *British* pledge – why were we not fulfilling it? The House swung against Chamberlain again. Winston Churchill, I saw, was getting whiter and grimmer. He turned round to look at Eden, who nodded as if to say, "You speak, I'll follow." I know that Churchill was about to move a vote of censure on the Government – which would have fallen. But Chamberlain looked across at Churchill: "I'm playing straight," his glance seemed to say, "there really *are* reasons for delay." Churchill sat back, relaxed, uneasy.

Then James Maxton, the pacifist, rose, gaunt, a Horseman from the Apocalypse, doom written across his face: "Don't let's talk of national honour: what do such phrases mean? The plain fact is that war means the slaughter of millions. If the Prime Minister can still maintain the peace he will have saved those lives, he mustn't be rushed." Again the House swung and was poised. We all thought in the curious hush: What if the gaunt figure of doom were right after all? Slaughter – misery – ruin – was he right? But the alternative: Hitler trading on our fears, Germany treading on freedom, Europe under terror. The whole House was swayed in unison with the drama which itself was living.

Another back-bencher spoke: "We must keep our pledge – Hitler must be stopped." Once again we were swinging against Chamberlain, when Margesson, damp and shapeless, rose to move the adjournment. In a kind of daze it was carried.

We broke up, some feeling sick from the reaction – two members *were* sick – all were uneasy and ashamed. I went home, lay awake all night, slept a bit towards morning, and was awakened by the air-raid warning. Had the Germans read the feelings of the country? Were they attacking first?

## BRITAIN DECLARES WAR ON GERMANY, 3 SEPTEMBER 1939

### *Neville Chamberlain*

*The text of the Prime Minister's speech, broadcast on the fine late summer's morning of 3 September.*

I am speaking to you from the Cabinet Room at 10, Downing Street.

This morning the British Ambassador in Berlin handed the German Government a final Note stating that, unless we heard from them by 11 o'clock that they were prepared at once to withdraw their troops from Poland, a state of war would exist between us.

I have to tell you now that no such undertaking has been received, and that consequently this country is at war with Germany. You can imagine what a bitter blow it is to me that all my long struggle to win peace has failed. Yet I cannot believe that there is anything more or anything different that I could have done and that would have been more successful.

Up to the very last it would have been quite possible to have arranged a peaceful and honourable settlement between Germany and Poland, but Hitler would not have it. He had evidently made up his mind to attack Poland whatever happened and although he now says he put forward reasonable proposals which were rejected by the Poles, that is not a true statement.

The proposals were never shown to the Poles, nor to us, and, though they were announced in a German broadcast on Thursday night, Hitler did not wait to hear comments on them, but ordered his troops to cross the Polish frontier. His action shows convincingly that there is no chance of expecting that this man will ever give up his practice of using force to gain his will. He can only be stopped by force.

We and France are today, in fulfilment of our obligations, going to the aid of Poland, who is so bravely resisting this wicked and unprovoked attack on her people. We have a clear conscience. We have done all that any country could do to establish peace. The situation in which no word given by Germany's ruler could be trusted and no people or country could feel themselves safe has become intolerable. And now that we have resolved to finish it, I know that you will all play your part with calmness and courage.

At such a moment as this the assurances of support that we have received from the Empire are a source of profound encouragement to us.

When I have finished speaking certain detailed announcements will be made on behalf of the Government. Give these your closest attention. The Government have made plans under which it will be possible to carry on the work of the nation in the days of stress and strain that may be ahead. But these plans need your help.

You may be taking your part in the fighting services or as a volunteer in one of the branches of Civil Defence. If so you will report for duty in accordance with the instructions you have received. You may be engaged in work essential to the prosecution of war for the maintenance of the life of the people – in factories, in transport, in public utility concerns, or in the supply of other necessaries of life. If so, it is of vital importance that you should carry on with your jobs.

Now may God bless you all. May He defend the right. It is the evil things that we shall be fighting against – brute force, bad faith, injustice, oppression and persecution – and against them I am certain that the right will prevail.

# LONDON AT WAR, 3 SEPTEMBER 1939

## *Mollie Panter-Downes*

*Mollie Panter-Downes was the London correspondent for the* New Yorker.

For a week everybody in London had been saying every day that if there wasn't a war tomorrow there wouldn't be a war. Yesterday people were saying that if there wasn't a war today it would be a bloody shame. Now that there is a war, the English, slow to start, have already in spirit started and are comfortably two laps ahead of the official war machine, which had to await the drop of somebody's handkerchief. In the general opinion, Hitler has got it coming to him – or, in the local patois, " 'E's fair copped it."

The London crowds are cool – cooler than they were in 1914 – in spite of thundery weather that does its best to scare everybody by staging unofficial rehearsals for air raids at the end of breathlessly humid days. On the stretch of green turf by Knightsbridge Barracks, which used to be the scampering ground for the smartest terriers in London, has appeared a row of steam shovels that bite out mouthfuls of earth, hoist it aloft, and dump it into lorries; it is then carted away to fill sandbags. The eye has now become accustomed to sandbags everywhere, and to the balloon barrage, the trap for enemy planes, which one morning spread over the sky like some form of silvery dermatitis. Posting a letter has acquired a new interest, too, since His Majesty's tubby, scarlet pillar boxes have been done up in squares of yellow detector paint, which changes color if there is poison gas in the air and is said to be as sensitive as a chameleon.

Gas masks have suddenly become part of everyday civilian equipment and everybody is carrying the square cardboard cartons that look as though they might contain a pound of grapes for a sick friend. Bowlegged admirals stump jauntily up Whitehall with their gas masks slung neatly in knapsacks over their shoulders. Last night London was completely blacked out. A few cars crawled through the streets with one headlight out and the other hooded while Londoners, suddenly become homebodies, sat under their shaded lights listening to a Beethoven Promenade concert interspersed with the calm and cultured tones of the BBC telling motorists what to do during air raids and giving instructions to what the BBC referred to coyly as expectant mothers with pink cards, meaning mothers who are a good deal more than expectant.

The evacuation of London, which is to be spaced over three days, began yesterday and was apparently a triumph for all concerned. At seven o'clock in the morning all inward traffic was stopped and AA scouts raced through the suburbs whisking shrouds of sacking off imposing bulletin boards, which informed motorists that all the principal routes out of town were one-way streets for three days. Cars poured out pretty steadily all day, yesterday and today, packed with people, luggage, children's perambulators, and domestic pets, but the congestion at busy points was no worse than it is at any other time in the holiday season. The railways, whose workers had been on the verge of going out on strike when the crisis came, played their part nobly and the London stations, accustomed to receiving trainloads of child refugees from the Third Reich, got down to the job of dispatching trainload after trainload of children the other way – this time, cheerful little cockneys who ordinarily get to the country perhaps once a year on the local church outing and could hardly believe the luck that was sending them now. Left behind, the mothers stood around rather listlessly at street corners waiting for the telegrams that were to be posted up at the various schools to tell them where their children were.

All over the country the declaration of war has brought a new lease of life to retired army officers, who suddenly find themselves the commanders of battalions of willing ladies who have emerged from the herbaceous borders to answer the call of duty. Morris 10s, their windshields plastered with notices that they are engaged on business of the ARP or WVS (both volunteer services), rock down quiet country lanes propelled by firm-lipped spinsters who yesterday could hardly have said "Boo!" to an aster.

Although the summer holiday is still on, village schools have reopened as centers where the evacuated hordes from London can be rested, sorted out, medically examined, refreshed with tea and biscuits, and distributed to their new homes. The war has brought the great unwashed right into the bosoms of the great washed; while determined ladies in white VAD overalls search the mothers' heads with a knitting needle for unwelcome signs of life, the babies are dandled and patted on their often grimy diapers by other ladies, who have been told to act as hostesses and keep the guests from pining for Shoreditch. Guest rooms have been cleared of Crown Derby knick-knacks and the best guest towels, and the big houses and cottages alike are trying to overcome the traditional British dislike of strangers, who may, for all anybody knows, be parked in them for a matter of years, not weeks.

Everybody is so busy that no one has time to look up at the airplanes that pass overhead all day. Today was a day of unprecedented activity in the air. Squadrons of bombers bustled in all directions and at midday an enormous number of vast planes, to which the knowing pointed as troop-carriers, droned overhead toward an unknown destination that was said by two sections of opinion to be (a) France and (b) Poland. On the ground, motor buses full of troops in bursting good humor tore through the villages, the men waving at the girls and howling "Tipperary" and other ominously dated ditties that everybody has suddenly remembered and found to be as good for a war in 1939 as they were in 1914.

London and the country are buzzing with rumours, a favorite one being that Hitler carries a gun in his pocket and means to shoot himself if things don't go too well; another school of thought favors the version that he is now insane and Göring has taken over. It is felt that Mussolini was up to no good with his scheme for holding a peace conference and spoiling what has become everybody's war. The English were a peace-loving nation up to two days ago, but now it is pretty widely felt that the sooner we really get down to the job, the better.

# A POLISH CADET IN INACTION, SEPTEMBER–OCTOBER 1939

## K.S. Karol

*Karol was a fifteen-year-old schoolboy undergoing a compulsory military course when Germany attacked Poland.*

The camp's commander . . . announced that the war would be a long one and that we would have a chance to fight when we reached eighteen or even twenty-one years of age. For now, however, he wanted some volunteers to protect public buildings, perhaps in Warsaw, thereby freeing a company of the regular army for duty on the front. Every one of us a patriot, we all took a step forward. I imagine that we resembled closely those schoolboys of the Kaiser's Germany, described so well by Erich Maria Remarque in *All Quiet on the Western Front*. Just as with them, patriotic ardor glazed over our eyes. For Jurek, Rysiek, and myself – Stefan Wegner's three protégés – enthusiasm consisted above all of antifascist élan. I also promised myself that in the Hour of Victory, after crushing the Germans, I would redirect my gun at the oppressor regime in Poland. But guarding public buildings would do until then: our army at the front had to have its rear guard well secured.

The only problem was that the front seemed to be everywhere, beginning with the road we took to Warsaw. In undisputed command of the air, the Luftwaffe bombed everything that moved, at least in western Poland. In the beginning, we were terrified. During the first raid, Sergeant Major Bartczak, a stupid and cruel man, even ordered a peasant woman to strangle her baby so that it would stop exposing us to risk with its crying. Fortunately the brave woman refused. Slowly we became used to the Luftwaffe; it had claimed no victims among our little troop, which comprised a hundred "auxiliary soldiers" and ten or so regular soldiers who flanked us. The real problems were slow progress in marching and the palpable lowering of morale, prompted by the fear that perhaps we weren't on the winning side after all.

Where were *our* planes? Did Poland have any planes? Some of us took comfort from pretending that our air force was active on the front, unlike the Luftwaffe, which was being used against civilians, including women and children. But this explanation, based on trust in the moral superiority of our pilots, collapsed when, on September 5, we at last reached the suburbs of the capital. Muffled rumblings of artillery fire convinced us that the front couldn't be very far away; and, alas, there wasn't a Polish plane in sight. Worse still, nourished by the myth of the combined might of France and Great Britain, we half expected to see their squadrons flying above our country. Instead, they were conspicuous by their absence.

Things were bad – much worse than our most pessimistic fears. The weary eyes of our camp commander betrayed fatigue and confusion; in Warsaw they hadn't any need of us, and it was too late to send us back to Lodz, which was now occupied by the Germans. Our leader recovered his verve only after meeting a group of officers among whom was a major who agreed to speak to him, to help him, to help us. I remember that after their conversation they separated on a perky note: "See you again, after another miracle on the Vistula." I too was sure that the Polish Army still had the capacity to wage a victorious battle on the outskirts of the capital. Hadn't my mother told me that in the hour of danger our people were capable of surpassing themselves, of revealing unsuspected reserves of heroism?

Nevertheless, our small troop was not supposed to contribute to this exploit. Our leader, after assembling our supplies and receiving his instructions, ordered us to march – singing – in the direction of Lublin. In our song, even the trees were supposed to salute us, because it was "for our Poland" that we were going into combat.

In reality, neither man nor beast nor any other living thing paid us any honor and we didn't have the opportunity to fire a single shot. The enemy always came from the air, and even when they flew very low, they were still beyond the range of our old Mausers. The spectacle of the war therefore rapidly became monotonous; day after day we saw the same scenes: civilians running to save themselves from air raids, convoys dispersing, trucks or carts on fire. The smell along the road was unchanging, too. It was the smell of dead horses that no one had bothered to bury and that stank to high heaven. We moved only at night and we learned to sleep while marching; smoking was forbidden out of fear that the glow of a cigarette could bring down on us the all-powerful Luftwaffe.

It was a marvelous month, that September of 1939: mild, sunny, worthy of the end of an Italian summer, and we weren't cold.

Two weeks after our departure from Warsaw, when we had already gone well beyond Lublin, our leader suddenly ordered us to make an about-face. We were going back toward the west, toward Chelm. What had happened? Had the miracle on the Vistula materialized? Were we finally going to protect the public buildings of Warsaw? In an army, orders are never explained – and the Polish Army was no exception to the rule. But along the roads, day or night, we were never alone; other soldiers and civilians were also on the march, and thanks to the ubiquitous rumor mill called in some parts of the West the "Arab telephone" and in the USSR "Radio Yerevan," we learned that no miracle had taken place. We were heading west because the Russians were arriving from the east. And not to come to our aid, either, to fight "in a consistent manner against the Nazis" as my Communist brother's old formula had it! "Stalin and his loyal comrades" were coming quite simply to gobble up their share of Poland.

Rysiek, Jurek, and I were seized with consternation. If the Bolsheviks had become friends with the Nazis, then principles no longer mattered; there was no longer any hope for our poor Poland. On the other hand, why should we go to meet the Germans, who had attacked us first, rather than toward the Russians, who, as far as one could tell, were neither bombing nor destroying everything in their way? Should we talk to our leader about his decision? Such a step would certainly have yielded nothing and would have marked us as Communist sympathizers – which, in Poland, even at this moment of total disarray, could only lead to unfortunate results. What, then, if all three of us took off to try to join up with the Russians? But this solution didn't have much to recommend it, either. After much discussion, we decided that if there was a way out of the trap that enclosed us, it was still our commander who had some hope of finding it. So we followed him to the end, but we were bitterly disappointed at having been betrayed by all sides: by the Western powers, by the Russians, and by our own government, which had already bolted to Romania.

While still marching, I began to sleep more and more deeply.

I began to dream as if I were in bed. One night I saw the sky fill with countless Soviet squadrons. They were coming to deliver us from the Nazis, and our commander thanked them, as a comrade-in-arms who knows how to appreciate fraternal bravery and help. Even Sergeant Major Bartczak, a vitriolic anti-Bolshevik who never missed an opportunity to curse the Reds, ignoring the fact that it was the Germans who had attacked us, embraced the Russian tank drivers as they rolled down the road in their powerful armored vehicles. Bartczak cried out. "We are all part of the same Slav family." Our Soviet liberators also had an enormous tank of fresh cream, which they were distributing generously, as if to show just how wrong my father had been to think that there wasn't any to be had under the Bolshevik regime.

"Are you crazy or what?" Jurek asked, pulling me toward a gully as some Luftwaffe planes roared over our heads. According to Jurek, I replied that they were Soviet squadrons, but I don't remember anything of this. Ever since this rudely interrupted dream of the great Russo-Polish antifascist reconciliation, however, I have talked in my sleep, and I even reply, apparently, to questions, just as if I were awake.

We marched around in circles for one week more. Warsaw surrendered on September 27, but we continued our march until October 5, when we found ourselves encircled, along with some detachments of the regular army, by the Germans, near the village of Krzywda (Injustice). The Wehrmacht, for its own amusement or to encourage us to lay down our arms more quickly, sprayed us copiously with bursts of machine-gun fire and bombarded us with grenades. I caught something in the eye almost without noticing it, and without feeling any pain. My right eye simply closed and I could no longer open it except with the help of my fingers, by forcing the eyelid. I didn't make a fuss about it, believing that it would pass, and I took part in all of the farewell ceremonies. A high-ranking Polish officer, a colonel or perhaps even a general, had been authorized by our German captors to make a speech to us in which he said that the war was not over, that the Polish Army, under the command of General Sikorski, fought on in France, and that our powerful Western allies were more than ever at our side. Our camp commander also came to say good-bye; the Germans were separating the officers from the NCOs and the rank-and-file troops.

We were taken to Demblin Fortress, on the Vistula. I would spend ten days there before being sent to a hospital in Random. It wasn't a camp like the one I had seen in Jean Renoir's film *La Grande Illusion*, replete with barracks, beds, and even a theater. In Demblin we were shut up in a large depot full of racks for arms – emptied, obviously – and were allowed out only to line up, in the rain, in front of an improvised, open-air kitchen. At night we arranged bunks as best we could with boards torn from the partitions and placed on the racks because, without them, there wouldn't even have been enough space for everyone on the ground. Our bunks, however, had an unfortunate tendency to collapse, which often provoked a good deal of stumbling and swearing in the darkness. The Germans would arrive forthwith, hurling abuse and insults, the wealth and variety of which far exceeded anything I had learned at Skorupka High School. Blows struck with rifle butts landed here and there on the heads of these *"polnische Schweinerhunde"* but I was lucky enough to avoid them.

We waited for them to take a census of their prisoners, so that we could explain our peculiar situation as student auxiliaries, but they didn't seem to be in any hurry. Instead, we were subjected to another sort of census altogether. One rainy morning, one of the Wehrmacht loud-mouths came into our depot, screaming, *"Alles was Jude ist, aufstehen."* ("Anyone who is Jewish, stand up.") "These savages only know how to speak the most brutal German," remarked Jurek, who was one-hundred-percent Aryan but who was still more afraid than I, because he had a bronze tint and a flattish nose that had earned him the nickname "golliwog" at the high school.

## POLAND: INSIDE FALLEN WARSAW, OCTOBER 1939

### Joseph W. Grigg

*Warsaw was encircled by German forces on 17 September; to persuade the garrison into surrender, it was bombed and shelled for ten days, when the defenders capitulated.*

I WAS a member of the first group of foreign newspapermen to reach Warsaw. We arrived there on October 5th, the day on which Hitler held his victory parade amid the ruins of the former Polish capital. Such devastation would be difficult to imagine. The whole center of the city had been laid in ruins by the two-day fury of the German bombardment and air bombing. Dead horses still lay rotting in the parks, their carcasses half hacked up by starving Polish troops during the siege. New graves bulged the grass along side street car tracks. Bomb craters made it difficult to drive along some of the main streets. The brand new central railway station was scarcely recognizable. The Polish population looked bewildered and stunned.

For an hour we stood alongside Hitler as tank after tank, motorized infantry, guns, and more tanks thundered past along the tree-lined avenue where most of the foreign embassies and legations are situated.

No Pole saw that victory parade. The street where Hitler stood and those along which the gray German columns rolled had been cordoned off and no Pole was allowed nearer than a block distant. The tanks were clean and in parade-ground condition. The troops were fresh and clear-eyed. The dull steel armor of the new Nazi *Wehrmacht* had scarcely been dented by its first blitz campaign.

That was the lesson of the conquest of Poland. Overwhelming superiority in tanks, overwhelming superiority in the air from the outset, use of the dive bomber as the new "super-artillery" of the future, and complete co-ordination between Army and Air Force. And the new strategy – lightning attack to gain the advantage of surprise and use of the swift, overlapping armored spearheads to split the enemy, encircle him and crush him in an iron ring from which there is no escape.

Later that afternoon on the Warsaw airport a dozen or so foreign newspapermen were presented to Hitler. His face was pallid and unhealthy-looking but his mood was that of a triumphant conqueror.

"Gentlemen," he said, "you have seen the ruins of Warsaw. Let that be a warning to those statesmen in London and Paris who still think of continuing this war."

With a quick Nazi salute he turned from us and walked towards the plane that was to carry him back to Berlin. He had used this chance meeting with our small group of foreign correspondents to send back to London and Paris the warning: "Remember the ruins of Warsaw. Remember what your own fate may be."

## A GERMAN TANK GUNNER TRAINS FOR WAR, LANGWASSER, AUTUMN 1939

### *Karl Fuchs, 25th Panzer Regiment, 7th Panzer Division*

*Fuchs was a schoolteacher conscripted into the* Wehrmacht *in October 1939.*

*Langwasser Training Camp*

Dear Father,

A week has gone by and we're now settled in at the military installation. The entire compound is superb! We have had our psychological examinations and, based upon these tests, I was assigned as a tank gunner. Now, of course, we have to learn and train until we perfect all of our skills. Infantry training is almost behind us and in eight weeks we have to be fit for combat. You, as an old soldier, know best what this means. The intensity of training is tremendous and there is no rest for anyone. All of us are eager to make progress and no one complains, least of all your son. You won't ever have to be ashamed of me; you can depend on me.

Several days ago I had to report to the captain of our company and speak to him about my plans for officer training. Today for the first time we had to practice pistol shooting – five shots and five bull's-eyes for me! Next week we have training in shooting with rifles and machine guns. The recruits are looking forward to this training. All of us tank gunners need to be crack shots.

Next week we'll be able to climb into our tanks for the first time. Operating the vehicle will have to become second nature to us. Tanks are really awesome!

For the time being we will have no furlough, at least not until New Year's. Christmastime will be spent in our barracks. I hope that all is well at home. Please write to me if you are able to come and visit. One more request; please take care of Madi so that she doesn't feel so alone.

That's all for today. Sieg Heil and on to old England!

Your loyal son, Karl

# FINLAND: GUERILLA WAR IN THE SNOW, 2 FEBRUARY 1940

## *Virginia Cowles*

*The Soviet Union invaded Finland on 30 November 1939. The main attack fell on the "waist" of Finland in the Suomussalmi area and on the Karelian Isthmus, and was intended to crack the fortified Mannerheim Line. Despite being outnumbered 5 to 1, Finnish troops resisted until 12 March 1940, taking – by virtue of superior tactics and training – 200,000 Russian lives for the loss of 25,000 Finns. Cowles was a reporter for* The Sunday Times *and* New York Herald Tribune.

Here in the slender waistline of Finland some of the fiercest fighting of the war is taking place. During the last two months more than 100,000 Russian troops have crossed the frontier, in this sector alone, in repeated attempts to cut Finland in two.

The Finns have succeeded in repulsing the onslaught with some of the most spectacular fighting in history. They have annihilated entire divisions and hurled back others thirty and forty miles to the border from whence they came. They have done it not by ordinary methods of trench warfare but by desperate guerilla fighting.

To understand how the Finnish soldiers, hopelessly outnumbered, have stemmed the heavy Russian advance, you must picture a country of thick snow-covered forests and ice-bound roads. You must visualize heavily armed ski patrols sliding ghostlike through the woods, cutting their communications until entire battalions are isolated, then falling on them in furious surprise attacks. This is a war in which skis have outmanœuvred tanks, sleds competed with lorries, and knives even challenged rifles.

I have just returned from a trip to a front-line position on the Finnish-Russian frontier, where I saw the patrols at work and had my first taste of Soviet artillery fire. I left the small town which serves as General Headquarters for the north-central front with four English and American correspondents and a young Finnish Army lieutenant.

We started off with the idea of perhaps accompanying one of the Finnish border patrols on a quick jaunt into Russia and back. Not that any of us imagined that the frozen Russian landscape would prove interesting but we all thought it would be fun to step into the Soviet Union without the formality of getting a visa.

We left at four o'clock in the morning, hoping to arrive at the front before dawn, but the roads were so slippery that our car skidded into the ditch three times, which delayed us considerably but gave us a small idea of what the mechanized Russian units are up against. We arrived near the village of Suomussalmi just as dawn was breaking and here I witnessed the most ghastly spectacle I have ever seen.

It was in this sector that the Finns, a little over a month ago, annihilated two Russian divisions of approximately 30,000 men. The road along which we drove was still littered with frozen Russian corpses, and the forests on either side are now known as "Dead Man's Land". Perhaps it was the beauty of the morning that made the terrible Russian débâcle all the more ghastly when we came upon it. The rising sun had drenched the snow-covered forest, and the trees like lace Valentines, with a strange pink light that seemed to glow for miles. The landscape was marred only by the charred framework of a house; then an overturned truck and two battered tanks.

Then we turned a bend in the road and came upon the full horror of the scene. For four miles the road and forests were strewn with the bodies of men and horses; with wrecked tanks, field kitchens, trucks, gun carriages, maps, books and articles of clothing. The corpses were frozen as hard as petrified wood, and the colour of the skin was mahogany. Some of the bodies were piled on top of each other like a heap of rubbish, covered only by a merciful blanket of snow; others were sprawled against the trees in grotesque attitudes.

All were frozen in the positions in which they huddled. I saw one with his hands clasped to a wound in his stomach; another struggling to open the collar of his coat, and a third pathetically clasping a cheap landscape drawing, done in bright childish colours, which had probably been a prized possession that he had tried to save when he fled into the woods.

What these troops must have suffered in the cold is not difficult to imagine. They were wearing only ordinary knitted hoods with steel helmets over them, and none of them had his gloves on. This is accounted for by the fact that the Russians do not wear "trigger-finger" mittens such as the Finns do; they wear only ordinary mittens which they must take off to fire their rifles.

Some miles further we arrived at our destination. A white-clad sentry stepped out of the forest into the roadway and motioned us to stop. The car was backed into a clearing between the trees and as we followed our guide through the twisting paths, the woods suddenly became alive with stalwart Finnish soldiers with only their black rifles visible against the snow, moving noiselessly in and out among the trees.

The major's hut was built of logs half underground and covered with snow. The camouflage was so clever that the only indication we had was by the skis stacked up against the trees. We crawled in the shelter, which was furnished with two beds, a long desk covered with maps, and a small stove that kept the temperature at thirty degrees.

The major greeted us warmly and told us breakfast was ready; he motioned us towards a table laden with coffee, bread and butter, reindeer meat, cheese and pickled fish. A few minutes later we were interrupted by the whine of an engine, which broke into a loud roar as a Russian plane passed only a few hundred feet above our heads. The major said the Russian planes patrolled the forests for several hours each day and often did a considerable amount of machine-gunning. "That's what we want," he said. "Planes."

Then he asked us if we thought the outside world would send any to Finland and searched our faces eagerly for our replies. "If only," he murmured, "it were possible for some kind old ladies to knit us some aeroplanes and crochet us some anti-tank guns. We should be very happy."

When we asked him if there was any possibility of our sneaking across the frontier into Russia he smiled and said he would send us up to the observation post, where we could have a look at the situation, and if we still wanted to go, it was ours for the asking. He then detailed a captain to look after us.

The captain's hut was some distance away; it was made of beaver-board built around the trunk of a tree so that the smoke from the stove would be diffused by the thick branches. The captain was a gay fellow who showed us with great relish the huge Russian samovar that he had captured in the Suomussalmi battle. He also had a pair of field glasses he had taken from a Russian officer, but his most prized possession was a machine-gun from a Russian tank. He said that every time a plane went by he took a pot shot at it, adding that it wasn't exactly his business but with the gun so handy it was difficult to resist.

The captain led us through the woods to the observation post. It was some distance away and we were accompanied by a ski patrol of eight men equipped with rifles and wicked-looking machine pistols. They slipped in and out through the trees like ghosts, managing their skis with astonishing agility. One moment they slipped behind the trees and we thought they were lost; a few seconds later they were on the path in front of us.

The observation post consisted merely of a shallow pit dug in the snow; in it there was an observer with a pair of field glasses and a telephone. But we did not need glasses to see the Soviet Union. Only three hundred yards away across an icebound lake, lay the frozen landscape of Russia.

We had been in the pit only a few minutes when the Finnish soldiers in our rear opened up artillery fire. A fountain of ice and snow shot up as several shells fell in the lake. The observation officer corrected the range and soon they were disappearing neatly into the trees on the other side. The Russians were not slow to reply, and a few minutes later the air resounded to the nasty whine of three-inch shells, and the pine trees were singing with the moan of grenades and the dull thud of mortars.

Twice, tree branches chipped by grenades fell down on us, and when two shells landed uncomfortably close, wounding two Finnish soldiers, the captain declared we had better go back to the hut.

Before we left he gave us a cup of tea. While we were drinking it a husky Finnish soldier crawled into the shelter. His cheeks were red with the cold but his blue eyes shone with excitement. He had just come in from a five-hour patrol behind the Russian lines and had penetrated as far back as three miles. He took out a map and explained to the captain the various changes in the enemy positions.

We learned that the boy was a farmer in ordinary life, but had distinguished himself as one of the bravest men in the patrol. The captain said that during the Suomussalmi battle he had destroyed a tank by jumping on top of it, prising the lid open with a crow-bar, and throwing a hand grenade inside.

When the boy departed another Finnish soldier came into the hut to say that a Russian patrol of two hundred men was heading toward the Finnish lines. The captain ordered him to start with a detachment and meet them on the way.

We could see that things were going to be pretty busy soon, so we decided that it was best to leave. Outside the hut a group of soldiers were already strapping on their rifles and adjusting their skis. When we shook hands with the captain he said: "Well, what about Russia? If you want to join the patrol just starting out, you have my permission."

We thanked him very much, but I for one said I was quite happy where I was.

## NORWAY: GERMAN PARATROOPS MARCH INTO OSLO, 9 APRIL 1940

### Leland Stowe

*The "Phoney War" or "Sitzkrieg" came to an abrupt end on the morning of 9 April 1940 when Germany launched a full-scale invasion of neutral Norway, principally to gain control of the iron-ore port of Kiruna and secure Atlantic bases for her U-boats. Overwhelmed, the Norwegian government requested military aid from Britain and France. Between 18 and 23 April 12,000 Allied troops were put ashore. The German navy suffered a sharp defeat at Narvik, losing ten destroyers to the Royal Navy and a large part of its invasion force, the survivors making a fighting retreat to the Swedish border under General Dietl. Elsewhere, German invasion troops, landing by sea and air, were almost entirely successful, helped in part by Norwegian pro-Nazis fifth columnists. The campaign in Norway was brought to a premature end in May when the Allies withdrew their troops through Narvik to stem the* Wehrmacht's *Blitzkrieg in France.*

At three minutes after three the rumble of the crowd, far down the boulevard, suddenly warned us that the Germans were coming at last. We saw a thin column, marching three abreast, swing into the Karl Johnsgade at the foot of the Palace hill. Six mounted Norwegian policemen led the way. We would scarcely believe our eyes. They were escorting the Germans in, and here they came. Directly behind the mounted police strode a German general and two other officers. We later learned that the commander was General Nikolaus von Falkenhorst. The German regulars marched behind them – three abreast to make the line look longer – granite-faced and loaded with equipment. Some had machine-guns on their shoulders and others carried rifles, also slung on their shoulders. As they came nearer we saw that virtually every man carried an aluminum kit or some kind of briefcase in his left hand, in addition to heavy knapsacks on the backs of all. Not a single soldier held his gun in his hand ready to use it.

For a victory parade it was extremely short and over very quickly. Less than fifteen hundred German soldiers had occupied Norway's capital while thousands of dazed, bewildered citizens looked dumbly on. Not a bomb had been dropped inside Oslo. Not a shot was fired. Not a hand or a voice had been lifted – and not a single Nazi soldier had yet reached this captured city by ship. This handful of troops had arrived by air, since daybreak that morning. They had only small weapons – but absolutely incredible discipline and nerve. They were an amazingly tiny band of men, but they marched in like conquerors. They were.

## NORWAY: THE ROUT OF THE BRITISH EXPEDITIONARY FORCE, 14 APRIL–5 MAY 1940

### General Sir Adrian Carton de Wiart

Shortly after the Germans made their first landing in Norway, we responded by a gallant failure at Narvik. In the middle of one night there was a telephone message for me to report to the War Office. It dawned on me the reason might be Norway, especially as I had never been there and knew nothing about it. Norway it was, and I was ordered to go there immediately to take command of the Central Norwegian Expeditionary Force. Unfortunately I was not to take my own division, the 61st, for the Force was to consist of a brigade and some odd troops sent from Northern Command, together with a French force composed of Chasseurs Alpins under General Audet. These troops were to proceed to Namsos.

Having got my orders, I collected my kit and flew up to Scotland the next day, 13 April. We were to fly across to Norway the same night but were delayed by a blizzard, and took off next morning in a Sunderland.

The Norwegian coastline was lovely to look at, with the majesty of its rough mountains covered in snow, but from a fighting angle the view had no attraction for me, as obviously in this type of country one would need very specialized troops.

We reached Namsos in the evening and started to disembark troops at once. It was soon evident that the officers had little experience in handling men, although they had a first-class commander in Brigadier G.P. Phillips.

In Norway, at that time of the year, there were only about three hours of darkness, and landing troops with the whole country under snow, and a vigilant and attentive enemy, was no easy matter.

The troops were only too anxious to do what they were told, and to be quick about it, and it says much for them that not only did they succeed in landing, but they completely obliterated all traces of their landing. The Germans who flew over next morning suspected nothing.

My orders were to take Trondheim whenever a naval attack took place. The date was unnamed but I moved my troops up to Verdael and Steinjaer (both near Trondheim), from where I would lose no time in synchronizing with the naval attack when it came.

The following night we had to land French troops – the Chasseurs Alpins under General Audet. Although far better trained than we were, and experienced at looking after themselves, they did not obliterate the traces of their landings. The next morning the Germans saw that troops had been put ashore, and the French made themselves still more noticeable by loosing off their machine-guns at them, which succeeded in making matters much worse. The Germans responded by more and more bombs, and in a matter of hours Namsos was reduced to ashes. The casualties were not heavy, as by that time my troops were all forward, and the French were bivouacked outside the town. I went up to the front with Peter Fleming soon after the bombing started, and by the time we returned there was little of Namsos left.

The French Chasseurs Alpins were a fine body of troops and would have been ideal for the job in hand, but ironically they lacked one or two essentials, which made them completely useless to us. I had wanted to move them forward, but General Audet regretted they had no means of transport, as their mules had not turned up. Then I suggested that his ski-troops might move forward, but it was found that they were lacking some essential strap for their skis, without which they were unable to move. Their other equipment was excellent; each man carried some sixty pounds and managed his load with the utmost ease. They would have been invaluable to us if only I could have used them.

The British troops had been issued with fur coats, special boots and socks to compete with the cold, but if they wore all these things they were scarcely able to move at all and looked like paralyzed bears.

As far as planes, guns and cars went, I had no trouble at all, for we had none, though we commandeered what cars we could. Landing facilities were conspicuous by their absence, and to make matters worse we were being supplied by ships larger than the harbour could take. How the sailors got them in and out of these harbours remains a mystery never to be understood by a mere landsman.

The Hun bombers destroyed our small landing-stage. They had the time of their lives with no opposition whatsoever. Some of the ships carried AA guns, and a few days before the evacuation I was sent some Bofors guns. The Bofors never actually shot down a Hun plane, but they managed to disconcert them and had a nuisance value, at the same time giving us a fillip at being able to shoot at them.

On one of our more hopeful days an aircraft carrier miraculously cleared the skies of German planes and stayed several hours, but as there were German submarines about it was not able to remain close to the land, and had to go out to sea again where some of the planes could not return to it.

My headquarters in Namsos was one of the few houses to escape destruction, but after the bombardment I moved out to a small farm on the south side of the River Namsen, where we were not bothered much by the enemy, and it was easier for me to get to the front-line troops.

Two or three days after we had occupied Steinjaer and Verdael, about forty or fifty miles south of Namsos, the German Navy gained its one and only victory of the war, for their destroyers came up Trondheim Fjord and shelled my troops out of these two places. We had rifles, a few Bren guns and some 2-inch smoke bombs, but none of them were either comforting or effective against a destroyer.

The troops at Verdael had a particularly bad time. The road ran through the town on the shore of the fjord in full view of the ships, and the troops had to take to the snow-covered hills, ploughing through unknown country in eighteen inches of snow, only to be attacked by German ski-troops. There is no doubt that not many of them would have survived had it not been for the handling of the situation by Brigadier Phillips.

We retired to positions north of Steinjaer and out of reach of the German naval guns, where we were able to hold on. Steinjaer was being heavily bombed and shelled, and it was not surprising that the population in these small towns lived in deadly terror of our arrival. Our intentions were excellent, but our ideas of ultimate deliverance invariably brought the whole concentrated weight of bombing on top of the heads of the population. At the time I felt irritated by their lack of interest in us, but afterwards I realized that, unused as they were to the horror of war, they were stunned by the invasion, and had not had time to come round.

Still I waited for news of our naval attack which was to be my signal to take Trondheim, but still it did not come. Hourly it became more and more obvious to me that with my lack of equipment I was quite incapable of advancing on Trondheim, and could see very little point in remaining in that part of Norway sitting out like rabbits in the snow. I wired the War Office to tell them my conclusions, only to get back the reply that for political reasons they would be glad if I would maintain my positions. I agreed, but said that it was about all I could do. They were so relieved that they actually wired me their thanks.

Now that my chances of taking Trondheim had gone, I sent Peter Fleming to the War Office to find out their future plans. He came back after a couple of days and told me that plans and ideas about Norway were somewhat confused, and adding, "You can really do what you like, for they don't know what they want done."

About this time a complete staff turned up, but I was not very pleased to see them. They took up a lot of unavailable space, there was not much for them to do, and Peter Fleming and Martin Lindsay had more than fulfilled my requirements. We had already been given one most useful addition – Major R. Delacombe – and I felt that soon we would be all staff and no war.

During these last few days I was offered more men. Lack of accommodation and the fact that my only line of communication was a single road and a small railway line functioning spasmodically forced me to refuse them. They were the type of troops that I should have been delighted to have under me, for they were Poles and the French Foreign Legion, but if I had accepted them it would have made evacuation still more difficult.

Several staff officers were sent over in the role of liaison officers, but I don't think they cared much about the job, for they seemed very intent on departing as soon as they could. One of them was particularly amusing: he was so anxious that his plane should not go off without him that he thought he would like to go and sit quite near it in a sloop which was in the fjord. A Hun promptly dropped a bomb on the sloop and sank it, but the gallant officer was not drowned and made a safe return to England, where his report must have been illuminating.

My farmhouse headquarters provided us with some amusement and excitement from the air. My new staff had not seen these air antics played by the Hun, and were startled one day when a German plane came down the road, flying very low and machine-gunning us. It is a most unnerving and unpleasant sensation to be peppered at from a plane bearing straight down on one, and takes a lot of getting used to.

Just as we had settled to an uneventful routine with my troops in their new positions, wires started to flash to and from the War Office. First to evacuate, then to hold on, then to evacuate, then suddenly it was suggested that I should retire on Mosjoen, about a hundred miles to the north of Namsos. I knew the road to be covered in deep snow and impassable for infantry, and I could see no point in the move and wired the War Office to that effect. Meanwhile I sent Peter Fleming and Martin Lindsay to reconnoitre the route in a car, and they took twelve hours to cover forty miles.

I believe the War Office considered me very unenterprising for opposing their suggestion, but I felt at that moment the move only looked feasible on a map.

More orders came to evacuate, and this time I started to set about it. General Audet came to see me and begged me not to leave his troops until the last when the hour came to embark. He seemed much moved, and on my assuring him that not a single British soldier would be embarked until every Frenchman was on board ship, I had a narrow escape from being embraced and was told that I was *un vrai gentleman*.

Gradually we retired towards Namsos, where we were to embark. The evacuation was to take place on two consecutive nights. I intended sending the French troops off the first night, and they had all gone down at dusk to be ready to embark. We waited – no ships turned up. There was no word from the Navy, and I must admit to feeling anxious. Just before dawn I had to move the troops up into their positions again, leaving them, depressed and disappointed, to await another night.

I was getting more and more anxious as Mr. Neville Chamberlain had told the House of Commons that General Paget's force had been evacuated from Andalsnes, which left me the only unenvied pebble on the beach. Alone against the might of Germany.

In the course of that last endless day I got a message from the Navy to say that they would evacuate the whole of my force that night. I thought it was impossible, but learned a few hours later that the Navy do not know the word.

Apparently there was a dense sea mist quite unsuspected by us on shore, and this had prevented their coming in the night before, but Lord Mountbatten managed to feel his way into the harbour, and the other ships followed him in. It was a tremendous undertaking to embark that whole force in a night of three short hours, but the Navy did it and earned my undying gratitude.

As day was breaking the Germans spotted us leaving the fjord and bombed us heavily. We lost the *Afridi* and a French destroyer and I lost my chance of being sunk. Having known the *Afridi* so well I asked to go on board, but had been told she was not coming in that night. When I found that she had come in after all I asked again to go in her, only to be told that my kit had been put on the *York* and it would be best for me to go in her instead. I did, and missed a very great experience. Unfortunately the wounded from the French destroyer had been put on board the *Afridi* and nearly all of them were drowned.

On my sixtieth birthday, 5 May, we arrived back at Scapa Flow exactly eighteen days after we had set forth. Captain Portal, who commanded the *York*, thought it was a most fitting occasion for a bottle of champagne. He must have known that to me the taste is extra good after a surgical operation or a major disaster.

# THE HOME FRONT: THE PROTECTION OF YOUR HOME AGAINST AIR RAIDS

## *Sir John Anderson*

*A Home Office pamphlet, 1940.*

If air raids ever come to this country . . . do not hesitate to ask for advice if you need it. A local Air Raid Precautions organisation has been established in your district and Air Raid Wardens have been appointed to help you. For any help you need, apply to your Warden or to your local Council Offices.

All windows, skylights, glazed doors or other openings in parts of the house where lights are used must be completely screened after dusk so that no light is visible from outside. All lights near an outside door must be screened.

Clear the loft, attic or top floor of all inflammable material – paper, litter, lumber, etc. – to lessen the danger of fire and prevent fire from spreading.

If you live in a large town think whether you can make arrangements for pets to be sent away the moment danger threatens. Animals will help to use up the supply of air in a room. Count two dogs or cats as one person in choosing the size of your refuge room.

Wounded and gas-contaminated casualties who can should walk direct to the nearest First-aid Post. Remove the affected garment, then wash yourself immediately. Stretcher cases will be taken immediately to hospital.

# OPERATION YELLOW: HITLER ADDRESSES HIS TROOPS ON THE EVE OF THE INVASION OF THE LOW COUNTRIES AND FRANCE, 9 MAY 1940

## *Adolf Hitler*

*Hitler ordered a western offensive as early as 27 September 1939, although foot-dragging by elements of the* Wehrmacht's *General Staff postponed, revised, denied* Fall Gelb *(Operation Yellow) until spring 1940. On 9 May Hitler addressed his troops and charged them with the fate of Germany. In the dawn of the next day, 10 May, Hitler sent Army Group B (28 divisions) rolling into Belgium and Holland, while Army Group A (44 divisions) sliced through the Ardennes. Although outnumbered in soldiery, the Germans had a crucial 3 to 1 advantage in tanks and aircraft.*

The hour has come for the decisive battle for the future of the German nation. For three hundred years the rulers of England and France have made it their aim to prevent any real consolidation of Europe and above all to keep Germany weak and helpless. With this your hour has come. The fight which begins today will decide the destiny of the German people for a thousand years. Now do your duty.

## OPERATION YELLOW: THE GERMAN ATTACK ON ROTTERDAM, 10–11 MAY 1940

### *Dirk van der Heide*

*Holland, a neutral country, had the misfortune of being an easy way around Belgium water-obstacles. Possessing only ten divisions, the Dutch – who had not fought a European war in 100 years – had small chance against the Blitzkrieg which befell them. At Rotterdam, Holland's major port, German troops attacked from merchantmen in the harbour and by parachute from the sky. On 13 May with the city almost in their hands, the Germans (perhaps by accident) bombed the city centre flat, killing some 900 civilians. Whatever the reason, two days later Holland capitulated. Dirk van der Heide was a 12-year-old Dutch boy.*

### Rotterdam: Friday, 10 May

Something terrible happened last night. War began!!! Uncle Pieter was right. The city has been bombed all day. . . . At first most people thought the noise was only practice. All the time people kept running outside and coming back with news. It was war all right and the radio was giving the alarm and calling all the time for all men in the reserves to report for duty at the nearest place. The radio said this over and over. It was very exciting. The bombing kept on all the time, boom-boom-boom, and everyone said they were falling on Waalhaven, the air-port, which is only about five miles away. The Baron went upstairs and began telephoning. The voices on the radio sounded strange and terribly excited. Father put Keetje into Mother's arms and went away. A few minutes later he came back dressed and carrying a gas mask and a knapsack. He kissed Mother and Keetje and me very hard and then hurried out. He shouted something about taking care of his animals and Mother nodded and told him to be careful, please.

### Saturday, 11 May

Soldiers are patrolling our little street, just going up and down which is patrolling. There are some soldiers on the housetops farther away. A few people have tin or steel helmets like the soldiers but I wore a kettle over my head and so did many other people. We do this to keep from getting hit by shrapnel from the anti-aircraft guns and machine-guns.

People look funny going around wearing kettles and pots over their heads and Keetje's keeps falling off all the time. The trolley cars have stopped running, to save electricity, the Baron says, and there is no drinking water in any of the houses in our section because the Germans blew up some of the water pipes yesterday. The telephone is not working either and all letters and telegrams have stopped coming. This is because of the traitors and parachutists. The radio says that no one is to go on the streets after 8:30 to-night unless he has the proper papers and not to go anywhere unless it's absolutely necessary. There were seven air raid alarms between nine this morning and supper. The radio says not to depend on sirens for warning because some of the traitors are giving false alarms. Uncle Pieter is furious about this and says he will shoot all traitors on sight and he has an army pistol to do it with too. He carries it inside his coat. There are not so many people here to-night because some of them were called out to fight fires and stand guard and help rescue and dig for people in fallen buildings. I wish I could do more.

This afternoon we saw our first parachutist. We were pasting strips of paper across the Baron's windows – the ones not broken – and across the windows of our own house so they won't break any more when the bombs come. About half of them were broken in all the houses around here yesterday. The parachutist came down at three o'clock. About fifty came down at once. This one was separated from the others. We saw the planes drop them but they seemed far away at first. Keetje was the first to see him because she was not doing much work. Mijnheer van Helst was near Keetje and when he saw the parachutist he called out to the women to go inside and then ran toward the man. The man came down behind the Baron's barn. We saw Mijnheer van Helst take out his pistol and aim and then he fired three times. He came back a moment later looking very sad and said the German was shot. The Baron and several others ran forward to see the German but Brenda kept me from going. Heintje Klaes went and came back and said the German was really dead and he was glad. Mijnheer van Helst didn't look glad and his hands were trembling. He is an old and very kind man and not used to shooting people the way regular soldiers do . . .

The worst air-raid of all has just come. About half the houses on our street are gone. One bomb landed on the lawn by our air-shelter and one side of the shelter is caved in but the Baron and others are repairing it now. Mevrouw Hartog broke down and cried during the air-raid and got everyone very nervous when she yelled. I think she almost went crazy.

Heintje Klaes was killed! He went outside to see the light from the big flares and incendiary bombs and didn't come back. He slipped out. Heintje was not afraid of anything but the bombs got him. The whole house rocked when the bombs came close. We put our fingers in our ears but it didn't help much. The fire engines are working outside now and half the people in the air-shelter including Uncle Pieter have gone out. I went out for a while and they were taking dead people out of the bombed houses. Uncle Pieter sent me back to stay with Keetje. There is a funny smell in the air like burnt meat and a funny yellow light all over the country from the incendiary bombs. Three men were killed trying to get a bomb away that hadn't gone off yet. One of the men was our postmaster and I loved him very much. He gave me my first bicycle ride. It is awful to watch the people standing by their bombed houses. They don't do much. They just walk around and look at them and look sad and tired. I guess there isn't anything else they can do but it seems awful . . .

At the end of our street the water is coming in where the canal locks were hit and I guess it will just keep running over the land until it is fixed. No one does anything about it because there are too many people to be helped and fires to fight. Twelve people on our street were killed and I knew every one of them but I knew Heintje best. Mevrouw Klaes has been crying ever since the bombing. Some people prayed all the time and some sang the national anthem and some just sat and stared. A woman who is very sick with a bad heart looked as if she might die. She was very pale when she came and still is. Jan Klaes is Mevrouw Klaes' other son and he is fighting somewhere like my father is. I said a prayer to myself for Father and I hope God heard it in spite of all the noise. I told Uncle Pieter I had prayed but he didn't say anything, just laid his hand on my shoulder. Uncle Pieter has gone off to the hospital to try to find Mother. It is getting late and he is worried, I think. I know he will find her. Keetje has gone to sleep again but she talks in her sleep and wakes up all the time asking if the war is over and things like that. Poor Keetje, she is so little and doesn't know what is happening. I think I do and it is worse than anything I ever heard about and worse than the worst fight in the cinema. The ambulances coming and going and so many dead people make it hard for me not to cry. I did cry some while the bombing was going on but so many other little children were that no one noticed me, I think. I just got into bed with Keetje and hid my face. I was really frightened this time.

Later:

Uncle Pieter came back. He didn't find Mother because she is dead. I can't believe it but Uncle Pieter wouldn't lie. We aren't going to tell Keetje yet. The ambulances are still screaming. I can't sleep or write any more now or anything.

# OPERATION YELLOW: CROSSING THE MEUSE, FRANCE, 13 MAY 1940

## *Erwin Rommel, 7th Panzer Division*

*The masterstroke of* Fall Gelb *was its by-passing of France's 87-mile-long Maginot Line (a concrete "Western Front"); the Germans simply came round its top, through Belgium and Holland. The* Schwerpunkt *of the German onslaught was in the forests of the Ardennes, assumed impassable to tanks. No less than 1,800* Wehrmacht *panzers filed through its thickets and woodland. There was some hope that the River Meuse would contain the juggernaut; this was rudely shattered by General Erwin Rommel of the 7th Panzer Division. His opponents, the French 2nd and 9th Armies, were typical of France's lack of modern equipment; they had not an anti-tank gun between them.*

On 13 May, I drove off to Dinant at about 04.00 hours with Captain Schraepler. The whole of the divisional artillery was already in position as ordered, with its forward observers stationed at the crossing points. In Dinant I found only a few men of the 7th Rifle Regiment. Shells were dropping in the town from French artillery west of the Meuse, and there were a number of knocked-out tanks in the streets leading down to the river. The noise of battle could be heard from the Meuse valley.

There was no hope of getting my command and signals vehicle down the steep slope to the Meuse unobserved, so Schraepler and I clambered down on foot through the wood to the valley bottom. The 6th Rifle Regiment was about to cross to the other bank in rubber boats, but was being badly held up by heavy artillery fire and by the extremely troublesome small arms fire of French troops installed among the rocks on the west bank.

The situation when I arrived was none too pleasant. Our boats were being destroyed one after the other by the French flanking fire, and the crossing eventually came to a standstill. The enemy infantry were so well concealed that they were impossible to locate even after a long search through glasses. Again and again they directed their fire into the area in which I and my companions – the commanders of the Rifle Brigade and the Engineer Battalion – were lying. A smoke screen in the Meuse valley would have prevented these infantry doing much harm. But we had no smoke unit. So I now gave orders for a number of houses in the valley to be set alight in order to supply the smoke we lacked.

Minute by minute the enemy fire grew more unpleasant. From up river a damaged rubber boat came drifting down to us with a badly wounded man clinging to it, shouting and screaming for help – the poor fellow was near to drowning. But there was no help for him here, the enemy fire was too heavy.

Meanwhile the village of Grange [$1\frac{1}{4}$ miles west of Houx (and the Meuse), and 3 miles north-west of Dinant] on the west bank had been taken by the 7th Motor-cycle Battalion, but they had not cleaned up the river bank as thoroughly as they should have done. I therefore gave orders for the rocks on the west bank to be cleared of the enemy.

With Captain Schraepler, I now drove south down the Meuse valley road in a Panzer IV to see how things were going with the 7th Rifle Regiment. On the way we came under fire several times from the western bank and Schraepler was wounded in the arm from a number of shell splinters. Single French infantrymen surrendered as we approached.

By the time we arrived the 7th Rifle Regiment had already succeeded in getting a company across to the west bank, but the enemy fire had then become so heavy that their crossing equipment had been shot to pieces and the crossing had had to be halted. Large numbers of wounded were receiving treatment in a house close beside the demolished bridge. As at the northern crossing point, there was nothing to be seen of the enemy who were preventing the crossing. As there was clearly no hope of getting any more men across at this point without powerful artillery and tank support to deal with the enemy nests, I drove back to Division Headquarters, where I met the Army commander, Colonel-General von Kluge and the Corps commander, General Hoth.

After talking over the situation with Major Heidkaemper and making the necessary arrangements, I drove back along the Meuse to Leffé [a village on the outskirts of Dinant] to get the crossing moving there. I had already given orders for several Panzer IIIs and IVs and a troop of artillery to be at my disposal at the crossing point. We left the signals vehicle for the time being at a point some 500 yards east of the river and went forward on foot through deserted farms towards the Meuse. In Leffé we found a number of rubber boats, all more or less badly damaged by enemy fire, lying in the street where our men had left them. Eventually, after being bombed on the way by our own aircraft, we arrived at the river.

At Leffé weir we took a quick look at the footbridge, which had been barred by the enemy with a spiked steel plate. The firing in the Meuse valley had ceased for the moment and we moved off to the right through some houses to the crossing point proper. The crossing had now come to a complete standstill, with the officers badly shaken by the casualties which their men had suffered. On the opposite bank we could see several men of the company which was already across, among them many wounded. Numerous damaged boats and rubber dinghies lay on the opposite bank. The officers reported that nobody dared show himself outside cover, as the enemy opened fire immediately on anyone they spotted.

Several of our tanks and heavy weapons were in position on the embankment east of the houses, but had seemingly already fired off almost all their ammunition. However, the tanks I had ordered to the crossing point soon arrived, to be followed shortly afterwards by two field howitzers from the Battalion Grasemann.

All points on the western bank likely to hold enemy riflemen were now brought under fire, and soon the aimed fire of all weapons was pouring into rocks and buildings. Lieutenant Hanke knocked out a pill-box on the bridge ramp with several rounds. The tanks, with turrets traversed left, drove slowly north at fifty yards' spacing along the Meuse valley, closely watching the opposite slopes.

Under cover of this fire the crossing slowly got going again, and a cable ferry using several large pontoons was started. Rubber boats paddled backwards and forwards and brought back the wounded from the west bank. One man who fell out of his boat on the way grabbed hold of the ferry rope and was dragged underwater through the Meuse. He was rescued by Private Heidenreich, who dived in and brought him to the bank.

I now took over personal command of the 2nd Battalion of the 7th Rifle Regiment and for some time directed operations myself.

With Lieutenant Most I crossed the Meuse in one of the first boats and at once joined the company which had been across since early morning. From the company command post we could see Companies Enkefort and Lichter were making rapid progress.

I then moved up north along a deep gully to the Company Enkefort. As we arrived an alarm came in: "Enemy tanks in front". The company had no anti-tank weapons, and I therefore gave orders for small arms fire to be opened on the tanks as quickly as possible, whereupon we saw them pull back into a hollow about 1,000 yards north-west of Leffé. Large numbers of French stragglers came through the bushes and slowly laid down their arms.

## CHURCHILL OFFERS "BLOOD, TOIL, TEARS AND SWEAT", HOUSE OF COMMONS, 13 MAY 1940

### *Winston Churchill*

*The text of Churchill's first speech to the Commons as Prime Minister, having replaced the discredited Chamberlain.*

On Friday evening last I received His Majesty's Commission to form a new Administration. It was the evident wish and will of Parliament and the nation that this should be conceived on the broadest possible basis and that it should include all parties, both those who supported the late Government and also the parties of the Opposition. I have completed the most important part of this task. A War Cabinet has been formed of five Members, representing, with the Opposition Liberals, the unity of the nation. The three party Leaders have agreed to serve, either in the War Cabinet or in high executive office. The three Fighting Services have been filled. It was necessary that this should be done in one single day, on account of the extreme urgency and rigour of events. A number of other positions, key positions, were filled yesterday, and I am submitting a further list to His Majesty to-night. I hope to complete the appointment of the principal Ministers during tomorrow. The appointment of the other Ministers usually takes a little longer, but I trust that, when Parliament meets again, this part of my task will be completed, and that the administration will be complete in all respects.

I considered it in the public interest to suggest that the House should be summoned to meet to-day. Mr. Speaker agreed, and took the necessary steps, in accordance with the powers conferred upon him by the Resolution of the House. At the end of the proceedings to-day, the Adjournment of the House will be proposed until Tuesday, 21st May, with, of course, provision for earlier meeting, if need be. The business to be considered during that week will be notified to Members at the earliest opportunity. I now invite the House, by the Resolution which stands in my name, to record its approval of the steps taken and to declare its confidence in the new Government.

To form an Administration of this scale and complexity is a serious undertaking in itself, but it must be remembered that we are in the preliminary stage of one of the greatest battles in history, that we are in action at many other points in Norway and in Holland, that we have to be prepared in the Mediterranean, that the air battle is continuous and that many preparations, such as have been indicated by my honourable Friend below the Gangway, have to be made here at home. In this crisis I hope I may be pardoned if I do not address the House at any length to-day. I hope that any of my friends and colleagues, or former colleagues, who are affected by the political reconstruction, will make allowance, all allowance, for any lack of ceremony with which it has been necessary to act. I would say to the House, as I said to those who have joined this Government: "I have nothing to offer but blood, toil, tears and sweat."

We have before us an ordeal of the most grievous kind. We have before us many, many long months of struggle and of suffering. You ask, what is our policy? I will say: It is to wage war, by sea, land and air, with all our might and with all the strength that God can give us; to wage war against a monstrous tyranny, never surpassed in the dark, lamentable catalogue of human crime. That is our policy. You ask what is our aim? I can answer in one word: It is victory, victory at all costs, victory in spite of all terror, victory, however long and hard the road may be: for without victory, there is no survival. Let that be realised; no survival for the British Empire, no survival for all that the British Empire has stood for, no survival for the urge and impulse of the ages, that mankind will move forward towards its goal. But I take up my task with buoyancy and hope. I feel sure that our cause will not be suffered to fail among men. At this time I feel entitled to claim the aid of all, and I say, "Come then, let us go forward together with our united strength."

## THE BATTLE OF FRANCE: 7TH PANZER DIVISION BREAK OUT, 15 MAY 1940

### General Erwin Rommel, GOC 7th Panzer Division

The way to the west was now open. The moon was up and for the time being we could expect no real darkness. I had already given orders, in the plan for the break-through, for the leading tanks to scatter the road and verges with machine and anti-tank gunfire at intervals during the drive to Avesnes, which I hoped would prevent the enemy from laying mines. The rest of the Panzer Regiment was to follow close behind the leading tanks and be ready at any time to fire salvoes to either flank. The mass of the division had instructions to follow up the Panzer Regiment lorry-borne.

The tanks now rolled in a long column through the line of fortifications and on towards the first houses, which had been set alight by our fire. In the moon-light we could see the men of 7th Motor-cycle Battalion moving forward on foot beside us. Occasionally an enemy machine-gun or anti-tank gun fired, but none of their shots came anywhere near us. Our artillery was dropping heavy harassing fire on villages and the road far ahead of the regiment. Gradually the speed increased. Before long we were five hundred – a thousand – two thousand – three thousand yards into the fortified zone. Engines roared, tank tracks clanked and clattered. Whether or not the enemy was firing was impossible to tell in the ear-splitting noise. We crossed the railway line a mile or so south-west of Solre le Château, and then swung north to the main road which was soon reached. Then off along the road and past the first houses.

The people in the houses were rudely awaken by the din of our tanks, the clatter and roar of tracks and engines. Troops lay bivouacked beside the road, military vehicles stood parked in farmyards and in some places on the road itself. Civilians and French troops, their faces distorted with terror, lay huddled in the ditches, alongside hedges and in every hollow beside the road. We passed refugee columns, the carts abandoned by their owners, who had fled in panic into the fields. On we went, at a steady speed, towards our objective. Every so often a quick glance at the map by a shaded light and a short wireless message to Divisional H.Q. to report the position and thus the success of the 25th Panzer Regiment. Every so often to look out of the hatch to assure myself that there was still no resistance and that contact was being maintained to the rear. The flat countryside lay spread out around us under the cold light of the moon. We were through the Maginot line.* It was hardly conceivable. Twenty-two years before we had stood for four and a half long years before this self-same enemy and had won victory after victory and yet finally lost the war. And now we had broken through the renowned Maginot Line and were driving deep into enemy territory. It was not just a beautiful dream. It was reality.

Suddenly there was a flash from a mound about three hundred yards away to the right of the road. There could be no doubt what it was, an enemy gun well concealed in a concrete pill-box, firing on the 25th Panzer Regiment from the flank. More flashes came from other points. Shell bursts could not be seen. Quickly informing Rothenburg of the danger – he was standing close beside me – I gave orders through him for the regiment to increase speed and burst through this second fortified line with broadsides to right and left.

Fire was opened quickly, the tank crews having been instructed in the method of fire before the attack. Much of our ammunition was tracer and the regiment drove on through the new defence line spraying an immense rain of fire into the country on either side. Soon we were through the danger area, without serious casualties. But it was not now easy to get the fire stopped and we drove through the villages of Sars Poteries and Beugnies with guns blazing. Enemy confusion was complete. Military vehicles, tanks, artillery and refugee carts packed high with belongings blocked part of the road and had to be pushed unceremoniously to the side. All around were French troops lying flat on the ground, and farms everywhere were jammed tight with guns, tanks and other military vehicles. Progress towards Avesnes now became slow. At last we succeeded in getting the firing stopped. We drove through Semousies. Always the same picture, troops and civilians in wild flight down both sides of the road.

* Rommel was mistaken; 7th Panzer had broken through an extension to the Maginot Line, which lay to the south.

*A week later, 7 p.m. on 20 May, the panzers of German Army Group A reached the mouth of the Seine at Abbeville, cutting the Allied army in half. The panzers would have reached the Channel sooner had a nervous Hitler not ordered a two-day halt. It was a poor strategic decision; the stop order enabled the encircled British Expeditionary Force to beat a retreat to the coast at Dunkirk from where it would be evacuated.*

## THE BATTLE OF FRANCE: A BRITISH SOLDIER'S DIARY, 15–21 MAY 1940

### *Sergeant L.D. Pexton*

*Pexton was a member of the 13-division-strong British Expeditionary Force (BEF) sent to France to counter German invasion.*

*Diary 15 May 1940.* [Cambrai, Northern France] Stood to at 3.30 a.m. Very quiet up to 4.15. German spotting plane came over pretty low. 6.30 a.m. First taste of bombers. 68 of them all trying to create hell upon earth together. What a day – just about blew us all out the ground. Got shelled all day too. Getting very warm round here now. Don't mind the bombs so much as the planes' machine-guns. They're wicked.

*16 May.* Stood to again at dawn. Quiet. Told they had come through Luxemburg with four armoured divisions, but that they could only last till Sunday with petrol. "*Must* hold them at all costs." Still more shelling. Cambrai must be in a mess by now. Got some more bombs today.

*17 May.* Dawn again. Lovely morning. Can't believe that war is anywhere near. Refugees still pouring out of Cambrai. I am only fifty yards from the main Cambrai–Arras road. Big steel bridge not far from my dug-out. Heard from Coy Commander today that Engineers will blow it up if he gets too near.

*18 May.* Stood to again. Pretty cold this morning. Spotter came over again at 4.30 a.m. Started getting a bit deeper into Mother Earth ready for his mates to come. They came all right. One hundred and seventeen bombers and fighters. Quite sticky while it lasted. The village that was in our rear just isn't now. Fighters began to machine-gun from the main road. What a mess. Be glad when night comes.

*19 May.* 2.45 a.m. Hell of a bang. They have blown the bridge up. He must be advancing again. Shells coming all over the place. Just in front of our position. Hope when he lifts he goes well over our heads.

Lots of dud shells coming. Went to see the bridge at 9.30 a.m.: Lots of dead there – must have gone up with it. Took a chance in between shells and dived in cafe. Got a bottle of Rum and two bottles of Vin Rouge. Didn't stay long. Good job, as cafe went west five minutes later. Direct hit. Shells are giving us some stick now, 12 noon. Afraid we shall have to retire soon. Can't hold tanks with rifles or bren-guns. 4 p.m. We HAVE to hold on till 8 p.m. and then retire. Roll on 8 p.m. It's been hell all day. Air battles have been worth looking at though. Got out at 8 p.m. and marched 6 kilometres and got some lorries. Arrived at small village at 3 a.m.

*20 May.* Slept till 8 a.m. Went out of barn to see what was happening and if possible scrounge some grub. Found that some grub was going on in one of the lorries but had to wait for the next party. Don't know where they are going. Refugees still coming through from somewhere. Saw two men running down the road. Refugees said they were Parachutists. Captain Martin and myself called on them to halt but they didn't. Not immediately. Dropped them. Both dead when we got to them. 10 a.m. Fun began. Germans came from nowhere. Properly surprised us. Got down to it in the open and fought for all we knew how. Getting wiped out this time all right. Got back out of the farm buildings, and he's sending everything he has at us. 11 a.m. Still holding out and there's a bit of a lull. Kid on my right will keep sticking his head up above the clover. He's sure to get his soon, I'm thinking. Can't really remember much about the next hour. Remember the order "Cease fire" and that the time was 12 o'clock. Stood up and put my hands up. My God, how few of us stood up. German officer came and spoke in English. Told to pick up the wounded and carry them to the road. There aren't many that need carrying. We have to leave our dead. Took us off the road into another field. I expected my last moments had come and lit a fag. Everyone expected to be shot there and then. Patched up our wounded as best we could and were taken back about two miles. Stayed the night in a Roman Catholic church. Learned that this village is called Ficheaux. Note: out of appr. 1,400 men only 425 spent the night in this church.

*21 May.* Roused out of it at 6 a.m. and put on road. I'm just beginning to realize that I'm a prisoner. We have had nothing to eat since Sunday and today is Tuesday. My water-bottle is empty now. Hope they give us something to eat soon. Got nothing to eat today.

# DUNKIRK: THE VIEW FROM THE BEACHES, 30 MAY 1940

## *Captain Richard Austin, BEF*

*Encircled, the British Expeditionary Force under the leadership of Lord Gort withdrew to the French coast at Dunkirk where, from 26 May to 3 June, some 340,000 British and French troops were evacuated despite the best attentions of the* Wehrmacht *and* Luftwaffe.

We were now in the region of the dunes, which rose like humps of a deeper darkness. And these in their turn were dotted with the still blacker shapes of abandoned vehicles, half-sunk in the sand, fantastic twisted shapes of burned-out skeletons, and crazy-looking wreckage that had been heaped up in extraordinary piles by the explosions of bombs. All these black shapes were silhouetted against the angry red glare in the sky, which reflected down on us the agony of burning Dunkirk.

Slowly we picked our way between the wreckage, sinking ankle-deep in the loose sand, until we reached the gaunt skeletons of what had once been the houses on the promenade. The whole front was one long continuous line of blazing buildings, a high wall of fire, roaring and darting in tongues of flame, with the smoke pouring upwards and disappearing in the blackness of the sky above the roof-tops. Out seawards the darkness was as thick and smooth as black velvet, except for now and again when the shape of a sunken destroyer or paddle-steamer made a slight thickening on its impenetrable surface. Facing us, the great black wall of the Mole stretched from the beach far out into the sea, the end of it almost invisible to us. The Mole had an astounding, terrifying background of giant flames leaping a hundred feet into the air from blazing oil tanks. At the shore end of the Mole stood an obelisk, and the high-explosive shells burst around it with monotonous regularity.

Along the promenade, in parties of fifty, the remnants of practically all the last regiments were wearily trudging along. There was no singing, and very little talk. Everyone was far too exhausted to waste breath. Occasionally out of the darkness came a sudden shout:

"A Company, Green Howards . . ."

"C Company, East Yorks . . ."

These shouts came either from stragglers trying to find lost units, or guides on the look-out for the parties they were to lead on to the Mole for evacuation.

The tide was out. Over the wide stretch of sand could be dimly discerned little oblong masses of soldiers, moving in platoons and orderly groups down towards the edge of the sea. Now and again you would hear a shout:

"Alf, where are you? . . ."

"Let's hear from you, Bill . . ."

"Over this way, George . . ."

It was none too easy to keep contact with one's friends in the darkness, and amid so many little masses of moving men, all looking very much alike. If you stopped for a few seconds to look behind you, the chances were you attached yourself to some entirely different unit.

From the margin of the sea, at fairly wide intervals three long thin black lines protruded into the water, conveying the effect of low wooden breakwaters. These were lines of men, standing in pairs behind one another far out into the water, waiting in queues till boats arrived to transport them, a score or so at a time, to the steamers and warships that were filling up with the last survivors. The queues stood there, fixed and almost as regular as if ruled. No bunching, no pushing, nothing like the mix-up to be seen at the turnstiles when a crowd is going to a football match. Much more orderly, even than a waiting theatre queue.

About this time, afraid that some of our men might be trailing off, I began shouting, "2004th Field Regiment . . . 2004th Field Regiment . . ." A group of dead and dying soldiers on the path in front of us quickened our desire to quit the promenade. Stepping over the bodies we marched down the slope to a dark beach.

We tacked ourselves on to the rear of the smallest of the three queues, the head of which was already standing in water up to the waist. Half an hour passed. Suddenly a small rowing boat appeared. The head of the queue clambered in and was rowed away into the blackness . . .

Along the entire queue not a word was spoken. The men just stood there silently staring into the darkness, praying that a boat would soon appear, and fearing that it would not. Heads and shoulders only showing above the water. Fixed, immovable, as though chained there. It was, in fact, practically impossible to move, even from one foot to another. The dead-weight of water-logged boots and sodden clothes pinned one down. My breeches seemed to be ballooned out with water as heavy as mercury. I was filled with a dread that when the time did come I should be unable to move.

Suddenly out of the blackness, rather ghostly, swam a white shape which materialised into a ship's lifeboat, towed by a motorboat. It moved towards us and came to a stop twenty yards in front of the head of our queue.

"Hi! Hi!" we all hailed, dreading they hadn't seen us.

"Ahoy! Ahoy!" came the lusty response.

"Come in closer," we shouted.

"We can't. It's unsafe. Might upset the boat." But they risked a few more yards . . .

Four sailors in tin-hats began hoisting the soldiers out of the water. It was no simple task. Half the men were so weary and exhausted that they lacked strength to climb into the boat unaided. The sailors judged the situation perfectly, as being one for rough words, threats, and bullying methods. The only spur sufficient to rouse our worn-out bodies to one last supreme effort.

"Come on you bastards . . ."

"Wake up, blast you . . ."

"Get a move on, Dopey . . ."

The gunwhale of the lifeboat stood three feet above the surface of the water. Reaching up, I could just grasp it with the tips of my fingers. When I tried to haul myself up I couldn't move an inch. The weight of my waterlogged clothes, especially my cherished greatcoat, beat me completely, desperately though I fought. I might have been a sack of lead. A great dread of being left behind seized me.

Two powerful hands reached over the gunwhale and fastened themselves into my arm-pits. Another pair of hands stretched down and hooked-on to the belt at the back of my greatcoat. Before I had time to realise it I was pulled up and pitched head-first into the bottom of the boat.

"Come on, you b—. Get up and help the others in," shouted a sailor, as I hit the planks with a gasp. It was rough medicine. But the right medicine for the moment.

The moment came when the lifeboat could not hold another soul.

"Carry on, Mr Jolly. Carry on," cried the sailor at our helm to someone in the motor-boat. And we got under weigh, leaving the rest of the queue behind to await the next boat.

## DUNKIRK: THE VIEW FROM THE BOATS, 1 JUNE 1940

### Commander C.H. Lightoller, RNR (Retd)

*The evacuation was carried out by an armada of 222 naval units and 665 civilian craft. These vessels succeeded in bringing back to Britain 224,585 British and 112,546 French and Belgian troops. Among the civilian vessels was the yacht* Sundowner *owned by Commander Lightoller. Lightoller had been in history once before: as the senior surviving officer of the* Titanic.

Half-way across we avoided a floating mine by a narrow margin, but having no firearms of any description – not even a tin-hat – we had to leave its destruction to someone better equipped. A few minutes later we had our first introduction to enemy aircraft, three fighters flying high. Before they could be offensive, a British destroyer – *Worcester*, I think – overhauled us and drove them off. At 2.25 p.m. we sighted and closed the twenty-five-foot motor-cruiser *Westerly*, broken down and badly on fire. As the crew of two (plus three naval ratings she had picked up in Dunkirk) wished to abandon ship – and quickly – I went alongside and took them aboard, giving them the additional pleasure of again facing the hell they had only just left.

We made the fairway buoy to the Roads shortly after the sinking of a French transport with severe loss of life. Steaming slowly through the wreckage we entered the Roads. For some time now we had been subject to sporadic bombing and machine-gun fire, but as the *Sundowner* is exceptionally and extremely quick on the helm, by waiting till the last moment and putting the helm hard over – my son at the wheel – we easily avoided every attack, though sometimes near lifted out of the water.

It had been my intention to go right on to the beaches, where my second son, Second-Lieutenant R.T. Lightoller, had been evacuated some forty-eight hours previously; but those of the *Westerly* informed me that the troops were all away, so I headed up for Dunkirk piers. By now divebombers seemed to be eternally dropping out of the cloud of enemy aircraft overhead. Within half a mile of the pierheads a two-funnelled grey-painted transport had overhauled and was just passing us to port when two salvoes were dropped in quick succession right along her port side. For a few moments she was hid in smoke and I certainly thought they had got her. Then she reappeared, still gaily heading for the piers and entered just ahead of us.

The difficulty of taking troops on board from the quay high above us was obvious, so I went alongside a destroyer (*Worcester* again, I think) where they were already embarking. I got hold of her captain and told him I could take about a hundred (though the most I had ever had on board was twenty-one). He, after consultation with the military C.O., told me to carry on and get the troops aboard. I may say here that before leaving Cubitt's Yacht Basin, we had worked all night stripping her down of everything movable, masts included, that would tend to lighten her and make for more room.

My son, as previously arranged, was to pack the men in and use every available inch of space – which I'll say he carried out to some purpose. On deck I detailed a naval rating to tally the troops aboard. At fifty I called below, "How are you getting on?" getting the cheery reply, "Oh, plenty of room yet" At seventy-five my son admitted they were getting pretty tight – all equipment and arms being left on deck.

I now started to pack them on deck, having passed word below for every man to lie down and keep down; the same applied on deck. By the time we had fifty on deck I could feel her getting distinctly tender, so took no more. Actually we had exactly a hundred and thirty on board, including three *Sundowners* and five *Westerlys*.

During the whole embarkation we had quite a lot of attention from enemy planes, but derived an amazing degree of comfort from the fact that the *Worcester*'s A.A. guns kept up an everlasting bark overhead.

Casting off and backing out we entered the Roads again; there it was continuous and unmitigated hell. The troops were just splendid and of their own initiative detailed lookouts ahead, astern, and abeam for inquisitive planes, as my attention was pretty wholly occupied watching the steering and giving orders to Roger at the wheel. Any time an aircraft seemed inclined to try its hand on us, one of the lookouts would just call quietly, "Look out for this bloke, skipper", at the same time pointing. One bomber that had been particularly offensive, itself came under the notice of one of our fighters and suddenly plunged vertically into the sea just about fifty yards astern of us. It was the only time any man ever raised his voice above a conversational tone, but as that big black bomber hit the water they raised an echoing cheer.

My youngest son, Pilot Officer H.B. Lightoller (lost at the outbreak of war in the first raid on Wilhelmshaven), flew a Blenheim and had at different times given me a whole lot of useful information about attack, defence and evasive tactics (at which he was apparently particularly good) and I attribute in a great measure our success in getting across without a single casualty to his unwitting help.

On one occasion an enemy machine came up astern at about a hundred feet with the obvious intention of raking our decks. He was coming down in a gliding dive and I knew that he must elevate some ten to fifteen degrees before his guns would bear. Telling my son "Stand by," I waited till, as near as I could judge, he was just on the point of pulling up, and then "Hard a-port." (She turns 180 degrees in exactly her own length.) This threw his aim completely off. He banked and tried again. Then "Hard a-starboard," with the same result. After a third attempt he gave it up in disgust. Had I had a machine-gun of any sort, he was a sitter – in fact, there were at least three that I am confident we could have accounted for during the trip.

Not the least of our difficulties was contending with the wash of fast craft, such as destroyers and transports. In every instance I had to stop completely, take the way off the ship and head the heavy wash. The M.C. being where it was, to have taken one of these seas on either the quarter or beam would have at once put paid to our otherwise successful cruise. The effect of the consequent plunging on the troops below, in a stinking atmosphere with all ports and skylights closed, can well be imagined. They were literally packed like the proverbial sardines, even one in the bath and another on the WC, so that all the poor devils could do was sit and be sick. Added were the remnants of bully beef and biscuits. So that after discharging our cargo in Ramsgate at ten p.m., there lay before the three of us a nice clearing-up job.

## ONE MAN'S WAR: PRIVATE JACK TOOMEY IN FRANCE, MAY–JUNE 1940

### Private Jack Toomey, 42nd Postal Unit, British Army

*Toomey writes to his cousins, shortly after his evacuation from Dunkirk.*

Dear Folks,

Just a line to let you know that I am still knocking about, had a letter from Mum this morning and was glad to hear that Aunt Edie was a lot better.

Things up here aren't too bad, we are billeted in a British Legion Club – beer downstairs blankets upstairs. An air raid warning twice nightly but such things don't bother us veterans who have been bombed from dawn to dusk nearly every day for three weeks, well, not much anyway.

Would you like to hear all about the War straight from the horses mouth. You wouldn't, good 'cos you are going to.

Before the war started we were enjoying a pleasant tour of France. Landed at Cherbourg, went south to Laval, in Mayeuse, had one or two trips into Le Mans with mails. From there we went N.E. to Evreux, stayed the night then onto Amiens here we stayed a week or so and moved on to the Belgium border at a place called Vervique-Sud on the Lys, to the south-east of Lille, and about ten klms south of Armentiers, we were staying here when the war started, after that we moved so fast and often that I didn't have time to take any notice of names.

Well, it started and after two days and nights of constant "alert" and all clears, we drunk a bottle of rum and another of Cognac biscuit to get some sleep, the air raid siren was in a church tower opposite and about twenty feet from our window. We were determined to sleep somehow. I was still drunk when I woke next day. A day or so later we were in a chateau farmhouse affair when a dog fight developed about a thousand feet above us Messerschmidts, Hurricanes and Spitfires were having a hell of a good time. I don't know who won, I was too busy dodging planes, bullets, and AA. shrapnel. From that day onwards my tin hat stayed on my head – even in bed sometimes. Another day a twin Messerschmidt came in to M.G. an AA post near us only they got him first he hit the dirt at about 300 mph – very little was left of the plane, the pilot and observer was buried by the road with a propblade stuck over them. At another place they flew up and down the street, machine gunning as they went, nice quiet clean fun. At another place, the last before we made the Dunkirk dash, the dive bombers came over and bombed us in the afternoon. Never look a dive-bomber* in the face, Bill, cos if you do you can bet your sweet life things are going to hum soon, but pray and pray hard and run, run like hell for the nearest ditches and dive into them. I got quite used to diving in the end, could make a flat dive from the middle of the road or a power dive from a lorry in one motion. Well, after the bombers had gone and we took stock of the wreckage and found we were all alive, they came back and threw out leaflets for our use.

Then came the order to move and a rumour had it that we were making for Dunkirk. Off we went, about half-a-mile in front of Jerry, after an hour we stopped and everyone went into the ditch, that is, except another bloke and myself who were jammed in the back of the lorry. We could hear M.G. fire and thought it was a quiet shoot up by Jerry planes but when tracer shells started coming through the roof of our lorry, I knew I was wrong. Two shells took a knapsack from the box next to my head and threw it out of the back looking like cotton waste, another went past my ear so close that I felt the wind of it. All the time M.G. bullets were smacking and rickshetting off the struts. I just sat and gave up all hope of coming out of that lorry alive. However I heard a noise of a tank chugging past the lorry and the shooting stopped for us. The bloke driving the tank saw us in the lorry and calmly tossed a hand grenade under the tailboard! After it had gone off and we found we were still alive we came out of that lorry with our hands in the clouds. There are pleasanter ways of committing suicide than fighting five tanks, an armoured wireless car and a plane, with a rifle. Well, they took us prisoners and while we were looking after the wounded the French opened fire and we were between the two fires, so back into the ditch we went. The main body of prisoners were run

---

* The Ju 87 dive-bomber ("Stuka"), an essential instrument of *Blitzkrieg*.

off to a nearby village. We lay in the ditch in a thunderstorm for two hours and then went back to our own lines. So much for my "escape", more of a case of getting left behind. The engine of our wagon was so shot up that it fell out when we pressed the self starter. We managed to get a tow from our Ordance and after ten hours we slung it into the ditch. We had got separated from our crowd and were alone in the middle of the night in France or was it Belgium, anyway we were lost, so we just ambled on until something came along – it did – one of our artillery crowds so we joined the arty for a spell. Then as dawn came up we found the main Dunkirk road and what a jam, after about ten hours of stopping and starting driving into ditches and back into lorries we got near Dunkirk, and here we had to dash thru' a barrage of shrapnel so we slammed the old bus into top and went flat-out down the road. When all was clear and we were on the outskirts of Dunkirk we stopped on a long raised road with the canal on either side and nice big trees sheltering us from the air. We got out and looked up – there were about seventy bombers (German make, naturally, we hadn't seen one of our planes for three weeks!!!) knocking hell out of the docks or what was left of them. From there to the beaches and they were black with troops waiting to go aboard only there were no boats. They gave us a raid that afternoon and evening and the following day they gave us a raid that lasted from dawn till dusk, about 17 hours. The fellows laid down on open beaches with the bombs falling alongside us, lucky it was sand, it killed the effect of the bombs. At the end of the day there were about 8 fellows killed and injured out of about 100,000.

The following day dawn broke and we saw the most welcome sight of all about a dozen destroyers off the beaches and more coming up – boats of all shapes and sizes, barges, Skylarks, life-boats and yachts. Fortunately the day was cloudy and misty, the bombers only came once and as they came low beneath the clouds the Navy let 'em have it. They slung up everything, the guns, I never saw this action, I was scrounging for a drink, we hadn't had water for a fortnight it was too risky to drink and all we could get was champagne and wines. Spirits only made me thirstier. However on this morning I had a drink of vin blanc and had to sit down. I was drunk as a lord, the last time I had anything to eat was about three days off, and on an empty stomach the wine had a devastating effect. That evening we went aboard after making dash after dash up the jetty to dodge shrapnel – Jerry had got close enough for his light artillery to shell us.

We got aboard and started, there were about 800 of us on one small destroyer. The Navy rallied round and dished out cocoa, tins of bully, and loaves of new bread. This was the first grub some of us had for nearly four days and the first bread we had for a fortnight.

When we were about an hour's run off Dover and thought we were safe a bomber came down and slammed three bombs at us – missed us by six feet and put all the lights out downstairs. We got to Dover at 2 am and climbed aboard a train, we were still scared to light cigarettes, a light on the beaches meant a hail of bombs, and we just drowsed, at Reading we got out and shambled to the road outside, it was about 8 am and people just going to work stopped and stared, we must have look a mob, none of us shaved or wash for a week, our uniform was ripped and torn, with blood and oil stains. I had no equipment bar a tin hat and gas mask, a revolver I picked up from somewhere stuck out of my map pocket. One or two old dears took one look at us and burst into tears. I dont blame them, I frightened myself when I looked into a mirror.

They had buses to run us to the barracks, we could just about shuffle to them, we were so done up. At the barracks breakfast was waiting and they apologised because it was tinned salmon and mashed potatoes, we, who had been on half or no rations for nearly three weeks were too busy eating. After grub we slept for a few hours and had dinner, got paid and changed our money to English, changed our uniform for a clean lot, had a shave, shampoo, haircut, and bath and breezed out for a drink of beer. We stayed here for a week and went to Bournemouth to be re-equipped. At Bournemouth, three Spitfires roared overhead one day just above the pier and over the beach. I was on the beach, laying flat on my face before you could say "Scarp". I just couldn't help it. Leaves a self preservation instinct or something.

From there we were sent up to here, nothing much has happened, we work in the P.O. doing much the same as we do in civilian life. They, the army, did try to get us out of it into the country under canvas but we told them we couldn't work without a post office near us so they let us stay.

Thus ends my little bit of the epic of the battle of Northern France and Dunkirk.

The times were rather tough and altho' I was scared stiff for three weeks it was something I wouldn't want to have missed. My only regret was that one of our Rover Scouts was left behind.

Still, c'est la guerre.

Chin, chin,
Love to all,
Jack.

## PARIS FALLS, 14 JUNE 1940

### *Demaree Bess*

*The author was an American war correspondent.*

We watched the Germans, almost literally with their hands in their pockets, walk into Paris. On that warm morning of June fourteenth, they hung the swastika flag on the Eiffel Tower and on the Arc de Triomphe. They made military headquarters of the Hotel Crillon, next door to the American Embassy; and press headquarters of the Hotel Scribe, around the corner from the American Express. They staged their ceremonial review in the Place de la Concorde, where two German planes alighted spectacularly and delivered that morning's Berlin newspapers.

But very few Parisians witnessed the scenes of that historic day. Because the Germans had conquered an almost abandoned city. They had walked into a Paris whose population was less than it ever has been in modern times, into a city where most of the responsible men had run away from their responsibilities. And that is one reason why the Germans came.

It is not yet possible to tell the full story of what occurred in France during those five dramatic weeks between the launching of the German Blitzkrieg and the occupation of Paris. The heavy smoke screen of the French censorship obscured the march of events, hiding what went on not only from the outside world but also from the French people themselves. A score of years from now old men publishing their memoirs will still be giving us additional details.

At this time, we can only report what we personally saw and heard of the Blitzkrieg in Paris. We can tell how doubt and suspicion and fear grew in the minds of the people, as they were deserted by their employers, as they observed politicians resuming their bitter personal quarrels in the hour of France's great danger, and as they heard sinister rumors of incompetence and treachery in the army high command.

During those days we encountered bewildered French junior officers who had been stationed on the front beyond the Meuse River, where the German break-through came. They reported that, instead of attempting to stop this invasion, a general withdrawal order had been issued. They had seen with their own eyes that, during this retreat, vital bridges had not been blown up – and they could not understand why. They knew that a number of French officers on that front had been executed – for reasons which were not clear. And, in spite of the confusion which began to spread from those earliest days, they had seen their friends fighting bravely and going to their death.

It was stories of this sort which began to percolate through Paris before the King of the Belgians surrendered, before the campaign in Flanders ended. It was such reports which distracted the French soldiers, even before the Germans turned their powerful striking force against the army on the Somme. It was these doubts and fears which laid the foundations for the panic which finally engulfed Paris.

The people of Paris were close to panic many times during those weeks. The war communiqués told them that their British allies were being driven across the Channel, that some of the finest troops of France were cut off in Belgium. They recognized that the stand on the Somme was a desperate hope, and that Paris would be one of the first German objectives. But in those days, the government took strong measures to stem the panic, and ordinary people responded courageously. They went about their business as cheerfully as they could, so long as their leaders stood by and directed their affairs. But when this leadership dissolved, Paris lapsed into chaos.

The evacuation panic started on June ninth. That night was black and sultry, uneasy with ominous lights and noises. There was the soft gulping sound of bomb explosions; the sharper barking of anti-aircraft guns; the dull hum of cannon on the all-too-near battlefields. And each sound was accompanied by strange lights; sudden white brilliance each time a bomb exploded; orange-colored flashes each time an anti-aircraft gun released its flame; and always the questing searchlights, sending long thin shafts of radiance, sweeping the skies, hunting for the enemy.

By dawn on Monday, the streets were thick with people. They had been packing their belongings all through that frightening night, and by four o'clock in the morning they were in full flight. Every vehicle with wheels was pressed into service. Some of the automobiles which passed our windows must have come from museums. Long queues stood at the taxi garages; there were two thousand people waiting at the depot nearest our hotel. But most Parisians had no motor vehicles, nor hope of hiring any. They left their homes on foot, pushing baby carriages and laden bicycles, carrying packs on their backs, leading a child by one hand, and clutching a dog or a gas mask with the other.

At twilight on Monday, Paris was blotted out by a blanket of black smoke. Was the wind blowing the cannon fumes from the adjacent battlefields? Was this smoke screen a clever device to protect our city? Or was the French army destroying its oil supply before it fell into German hands? No one knew. The French government itself had evacuated during the day, and no one remained behind to answer the anxious questions of the people.

There were no more guns or bombs the next day, but the pitiful procession of men with bundles and women with bread and babies continued endlessly. Where were they going? Many of them said they were going to their families on farms. Would they be able to reach these ancestral homes? Most unlikely. The trains were loaded beyond capacity and by this time no longer attempted to collect tickets. Reports came back that the roads around Paris were clogged not only with civilian refugees and thirsty cattle but also with wounded soldiers and the advancing German army. Then why were Parisians rushing out into this mad bedlam? Most of them did not know. Sheep without a shepherd, they followed one another, because no one directed them otherwise.

From what was happening in the small hotel which we occupied, we could tell what was happening in private enterprises everywhere in Paris that week. The owner of this hotel, its manager and its chief accountant had all been mobilized when war was declared in September. Although mobilization had thus deprived the organization of most of its brains, the hotel continued to operate during the winter on its inherited energy. Many of the staff had been on the job for years and they continued to function fairly well under the direction of the concierge, a wounded veteran of the last war. The concierge told us, in fact, that the hotel had never enjoyed such a busy winter season. The profits from this season were paid to the aged mother of the owner.

On June tenth, however, the old lady caught the contagion of fear which was infecting Paris. She sought advice from the municipal authorities, but none was to be had. Suddenly, deciding to seek safety in the country, she paid the hotel employees their wages and left them to fend for themselves. Most of the guests of the hotel were also departing, and this decision to close the hotel confirmed the doubts of any who had considered remaining. All joined the stampede southward.

But, as we had decided to remain in Paris, we asked permission to keep our own apartment in this otherwise sealed hotel, and this request was granted. We then recruited a maid and a cook and laid in a little supply of food for ourselves. Several other members of the hotel staff, when they heard that we were staying, begged us to provide work for them also, and we did set two of them to cleaning up the rooms of some of the guests who had departed, leaving their rooms in wildest confusion.

No one remotely guessed what actually did happen. No one foresaw that German troops would come into Paris as peacefully and quietly as they came into Copenhagen or Oslo. No one predicted that Parisians would watch the German entry with the same appearance of bewildered incomprehension the Danes and Norwegians had shown.

We first became aware that Germans were in occupation of the city when Paris fire trucks, manned by Frenchmen, stopped below our hotel on Friday morning and we watched them haul down the four big French flags which encircled the Rond-Point des Champs Elysées. Then they began to tear down posters which urged Frenchmen to buy armament bonds.

We went out then to meet the incoming troops, advancing along the Rue Lafayette, past the Madeleine into the Place de la Concorde. The German high command knew, of course, the conditions which awaited the arrival of their army in Paris. They knew they were coming into an almost empty city. They knew that French gendarmes had been left behind to guard against disorderly incidents.

Nevertheless, it was startling to observe the nonchalance with which those Germans marched through the heart of Paris. They were still at war with France, but they did not even bother to assign guards along the boulevards through which they advanced.

Those first German troops were young and alert and freshly shaved. They had rested during the night in the suburbs and they did not seem tired. To the amazement of Parisians, who had read so much of Germany's mechanized army, those first units were all drawn by horses. We stood at the Madeleine on that sunny morning amid small clusters of Frenchmen and watched the Germans pass. They looked about them with a lively curiosity at the beautiful city which most of them were viewing for the first time. They might have been tourists, out to see the sights, for anything their manner showed. If they felt a sense of exultation, they carefully suppressed demonstrations of triumph. The French people around us watched the procession in silence, bearing themselves with that dignity and sang-froid which their authorities had recommended.

For several days after the occupation the German army authorities simply ignored the population of Paris. The disorganized French civil administration very slowly pulled itself together again. We had curfew at nine o'clock and the blackout continued. And Paris, for the first time since the war began, took on the appearance of a military city. There were continuous troop parades up and down the boulevards, there were military band concerts, there was the incessant roar of planes flying low over the city. We had seen none of these things in Paris during the previous nine months of the war.

On the afternoon of the second day of occupation, as we stood near the American Embassy, the first French prisoners went by in trucks through the Place de la Concorde. The crowds had become larger then, and they surged toward their defeated men. Girls and women ran after them, a few weeping, but most of them shouting encouragement and questions. The Germans did not attempt to hold them back.

Sunday the sixteenth, the third day of the occupation, was a cool sunny day. By this time Paris had become accustomed to the steady roll of army vehicles, carrying German troops and guns and supplies along the boulevards toward the battle lines in the south. We were incapable of astonishment now, even when we saw sight-seeing busses commandeered in Holland and Belgium and Northern France conveying infantrymen to the swiftly shifting front. They looked like some gigantic excursion party, and the eagerness with which the Germans soldiers snatched their brief view of Paris enhanced the illusion.

# FRANCE SURRENDERS, 21 JUNE 1940

## William Shirer, war correspondent

*In early June, the French government evacuated to Tours, before moving to Bordeaux, after a desperate east-west defensive position across the country from the Seine to the Maginot Line failed to stop the* Wehrmacht *moving south. (Paradoxically, the more the French military stared at defeat the harder it fought; at Samur the cadets held the bridges over the Loire until their ammunition ran out.) The trials of France were only added to when Mussolini, anxious for some spoils of war, declared hostilities and moved against the Riviera. With its enemies closing in, the French government pondered indecisively until all direction and will departed it. Only old Marshal Petain had a clear policy: armistice. Accordingly on 16 June the accommodationist Petain – more fearful that disorder would allow the Left into French government than the Nazis – asked France's "adversary" for a cessation of hostilities. The formal surrender came on 21 June in the railroad carriage at Compiègne – where Marshal Foch had dictated terms to the Germans in 1918. William Shirer, the Berlin correspondent of CBS, was there.*

On the exact spot in the little clearing in the Forest of Compiègne where, at five a.m. on 11 November 1918, the armistice which ended the World War was signed, Adolf Hitler today handed *his* armistice terms to France. To make German revenge complete, the meeting of the German and French plenipotentiaries took place in Marshal Foch's private [railway] car, in which Foch laid down the armistice terms to Germany twenty-two years ago. Even the same table in the rickety old *wagon-lit* car was used. And through the windows we saw Hitler occupying the very seat on which Foch had sat at that table when he dictated the other armistice.

The humiliation of France, of the French, was complete. And yet in the preamble to the armistice terms Hitler told the French that he had not chosen this spot at Compiègne out of revenge; merely to right an old wrong. From the demeanour of the French delegates I gathered that they did not appreciate the difference . . .

The armistice negotiations began at three fifteen p.m. A warm June sun beat down on the great elm and pine trees, and cast pleasant shadows on the wooded avenues as Hitler, with the German plenipotentiaries at his side, appeared. He alighted from his car in front of the French monument to Alsace-Lorraine which stands at the end of an avenue about 200 yards from the clearing where the armistice car waited on exactly the same spot it occupied twenty-two years ago.

The Alsace-Lorraine statue, I noted, was covered with German war flags so that you could not see its sculptured work nor read its inscription. But I had seen it some years before – the large sword representing the sword of the Allies, and its point sticking into a large, limp eagle, representing the old Empire of the Kaiser. And the inscription underneath in French saying: "TO THE HEROIC SOLDIERS OF FRANCE . . . DEFENDERS OF THE COUNTRY AND OF RIGHT . . . GLORIOUS LIBERATORS OF ALSACE-LORRAINE."

Through my glasses I saw the Führer stop, glance at the monument, observe the Reich flags with their big swastikas in the centre. Then he strode slowly towards us, towards the little clearing in the woods. I observed his face. It was grave, solemn, yet brimming with revenge. There was also in it, as in his springy step, a note of the triumphant conqueror, the defier of the world. There was something else, difficult to describe, in his expression, a sort of scornful, inner joy at being present at this great reversal of fate – a reversal he himself had wrought.

Now he reaches the little opening in the woods. He pauses and looks slowly around. The clearing is in the form of a circle some 200 yards in diameter and laid out like a park. Cypress trees line it all round – and behind them, the great elms and oaks of the forest. This has been one of France's national shrines for twenty-two years. From a discreet position on the perimeter of the circle we watch.

Hitler pauses, and gazes slowly around. In a group just behind him are the other German plenipotentiaries: Göring, grasping his field-marshal's baton in one hand. He wears the sky-blue uniform of the air force. All the Germans are in uniform, Hitler in a double-breasted grey uniform, with the Iron Cross hanging from his left breast pocket. Next to Göring are the two German army chiefs – General Keitel, chief of the Supreme Command, and General von Brauchitsch, commander-in-chief of the German army. Both are just approaching sixty, but look younger, especially Keitel, who has a dapper appearance with his cap slightly cocked on one side.

Then there is Erich Raeder, Grand Admiral of the German Fleet, in his blue naval uniform and the invariable upturned collar which German naval officers usually wear. There are two non-military men in Hitler's suite – his Foreign Minister, Joachim von Ribbentrop, in the field-grey uniform of the Foreign Office; and Rudolf Hess, Hitler's deputy, in a grey party uniform.

The time is now three eighteen p.m. Hitler's personal flag is run up on a small standard in the centre of the opening.

Also in the centre is a great granite block which stands some three feet above the ground. Hitler, followed by the others, walks slowly over to it, steps up, and reads the inscription engraved in great high letters on that block. It says: "HERE ON THE ELEVENTH OF NOVEMBER 1918 SUCCUMBED THE CRIMINAL PRIDE OF THE GERMAN EMPIRE . . . VANQUISHED BY THE FREE PEOPLES WHICH IT TRIED TO ENSLAVE."

Hitler reads it and Göring reads it. They all read it, standing there in the June sun and the silence. I look for the expression on Hitler's face. I am but fifty yards from him and see him through my glasses as though he were directly in front of me. I have seen that face many times at the great moments of his life. But today! It is afire with scorn, anger, hate, revenge, triumph. He steps off the monument and contrives to make even this gesture a masterpiece of contempt. He glances back at it, contemptuous, angry – angry, you almost feel, because he cannot wipe out the awful, provoking lettering with one sweep of his high Prussian boot. He glances slowly around the clearing, and now, as his eyes meet ours, you grasp the depth of his hatred. But there is triumph there too – revengeful, triumphant hate. Suddenly, as though his face were not giving quite complete expression to his feelings, he throws his whole body into harmony with his mood. He swiftly snaps his hands on his hips, arches his shoulders, plants his feet wide apart. It is a magnificent gesture of defiance, of burning contempt for this place now and all that it has stood for in the twenty-two years since it witnessed the humbling of the German Empire . . .

It is now three twenty-three p.m. and the Germans stride over to the armistice car. For a moment or two they stand in the sunlight outside the car, chatting. Then Hitler steps up into the car, followed by the others. We can see nicely through the car windows. Hitler takes the place occupied by Marshal Foch when the 1918 armistice terms were signed. The others spread themselves around him. Four chairs on the opposite side of the table from Hitler remain empty. The French have not yet appeared. But we do not wait long. Exactly at three thirty p.m. they alight from a car. They have flown up from Bordeaux to a nearby landing field. They too glance at the Alsace-Lorraine memorial but it's a swift glance. Then they walk down the avenue flanked by three German officers. We see them now as they come into the sunlight of the clearing.

General Huntziger, wearing a bleached khaki uniform, Air General Bergeret and Vice-Admiral Le Luc, both in dark blue uniforms, and then, almost buried in the uniforms, M Noël, French Ambassador to Poland. The German guard of honour, drawn up at the entrance to the clearing, snaps to attention for the French as they pass, but it does not present arms.

It is a grave hour in the life of France. The Frenchmen keep their eyes straight ahead. Their faces are solemn, drawn. They are the picture of tragic dignity.

They walk stiffly to the car, where they are met by two German officers, Lieutenant-General Tippelskirch, Quartermaster General, and Colonel Thomas, chief of the Führer's headquarters. The Germans salute. The French salute. The atmosphere is what Europeans call "correct". There are salutes, but no handshakes.

Now we get our picture through the dusty windows of that old *wagon-lit* car. Hitler and the other German leaders rise as the French enter the drawing-room. Hitler gives the Nazi salute, the arm raised. Ribbentrop and Hess do the same. I cannot see M Noël to notice whether he salutes or not.

Hitler, as far as we can see through the windows, does not say a word to the French or to anybody else. He nods to General Keitel at his side. We see General Keitel adjusting his papers. Then he starts to read. He is reading the preamble to the German armistice terms. The French sit there with marble-like faces and listen intently. Hitler and Göring glance at the green table-top.

The reading of the preamble lasts but a few minutes. Hitler, we soon observe, has no intention of remaining very long, of listening to the reading of the armistice terms themselves. At three forty-two p.m., twelve minutes after the French arrive, we see Hitler stand up, salute stiffly, and then stride out of the drawing-room, followed by Göring, Brauchitsch, Raeder, Hess, and Ribbentrop. The French, like figures of stone, remain at the green-topped table. General Keitel remains with them. He starts to read them the detailed conditions of the armistice.

Hitler and his aides stride down the avenue towards the Alsace-Lorraine monument, where their cars are waiting. As they pass the guard of honour, the German band strikes up the two national anthems, *Deutschland, Deutschland über Alles* and the *Horst Wessel* song. The whole ceremony in which Hitler has reached a new pinnacle in his meteoric career and Germany avenged the 1918 defeat is over in a quarter of an hour.

*According to the terms of the armistice, the Petain government (soon to be based at the spa town of Vichy) was to remain sovereign and French colonial possessions stayed under its control. However, Paris, northern France and the Atlantic border became a German zone of occupation. Italy got a 50-kilometre slice of France along their joint border. The cost of the German occupation was to be borne by the French. All prisoners taken in the campaign – two million men – went into captivity. It was humiliation upon humiliation.*

*Not all Frenchmen and women were prepared to accept. Already an obscure general, Charles de Gaulle, had departed France to London to form the "Free French Army". Inside France, a Resistance movement would soon begin.*

## BATTLE OF BRITAIN: A BRITISH FIGHTER PILOT'S DIARY, 19 AUGUST – 7 OCTOBER 1940

### P/O D.H. *Wissler RAF*

*France conquered, Hitler turned to the invasion of Britain. This was predicated upon the defeat of the RAF's Fighter Command, which would thus clear the skies above the Channel for the safe passage of the* Wehrmacht's *invasion barges. Herman Goering, head of the* Luftwaffe, *announced that it would take his fighters, now operating from bases in occupied France, just four days to extirpate Fighter Command. Numerical advantage lay with the* Luftwaffe, *which possessed some 980 fighters against the RAF's 700. But the range of the principal German fighter, the Messerschmitt Bf109, was limited; crucially, it could only protect German bombers for about ten minutes over the main field of battle, the south-east corner of England. In retrospect, the Battle of Britain fell into three main phases: mid-July until 11 August, when the* Luftwaffe *attacked Channel shipping; 12 August until 6 September, when the* Luftwaffe *targeted the RAF and its airfields; then 7 September to 30 October when its offensive effort switched to London. A Hurricane pilot, Wissler fought throughout the battle.*

### Monday, 19 August

I was recalled from leave today . . . The squadron is moving to TANGMERE. I flew "X", which was due for an inspection to Debden. "V", my own plane not ready so I spent the night in a comfortable bed for a change . . .

**Tuesday, 20 August**

I took off from Debden at about 10.15 and flew to Tangmere. I navigated my way ok but being on the coast this wasn't very hard. Tangmere is in a shocking state. The buildings being in an awful shambles, several 1000lb bombs having fallen. We were put to 30 mins at 1, and did nothing for the rest of the day. The dispersal hut is most cozy and puts ours at Debden to shame.

**Wednesday, 21 August**

We did five flying patrols today . . . but the Flight commander only saw one E/A [enemy aircraft] and then only for a second when it was between some clouds. The other section in our flight shot down a Ju88 as did yellow section in "A" flight. After it got dark we were sent up on patrol but having got to 7000 ft over the aerodrome we were recalled.

**Friday, 23 August**

I did not fly at all today, in fact it was very quiet. We were released at 1 p.m. and went up [to London] on train. I went home.

**Saturday, 24 August**

There was an air raid warning in Blackheath and thought I should miss my train. However, we caught it and arrived back ok. In the afternoon we went up on a flight and saw dozens of E/A going out to sea, however did not fire although the CO and P/O Stevens got an Hel 11. We had one very short patrol after this, but nothing was seen.

**Sunday, 25 August**

This was a hard day being at 15 mins and readiness the day long. At about half past seven we had a hell of a scrap over Portland in which 100 a/c were engaged. F/L Bayne made an attack below and astern quarter. The ME110 whipped up in a slow turn and I gave him a long burst while he was in a stalled condition, it fell over and went down. I then went on my own and made an Me111 break formation. I gave it another burst and it went towards the sea. F/L Bayne shot down but ok. F/L Williams lost wing. Shot off.

**Saturday, 31 August**

We did four patrols today ending up with one in which we intercepted about 30 Do. 17s and 20–30 Me. 109s. I got on an Me 109's tail, after an ineffectual attack on the bombers, and got in several long bursts at about 300 yards, however nothing was observed in the way of damage. Another got on my tail and I had to break away. I succeeded in throwing him off in a steep turn but not before he had put explosive bullet through my wing. Sgt Stewart was shot down, but was safe. I lost another tail wheel today.

### Tuesday, 3 September
We did two patrols, in the first intercepted about 100 E/A (Do.215 and Me 110). F/Lt Bayne and I got on an Me 110's tail and firing together sent it down in flames. We then attacked a Do 215, [?] Leary finishing the attack and the bomber crashed in a field just North of the River Crouch. I collected a bullet in the radiator and got covered with glycol, force landing at Castle Camps. Collected a Hurricane off 111 Sqd., flew back to Debden . . . We did one more patrol over the Thames. Then in the night I was aerodrome Control Pilot.

### Saturday, 7 September
I did two types again today, the one in the morning was uneventful, the second at 5.30, on which we used V.H.F. for the first time, we saw four huge enemy formations but as we were only 6 we did not engage. We had one short scrap with Me 109's, but I only had one short burst – with no effect. These raids created a lot of damage in London. The provisional casualty list say 400 dead, 15000 seriously injured: what complete swine these Jerries are.

### Sunday, 8 September
Did not fly today and got afternoon off. Went on 4 days leave. Air raids have messed up London quite a bit.

### Sunday, 15 September
I flew once today but missed the Big Blitz owing to my a/c being unservicable. Nothing was claimed by anyone because there were so many Jerries, over 200 in all. I am at 15 mins readiness tonight, and will be second off, if we have to fly. The RAF claimed 117 e/a destroyed, boy oh boy what a total. We had the station dance band in the mess tonight, and it turned into quite a party. Czernin is now DFC.

### Tuesday, 17 September
We did a couple of patrols today but neither came to anything. I feel very depressed tonight. I don't know why, just a passing mood. Alf Bayne's engine cut taking off, and he had a glorious pile up, completely wrecking the Hurricane but only getting an odd bruise himself.

### Wednesday, 18 September
We did four patrols today of over an hour each. On the first we saw lots of Huns way above us we could not engage, and anyway they were

fighters. Nothing happened on any of the other patrols although there appear to have been lots of e/a about. We tried most unsuccessfully to play a game of snooker in the evening but the lights kept going out: switched out by the Control room when a hun is about, how they flap here!!

**Friday, 20 September**
I went to the Sergeants' Mess this evening for a party and got to know a sweet little W.A.A.F. named Margaret Cameron and we had quite a kissing session after the party was over.

**Tuesday, 24 September**
I had just one (patrol) and one blitz only (8.30). We were attacked by ME 109s and having made our attack on an Me 109 I was making a second . . . when I realized I should let it all go. I levelled off. Suddenly there was a bloody flash on my port wing and I felt a hell of a blow on my left arm, and the blood running down. I went into a hell of a dive and came back to Debden. A cannon shell had hit my wing and a bit of it had hit me just above the elbow and behind. The shell had blown away most of my port flap. So I tried to land without flaps and I could not stop and crashed into a pile of stones just off the field, hitting my face and cutting it in two places. I was taken to Saffron Walden General Hospital, they operated but had to leave small pieces in . . .

**Thursday, 26 September**
Hospital.

**Sunday, 29 September**
Did nothing during the day but there was the usual band in the mess and when they packed up I completed the party at the Sergeants' Mess. Met Edith Heap and fell in love with her at sight. I rather cut Margaret Cameron and I am not as popular as I was!!!

**Monday 7 October**
Returned to Debden, had grand party, and met Edith Heap, my God it seems to be the real thing this time. She is so sweet and seems to like me as much as I like her.

*PO Wissler was posted missing in November 1940.*

# BATTLE OF BRITAIN: DOGFIGHT OVER SOUTH-EAST ENGLAND, 2 SEPTEMBER 1940

## *P/O Roger Hall, 152 Squadron RAF*

We were ready to attack. We were now in the battle area and three-quarters of an hour had elapsed since we had taken off.

The two bomber formations furthest from us were already being attacked by a considerable number of our fighters. Spitfires and Hurricanes appeared to be in equal numbers at the time. Some of the German machines were already falling out of their hitherto ordered ranks and floundering towards the earth. There was a little ack-ack fire coming from up somewhere on the ground although its paucity seemed pathetic and its effect was little more than that of a defiant gesture.

We approached the westernmost bomber formation from the front port quarter, but we were some ten thousand feet higher than they were and we hadn't started to dive yet. Immediately above the bombers were some twin-engined fighters, M.E. 110's. Maida Leader let the formation get a little in front of us then he gave the order "Going down now Maida aircraft," turning his machine upside-down as he gave it. The whole of "A" Flight, one after the other, peeled off after him, upside-down at first and then into a vertical dive.

When they had gone "B" Flight followed suit. Ferdie and I turned over with a hard leftward pressure to the stick to bring the starboard wing up to right angles to the horizon, and some application to the port or bottom rudder pedal to keep the nose from rising. Keeping the controls like this, the starboard wing fell over until it was parallel to the horizon again, but upside-down. Pulling the stick back from this position the nose of my machine fell towards the ground and followed White one in front, now going vertically down on to the bombers almost directly below us. Our speed started to build up immediately. It went from three hundred miles per hour to four and more. White one in front, his tail wheel some distance below me but visible through the upper part of my windscreen, was turning his machine in the vertical plane from one side to the other by the use of his ailerons. Red Section had reached the formation and had formed into a loosened echelon to starboard as they attacked. They were coming straight down on top of the bombers, having gone slap through the protective M.E. 110 fighter screen, ignoring them completely.

Now it was our turn. With one eye on our own machines I slipped out slightly to the right of Ferdie and placed the red dot of my sight firmly in front and in line with the starboard engine of a Dornier vertically below me and about three hundred yards off. I felt apprehensive lest I should collide with our own machines in the mêlée that was to ensue. I seemed to see one move ahead what the positions of our machines would be, and where I should be in relation to them if I wasn't careful. I pressed my trigger and through my inch thick windscreen I saw the tracers spiralling away hitting free air in front of the bomber's engine. I was allowing too much deflection. I must correct. I pushed the stick further forward. My machine was past the vertical and I was feeling the effect of the negative gravity trying to throw me out of the machine, forcing my body up into the perspex hood of the cockpit. My Sutton harness was biting into my shoulders and blood was forcing its way to my head, turning everything red. My tracers were hitting the bomber's engine and bits of metal were beginning to fly off it. I was getting too close to it, much too close. I knew I must pull away but I seemed hypnotised and went still closer, fascinated by what was happening. I was oblivious to everything else. I pulled away just in time to miss hitting the Dornier's starboard wingtip. I turned my machine to the right on ailerons and heaved back on the stick, inflicting a terrific amount of gravity on to the machine. I was pressed down into the cockpit again and a black veil came over my eyes and I could see nothing.

I eased the stick a little to regain my vision and to look for Ferdie. I saw a machine, a single Spitfire, climbing up after a dive about five hundred yards in front of me and flew after it for all I was worth. I was going faster than it was and I soon caught up with it – in fact I overshot it. It was Ferdie all right. I could see the "C" Charlie alongside our squadron letters on his fuselage. I pulled out to one side and back again hurling my machine at the air without any finesse, just to absorb some speed so that Ferdie could catch up with me. "C" Charlie went past me and I thrust my throttle forward lest I should lose him. I got in behind him again and called him up to tell him so. He said: "Keep an eye out behind and don't stop weaving." I acknowledged his message and started to fall back a bit to get some room. Ferdie had turned out to the flank of the enemy formation and had taken a wide sweeping orbit to port, climbing fast as he did so. I threw my aircraft first on to its port wing-tip to pull it round, then fully over to the other tip for another steep turn, and round again and again, blacking out on each turn. We were vulnerable on the climb, intensely so, for we were so slow.

I saw them coming quite suddenly on a left turn; red tracers coming towards us from the centre of a large black twin-engined M.E. 110 which wasn't quite far enough in the sun from us to be totally obscured, though I had to squint to identify it. I shouted to Ferdie but he had already seen the tracers flash past him and had discontinued his port climbing turn and had started to turn over on his back and to dive. I followed, doing the same thing, but the M.E. 110 must have done so too for the tracers were still following us. We dived for about a thousand feet, I should think, and I kept wondering why my machine had not been hit.

Ferdie started to ease his dive a bit. I watched him turn his machine on to its side and stay there for a second, then its nose came up, still on its side, and the whole aircraft seemed to come round in a barrel-roll as if clinging to the inside of some revolving drum. I tried to imitate this manoeuvre but I didn't know how to, so I just thrust open the throttle and aimed my machine in Ferdie's direction and eventually caught him up.

The M.E. 110 had gone off somewhere. I got up to Ferdie and slid once more under the doubtful protection of his tail and told him that I was there. I continued to weave like a pilot inspired, but my inspiration was the result of sheer terror and nothing more.

All the time we were moving towards the bombers; but we moved indirectly by turns, and that was the only way we could move with any degree of immunity now. Four Spitfires flashed past in front of us, they weren't ours, though, for I noticed the markings. There was a lot of talking going on on the ether and we seemed to be on the same frequency as a lot of other squadrons. "Hallo Firefly Yellow Section – 110 behind you" – "Hallo Cushing Control – Knockout Red leader returning to base to refuel." "Close up Knockout 'N' for Nellie and watch for those 109's on your left" – "All right Landsdown Squadron – control answering – your message received – many more bandits coming from the east – over" – "Talker White two where the bloody hell are you?" – "Going down now Sheldrake Squadron – loosen up a bit" – "You clumsy clot – Hurricane 'Y' Yoke – what the flaming hades do you think you are doing?" – "I don't know Blue one but there are some bastards up there on the left – nine o'clock above" – Even the Germans came in intermittently: "Achtung, Achtung – drei Spitfeuer unter, unter Achtung, Spitfeuer, Spitfeuer." "Tally Ho – Tally Ho – Homer Red leader attacking now." "Get off the bastard air Homer leader" – "Yes I can see Rimmer leader – Red two answering – Glycol leak I think – he's getting out – yes he's baled out he's o.k."

And so it went on incessantly, disjointed bits of conversation coming from different units all revealing some private little episode in the great battle of which each story was a small part of the integral whole.

Two 109's were coming up behind the four Spitfires and instinctively I found myself thrusting forward my two-way radio switch to the transmitting position and calling out "Look out those four Spit-fires – 109's behind you – look out." I felt that my message could hardly be of less importance than some that I had heard, but no heed was taken of it. The two 109's had now settled themselves on the tail of the rear Spitfire and were pumping cannon shells into it. We were some way off but Ferdie too saw them and changed direction to starboard, opening up his throttle as we closed. The fourth Spitfire, or "tail end Charlie", had broken away, black smoke pouring from its engine, and the third in line came under fire now from the same 109. We approached the two 109's from above their starboard rear quarter and, taking a long deflection shot from what must have been still out of range, Ferdie opened fire on the leader. The 109 didn't see us for he still continued to fire at number three until it too started to trail Glycol from its radiator and turned over on its back breaking away from the remaining two. "Look out Black one – look out Black Section Apple Squadron – 109's–109's came the belated warning, possibly from number three as he went down. At last number one turned steeply to port, with the two 109's still hanging on to their tails now firing at number two. They were presenting a relatively stationary target to us now for we were directly behind them. Ferdie's bullets were hitting the second 109 now and pieces of its tail unit were coming away and floating past underneath us. The 109 jinked to the starboard. The leading Spitfire followed by its number two had now turned full circle in a very tight turn and as yet it didn't seem that either of them had been hit. The 109 leader was vainly trying to keep into the same turn but couldn't hold it tight enough so I think his bullets were skidding past the starboard of the Spitfires. The rear 109's tail unit disinte-grated under Ferdie's fire and a large chunk of it slithered across the top surface of my starboard wing, denting the panels but making no noise. I put my hand up to my face for a second.

The fuselage of the 109 fell away below us and we came into the leader. I hadn't fired at it yet but now I slipped out to port of Ferdie as the leader turned right steeply and over on to its back to show its duck-egg blue belly to us. I came up almost to line abreast of Ferdie on his port side and fired at the under surface of the German machine, turning upside-down with it. The earth was now above my perspex hood and I was trying to keep my sights on the 109 in this attitude, pushing my stick forward to do so. Pieces of refuse rose up from the floor of my machine and the engine spluttered and coughed as the carburettor became temporarily starved of fuel. My propeller idled helplessly for a second and my harness straps bit into my shoulders again. Flames leapt from the engine of the 109 but at the same time there was a loud bang from somewhere behind me and I heard "Look out Roger" as a large hole appeared near my starboard wing-tip throwing up the matt green metal into a ragged rent to show the naked aluminium beneath.

I broke from the 109 and turned steeply to starboard throwing the stick over to the right and then pulling it back into me and blacking out at once. Easing out I saw three 110's go past my tail in "V" formation but they made no attempt to follow me round. "Hallo Roger – Are you O.K.?" I heard Ferdie calling. "I think so – where are you?" I called back.

"I'm on your tail – keep turning" came Ferdie's reply. Thank God, I thought. Ferdie and I seemed to be alone in the sky. It was often like this. At one moment the air seemed to be full of aircraft and the next there was nothing except you. Ferdie came up in "V" on my port side telling me at the same time that he thought we had better try to find the rest of the squadron.

The battle had gone to the north. We at this moment were somewhere over the western part of Kent, and a little less than a quarter of an hour had elapsed since we had delivered our first attack on the bombers. Ferdie set course to the north where we could see in the distance the main body of aircraft. London with its barrage balloons floating unconcernedly, like a flock of grazing sheep, ten thousand feet above it, was now feeling the full impact of the enemy bombers. Those that had got through – and the majority of them had – were letting their bombs go. I recalled for an instant Mr Baldwin's prophecy, not a sanguine one, made to the House of Commons some five years before when he said that the bomber will always get through.

Now it was doing just that. I wondered if it need have done. As we approached South London the ground beneath us became obscured by smoke from the bomb explosions which appeared suddenly from the most unlikely sort of places – an open field, a house, a row of houses, a factory, railway sidings, all sorts of things. Suddenly there would be a flash, then a cloud of reddish dust obscuring whatever was there before and then drifting away horizontally to reveal once more what was left of the target.

I saw a whole stick of bombs in a straight line advancing like a creeping barrage such as you would see on the films in pictures like "Journey's End" or "All quiet on the Western Front", but this time they were not over the muddy desolation of No-Man's. Land but over Croydon, Surbiton and Earl's Court. I wondered what the people were like who were fighting the Battle of Britain just as surely as we were doing but in a less spectacular fashion. I thought of the air raid wardens shepherding their flocks to the air raid trenches without a thought of their own safety; the Auxiliary Firemen and the regular fire brigades who were clambering about the newly settled rubble strewn with white-hot and flaming girders and charred wood shiny black with heat, to pull out the victims buried beneath; the nurses, both the professional ones and the V.A.D.'s in their scarlet cloaks and immaculate white caps and cuffs, who were also clambering about the shambles to administer first aid to the wounded and give morphine to the badly hurt; the St John Ambulance brigade who always were on the spot somehow no matter where or under what circumstances an accident or emergency occurred, helping, encouraging and uplifting the victims without thought for themselves; the Red Cross and all the civilian volunteers who, when an emergency arises, always go to assist. Not least I thought of the priests and clergy who would also be there, not only to administer the final rites to the dying but to provide an inspiration to those who had lost faith or through shock seemed temporarily lost. The clergy were there all right and showed that their job was not just a once-a-week affair at the Church, but that religion was as much a part of everyday living as was eating and sleeping.

I felt humble when I thought of what was going on down there on the ground. We weren't the only people fighting the Battle of Britain. There were the ordinary people, besides these I've mentioned, all going about their jobs quietly yet heroically and without any fuss or complaint. They had no mention in the press or news bulletins, their jobs were routine and hum-drum and they got no medals.

We were now in the battle area once again and the fighting had increased its tempo. The British fighters were becoming more audacious, had abandoned any restraint that they might have had at the outset, and were allowing the bombers no respite at all. If they weren't able to prevent them from reaching their target they were trying desperately to prevent them from getting back to their bases in Northern France. The air was full of machines, the fighters, British and German, performing the most fantastic and incredibly beautiful evolutions. Dark oily brown streams of smoke and fire hung vertically in the sky from each floundering aircraft, friend or foe, as it plunged to its own funeral pyre miles below on the English countryside. The sky, high up aloft, was an integrated medley of white tracery, delicately woven and interwoven by the fighters as they searched for their opponents. White puffs of ack-ack fire hung limply in mid-air and parachute canopies drifted slowly towards the ground.

It was an English summer's evening. It was about a quarter to six. We had been in the air now for about an hour and a quarter and our fuel would not last much longer. We had failed to join up with the rest of the flight, but this was understandable and almost inevitable under the circumstances. I don't suppose the others were in any formation other than sections now.

Beneath us at about sixteen thousand feet, while we were at twenty-three, there were four Dorniers by themselves still going north and I presumed, for that reason, they hadn't yet dropped their bombs. Ferdie had seen them and was making for them. Three Hurricanes in line astern had seen the same target, had overtaken them, turned, and were delivering a head-on attack in a slightly echeloned formation. It was an inspiring sight, but the Dorniers appeared unshaken as the Hurricanes flew towards them firing all the time. Then the one on the port flank turned sharply to the left, jettisoning its bomb load as it went. The leading Hurricane got on to its tail and I saw a sheet of flame spring out from somewhere near its centre section and billow back over the top surface of its wing, increasing in size until it had enveloped the entire machine except the extreme tips of its two wings. I didn't look at it any more.

We were now approaching the remaining three Dorniers and we came up directly behind them in line astern. "Get out to port, Roger," cried Ferdie "and take the left one." I slid outside Ferdie and settled my sight on the Dornier's starboard engine nacelle. We were not within range yet but not far off. The Dorniers saw us coming all right and their rear-gunners were opening fire on us, tracer bullets coming perilously close to our machines. I jinked out to port in a lightning steep turn and then came back to my original position and fired immediately at the gunner and not the engine. The tracers stopped coming from that Dornier. I changed my aim to the port engine and fired again, one longish burst and my "De-Wilde" ammunition ran up the trailing edge of the Dornier's port wing in little dancing sparks of fire until they reached the engine. The engine exploded and the machine lurched violently for a second as if a ton weight had landed on the wing and then fallen off again for, as soon as the port wing had dropped it picked up again and the bomber still kept formation despite the damage to its engine. The engine was now totally obscured by thick black smoke which was being swept back on to my windscreen. I was too close to the bomber now to do anything but break off my attack and pull away. I didn't see what had happened to the Dornier that Ferdie had attacked and what's more I could no longer see Ferdie.

I broke off in a steep climbing turn to port scanning the sky for a single Spitfire – "C" Charlie. There were lots of lone Spitfires, there were lots of lone Hurricanes and there were lots of lone bombers but it was impossible now and I thought improvident to attempt to find Ferdie in all this mêlée. I began to get concerned about my petrol reserves as we had been in the air almost an hour and a half now and it was a long way back to base.

I pressed my petrol indicator buttons and one tank was completely empty, the other registering twenty-two gallons. I began to make some hasty calculations concerning speed, time and distance and decided that if I set course for base now and travelled fairly slowly I could make it. I could put down at another airfield of course and get refuelled, but it might be bad policy, especially for a new pilot.

I called up Ferdie, thinking, not very hopefully, that he might hear me, and told him what I was doing. Surprisingly he came back on the air at once in reply and said that he was also returning to base and asked me if I thought I had got enough fuel. He said that he thought it ought to be enough and added as an after-thought that I should make certain that my wheels and flaps were working satisfactorily before coming too low, for they could be damaged. I thanked him for his advice and listened out. I was by myself now and still in the battle area and I was weaving madly for I realised how vulnerable I was. I was easy meat to German fighters, just their cup of tea, particularly if there should be more than one of them, for the Germans always seemed to fancy themselves when the odds were in their favour, particularly numerical odds. It was past six o'clock now and the sun was getting lower in the west, the direction I was travelling in. If I were going to be attacked from the sun, then it would be a head on attack. I felt fairly secure from behind, provided I kept doing steep turns.

## BATTLE OF BRITAIN: A BURN VICTIM, 3 SEPTEMBER 1940

### Richard Hillary, 603 Squadron RAF

*Hillary was badly burned when he baled out of his Spitfire over the North Sea.*

I was falling. Falling slowly through a dark pit. I was dead. My body, headless, circled in front of me. I saw it with my mind, my mind that was the redness in front of the eye, the dull scream in the ear, the grinning of the mouth, the skin crawling on the skull. It was death and resurrection. Terror, moving with me, touched my cheek with hers and I felt the flesh wince. Faster, faster . . . I was hot now, hot, again one with my body, on fire and screaming soundlessly. Dear God, no! No! Not that, not again. The sickly smell of death was in my nostrils and a confused roar of sound. Then all was quiet. I was back.

Someone was holding my arms.

"Quiet now. There's a good boy. You're going to be all right. You've been very ill and you mustn't talk."

I tried to reach up my hand but could not.

"Is that you, nurse? What have they done to me?"

"Well, they've put something on your face and hands to stop them hurting and you won't be able to see for a little while. But you mustn't talk: you're not strong enough yet."

Gradually I realized what had happened. My face and hands had been scrubbed and then sprayed with tannic acid. The acid had formed into a hard black cement. My eyes alone had received different treatment: they were coated with a thick layer of gentian violet. My arms were propped up in front of me, the fingers extended like witches' claws, and my body was hung loosely on straps just clear of the bed.

I can recollect no moments of acute agony in the four days which I spent in that hospital; only a great sea of pain in which I floated almost with comfort. Every three hours I was injected with morphia, so while imagining myself quite coherent, I was for the most part in a semi-stupor. The memory of it has remained a confused blur.

Two days without eating, and then periodic doses of liquid food taken through a tube. An appalling thirst, and hundreds of bottles of ginger beer. Being blind, and not really feeling strong enough to care. Imagining myself back in my plane, unable to get out, and waking to find myself shouting and bathed in sweat. My parents coming down to see me and their wonderful self-control.

They arrived in the late afternoon of my second day in bed, having with admirable restraint done nothing the first day. On the morning of the crash my mother had been on her way to the Red Cross, when she felt a premonition that she must go home. She told the taxi-driver to turn about and arrived at the flat to hear the telephone ringing. It was our Squadron Adjutant, trying to reach my father. Embarassed by finding himself talking to my mother, he started in on a glamorized history of my exploits in the air and was bewildered by mother cutting him short to ask where I was. He managed somehow after about five minutes of incoherent stuttering to get over his news.

They arrived in the afternoon and were met by Matron. Outside my ward a twittery nurse explained that they must not expect to find me looking quite normal, and they were ushered in. The room was in darkness; I just a dim shape in one corner. Then the blinds were shot up, all the lights switched on, and there I was. As my mother remarked later, the performance lacked only the rolling of drums and a spotlight. For the sake of decorum my face had been covered with white gauze, with a slit in the middle through which protruded my lips.

We spoke little, my only coherent remark being that I had no wish to go on living if I were to look like Alice. Alice was a large country girl who had once been our maid. As a child she had been burned and disfigured by a Primus stove. I was not aware that she had made any impression on me, but now I was unable to get her out of my mind. It was not so much her looks as her smell I had continually in my nostrils and which I couldn't dissociate from the disfigurement.

They sat quietly and listened to me rambling for an hour. Then it was time for my dressings and they took their leave.

The smell of ether. Matron once doing my dressing with three orderlies holding my arms; a nurse weeping quietly at the head of the bed, and no remembered sign of a doctor. A visit from the lifeboat crew that had picked me up, and a terrible longing to make sense when talking to them. Their inarticulate sympathy and assurance of quick recovery. Their discovery that an ancestor of mine had founded the lifeboats, and my pompous and unsolicited promise of a subscription. The expectation of an American ambulance to drive me up to the Masonic Hospital (for Margate was used only as a clearing station). Believing that I was already in it and on my way and waking to the disappointment that I had not been moved. A dream that I was fighting to open my eyes and could not: waking in a sweat to realize it was a dream and then finding it to be true. A sensation of time slowing down, of words and actions, all in slow motion. Sweat, pain, smells, cheering messages from the Squadron, and an overriding apathy.

Finally I was moved. The ambulance appeared with a cargo of two somewhat nervous ATS women who were to drive me to London, and, with my nurse in attendance, and wrapped in an old grandmother's shawl, I was carried aboard and we were off. For the first few miles I felt quite well, dictated letters to my nurse, drank bottle after bottle of ginger beer, and gossiped with the drivers. They described the countryside for me, told me they were new to the job, expressed satisfaction at having me for a consignment, asked me if I felt fine. Yes, I said, I felt fine; asked my nurse if the drivers were pretty, heard her answer yes, heard them simpering, and we were all very matey. But after about half an hour my arms began to throb from the rhythmical jolting of the road. I stopped dictating, drank no more ginger beer, and didn't care whether they were pretty or not. Then they lost their way. Wasn't it awful and shouldn't they stop and ask? No, they certainly shouldn't: they could call out the names of the streets and I would tell them where to go. By the time we arrived at Ravenscourt Park I was pretty much all-in. I was carried into the hospital and once again felt the warm September sun burning my face. I was put in a private ward and had the impression of a hundred excited ants buzzing around me. My nurse said good-bye and started to sob. For no earthly reason I found myself in tears. It had been a lousy hospital, I had never seen the nurse anyway, and I was now in very good hands; but I suppose I was in a fairly exhausted state. So there we all were, snivelling about the place and getting nowhere. Then the charge nurse came up and took my arm and asked me what my name was.

"Dick," I said.

"Ah," she said brightly. "We must call you Richard the Lion Heart."

*Hillary recovered and returned to active service but was killed in action later in the war.*

## THE BATTLE OF BRITAIN: THE BLITZ, LONDON, SEPTEMBER–OCTOBER 1940

*Thwarted in its attempt to destroy the RAF, the* Luftwaffe *switched to mass bombing raids on London. The first of the big raids came on 7 September, when 375 bombers unloaded their ordnance on the British capital – a happenstance Londoners nicknamed "the Blitz".*

### Desmond Flower

#### 7 September, London Docks

Suddenly we were gaping upwards. The brilliant sky was criss-crossed from horizon to horizon by innumerable vapour trails. The sight was a completely novel one. We watched, fascinated, and all work stopped. The little silver stars sparkling at the heads of the vapour trails turned east. This display looked so insubstantial and harmless; even beautiful. Then, with a dull roar which made the ground across London shake as one stood upon it, the first sticks of bombs hit the docks. Leisurely, enormous mushrooms of black and brown smoke shot with crimson climbed into the sunlit sky. There they hung and slowly expanded, for there was no wind, and the great fires below fed more smoke into them as the hours passed.

On Friday and Saturday morning the sky grew darker and darker as the oily smoke rose and spread in heavy, immobile columns, shutting out the sun.

At the barracks, drill quickly became monotonous. We had work to do, and we weren't the target. But we couldn't keep our eyes off those sickening, solid columns climbing up like the convolutions of a lazy snake into a torpid sky.

I suppose our masters felt that, although the Battle of Britain had begun, the worst might already be over – I don't know; but they decided to put us recruits in the hat and draw out three for week-end leave. My name came out of the hat first, and I sent a wire to my parents in Sevenoaks to say that I was coming home. My pass was from midday on Saturday, and I got down to the centre of London by Underground. Bombers were coming over at monotonously regular intervals. I walked down to Charing Cross. There was a lot of noise still, and a lot of smoke. As I entered the station the loudspeakers were ordering everyone out because planes were overhead and they were frightened of casualties if the place were hit. I strolled out to the top of that long flight of stone steps down into Villiers Street and sat on the balustrade watching.

Up in the lonely sky there was still one bomber, gleaming silver, and then he dropped a stick just across the Thames from us. Back in the station the loudspeaker announced that the main line was gone and that there wouldn't be any more trains out for hours. Hundreds of people stood around like a flock of sheep which is frightened and can't make up its mind which way to turn. You could see the dead mask of indecision on their faces as they looked about, hoping someone would tell them what to do. I walked out of the station and decided to hitch-hike home. I was lucky; somewhere on the south bank of the river I met a man on a motor-cycle who was going through Blackheath, and he took me on his pillion.

Now we were nearer to the docks. The columns of smoke merged and became a monstrous curtain which blocked the sky; only the billows within it and the sudden shafts of flame which shot up hundreds of feet made one realize that it was a living thing and not just the backdrop of some nightmare opera. There were fire-hoses along the side of the road, climbing over one another like a helping of macaroni, with those sad little fountains spraying out from the leaks, as they always seem to do from all fire-hoses. Every two or three minutes we would pull into the gutter as a fire-bell broke out stridently behind us and an engine in unfamiliar livery tore past at full tilt: chocolate or green or blue, with gold lettering – City of Birmingham Fire Brigade, or Sheffield, or Bournemouth. The feeling was something you had never experienced before – the excitement and dash of fire-engines arriving to help from so far away, and the oily, evil smell of fire and destruction, with its lazy, insolent rhythm.

It looked terrible and hopeless, but there was a kind of *Götter-dämmerung* grandeur about it.

## Virgina Woolf

### Diary, 10 September

Back from half a day in London – perhaps our strangest visit. When we got to Gower Street a barrier with diversion on it. No sign of damage. But coming to Doughty Street a crowd. Then Miss Perkins at the window. Mecklenburgh Square roped off. Wardens there. Not allowed in. The house about 30 yards from ours struck at one in the morning by a bomb. Completely ruined. Another bomb in the square still unexploded. We walked round the back. Stood by Jane Harrison's house. The house was still smouldering. That is a great pile of bricks. Underneath all the people who had gone down to their shelter. Scraps of cloth hanging to the bare walls at the side still standing. A looking glass I think swinging. Like a tooth knocked out – a clean cut. Our house undamaged. No windows yet broken – perhaps the bomb has now broken them. We saw Bernal with an arm band jumping on top of the bricks. Who lived there? I suppose the casual young men and women I used to see from my window; the flat dwellers who used to have flower pots and sit in the balcony. All now blown to bits. The garage man at the back – blear eyed and jerky – told us he had been blown out of his bed by the explosion: made to take shelter in a church. "A hard cold seat," he said, "and a small boy lying in my arms. I cheered when the all clear sounded. I'm aching all over." He said the Jerries had been over for three nights trying to bomb Kings Cross. They had destroyed half Argyll Street, also shops in Grays Inn Road. Then Mr Pritchard ambled up. Took the news as calm as a grig. "They actually have the impertinence to say this will make us accept peace . . .!" he said: he watches raids from his flat roof and sleeps like a hog. So, after talking to Miss Perkins, Mrs Jackson – but both serene – Miss P. had slept on a camp bed in her shelter – we went on to Grays Inn. Left the car and saw Holborn. A vast gap at the top of Chancery Lane. Smoking still. Some great shop entirely destroyed: the hotel opposite like a shell. In a wine shop there were no windows left. People standing at the tables – I think drink being served. Heaps of blue-green glass in the road at Chancery Lane. Men breaking off fragments left in the frames. Glass falling. Then into Lincoln's Inn. To the *New Statesman* office: windows broken, but house untouched. We went over it. Deserted. Wet passages. Glass on stairs. Doors locked. So back to the car. A great block of traffic. The Cinema behind Madame Tussaud's torn open: the stage visible; some decoration swinging. All the Regent's Park houses with broken windows, but undamaged. And then miles and miles of orderly ordinary streets – all Bayswater, and Sussex Square as usual – streets empty – faces set and eyes bleared. In Chancery Lane I saw a man with a barrow of music books. My typist's office destroyed. Then at Wimbledon a siren; people began running. We drove, through almost empty streets, as fast as possible. Horses taken out of the shafts. Cars pulled up. Then the all clear. The people I think of now are the very grimy lodging house keepers, say in Heathcote Street: with another night to face: old wretched women standing at their doors; dirty, miserable. Well – as Nessa said on the phone, it's coming very near: I had thought myself a coward for suggesting that we should not sleep two nights at 37. I was greatly relieved when Miss P. telephoned advising us not to stay, and L. agreed.

## Edward R. Murrow, CBS war correspondent

### 13 September, London

This is London at 3:30 in the morning. This has been what might be called a "routine night" – air-raid alarm at about 9 o'clock and intermittent bombing ever since. I had the impression that more high explosives and few incendiaries have been used tonight. Only two small fires can be seen on the horizon. Again the Germans have been sending their bombers in singly or in pairs. The anti-aircraft barrage has been fierce but sometimes there have been periods of twenty minutes when London has been silent. Then the big red busses would start up and move on till the guns started working again. That silence is almost harder to bear. One becomes accustomed to rattling windows and the distant sound of bombs and then there comes a silence that can be felt. You know the sound will return – you wait, and then it starts again. That waiting is bad. It gives you a chance to imagine things. I have been walking tonight – there is a full moon, and the dirty-gray buildings appear white. The stars, the empty windows, are hidden. It's a beautiful and lonesome city where men and women and children are trying to snatch a few hours' sleep underground.

In the fashionable residential districts I could read the TO LET signs on the front of big houses in the light of the bright moon. Those houses have big basements underneath – good shelters, but they're not being used. Many people think they should be.

The scale of this air war is so great that the reporting is not easy. Often we spend hours traveling about this sprawling city, viewing damage, talking with people, and occasionally listening to the bombs coming down, and then more hours wondering what you'd like to hear about these people who are citizens of no mean city. We've told you about the bombs, the fires, the smashed houses, and the courage of the people. We've read you the communiques and tried to give you an honest estimate of the wounds inflicted upon this, the best bombing target in the world. But the business of living and working in this city is very personal – the little incidents, the things the mind retains, are in themselves unimportant, but they somehow weld together to form the hard core of memories that will remain when the last "all-clear" has sounded. That's why I want to talk for just three or four minutes about the things we haven't talked about before; for many of these impressions it is necessary to reach back through only one long week. There was a rainbow bending over the battered and smoking East End of London just when the "all-clear" sounded one afternoon. One night I stood in front of a smashed grocery store and heard a dripping inside. It was the only sound in all London. Two cans of peaches had been drilled clean through by flying glass and the juice was dripping down onto the floor.

There was a flower shop in the East End. Nearly every other building in the block had been smashed. There was a funeral wreath in the window of the shop – price: three shillings and sixpence, less than a dollar. In front of Buckingham Palace there's a bed of red and white flowers – untouched – the reddest flowers I've ever seen.

Last night, or rather early this morning, I met a distinguished member of Parliament in a bar. He had been dining with Anthony Eden and had told the Secretary for War that he wouldn't walk through the streets with all that shrapnel falling about, and as a good host Eden should send him home in a tank. Another man came in and reported, on good authority, that the Prime Minister had a siren suit, one of those blue woolen coverall affairs with a zipper. Someone said the Prime Minister must resemble a barrage balloon when attired in his siren suit. Things of that sort can still be said in this country. The fact that the noise – just the sound, not the blast – of bombs and guns can cause one to stagger while walking down the street came as a surprise. When I entered my office today, after bombs had fallen two blocks away, and was asked by my English secretary if I'd care for a cup of tea, that didn't come as much of a surprise.

Talking from a studio with a few bodies lying about on the floor, sleeping on mattresses, still produces a strange feeling but we'll probably get used to that. Today I went to buy a hat – my favorite shop had gone, blown to bits. The windows of my shoe store were blown out. I decided to have a haircut; the windows of the barbershop were gone, but the Italian barber was still doing business. Someday, he said, we smile again, but the food it doesn't taste so good since being bombed. I went on to another shop to buy flashlight batteries. I bought three. The clerk said: "You needn't buy so many. We'll have enough for the whole winter." But I said: "What if you aren't here?" There were buildings down in that street, and he replied: "Of course, we'll be here. We've been in business here for a hundred and fifty years."

But the sundown scene in London can never be forgotten – the time when people pick up their beds and walk to the shelter.

## J.B. Priestley

### BBC broadcast 15 September

A lot of us, especially if we were from the North and thought we knew everything, imagined that the old cockney spirit was dead and gone. We thought the Londoner of today, catching his tubes and electric trains, was a different kind of fellow altogether, with too many of his corners rubbed off, too gullible, easily pleased, too soft; and we were wrong. This last grim week has shown us how we can take it. The Londoners, as the Americans are saying, can take it . . . There was a time when, like many North-countrymen who came South, I thought I disliked London; it had vast colourless suburbs that seemed to us even drearier than the ones we had left behind. We hated the extremes of wealth and poverty that we found cheek by jowl in the West End, where at night the great purring motor cars filled with glittering women passed the shadowy rows of the homeless, the destitute, the down-and-out . . . But on those recent nights, when I have gone up to high roofs and have seen the fires like open wounds on the vast body of the city, I've realised, like many another settler here, how deeply I've come to love London, with its misty, twilit charm, its hidden cosiness and companionship, its smoky magic . . . This then is a wonderful moment for us who are here in London, now in the roaring centre of the battlefield, the strangest army the world has ever seen, an army in drab civilian clothes, doing quite ordinary things, an army of all shapes and sizes and ages of folk, but nevertheless a real army, upon whose continuing and defiant spirit the world's future depends.

## THE BATTLE OF BRITAIN: THE VIEW FROM THE OPERATIONS ROOM, NO. 11 FIGHTER GROUP RAF, UXBRIDGE, 15 SEPTEMBER 1940

### Winston S. Churchill MP

We must take 15th September as the culminating date. On this day the Luftwaffe, after two heavy attacks on the 14th, made its greatest concentrated effort in a resumed daylight attack on London.

It was one of the decisive battles of the war, and, like the Battle of Waterloo, it was on a Sunday. I was at Chequers. I had already on several occasions visited the headquarters of No 11 Fighter Group in order to witness the conduct of an air battle, when not much had happened. However, the weather on this day seemed suitable to the enemy, and accordingly I drove over to Uxbridge and arrived at the Group Headquarters. No 11 Group comprised no fewer than twenty-five squadrons covering the whole of Essex, Kent, Sussex, and Hampshire, and all the approaches across them to London. Air Vice-Marshal Park had for six months commanded this group, on which our fate largely depended. From the beginning of Dunkirk all the daylight actions in the South of England had already been conducted by him, and all his arrangements and apparatus had been brought to the highest perfection. My wife and I were taken down to the bombproof Operations Room, fifty feet below ground. All the ascendancy of the Hurricanes and Spitfires would have been fruitless but for this system of underground control centres and telephone cables, which had been devised and built before the war by the Air Ministry under Dowding's advice and impulse. Lasting credit is due to all concerned. In the South of England there were at this time No 11 Group HQ and six subordinate Fighter Station Centres. All these were, as has been described, under heavy stress. The Supreme Command was exercised from the Fighter Headquarters at Stanmore, but the actual handling of the direction of the squadrons was wisely left to No 11 Group, which controlled the units through its Fighter Stations located in each county.

The Group Operations Room was like a small theatre, about sixty feet across, and with two storeys. We took our seats in the Dress Circle. Below us was the large-scale map-table, around which perhaps twenty highly-trained young men and women, with their telephone assistants, were assembled. Opposite to us, covering the entire wall, where the theatre curtain would be, was a gigantic blackboard divided into six columns with electric bulbs, for the six fighter stations, each of their squadrons having a sub-column of its own, and also divided by lateral lines. Thus the lowest row of bulbs showed as they were lighted the squadrons which were "Standing By" at two minutes' notice, the next row those at "Readiness", five minutes, then at "Available", twenty minutes, then those which had taken off, the next row those which had reported having seen the enemy, the next – with red lights – those which were in action, and the top row those which were returning home. On the left-hand side, in a kind of glass stage-box, were the four or five officers whose duty it was to weigh and measure the information received from our Observer Corps, which at this time numbered upwards of fifty thousand men, women, and youths. Radar was still in its infancy, but it gave warning of raids approaching our coast, and the observers, with field-glasses and portable telephones, were our main source of information about raiders flying overland. Thousands of messages were therefore received during an action. Several roomfuls of experienced people in other parts of the underground head-quarters sifted them with great rapidity, and transmitted the results from minute to minute directly to the plotters seated around the table on the floor and to the officer supervising from the glass stage-box.

On the right hand was another glass stage-box containing Army officers who reported the action of our anti-aircraft batteries, of which at this time in the Command there were two hundred. At night it was of vital importance to stop these batteries firing over certain areas in which our fighters would be closing with the enemy. I was not unacquainted with the general outlines of this system, having had it explained to me a year before the war by Dowding when I visited him at Stanmore. It had been shaped and refined in constant action, and all was now fused together into a most elaborate instrument of war, the like of which existed nowhere in the world.

"I don't know," said Park, as we went down, "whether anything will happen today. At present all is quiet." However, after a quarter of an hour the raid-plotters began to move about. An attack of "40 plus" was reported to be coming from the German stations in the Dieppe area. The bulbs along the bottom of the wall display-panel began to glow as various squadrons came to "Stand By". Then in quick succession "20 plus", "40 plus" signals were received, and in another ten minutes it was evident that a serious battle impended. On both sides the air began to fill.

One after another signals came in, "40 plus", "60 plus"; there was even an "80 plus". On the floor-table below us the movement of all the waves of attack was marked by pushing discs forward from minute to minute along different lines of approach, while on the blackboard facing us the rising lights showed our fighter squadrons getting into the air, till there were only four or five left "At Readiness". These air battles, on which so much depended, lasted little more than an hour from the first encounter. The enemy had ample strength to send out new waves of attack, and our squadrons, having gone all out to gain the upper air, would have to refuel after seventy or eighty minutes, or land to rearm after a five-minute engagement. If at this moment of refuelling or rearming the enemy were able to arrive with fresh unchallenged squadrons some of our fighters could be destroyed on the ground. It was therefore one of our principal objects to direct our squadrons so as not to have too many on the ground refuelling or rearming simultaneously during daylight.

Presently the red bulbs showed that the majority of our squadrons were engaged. A subdued hum arose from the floor, where the busy plotters pushed their discs to and fro in accordance with the swiftly-changing situation. Air Vice-Marshal Park gave general directions for the disposition of his fighter force, which were translated into detailed orders to each Fighter Station by a youngish officer in the centre of the Dress Circle, at whose side I sat. Some years after I asked his name. He was Lord Willoughby de Broke. (I met him next in 1947, when the Jockey Club, of which he was a Steward, invited me to see the Derby. He was surprised that I remembered the occasion.) He now gave the orders for the individual squadrons to ascend and patrol as the result of the final information which appeared on the map-table. The Air Marshal himself walked up and down behind watching with vigilant eye every move in the game, supervising his junior executive hand, and only occasionally intervening with some decisive order, usually to reinforce a threatened area. In a little while all our squadrons were fighting, and some had already begun to return for fuel. All were in the air. The lower line of bulbs was out. There was not one squadron left in reserve. At this moment Park spoke to Dowding at Stanmore, asking for three squadrons from No 12 Group to be put at his disposal in case of another major attack while his squadrons were rearming and refuelling. This was done. They were specially needed to cover London and our fighter aerodromes, because No 11 Group had already shot their bolt.

The young officer, to whom this seemed a matter of routine, continued to give his orders, in accordance with the general directions of his Group Commander, in a calm, low monotone, and the three reinforcing squadrons were soon absorbed. I became conscious of the anxiety of the Commander, who now stood still behind his subordinate's chair. Hitherto I had watched in silence. I now asked: "What other reserves have we?" "There are none," said Air Vice-Marshal Park. In an account which he wrote about it afterwards he said that at this I "looked grave". Well I might. What losses should we not suffer if our refuelling planes were caught on the ground by further raids of "40 plus" or "50 plus"! The odds were great; our margins small; the stakes infinite.

Another five minutes passed, and most of our squadrons had now descended to refuel. In many cases our resources could not give them overhead protection. Then it appeared that the enemy were going home. The shifting of the discs on the table below showed a continuous eastward movement of German bombers and fighters. No new attack appeared. In another ten minutes the action was ended. We climbed again the stairways which led to the surface, and almost as we emerged the "All Clear" sounded.

*15 September was the* Luftwaffe's *day of disaster; it lost nearly sixty bombers on its raids on London. The Blitz continued, with the* Luftwaffe *supplanting night bombing for daylight raids, but the threat of invasion had gone. On 17 September Hitler cancelled*

*Operation Sealion indefinitely. "The Few", the 2,500 pilots of Fighter Command, deserved their plaudits. They had shot down 1,268 aircraft for the loss of 832, and inflicted upon Nazi Germany its first defeat. Britain stood alone against Hitler – but it was at least still standing.*

## THE HOME FRONT: A CHILD'S VIEW, SHEFFIELD, AUTUMN 1940

### George Macbeth

In the morning, I would walk along Clarkehouse Road with my eyes glued to the pavement for shrapnel. It became the fashion to make a collection of this, and there were few days when I came home without a pocketful of jagged, rusting bits, like the unintelligible pieces from a scattered jigsaw of pain and violence.

Of course we didn't see them as this at the time. They were simply free toys from the sky, as available and interesting as the horse chestnuts in the Botanical Gardens, or the nippled acorns in Melbourne Avenue.

It must have been about this time that the British Restaurants were opening, with their austerity jam roll and meat balls; and our own meals were beginning to rely rather more on rissoles and home-made apple sponge. But my mother was always a good manager, and I have no sense of any sudden period of shortage or of going hungry.

Sweets were the great loss. There was no longer an everlasting, teeth-spoiling fountain of sherbet and liquorice, or of Boy Blue cream whirls, or of Cadbury's Caramello. Sweets were hard to come by, and then limited to a fixed ration.

One of the worst casualties was chocolate. The traditional division into milk and plain disappeared, and an awful intervening variety known as Ration Chocolate was born, issued in semi-transparent grease-proof wrappers, and about as appetising as cardboard. In spite of a lifelong sweet tooth, I could never eat it.

# Part Two

---

*The Battle of the Atlantic: 1939–43*

# INTRODUCTION

The cruel waters of the Atlantic were always destined to be a major battlefield of World War II. An overpopulated island, Britain was peculiarly needy of imports; in 1939 over half its food was imported. So was all of its oil, and much of its non-ferrous metal. All were conveyed to the island by the largest merchant fleet in the world. Cognizant of lessons learned in World War I, when hostilities commenced in 1939 the Royal Navy organized merchantmen into trans-Atlantic convoys under the protection of its 220 escort vessels (mostly destroyers).

Cognizant, meanwhile, of Britain's dependence on its waterly supply line it became German strategy to disrupt, better still destroy, this self-same supply line. There were occasional raids on sea lanes by the battleships of the *Kriegsmarine* (although Hitler was almost paranoically scared of squandering his big sea guns) and E-boats were a constant menace in British coastal waters. Much the most effective, however, of Germany's weapons was the *Unterseeboot*: the U-boat. Admiral Karl Donitz began the war with just 57 U-boats; by July 1942 the U-boat fleet had reached 300 strong and was sinking 7 million tons annually. Small wonder that Churchill, after victory, declared that "the only thing that really frightened me during the war was the U-boat peril." Disaster for Britain was only averted by the entry of the US into the war (Uncle Sam was soon building three "Liberty" merchant ships a day for the Atlantic supply route), the breaking of German U-boat wireless "traffic" by the cryptographers at Bletchley Park (henceforth U-boats could more easily be obviated or hunted) and advances in avionics which allowed the RAF to patrol greater and greater distances into the Atlantic. Depite reactive improvements in U-boat tactics and technology, notably the invention of the *schnorkel* which allowed U-boats to cruise submerged whilst using their diesel engines, the tide of the Atlantic war turned ineluctably against the *Kriegsmarine*. In 1943 twice as many U-boats were sunk as were built. The chance to starve Britain into submission had gone.

# THE *ROYAL OAK* IS TORPEDOED, SCAPA FLOW, 13 OCTOBER 1939

## *Gunther Prien*

*The Second World War was barely six weeks old when a German submarine U-47, commanded by Gunther Prien, penetrated the defences of the Royal Navy's base at Scapa Flow and sank the battleship* Royal Oak.

. . . We are in Scapa Flow.

*14.10.39.* It is disgustingly light. The whole bay is lit up. To the south of Cava there is nothing. I go farther in. To port, I recognize the Hoxa Sound coastguard, to which in the next few minutes the boat must present itself as a target. In that event all would be lost; at present south of Cava no ships are to be seen, although visibility is extremely good. Hence decisions.

South of Cava there is no shipping, so before staking everything on success, all possible precautions must be taken. Therefore, turn to port is made. We proceed north by the coast. Two battleships are lying there at anchor, and further inshore, destroyers. Cruisers not visible, therefore attack on the big fellows.

Distance apart, 3,000 metres. Estimated depth, seven and a half metres. Impact firing. One torpedo fired on northern ship, two on southern. After a good three and a half minutes, a torpedo detonates on the northern ship; of the other two nothing is to be seen.

About! Torpedo fired from stern; in the bow two tubes are loaded; three torpedoes from the bow. After three tense minutes comes the detonation on the nearer ship. There is a loud explosion, roar, and rumbling. Then come columns of water, followed by columns of fire, and splinters fly through the air. The harbour springs to life. Destroyers are lit up, signalling starts on every side, and on land, 200 metres away from me, cars roar along the roads. A battleship had been sunk, a second damaged, and the other three torpedoes have gone to blazes. All the tubes are empty. I decide to withdraw, because: (1) With my periscopes I cannot conduct night attacks while submerged . . . (2) On a bright night I cannot manoeuvre unobserved in a calm sea. (3) I must assume that I was observed by the driver of a car which stopped opposite us, turned around, and drove off towards Scapa at top speed. (4) Nor can I go farther north, for there, well hidden from my sight, lie the destroyers which were previously dimly distinguishable.

At full speed both engines we withdraw. Everything is simple until we reach Skildaenoy Point. Then we have more trouble. It is now low tide. The current is against us. Engines at slow and dead slow; I attempt to get away. I must leave by the south through the narrows, because of the depth of the water. Things are again difficult. Course, 058°, slow – ten knots. I make no progress. At full speed I pass the southern blockship with nothing to spare. The helmsman does magnificently. Full speed ahead both, finally three-quarter speed and full ahead all out. Free of the blockships – ahead a mole! Hard over and again about, and at 02.15 we are once more outside. A pity that only one was destroyed. The torpedo misses I explain as due to faults of course, speed and drift. In tube 4, a misfire. The crew behaved splendidly throughout the operation.

# THE BATTLE OF THE RIVER PLATE, 13 DECEMBER 1939

## *Lieutenant-Commander R.E. Washbourn RN, HMNZS Achilles*

*The German pocket battleship* Graf Spee *left Wilhelmshaven on 23 August 1939 on a spree of sinkings in the Atlantic and Indian Oceans, until tracked down by HMS* Ajax, *HMS* Exeter *and HMNZS* Achilles *to the mouth of the River Plate.*

From the personal point of view it was a tremendous moment when we suddenly realised that we had bumped up against her [*Graf Spee*], and that *this* time it was the real thing. I was PCO at the time. I would be. The captain was on the bridge, and we turned to each other and said simultaneously, "My God, it's a pocket battleship!" I legged it as hard as I could go for my box of tricks, and just had time to wonder if there was anything in this gunnery business after all, and where I should be in half an hour's time, before all my lamps lit up and I was able to say "SHOOT" for the first time in anger. Four minutes only, though most of the sailors were enjoying their very necessary beauty sleep at the time and we were only at cruising stations. We were rather proud of that, even though *Exeter* did beat us to it.

After that my impressions are rather confused. There were a lot of splashes growing up around that target and it wasn't a bit easy picking out my own. I can remember feeling a quite illogical resentment every time he put his great eleven-inch cannon on us, when I saw those damn great pieces belching their unpleasantness at myself and I can remember feeling unspeakably grateful to poor old *Exeter* every time I saw them blazing in her direction.

He came at us for about a quarter of an hour, very obligingly thinking that we were a couple of destroyers in company with *Exeter*. That covered the rather unpleasant stretch of water in which he could outrange us.

He scored a pretty little straddle after twenty minutes and his HE burst on the surface of the water and the pieces peppered us. There weren't as many casualties as one would expect. Our captain acquired a sizish hole in both legs and the chief yeoman on the bridge had a leg smashed up. In my DCT we had rather more than our share. Six pieces came inside. With my usual fantastic luck three pieces impinged on my ample anatomy (and I regret that it grows even ampler as the years go on despite my efforts to squash it out), but caused me little inconvenience, apart from a certain mental vagueness of the ensuing minute or two. Three died quite quickly and definitely, two of whom were actually in physical contact with me, and three were wounded. I don't expect that names mean anything to you at this distance of time, but one of the casualties was an old "*Diomede*", Archibald Cooper Hirst Shaw. E.V. Shirley, another old "*Diomede*", was one of the very severely wounded. The others had the common misfortune of being imperial ratings (NZ).

The survivors behaved just as one expected and hoped. They took no notice of the shambles (and it looked more like a slaughter-house on a busy day than a Director Control Tower) and took over the jobs of those who had been put out as if nothing had happened. One youngster had to seat himself on the unpleasantness that very shortly before had been a very efficient GO's writer and carry out his job. He was a little wide-eyed after we had disengaged but otherwise unmoved. A splinter had jammed the door and prevented the medical parties from reaching us. The wounded never murmured. Shirley quietly applied a tourniquet to himself and saved his life thereby. A sergeant of Marines who was sitting right alongside me never let on that he was wounded. I didn't discover it until the first lull, an hour later, when he nearly fainted from loss of blood.

I learnt this lesson – though it's a difficult one to put into words – that one can wish for nothing better than these troops of ours. They may be a bit of a nuisance in the easy times of peace, but one can't improve on them when things get a bit hot. A spot of trouble of this sort completely changes one's attitude to the troops. I felt very proud of my fellow countrymen. [Washbourn is a New Zealander.]

*Exeter*, as you know, bore the brunt. We had the attentions of the 5.8s all the time, but they weren't very effective. I think that we shot up their control fairly early on, and put at least two of the starboard battery out of action.

Tactically my only criticism is that we should have gone in earlier, but that certainly would have meant more damage and casualties than we actually received, and we did achieve the object of the exercise without it.

It was a plain straightforward scrap, with none of the "hit-and-run" tactics which the Yellow Press credited us with. We hammered away for an hour and a half, and then hauled off under smoke. I must admit to a certain feeling of being baulked of my prey when we were ordered to turn away, because the last twenty minutes at really effective range had been most enjoyable. It turned out to be the psychologically correct moment. We had damn little ammunition left and, as it proved, the job was done. It didn't seem like it at the time. I was very depressed. We had expended most of our bricks and our enemy looked disappointingly undamaged. The after turret was temporarily out of action, and we had seen one fire on board, and he was running like a frightened rabbit, but his fire was distressingly accurate, and his speed was the same as ever, and there was no sign of structural damage.

We shadowed all day. Once or twice we ventured a bit too close and he swung round and let us have it, but he was out of our range and we didn't reply.

In the evening we gave the Uruguayans the thrill of their lives by another little brush just at sunset when we were closing the range to keep him in sight as the visibility lessened. Four times later, during the advancing twilight, he took exception to our presence, but these last Parthian shots were merely gestures.

The morale was magnificent while we were waiting for him to emerge from his hole. The fantastic fleets that Winston, ably aided and abetted by the BBC, built up outside Montevideo gave us great pleasure. We were pleased to see *Cumberland*, not for any great confidence in her fighting abilities, but from the point of view that she would again provide the first target for *Graf Spee*'s attentions.

We stayed at action stations all night, with the usual "Hula" parties keeping us amused and awake with their Maori songs. Do you remember Gould, with his guitar and his indiarubber hips?

On the Sunday evening we three went in to finish the job off. *Graf Spee* was just visible at sunset when *Ajax*'s aircraft reported that she had blown herself up. Another big moment. We steamed up close past *Ajax*, who was leading us in. Both ships had ordered "All hands on deck", and were black with bodies who had emerged to see the last of the old enemy. Another big moment. We shouted ourselves hoarse, both ships. The "Diggers" did their "Hakas", and sang their songs, and the *Ajax* cheered in reply.

And that was that.

# SURVIVAL, THE ARCTIC, 8–11 JUNE 1940

## *Ronald Healiss, Royal Marines*

*At 4.30 p.m. on 9 June the aircraft carrier HMS* Glorious, *returning from the Narvik landings, was intercepted by the German battle cruisers* Scharnhorst *and* Gneisenau. *Ninety minutes later* Glorious *was no more. Of her 1,700 crew many were already dead, but hundreds took to the icy waters grabbing hold of any floatable device they could or scrambling aboard life rafts.*

Around me, those who had survived the shelling were laughing and swearing as they peeled off their outer garments and prepared themselves for the shock of the icy water.

Down below me, men were already struggling in the water, reaching out for the few floatable things we had been able to throw overboard. The ship's propeller blades, half out of the water, were churning slowly right underneath me. But it was my turn to go and I had to jump from where I was.

I took a deep breath and shoved against the deck with all my strength. Then I sailed out in a great arc above the propeller.

The thirty feet down to the water seemed like a thousand. There was a terrific jolt, then I was going down with an icy hand slowly squeezing the breath from my lungs. Things grew a little muddled.

I broke surface and gulped air. The icy water was already taking a grip on me and I looked around for something to float on.

The sea, calm a few hours before, now boiled with a sort of cold fury. As the waves lifted me I saw hundreds of my shipmates floating round me. The chances of finding a place on a raft seemed slim, but mechanically I began to swim, held up by my lifebelt.

After about five minutes I saw an air-cushion from one of the lifeboats and made for it as fast as my failing strength would allow. As I bobbed up and down I saw that four other men were swimming toward it, too. Three of them reached it with me. The fourth just disappeared.

We floated around on that air-cushion for about an hour, while the cold and cramp ate into us. Then I caught sight of what I thought to be a Carley float. My three companions hanging on to the cushion already had cramp and couldn't move their limbs, so I began to strike out in a sort of mad frenzy with one hand, using the other to drag the air-cushion behind me with the others hanging on.

I knew I was attempting the impossible in those seas. After a long, futile struggle with the waves, against which I made no progress, I told the others that I was going to make a try on my own. I let the cushion go and struck out for the float.

The distance was only about fifty yards. It seemed like fifty miles. My strokes became slower and weaker as the cold bit deeper. I knew I couldn't carry on much longer.

Then I heard a voice I knew. "Wotcher, Tubby! Trying to swim home?" it said.

I looked up and saw a fellow Marine clinging to an oar. He grinned cheerfully and I grinned back – and the strength came back into my arms.

The "float" turned out to be one of our motor-boats, badly damaged and well down in the water. Somehow I clambered over the side and flopped down inside it, rigid with cold.

There were already about twenty men in the boat, including the Surgeon-Commander, the Surgeon-Lieutenant and a couple of Marines I knew.

They had lashed themselves with rope to avoid being carried away by the heavy seas which were breaking over them. I followed suit, leaving enough slack on the rope to keep me on top of each wave.

In the next four hours I saw all those men die.

Many of them were already far gone from exposure when I clambered aboard and, as we floated helplessly around with the seas breaking over us, they became more and more silent.

I watched them go, one by one, sliding silently into death, glassy-eyed and motionless, except when the waves lifted them in their ropes and flopped them back into the boat.

The Surgeon-Commander was the last to go. I watched him silently as his movements grew slower. The cold now had bitten into my own body and it was getting increasingly difficult to brace myself against the waves.

I began to wonder which of us death would leave until last, but when the Surgeon-Commander answered my unspoken thought I was shocked beyond measure.

"I'll be the next to go, lad," he said. "Do what you can for those others. Cut them loose and let them go to their final rest. And do the same for me when I'm gone."

He watched while I summoned all my strength and dragged myself about the boat, cutting the bodies free one by one and letting the waves carry them away.

As the last one sank into those black waters, I heard the Commander mutter: "Good lad, now – do it – for me." When I reached him he had gone, and a wave had carried him over the side.

I cut the rope wrapped round his wrists and his body glided gently beneath the surface. I was alone.

Boxes and bits of wreckage floated by. The Huns were still shelling what remained of the *Glorious*. I lost count of time.

At last the bits of flotsam thinned out, then ceased to float by. There was nothing but sea and cold silence. The intolerable loneliness ate into me as much as the cold.

I don't know how long I'd been alone in that boat when I saw what looked like a couple of floats, full of men, drifting about a mile away. The sight of human beings in that waste of water did something to me. On an impulse I decided to try to reach them.

I deflated my lifebelt so that if cramp or exhaustion overtook me I shouldn't linger, then cut myself loose and went over the side.

I seemed to be swimming for hours. My legs gradually grew stiff, first at the feet, then the calves, the knees, the thighs. My stomach seemed knotted with an intolerable pain. I knew, as I rose and fell in the waves, that my time had come.

It's true that when you see death approaching your past life passes before your eyes. I remembered my boyhood, the day I joined the Royal Marines. I could see my mother clearly. And the girl who would have been my wife in a few short days.

In my trouser-pocket there had been a little leather case in which I always carried a picture of my parents and my girl. I felt about me with a frozen hand. The case was still there.

I took it out while I floated, intent on bidding them goodbye. But I couldn't. The faces were too real. The sodden photographs smiled up at me and I knew I couldn't die without seeing those three people again.

I thrust the wallet back in my pocket and struck out again with fresh strength.

Then a wave lifted me and, as I floundered on top of it, I saw the rafts not ten yards away. Somebody shouted to me. I reached one of the rafts – I don't know how – and was dragged aboard.

I wanted to cry, but I was too cold. I closed my eyes and thanked God for deliverance.

There were a lot of us on board the raft that first night. As the Northern Lights flashed around us, we discussed among ourselves the chances of being picked up.

The Signal Boatswain was aboard and told us that distress signals had been sent off before we abandoned ship. We started guessing how long it would be before help came. The optimists said twelve hours. The pessimists had no hope at all.

I judged it was about midnight when the first of my comrades started dying from exposure. In the next hours many more of them followed. Only two of us had enough strength left to thump each other to keep the circulation going.

At first we moved about the raft as our shipmates died and passed them over the side to their final resting-place. But our own strength was soon too far gone and we could do nothing but watch them die and let their bodies rest at the bottom of the float.

And so another day and another night passed. People ask me how it was that I survived those terrible hours. I can't tell. Time had no real meaning. The bodily agony became something remote. I just knew that whatever happened I had to stay alive.

On the third morning, only three of us were left alive, and one was already demented. He writhed and shouted while the other two of us made feeble efforts to quieten him.

But there was nothing we could do for him. We watched, horrified, as he suddenly raised himself to his feet on the side of the raft and hurled himself into the black water with a scream that haunts me still.

My fellow survivor was a Fleet Air Arm pilot, Petty Officer Leggett. As that last awful day dragged by he tried to work out our direction of drift. According to his deductions we were nearing the Gulf Stream, which would carry us down toward the Norwegian coast.

Some hundreds of yards away we could see another raft. Several times we waved, but there was no response and at last we gave up trying to establish contact with what were only too obviously dead bodies.

The weather now had calmed a little and once, through the slight haze, we thought we could see the British Fleet. But it disappeared and our hopes sank again.

Then, miraculously, there was the drone of an aeroplane. It sang out of the blue sky and roared over our heads while we waved and shouted like maniacs. I could see it was a Walrus such as we had on the *Glorious*. But it banked away and in a few seconds was lost to sight.

We settled back on the float, stupefied with disappointment.

After a while, another Walrus passed overhead, but we had convinced ourselves that it was just imagination – the first signs of the madness that had already claimed one of our shipmates.

We told ourselves we could last another day at most, and then took it in turns to snatch our first sleep for three days, in spells of a few minutes each. In that temperature, any lengthy inaction would have stilled the blood in our veins for ever.

As I lay there watching the spout of whales not far away, something else attracted my attention – something wispy and indeterminate on the horizon. I sat up and peered hard. There was no doubt about it.

Smoke! We thought it might be a German ship, though we didn't care much. But as the masts and then the hull appeared we saw it was a trawler. Frantically we waved.

Twice that ship stopped and changed course while our hearts choked us, but at last there was no doubt that she had sighted us. Oh, the delicious agony of those last moments as we saw her steaming straight for us!

The rest is any shipwrecked sailor's story. A rope ladder came over the side and the husky Norwegians dragged my fellow survivor aboard. I remember trying to climb the ladder myself, then I passed out.

When I came round I was lying in front of the galley fire. A sailor passed over some hot spirits and I drifted back into unconsciousness for many hours. When I awoke, it was to find myself in a bunk with another survivor, a stoker.

Altogether, I believe that ship picked up about thirty men – the bulk of those who survived.

It took us three days to reach land – three days that seemed like three weeks. We drank the ship's freshwater supply in twenty-four hours and then they started making it for us down in the engine-room. None of us could eat solid food, not even the soup those fine fellows made for us.

We were a sorry lot when we made the Faroe Islands. Some were able to walk ashore between two sailors. Others, like myself, came off on a stretcher.

It isn't possible to describe how we felt as each stage of our rescue brought us nearer and nearer to home and those we loved, and I'm not going to try. Nor can any of us express our thanks to the many people, Danes, Norwegians, Scots, English, who looked after us with such care as we passed through their hands.

For my part, I spent fourteen weeks in hospital with hands and feet badly frost-bitten, swollen to twice their normal size and blistered into shapelessness.

But it was a small price to pay for deliverance. The pain that still sears periodically through my feet and the bitterness of my soul when I think of those three awful days are nothing.

Hundreds upon hundreds of my shipmates of the *Glorious* who did their duty, simply and straightforwardly as I tried to do mine, perished in those frightful waters while the Hun sailed by, unmoved.

I am alive. I thank God for it, though I do not pretend to understand His ways.

# U-99 ATTACKS A CONVOY, THE ATLANTIC, 18–19 OCTOBER 1940

## Kapitan-Leutnant Otto Kretschmer, U-99

*Kretschmer was the leading U-boat ace of World War II, sinking 350,00 tons of Allied shipping. Below is Kretschmer's log detailing U-99's initial attack on convoy SC7. The U-boat did not operate alone but in concert with several others – a classic example of Donitz's "wolf-pack" tactic.*

*18th October* 9.24 PM. Exchange recognition signals with *U123*. Convoy again in sight. I am ahead of it, so allow my boat to drop back, avoiding leading destroyers. Destroyers are constantly firing starshells. From outside, I attack the right flank of the first formation.

10.02 PM. Weather, visibility moderate, bright moon-light. Fire bow torpedo by director. Miss.

10.06 PM. Fire stern tube by director. At 700 metres, hit forward of amidships. Vessel of some 6,500 tons sinks within 20 seconds. *I now proceed head-on into the convoy.*

10.30 PM. Fire bow tube by director. Miss because of error in calculation of gyro-angle. I therefore decide to fire rest of torpedoes without director, especially as the installation has still not been accepted and adjusted by the Torpedo Testing Department. Boat is soon sighted by a ship which fires a white star and turns towards us at full speed continuing even after we alter course.

I have to make off with engines all out. Eventually the ship turns off, fires one of her guns and again takes her place in the convoy.

11.30 PM. Fire bow torpedo at a large freighter. As the ship turns towards us, the torpedo passes ahead of her and hits an even larger ship after a run of 1,740 metres. This ship of 7,000 tons is hit abreast the foremast and the bow quickly sinks below the surface, as two holds are apparently flooded.

11.55 PM. Fire a bow torpedo at a large freighter of 6,000 tons at a range of 750 metres. Hit abreast foremast. Immediately after the torpedo explosion there is another explosion, with a high column of flame from bow to bridge. Smoke rises 200 metres. Bow apparently shattered. Ship continues to burn with green flame.

*19th October.* 12.15 AM. Three destroyers approach the ship and search area in line abreast. I make off at full speed to the south-west and again make contact with the convoy. Torpedoes from other boats are constantly heard exploding. The destroyers do not know how to help and occupy themselves by constantly firing starshells which are of little effect in the bright moonlight. I now start attacking the convoy from astern.

*Over the next few hours Kretschmer sank another four ships in convoy SC7.*

## HUNTING U-BOATS, 17 MARCH 1941
### *Captain Donald Macintyre RN, HMS* Walker

In the next hour five ships were torpedoed. I was near to despair and I racked my brains to find some way to stop the holocaust. While the convoy stayed in impeccable formation, we escorts raced about in the exasperating business of searching in vain for the almost invisible enemy. Our one hope was to sight a U-boat's telltale white wake, give chase to force her to dive, and so give the Asdics* a chance to bring our depth-charges into action. Everything had to be subordinated to that end and so, with binoculars firmly wedged on a steady bearing, I put *Walker* into a gently curving course, thereby putting every point of the compass under a penetrating prove. It worked.

As her bows swung, a thin line of white water came into the lens of my glasses, a thin line which could only be the wake of a ship. There were none of ours in that direction; it had to be a U-boat! I shouted orders increasing speed to thirty knots and altered course towards the target. Suddenly, the U-boat spotted us and in a cloud of spray he crash-dived. A swirl of phosphorescent water still lingered as we passed over the spot and sent a pattern of ten depth-charges crashing down. We could hardly have missed; it had been so quick we must have dropped them smack on top of him. Then the depth-charges exploded with great cracking explosions and giant water-spouts rose to masthead height astern of us. Two and a half minutes later another explosion followed and an orange flash spread momentarily across the surface. We had every reason to hope that this was our first "kill".

Though we learned that this was not so, for our charges had exploded too deeply to do him fatal damage, we felt almost certain at the time when our Asdic search showed no trace of a contact. *Vanoc* came racing past to rejoin the convoy and offered assistance. I refused this, convinced as I was that we could safely leave the scene with a "probable" marked down in the log-book, and ordered her back to her station.

However, no U-boat was officially recorded as destroyed without tangible evidence and I continued the Asdic search until such time as wreckage should come to the surface.

* Asdic – the abbreviation of Allied Submarine Detection Investigation Committee – was the echo-sounding equipment used by surface vessels to detect submerged U-boats.

It was just as well. For half an hour later we gained contact with a certain U-boat. Our prey had not been "killed"; he was, in fact, sneaking back towards the convoy, still bent on attack.

Recalling *Vanoc* to assist in the hunt, we set about our target with a series of carefully aimed patterns of depth-charges.

Taking it in turns to run in to the attack, pattern after pattern of depth-charges went down as we tried to get one to within the lethal range of about twenty feet of our target. But he was a wily opponent and, dodging and twisting in the depths, he managed to escape destruction though heavily damaged.

Soon the waters became so disturbed by the repeated explosions, each one of which sent back an echo to the Asdic's sound beam, that we could no longer distinguish our target from the other echoes and a lull in the fight was forced upon us.

I had for some time past noticed in the distance the bobbing lights from the lifeboats of one of our sunken ships, but with an enemy to engage there was nothing for it but to harden my heart and hope that the time might come later when I could rescue the crews. This lull seemed a good opportunity and perhaps if we left the area temporarily the U-boat commander might think he had shaken us off and be tempted into some indiscretion. So, the *Vanoc* steaming round us in protection, we stopped and picked up the master and thirty-seven of the crew of the ss *J.B. White*.

This completed, the time was ripe to head quietly back to where the U-boat had last been located and perhaps catch him licking his wounds on the surface.

We had hardly got under way when I noticed that *Vanoc* was drawing ahead fast and thought perhaps she had misread the signal ordering the speed to be maintained. As I ordered a signal to be made to her, Yeoman of Signals Gerrard said, "She's signalling to us, sir, but I can't read it as her light is flickering so badly." I realised that *Vanoc* must be going ahead at her full speed and being, like *Walker*, an old veteran, her bridge would be shaking and rattling as her 30,000 hp drove her forward through the Atlantic swell.

Rupert Bray, on the bridge beside me, said, "She must have sighted the U-boat." Even as he spoke, *Vanoc* came on the air with his radio telephone, with the laconic signal: "Have rammed and sunk U-boat."*

What a blissful moment that was for us, the successful culmination of a long and arduous fight. Something in the way of revenge for our losses in the convoy had been achieved.

There was grim joy on board *Walker*, and not least amongst the

---

* This was U-100, captained by Joachim Schepke

merchant seamen from the *J.B. White*, who felt they had a personal score to settle. But for the moment our part was confined to circling *Vanoc* in protection, while she picked up the few survivors from the U-boat and examined herself for damage. We were glad of this breathing space, as, with all the depth-charges carried on the upper deck expended, the depth-charge party, led by Leading Seaman Prout, were struggling to hoist up more of these awkward heavy loads from the magazine, with the ship rolling in the Atlantic swell, and often with water swirling round their waists. They were not a moment too soon, for, as we circled *Vanoc*, I was electrified to hear the Asdic operator Able Seaman Backhouse excitedly reporting, "Contact, contact." But I could hardly credit it, for not only was it unbelievable that in all the wide wastes of the Atlantic a second U-boat should turn up just where another had gone to the bottom, but I knew that there were sure to be areas of disturbed water persisting in the vicinity from our own and *Vanoc*'s wakes. The echo was not very clear and I expressed my doubts to John Langton, but Backhouse was not to be disheartened. "Contact definitely submarine", he reported, and as I listened to the ping the echo sharpened and there could be no further doubt. With a warning to the men aft to get any charges ready that they had managed to hoist into the throwers and rails, we ran into the attack. It was a great test for John Langton, for, with the maddening habit of the beautiful instruments of precision provided for us, they all elected to break down at the crucial moment. But much patient drill against just such an emergency now brought its reward. Timing his attack by the most primitive methods Langton gave the order to fire. A pattern of six depth-charges – all that could be got ready in time – went down. As they exploded, *Walker* ran on to get sea-room to turn for further attacks, but as we turned came the thrilling signal from *Vanoc* – "U-boat surfaced astern of me."

A searchlight beam stabbed into the night from *Vanoc*, illuminating the submarine U-99 which lay stopped. The guns' crews in both ships sprang into action and the blinding flashes from the four-inch guns and tracers from the smaller weapons made a great display, though I fear their accuracy was not remarkable. Destroyer night gunnery in such a mêlée is apt to be pretty wild and in those days, when flashless cordite was not issued to us, each salvo left one temporarily blinded. In *Walker* confusion soon reigned around the guns, for the enthusiasm of our guests from *J.B. White* knew no bounds. Joining up with the ammunition supply parties, shells came up at such a phenomenal rate that the decks were piled high with them till the guns' crews were hardly able to work their guns. But fortunately we were able very soon to cease fire as a signal lamp flashing from the U-boat, "We are sunking" [*sic*], made it clear that the action was over. Keeping end on to the U-boat in case he still had some fight left, we prepared to lower a boat in case there was a chance of a capture, but even as we did so the crew of the U-boat abandoned ship and she plunged to the bottom.

I manœuvred *Walker* to windward of the swimming Germans and as we drifted down on to them, they were hauled on board. Some of them were in the last stages of exhaustion from the cold of those icy northern waters by the time we got them on board. Some indeed would never have made safety had not Leading Seaman Prout gone over the side fully clothed to aid them.

The last to come over the side was obviously the captain, as he swam to *Walker* still wearing his brass-bound cap. We were soon to find out that we had made indeed a notable capture, for the captain was Otto Kretschmer, leading ace of the U-boat arm, holder of the Knight's Cross with oak leaves and top scorer in terms of tonnage sunk.

# HMS *HOOD* IS SUNK, 24 MAY 1941

## *Lieutenant Esmond Knight RNVR,* HMS **Prince of Wales**

*On 18 May 1941 the German battleship* Bismarck *slipped her berth in occupied Norway on a hunt for Allied shipping. She was intercepted in the Denmark Strait by HMS* Suffolk, *HMS* Norfolk, *HMS* Prince of Wales *and HMS* Hood *six days later.*

After minutes of staring at the blank distance, suddenly – and one could scarcely believe one's eyes – there appeared the topmasts of two ships! Again that phrase was shouted by the first man who could find his voice – "Enemy in sight!" Silently, but as if controlled by one main switch, the director towers of the main and secondary armaments swung in that direction, immediately followed by the great fourteen-inch guns and the 5.25s on the starboard side. The minutes raced by, but time during those unendurable moments seemed to be standing still. There they were, in deep sharp silhouette on the horizon – *Bismarck* and *Prinz Eugen*, steaming in smokeless line ahead, unperturbed and sinister. "Ye gods! – what a size!" I heard someone mutter. On we raced, keeping the same course. The range was now closing at an alarming speed, and we on the bridge began to look at each other and wonder what the next move was to be. I must say I was rather relieved at this time to see that even old George was looking a trifle – but only a trifle – paler. The two enemy ships, travelling at probably about thirty knots, were now practically crossing our bows, still on the horizon, while we were closing to a range which should be deadly. Had anything gone wrong?

Had the admiral decided to change his plan at the last moment? Why had we not opened fire?

All those thoughts raced through one's head as the great guns of the *Hood* and *Prince of Wales* followed the enemy steadily as the relative positions changed.

At last it came – a signal flashed from *Hood* – "Open fire!" Almost immediately after there were the great orange flashes and huge clouds of black smoke belching from the for'ard turrets of the *Hood* as she fired her first salvo. This was the great moment everyone had been waiting for. A few more seconds of agonising waiting and then that ding-ding ringing up in the fourteen-inch director tower which told us that our own guns were about to open fire.

Two more moments of unendurable ecstasy, then that pulverising crashing roar, which for a second seems to knock one senseless – we had opened fire! We were blinded by a dense sheet of flame which rose before us, mixed with clouds of black, bitter-smelling smoke. For a second we closed our eyes till it dispersed: then, peering through binoculars we gazed anxiously to see where the first salvo had fallen. At this moment nothing was visible except the serene forms of the enemy ships. There was no change in what we saw; for our own shells were actually still in the air, hurtling towards the enemy, while they had not yet opened fire.

The first salvo from *Hood* fell just astern – one could see the great towering columns of water spurting into the air. Almost simultaneously we saw those brilliant flashes and the same jet-black smoke belching from *Bismarck*, as she, in turn, opened with her first returning salvo. Now followed the most exciting moments that I am likely to experience – those desperate and precious seconds racing past while guns were reloaded and the enemy's first salvo was roaring to meet us. Suddenly one became conscious of that unmistakable noise, which produced a horrid sinking feeling inside one – a noise growing in a gradual crescendo – something like the approach of an underground train, getting louder and louder and filling the air, suddenly to cease as the first great spouts of water rose just astern of *Hood*. I looked over at George – he was thinking the same as I was – just a little too close to be comfortable, wasn't it? The next moment might have taken minutes, may have taken hours; it was impossible to measure time, except that one could remember that heavy concussion as we got off salvo after salvo. I could see that our own falls of shot must have been embarrassing to the enemy, since they were certainly falling in line, but a little towards their stern. Then again that horrible rushing noise, and suddenly an enormous geyser of sea-water rising on our starboard side as a shell from *Bismarck* fell just short. This seemed to hang in the air for a second or two, then fell in a soaking cascade across the bridge. At intervals there was an ear-splitting crack as HE shells from *Prinz Eugen*, exploding practically overhead, rained showers of shrapnel on to the decks and into the sea around. The enemy had certainly got the range taped.

We were racing on, on the same course, and tearing my eyes from the great form of the *Bismarck*, which now appeared in clear detail in my glasses, I ran to the other side of the ship, where, to my horror, I saw a great fire burning on the boat-deck of the *Hood*. They would have a job to put that out. Then, as one looked . . . the incredible happened: there had been that rushing sound which had ominously ceased, and then, as I looked a great spouting explosion issued from the centre of the *Hood*, enormous reaching tongues of pale-red flame shot into the air, while dense clouds of whitish-yellow smoke burst upwards, gigantic pieces of brightly burning debris being hurled hundreds of feet in the air. I just did not believe what I saw – *Hood* had literally been blown to pieces, and just before she was totally enveloped in that ghastly pall of smoke I noticed that she was firing her last salvo. I felt quite sick inside and turned away and looked towards George, where he was standing with his hands limply to his sides, staring like a man in a dream. "Well, that's the end of her." "What's that?" "*Hood*'s gone!" I turned back and looked again, with a weak feeling in my knees – the smoke had cleared and the *Hood* was no more; there was nothing to be seen of her. It was fantastic, one just couldn't grasp it.

*Just three of the* Hood's *crew survived the engagement.*

## THE PURSUIT OF THE *BISMARCK*, 24–27 MAY 1940

### *Lieutenant Ludovic Kennedy RN, HMS* Tartar

I had the first watch that May evening, a day out from the Clyde. With *Somali, Eskimo* and *Mashona* we were escorting the troopship *Britannic* and the battleship *Rodney* westward across the Atlantic. It was, as I recall, an uneventful watch, and at about 9 p.m. while checking bearings and distance from *Rodney* for perhaps the sixth time. I heard the buzzer from the wireless office. Signalman Pearson, with whom I was sharing the watch, a barrel-shaped fellow partial to chocolate "Nutty," thrust his flabby fist into the voicepipe and hauled up the signal box.

"U-boat Disposition Report, I expect," he said.

He unraveled the signal, scanned it, then handed it to me. It was prefixed MOST IMMEDIATE, came from the cruiser *Norfolk* and went something like this: IBS ICR 66.40N 28.22W Co220 Sp 30.

"Pearson," I said, "does that mean what I think it means?"

"Yes, sir. One enemy battleship, one enemy cruiser, position sixty-six forty North, twenty-eight twenty-two West, course 220, speed 30 knots."

"Christ!" I said, and pressed the captain's buzzer.

In such a manner did I learn of the break-out into the Atlantic of the giant *Bismarck* together with the *Prinz Eugen*, an event followed by the most exciting week of my life. A glance at the chart showed that the German ships had been picked up in the Denmark Strait, the stretch of water that lies between Greenland and the north of Iceland. Although of intense interest the news did not then affect us personally, as we were 600 miles away and fully occupied with protecting *Rodney* and *Britannic* against U-boats. But it was the one topic of conversation throughout the ship. In the wardroom that night we discussed the likely eventualities into the early hours, and when my servant called me with tea at 7.30 next morning, I was already awake.

"Heard the news, sir?"

"No."

"*Hood*'s gone."

"*No!*"

"Yes, and *Prince of Wales* damaged."

The *Hood* gone – the most famous, most loved of British warships, the one above all others that epitomized the Navy and the country? It seemed impossible to believe. And the brand new battleship *Prince of Wales* damaged! If this is what the *Bismarck* could do in six minutes flat, what might she not achieve against the convoys from America? The question-mark that had arisen at the time of Dunkirk rose again. Loose in the Atlantic and supported by supply ships and tankers, she could prey on our shipping for months and cut the supply line on which we depended for survival.

After breakfast I went to the charthouse where Spider had put up a large scale chart of the Atlantic, and penciled on it the position of the first sighting of the German squadron, the location of the sinking of *Hood*, and the squadron's present position as received from the signals of the pursing *Norfolk*, *Suffolk* and wounded *Prince of Wales*. He had also marked the positions of the British ships closing in on *Bismarck*, and as the day passed and assuming she kept her present course and speed, it looked as though the commander-in-chief, Admiral Tovey, in his flagship *King George V* with the battlecruiser *Repulse* would be the first to engage her in the morning and (if the result was inconclusive) that we would be the second.

*Eskimo* and *Britannic* went off to the west, while we steamed south-westward all day, the seas getting higher, the wind rising hourly. Inevitably that evening, as the gap between us gradually narrowed, one's thoughts turned to the action that lay ahead. Inevitably too one had mixed feelings, partly a desire to stop the *Bismarck* at all costs and by so doing perhaps win honor and glory, partly – and I'm not sure if it wasn't the stronger part – a reluctance to get embroiled at all. Our task, if we met, was to close in to some 6000 yards to deliver our four torpedoes. With *Rodney* soon outdistanced by the swifter enemy, we would have to undergo the full weight of his broadsides during the run-in; and we knew, without having to say it, that if we survived that, it would be a miracle.

When I came on watch again at midnight, it was blowing a gale. We had had to reduce speed to 15 knots, while *Rodney* with her long dachshund's snout pushing through the crests had lumbered past at her maximum 22 knots and was now out of sight ahead. I think that was the most uncomfortable watch I ever kept. The motion was like that of a hovercraft in a bumpy sea, greatly magnified, for we lunged at the waves rather than rode them. Throughout the watch the signals from the shadowers kept coming in, and it looked as though the commander-in-chief would make contact with the enemy at around noon. When I reached my cabin via the engine-room and boiler-room (for there was a danger of being washed overboard along the upper deck) I found the place a shambles – books, wireless and broken water carafe strewn about the deck. I left them where they were and clambered into bed.

"Sir?"

Where was I?

"Seven-thirty. Here's your tea. I've cleaned up the mess on the deck. And Jerry's done a bunk."

I thought sleepily, this man has got his priorities right.

"Lost contact, have we?"

"Not a whisper since you came off watch. Can't say I'm altogether sorry."

This is not the place to recount the changing events and fortunes of either side during the rest of the operation, for we had little knowledge of them at the time . . . Suffice it to say that two days later when we had begun to think that *Bismarck* had disappeared off the face of the waters, she was spotted alone (for she had detached *Prinz Eugen* for independent warfare) some 700 miles north-west of Brest. Her speed was down to 20 knots which suggested damage or a fuel problem (it was both) but which would bring her under German air cover within twenty-four hours. At that time *Rodney*, *Tartar* and *Mashona* (*Somali* had left us to refuel) were still bucketing around the ocean at high speed, but we were some 150 miles to the north of her, and with only a couple of knots' advantage had virtually no chance of catching up.

There was still however one British group between *Bismarck* and France, Vice-Admiral Somerville's Force H. steaming north from Gibraltar; it included the aircraft-carrier *Ark Royal*, and if one of her torpedo-planes could slow down *Bismarck* a little more, there might still be a faint chance of bringing her to book. At six that evening Admiral Tovey in *King George V* thundered over the horizon to join us, and took station in the van.

Presently a signal lamp began flashing from the flagship's bridge. "To *Rodney*," sang out our signalman, "from C-in-C. What is your best speed?"

Then it was *Rodney*'s turn.

"To C-in-C. From *Rodney*. Twenty-two knots."

Gradually the distance between the two ships lengthened and *Rodney*'s lamp began flashing again.

"To C-in-C," shouted the signalman, "from *Rodney*. I am afraid that your twenty-two knots is faster than mine."

The flagship dropped back, and we all steamed on, less with any real hope of *Bismarck* being delivered to us than for the lack of any alternative; if failure had to be admitted, let it not be admitted until the last possible moment. At 6.30 p.m. Tovey signaled the Admiralty that unless *Bismarck*'s speed had been reduced by midnight, *King George V* would have to return to harbor for lack of fuel; *Rodney*, with *Tartar* and *Mashona* also very short of fuel, could continue until eight the next morning. A little later came a report from Admiral Somerville that he had launched a torpedo attack with Swordfish aircraft, but they had registered no hits: if the light held, he aimed to launch another. For two hours we waited in anticipation of this, praying, hoping that it might be successful. Then came a second signal: "Attack completed. Estimate no hits."

So that was it. The long week's night was over: we had lost *Hood* and gained nothing in exchange, and *Bismarck* was freed to fight another day. In *Rodney* the captain told the crew over the public address system that their last chance of bringing the enemy to action had gone, and his commander ordered guns' crews to stand down. As for *Tartar*, it is difficult to convey the extent of the gloom in which we sat down to supper in the wardroom; nor, now that the week-long tension had been broken and the banging and buffeting were almost over, the overwhelming sense of exhaustion we all felt.

And then a most extraordinary thing happened. A signal was received from the cruiser *Sheffield*, shadowing *Bismarck* from astern:

"Enemy's course 340°." Now 340° was almost due north, toward us, almost the opposite of the course of around 120° which she had been steering for Brest. On the bridge the general feeling was that the captain of the *Sheffield* must have made a mistake and thought *Bismarck* was steaming from right to left instead of left to right, understandable enough in the prevailing weather. But a few minutes later came a confirmatory signal, "Enemy's course North," and when further signals came in saying her speed was no more than a few knots, we all realized that *Bismarck* had been crippled by the last Swordfish attack (one torpedo had hit and jammed her rudder) and that she was going to be delivered to us after all.

So we made preparations for a battle which – unless *Bismarck* was able to slip away in the night – now looked inevitable; I stowed away all things breakable in my cabin, put on clean underwear and filled the brandy flask, mounted to my action station at the pom-pom, and wondered how it might be when the time came.

And then an odd thing occurred. An army officer, what the Navy calls a pongo, had come aboard when we first sailed as a wardroom guest; he had been given a week's leave, was hoping for a spot of sea breezes, had not thought to get involved in this. After dinner, not knowing the rules and having nothing to do, he had got rather tipsy, and now he appeared on the upper deck singing to the wild night his repertoire of pongo songs. When it was reported to the captain, he was ordered to go to his cabin and stay there. In former times, I suppose, he would have been clapped in irons or shot.

The weather worsened as the night wore on. The same head-wind into which *Bismarck* had involuntarily turned gave us a following sea; one in which the bows yawed sideways like a car in a skid, so that the ship leaned heavily to starboard and stayed there like a determined drunk until the quartermaster gradually eased her back to the given course. All night long we stayed at action stations while the ship slewed first one way and then the other and great rafts of spray, flung up from the bows, slapped at our oilskins and sou 'westers. At first I had turned over in my mind what our role might be – perhaps a night torpedo attack – but soon anything beyond the next five or ten minutes seemed remote and irrelevant. After what felt like an eternity dawn came, with curling wave-tops, a leaden sky, wretched visibility. Presently the commander-in-chief sent a signal asking *Tartar* and *Mashona* their fuel situation. When he had been told, he sent another signal: "On receipt of executive signal, proceed as convenient to refuel at Plymouth or Londonderry." Were we not going to be allowed to be in at the kill?

During the morning watch guns crews were allowed to go off in ones and twos for breakfast, and around 8 a.m. I went down to the wardroom for mine. Returning, I saw that *Rodney* and *King George V* had drawn well ahead of us, so popped up to the bridge for the latest news. There I found long faces and silence. I looked at the Yeoman of Signals quizzically and he handed me the signal log. "*Tartar* and *Mashona* from C-in-C," I read. "Proceed in execution of previous orders." So, thanks to our critical fuel situation (for if ordered in to a torpedo attack at speed, we would use up a great deal more), we were to be denied any part in the battle. But Tovey's original signal had said to proceed to refuel *as convenient* – "and what I'm going to find convenient," said the captain, "is to stick around for a bit and watch." I had reason for disappointment too. I had with me both my grandmother's Kodak and also a 16-millimeter Bell and Howell movie camera lent me by the father of a girl-friend; and with the pom-pom gun having no role to play, I could, had we been sent in on a torpedo attack, have obtained some unique footage.

A moment later I saw a big puff of cordite smoke above *Rodney*'s main armament and a second later heard the thud of her guns. Through my binoculars I saw in the distance, on the edge of a patch of rainfall, the dull smudge of a ship. There she was at last, the vessel that these past six days had filled our waking thoughts, been the very marrow of our lives. And, as the rain faded, what a ship! Broad in the beam, with long raked bow and formidable superstructure, two twin 15-inch gun turrets forward, two aft, symmetrical, massive, elegant, she was the largest, most handsome warship I, or any of us, had ever seen, a tribute to the skills of German shipbuilding. Now there came flashes from her guns and those of *King George V*. The final battle had begun.

In all my life I doubt if I will remember another hour as vividly as that one. It was the color contrasts I recall most, so rare in the eternal grayness of voyaging at sea. The sun appeared for the first time in days, shining from a blue sky between white, racing clouds; and the wind, still strong, was marbling and stippling the green water, creaming the tops of the short, high seas. There was the somber blackness of *Bismarck* and the gray of the British ships, the orange flashes of the guns, the brown of the cordite smoke, shell splashes tall as houses, white as shrouds.

It was a lovely sight to begin with, wild, majestic as one of our officers called it, almost too clean for the matter in hand. It seemed strange to think that within those three battleships were five thousand men; it seemed almost irrelevant, for this was a contest between ships not men. And who was going to win? None of us had any illusions about the devastating accuracy of *Bismarck*'s gunfire. She had sunk *Hood* with her fifth salvo, badly damaged *Prince of Wales*, straddled *Sheffield* and killed some of her crew the evening before, and hit an attacking destroyer in the course of the previous pitch-black night. But there were factors we had not reckoned with: the sheer exhaustion of her crew who had been at action stations for the past week, the knowledge as they waited through that long, last dreadful night that the British Navy was on its way to exact a terrible revenge, that they were virtually a sitting target.

*Rodney* was straddled with an early salvo but not hit, then with her fire divided, *Bismarck*'s gunnery sharply fell off. But that of *Rodney* and *King George* V steadily improved. As they moved in ever closer, we observed hit after hit. The hydraulic power that served the foremost turret must have been knocked out early, for the two guns were drooping downward at maximum depression, like dead flowers. The back of the next turret was blown over the side and one of its guns, like a giant finger, pointed drunkenly at the sky. A gun barrel in one of the two after turrets had burst, leaving it like the stub of a peeled banana. The main director tower had been smashed in and part of the foremost was in shreds. Through holes in the superstructure and hull we could see flames flickering in half a dozen places. But still her flag flew; still, despite that fearful punishment, she continued, though now fitfully, to fire.

It was not a pretty sight. *Bismarck* was a menace that had to be destroyed, a dragon that would have severed the arteries that kept Britain alive. And yet to see her now, this beautiful ship, surrounded by enemies on all sides, hopelessly outgunned and outmaneuvered, being slowly battered to a wreck, filled one with awe and pity. As Tovey said in his dispatch: "She put up a most gallant fight against impossible odds, worthy of the old days of the Imperial German Navy." And George Whalley, our Canadian lieutenant, wrote, "What that ship was like inside did not bear thinking of; her guns smashed, the ship full of fire, her people hurt; and surely all men are much the same when hurt." It was a thought shared by many British sailors that day, yet one rarely expressed by airmen who incinerate cities or by soldiers of those they kill in tanks.

By 10 a.m. the last of *Bismarck*'s guns had fallen silent. She was still making headway through the water, though now listing heavily to port. The fires had spread, and now smoke was issuing from a hundred cracks and crevices in the deck. And then, as we looked at this silent, deadweight shambles of a ship, we saw for the first time what had previously existed only in our imagination, the enemy in person, a little trickle of men in ones and twos, running or hobbling toward the quarterdeck to escape from the inferno that was raging forward; and as we watched they began to jump into the sea.

We had seen enough. It was time – way beyond time – to go home.

# ONE MAN'S WAR: THE DIARY OF AN ASDIC OPERATOR, 19 JANUARY–13 FEBRUARY 1942

## *Frank Curry RCN, HMCS* Kamsack

*Curry served as an Asdic operator with a Canadian corvette escorting convoys across the Atlantic.*

### Monday-January 19 [1942]

This morning spent doing a final check on the Asdic. We sailed at 1600, picking up oil from the *Teakwood* on the way out. Headed for the open Atlantic at dusk. Rounded up convoy of 78 ships and we took up our screening position on the port beam . . . here we go again.

### Tuesday-January 20

Weather not too bad as we plunge ahead. Sea quite heavy and kicking us around a fair bit. We are operating Asdic 2 on and 4 off. No sign of an echo so far. Tough time holding onto the convoy in the pitch dark. Thinking a lot of home so far away.

### Wednesday-January 21

We are steaming north-east with our large convoy. Heavy seas running, operating and watches down to a routine. So far not a sign of any trouble. Feeling pretty good – so far. Eating everything in sight – an enormous appetite. So it goes – where are we headed???

### Thursday-January 22

Operating 2 on and 4 off. Visibility closed down to one half mile. Picked up a sub echo at 0530 and we gave it two solid patterns . . . resumed position at 0700.

### Friday-January 23

Headed more easterly now – our convoy is steaming right along and for a change things are going very smoothly. Not a sign of trouble so far. Sighted two American destroyers and a patrol bomber off the port wing of the convoy . . . something to break the monotony.

### Saturday-January 24

Seas are running much rougher and huge swells are rolling us 40 and 50 degrees at a roll. We are warned to be on the lookout for Hudson bomber down in the Atlantic in our vicinity. What a hope in all this water. No sign of subs since that echo of several days ago.

**Sunday-January 25**
Greek ship on the far side of our convoy was torpedoed at 0500 this morning, nothing doing on our wing. HMCS *Rimouski* picked up some survivors. Sure feel tense when I am operating Asdic, knowing that subs are close by. Split my knee going to action stations when I skidded on the icy decks. Depth charges going off all round the convoy. We haven't had a contact yet.

**Monday-January 26**
Looks as if we might be getting off lightly this time as we have not lost any more ships. Things quietened down considerably – perhaps it is the huge seas that are running. We are bouncing around like a top. My knee is driving me crazy with throbbing. Still heading east, ever east.

**Tuesday-January 27**
Well, we are still rolling – and I do mean rolling – due east. How vast this old Atlantic appears to be to an awed landlubber like myself when I gaze out in all directions day after day and see nothing but turbulent waters as far as I can see – never dreamt a few short years ago that this is what my future would bring.

**Wednesday-January 28**
Boy – are there ever huge seas running. I never expected to see them this big – ever. We are still keeping the port beam of our convoy covered and heading ever east. We run out of spuds today. Rice from now on. Double lookouts on watch for long-range German Junker aircraft which are spotting allied convoys.

**Thursday-January 29**
Huge seas still running. We ran out of bread today and it will be a diet of hardtack from here on in. British escort arrived at dusk as we are now off the north-west coast of Ireland. We five corvettes gladly turned over our convoy to them and we – the *Kamsack*, *Rimouski*, *Trail*, *Trillium* and *Napanee* headed on alone at full speed.

**Friday-January 30**
Great seas still pounding us. We are close to the coast of Ireland as I write this. What a wonderful feeling after two solid weeks at sea. German air activity in the Irish sea reported, and we got a red

warning in our vicinity. Everyone highly enthused about getting near land. What a life.

### Saturday-January 31
Today is a great day – a wonderful day. At dawn, even before darkness lifted, we could smell that wonderful smell of land, earth, long before we could see it. In the early dawn we slipped quietly into Loch Foyle. Immediately went alongside a British tanker where we filled our near-empty oil tanks brimming. Ireland looks beautiful. Guess any solid earth looks beautiful at a moment like this. We sailed twenty miles up Loch Foyle and at dusk tied up in Londonderry. Everyone busy buying fresh cream, live chickens for packages of cigarettes. I headed ashore for the first time in Ireland – went along with Yearsley, and we wandered around in the blackout and rain, finally finding a chip shop where we had a feed of chips. Returned early – drew two pound casual.

### Tuesday-February 3
Morning spent lugging on board sacks and baskets of those huge Irish loaves of bread. We left Londonderry at 1300 and headed down Loch Foyle. Went alongside tanker at Moville. Rumor has it that we shall be boarded tonight.

### Wednesday-February 4
Up anchor at 0400 (no boarding during the night) and sailed with St. Laurent and four other corvettes. Out of Loch Foyle and so off to sea facing us as a rather unpleasant prospect. Feeling pretty grim as we plunge our way out into the Atlantic. Headed north-west, where to, know not we. Heavy seas running, and already our little ship is a mess . . .

### Thursday-February 5
A weird feeling to see it pitch dark at 0900 and a full moon shining down on us . . . we are heading to the north with our large westbound convoy, in the hope of eluding subs; operating steadily, with the seas having levelled off just a little, much to the relief of everyone on board.

### Friday-February 6
Thick fog has settled down around us – rather a queer feeling to be escorting a convoy that is invisible – a huge convoy of 73 ships. Suddenly at 1500 we cleared the fog and it was an amazing sight to gaze on our convoy in the brilliant sunshine. Lots of time off watch spent behind the funnel, the gathering place for the Funnel Gang – off watchers.

**Saturday-February 7**
Sea smooth as silk – there has been trouble close by. We sighted several large pieces of wreckage and then we came upon two machine-gun-riddled life boats, two dead seamen in one – nothing we could do about it – a terrible sight and I feel it very deeply. Action stations in the noon hour and the *Rimouski*, our old winger, is going at it hot and heavy on the other side of the convoy with a sub contact. No contacts for us, but I feel pretty tense every minute I am operating on the old Asdic set.

**Sunday-February 8**
Beautiful sunrise as I operated on the 0400–0600 watch. Something to remember, just to sit high on the bridge and gaze out on such a magnificent scene, with a brilliant sun coming up in the east and our great convoy steaming quietly on its way, with little corvettes spotted out on all wings. Still smooth as anyone could wish for – everyone amazed and happy about it. We picked up a good sub echo on the Asdic at 1925 and threw four patterns of depth charges at it – crew pretty tense, not to mention one FC.

**Monday-February 9**
A bit rough today, but really nothing to moan about. We are ploughing right ahead with our large convoy and making good progress. We have certainly swung far to the north with this one, and are now well up between Iceland and Greenland . . . must be method in this madness . . .

**Tuesday-February 10**
Seas have flattened out again, and we are steaming right along, with nothing out of the ordinary for the last couple of days. Just a constant alterness for something to happen . . .

**Wednesday-February 11**
Still (I repeat still) smooth as smooth. Grand warm sun came out and poured down on us all this long day. If you were trying to convince anyone back home that winter in the north Atlantic was not exactly a picnic, you would have a tough time today. Seems more like a summer cruise in the Caribbean. But we are not complaining a bit . . .

**Thursday-February 12**
Does not take it long to change. This morning it is rather rough and much, much colder. Guess we have moved out of the Gulf Stream and are now getting closer to the dear shores of Newfoundland. Feeling in

an awful mood, and thought I would go raving mad on the 2400–0400 watch. Staggered through it somehow.

# VOYAGE TO MURMANSK, SEPTEMBER 1942
## *Able Seaman Robert Carse, Merchant Navy*

*With the 1941 entry of the Soviet Union into the war, Britain was posed with a new problem: conveying war* materiel *to its hard-pressed new ally. The main route, to Murmansk and Archangel, was off the coast of occupied Norway and thus in easy range of both the* Kriegsmarine *and the* Luftwaffe. *When the USA also began supplying the Soviet Union with tanks (to the tune of 4,700), planes (7,800), boots (millions) and steel (a million tons plus) the "North Russia run" became the graveyard of thousands of Allied sailors. Carse was an American able seaman (and tyro gunner) on a merchantman bound from Scotland to Murmansk.*

We came one day into another port. This was no place like our anchorage in the Clyde and was used only for the purposes of war. More ammunition was brought out to us for our machine guns, and we cleared and inspected our P.A.C. rockets, the ingenious and skillful device by which, through rocket fire, 500 feet of piano wire is suspended above the ship between two small parachutes to slice the wing right off a diving Nazi plane or wind and wind, snarling around his propeller blades. On our 'midships and after decks also were huge smoke-screen cans which would protect us from the enemy we were very soon to meet . . .

From that port, again in convoy, we ran North. There was talk of the *Tirpitz* again, and of the *Admiral Scheer*, but we held to our course and came in good order up to that island which is one huge, smoky mountain thrusting from the fog swirl and surf rush of the sea. One more time we went to anchor, back in the tremendous depths of the harbor.

Our own bombers and patrol planes were overhead there. Our own battle wagons, cruisers, and destroyers and submarines came and went out again in ceaseless operation. We watched them, learning, studying, for we were with the Navy now, would fight with it. On the bleak shore, where the shaggy little Iceland ponies ran among the sod-walled houses and the humped khaki shapes of the fabricated huts, our Army jeeps jumped the ruts of the roads, and we could hear the racketing of machine-gun fire on the ranges; at night, sometimes see the enormous white lances of the Marine Corps anti-aircraft search-lights in the sky, hear a salvo burst in practice fire . . .

Fog closed some hours after that, bringing obscurity and a kind of fulginous darkness. Allen and I were in our bunks in our room at two-thirty when blond Olë and "Sensation," the wild-eyed ordinary, came running to the door. "Get up on deck," they said, the same note of shock and horror in their voices. "The *So-and-So* has just got it. She's sinking."

We grabbed our shoes and coats and ran for deck. The *So-and-So* was over on our starboard hand, two columns away from us to the inboard. Fog was close about her, dimming her, but her hull still showed black against the gray shoulders of the sea.

That hull was in two pieces. She had broken in half 'midships, was sinking. The explosion we had dully heard as we ran up the companion ladder was her cargo of T.N.T., and she carried a lot of the stuff. Vapor in a low and white and then broad and high cloud rose from her as her cylinder tops and boilers gave.

She sank, and those two black halves went into the sea like swiftly withdrawn fingers. We stood there, the wind hard against us, the fog clammy on our faces and coat collars, the deck slightly areel under us, but firm, shaken only by the strong turning of our screw. We didn't speak. The horror and the sorrow were too great. They were dead, and we were alive, and our brains could take no more . . .

During the fog, after the *So-and-So* had got it, the cruisers had pulled out of the convoy. Warning had been received by them that German surface raiders were out, and it was their task to find them. So that day and in all the rest of the battle we fought without the great aid of the cruisers' gunfire.

Raid after raid was made on us. The Messerschmitts were back, the jobs that had been on us yesterday and the same type that had done so much damage to London and the other cities in the Battle of Britain. But today, too, we had the Heinkel 111 K's, the twin-motored medium bombers that here were being used as aerial torpedo carriers.

They slanted down from the low ceiling at us through the snow and the sleet, and we hardly had our guns on them before they'd released their torpedoes and were up and away again. Those torpedoes they carried had a 21-inch warhead and weighed half a ton. In the air, they held the speed of the plane, 274 knots an hour. In the water, they made a speed of 35 knots, were fired from an approximate distance of 500 yards.

Our Commodore had warned us against them. We crouched tense watching for them, knowing just one would finish everything. The Heinkels came in a roaring dive, straight in the first part of it in the fashion of the dive-bombers. But then, as they released the torpedoes, they made a peculiar upward, flipping motion, and from under their broad wings the torpedoes took the sea.

There was a white splatter of spume as the torpedoes rushed into the

sea. Then they went beneath the surface to leap and broach at
intervals, porpoise-wise, as they raced towards the ships. We swung
with hard right helm, hard left helm back and away from them. Our
gunners, waiting, waiting, let go at the Heinkels just in that moment
when they executed that upward-flipping swing.

Visibility was bad, though, and it was hard for us to see our
enemy; the same for them. There were a lot of near misses that day
from torpedoes, from bombs, and from the floating mines the Nazi
planes dropped, but all of our ships came through safe. Tuesday was
another good day for us. We had done all right. Yet the Nazis had
discovered one major fact that a lot of us overlooked as we sat in our
messroom after the "All Clear" was given: the cruisers were no
longer with us. Our fire power was greatly reduced, particularly at
high altitudes.

The snow and the sleet squalls passed. Wednesday gave a clear
cerulean sky, a blue and gleaming sea, very little horizon or zenith
cloud. This was their day, the Nazis', we knew. We dragged our
ammunition cases closer to the guns; got ready as well as we could.

They came early: the Heinkels, the Messerschmitts, the Stukas, the
Junkers 89's, and all told there were 105 of them over us during that
day's fight that was to last twenty hours. They used everything: 1,100-
pounders, 550's, 250's, aerial torpedoes, mines, their cannons, and
their machine guns; while outside, always trying to get in, their
submarines rushed our escort.

That was hell. There is no other word I know for it. Everywhere you
looked aloft you saw them, crossing and recrossing us, hammering
down and back, the bombs brown, sleek in the air, screaming to burst
furiously white in the sea. All around us, as so slowly we kept on going,
the pure blue of the sea was mottled blackish with the greasy patches
of their bomb discharges. Our ship was missed closely time and again.
We drew our breaths in a kind of gasping choke.

At about half-past ten that morning, the long-shanked Fourth Mate
and I were on the after guns on the poop. Two Messerschmitts came
after us, off the bank of broken cirrus cloud on the Northern horizon.
Since Monday, the Messerschmitt squadrons had given our ship a lot
of attention, no doubt remembering their pal that we had nailed.

This pair came down in one-two formation, the aftermost perhaps
three hundred feet behind his partner. At the start of their direct dive
on us they had about two thousand foot altitude.

It was my first time to fire at them, and, eager and excited, I shot
too soon. My tracers curved off; I was out of range, so I cut the guns.
But they kept on coming, bigger and bigger in the ring sights, their
wings growing from thin lines to thick fierceness from which lanced

gun flame. We could see the bombs in the racks; we could see the bombardiers. Together, the Fourth Mate and I cut in at them.

We were leaning far back, knees bent, hands hard on the rubber grips, fingers down on the triggers, eyes to the ring sights. We were no longer conscious of the empties clacketing out underfoot, of the cold, the trembling motion of the ship as the other bombs burst. Here was death, and we were throwing death back to meet it.

The aftermost plane peeled off, banking towards the ship astern. The other kept on, right into our fire, smack for us. Then he dropped it, a 550-pounder. He was gone, away from our fire, and, hanging to the guns, all we could do was look up at that bomb.

It fell, slanting with the pull of the plane's speed. It whirled, screaming and howling in the air directly overhead. We could very clearly see the cylindrical khaki shape, the fins, even the white blur that was the serial markings on the side. This was for us, we thought. This was death. Even should it miss, the concussion will take the T.N.T.

There was nothing to do but hang on tighter to the gun grips. We said good-by to each other, but the bomb held our ears, the sound of it seemed to possess all sound.

Then in some sudden and not-yet-strong gust of wind it veered a bit. It struck the sea no more than twenty-five feet astern of us. There was the impact of passage into the sea, an immense, rushing smack, then the detonation. My wife's image was before my eyes. I stood there waiting for the T.N.T.

Water went tumbling over me in a dousing, blinding column. The ship rose and fell, groaning, terribly shaking. Empty cartridges jumped under the shock, pitched off into the sea. Beneath my feet, as the ship still jarred from that awful violence, the deck seams opened, and the oakum lay loose.

Water dripped from my helmet brim into my eyes. I was soaked from the collar of my sheepskin coat to my felt-lined boots. Beside me, still at his station between me and the Fourth Mate's guns, was old Ben. He was the oldest A.B. in the ship; Ben, a Baltimore man, who in the last war had seen service at the front in France. He might have run as that bomb fell, taken out forward for the life boats on the boat deck, anywhere away from the bomb. But he stayed there; he just bent his knees and set himself and waited, empty-handed and where he belonged.

For that moment of steadfastness, I loved Ben, and I always shall. We looked staring, shaking, just about conscious, into each other's eyes, and as the frightful tightness gave from our stomachs and lungs, spoke to each other. I forget what we said, and I guess it doesn't matter. We talked as shipmates, that was all.

Allen, my partner, was the next man up there. He had been coming up the companion ladder from the fo'c'sle below, and the shock had all but hurled him back down the steps. He helped me dry and reload my guns, and we tried them and they were all right. The ship was still going on, although now there was a great, grinding thump from the propeller under us. We were in a bad way, we knew. We had been damaged plenty below.

The Chief, quiet and bespectacled, came aft to look at her and told us that nine of the ten main bearings on the shaft had been shattered. There was a bad twist in the tail-shaft itself, and plates had been stove in the shaft alleyway. She was taking water there, but, for the time being, the pumps could handle that. We kept on going up to Russia.

# A U-BOAT IS DEPTH-CHARGED, MID-ATLANTIC 1942
## *Midshipman Heinz Schaefer, U-977*

*The crew of U-264 were lucky. Over the course of World War II, the Kriegsmarine, in addition to other vessels, lost 696 U-boats, almost all in the Atlantic. The fatality rate for U-boat crews was 63 per cent. No other service, of any type, of any combatant nation, suffered such a loss of life.*

The night, which was pitch dark without a moon, was in our favour. But some U-boats were failing to show up. As far as we could judge from the reports we got we might be six in all by dawn. It was an important convoy – fifty ships with war materials bound for England.

"Make call-signs," the Commander ordered.

Rather a nerve, sending out wireless messages right in among the enemy ships. If our wavelength was known we were finished. But it couldn't be helped, we had to have more U-boats.

Wireless operator to Commander: "U X has contacted the convoy."

Next thing we learned was that another of our boats had done so too.

So we were now three in all, and our Commander decided to attack. Bearing indications to the other ships were no longer required, as you can see the flash of a torpedo miles away, and if one ship went up in flames it would light the way for the other U-boats. We wanted to torpedo four ships, so we picked out the big ones, preparing to attack the furthest first and the rest afterwards, allotting two torpedoes to the largest ship, and one each to the others. If possible all four must hit simultaneously, so as to leave no time for alterations of course. We were quite close to the nearest ship already – 650 metres perhaps.

"*Fire!*"

The ship throbbed five times – we were using our after tube along with the rest. In fifteen seconds the torpedoes should hit. We grew impatient; they seemed such very long seconds. Perhaps the tinfish hadn't run properly. Was anything wrong?

A spurt of flame and then two thuds. Sound travels through water faster than through the air. One more explosion aboard the same ship. She was breaking apart now, and in a moment she had gone down. There could be few survivors. Then came two more explosions – one torpedo had evidently missed. In a moment the convoy which had been peacefully pursuing its course sprang to action with much flashing of red and blue lights and signals to change course. The British knew their job. To handle blacked-out ships in convoy at night is no easy task, yet there was no collision. A pity for us, it would have saved us extra work.

The destroyers now pounced on their prey. Searchlights switched on, guns opened fire, depth-charges detonated. But we were not discovered, for we were still in among the convoy, which was probably the last place they expected to find us. Instead of making off or diving we went further in. Our Commander guessed they'd overlook us there, and he was right. With a small range of vision you can easily overlook a submarine from the high bridge of a merchant-ship. It's hard to make out that dark streak on the water, to distinguish it from the shadows cast by the higher waves.

The rear doors of the torpedo tubes swung open, one torpedo after another sliding in. The crew were bathed in sweat, working like mad. It was a matter of life and death, no time or place for reflection. If they found us now we were utterly lost, for without our torpedoes secured we couldn't dive. This was war – "Go in and sink".

It lasted thirty-five minutes. Already we were making ready for the next attack.

Torpedo control officer to Commander: "Tubes one to four ready!"

Heavy explosions. Ships were breaking up, others letting off steam and coming to a standstill, thick smoke mounting skywards. Searchlights played on the dark water and the starry blaze of oil. SOS calls never stopped going out on the 600-metre wavelength. More U-boats were coming up. Still more explosions.

"Hope we don't buy one of the 'overs'," said the second officer of the watch. "It would be the limit if our own people sent us all to hell."

And it might so easily happen, seeing that we were all mixed up with the escort ships.

At last the convoy was really breaking up, ships making off in all directions. That was bad for us for we could only take one target at a time now. Besides, they'd had their warning – some were zig-zagging, others steaming on a circular course.

Hard a-starboard. Our next victim, an 8,000-ton ship, was held in the crosswires. "*Fire!*" Almost simultaneously with this fresh command a flash went up from her. But we only scored one hit, though she was listing heavily aft.

"Object ahead!"

We tried to get away – but the object moved more quickly than we could. Gradually it loomed larger. "Watch out! They're after us!" As we rushed below we heard more explosions. We were just robots. Things were happening spontaneously, events taking charge of us.

Our High Command had warned us about fast launches shipped aboard the convoys and launched when U-boats attacked at night. Their strength lay in their small size, amazing speed and strong armament of quick-firing guns. You could only see these craft when they were right on top of you, if you saw them at all.

Down to 50 fathoms. With 40 degrees load and all our power we sank into the depths . . . Was our engineer by any chance related to a fish? He dived the boat to the exact depth, put her on an even keel, closed the vents and finally reported "All clear".

"Well done," the Commander congratulated him.

Our friend the enemy had always got a new card up his sleeve. Well, the war would be very dull if he hadn't. Anyhow, we'd know better next time. The watch on the bridge were pretty alert in my opinion.

The first depth-charges were exploding now, but a long way off. We were still too close to the convoy and the destroyers couldn't pick us up because of all the other din – a happy state that could hardly last long. The Commander gave the order to proceed at silent speed. The electric engines were almost inaudible, and the auxiliaries shut off; words of command whispered, the ratings went around in felt shoes. Everybody not needed for immediate duty went off to lie down, as in that way we expended less oxygen. Nobody knew how long we would have to survive on what we had, and you consume less lying down than standing up and talking.

The convoy was steaming away now, its propellers barely audible. But three destroyers were after us, and before long the sound of their Asdic, like fingernails run over a comb, grew all too familiar. Another of their Asdic devices rattled like peas in a tin, a third screeched like an ancient tramcar taking a curve. We weren't likely to forget this experience. I thought of the man who went out to discover what fear meant. He should have been there.

The destroyers surrounded us, their explosions sounding closer and closer, usually in threes. My action-station was cramped up aft at the speaking-tube, and every time a charge exploded I had to report if there was any damage. The tube ran between the hull and the torpedo tube, and in this minute space I had to support myself leaning on one hand and aching in every limb. There was an almighty roar, and the boat sank like a stone for 20 metres: the light went out, and the emergency lighting came on automatically. It was no joke, when the enemy had us held like this on the dials of his instruments. Engine noises got louder – and the depth-charges ever nearer. The electricians were moving about the boat repairing damage: meanwhile the lights were switched over to the second of the two ring-main electrical circuits with which the boat was fitted. It went on for hours. Our wireless operators maintained contact with the destroyers, and kept the Commander posted; when they came closer he went to the wireless room himself to give orders.

Every time a destroyer was on top of us we altered course – you have to react instinctively. Fortunately our Commander knew exactly what he was about. He betrayed no feeling, and indeed everyone gave an appearance of self-control, but we were all uneasy, myself not least. It had never been as bad as this – we couldn't see, we couldn't shoot, we just had to last it out, though it was almost more than we could stand. We counted sixty-eight depth-charges.

How long could this unreal combat, not man to man or even weapon against weapon, this inhuman strain go on, this mixture of luck, blind tactics and instinctively doing the right thing at the right time? We were caught up in a mechanism, everyone getting down to their work in a dead, automatic silence. There was something un- canny about the whole atmosphere aboard. The ratings looked like phantoms.

There is a frightful crack, just as if the boat has been struck by a gigantic hammer. Electric bulbs and glasses fly about, leaving frag- ments everywhere. The motors have stopped. Reports from all stations show, thank God, that there are no leaks – just the main fuses blown. The damage is made good. We are now using special breathing apparatus to guard against the deadly carbon-monoxide which may be in the boat. The rubber mouthpiece tastes horrible. This is war all right, real war, not a film-war of waving flags and blaring music.

Yet the instinct of self-preservation is active in every man of us, and if we had been asked if we really felt frightened I doubt if we could have given a plain yes or no in reply.

The hundredth depth-charge bursts. Beads of sweat stand out on every forehead. As our last hope we discharge the *Bold* – the Asdic decoy to which so many U-boats owe their survival, its chemical components creating a film which hangs like a curtain in the water and gives an echo like a submarine to the destroyer's Asdic.

Our tactics then are to turn, intentionally, broadside on to our hunters, so as to make sure they get our echo, then turn away sharply and show them our stern, sneaking away and leaving the *Bold* for the hunting pack to worry.

Our *Bold* evidently helped us, for fewer depth-charges were exploding now, and it did seem the enemy had been tricked. After counting one hundred and sixty-eight charges in eight hours, we at last began to breathe again. The destroyers were steaming away. They had to pick up their convoy, for it needed an escort for the coming night. If every U-boat had pinned down three destroyers, then only one of the ten could still be with the convoy, and things would be easier for other U-boats.

Our kind of warfare is not what the layman thinks it is, just slinking up under water, shooting and stealing away like a thief in the night. On the contrary, most ships are torpedoed in an escorted convoy by a surfaced submarine; and although the size of a destroyer doesn't allow for an unlimited number of depth-charges – I imagine that they must make do with about eighty – what they have can make things hot enough while the action lasts.

We waited for an hour and then we surfaced.

Full speed ahead.

# FATAL SIX WEEKS: THE LOG OF A U-BOAT KILLER, 31 JANUARY–19 FEBRUARY 1944

## *Commander DEG Wemyss RN, HMS* Wild Goose

*The Second Escort Group killed no less than six U-boats in six weeks at the beginning of 1944. By then the Battle of the Atlantic had clearly been won and most U-boat operations were virtual suicide missions.*

### I. U-592. 31st JANUARY

The U-boat was abaft my beam when I started to turn towards her, and the noise of a number of ship's propellers in her hydrophones must have drowned the sound of my ship's increase of speed at the start of the attack. At any rate she made no move to get out of the way, nor did she get off her torpedoes in a hurry as I came charging in, and it looked as though the attack was unexpected up to the last moment. Then I imagine there came a cry from the U-boat's hydrophone operator of: "Propellers . . . Fast . . . Loud . . . Getting louder!" and a *"Himmel"* from the captain as he swung his periscope round and caught sight of us coming. He acted fast and in time, for he dodged my pattern of depth-charges all right. His mind, however, was no longer occupied with thoughts of attacking and sinking anyone, which meant that we had achieved our first objective. His next intention, to get safely away out of all this, could be dealt with in the manner we liked best, in slow time.

My chief fear during the run in to attack was that I should get there too late to put the enemy off his stroke. The Asdic contact was grand, and the attack more or less ran itself, but try as I could to stop them, those big ships would come on. Of course, the whole thing was very quickly over, though it seemed to take ages at the time, and the depth-charges produced an immediate response. With delight I saw the carriers turn and present their sterns, which meant that even if torpedoes had been fired they would now miss. With fresh heart we were now free to proceed with the second part of the programme.

There is not much more to tell. Conditions were very good indeed, and the enemy proved strangely docile after his early show of spirit. We regained our contact after the attack and had it confirmed, first by the *Magpie* and then by the Boss in the *Starling*. The *Magpie* had a go, but missed and was told to rejoin the screen. The Boss then ordered an "Extra Special" and charges rained down. Debris and oil appeared in sufficient quantity, and that was the end of the hunt.

### 2. U-762. 8th FEBRUARY

The weather held wonderfully fine, and the night of 9th February was clear and moonlit. My ship was out in the deep field on the convoy's port bow when a shout from the port look-out drew the officer of the watch's attention to a U-boat on the surface. It was a nice bit of work, as the enemy was fully a mile and a half away, with little but the conning tower showing, and I am glad to say that the lookout, Able Seaman J. G. Wall, was decorated for it.

We turned towards her at once, but before I had got to the bridge, or the guns had opened fire, she dived. The Asdic team, however, did their stuff and it was not long before we had contact, had told the Boss about it, and had been ordered to hang on until he could team up as usual. The U-boat made no use of speed or violent manœuvre to shake us off, while, since we knew that she had a long way to go before she became a danger to the convoy, we kept quiet as well. The two ships approached one another in this leisurely manner on opposite courses until it was clear that the U-boat would pass more or less directly underneath the ship. I do not suppose the U-boat realised that she had been spotted before diving, nor, apparently, did she hear anything on her hydrophones, as her next action caught us completely by surprise and made me feel extremely foolish. She put up her periscope not more than twenty yards from the ship. The look-out saw it and let out a yell: I followed his pointing arm and there it was in the moonlight, a good two feet of it. The U-boat captain evidently intended to have a good look round, and I trust he was even more surprised at what he saw than we were.

My first reaction was to go full ahead and drop a pattern: a really good shot with the port thrower would score a bull on that periscope. I had hardly got out the orders to the engines, and the depth-charge party had only started to take action, when I looked in the water alongside and realised we could never make it. We might damage the U-boat, but we could certainly never get enough way on the ship to avoid blowing our own stern off. She was too close for the four-inch guns, and the only action was the result of some quick thinking on the part of the men stationed at the close range weapons. Ordinary Seaman R. W. Gates on one Oerlikon got off a pan of ammunition, and I think the stripped Lewis-gun got off some rounds; at any rate tracer hopped all round that periscope, we thought we saw sparks fly from it, we hoped the fellow at the other end got an eye-bath, and then it disappeared.

Having persuaded the depth-charge party not, repeat NOT, to fire, we tried to withdraw to a more convenient range to collect ourselves, and continue to carry out the Boss's orders, but found that the enemy had made up his mind to beat it in exactly the same direction. We simply could not get away from him, and the situation seemed to be getting out of hand when order was restored by the arrival of the *Woodpecker*. She had been told to join in the hunt as well, and had beaten the *Starling* to it. When she had got contact there were two of us on the job and matters could proceed properly. She ran in for the first attack, dropped her charges, and the contact disappeared. Up came the *Starling*, and was directed to the spot. "Come over here," signalled Captain Walker to Commander Pryse, "and look at the mess you have made." I circled round the two of them while they examined her handiwork, and then we dispersed to our stations again.

### 3. U-734. 9th FEBRUARY

That action finished at about 1 am. Not long after 4 am I was once more flying up to the bridge to learn that Able Seaman J. D. Hunt, on radar watch, had detected another U-boat on the surface. The sequence of events was the same as before; she dived before we could get the guns off, we got Asdic contact, told the world and were told by the Boss that he was coming. I knew, however, that this time he was a good way off and would be a couple of hours reaching me. Hang on as I would, but be stared at through a periscope twice in one night was more than anyone could stand, and so I determined to have a smack at this one right away. We might lose contact in the commotion, but we should just have to pick it up again if we missed, and anyway it would keep her quiet until we could attend to her properly. It worked out according to this plan. The pattern produced no evidence of damage, but we picked up the trail after our attack and followed it without trouble as the U-boat made no real effort to shake us off. The Boss turned up at 6.30 am and between us we put in two "Extra Specials". The first one winged her, and after that she left a trail of oil wherever she went; the second one got her. Again we got debris, but no survivors.

#### 4. U-238. 9th FEBRUARY

As soon as the Boss was satisfied, we were on our way again to a fresh "incident". From snatches of intercepted signals we gathered that the *Kite* had picked up another U-boat at about the same time as our second, which, with the *Magpie* to help, she had been hammering ever since. This enemy had proved a tougher and more wily opponent than the other two, so that all their patience and perseverance had not managed to hurt her much, although she had not succeeded in getting away and losing herself either. We sped along at a brisk pace to the scene of this struggle, a matter of thirty miles away, and on arrival I was put on patrol to keep the ring, while the Boss mixed it with the others in the middle. After all the drama of the night this was a welcome spell of quiet, though it was good to see our leader going at it with undiminished vigour. There was some hard slogging still for him to do, with this agile customer sidestepping attack after attack. The *Kite* had to be pulled out of the struggle to join me as ring-keeper because she was practically out of depth-charges. Then, at last, the end came. Our scientists ashore may not have been best pleased at the way in which it was done, but that is a technical joke not worth telling here. Sufficient to say that the *Magpie* was duly blooded, and the Group's third victim within fifteen hours was safely gathered in.

#### 5. U-424. 11th FEBRUARY

It was just before midnight on the following night, as we reached the end of our beat, that we found one, and once again my ship was in luck. The moment was an awkward one, as the Group was engaged in the manœuvre of changing the direction of search, which meant that we were not in a formation to keep clear of one another. I told the rest what I had found, and our new senior officer tried to confirm the contact, at first without success. Still under the influence of what I can only describe as a "Won't be stared at through periscopes" complex, I then made to attack, and went through a hair-raising time, as I had to break off and stop the ship to avoid a colleague, and then re-start the attack from only 400 yards range. The explosion of the pattern lifted the stern of the ship, but she still held together, and the instruments still worked so the battle could proceed. Conditions for some reason were not as good as usual, and an uncomfortable time followed while we lost and regained and lost contact again while trying to follow the U-boat, which was snaking freely. The *Woodpecker* got contact firmly, though she was not sure that she had a genuine submarine echo, and only attacked it for luck, without result. They then lost it altogether, and it looked as though this whole operation would turn out a frost until Wilkinson, promoted to leading seaman, and his Asdic team, announced a firm contact at last, well clear of consorts. It was astern and at long range, which sounded on the face of it unlikely, but Leading Seaman Wilkinson was so confident that I begged to be excused, and went back after it. It got better as we got closer, until we were not only sure that we had got hold of the real thing, but knew enough about it to attack. The proper thing would have been to wait for a colleague to confirm, but this groping around, dot and carry one business was tiring people out without getting anywhere, and so in we went. We lost contact again on the way in, but were determined to have a bang, and completed the attack. After that we waited.

There was no contact, but instead we were rewarded with sounds. First of all I was told my listeners could hear a noise as though someone was hitting a bit of metal with a hammer. That went on intermittently for some minutes, and then there followed a sharp crack: two more bangs like muffled explosions came next, and then silence.

We had heard of what the submariners call "breaking up noises", which came from a ship as she sinks after disappearing from view. It seemed fair to assume that what we had been listening to were breaking up noises from a U-boat, and, since other ships present had also heard them, and none of us now had a contact, it was decided not to hunt further, but to patrol around this spot until daylight and see if any evidence could be found then. We told the Boss what we had done, and gathered from his reply that he was hastening back; having replenished his stock of depth-charges, and would give us his verdict when he had seen the evidence.

The investigation at dawn was rather disappointing. There were patches of oil, of which we picked up samples for analysis, since the light diesel oil that the submarines use is different from the oil burnt in ship's boilers, and there was some wooden debris painted grey, but of a nondescript character that might have come from any kind of vessel.

The Boss turned up about ten o'clock and was justifiably uncon-
vinced, but I was so insistent with my story of the bangs that he gave
us the benefit of the doubt, and decreed that we would all go away and
return before dark, when he would give us his decision. We formed up
and away we went. It was a long and tiresome day, and I, for one, got
my head down all the afternoon to make the time pass. At 5 pm we
were back, and what a sight met our eyes this time. An oil patch
covered several square miles of sea, in the middle of which floated a
convincing quantity of debris. "The U-boat is sunk," signalled the
*Starling*, "you may splice the main brace."

## 6. U-264. 19th FEBRUARY

At daybreak the convoy was clear of attack, but it was tolerably
certain that the discomfited U-boats would be found not far astern of
the convoy, and so that was where Captain Walker took the Group to
look for them. We started the search at 9 am and by 11 am the
*Woodpecker* had "found". She had plenty of depth-charges left, and so
she and the *Starling* hunted while the rest of us kept the ring. It was a
long hunt this time, of great interest to the people in the middle, but
dull for the rest of us until the climax came. A series of attacks had
damaged the U-boat until her leaks got beyond the capacity of her
crew to keep under. She was getting heavier and heavier and nothing
further could be done, so her captain decided to abandon ship. He
used the last of his high-pressure air to get to the surface, the crew got
out and the submarine sank at once. We got off some shots when she
broke surface, but soon realised it was a waste of ammunition and
ceased fire. The whole crew was picked up.

# Part Three

*The War in the Desert*
*North Africa, 1940–43*

# INTRODUCTION

The spillover of World War II from Europe into Africa was primarily caused by the territorial ambitions of Mussolini. With the vision of a new Roman Empire before him, the Italian Fascist leader first struck at Britain's East African colonies. This turned into an ignominious rout when British forces – primarily made up of colonial units – defeated the Italians at Keren, Eritrea, in March 1941 and promptly occupied Italy's colony of Ethiopia. Mussolini's offensive against Egypt and the strategically vital Suez Canal was no more auspicious. Launched from the Italian possession of Libya, the army of Marshal Rodolfo Graziani marched sixty miles into Egypt in three days – and then, enormously over-extended, collapsed at Sidi Barrani before a surprise attack on 9 December 1940 by Britain's Western Desert force. The counter-offensive subsequently rolled Graziani back 400 miles to Beda Fomm.

And so was set the pattern of war in the Western Desert. A running offensive (and retreat by the other side) along the single coastal road, with the pursuer attempting to hook around the pursued to cut off the retreat whilst also striking at his defended positions (essentially the ports of Tobruk, Gazala, Benghazi, El Aghelia, Tripoli). The war in the desert would probably have been over by spring 1941 had not Hitler sent Mussolini a rescuing knight in tank armour, Erwin Rommel. For eighteen months the conflict in the Western Desert swung back and forth along the 1,200-mile coastal strip until October 1942 when the British Eight Army, under the newly appointed Montgomery, landed a reeling blow at El Alamein which forced Rommel into headlong retreat towards Tunisia. Unfortunately for Rommel, Tunisia was no haven, because on 8 November an Anglo-America Army began to land in French North Africa in Operation

Torch. The Afrika Korps was squeezed between a rock and a hard place. Six months of dogged fighting later, 13 May 1943, Tunis fell to the Allies. The war in Africa was over.

# THE BATTLEGROUND: THE WESTERN DESERT, AUTUMN, 1940

### *Alan Moorehead, war correspondent*

Yellow rocks, saltbush, grey earth and this perfect beach was the eternal background wherever you looked in the north of the Western Desert. Except at spots along the coast and far inland it never even achieved those picturesque rolling sandhills which Europeans seem always to associate with deserts. It had fresh colours in the morning, and immense sunsets. One clear hot cloudless day followed another in endless progression. A breeze stirred sometimes in the early morning, and again at night when one lay on a camp bed in the open, gazing up into a vaster and more brilliant sky than one could ever have conceived in Europe. I found no subtle fascination there nor any mystery, unless it was the Bedouin who appeared suddenly and unexpectedly out of the empty desert as soon as one stopped one's car. But there was a sense of rest and relaxation in the tremendous silence, especially at night, and now the silence is still the best thing I remember of the desert, the silence, the cool nights, the clear hot days and the eternal flatness of everything.

The morning I drove towards Mersa Matruh, however, looking for Force quarters, a khamseen was blowing, and that of course changed everything. The khamseen sandstorm, which blows more or less throughout the year, is in my experience the most hellish wind on earth. It picks up the surface dust as fine as baking powder and blows it thickly into the air across hundreds of square miles of desert. All the way through Daba's tent-hospital base and past Fuka it gathered force along the road until at Bagush it blocked visibility down to half a dozen yards. In front of the car little crazy lines of yellow dust snaked across the road. The dust came up through the engine, through the chinks of the car-body and round the corners of the closed windows. Soon everything in the car was powdered with grit and sand. It crept up your nose and down your throat, itching unbearably and making it difficult to breathe. It got in your ears, matted your hair and from behind sandgoggles your eyes kept weeping and smarting. An unreal yellow light suffused everything. Just for a moment the billows of blown sand would open, allowing you to see a little farther into the hot solid fog ahead, and then it would close in again. Bedouin, their heads muffled in dirty rags, lunged weirdly across the track. You sweated, returned again and again to your water-bottle for a swig of warm sandy water, and lay back gasping. Sometimes a khamseen may blow for days, making you feel that you will never see light and air and feel coolness again . . .

More and more I began to see that desert warfare resembled war at sea. Men moved by compass. No position was static. There were few if any forts to be held. Each truck or tank was as individual as a destroyer, and each squadron of tanks or guns made great sweeps across the desert as a battle-squadron at sea will vanish over the horizon. One did not occupy the desert any more than one occupied the sea. One simply took up position for a day or a week, and patrolled about it with Bren-gun carriers and light armoured vehicles. When you made contact with the enemy you manœuvred about him for a place to strike, much as two fleets will steam into position for action. There were no trenches. There was no front line. We might patrol five hundred miles into Libya and call the country ours. The Italians might as easily have patrolled as far into the Egyptian desert without being seen. Always the essential governing principle was that desert forces must be mobile: they were seeking not the conquest of territory or position but combat with the enemy. We hunted men, not land, as a warship will hunt another warship, and care nothing for the sea on which the action is fought. And as a ship submits to the sea by the nature of its design and the way it sails, so these new mechanised soldiers were submitting to the desert. They found weaknesses in the ruthless hostility of the desert and ways to circumvent its worst moods. They used the desert. They never sought to control it. Always the desert set the pace, made the direction and planned the design. The desert offered colours in browns, yellows and greys. The army accordingly took these colours for its camouflage. There were practically no roads. The army shod its vehicles with huge balloon tyres and did without roads. Nothing except an occasional bird moved quickly in the desert. The army for ordinary purposes accepted a pace of five or six miles an hour. The desert gave water reluctantly, and often then it was brackish. The army cut its men – generals and privates – down to a gallon of water a day when they were in forward positions. There was no food in the desert. The soldier learned to exist almost entirely on tinned foods, and contrary to popular belief remained healthy on it. Mirages came that confused the gunner, and the gunner developed precision-firing to a finer art and learned new methods of establishing observation-posts close to targets. The sandstorm blew, and the tanks, profiting by it, went into action under the cover of the storm. We made no new roads. We built no houses. We did not try to make the desert livable, nor did we seek to subdue it. We found the life of the desert primitive and nomadic, and primitively and nomadically the army lived and went to war.

The Italians failed to accept these principles, and when the big fighting began in the winter it was their undoing. They wanted to be masters of the desert. They made their lives comfortable and static. They built roads and stone houses and the officers strode around in brilliant scented uniforms. They tried to subdue the desert. And in the end the desert beat them.

## THE ITALIANS SURRENDER AT BEDA FOMM, 7 FEBRUARY 1941

### Cyril Joly, 7th Armoured Division

*A breakneck march by the British 7th Armoured Division saw them hook around behind the retreating Italian 10th Army, which was then trapped at Beda Fomm between the "Desert Rats" and the 6th Australian Division.*

Before first light the leaguers were astir, and as the dawn reddened the eastern sky behind us, it lit the long, straggling, inert mass of the Italian column where it lay still in its positions of the previous day. The Italians had been harassed throughout the night by our guns and a number of roving infantry fighting patrols which had kept them on the alert and deprived them of rest and any chance to reorganize. From my position on the dune I watched an attack which was launched soon after dawn by about thirty Italian tanks against the position on the road. This was beaten off quickly and with little difficulty.

For a time there was silence on both sides. For all the efforts of the previous day, the Italian column still looked huge and threatening. I watched with apprehension the movements of the mass of vehicles before me. On either side of me, hidden behind the crests of other dunes and ridges, I knew that there were other eyes just as anxious as mine, surveying the scene before them. In the mind of each one of us was the sure knowledge that we were well outnumbered. Each of us knew by what slim margin we still held dominance over the battlefield. Our threat was but a façade – behind us there were no more reserves of further troops. Even the supplies of the very sinews which could keep us going had almost run out. If we lost now we were faced with capture or a hopeless retreat into the empty distances of the inner desert. It was a sobering thought. I felt that the day, with all its black, wet dullness, was heavy with ominous foreboding. The scene before me was made gloomy enough to match my mood by the black clouds of acrid smoke which shrouded the battlefield like a brooding pall.

Gradually I became aware of a startling change. First one and then another white flag appeared in the host of vehicles. More and more became visible, until the whole column was a forest of waving white banners. Small groups of Italians started to move out hesitantly towards where they knew we lay watching them. Larger groups appeared, some on foot, some in vehicles.

Still not able to believe the evidence of his own eyes, the Colonel warned, ". . . Don't make a move. This may be a trap. Wait and see what happens. Off."

But it was no trap. Italians of all shapes and sizes, all ranks, all regiments and all services swarmed out to be taken prisoner. I felt that nothing would ever surprise me again after my loader suddenly shouted: "Look, sir, there's a couple of bints there coming towards us. Can I go an' grab 'em, sir? I could do with a bit of home comforts." We took the two girls captive, installed them in a vehicle of their own and kept them for a few days to do our cooking and washing. I refrained from asking what other duties were required of the women, but noted that they remained contented and cheerful.

Out of the first confusion, order was slowly restored. Each squadron was given a part of the battlefield where we were to collect the prisoners and equipment and to keep careful tally of the captures. It was a novel but exhausting task, and Kinnaird, anxious to be done with it as soon as possible, pushed and harried us to clear our portion of the area.

The battlefield was an amazing sight. It was strewn with broken and abandoned equipment, tattered uniforms, piles of empty shell and cartridge cases. It was littered with paper, rifles and bedding. Here and there small groups of men tended the wounded who had been gathered together. Others were collecting and burying the dead. Still others, less eager to surrender than the majority, stood or lay waiting to be captured. Some equipment was still burning furiously, more was smouldering. There were many oil and petrol fires emitting clouds of black smoke.

There were few incidents. Soon the generals and the high-ranking officers had been discovered and taken away. The remaining officers were piled unceremoniously into Italian lorries and driven off. The thousands of men were formed into long columns guarded at head and tail by only one or two of our impassive, imperturbable and perpetually cheerful soldiers, who shouldered the unaccustomed new duties with the same confident assurance with which they had met and mastered all the other trials of the campaign.

It was the work of some days to clear the battlefield of all that was worth salvaging and to muster and despatch on their long march to the prison camps in Egypt the thousands of prisoners.

# ENTER ROMMEL, FEBRUARY–JULY 1941

## *Leutnant Heinz Werner Schmidt, Afrika Korps*

*Born in 1891, Rommel first distinguished himself in World War I, winning a Pour le Merite. An early Nazi sympathiser, he commanded the Fuhrer's escort battalion during the Austrian, Sudetenland and Czech occupations and the Polish campaign. During the invasion of France, he commanded the 7th Panzer Division to such great distinction that he earned himself promotion to commander of the Afrika Korps. Although he only arrived in North Africa on 12 February 1941, and knew nothing of desert warfare, he was a born master of mobile operations – so garnering the nickname "The Desert Fox" by an admiring enemy – and by 24 March was on the offensive. After unceremoniously ejecting the British from Beda Fomm he went eastwards at lightning speed and by 11 April was almost at the start line of O'Connor's December 1940 offensive.*

We went for the little fort in the desert, and the British positions round it, from three directions. The engagement was sharp but lasted only a couple of hours. We took the British commander, Major-General Gambier-Parry, in his tent. The haul of prisoners numbered almost three thousand. We had a further spectacular success. A mobile force of motor-cyclists caught up with the British column moving eastward across the desert below the Jebel Akhdar nearby, and to their astonishment held up the two heroes of the British advance to Benghazi: Lieutenant-General Sir Richard O'Connor, who had just been knighted for his successes against the Italians, and Lieutenant-General Sir Philip Neame, V.C. So we had three generals in the bag.

Mechili landing-ground was littered with destroyed planes. British machines swooped down to attack it afresh at short intervals. At the height of one assault, "my" Fieseler Storch dropped in out of the sky. Out stepped Rommel, smiling buoyantly, fresh from a personal reconnaissance of the desert scene.

The command trucks of the captured British generals stood on a slight rise. They were large, angular vehicles on caterpillar tracks, equipped inside with wireless and facilities for "paper" work. We christened them "Mammoths" then, but I did not realize that these useful trucks would be used by Rommel and his staff and commanders right through the long struggle that was now beginning in the desert.

Rommel inspected the vehicles with absorbed interest after a brief interview with the captured British generals. He watched them emptied of their British gear. Among the stuff turned out he spotted a pair of large sun-and-sand goggles. He took a fancy to them. He grinned, and said, "Booty – permissible, I take it, even for a General." He adjusted the goggles over the gold-braided rim of his cap peak.

Those goggles for ever after were to be the distinguishing insignia of the "Desert Fox".

### General Erwin Rommel, Afrika Korps

*Rommel writes to his wife.*

3 April 1941

DEAREST LU, – We've been attacking since the 31st with dazzling success. There'll be consternation amongst our masters in Tripoli and Rome, perhaps in Berlin too. I took the risk against all orders and instructions because the opportunity seemed favourable. No doubt it will all be pronounced good later and they'll say they'd have done exactly the same in my place. We've already reached our first objective, which we weren't supposed to get until the end of May. The British are falling over each other to get away. Our casualties small. Booty can't yet be estimated. You will understand that I can't sleep for happiness.

### Brigadier James Hargest, 5th New Zealand Infantry Brigade

*Hargest was captured at Sidi Azis in July.*

There was a little stir among the Germans and another appeared. It was Rommel. He sent for me. I bowed to him. He stood looking at me coldly. Through an interpreter he expressed his displeasure that I had not saluted him. I replied that I intended no discourtesy, but was in the habit of saluting only my seniors in our own or allied armies. I was in the wrong, of course, but had to stick to my point. It did not prevent him from congratulating me on the fighting quality of my men.

"They fight well," he said.

"Yes, they fight well," I replied, "but your tanks were too powerful for us."

"But you also have tanks."

"Yes, but not here, as you can see."

"Perhaps my men are superior to yours."

"You know that is not correct."

Although he had been fighting for over a week and was travelling in a tank, he was neat and clean, and I noticed that he had shaved before entering the battle that morning.

## A TANK IS "BREWED-UP", LIBYA, 15 JUNE 1941

### *Cyril Joly, 7th Armoured Division*

"Driver, halt," I ordered. "Gunner, 2-pounder – traverse left – on – tank – German Mark III – eight five zero yards. Fire." I watched Basset carefully turn the range-drum to the right range, saw him turn to his telescope and aim, noticed out of the corner of my eye that King was ready with the next round, and then the tank jolted slightly with the shock of the gun firing. Through the smoke and dust and the spurt of flame I watched intently through my binoculars the trace of the shot in flight. It curved upwards slightly and almost slowly, and then seemed to plunge swiftly towards the target. There was the unmistakable dull glow of a strike of steel on steel. "Hit, Basset! Good shot! Fire again," I called. Another shot and another hit, and I called, "Good shot; but the bastard won't brew."

As I spoke I saw the flame and smoke from the German's gun, which showed that he was at last answering. In the next instant all was chaos. There was a clang of steel on the turret front and a blast of flame and smoke from the same place, which seemed to spread into the turret, where it was followed by another dull explosion. The shock-wave which followed swept past me, still standing in the cupola, singed my hands and face and left me breathless and dazed. I looked down into the turret. It was a shambles. The shot had penetrated the front of the turret just in front of King, the loader. It had twisted the machine-gun out of its mounting. It, or a jagged piece of the torn turret, had then hit the round that King had been holding ready – had set it on fire. The explosion had wrecked the wireless, torn King's head and shoulders from the rest of his body and started a fire among the machine-gun boxes stowed on the floor. Smoke and the acrid fumes of cordite filled the turret. On the floor, licking menacingly near the main ammunition stowage bin, there were innumerable small tongues of flame. If these caught on, the charge in the rounds would explode, taking the turret and all in it with it.

I felt too dazed to move. My limbs seemed to be anchored, and I wondered vaguely how long I had been standing there and what I ought to do next. It was a miracle that the explosion had left me unharmed, though shaken. I wondered what had happened to Basset and bent into the cupola to find out. Shielded behind the gun and the recoil guard-shield, Basset, too, had escaped the main force of the explosion. The face that turned to look at me was blackened and scorched and the eyes, peering at me from the black background, seemed to be unnaturally large and startlingly terrified. For once Basset's good humour had deserted him, and the voice which I heard was shaking with emotion.

"Let's get out of 'ere, sir. Not much we can do for King, poor bastard! – 'e's 'ad it and some. An' if we 'ang around we'll catch a packet too. For Gawd's sake let's—off quick."

At last I awoke from my daze. "O.K., Basset. Tell Newman to bale out, and be bloody quick about it."

As Basset bent to shout at the driver the tank was struck again, but this time on the front of the hull. When the smoke and dust cleared, Basset bent again to shout at Newman. A moment later he turned a face now sickened with horror and disgust and blurted out:

"'E's ad it too, sir. It's took 'alf 'is chest away. For—'s sake let's get out of 'ere." In a frenzy of panic he tried to climb out of the narrow cupola past me, causing me to slip and delaying us both. Through my mind there flashed the thought that the German would still continue to fire until he knew that the tank was knocked out, and as yet no flames would be visible from the outside. Inside the turret there was now an inferno of fire.

Without knowing how I covered the intervening distance, I found myself lying in a small hollow some twenty yards from my stricken tank, watching the first thin tongues of flame and black smoke emerging from the turret top.

## ONE MAN'S WAR: DESERT WEARINESS, OCTOBER 1941

### Private R.L. Crimp, 7th Armoured Division

*18 October 1941.* Just lately I've been feeling a bit browned off. There's a sort of psychological complaint some chaps get after long exposure on the Blue called "desert weariness", though I can hardly claim to have reached that yet. But for months now we've been cut off from nearly every aspect of civilized life, and every day has been cast in the same monotonous mould. The desert, omnipresent, so saturates consciousness that it makes the mind as sterile as itself. It's only now that you realize how much you normally live through the senses. Here there's nothing for them. Nothing in the landscape to rest or distract the eye; nothing to hear but roaring truck engines; and nothing to smell but carbon exhaust fumes and the reek of petrol. Even food tastes insipid, because of the heat, which stultifies appetite. The sexual urge, with nothing to stir it, is completely dormant, and there's nothing to encourage its sublimation except, perhaps, this crack-pot journal.

Then over and above the physical factors, there's the total lack of change or relaxation; nothing really certain even to look forward to, that, after a term of such vacuum-living, would make it tolerable. In civvy-street, when day's work is done, there's always an hour or two watching Rita Hayworth, a couple of drinks at the "Spread Eagle", a chair by the fire and a Queen's Hall prom, or a weekend's hike on the North Downs. Even in camp there's Garrison Theatre, or Shafto's Shambles, and the ubiquitous NAAFI. But here there's no respite or getting away from it all. For weeks, more probably months, we shall have to go on bearing an unbroken succession of empty, ugly, insipid days. Perhaps, eventually, a chance will come of a few days' leave in Cairo, but that's too vague and remote to be worth setting tangible hopes upon. Anything might happen in the meantime. But the one thing that keeps the chaps going, that gives them a sort of dogged persistence in living through these interim days, is the thought of Home.

The immediate present effect, however, is extreme mental sluggishness, sheer physical apathy, and a vast aversion to exertion in every form. The most trivial actions, such as cleaning the sand off weapons, making a fire for a brew, or, when you're lying down by the truck, moving position into the patch of shade that the surf has shifted, seem utterly not worthwhile and require a tremendous effort to perform. It all seems so futile.

Then, of course, there are the flies. Lord Almighty, that such pests should ever have been created! Bad enough in any climate, the Egyptian sort are militant in the extreme, almost a different type, imbued with a frenzied determination to settle on human flesh. This may be due to the aridity of the terrain and to the fact that the only moisture available is human sweat. Soon after sunrise they arrive in hordes from nowhere, then plague us with malign persistence all through the day, swarming and buzzing around, trying desperately to land on our faces, in our eyes, ears and nostrils, on our arms, hands, knees and necks. And once settled, they bite hard. Desert sores, oases of succulence, draw them like magnets. In fact everything unwholesome, filthy and putrefied is manna to them. That's why we have to make our latrines completely sealed and burn out our refuse dumps with petrol daily. It's the devil's own job keeping our food from their clutches, and as soon as a meal's on the plates they always get the first nibble. At the moment of writing this there are five crawling over my hands and I'm spitting as many again away from my mouth. You can whack them a hundred times, and still they'll come back. It is a blessed relief at sunset, when, as at some secret signal, they all simultaneously disappear.

## PANZER LIED: "HEISS UBER AFRIKAS BODEN"

*A favourite song of the Afrika Korps tank divisions.*

**The sun is glowing hot over the African soil**

Crossing the Schelde, the Meuse and the Rhine,
The tanks pushed into France,
Huzzars of the Führer dressed in black,
They have overrun France by assault.

*Refrain*:
**The treads are rattling**
**The engine is droning**
**Tanks are advancing in Africa**
**Tanks are advancing in Africa**

The sun is glowing hot over the African soil,
Our tank engines sing their song,
German tanks under the burning sun,
Stand in battle against England,
**The treads are rattling, the engine is droning,**
**Tanks are advancing in Africa**

Tanks of the Führer, British beware,
They are intended to annihilate you,
They don't fear death or the devil,
On them the British arrogance breaks,
**The treads are rattling, the engine is droning,**
**Tanks are advancing in Africa**

The sun is glowing hot over the African soil,
Our tank engines sing their song,
German tanks under the burning sun,
Stand in battle against England,
**The treads are rattling, the engine is droning,**
**Tanks are advancing in Africa**

# OPERATION CRUSADER: TANK BATTLE AT SIDI REZEGH, 28 NOVEMBER 1941

## Captain Robert Crisp, 3rd Royal Tank Regiment, 4th Armoured Brigade

*In November 1941 desert warfare reached a new pitch of intensity when the British Western Desert Force (newly rechristened the Eighth Army) went on the offensive against Rommel in Operation Crusader, not the least objective of which was the relief of Tobruk in Rommel's rear, garrisoned by the 9th Australian Division. Crusader, which began on 18 November, dispatched 700 tanks against 400 German-Italian. Some of the fiercest tank fighting of the war ensued around the airfield at Sidi Rezegh, south of Tobruk.*

As my Honey\* edged up to the final crest I was immediately aware of the dense throng of transport in front of me. The Trigh was black and broad and moving with packed trucks and lorries. Over it all hung a thick, drifting fog of dust so that only the nearest stream of vehicles was clearly discernable. There was not a panzer in sight. The tail of the enemy column was just on our right front, and it looked as though we could not have timed it better. The Germans gave no sign of having seen us, or of being aware of our tanks poised for the strike within a thousand yards of them. They moved slowly westwards wondering, no doubt, what the devil Rommel thought he was playing at with these mad rushes up and down the desert, and beefing like hell about the dust.

I looked approvingly to right and left, where the rest of the squadron were lined up following the curve of the contour. From each turret top poked the head and shoulders of the commander, eyes glued to binoculars trained on that enemy mass. It must have been quite a sight to somebody only a week out from base camp in England. I got on the air to the C.O. with a quick, formal announcement that "C" Squadron was in position and ready. From my left the other squadron did the same. Within a minute the reply came: "Hullo JAGO, JAGO calling. Attack now. Alec sends a special message 'Go like hell and good luck'. Good luck from me too. JAGO to JAGO, off."

The order went through all the intercoms, from commander to crew: "Driver, advance. Speed up. Gunner, load both guns." The Honeys positively leapt over the top of the ridge and plunged down the steady incline to the Trigh. I knew my driver, who was getting used to this sort of thing, would have his foot hard down on the accelerator, straining his eyes through the narrow slit before him to

---

\* "Honey": a M3 Light Cavalry Tank or "Stuart".

avoid the sudden outcrops of rock or the slit trenches that littered this oft-contested terrain. On each side the Honeys were up level with me. That was good. My wrist-watch showed 1 o'clock as I gripped hard on the edge of the cupola and pressed back against the side to ride the bucking tank.

We were half-way down the slope and going like bats out of hell in the bright sunlight before the Jerries realised what was happening. Then the familiar pattern of alarm and confusion and panic-flight away from us at right angles to the road. There was no slackening of speed, and within another minute we had hit the soft sand of the well-worn desert highway and become absorbed into the cloud of dust and that frightened herd of vehicles stampeding blindly northwards.

I had the same intention in my mind as on a previous occasion – to go right through them, turn about and cut off as many as possible, shooting up everything that tried to get past. I put the mike close to my lips and told my tank commanders briefly to start shooting. My own gunner pulled the trigger immediately and within seconds the dust was full of the criss-cross pattern of tracers drawing red lines through the yellow cloud and puncturing the fleeing dark shapes wiht deadly points. From the turret tops we let go with tommy-guns and revolvers, and every now and again the whip-crack of the 37-mm. interjected the staccato chatter of the Brownings. I could still see a Honey or two racing alongside, but what was happening beyond the narrow limits of vision I could only guess. And my guess was that the whole squadron was there. Another minute perhaps, I thought, and then I would give the order to turn about.

Suddenly, through the dust, I saw the flat plane of the ground disappear into space. I yelled like mad at the driver to halt. He had seen the danger only a fraction of a second after I had, and jerked back on the brakes even while I was shouting at him. The tracks locked fast and tore up sand, rock and scrub in a brief and frantic struggle to stop the momentum of the tank. We skidded to a violent stop with the front sprockets hanging over a sharp drop that started the descent of a steep escarpment.

The first thing I saw, through popping eyes, ten yards in front and below me, was a motor-cycle combination lying on its side with three German soldiers standing stiffly to attention in a row beside it, their backs towards me and their hands stretched high above their heads. I rejected immediately a quick impulse to shoot them. While my mind was still trying to absorb this apparition, I became aware of the astonishing scene at the foot of the escarpment, where it levelled out into a broad wadi. Vehicles of all shapes and sizes were everywhere – some upright and still moving away as fast as they could; others stationary and bewildered; many lying on their sides or backs with wheels poking grotesquely upwards. Dark figures of men darted wildly about.

Even as I watched, a great lorry went plunging down the escarpment out of control; it struck some outcrop and leapt high in the air, somersaulting to the bottom in a fantastic avalanche of earth, rock and scrub and odd-shaped bundles of men integrated with jagged pieces of wood and metal. The concentration of transport in the wadi below was a wonderful target. I said quickly into the mouthpiece: "Both guns. Men and vehicles. Fire with everything you've got."

The bullets went zipping inches above the heads of the three immovable figures in front of the tank. They never twitched a muscle. When the 37-mm. cannon suddenly went off they jumped involuntarily, but none of them turned their heads or gave any indication that I could see of fear or curiosity. They just stood there, three backs and three pairs of arms while the tracers went streaming in flat, straight lines into the dusty turmoil below. I wondered idly where the rest of the Honeys were, and if they were having as good a time as mine was.

Suddenly there was a fearful bang, and simultaneously I was drenched from head to foot in an astonishing cascade of cold water. For a moment or two I was physically and mentally paralysed. I just could not believe that anything like that could happen. Then realisation came swiftly and terribly . . . the water tins on the back of the tank had been hit. It could mean only one thing. As I looked backwards I was already giving the order to the gunner to traverse the turret as fast as he bloody well could. In one comprehensive flash I saw it all, and the fear leapt up in me. Not fifty yards away a 50-mm. anti-tank gun pointed straight at the Honey, pointed straight between my eyes. Beyond it were other guns and then as the dust drifted over the scarp the sight I had dreaded most – a number of motionless Honeys and the huddled figures of black-bereted men crouched on the sand or stretched out in the agony of death.

It took less than a second for the whole scene and its awful meaning to register in my mind. I could see the German gunners slamming the next shell into the breech as the turret whirled. I yelled "On. Machine gun. Fire." In the same moment I saw the puff of smoke from the anti-tank gun and felt and heard the strike on the armour-plating. Quickly I looked down into the turret. A foot or two below me the gunner was staring at his hand, over which a dark red stain was slowly spreading. Then he gave a scream and fell grovelling on the floor. In the top right hand corner of the turret a jagged hole gaped, and through it, like some macabre peepshow, I could see the gun being reloaded. I knew that in another few seconds I would be dead, but something well beyond reason or sanity impelled my muscles and actions.

I leaned down and pulled the trigger, and kept my finger there until the gun jammed. God knows where the bullets went. Twice I felt the Honey shudder and the second time more water came pouring in. When the Browning stopped and my mind leapt about searching for some ways to stay alive I suddenly saw the slim chance. If the tank would move at all, and we could drop over the edge of the escarpment, we would be out of sight of those blasted anti-tank guns. I could see them framed in that jagged hole, the gunners working feverishly, their faces strained and vicious. I said urgently into the mike: "Driver, advance. Over the edge. Quick!"

Nothing. I thought "My God, Whaley's had it. We've all had it," and screamed down into the turret "Driver advance. For Christ's sake advance!" Then I saw what had happened. In falling, the gunner had jerked back on the intercom leads to the driver's earphones. The cords had tightened round his neck, pulling him backwards over the driving seat and half-strangling him. He wrestled frantically with his earphones and ripped them off. He didn't need them to hear my panic bellowing.

I felt the gears engage, and for a split second the world stood still. Then the engine revved, and the Honey heaved forward and dropped with a violent crash over the escarpment. In the turret we were hurled about like corks, and then the bouncing stopped and we rode smoothly down the slope. We were out of sight of the guns on top of the escarpment, and with a great rush of unbelief I knew we were going to get away with it. The three German motor-cyclists still stood motionless. The tank could not have missed them by more than a few inches, yet they still had their hands in the air. Down in the driving compartment Whaley was wrestling with the sticks to keep the tank on a diagonal course that would take him to the bottom of the slope away from the enemy. When the ground levelled out a bit I ordered him to turn right to run into a little wadi that offered a safe way out to the south. We were travelling with the turret back to front, and I prodded the operator with my foot as he bent over the prostrate gunner and indicated to him that I wanted the turret traversed back to the normal position. While he was turning the handle I could not resist a last backward look at those three men. Incredibly, they were still standing as we had left them. I began to think they had become literally petrified with fright and would stay there down the centuries in some miraculous monument.

So much had happened in a few minutes, or a few hours it might have been, and I had looked so closely into the valley of the shadow, that I found it difficult to return to reality. I just could not fully absorb our situation. I had to grip the hardness of the armour-plating and see the familiar figures of the tank crew to realise that we were still alive, and that we were going to stay alive. The gunner lay there groaning in pain and sobbing in fear. There was nothing much wrong with him, and I shouted at him roughly to pull himself together. My thoughts went out to the rest of the squadron. Where were they? What had happened to them? Were they all dead? It was something I had to find out.

We were chugging along casually through the deserted silence of the wadi. It was uncanny after the tumult and terror just behind us, and the thought kept on intruding that we were no longer on earth, that we were driving in some ghost tank on another level of existence . . . that we were all dead. When I put the mouthpiece to my lips I was half-prepared to hear no voice come out. The unreality persisted when the Honey swung right in response to my order, and moved slowly up the slope to the crest. As soon as my eyes were above the lip of the escarpment we halted, and the full picture of horror burst on me immediately.

Not much more than 500 yards away, like a projection on a cinema screen, lay the battlefield. My eyes lifted to the tall black columns, leaning slightly with the wind, and followed them down to the Honeys gasping smoke. Four of my tanks were blazing infernos; three others just sat there, sad and abandoned. A line of anti-tank guns with their crews still manning them expectantly, lined the edge of the drop. The whole scene was silhouetted sharply against the yellow clouds of dust which rose in a thick fog from the wadi bank. I could see many men running about between guns and tanks and vehicles. My heart ached as I picked out the familiar bereted figures of our own troops, huddled in disconsolate groups or being shepherded by gesticulating Germans.

Was there nothing I could do? My mind moved round the prospect of a sudden charge into that line of anti-tank guns, over-running them before they could get their sights on me. If I had had a gunner to fire the Browning, perhaps I might have. As it was I was grateful for the opportunity of rejecting it as impossible, and so prolonging my life and those of my crew. But who knows? It might have come off.

As a concession to my own great distress and impotency I stood up on the turret and waved my beret. There was a chance that some gunner, operator or driver, one of the commanders perhaps, might have been lying crouched in the scrub, waiting for the night or the unbidden moment to make a break for it. But it was more of a gesture of complete despair, and when I heard the whishing past my ears, followed by the quick barking of the machine guns, I dropped back into the turret. I said wearily over the intercom: "O.K., Whaley. There's nothing we can do. Let's go back."

We followed the wadi southwards as it grew shallower and shallower, eventually disgorging us unobtrusively on to the plateau over which we had charged so bravely . . . when? ten minutes ago? an hour ago? today? yesterday? and how many lives ago? My wrist-watch was staring me in the face as we paused on the rim of the depression. The hands pointed to 17 minutes past one. 17 minutes.

# IN THE CAULDRON, 12 JUNE 1942

## *Anonymous British Gunner*

*The pendulum of the desert war swung hard against the British Eighth Army in May 1942 when Rommel launched an all-out offensive on their Gazala Line positions. Rommel personally led his panzers into the British position, repelling all assaults in the battle of the "Cauldron".*

As darkness approached, the fighting intensified, the shelling increased and brew-ups flared up all round. At last light a Jat battalion drove out to take up a position on the ridge six hundred yards in front. It was caught as it was deploying; all the officers were killed and what was left melted away. The night was very dark and every man on the guns "stood to" in view of the infantry attack that had seemed to be boiling up when darkness fell.

As the tanks rumbled off to their rallying point, quiet descended on the Cauldron and it was possible to take stock of the situation. All ammunition was brought up and spread round the guns. The wounded were loaded up in fifteen-hundredweights and sent off eastwards. The men had a substantial, though cold, meal. Most of the guns were still in action, but many had been hit, and gun detachments were made up to at least three men per gun . . .

On the left the Baluchis, commanded by a most capable and phlegmatic colonel, had dug in and prepared to meet any onslaught. In rear as night fell Gurkhas could be seen digging in hard, and on the right rear another infantry battalion seemed to be arriving. There was also a company of those most excellent and experienced machine-gunners the Northumberland Fusiliers, who in the days of peace had challenged the Abbasia gunners at every sport. One of their officers, just arrived back from Cairo, brought a very opportune parcel of food and drink. Arriving at dusk in the midst of heavy shelling, he threw it out and drove off to his company.

The night passed quietly enough with spasmodic shelling, and at dawn everyone brewed up and had a good breakfast. The day had every promise of being exciting and the Gunners were thrilled at the certain prospect of a tank shoot. They wanted badly to get their own back for the shelling they had had to put up with, for the incessant dive-bombing and for all the good chaps dead . . .

Meanwhile the Germans had been massing their tanks and lorried infantry in the gap a few thousand yards westwards. As the dawn spread quickly over the desert the shelling started once more and our guns answered back. Our O.Ps attempted to get forward on to the high ground again but in the absence of our own armour found it already occupied by German tanks, with of course *their* O.Ps. More and more German tanks appeared in the west and spread round the position in a double ring, shooting up the F.O.Os in their Honeys, but remaining just out of range of our 25-pounder solid shot. They gave the impression of hounds holding a stag at bay, but not daring to go in.

Suddenly at 8.30 a.m. the enemy fire was concentrated on Birkin's battery, then into the Baluchis. The German tanks moved in, making for E Troop of 425th, and a brisk and deadly exchange took place. Then, as the dust and smoke cleared away, the enemy withdrew, leaving ten tanks behind, knocked out a few hundred yards from the guns of 425th Battery. The Gunners were delighted and settled down to await the next attack. It was not long in coming. The enemy moved farther west, to attack the units on 425th's left flank. A few minutes of intense small arms and machine-gun fire – and then dead silence. The position had been overrun. A handful of men were seen staggering off under heavy escort. This left 425th Battery with an exposed flank, and a hasty rearrangement had to be made. But a little later Stukas flew over the position and the ring of purple smoke sent up by the enemy to show his forward positions to the planes made it clear that the box was now completely surrounded.

Never for a moment did the shelling stop. Casualties became heavier and heavier. Vehicles were burning everywhere. The enemy with their guns just out of sight could direct their fire with great accuracy on the mass of men and vehicles and guns in the Cauldron below. Captain Bennett, hit through the leg, arrived at the Command Post to report his troop position untenable. Three of his gun detachments had been knocked out, but the guns themselves were intact. B.S.M. Hardy and a driver were immediately despatched in a quad to pull the guns in four hundred yards, a feat which they accomplished most gallantly in spite of heavy machine-gun fire.

Ammunition was now running short, particularly A.P., and orders were given for all fire to be held until the attack came in to close quarters. The position was exceedingly unhealthy and on the left flank had every prospect of soon becoming untenable. It was suggested to

Colonel de Graz, commander of the Support Group, that the whole force should move back to the Knightsbridge Ridge, some three and a half miles to the east, and so have its flanks assured on the minefield before it was completely surrounded. But in view of the orders given him, he would not contemplate it.

More and more enemy tanks kept spreading round the area and presently a large column many miles long (actually the German 90 Light Division) appeared from the south behind the position, thus sealing the fate of this luckless brigade.

About 10 a.m. there was a very welcome lull – but it was short-lived. Down came the shells again, and a number of the Command Post staff were hit.

The Germans could now observe our every move. At about this time Colonel de Graz and Colonel Seely held a small conference at the Regimental Command Post, roughly in the centre of the box, and though there were only some ten people present the enemy at once started shelling.

The next attack came in very quickly and soon German tanks had overrun the infantry battalion in the rear and were nosing about amongst the burning vehicles round the Bir. Captain Trippier and his Northumberland Hussars were quite magnificent. Under heavy fire they man-handled their anti-tank guns across to try to safeguard our rear, but they were all knocked out. He then drove back with his truck full of badly wounded men to report that he had not a man left. As he spoke a shell exploding beside him wounded him severely. Events moved quickly now and amazing things happened as the fighting raged at close quarters. A sergeant of the Recce Regiment with what was left of his section leaped on a German tank, trying to ram hand grenades through the turret. They were killed to a man. The machine-gun fire was intense. Cartridge boxes went up in a sheet of flame. Four lorry loads of Germans in British three-tonners drove straight past the guns untouched. A staff car and two generals drove up to the Command Post, and as the gunners jumped at it, accelerated and got away. The doctor and his orderly worked unceasingly in a murderous fire round the Command Post, which was a shambles of dead and wounded. As the gun detachments were killed signallers, drivers and Northumberland "Geordies" crawled over to take their places.

Colonel Seely, who had been constantly on the move around his Regiment in his Honey tank, encouraging the men by his splendid example, arrived at 426th Battery Command Post during the early afternoon and suddenly observed three German infantry lorries appearing over the escarpment about a thousand yards north of F

Troop. The German infantry jumped out, but before they could get into action with their light automatics they were met by the concentrated fire of F Troop, the 6-pounder anti-tank guns of the Northumberland Hussars and the small arms of the Recce Regiment. In a few moments the lorries were in flames and the scattered German survivors rounded up.

About 3 p.m. the Germans were attacking the right of the position. Of the anti-tank guns one only now remained, but there was no one to man it until a young lance-bombardier, with one arm blown off at the elbow, crawled out in a vain attempt to reach it. Colonel de Graz walked over from his blazing and useless vehicle, but was killed immediately as he tried to fire the anti-tank gun. Communication still remained. For sixteen hours the Signal Sergeant had sat in his vehicle keeping on the air to Brigade. The second-in-command spoke to the Brigadier and told him that if he would get some ammunition through with some tanks, we could hold out until dark. The Brigadier wished him luck, but at that moment the vehicle was hit and up it went.

As evening approached, everywhere the German tanks were moving in. The Indian Infantry Brigade was completely overrun – there was nothing left. Nearly every vehicle was burning and heavy smoke obliterated the sky. Still the South Notts Hussars held out and kept the tanks at bay. Guns were facing every direction – wherever a tank could be seen working up through the smoke. Solid shot tore up the ground all round. As a last desperate measure it was decided to move the guns of Captain Pringle's E Troop to the rear, despite the enemy's immediate reaction to any sign of movement.

The quads drove up and the men – all that were left of them – leapt to hook in the guns. But before they had gone two hundred yards all four of the quads went up in flames. Major Birkin, hurrying to see what could be done, had his armoured car hit by an A.P. shot and his invaluable B.S.M. Hardy killed beside him. By the time he had regained his remaining A Troop, of which only two guns were still in action, the enemy tanks were on top of the position and the gallant fight of the 425th Battery was over.

Down in the hollow, Alan Chadburn's guns were still intact, but on all sides the German tanks were closing in, machine-guns blazing. Colonel Seely and Bish Peal, his adjutant, who had continued to ply indomitably about the battle-field, had their tank hit and set on fire. Both died later in enemy hands. The end was very near now. 426th Battery Command Post fell to the advancing tanks; and though in a last defiant gesture Chadburn's F Troop scored two direct hits at eight hundred yards they could do no more. The groups of British prisoners appearing over the escarpment put further firing out of the question, and the survivors of 426th Battery turned sadly to their final task – the battering of their gun sights. For a few moments more the air sang with machine-gun bullets; then all was quiet, and that deep silence that descends on a battlefield when the contest is over spread over the Cauldron.

# THE FALL OF TOBRUK, 20–21 JUNE 1942

## *General von Mellenthin, Afrika Korps*

*After losing the battle of the Cauldron, the British withdrew eastwards to Alam Halfa, leaving Tobruk as a garrisoned thorn in Rommel's side. After a mere week of siege, however, the 2nd South African Division surrendered the port to the enemy. Churchill was mortified ("Defeat is one thing; disgrace is another"), Hitler joyous and awarded Rommel a field-marshal's baton.*

At 05.00 [20 June] I stood with Rommel on the escarpment to the north-east of El Adem; Battle Headquarters had been set up there and when daylight came we had excellent observation as far as the Tobruk perimeter. Promptly at 05.20 the Stukas flew over. Kesselring had been as good as his word and sent hundreds of bombers in dense formations; they dived on to the perimeter in one of the most spectacular attacks I have ever seen. A great cloud of dust and smoke rose from the sector under attack, and while our bombs crashed on to the defences, the entire German and Italian Army artillery joined in with a tremendous and well co-ordinated fire. The combined weight of the artillery and bombing was terrific, and as we soon realized, had a crushing effect on the morale of the Mahratta battalion in that sector. The Stukas kept it up all day, flying back to the airfields at Gazala and El Adem, replenishing with bombs, and then returning to the fray. On this occasion the Air Force bombing was directed through the Operations Section of Army Headquarters, with very fruitful results.

After a time the assault engineers released orange smoke as a signal that the range should be lengthened, and at 06.35 the report came back that the wire had been cut in front of Strong Point 69. Group Menny, and the infantry of the Afrika Korps, now attacked the forward line of bunkers and made rapid progress against feeble resistance. At 07.03 Group Menny reported that a whole company of Indians had been taken prisoner, and by 07.45 a wide breach had been made and about ten strong points had been taken. Bridges were laid across the anti-tank ditch and the way was prepared for the tanks to enter the perimeter.

The weak resistance of the defenders was due primarily to the bombardment, and paradoxically to the excellent concrete shelters built by the Italians. Under the crushing weight of bombs and shells the Indians were driven below ground, where they were relatively secure, but could not bring any fire to bear on our attacking troops, who followed closely behind the barrage. Another important factor was the weakness of the defenders' artillery fire. There seeems to have been a complete lack of co-ordination of the various batteries; a few South African guns were firing during the break-through, but apparently the 25th Field Regiment R.A., which was in immediate support of 11 Indian Brigade, did not fire until 07.45. The guns of this regiment had been sited in an anti-tank role, and it appears that they were relying on the medium artillery to bombard the perimeter gap, and the German troops assembling beyond it. But the mediums remained silent, and it was not until 08.45 that the Afrika Korps reported that the enemy's fire was "increasing", particularly that of the "heavy calibres". I well remember our surprise, when watching the battle that morning, at the small volume of fire put down by the Tobruk artillery. Meanwhile Rommel had gone forward to take direct command of the break-through.

# TOBRUK: THE CONQUEROR ENTERS, 21 JUNE 1942

## General Erwin Rommel, Afrika Korps

At 05.00 hours on 21 June, I drove into the town of Tobruk. Practically every building of the dismal place was either flat or little more than a heap of rubble, mostly the result of our siege in 1941. Next I drove off along the Via Balbia to the west. The staff of 32 British Army Tank Brigade offered to surrender, which brought us thirty serviceable British tanks. Vehicles stood in flames on either side of the Via Balbia. Wherever one looked there was chaos and destruction.

At about 09.40 hours, on the Via Balbia about four miles west of the town, I met General Klopper, G.O.C. 2 South African Infantry Division and Garrison Commandant of Tobruk. He announced the capitulation of the fortress of Tobruk. He had been unable to stave off the defeat any longer, although he had done all he could to maintain control over his troops.

I told the General, who was accompanied by his Chief of Staff, to follow me in his car along the Via Balbia to Tobruk. The road was lined with about ten thousand prisoners of war.

On arrival at the Hotel Tobruk, I talked for a while with General Klopper. It seemed that he had no longer been in possession of the necessary communications to organize a break-out. It had all gone too quickly. I instructed the South African general to make himself and his officers responsible for order among the prisoners, and to organize their maintenance from the captured stores.

## LILI MARLENE

*The melancholic song, played incessantly by Nazi radio stations, which became the favourite of the Afrika Korps and eventually soldiers everywhere.*

Vor der Kaserne, vor dem grossen Tor
Steht eine Laterne, und steht sie noch davor.
Wenn sich die späten Nebel drehn,
Bei der Laterne woll'n wir stehn
Wie einst Lili Marlene
Wie einst Lili Marlen'.

## MONTGOMERY TAKES OVER AS COMMANDER EIGHTH ARMY, AUGUST 1942

### *General Bernard Montgomery, Commander Eighth Army*

*After the debacle that was the surrender of Tobruk, Churchill insisted on new brooms in the desert campaign. Alexander replaced Auchinleck (Churchill: "You know it is like killing a magnificent stag") as Commander-in-Chief Middle East, with the wiry and ascetic Bernard Montgomery as Commander Eighth Army under him.*

My orders from Alexander were quite simple; they were to destroy Rommel and his Army. I understood Rommel was expected to attack *us* shortly. If he came soon it would be tricky, if he came in a week, all right, but give us two weeks and Rommel could do what he liked; he would be seen off and then it would be our turn. But I had no intention of launching *our* attack until we were ready. . . .

I had taken command of truly magnificent material; it did not take me long to see that. The Eighth Army was composed of veteran fighting divisions. But the officers and men were bewildered at what had happened and this had led to a loss of confidence. "Brave but baffled" the Prime Minister had called them.

This loss of confidence, combined with bellyaching which went on and which was partly the cause of it, were becoming dangerous and could only be eradicated by a successful battle: a battle in which Rommel was defeated easily, and must be seen to have been beaten, with few casualties to the Eighth Army.

I could not myself attack; Rommel must provide that opportunity for me. But in order to reap the full benefit, I must correctly forecast the design of his expected attack and determine in advance how we would defeat it. This was not difficult to do. . . .

The design of Rommel's attack was exactly as had been forecast; we fought the battle* as I had laid down. Once Rommel's forces had beaten up against our strong positions from the New Zealand Division area eastwards, they became unable to move. We then concentrated on shooting them up from all directions and the Desert Air Force in attacking them from the air. This was very successful and after a few days the enemy losses in tanks and soft-skinned vehicles were so severe that he had to consider a withdrawal. A most important factor which forced his eventual withdrawal was the action of the Desert Air Force under Air Marshal Coningham. Army and Air Force worked on one plan, closely knitted together, and the two headquarters were side by side.

A major factor in the overall air plan was Tedder's decision to send his Wellingtons to bomb Tobruk behind Rommel's attack, so that his last quick hope of re-supply vanished. This was the operative point in Rommel's decision to call off the attack; he was already beaten, and lack of petrol meant that he couldn't resume the attack. Tedder bit his tail.

Rommel's attack came on the night of 31st August. I had gone to bed at my usual time and was asleep when the attack began soon after midnight. De Guingand tells his own story about that night. He decided he should wake me up up and tell me the news; he said I merely replied, "Excellent, couldn't be better" and went to sleep again at once, and had breakfast at the usual time in the morning. I don't remember but am prepared to believe him. I was confident that if everyone obeyed orders, we must win this battle; my main preoccupation was to see, in this my first battle with the Eighth Army, that it was fought in complete accord with my master plan.

When I saw that Rommel's forces were in a bad way, I ordered a thrust southwards from the New Zealand Division area to close the gap through which they had entered our positions. The enemy reaction was immediate and violent; they began to pull back quickly to the area of our minefield through which they had originally come. We left them there and I called off the battle. Knowing what lay ahead, I pinned up three quotations in my caravan when the battle was over. They remained there during the long journey from Alamein to Berlin and are still there. The quotations were as follows:

* Alam Halfa

PRAYER OF SIR FRANCIS DRAKE
ON THE MORNING OF THE ATTACK ON CADIZ
1587

O Lord God, when thou givest to Thy servants to endeavour any great matter, grant us also to know that it is not the beginning, but the continuing of the same, until it be thoroughly finished, which yieldeth the true glory.

JAMES GRAHAM, MARQUIS OF MONTROSE
1612–50

He either fears his fate too much,
Or his deserts are small,
Who dare not put it to the touch,
To win or lose it all.

HENRY V, ACT IV, SCENE I

O God of battles! steel my soldiers' hearts.

## ROMMEL'S AILING HEALTH, 26 AUGUST 1942
### *Leutnant Alfred Berndt, Afrika Korps*

*Berndt writes to Rommel's wife in Germany. The Field Marshal suffered from a persistent stomach malady during the African campaign.*

Dear Frau Rommel,                                  26 August 1942
  You'll no doubt be surprised at hearing from me from Africa. . . . The reason for my letter is to inform you about the state of the Marshal's health. Your husband has now been nineteen months in Africa, which is longer than any other officer over forty has stood it so far, and, according to the doctors, an astonishing physical feat. After the rigours of the advance, he has had to carry the immense responsibility of the Alamein front, anxiety for which has for many nights allowed him no rest. Moreover, the bad season has come again.
  All this has, in the nature of things, not failed to leave its mark, and thus, in addition to all the symptoms of a heavy cold and the digestive disturbances typical of Africa, he has recently shown signs of exhaustion which have caused great anxiety to all of us who were aware of it. True, there is no immediate danger, but unless he can get a thorough rest some time, he might easily suffer an overstrain which could leave organic damage in its train.
  The doctor who is treating him, Professor Dr. Horster of

Würzburg University – one of the best-known stomach specialists in Germany – is constantly available to him for medical advice and to watch over his health. The Führer has been informed, and it has been agreed that he will receive a long period of sick leave in Europe once the future of this theatre has been decided. Until that time, we will do everything we can to make his life easier and to persuade him to look after himself. We prepare and keep handy everything he needs for his health. I have installed a small kitchen and obtained a good cook. Fresh fruit and vegetables arrive by air daily. We fish, shoot pigeons, obtain chickens and eggs, etc., in order to keep his strength up.

Lieutenant Alfred Ingemar Berndt

*Rommel was invalided to Germany on 22 September and replaced by Georg Stumme. A month into his convalescence, Rommel was telephoned by Hitler with the words "There is bad news from Africa" and asked to return. The bad news was the Eighth Army offensive at El Alamein.*

# EL ALAMEIN: THE PLAN, SEPTEMBER 1942

## *General Bernard Montgomery, Eighth Army*

Alam Halfa\* had interfered with the preparations for our own offensive, and delayed us. But the dividend in other respects had been tremendous. Before Alam Halfa there was already a willingness from below to do all that was asked, because of the grip from above. And for the same reason there was a rise in morale, which was cumulative. I think officers and men knew in their hearts that if we lost at Alam Halfa we would probably have lost Egypt. They had often been told before that certain things would happen; this time they wanted to be shown, not just to be told. At Alam Halfa the Eighth Army had been told, and then shown; and from the showing came the solid rocklike confidence in the high command, which was never to be lost again.

The basic problem that confronted us after the Battle of Alam Halfa was a difficult one. We were face to face with Rommel's forces between the sea and the Qattara Depression, a distance of about 45 miles. The enemy was strengthening his defences to a degree previously unknown in the desert, and these included deep and extensive minefields. There was no open flank. The problem was:

First – to punch a hole in the enemy positions.

Second – to pass 10 Corps, strong in armour and mobile troops, through this hole into enemy territory.

\* Alam el Halfa, fought 31 August–7 September 1942 when Rommel launched an offensive against the ridge of that name.

Third – then to develop operations so as to destroy Rommel's forces.

This would be an immense undertaking. How could we obtain surprise?

It seemed almost impossible to conceal from the enemy the fact that we intended to launch an attack. I decided to plan for tactical surprise, and to conceal from the enemy the exact places where the blows would fall and the exact times. This would involve a great deception plan . . .

Next, a full moon was necessary. The minefield problem was such that the troops must be able to see what they were doing. A waning moon was not acceptable since I envisaged a real "dog-fight" for at least a week before we finally broke out; a waxing moon was essential. This limited the choice to one definite period each month. Owing to the delay caused to our preparations by Rommel's attack, we could not be ready for the September moon and be sure of success. There must be no more failures. Officers and men of the Eighth Army had a hard life and few pleasures; and they put up with it. All they asked for was success, and I was determined to see they got it this time in full measure. The British people also wanted real success; for too long they had seen disaster or at best only partial success. But to gain complete success we must have *time*; we had to receive a quantity of new equipment, and we had to get the army trained to use it, and also rehearsed in the tasks which lay ahead. I had promised the Eighth Army on arrival that I would not launch our offensive till we were ready. I could not be ready until October. Full moon was the 24th October. I said I would attack on the night of 23rd October, and notified Alexander accordingly. The comeback from Whitehall was immediate. Alexander received a signal from the Prime Minister to the effect that the attack must be in September, so as to synchronise with certain Russian offensives and with Allied landings which were to take place early in November at the western end of the North African coast (Operation TORCH). Alexander came to see me to discuss the reply to be sent. I said that our preparations could not be completed in time for a September offensive, and an attack then would fail: if we waited until October, I guaranteed complete success. In my view it would be madness to attack in September. Was I to do so? Alexander backed me up whole-heartedly as he always did, and the reply was sent on the lines I wanted. I had told Alexander privately that, in view of my promise to the soldiers, I refused to attack before October; if a September attack was ordered by Whitehall, they would have to get someone else to do it. My stock was rather high after Alam Halfa! We heard no more about a September attack.

# EL ALAMEIN: THE VIEW FROM THE AFRIKA KORPS, 24–27 OCTOBER 1942

## *Field Marshal Erwin Rommel, Afrika Korps*

*The battle of El Alamein began – while Rommel was still convalescing in Germany – at 21.40 on the still moonlit night of 23 October, with a 1,000 gun British barrage. Eventually, the British would commit 195,000 men and over 1,000 tanks to the battle; the Akrika Korps, with its Italian ally, mustered 104,000 men and 489 tanks.*

On the afternoon of the 24th, I was rung up on the Semmering [Germany, where Rommel had been on leave for his health] by Field Marshal Keitel, who told me that the British had been attacking at Alamein with powerful artillery and bomber support since the previous evening. General Stumme was missing. He asked whether I would be well enough to return to Africa and take over command again. I said I would. Keitel then said that he would keep me informed of developments, and would let me know in due course whether I was to return to my command. I spent the next few hours in a state of acute anxiety, until the evening, when I received a telephone call from Hitler himself. He said that Stumme was still missing – either captured or killed – and asked whether I could start for Africa immediately. I was to telephone him again before I actually took off, because he did not want me to interrupt my treatment unless the British attack assumed dangerous proportions. I ordered my aircraft for seven o'clock next morning and drove immediately to Wiener Neustadt. Finally, shortly after midnight, a call came through from the Führer. In view of developments at Alamein he found himself obliged to ask me to fly back to Africa and resume my command. I took off next morning. I knew there were no more laurels to be earned in Africa, for I had been told in the reports I had received from my officers that supplies had fallen far short of my minimum demands. But just how bad the supply situation really was I had yet to learn.

On arriving at Rome at about 11.00 hours (25 October) I was met at the airport by General von Rintelen, Military Attaché and German General attached to the Italian forces. He informed me of the latest events in the African theatre. After heavy artillery preparation, the enemy had taken part of our line south of Hill 31; several battalions of 164th Division and of Italians had been completely wiped out. The British attack was still in progress and General Stumme still missing. General von Rintelen also informed me that only three issues of petrol remained in the African theatre; it had been impossible to send any more across in the last weeks, partly because the Italian Navy had not provided the shipping and partly because of the British sinkings. This

was sheer disaster, for with only 300 kilometres' worth of petrol per
vehicle between Tripoli and the front, and that calculated over good
driving country, a prolonged resistance could not be expected; we
would be completely prevented from taking the correct tactical
decisions and would thus suffer a tremendous limitation in our freedom of action. I was bitterly angry, because when I left there had been
at least eight issues for the Army in Egypt and Libya, and even this
had been absurdly little in comparison with the minimum essential of
thirty issues. Experience had shown that one issue of petrol was
required for each day of battle; without it, the army was crippled
and could not react to the enemy's moves. General von Rintelen
regretted the situation, but said that he had unfortunately been on
leave and had consequently been unable to give sufficient attention to
the supply question.

Feeling that we would fight this battle with but small hope of
success, I crossed the Mediterranean in my Storch and reached
headquarters at dusk (25 October). Meanwhile, General Stumme's
body had been found at midday and taken to Derna. He had
apparently been driving to the battlefield along the Alarm track
when he had suddenly been fired on in the region of Hill 21 by British
infantry using anti-tank and machine-guns. Colonel Buechting had
received a mortal wound in the head. The driver, Corporal Wolf, had
immediately swung the car round, and General Stumme had leapt out
and hung on to the outside of it, while the driver drove at top speed
out of the enemy fire. General Stumme must have suddenly had a
heart attack and fallen off the car. The driver had noticed nothing. On
Sunday morning the General had been found dead beside the Alarm
track. General Stumme had been known to suffer from high blood-
pressure and had not really been fit for tropical service.

We all deeply regretted the sudden death of Stumme. He had
spared no pains to command the army well and had been day and
night at the front. Just before setting off on his last journey on 24
October, he had told the acting Chief of Staff that he thought it would
be wise to ask for my return, since with his short experience of the
African theatre, and in view of the enormous British strength and the
disastrous supply situation, he felt far from certain that he would be
able to fight the battle to a successful conclusion. I, for my part, did
not feel any more optimistic.

General von Thoma and Colonel Westphal reported to me that
evening on the course of the battle to date, mentioning particularly
that General Stumme had forbidden the bombardment of the enemy
assembly positions on the first night of the attack, on account of the
ammunition shortage. As a result the enemy had been able to take

possession of part of our minefield and to overcome the occupying troops with comparatively small losses to himself. The petrol situation made any major movement impossible and permitted only local counter-attacks by the armour deployed behind the particular sector which was in danger. Units of the 15th Panzer Division had counter-attacked several times on 24 and 25 October, but had suffered frightful losses in the terrible British artillery fire and non-stop RAF bombing attacks. By the evening of the 25th, only 31 of their 119 tanks remained serviceable.

There were now only very small stocks of petrol left in North Africa and a crisis was threatening. I had already – on my way through Rome – demanded the immediate employment of all available Italian submarines and warships for the transport of petrol and ammunition. Our own air force was still unable to prevent the British bombing attacks, or to shoot down any major number of British aircraft. The RAF's new fighter-bombers were particularly in evidence, as is shown by the fact that every one of the captured tanks belonging to the *Kampfstaffel* had been shot up by this new type of aircraft.

Our aim for the next few days was to throw the enemy out of our main defence line at all costs and to reoccupy our old positions, in order to avoid having a westward bulge in our front.

That night our line again came under a heavy artillery barrage, which soon developed into one long roll of fire. I slept only a few hours and was back in my command vehicle again at 05.00 hours [26 October], where I learnt that the British had spent the whole night assaulting our front under cover of their artillery, which in some places had fired as many as 500 rounds for every one of ours. Strong forces of the Panzer divisions were already committed in the front line. British night-bombers had been over our units continuously. Shortly before midnight the enemy had succeeded in taking Hill 28, an important position in the northern sector. [Called by the British "Kidney Ridge".] He had then brought up reinforcements to this point ready to continue the attack in the morning with the object of extending his bridge-head west of the minefields.

Attacks were now launched on Hill 28 by elements of the 15th Panzer Division, the Littorio and a Bersaglieri Battalion, supported by the concentrated fire of all the local artillery and A.A. Unfortunately, the attack gained ground very slowly. The British resisted desperately. Rivers of blood were poured out over miserable strips of land which, in normal times, not even the poorest Arab would have bothered his head about. Tremendous British artillery fire pounded the area of the attack. In the evening part of the Bersaglieri Battalion succeeded in occupying the eastern and western edges of the hill. The hill itself remained in British hands and later became the base for many enemy operations.

I myself observed the attack that day from the north. Load after load of bombs cascaded down among my troops. British strength round Hill 28 was increasing steadily. I gave orders to the artillery to break up the British movement north-east of Hill 28 by concentrated fire, but we had too little to do it successfully. During the day I brought up the 90th Light Division and the *Kampfstaffel*, in order to press home the attack on Hill 28. The British were continually feeding fresh forces into their attack from Hill 28 and it was clear that they wanted to win through to the area between El Daba and Sidi Abd el Rahman. I therefore moved the Trieste into the area east of El Daba. Late in the afternoon German and Italian dive-bomber formations made a self-immolating attempt to break up the British lorry columns moving towards the north-west. Some 60 British fighters pounced on these slow machines and forced the Italians to jettison their bombs over their own lines, while the German pilots pressed home their attack with very heavy losses. Never before in Africa had we seen such a density of anti-aircraft fire. Hundreds of British tracer shells criss-crossed the sky and the air became an absolute inferno of fire.

British attacks supported by tanks tried again and again to break out to the west through our line south of Hill 28. Finally, in the afternoon, a thrust by 160 tanks succeeded in wiping out an already severely mauled battalion of the 164th Infantry Division and penetrated into our line towards the south-west. Violent fighting followed in which the remaining German and Italian tanks managed to force the enemy back. Tank casualties so far, counting in that day's, were 61 in the 15th Panzer Division and 56 in the Littorio, all totally destroyed.

Following on their non-stop night attacks, the RAF sent over formations of 18 to 20 bombers at hourly intervals throughout the day, which not only caused considerable casualties, but also began to produce serious signs of fatigue and a sense of inferiority among our troops.

The supply situation was now approaching disaster. The tanker *Proserpina*, which we had hoped would bring some relief in the petrol situation, had been bombed and sunk outside Tobruk. There was only enough petrol left to keep supply traffic going between Tripoli and the front for another two or three days, and that without counting the needs of the motorized forces, which had to be met out of the same stocks. What we should really have done now was to assemble all our motorized units in the north in order to fling the British back to the main defence line in a concentrated and planned counter-attack. But we had not the petrol to do it. So we were compelled to allow the armoured formations in the northern part of our line to assault the British salient piecemeal.

Since the enemy was operating with astonishing hesitancy and caution, a concentrated attack by the whole of our armour could have been successful, although such an assembly of armour would of course have been met by the heaviest possible British artillery fire and air bombardment. However, we could have made the action more fluid by withdrawing a few miles to the west and could then have attacked the British in an all-out charge and defeated them in open country. The British artillery and air force could not easily have intervened with their usual weight in a tank battle of this kind, for their own forces would have been endangered.

But a decision to take forces from the southern front was unthinkable with the petrol situation so bad. Not only could we not have kept a mobile battle going for more than a day or two, but our armour could never have returned to the south if the British had attacked there. I did, however, decide to bring the whole of the 21st Panzer Division up north, although I fully realized that the petrol shortage would not allow it to return. In addition, since it was now obvious that the enemy would make his main effort in the north during the next few days and try for a decision there, half the Army artillery was drawn off from the southern front. At the same time I reported to the Führer's HQ that we would lose the battle unless there was an immediate improvement in the supply situation. Judging by previous experience, there was very little hope of this happening.

Relays of British bombers continued their attack throughout the night of the 26th. At about 02.00 hours a furious British barrage by guns of every caliber suddenly began in the northern sector. Soon it was impossible to distinguish between gun-fire and exploding shells and the sky grew bright with the glare of muzzle-flashes and shell-bursts. Continuous bombing attacks seriously delayed the approach march of the 21st Panzer Division and a third of the Ariete. By dawn the 90th Light Division and the Trieste had taken up position round the southern side of Sidi Abd el Rahman.

That morning [27 October] I gave orders to all formations to pin down the British assault forces during their approach by all-out fire from every gun they could bring to bear.

The tactics which the British were using followed from their apparently inexhaustible stocks of ammunition. Their new tank, the General Sherman, which came into action for the first time during this battle, showed itself to be far superior to any of ours.

Attacks against our line were preceded by extremely heavy artillery barrages lasting for several hours. The attacking infantry then pushed forward behind a curtain of fire and artificial fog, clearing mines and removing obstacles. Where a difficult patch was struck they frequently switched the direction of their attack under cover of smoke. Once the infantry had cleared lanes in the minefields, heavy tanks moved forward, closely followed by infantry. Particular skill was shown in carrying out this manoeuvre at night and a great deal of hard training must have been done before the offensive.

In contact engagements the heavily gunned British tanks approached to a range of between 2,000 and 2,700 yards and then opened concentrated fire on our anti-tank and anti-aircraft guns and tanks, which were unable to penetrate the British armour at that range. The enormous quantities of ammunition which the enemy tanks used – sometimes they fired over 30 rounds at one target – were constantly replenished by armoured ammunition carriers. The British artillery fire was directed by observers who accompanied the attack in tanks.

In the early hours of 27 October, the British attacked again towards the south-west at their old break-in point south of Hill 28. At about 10 a.m. I went off to Telegraph Track. Two enemy bomber formations, each of 18 aircraft, dropped their bombs inside ten minutes into our defence positions. The whole front continued to lie under a devastating British barrage.

Local counter-attacks were due to be launched that afternoon by the 90th Light Division on Hill 28 and by the 15th and 21st Panzer Divisions, the Littorio and a part of the Ariete, against the British positions between minefields L and I.

At 14.30 hours I drove to Telegraph Track again, accompanied by Major Ziegler. Three times within a quarter of an hour units of the 90th Light Division, which had deployed and were standing in the open in preparation for the attack, were bombed by formations of eighteen aircraft. At 15.00 hours our dive-bombers swooped down on the British lines. Every artillery and anti-aircraft gun which we had in the northern sector concentrated a violent fire on the point of the intended attack. Then the armour moved forward. A murderous British fire struck into our ranks and our attack was soon brought to a halt by an immensely powerful anti-tank defence, mainly from dug-in anti-tank guns and a large number of tanks. We suffered considerable losses and were obliged to withdraw. There is, in general, little chance of success in a tank attack over country where the enemy has been able to take up defensive positions; but there was nothing else we could do. The 90th Light Division's attack was also broken up by heavy British artillery fire and a hail of bombs from British aircraft. A report from the division that they had taken Hill 28 unfortunately turned out to be untrue.

That evening further strong detachments of the Panzer divisions had to be committed in the front to close the gaps. Several of the 90th Light Division's units also went into the line. Only 70 tons of petrol had been flown across by the *Luftwaffe* that day, with the result that the army could only refuel for a short distance, for there was no knowing when petrol would arrive in any quantity and how long the divisions would have to get along with the few tons we could issue to them. The watchword "as little movement as possible" applied more than ever.

In the evening we again sent SOSs to Rome and the Führer's HQ. But there was now no longer any hope of an improvement in the situation. It was obvious that from now on the British would destroy us bit by bit, since we were virtually unable to move on the battlefield. As yet, Montgomery had only thrown half his striking force into the battle.

*On 2 November Montgomery "directed two hard punches at the 'hinges'" which knocked a gap in the enemy position. Rommel prepared to retreat on 3 November but was forbidden to do so by Hitler. The Afrika Korps made one last desperate bid to plug the hole, even throwing General Ritter von Thoma's HQ staff into the battle*

# EL ALAMEIN: GERMAN PRISONERS, 2 NOVEMBER 1942
## *Keith Douglas, Eighth Army*

"There they are!" cried the infantryman suddenly. A few yards from the left of the tank, two German soldiers were climbing out of a pit, grinning sheepishly as though they had been caught out in a game of hide and seek. In their pit lay a Spandau machine-gun with its perforated jacket. So much, I thought with relief, for the machine-gun nest. But men now arose all round us. We were in a maze of pits. Evan flung down the Besa machine-gun, cried impatiently, "Lend us your revolver, sir," and snatching it from my hand, dismounted. He rushed up and down calling "Out of it, come on out of it, you bastards," etc. The infantry officer and I joined in this chorus, and rushed from trench to trench; I picked up a rifle from one of the trenches and aimed it threateningly, although I soon discovered that the safety-catch was stuck and it would not fire. The figures of soldiers continued to arise from the earth as though dragons' teeth had been sown there. I tried to get the prisoners into a body by gesticulating with my useless rifle. To hurry a man up, I pointed a rifle at him, but he cowered to the ground, like a puppy being scolded, evidently thinking I was going to shoot him on the spot. I felt very embarrassed, and lowered the rifle: he shot away after his comrades as though at the start of a race. I began to shout: "Raus, raus, raus," with great enthusiasm at the occupants of some trenches further back, who were craning their necks at us in an undecided way. Evan unluckily discouraged them by blazing off at them with a Spandau which he had picked up, and some high explosive began to land near the tank, which was following us about like a tame animal. Evan now found a man shamming dead in the bottom of a pit and was firing at his heels with my revolver, swearing and cursing at him. Another German lay on the ground on his back, occasionally lifting his head and body off the ground as far as the waist, with his arms stretched stiffly above his head and his face expressive of strenuous effort, like a man in a gymnasium. His companions gesticulated towards him and pointed at their heads, so that I thought he had been shot in the head. But when I looked more closely, I could see no wound, and he told me he was ill. Two of them assisted him away.

From the weapon pits, which were crawling with flies, we loaded the back of the tank with Spandaus, rifles, Luger pistols, Dienstglasse, the lightweight German binoculars, British tinned rations and the flat round German tins of chocolate.

As the main body of the prisoners was marched away under an infantry guard, the high explosive began to land closer to us. I did not feel inclined to attack the further position singlehanded, so I moved the tank back and tacked it on to the column of prisoners. The mortar stopped firing at us, and some of the infantry climbed on to the tank to ride back. I reported over the air that we had taken some prisoners. "Nuts five, how many prisoners?" asked what I presumed to be Andrew's voice. "Nuts five wait. Off." I said, counting, "Nuts five about figures four zero. Over." "Bloody good. Most excellent." Apparently it was the Colonel talking. "Now I want you to send these chaps back to our Niner" – he meant the Brigadier – "so that you'll get the credit for this." This was unfortunately more than my conscience would stand. I felt that all the work had been done by Evan and the infantry officer, and said so. This was a bad thing to say to Piccadilly Jim, because it showed him that I did not agree with him about snatching little gobbets of glory for the regiment whenever possible. The infantry were in another Brigade, as Piccadilly Jim knew. Evan said: "You were a bloody fool to say that, sir. You've as good as thrown away an M.C." I said shortly that if I had, it was an undeserved one.

The reaction on me of all this was an overpowering feeling of insignificance. I went over to the infantry officers who were searching the prisoners and said: "You did most of the dirty work, so you'd better take them back to your Brigade." The one who had ridden on my tank replied. "Yes, we had orders to," in such a supercilious way that I almost decided to insist on my right to escort them after all. The man with a bad head was lying groaning on the ground. He clutched his head and waved it from side to side. I think perhaps he had ostitis: the pain made him roll about and kick his legs like a baby.

The turret, after the removal of the Besa, and our leaping in and out of it, was in utter confusion. During our struggles with the machine-gun the bottom of an ammunition box had dropped out, and the belt of it was coiled everywhere. The empty belt fired from the biscuit box mounting had fallen in whorls on top of this. The microphones, spare headphones, gunner's headphones and all their respective flexes were inextricably entwined among the belts. Empty cartridge and shell cases littered the floor. On the surface of this morass of metal reposed the Besa itself, and an inverted tin of Kraft cheese, which had melted in the sunlight. I rescued a microphone and a pair of headphones, and got permission to retire and reorganize. On my way back I was to call at the Colonel's tank. This I duly did, but my ears were singing so loudly that I could scarcely hear his kind words. As soon as the tank moved away from the prisoners, we were again fired on by a mortar, which followed us as we moved back, dropping shells consistently a few yards behind us. We brewed up in dead ground to the enemy behind a ridge; the mortar continued to search this ground with fire, but never got nearer than thirty yards, and that only with one shot.

We examined our trophies, and were shocked to find that the infantry had stolen all our German binoculars while enjoying our hospitality as passengers on the tank. We all bitterly reproached them, and I regretted ever having wished to give them extra credit. We had left, however, a large stack of machine-guns and rifles, which we dumped. Three Luger pistols, which we kept: these are beautiful weapons, though with a mechanism too delicate for use in sandy country. There were a few odds and ends of rations, cutlery, badges, knives, etc., which we shared out, eating most of the extra rations there and then in a terrific repast, with several pints of coffee. At last I decided we ought to rejoin the squadron, and reported we were on our way back.

# EL ALAMEIN: THE DEFEAT OF THE AFRIKA KORPS, 4 NOVEMBER 1942

## General Fritz Bayerlein, Afrika Korps

It was eight o'clock before the British attacked, after approximately one hour's artillery preparation. Their main effort was directed against Tel el Mampsra. By committing all its forces the Afrika Corps was able to hold attacks by two hundred British tanks.

At eleven o'clock Lieutenant Hartdegen appeared at my command post and said:

"General von Thoma has sent me back, with the radio transmitter. He doesn't need it any more. All our tanks, anti-tank guns and ack-ack have been destroyed on Tel el Mampsra. I don't know what has happened to the general."

I immediately climbed into a small armoured reconnaissance car and drove off eastwards. Suddenly a hail of armour-piercing shot was whistling all about me. In the noontime haze I could see countless black monsters far away in front. They were Montgomery's tanks, the 10th Hussars. I jumped out of the armoured car and beneath the burning midday sun ran as fast as I could towards Tel el Mampsra. It was a place of death, of burning tanks and smashed flak guns, without a living soul. But then, about two hundred yards away from the sand-hole in which I was lying, I saw a man standing erect beside a burning tank, apparently impervious to the intense fire which criss-crossed about him. It was General von Thoma. The British Shermans which were closing up on Tel el Mampsra had halted in a wide half-circle. What should I do? The general would probably regard it as cowardice on my part were I not to go forward and join him. But to run through the curtain of fire which lay between General von Thoma and myself would have been to court certain death. I thought for a moment or two. Then the British tanks began to move forward once again. There was now no fire being put down on Tel el Mampsra. Thoma stood there, rigid and motionless as a pillar of salt, with his canvas bag still in his hand. A Bren carrier was driving straight towards him, with two Shermans just behind. The British soldiers signalled to Thoma. At the same time one hundred and fifty fighting vehicles poured across Tel el Mampsra like a flood.

. . . The Afrika Korps signals officer brought Rommel a decoded message, from the 10th Hussars to Montgomery, which our people had intercepted. It read:

"We have just captured a general named Ritter von Thoma."

The Field-Marshal took me aside, and said:

"Bayerlein, what we tried with all our might to prevent has now happened. Our front is smashed and the enemy is pouring through into our rear area. There can no longer be any question of obeying Hitler's order. We're withdrawing to the Fuka position so as to save what still can be saved.

. . . "Bayerlein," Rommel went on, "I'm putting you in command of the Afrika Korps. There's no one else to whom I can entrust it. And if it should happen later on that the Führer court-martials us for our disobedience, we'll both have to answer squarely for our decision to-day. Do your duty as best you can. All your orders to the troops carry my authority. You may say this to the senior commanders, in the event of your having any trouble with them."

"I shall do my best, sir," I replied. Then Rommel got into his armoured command vehicle, to visit the other units of his beaten army and to give the orders for the retreat.

## EL ALAMEIN: AFTER THE BATTLE, 4 NOVEMBER 1942

### *Keith Douglas, Eighth Army*

We began to creep forward, swinging west again to face the enemy. As we advanced, I remembered how we had sat so long during my first action within a stone's throw of enemy infantry, and I began to look very carefully at the trenches we passed. About two hundred yards from the German derelicts, which were now furiously belching inky smoke, I looked down into the face of a man lying hunched up in a pit. His expression of agony seemed so acute and urgent, his stare so wild and despairing, that for a moment, I thought him alive. He was like a cleverly posed waxwork, for his position suggested a paroxysm, an orgasm of pain. He seemed to move and writhe. But he was stiff. The dust which powdered his face like an actor's lay on his wide open eyes, whose stare held my gaze like the Ancient Mariner's. He had tried to cover his wounds with towels against the flies. His haversack lay open, from which he had taken towels and dressings. His water bottle lay tilted with the cork out. Towels and haversack were dark with dried blood, darker still with a great concourse of flies. This picture, as they say, told a story. It filled me with useless pity.

As the tank went gruffly past, the head of a living man was raised from the next pit; he had not strength to keep it raised, but lifted head and arm alternately, as a man lifts a hat on a stick to draw fire. As we went on moving past, an awful despair settled on his face. I halted the tank, realising suddenly that the driver had not seen him, and had the engine switched off. I got out of the turret and ran to him, hoping that there were no snipers about. I held a two-gallon can for him while he drank the warm, rusty water. Then he said: "Can you get me out of here?" He was a second lieutenant, I think of New Zealand infantry. His leg was hit in several places below the knee, and covered, like the dead man's wound, with a towel. "The one that got me got my water-bottle," he said. "I've been here two days. I've had about enough.

Can you get me out?" His voice broke and hesitated over the words. He suddenly added, remembering: "Do something for the chap in the next trench," and seeing my face, "Is he dead?" "Dead as a doornail," said my voice.

# ONE MAN'S WAR: THE DIARY OF A BRITISH SOLDIER AT EL ALAMEIN, 23 OCTOBER–10 NOVEMBER 1942

## *Corporal John Green, Military Police*

*Green supervised track laying for British armour during Alamein.*

*Diary: 23 Oct 1942.* 1600 hrs take position, my position West of Quartara Track, which means I am in front of our own artillery. 1730 hrs L/C Newton reports to me track all ready & lit nothing to do now only wait.

*App. 2140 hrs* British Barrage goes over, it is like hell let loose, shells are screaming over my head by the thousand. I don't think anybody ever experienced any thing like this before. It is terrific. The push is on.

*0000 hrs* Tanks are using my track now hundreds of them nose to tail they are going in, it is going to be a terrific battle. I am choked with dust and deafened by the noise of the guns.

*0200 hrs 24th Oct.* MT & tanks ease up on tracks to allow the stuff to get clear that went in front. Our bombers roaring overhead in one continuous stream & bombing Jerry's position. They are never going to stop. Barrage eased off about 0200 hrs. 0300 hrs. Traffic starts again Tanks, MT & Infantry going in 0400 hrs. Barrage bursts out again plastering Jerry with Shells. This continues until 0600 hrs All night our planes have been blasting Jerry's lines. 0730 I am relieved for breakfast & what a relief. Everybody is full of high spirits. The main topic is the barrage. Every one was impressed by the intensity of it, I should think the people most impressed are the Germans.

*24 Oct.* Go back to duty at 0930 hrs. We are right in the thick of it. German aircraft active today. 1730 back on the tracks, we are bombed. None of my gang hurt. A very similar night to last night, relieved at 0700 No sleep again tonight, duty again.

*25.10.42* Resume duty at 0930 hrs, plenty of activity over the whole front dozens of dogfights. Our planes continue to bomb enemy without stopping day & night. We also get bombed quite frequently. At 15.30 I am relieved to go back to Alamein Station. I take on duties of visiting NCO to visit every post on all Tracks. This visiting job is sticky being in a truck, I cannot hear enemy aircraft. They are on you before you know. I go to bed at 7.30 pm for the first time since the night of the 22nd. I am tired to death. We are bombed at intervals during the night, but I am too tired I just snuggle in my hole and hope for the best. *26.10.42.* I continue visiting each post on each track twice a day, these are very exciting days. On each journey I have to take cover and leave the truck at least a dozen times. We are bombed & straffed through the night. Bombs drop right across our laager, we are lucky again no one is injured. Reports say the battle is going in our favour.

*27th.* Same duty – visiting Tracks.

*28th* We move back a mile, it being too hot.

*29th* All these days are nearly alike busy all day & getting as much sleep as Jerry allows at night. I am used to it by now. We hear Jerry is retreating – slowly but surely although the din he makes doesn't seem much like it, but things are going in our favour.

*30th Oct.* Bombed again during last night at frequent intervals. Detailed for a special job I take 6 L/Cpls with me. I have to go forward as far as the second German minefield and light the gaps for our armours to (go) through at night. This takes me right into the forward zone about 4 miles west of Quatara Rd. The Germans were here only a few hours ago. All my past experiences were nothing compared to this. We are right amongst it.

*31st Oct.* We had Bacon, beans & Stukas for Breakfast. 21 of them dive bombing. Lucky we have each got a good dug out. We are shelled for 2 hours. Our artillery are behind us & are replying. We are shelled again in the afternoon. Jerry seems to have taken a personal dislike to us.

We spend most of the day in our holes. At night our dug outs are one continuous boom, owing to the guns. After a while you get used to it & find you can sleep without difficulty. We light up the gap tonight. The N.Z's go through the gap "Good Luck to Them".

*1st Nov.* Plenty of air raids 1st night also Jerry dropped his shells around us. It is a hot spot here. L/cpl.S looks like cracking up. He takes hold of himself fairly well. All day is the same as yesterday. Lighting the gap again tonight.

*Nov 2nd.* 2 German planes are shot down quite near us. We see 7 shot down altogether. S. is definitely "Bomb Happy" – he has been much worse today I have taken him off duty tonight & do his duty myself – the gap lighting is pretty sticky when within range of enemy guns.

*Nov 3rd.* More air raids last night. We have had them every night since the push started we are shelled again at intervals Jerry is definitely being pushed back. More prisoners pass us today. Shelling is worse this afternoon. 3 pm DR brings message. I have to hand over to S. African Police at 4 pm. We are all pleased to leave this joint. We pack our kit and make ready to move – Jerry is shelling again (as we) pull out. My dug out has got hit. Lucky I got out.

We go back to Alamein & dig in once again.

*Nov 4th.* More bombing last night flares by the thousand. I am informed that the whole company is moving forward. We move west of Quartara Rd on the coast Rd at 9 am. At 11.30 I am detailed along with my section to lengthen Diamond Track, running it 2 miles nearer Jerry's lines, Jerry is shelling the track all the time. At 5.00 pm Hopkinson is killed & Power & Varley badly injured, both Varley's feet are blown off. At 5.15 Varley dies. Power has about 11 wounds. We get our job finished about 6 pm, from 12.00 to 7 pm we were shelled, straffed & Stuka-ed continuously. It has been a trying day. Young Hopkinson has only been out here three weeks & Varley has a baby he hasn't seen. It shook me a bit today to see my own blokes get wiped out.

*Nov 5th.* We had air raids again last night but I didn't hear them. I had a deep hole & I slept well. I am back with Coy at the new location. I am not put on duty today so I spend the day digging myself a good dugout.

It is bonfire night & all the boys are firing flares & shooting tracers into the air. It was quite a display but Jerry put a stop to it at 8 pm. He came over & dropped flares of his own, he wasn't long before he dropped something else. He hit 2 ammo trucks near us.

*Nov 6th.* There are signs that Jerry is flapping back, but is fighting strong rearguard action. One or two daylight raids. I got 2 bottles of beer today. At 6 pm we hear Darba has fallen.

*Nov 7th.* We move up to Darba at 9 am We see lots of German & Italian dead on the way & learn they are putting mines under their own dead. Our chaps refuse to bury them, they are afraid of being blown up in the process.

Coy make location at Darba. Dozens of knocked out Jerry tanks & MT & planes here.

The Darba airfield is littered with German planes. Fuka has fallen today.

*Nov 8th.* I am sent to Fuka, 25 miles west of Darba, this morning, with a detachment to take charge of water point. This job is a little quieter than the ones I have had lately. Jerry is flapping & only fighting rear guard action. Our troops are advancing & doing fine. The RE are busy all day & work through the night to get water.

*Nov 9th.* Start pumping water at 6.30 am. I learn that this is the only water point for miles. 14 Italian soldiers come in from across the desert & give themselves up.

Later nine Germans come & surrender. I keep filling batches of prisoners all day. They are all short of water & look hungry. They say they have been drinking water from pools left by the recent rains.

*Nov 10th.* O.C. visits me today & says we have to take it easy, the whole Company have been pulled out to rest. The Coy is 25 miles behind us.

*Nov 11th.* I go for a look round to-day & find dozens of enemy tanks knocked out on the desert. The bodies are still in some of them. There are about 30 German planes all knocked out on Fuka landing ground.

Prisoners still coming in. Enemy aircraft visit us during the night, & few shells from very long range guns.

*Nov 12th.* Our rest doesn't last long, we are on a half hours notice to move. Jerry is going back faster now & we are to follow up. We move off at 11.30 hoping to make Mersa Matruh & if Jerry keeps running we shall be in Tobruk in a day or two.

## A MEETING WITH THE FÜHRER, RASTENBURG, 28 NOVEMBER 1942

### Field Marshal Erwin Rommel, Afrika Korps

*On 8 November, even as Rommel was in headlong retreat towards Tunisia, a strong Anglo-American force (the USA having joined World War II in December 1941) under*

*General Eisenhower landed in French North Africa in Operation Torch. Three days later, the invasion army had taken Casablanca, Algiers and Oran. Rommel was now squeezed between two gathering armies.*

At about 1700 I was ordered to the Fuehrer. There was a noticeable chill in the atmosphere from the outset. I described all the difficulties which the army had had to face during both the battle and the retreat. It was all noted and the execution of the operation was described as faultless and unique.

Unfortunately, I then came too abruptly to the point and said that, since experience indicated that no improvement in the shipping situation could now be expected, the abandonment of the African theatre of war should be accepted as a long-term policy. There should be no illusions about the situation and all planning should be directed towards what was attainable. If the army remained in North Africa, it would be destroyed.

I had expected a rational discussion of my arguments and intended to develop them in a great deal more detail. But I did not get so far, for the mere mention of the strategic question worked like a spark in a powder barrel. The Fuehrer flew into a fury and directed a stream of completely unfounded attacks upon us. Most of the F.H.Q. staff officers present, the majority of whom had never heard a shot fired in anger, appeared to agree with every word the Fuehrer said . . .

But there was no attempt at discussion. I began to realise that Adolf Hitler simply did not want to see the situation as it was, and that he reacted emotionally against what his intelligence must have told him was right. He said that it was a political necessity to continue to hold a major bridgehead in Africa. He would do everything possible to get supplies to me. The Reichsmarschall (Goering) was to accompany me to Italy. He would be vested with extraordinary powers and was to negotiate with the Italians and all responsible authorities. We, however, had had experience enough of these ventures.

After leaving the Fuehrer's H.Q., Goering and I travelled in a rail-car as far as Gumbinnen where we changed to Goering's special train for the journey to Rome. I was angry and resentful at the lack of understanding displayed by our highest command and their readiness to blame the troops at the front for their own mistakes. My anger redoubled when I was compelled to witness the antics of the Reichs-marschall in his special train. The situation did not seem to trouble him in the slightest. He plumed himself, beaming broadly at the primitive flattery heaped on him by imbeciles from his own court, and talked of nothing but jewellery and pictures. During the whole of this time my bitterest enemy was Goering. I think he wanted to get me sacked in order to realise his own plans in North Africa . . .

Flying back to Africa I realised that we were now completely thrown back on our resources and that to keep the army from being destroyed as the result of some crazy order or other would need all our skill.

# OPERATION TORCH: GI MEALS, NOVEMBER 1942

## Ernie Pyle, war correspondent

*Pyle was a reporter for the* Washington Daily News *in World War II.*

Our soldiers at the front learned quickly how to keep their stomachs filled during emergencies. Ordinarily, the soldier's food was prepared for him in army mess kitchens, but at the front many things could happen. Small parties went out for days at a time and had to carry their own rations. On the battle front, kitchen trucks came up only at night and sometimes not even then. With our mobile armies on the move it wasn't always possible for kitchen trucks to be in the right place at the right moment, and as a consequence every soldier learned how to feed himself. Every vehicle from jeep to tank had a few spare cans of rations hidden away somewhere.

Soldiers cooked their own meals when on the move. They made a fire in one of two ways, each involving the use of gasoline: For a short fire they dug a hole about the size of a man's hand, poured gasoline into it, sprinkled sand over the gasoline, and then threw in a match. The sand kept the gas from burning too quickly. On a small fire like that they could heat a canteen or cup of coffee. For a bigger fire, they filled a small can with gasoline and buried it even with the surface of the ground. They piled rocks around to set their cooking utensils on, and then tossed a match at the gas.

I never saw a real skillet, pan or stewpot. The soldiers made their own utensils out of those famous five-gallon gasoline tins. I don't believe there's anything in the world that can't be made out of a five-gallon gasoline tin.

The soldiers also learned not be lax about keeping their mess kits clean, for they found out by bitter experience that a dirty mess kit was the quickest way to violent nausea through poisoning. To wash their mess kits they scoured them with sand and then polished them with toilet paper – the best dishrag I've ever found.

Despite their primitive forms of cooking, the soldiers did eat well. They got either British or American rations, or a mixture of the two. Soldiers who were traveling actually preferred the British "compo" to our own famous C ration. The reason being that the C ration has so little variety that after three meals a man could hardly look a C can in the face.

The British compo was more diverse. It had such things as sausage, puddings, chocolate bars, salt, jam, butter, and cheese. It even included toilet paper.

Although a general order was issued against buying food from the Arabs, in order to avoid using up their supply, we bought it anyhow. Mess sergeants scoured the country and came back with eggs, sheep and chickens. You might say we lived partly off the country.

Of course ridiculous prices were paid to the Arabs, which infuriated the Europeans in North Africa because it ran up the prices for them too. But the Americans' attitude was usually expressed something like this: "Well, money means nothing to us here, and from the looks of most of the Arabs a few extra francs won't hurt them."

We had more eggs right at the front than anywhere else in the whole European and African theaters of war. The love of Americans for eggs has become almost a legend. Along the roads over which our motor convoys were passing constantly. Arabs stood by the score, even out on the limitless desert, holding up eggs for sale. The natives paid one franc for an egg. Mess sergeants paid three francs when buying in bulk, and individual soldiers paid five francs an egg.

## F BATTERY IN ACTION AT THALA: THE COMMANDER'S REPORT, 21 FEBRUARY 1943

### Major C. Middleton, F Battery, RA

*After being driven out of Libya (Tripoli fell to the Allies on 23 January), Rommel withdrew to Tunisia, where the Axis army was surrounded but far from defeated. On 14 February, Rommel launched a fierce assault on the Americans in the south, his Afrika Korps and 10th Panzer Division veterans shattering the untested US 2nd Corps at Kasserine Pass and driving through to threaten Allied advance airfields, supply dumps and TAC HQ First Army. A "thin red line" stand by a small British force, including F Battery, halted the German penetration.*

At first light on February 21st the Armoured Brigade, with 17th/21st Lancers on the right and 2nd Lothians with F Battery in support on the left, were in position astride the road about 20 miles east of Thala. The Leicesters were moving on to their position. It was a bright, sunny day and during the morning a certain amount of activity was observed. German infantry could be seen getting out of vehicles, but they were well outside the range of our guns. At about one o'clock a German tank attack developed, with SP guns in support. They were engaged and the armoured regiments, already much reduced in strength and armed with 2-pdr Valentines only and a few Crusaders with 6-pdrs, were leap-frogged back during the afternoon. Observed shooting was extremely difficult at this stage owing to the dust and the almost continuous smoke screen put down by the armoured regiments. The battery was at the same time leap-frogged back troop by troop, and about 30 minutes before dusk it passed back through the Leicesters' position and went into action about 1,500 yards in the rear. There had only been time for the very briefest of reconnaissances by the CPO and troop leaders and by the time the guns got into action it was dark. The position was extremely cramped, for guns were sometimes only 20 yards apart and no more than 150 yards separated the two troops, T Troop being in the front with V Troop behind them. At dusk the armoured regiments passed back through the Leicesters' position and went into leaguer.

Less than an hour later, while subsection meals were being got ready and the digging of slit trenches and preparations for the night were going on in the dark, some tanks came up the road and stopped, the leading one no more than 100 yards from the battery position. The situation was confused, some of our vehicles were lost and looking for their units, and the night was dark; but the identity of these tanks was suspect. Sergeant Ainslie, No. 1 of the nearest gun, went forward to reconnoitre and heard German voices. In the dark he got close up and found that the leading tank had apparently broken down with mechanical trouble. As he got back, a Bren carrier drove unsuspectingly up the road towards the leading tank, which opened at point-blank range and brewed it up. A small plan was made to deal with the immediate situation. Captain J. S. Pirie was to fire a Very light over the German tanks while Sergeant Ainslie laid his gun on the leader. Lieutenant J. G. Bagnall was to discourage any German from showing his head out of the turret by opening on him with a Bren. The first Very light misfired, but the second one was successful, and Sergeant Ainslie knocked out the leading tank with his first shot. It burst into flames. This stirred the remainder of the tanks into activity and they attempted to withdraw, firing as they went. Another tank was knocked out almost immediately by Sergeant Ainslie's gun and a third, which came off the road and moved round in front of T Troop's position, was dealt with by Sergeant Laurie. He and his detachment were taking cover from the small-arms fire in their shallow slit trenches when the silhouette of this tank was seen passing across the front of the gun position about 50 yards away. Sergeant Laurie immediately jumped up, laid, loaded and fired his gun himself and knocked out the tank.

The remainder of the tanks withdrew back down the road and sat on the high ground firing their machine guns, with tracer, indiscriminately down the road. At the same time a fierce exchange of firing broke out away on the right, where German tanks had penetrated into the leaguer of 17th/21st Lancers, and a number of tanks on both sides were knocked out in a confused engagement in the dark.

The situation was now highly obscure, but the one thing that was clear was that there was to be no withdrawal from this position. It soon became obvious that the Leicesters' position was no longer held and that the actual front line was T Troop's line of guns. There was a great deal to be done, and not much time to do it. Slit trenches had to be dug for each gun, arrangements made for local defence and the two guns on the right of the road moved to the main battery position. The command post, too, was re-sited by a small bridge at the side of the road close to the guns. When daylight came the position was not going to be healthy, as the guns were in a hollow overlooked from the high ground about 1,500 yards ahead. In addition, the road from Thala on to the gun position was completely exposed and so the quads were ordered to dump all their ammunition and, together with the remainder of the vehicles, get clear of the position by dawn. At any moment the position might be attacked by infantry.

By first light each gun and command post had a slit trench, and Captain I. Buchanan (a Canadian officer on attachment) had been established in an OP on a pimple to the left of the position. The area was shelled at frequent intervals throughout the morning and several tanks which appeared on the crest about 1,500 to 2,000 yards away were engaged furiously over open sights. When AP ran short, HE 119 "cap-on" was used. It is doubtful if any of the tanks were actually knocked out but they were certainly discouraged. OPS were also engaged over open sights. No infantry attack on the position developed during the day, but the shelling was heavy and obviously directed from the ridge in front, and casualties amounted to one killed and thirteen wounded, including Captain Pirie, who had been an inspiration throughout. During the day the battery was greatly heartened by a visit from the BRA, First Army, Brigadier Parham, who insisted on visiting each gun. While he was there a German motorcyclist with sidecar advanced down the ridge in front and after having been greeted with a hail of ill-directed small-arms fire was knocked out by a gun. Too late, and to our great regret, we discovered that he was a medical orderly who had clearly lost his way.

The road from Thala was under shellfire and during the day the quads had to run the gauntlet several times to bring up more ammunition. The evacuation of casualties was undertaken voluntarily by Gunners Kerr and Peters, the driver and wireless operator of one of the troop leader's trucks. They worked untiringly, often under shell-fire, and succeeded in getting all casualties, both our own and those of other nearby units, back to the ADS at Thala.

Another highlight of the day was Captain Buchanan's OP work. Practically all the time his line was out of action, as it was repeatedly cut by shellfire, but he was able to carry on sending fire orders by "voice control", which he enlivened with suitable words of encouragement. When his voice failed him he engaged enemy OPS with his rifle and claimed several hits. By the end of the day he could no longer speak. We were told later that his running commentary had been a great encouragement to a company of the Rifle Brigade who, unknown to us, had been in a position on our right.

## BLOWING UP TANKS BEHIND ENEMY LINES, TUNISIA, 25 FEBRUARY 1943
### Major Vladimir Peniakoff ("Popski"), PPA

*Peniakoff commanded the smallest independent unit in the British Army (23 men) which became officially christened Popski's Private Army when no-one could think of anything better. Like the other British special forces which blossomed in the desert war, the LRDG and the SAS, the job of the PPA was reconnaissance and general mayhem-making behind Axis lines.*

Between us and the road and running parallel with it was a narrow, flat-bottomed wadi, the sand of which appeared broken up with many tracks. We drove into it and found the unmistakable marks of at least twenty tanks which, we reckoned, had passed this way towards Gafsa not longer ago than the previous night. Better even, we found a board on a post marked Gafsa with an arrow. A tank by-pass, we concluded, had been designed along this wadi, to avoid driving them on the hard tarmac. Hurriedly we buried two lines of mines across the wadi and withdrew in some haste because our look-out on the hill reported a line of armed men deploying from the station building and advancing towards us, like beaters at a shoot. Night was falling fast. I stopped after we had crossed two ridges and gave instructions for our night trip back to Bir el Ater: I intended taking a more southerly route, where I thought the going might be better. We formed up and started: Waterson, who drove second, pushed up alongside my jeep to say that he heard a vehicle behind us. I stopped, waved the others on, looked back and, in the half light, saw two German armoured cars creeping on our tail; they halted 150 yards away. At that moment tracers from Waterson's half-inch Browning rushed past me: his third or fourth burst hit the foremost armoured car, which seemed to give a shudder and then puffed out black smoke. I drove a little further away from Waterson and turned round to allow Locke to open up with my twin .30 guns, spraying both armoured cars. Waterson hadn't bothered to turn his jeep round, but, seated on the bonnet, fired over the stern.

The second car turned tail after firing a few bursts and disappeared over a hill. I was annoyed that none of my other jeeps had opened up: my men, it seemed, had not yet got much battle sense and presumably they waited for someone to point out the objective and give them the order to fire!

Sapper Curtis, a new recruit to PPA, who was driving a jeep with us for the first time, came trotting up to me: he had tipped his jeep down a steep, very narrow gully in the dark, and he didn't think it could be got out without much digging. His breath came short with anxiety:

"I suppose you will give me the sack now, Sir. I have lost my jeep – and not through enemy action."

I told him to salvage his gun and as much as he could of his kit, set his incendiary bomb on the petrol tank and climb on to Davies's vehicle. We had to get back quickly with my information and I wouldn't spare the time to salvage Curtis's jeep; but I had no intention of dispensing with his services, as I believed he would turn out to be one of our outstanding recruits. I left him in doubt of his fate for the time being, which would do him and his companions no harm.

We went on in the dark over ground so bad that one of David Stirling's sergeants walked in front of my jeep to warn me of obstacles. For a long time we were accompanied by the noise of several armoured cars floundering behind us and we saw an occasional flash of a headlight. Then, as we reached higher and better ground, they gave up the chase. I called a halt on a hill to the south of the morass in which we had struggled on our way out and listened: after a while a mighty rumble approached from the north, grew and resolved itself into the manifold clangings of tanks on the move, some more of von Arnim's armour slipping away to the Mareth Line. We drove towards home: on our way Locke, who had become fanciful with the excitement of our little battle, heard so many bangs behind us that by his reckoning each of our mines must have gone off twice over.

# "FIGHTING LIKE THE DEVIL": THE US 26TH REGIMENT AT EL GUETTAR, 23 MARCH 1943

## Brigadier General Theodore Roosevelt Jr, 26th Regiment, US 1st Infantry Division

*Roosevelt, son of the 26th President of the US, commanded the 26th Regiment in both World Wars.*

North Africa, Mar. 25, 1943

Dearest Bunny:

Since I wrote of our attack on the unnamed city much has happened.

First we were ordered to attack again. We moved out for this show as usual under cover of darkness. We had only one road and two combat teams plus supporting arms to be brought down. That meant a truck movement covering twenty miles of road space. After we had done our best to give our directive to the unit commanders and laid on a schedule of movement for units timetable I went forward in my jeep. All went reasonably well. At the time I did not think so for I got furiously angry with countless idiocies that delayed the column.

By dawn the show was on – machine guns spluttered, artillery rumbled. We caught the Italians unprepared. On the north we came down on them from the mountains – a devilish climb. On the south we swept around their right flank. By then the original objectives were taken and crowds of prisoners were being marched to the rear. Our men don't take to all this "bitter hate" business – and all the Sherwoods, MacLeishes, Sarnoffs etc. with their swivel chairs, daintily fed bellies and soft safe beds can't change their natures. Our men will fight like the devil, but when the battle's over, it's over. They treat war like a football game – when the game's over let's all get drunk together. They gave the prisoners candy and cigarettes and roared with laughter.

Next day we pushed still further to new positions. Among our troubles were the dive bombers. They came down on us constantly. Once I was caught in a valley by a raid. A bomb hit within twelve paces of where I was lying. My helmet was struck by a fragment and knocked galley-west, but I was unhurt though a couple of men were killed. By the way, don't wear your helmet strap hooked. If I had my head would have gone rolling off inside the helmet.

The following day the enemy counter attack came. During

the night, which was clear with the bright moon of Africa lighting the arid country, the German tanks came into our position. We got vague rumors of them from our reconnaissance units, and soon I began to hear bursts of enemy m.g.s. I went forward to an O.P. on the front of our main line positions. At dawn the battlefield lay at my feet on a circular plain about seven miles in diameter. I could see it all.

The first move was a swing of German tanks to our right flank – 24 in all. We took them under artillery fire. On they came until they had nearly turned our position – the shells bursting around them. Then the going got too tough for them. They hesitated, milled around and withdrew, leaving two destroyed tanks nearly in our lines to mark the high tide of their advance. Meanwhile their artillery had been shelling us and their dive bombers were busy.

Whenever a flight of these appeared they were greeted by a fury of anti-aircraft and small arms. Incidentally, I did not see one shot down, though how they lived through that flood of lead is more than I can tell. From then on the day was a series of assaults, each repelled in turn. Once they brought forward their enormous Mark X tanks. The plain became a smoky, dusty dream, or rather nightmare. It was dotted with destroyed tanks and vehicles, some of them ours for they got in on some of our artillery and our Tank Destroyers made a costly and stupid sally.

Sometimes vehicles would hit mines and blow up. Once an enemy vehicle towing a 37 m.m. gun ran down the road practically into our lines. It was hit by mortar-fire and burst into flames. A couple of men got out and started to run. The m.g.s got them.

The final assault came at five. It was preceded by four dive bombing attacks and artillery. It was composed of tanks and infantry. Just in front of me was a German unit of 400 men. We took them under fire and they went to ground behind some sand dunes. The artillery went after them with time-shells and air-bursts. In no time they were up running to the rear, khaki figures reeling and falling with black bursts over their heads. That was the last of the day. Nightfall brought us rest. We'd thrown back a Panzer division with heavy loss. I never expect to see anything like this again – a battle fought at my feet while I commanded by telephone as I saw the developments before my eyes. Incidentally, I was two days without sleep, washing or even brushing my teeth.

Now we're at it again. We're all weary, but I guess the enemy is wearier than we are. In this war no units in the line get relief. We just go on and on. I believe that the very fierceness of this fighting means that later resistance will be softened.

I got a letter from Q. He sounds well and cheerful. He says he'll be fit for service towards the end of April. I hope he does not get back until the battle of Africa is finished. No letters from you any more. They've all stopped. Nothing since Q's wound more than a month ago. I guess they'll all come in a batch.

Much, much love.

Ted.

# TUNIS FALLS, 7 MAY 1943

## *Alan Moorehead, war correspondent*

*By the end of April 1943 the supply situation for the Axis army in Africa – of which there were still eleven divisions in fighting order – had become critical. So seriously disrupted were Italo-German air and sea convoys across the Mediterranean by Allied attacks that a bare quarter of necessary materiel was landing in Tunisia. At one point, panzer crews resorted to distilling local wines for fuel for their charges. The situation was untenable. The ports of Bizerte and Tunis both fell on 7 May.*

At Kilometre 9 all Tunis broke into view – the wide bay, flanked by mountains, the spreading town, one of the largest in Africa, not much harmed by bombs but smoking now with a score of large fires. We stood poised on the summit for a moment before we dipped down into the suburbs. I remember thinking over and over again as I stood in the rain, "Tunis has fallen." That simple thought seemed to be quite enough in itself, as complete as a curtain falling on a play, and if one had any sense of triumph I do not remember it. I can recall only a sense of relief and gratitude.

Someone, the retreating Germans probably, had piled brushwood round a bungalow and it was burning brightly. In all directions there were fires and occasional explosions. Clearly the enemy was destroying his dumps before he got away. More and more houses appeared. The crew of a tank had pulled into a piece of waste land and the crew were boiling a pot of tea with a ring of curious Arabs squatting around them . . .

Looking around I saw I was again among the Desert Rats. The Red Jerboa in the red circle was painted on the battered mudguards; the most famous symbol in the whole Desert War. And the men in the vehicles were the Eleventh Hussars, the reconnaissance unit that had led the Eighth Army across the desert since Wavell's time. With them were the Derbyshire Yeomanry, the men who had led the First Army through all the hard fighting in Tunisia, and they carried the symbol of the mailed fist . . .

The vehicles had pulled up and at the head of the line a British officer stopped us. "No farther," he said. "There are German snipers down the street. Wait until they are cleared up." We waited in the rain but no firing sounded and one or two of the armoured cars moved on again. In his excitement my driver tried to get ahead of the armoured cars but I held him back, as we were already third in line and the only unarmoured vehicle on the spot except for Keating's jeep. We waited until two tanks and a Bren-gun carrier had gone ahead and then we followed.

Quite suddenly the Avenue de Bardo sprang to life. Crowds of French people rushed into the street and they were beside themselves in hysterical delight. Some rushed directly at us, flinging themselves on the running-boards. A girl threw her arms round my driver's neck. An old man took a packet of cigarettes from his pocket and flung them up at us. Someone else brandished a bottle of wine. All the women had flowers that they had hastily plucked from their gardens. A clump of roses hit me full on the mouth and there were flowers all over the bonnet of the car. Everyone was screaming and shouting and getting in the way of the vehicles, not caring whether they were run over or not. A young Frenchman, his face working with excitement, hoisted himself on to the roof of our car with a Sten gun in his hand. He screamed that he was an escaped prisoner and something else in French I did not catch, but I pushed him off, not sure whether he was friend or enemy. There were Germans walking about all over the place. They stood gaping on the pavements, standing in groups, just staring, their rifles slung over their shoulders. A Bren-gun carrier shot past us and it was full of Germans whom the Tommies had picked up, and in their excitement the crowd imagined that these Germans in the British vehicle were British and so they threw flowers at them. The Germans caught the flowers, and they sat there stiffly in the Bren-gun carrier, each man with a little posy clutched in his hand.

The double doors of a big red building on the right-hand side of the street burst open and at first I could not understand – the men who ran out, scores, hundreds of them, were British in flat steel helmets and British battledress. Then it came to me – they were prisoners whom we had rescued. They stood in an undecided group for a moment on the sidewalk in the rain, filling their eyes with the sight of us. Then they cheered. Some of them had no heart to speak and simply looked. One man, bearded up to his eyes, cried quietly. The others yelled hoarsely. Suddenly the whole mass of men were swept with a torrent of emotional relief and wild joy. They yelled and yelled.

Handing out cigarettes we caught their story in broken phrases. "Four hundred of them, all officers and NCOS . . . due to sail for Italy today. Another big batch of them had sailed yesterday."

There was an Italian lying in blood at the doorway and I asked about him. A major answered. "He and another Italian were on guard over us. An hour ago a German armoured car went down this street and they put a burst of machine-gun bullets through the door, hoping to hit us. They didn't care about the Italian sentries and they hit this one in the head. He's dying. His friend went crazy. He rushed off down the street shooting any German he could see, and I think they killed him."

We drove on again. On our left there was a tall and ancient stone viaduct and piles of ammunition were burning at the base of the pillars. A railway line ran beside the road. On our right there was a four-storied red building, a brewery. We were just level with this when the shooting started.

It started with a stream of tracer bullets, about shoulder high, skidding across the road between my vehicle and the armoured car in front. We stopped and jumped for the gutters. The crowd melted from the street, the cheering died away with a sort of strangled sigh. After the first burst there came another and another, and soon there must have been half a dozen machine-guns firing at very close range. The trouble was that one had at first no notion of where it was coming from. This was my first experience of street fighting, but I felt instinctively I wanted to get up against the wall. There were five of us in our car, Austen, Buckley, the driver and Sidney Bernstein, none of us with arms, and we groped our way along one of the side walls of the brewery.

The shooting now was continuous. Three lads suddenly jumped out of the nearest armoured car with a Bren-gun. They dashed across the road, flung themselves down on the railway line, set up the gun and began firing. The Germans from the Bren-gun carrier had also jumped into the ditch beside the railway and they lay there on their backs, each man still holding his posy.

Looking up, I saw a line of bullets slapping against the brewery wall above us. As each bullet hit it sent out a little yellow flame and a spray of plaster came down on top of us. At the same moment my driver pointed up. Directly above us two German snipers were shooting out of the brewery, and we could see the barrels of their guns sticking out of a second-storey window. As yet the Germans had not seen us. Since at any moment they might look down, we crawled back to the main street. Keeping pressed against the wall, we edged our way from doorway to doorway until we reached the building where the British prisoners were kept. It was raining very heavily. There was now a second wounded man on the wooden floor. All this time the engine of our stationary car was running and the windscreen wipers were swishing to and fro. It was in a very isolated position and directly in the path of the shooting.

After ten minutes or so the firing eased off. The tank had let fly with a couple of heavy shells and that had sobered up the snipers. We began to edge back to the brewery, hoping to get our car before it caught fire from the tracers.

A German with blood pouring down his leg popped out of a doorway in front of me and surrendered. We waved him back towards the British prisoners. Two more Germans came out of a house with their hands up, but we were intent on getting to the car and took no notice. At the corner of the brewery two sergeants, one American and the other British, who were staff photographers, ran across the open road to their vehicle, grabbed their tommy-guns and began firing. They were enjoying the whole thing with a gusto that seemed madness at first. Yet I could understand it a little. This street fighting had a kind of Red Indian quality about it. You felt you were right up against the enemy and able to deal with him directly, your nimbleness and marksmanship against his. The American was coolly picking his targets and taking careful aim. The young Frenchman with the Sten gun turned up, and I realised now that he had been warning us about these snipers in the first place. He led the two sergeants into the brewery, kicking the door open with his foot and shooting from the hip. They sent a preliminary volley through the aperture. Presently the three of them came out with the two snipers who had been shooting above our heads. They had wounded one.

The sergeants then offered to cover us while we ran for our car. My driver was quick. He whizzed it backwards up the street, and we ran to the point a quarter of a mile back where the rest of the British column was waiting.

Clifford had been having a busy time at the cross-roads. He had stopped one car with two German officers in it. They had pointed to the red crosses on their arms, but Clifford found the vehicle full of arms and he lugged them out. At the same time two snipers had run across to the house on the corner. A Tommy with a neat burst killed them as they ran. Mad things were going on. Two Italian officers marched up and demanded, in the midst of this confusion, that they should be provided with transport to return to their barracks, where they had left their waterproof coats.

Meanwhile another patrol of armoured cars had taken the right fork, the Rue de Londres, down to the centre of the town. They took the city entirely unawares. Hundreds of Germans were walking in the streets, some with their girl friends. Hundreds more were sitting drinking aperitifs in a big pavement café. No one had warned them the British were near. The attack had gone so quickly that here in the town there had been no indication that the Axis line was broken. Now, suddenly, like a vision from the sky, appeared these three British armoured cars. The Germans rose from their seats and stared. The Tommies stared back. There was not much they could do. Three armoured cars could not handle all these prisoners. In the hair-dressing saloon next door more Germans struggled out of the chairs and, with white sheets round their necks and lather on their faces, stood gaping.

The three armoured cars turned back for reinforcements.

In this mad way Tunis fell that night. Here and there a German with desperate courage emptied his gun down on the streets and hurled a grenade or two. But for the most part these base troops in Tunis were taken entirely off their guard and there were thousands of them. All night there was hopeless confusion in the dark, Germans and British wandering about together, Italians scrambling into civilian clothes and taking refuge in the cellars, saboteurs starting new fires and igniting more dumps, men putting out to sea in rowing-boats, others grabbing bicycles and carts and making up the roads to Cape Bon, and others again, bewildered and afraid, simply marching along until they could find someone to whom they could surrender. All night the fires burned, and they were still going in the morning when the British infantry began to flood into the town in force.

An extraordinary scene of havoc and confusion was revealed by the morning light. The town itself was pretty well unscathed, but the waterfront had been savaged by bomb-fire out of all recognition. Six-storey buildings had collapsed like pancakes. For days hardly a man had dared to approach the docks. The port of La Goulette outside the town, near the site of ancient Carthage, was even worse. Ships or parts of ships were blown out of the sea and flung upon the hulks of their sister ships. The stone wharves were split up and pocked with immense craters.

At the two airfields scores of smashed German planes were lying about in the soaking rain – Messerschmitts, Dorniers, Macchis, Focke-Wulfs, Junkers, Stukas and communication machines of every possible sort.

My party had not stayed to explore these things. We had entered the city at fifteen minutes to three on May 7th. The street fighting had held us up until nearly dark, and then, through the evening, we made that endless tedious drive back to Thibar to send our messages. We were so tired we scarcely glanced up when a Spitfire crashed close by us at Medjez-el-Bab. On the way we heard that the Americans had reached Bizerta. It was just six months since the landing in North Africa, just on three years since the African war had begun.

*After the fall of Bizerte and Tunis the Axis army had almost no territory left to defend. There was sporadic resistance until 13 May when the last German and Italian units surrendered.*

*The two years of the desert war had cost the Axis powers over a million soldiers killed and taken prisoner.*

## ENVOI: "I WOULDN'T MISS THE EXPERIENCE I HAVE ENCOUNTERED FOR ANY AMOUNT OF MONEY", JULY 1943

### Sergeant Ray Salisbury, USAAF

Somewhere in North Africa
July 6, 1943

Dear Sis:

Patriotism in its true sense is difficult to define. According to Webster it is the feeling of undying faith that one bears for a cause. It is the willingness of a person to die in defense of an ideal. In my case, and many others, I AM NOT WILLING TO DIE. Dead, I would be of no further use to the Government. They realized that a long time ago – which is no doubt why they spend millions of dollars training soldiers to do a job skilfully. I can really appreciate the careful planning and foresight that went into my military education. Teamwork, initiative, willingness, cooperativeness, timing, skill and courage are the only requisites a soldier requires. Of course, sometimes the timing is faulty, or some member of a chain doesn't cooperate and casualties inevitably result. But on the whole, this war is being run like clock work with the pleasing results you read about in the newspaper. But behind all these successes, major or minor the underlying factor is an individual's bravery and guts. One person can provide the spark that causes an Army to do unheard of things. That's the true spirit of Americanism. That's why we as a Nation will never be beaten! We can complain to ourselves, grouse about conditions and yell about anything or everything but when something comes up that needs everyone's cooperation the Americans are there to do it. Then they go back to their complaining . . . Just to witness the ingenuity of soldiers who aren't provided with the comforts of home, to see them make crystals for their watches out of a turret canopy – to watch them repair their shoes with nails made from carpet tacks. There are countless other things they do. They do not complain because they are without facilities – they make their own . . . Here is where you get down to bed rock. Here is where you discover that you have pools of energy that have never been tapped – and because you live so closely with other men, YOU have to be a regular guy. I wouldn't miss the experience I have encountered for any amount of money. There's something new every day . . .

  Yours,

                Ray.

# Part Four

*Barbarossa*

*The German Invasion of Russia,
June 1941–February 1943*

# INTRODUCTION

---

Operation Barbarossa, Hitler's invasion of Russia launched on 22 June 1941, was a three-pronged attack: one offensive under General von Leeb drove through the Baltic states towards Leningrad; the main offensive, under von Bock, headed towards Moscow; and the third, under von Rundstedt, headed through southern Poland towards the Black Sea. It was not to be a war of conquest, but of destruction; the annihilation of a sub-human people whose land would eventually be colonised by Teutons. To this end, Hitler committed three million German soldiers – plus 43 divisions from pro-Nazi countries, principally Finland, Rumania and Italy – to Barbarossa. The Soviet Union had 170 divisions along its front line, but these suffered from poor leadership (Stalin had purged many Soviet officers) and worse communications. The Russians were also taken by surprise because Stalin refused to believe that his erstwhile ally Hitler, with whom he had happily carved up Poland, would turn against him.

## OPERATION BARBAROSSA: INVASION OF THE SOVIET UNION, 22 JUNE 1941
### Colonel-General Heinz Guderian, Panzer Group 2

*Guderian commanded Panzer Group 2, subordinated to Army Group Centre under von Bock, in the invasion.*

After Hitler's speech to the generals on June 14th I flew to Warsaw, on the 15th, where my staff was quartered. The days until the opening of the attack on June 22nd I spent visiting the troops and their jumping-off places and also the neighbouring units in order to ensure full co-operation. The march to the assembly areas and the final preparations for the attack passed smoothly enough. On June 17th I examined the course of the River Bug, which was our front line. On the 19th I visited General von Mackensen's III Army Corps, which was immediately to the right of my Panzer Group. On the 20th and 21st I visited the forward units of my corps to make sure that all preparations for the attack were satisfactorily completed. Detailed study of the behaviour of the Russians convinced me that they knew nothing of our intentions. We had observation of the courtyard of Brest-Litovsk citadel and could see them drilling by platoons to the music of a military band. The strong points along their bank of the Bug were unoccupied. They had made scarcely any noticeable progress in strengthening their fortified positions during the past few weeks. So the prospects of our attack achieving surprise were good and the question therefore arose whether the one hour's artillery preparation which had been planned was now necessary after all. I finally decided not to cancel it; this was simply a precaution lest unexpected Russian counter-measures cause us avoidable casualties.

On the fateful day of June 22nd, 1941, I went at 02.10 hrs. to my Group command post which was located in an observation tower south of Bohukaly, 9 miles north-west of Brest-Litovsk. It was still dark when I arrived there at 03.10 hrs. At 03.15 hrs. our artillery opened up. At 03.40 hrs. the first dive-bomber attack went in. At 04.15 hrs. advance units of the 17th and 18th Panzer Divisions began to cross the Bug. At 04.45 hrs. the leading tanks of the 18th Panzer Division forded the river. For this they were equipped with the waterproofing that had been tested for *Operation Sea-lion*, which enabled them to move through 13 feet of water.

At 06.50 hrs. I crossed the Bug in an assault boat in the neighbourhood of Kolodno. My command staff, consisting of two armoured wireless trucks, a number of cross-country vehicles and some motorcyclists, followed at 08.30 hrs. I began by following the tank tracks of 18th Panzer Division and soon reached the bridge over the Lesna, whose capture was important for the advance of XLVII Panzer Corps; there I found nobody except some Russian pickets. The Russians took to their heels when they saw my vehicles. Two of my orderly officers set off after them, against my wishes; unfortunately they both lost their lives as a result.

At 10.25 hrs. the leading tank company reached the Lesna and crossed the bridge. Next to arrive was the divisional commander, General Nehring. I accompanied the 18th Panzer Division in their advance until mid-afternoon. At 16.30 hrs. I returned to the bridgehead at Kolodno and from there I went at 18.30 hrs. to my command post.

We had managed to take the enemy by surprise along the entire Panzer Group front. To the south of Brest-Litovsk the XXIV Panzer Corps had captured the bridges over the Bug intact. To the north-west of the fortress our bridges were being built according to plan. The enemy, however, soon recovered from his initial surprise and put up a tough defence in his prepared positions. The important citadel of Brest-Litovsk held out with remarkable stubbornness for several days, thus depriving us of the use of the road and rail communications across the Bug and Muchaviec.

In the evening the Panzer Group was fighting around Maloryta, Kobryn, Brest-Litovsk, and Pruzana. At the last-named place the 18th Panzer Division became involved in the first tank battle of the campaign.

## "WE'RE GOING TO SHOW THOSE BOLSHEVIK BUMS WHO'S WHO": A GERMAN TANK GUNNER WRITES HOME, 25 JUNE 1941

### Sergeant Karl Fuchs, 25 Panzer Regiment

*Eastern Front*
*25 June 1941*

My dearest wife, my dear little Horsti,

After three days of heavy fighting we were finally granted a well-deserved day of rest. Unfortunately there is some maintenance work that has to be done.

How are you, my two loved ones? Since I received your postcard several days ago, I haven't heard from you. I suppose it's because of the postal delivery which, because of the huge distances now, only comes to us every three or four days. I myself am fine and healthy and today I received my first war decoration from our commander, namely, the tank assault medal. I wear it proudly and hope you are proud of me.

Up to now, all of the troops have had to accomplish quite a bit. The same goes for our machines and tanks. But, nevertheless, we're going to show those Bolshevik bums who's who around here! They fight like hired hands – not like soldiers, no matter if they are men, women or children on the front lines. They're all no better than a bunch of scoundrels. By now, half of Europe is mobilized. The entry of Spain and Hungary on our side against this Bolshevik archenemy of the world overjoyed us all. Yes, Europe stands under the leadership of our beloved Führer Adolph Hitler, and he'll reshape it for a better future.

The entry of all these volunteer armies into this war will cause the war to be over soon.

The impressions that the battles have left on me will be with me forever . . .

Your Korri

*Sergeant Fuchs was killed in action in November 1941.*

# THE *WEHRMACHT* ADVANCES INTO RUSSIA, JULY 1941

## *General Blumentritt*, Wehrmacht

*At the start of Barbarossa, some German units were advancing 50 miles a day and Hitler declared that he hoped to seize the Caucasus before the end of 1941. His more prescient generals, however, already understood that the* Wehrmacht *was in trouble.*

The infantry had a hard time keeping up. Marches of twenty-five miles in the course of a day were by no means exceptional, and that over the most atrocious roads. A vivid picture which remains of these weeks is the great clouds of yellow dust kicked up by the Russian columns attempting to retreat and by our infantry hastening in pursuit. The heat was tremendous, though interspersed with sudden showers which quickly turned the roads to mud before the sun reappeared and as quickly baked them into crumbling clay once again.

By 2 July the first battle was for all intents and purposes won. The haul was astounding. A hundred and fifty thousand prisoners taken, some 1,200 tanks and 600 guns captured or destroyed. First impressions revealed that the Russian was as tough a fighter as ever. His tanks, however, were not particularly formidable and his air force, so far as we could see, non-existent.

The conduct of the Russian troops, even in this first battle, was in striking contrast to the behaviour of the Poles and of the Western allies in defeat. Even when encircled, the Russians stood their ground and fought. The vast extent of the country, with its forests and swamps, helped them in this. There were not enough German troops available completely to seal off a huge encirclement such as that of Bialystok-Slonim. Our motorized forces fought on or near to the roads: in the great trackless spaces between them the Russians were left largely unmolested. This was why the Russians were able not infrequently to break out of our encirclements, whole columns moving by night through the forests that stretched away eastwards. They always attempted to break out to the east, so that the eastern side of each encirclement had to be held by our strongest troops, usually Panzer troops. Nevertheless, our encirclements were seldom entirely successful.

## STUKAS DIVE-BOMB THE SOVIET FLEET, 21 SEPTEMBER 1941

### Hans Ulrich Rudel, Luftwaffe

Brilliant blue sky, without a rack of cloud. The same even over the sea. We are already attacked by Russian fighters above the narrow coastal strip; but they cannot deflect us from our objective, there is no question of that. We are flying at 9000 feet; the flak is deadly. About ten miles ahead we see Kronstadt; it seems an infinite distance away. With this intensity of flak one stands a good chance of being hit at any moment. The waiting makes the time long. Dourly, Steen and I keep on our course. We tell ourselves that Ivan is not firing at single aircraft; he is merely putting up a flak barrage at a certain altitude. The others are all over the shop, not only in the squadrons and the flights, but even in the pairs. They think that by varying height and zigzagging they can make the A.A. gunners' task more difficult. There go the two blue-nosed staff aircraft sweeping through all the formations, even the separate flights. Now one of them loses her bomb. A wild helter-skelter in the sky over Kronstadt; the danger of ramming is great. We are still a few miles from our objective; at an angle ahead of me I can already make out the *Marat* berthed in the harbour. The guns boom, the shells scream up at us, bursting in flashes of livid colours; the flak forms small fleecy clouds that frolic around us. If it was not in such deadly earnest one might use the phrase: an aerial carnival. I look down on the *Marat*. Behind her lies the cruiser *Kirov*. Or is it the *Maxim Gorki?* These ships have not yet joined in the general bombardment. But it was the same the last time. They do not open up on us until we are diving to the attack. Never has our flight through the defence seemed so slow or so uncomfortable. Will Steen use his diving brakes today or in the face of this opposition will he go in for once "without"? There he goes. He has already used his brakes. I follow suit, throwing a final glance into his cockpit. His grim face wears an expression of concentration. Now we are in a dive, close beside each other. Our diving angle must be between seventy and eighty degrees. I have already picked up the *Marat* in my sights. We race down towards her; slowly she grows to a gigantic size. All their A.A. guns are now directed at us. Now nothing matters but our target, our objective; if we achieve our task it will save our brothers in arms on the ground much bloodshed. But what is happening? Steen's aircraft suddenly leaves mine far behind. He is travelling much faster. Has he after all again retracted his diving brakes in order to get down more quickly? So I do the same. I race after his aircraft going all out. I am right on his tail, travelling much too fast and unable to check my speed. Straight ahead of me I see the horrified face of W.O. Lehmann, Steen's rear-gunner. He expects every second that I shall cut off his tail unit with my propeller and ram him.

I increase my diving angle with all the strength I have got – it must surely be 90 degrees – sit tight as if I were sitting on a powder-keg. Shall I graze Steen's aircraft which is right on me or shall I get safely past and down? I streak past him within a hair's breadth. Is this an omen of success? The ship is centered plumb in the middle of my sights. My Ju 87 keeps perfectly steady as I dive; she does not swerve an inch. I have the feeling that to miss is now impossible. Then I see the *Marat* large as life in front of me. Sailors are running across the deck, carrying ammunition. Now I press the bomb release switch on my stick and pull with all my strength. Can I still manage to pull out? I doubt it, for I am diving without brakes and the height at which I have released my bomb is not more than 900 feet. The skipper has said when briefing us that the two thousand pounder must not be dropped from lower than 3000 feet as the fragmentation effect of this bomb reaches 3000 feet and to drop it at a lower altitude is to endanger one's aircraft. But now I have forgotten that! – I am intent on hitting the *Marat*. I tug at my stick, without feeling, merely exerting all my strength. My acceleration is too great. I see nothing, my sight is blurred in a momentary blackout, a new experience for me. But if it can be managed at all I must pull out. My head has not yet cleared when I hear Scharnovski's voice:

"She is blowing up, sir!"

Now I look out. We are skimming the water at a level of ten or twelve feet and I bank round a little. Yonder lies the *Marat* below a cloud of smoke rising up to 1200 feet; apparently the magazine has exploded.

"Congratulations, sir."

Scharnovski is the first. Now there is a babel of congratulations from all the other aircraft over the radio. From all sides I catch the words: "Good show!" Hold on, surely I recognize the Wing Commander's voice? I am conscious of a pleasant glow of exhilaration such as one feels after a successful athletic feat. Then I fancy that I am looking into the eyes of thousands of grateful infantrymen. Back at low level in the direction of the coast.

"Two Russian fighters, sir," reports Scharnovski.

"Where are they?"

"Chasing us, sir. – They are circling round the fleet in their own flak. – Cripes! They will both be shot down together by their own flak."

This expletive and, above all, the excitement in Scharnovski's voice are something quite new to me. This has never happened before. We fly on a level with the concrete blocks on which A.A. guns have also been posted. We could almost knock the Russian crews off them with our wings. They are still firing at our comrades who are now attacking the other ships. Then for a moment there is nothing visible through the pall of smoke rising from the *Marat*. The din down below on the surface of the water must be terrific, for it is not until now that a few flak crews spot my aircraft as it roars close past them. Then they swivel their guns and fire after me; all have had their attention diverted by the main formation flying off high above them. So the luck is with me, an isolated aircraft. The whole neighbourhood is full of A.A. guns; the air is peppered with shrapnel. But it is a comfort to know that this weight of iron is not meant exclusively for me! I am now crossing the coast line. The narrow strip is very unpleasant. It would be impossible to gain height because I could not climb fast enough to reach a safe altitude. So I stay down. Past machine guns and flak. Panic-stricken Russians hurl themselves flat on the ground. Then again Scharnovski shouts:

"A *Rata* coming up behind us!"

I look round and see a Russian fighter about 300 yards astern.

"Let him have it, Scharnovski!"

Scharnovski does not utter a sound. Ivan is blazing away at a range of only a few inches. I take wild evasive action.

"Are you mad, Scharnovski? Fire! I'll have you put under arrest." I yell at him!

Scharnovski does not fire. Now he says deliberately:

"I am holding fire, sir, because I can see a German ME coming up behind and if I open up on the *Rata* I may damage the Messerschmitt." That closes the subject, as far as Scharnovski is concerned; but I am sweating with the suspense. The tracers are going wider on either side of me. I weave like mad.

"You can turn round now, sir. The ME has shot down the *Rata*." I bank round slightly and look back. It is as Scharnovski says; there she lies down below. Now a ME passes groggily.

"Scharnovski, it will be a pleasure to confirm our fighter's claim to have shot that one down." He does not reply. He is rather hurt that I was not content to trust his judgment before. I know him; he will sit there and sulk until we land. How many operational flights have we made together when he has not opened his lips the whole time we have been in the air.

After landing, all the crews are paraded in front of the squadron tent. We are told by Flt./Lt. Steen that the Wing Commander has already rung up to congratulate the 3rd squadron on its achievement. He had personally witnessed the very impressive explosion. Steen is instructed to report the name of the officer who was the first to dive and drop the successful two thousand pounder in order that he may be recommended for the Knight's Cross of the Iron Cross.

With a side-glance in my direction he says:

"Forgive me for telling the Kommodore that I am so proud of the whole squadron that I would prefer it if our success is attributed to the squadron as a whole."

In the tent he wrings my hand. "You no longer need a battleship for special mention in despatches," he says with a boyish laugh.

The Wing Commander rings up. "It is sinking day for the 3rd. You are to take off immediately for another attack on the *Kirov* berthed behind the *Marat*. Good hunting!" The photographs taken by our latest aircraft show that the *Marat* has split in two. This can be seen on the picture taken after the tremendous cloud of smoke from the explosion had begun to dissipate. The telephone rings again:

"I say, Steen, did you see my bomb? I didn't and neither did Pekrun."

"It fell into the sea, sir, a few minutes before the attack."

We youngsters in the tent are hard put to it to keep a straight face. A short crackling on the receiver and that is all. We are not the ones to blame our Wing Commander, who is old enough to be our father, if presumably out of nervousness he pressed the bomb release switch prematurely. He deserves all praise for flying with us himself on such a difficult mission. There is a big difference between the ages of fifty and twenty five. In dive bomber flying this is particularly true.

Out we go again on a further sortie to attack the *Kirov*. Steen had a slight accident taxying back after landing from the first sortie: one wheel ran into a large crater, his aircraft pancaked and damaged the propeller. The 7th flight provides us with a substitute aircraft, the flights are already on dispersal and we taxi off from our squadron base airfield. Flt./Lt. Steen again hits an obstacle and this aircraft is also unserviceable. There is no replacement available from the flights; they are of course already on dispersal. No one else on the staff is flying except myself. He therefore gets out of his aircraft and climbs onto my wingplane.

"I know you are going to be mad at me for taking your aircraft, but as I am in command I must fly with the squadron. I will take Scharnovski with me for this one sortie."

Vexed and disgruntled I walk over to where our aircraft are overhauled and devote myself for a time to my job as engineer officer.

The squadron returns at the end of an hour and a half. No. 1, the green-nosed staff aircraft – mine – is missing. I assume the skipper has made a forced landing somewhere within our lines.

As soon as my colleagues have all come in I ask what has happened to the skipper. No one will give me a straight answer until one of them says: "Steen dived onto the *Kirov*. He was caught by a direct hit at 5000 or 6000 feet. The flak smashed his rudder and his aircraft was out of control. I saw him try to steer straight at the cruiser by using the ailerons, but he missed her and nose-dived into the sea. The explosion of his two thousand pounder seriously damaged the *Kirov*."

The loss of our skipper and my faithful Cpl. Scharnovski is a heavy blow to the whole squadron and makes a tragic climax to our otherwise successful day. That fine lad Scharnovski gone! Steen gone! Both in their way were paragons and they can never be fully replaced. They are lucky to have died at a time when they could still hold the conviction that the end of all this misery would bring freedom to Germany and to Europe.

## LENINGRAD DURING THE BLOCKADE, SEPTEMBER 1941–JANUARY 1944

### *Alexander Werth, war correspondent*

*Leningrad was besieged by the Germans for 890 days, during the course of which 630,000 Leningraders died of starvation and hypothermia and 200,000 were killed by German shells.*

The famine had peculiar physical effects on people. Women were so run down that they stopped menstruating . . . so many people died that we had to bury most of them without coffins. People had their feelings blunted, and never seemed to weep at the burials. It was all done in complete silence without any display of emotion. When things began to improve the first signs were when women began to put rouge and lipstick on their pale skinny faces. Yes, we lived through hell right enough; but you should have been here the day the blockade was broken – people in the streets wept for joy and strangers fell round each other's necks. And now, as you see, life is almost normal. There is this shelling, of course, and people get killed, but life has become valuable again. The other day I saw an unpleasant street accident: a man was knocked down by a tramcar and had his leg cut off by the wheels. Why, our Leningrad crowd nearly lynched the driver! It seemed so wrong that anyone who had lived through the Leningrad siege should lose a leg through the fault of another Leningrader; whose fault it was exactly I do not know, but you see the point? . . .

At the end of January and in February, frost also joined the blockade and lent Hitler a hand. It was never less than thirty degrees of frost! Our classes continued on the "Round the Stove" principle. But there were no reserved seats, and if you wanted a seat near the stove or under the stove pipe, you had to come early. The place facing the stove door was reserved for the teacher. You sat down, and were suddenly seized by a wonderful feeling of well-being; the warmth penetrated through your skin, right into your bones; it made you all weak and languid and paralysed your thoughts; you just wanted to think of nothing, only to slumber and drink in the warmth. It was agony to stand up and go to the blackboard. One wanted to put off the evil moment. It was so cold and dark at the blackboard, and your hand, imprisoned in its heavy glove, goes all numb and rigid, and refuses to obey. The chalk keeps falling out of your hand, and the lines are all crooked and the figures deformed . . . By the time we reached the third lesson there was no more fuel left. The stove went cold, and horrid icy draughts started blowing down the pipe. It became terribly cold. It was then that Vasya Pughin, with a puckish look on his face, could be seen slinking out and bringing in a few logs from Anna Ivanovna's emergency reserve; and a few minutes later one could again hear the magic crackling of wood inside the stove . . . During the break nobody would jump up because no one had any desire to go into the icy corridors . . .

One of the greatest examples of how Leningrad fought for its life was when in the spring 300,000 or 400,000 people came out into the street with shovels – people who were scarcely standing on their feet, so weak and hungry were they – and proceeded to clean up the town. All winter the drains and sewers had been out of action; there was a great danger of epidemics spreading with the coming of the warm weather. And in a few days these 300,000 or 400,000 weak, hungry people – many of them were very old people who had never handled a shovel in their lives – had shovelled away and dumped into the river and the canals all those mountains of snow and filth which, had they remained there, would have poisoned Leningrad. And it was a joy to see the city streets a few days later all clean and tidy. It had a great moral effect . . .

It was our people and not the soldiers who built the fortifications of Leningrad. If you added up all the anti-tank trenches outside Leningrad, made by the hands of our civilians, they would add up to as much as the entire Moscow-Volga canal. During the three black months of 1941, 400,000 people were working in three shifts, morning, noon and night, digging and digging. I remember going down to Luga during the worst days, when the Germans were rapidly advancing on Luga. I remember there a young girl who was carrying away earth inside her apron. It made no sense. I asked her what she was doing that for. She burst into tears, and said she was trying to do at least that – it wasn't much, but her hands simply couldn't hold a shovel any longer. And, as I looked at her hands, I saw that they were a mass of black and bloody bruises. Somebody else had shovelled the earth on to her apron while she knelt down, holding the corners of the apron with the fingers of her bruised, bloodstained hands. For three months our civilians worked on these fortifications. They were allowed one day off in six weeks. They never took their days off. There was an eight-hour working day, but nobody took any notice of it. They were determined to stop the Germans. And they went on working under shellfire, under machine-gun fire and the bombs of the Stukas.

# THE ARRIVAL OF "GENERAL WINTER", 13 NOVEMBER 1941
## *Heinrich Haape*, Wehrmacht

*Like another previous invader of Russia, Napoleon Bonaparte, Hitler found that winter would undo his plans.*

On 13 November we awoke and shivered. An icy blast from the north-east knifed across the snowy countryside. The sky was cloudless and dark blue, but the sun seemed to have lost its strength and instead of becoming warmer towards noon as on previous days, the thermometer kept falling and by sundown had reached minus twelve degrees Centigrade.

The soldiers, who up to now had not regarded the light frosts too seriously, began to take notice. One man who had been walking outside for only a short distance without his woollen *Kopfschutzer* or "head-saver" came into the sick bay. Both ears were white and frozen stiff.

It was our first case of frost-bite.

We gently massaged the man's ears, taking care not to break the skin, and they thawed out. We powdered them and covered them with cotton-wool and made a suitable head-dressing. Perhaps we had managed to save the whole of the ears; we should have to wait and see.

This minor case of frost-bite was a serious warning. The icy winds from Siberia – the breath of death – were blowing across the steppes; winds from where all life froze, from the Arctic ice-cap itself. Things would be serious if we could not house ourselves in prepared positions and buildings, and I stopped to think of the armies marching on Moscow across open country at this very moment. All that those men had received so far were their woollen *Kopfschutzers*; the winter clothing had still not arrived. What was happening to the men's feet, for the ordinary army boot retained very little warmth?

Then, too, the thermometer showed only twelve degrees below zero. Temperatures would drop to minus twenty-four degrees – minus thirty-six degrees – minus forty-eight degrees – perhaps even lower. It was beyond comprehension – a temperature four times colder than a deep freezer. To attempt any movement without warm clothing in those conditions would be sheer suicide. Surely the older generals had been right when, after the battle of Vyasma and Bryansk, they had counselled: "Dig in for the winter." Some of them were men with experience of Russia during the 1914–1918 War. At the most they had said, continue the war through the winter only with a few thoroughly-equipped and well-provisioned divisions. Make the big push in the spring.

If only the battle for Moscow had started fourteen days earlier, the city would now have been in our hands. Or even if the rains had held off for fourteen days. If – if – if. If Hitler had started "Barbarossa" six weeks earlier as originally planned; if he had left Mussolini on his own in the Balkans and had attacked Russia in May; if we had continued our sweeping advance instead of stopping at the Schutsche Lake; if Hitler had sent us winter clothing. Yes, if, if, if – but now it was too late.

Those Arctic blasts that had taken us by surprise in our protected positions had scythed through our attacking troops. In a couple of days there were 100,000 casualties from frost-bite alone; 100,000 first-class, experienced soldiers fell out because the cold had surprised them.

A couple of days later our winter clothing arrived. There was just enough for each company to be issued with four heavy fur-lined greatcoats and four pairs of felt-lined boots. Four sets of winter clothing for each company! Sixteen greatcoats and sixteen pairs of winter boots to be shared among a battalion of 800 men! And the meagre issue coincided with a sudden drop in the temperature to minus twenty-two degrees.

Reports reached us that the issue of winter clothing to the troops actually advancing on Moscow had been on no more generous scale. More and more reports were being sent to Corps and Army Head-quarters recommending that the attack on Moscow by a summer-clad army be abandoned and that winter positions be prepared. Some of these reports were forwarded by Central Army Group to the Führer's Headquarters, but no reply or acknowledgement ever came. The order persisted: "Attack!" And our soldiers attacked.

*The attacks of the* Wehrmacht *brought them to within five miles of Moscow's city limits during the first week of December; a Red Army counter-attack on 6 December began to drive the Germans back, and they would never come so close to the prize again.*

# ONE MAN'S WAR: A *WEHRMACHT* SOLDIER'S DIARY OF THE RUSSIAN FRONT, 31 MARCH–26 SEPTEMBER 1942

## *Private First Class Wolfgang Knoblich, 7th Company, 2nd Battalion, 513th Infantry Regiment*

Dedicated to My Dear Parents 25/3/42
"Conquer the heritage of your fathers
So that you may have the right to possess it.'

I chose to prefix this epigraph to my diary because I realize that life at the front compels one to assess at their true value those good things in life which we failed to appreciate while they came to us easily.

### 31 March 1942
The front must be about forty miles away. The latest news from there contains little to comfort us . . . At such moments it dawns upon us what insignificant pawns we are in the big chess game that is now in progress. One order and we go thither, another order and we go thence. Yes sir! 'Ten-shun! About-turn; quick march! You cannot escape the eternal doom of fate . . .

### 1 April
Both in Kharkov and here in our quarters we, to our great surprise, have found books on mathematics, physics, English and ancient history which attest to high mental culture. These are real cultural values. Evidently they did pay attention to public education.

### 2 April
The village where we are stationed is called Neopkrytoye. Comrades tell me that only about two weeks ago the Russians broke through as far as this place. At that time we had to blow up the guns sited in the forward section of our defence line. Many ran as fast as their legs would carry them, thinking only of saving their skins.

### 3 April
To-day it's a year since I joined the army. Just as I did a year ago, so to-day I feel greatly distressed, as if a stone were pressing on my heart. This feeling of embarrassment and maladjustment always weighs me down when I find myself in a new situation. Good for him who can adjust himself to a new environment with ease and without friction. So far my only enjoyment has been to recollect the past.

## 4 April

A host of new impressions, not always pleasant. They are still alluring because of their novelty and therefore interesting, but hardly for long. There is a baneful melancholy about the landscape and the service too will no doubt become in time intolerably dull.

## 5 April

. . . All Germany hopes and believes that this spring this horrible blood-letting war will at last take a decisive turn. We pray for victory and peace.

## 16 April

The sergeant who takes me through every possible course of instruction and wants to teach me gunnery possesses more conceit than knowledge.

## 22 April

The soldiers who have been in France and in the Balkans are anxious to get home, are impatiently waiting to be relieved. But their faith in our strength and their belief in victory are unlimited. This belief has its root in the consciousness of their superiority over the Russians.

## 12 May

To-day I can honestly state that I have experienced the horrors of the front. Nepokrytoye is the last fortified point on the line of defence before Kharkov. If it falls the road to Kharkov, which leads through open spaces, will be clear. It was still night when we were informed by our outpost at V. that Russian tanks were approaching. At daybreak eight of them actually loomed in sight. By that time I and a senior sergeant were already at our post in V. From early morning our batteries kept pouring a massed shell-fire into the array of enemy tanks. Results were not wanting. One tank was soon kaput. It remained immobile at its initial position. But the Russians were not slow to act. The height where post V. was stationed soon witnessed such a downpour of shells that we did not know where to be take ourselves. Besides, Russian bombers and fighters launched an attack to add to the frightfulness of the scene, but the worst was still to come.

The intense artillery bombardment had damaged both our lines and so we were cut off from all communications. Our actions could not be co-ordinated. The German artillery was silenced.

Then the Russian tanks launched an attack. Our infantry retreated. We made another frantic attempt to restore communications while our infantry was already stampeding to the rear. Then our turn came.

We made a rather unseemly dash for safety, taking along only our field telephones and carbines. Bullets whizzed close by our ears. Now our gunners could sight the tanks and opened fire. It took the enemy some time to ascertain where our gun emplacements were. But now that he had spotted them their heavies shelled our guns almost without a miss and the air was filled with flying fragments of deadly iron and steel . . .

I helped to bring up ammunition, just to have something to do. After many hours of this sustained rifle and artillery effort our ammunition gave out. We had fired more than 800 rounds and were now compelled to take cover in our blockhouses. The Russians also ceased firing. Finally a truck drove up with new supplies of shells and the firing recommenced with new vigour on both sides.

The Russian marksmanship is devilishly accurate. Our first and third guns were knocked into a heap of scrap by two direct hits. But the crews were not touched. All the commissioned and non-commissioned officers assembled around the second gun, the only one that still kept up the fight. I felt ill at ease when I saw this assemblage of people and decided to change position. It was fortunate I did so, for immediately afterwards two shells crashed in among them. Eight were killed outright while six severely wounded lay on the ploughed-up ground. We bandaged their wounds as best we could and hastened our departure. Our troops were beginning to retreat. I helped to carry the wounded and therefore had to jettison even the little I had prepared to take with me. All my belongings can now find room in the bag I used to use for biscuits and things. But I did manage to salvage my shelter tent, carbine and cartridges out of the general wreckage.

As we left the village we were rallied and thrown into the fight as infantry. But the Russian artillery was up to our game and its shells rained thick and fast right in our midst. And this was capped by an air attack that also exacted a heavy toll.

Time passed by; it was already 4 p.m and not a single German plane in the air and not a single German tank acting in support of our land troops! We had been compelled, with heavy heart, to abandon all our artillery. In such distressing circumstances I think we did right to retreat fighting.

At last we have come to a hollow. It was a relief to find some shelter from the unceasing whistle of bullets. Behind a copse we have called a halt to get our breath. Thank the Lord, twilight was coming on or the Russians would have shot us like rabbits while crossing the wide plain that lies before Kharkov. There are exactly twelve men left in our battery.

**21 May**
I have been made a private first class. I can hardly believe it . . . I am
exceedingly glad that I am rid now of those humdrum duties in the
battery that simply stupefy your mind. I am sure that back there I
would never have obtained my chevron.

**27 May**
We have again been transferred to a so-called reserve command. This
command includes lads who are still quite young and require drilling.
So we act as N.C.O.'s We do nothing all day except watch our
"charges" clean the horses. Naturally, such a job is not to our taste.

**5 June**
Life is not a bed of roses here. All kinds of malicious and unjust
complaints are made against us. The corporals and sergeants are
particularly mean. The last few days have shown that we are fully able
to cope with our duties.

**17 June**
Events come one after another with incredible rapidity. At 11 p.m.
while I happened to be on duty, I was called to the telephone. The
conversation started with the fateful words: "Well, Knoblich, tomorrow we go to the front." I was put down as signaller. I shall
have the doubtful pleasure of laying cables. I'm called out in the
middle of the night, and all because I am unfortunate enough to be a
"greenhorn" and can be assigned to any nasty job. I am sick and tired
of being kicked about like a stepchild. After an hour's sleep we are to
march for several miles. I must admit the start was not very auspicious. The same day we again changed position. I am fed up with this
by now. On the 12th we forced the Donets.

Again and again we had to flop down in the muck. The trench
mortar and artillery fire was so intense that it gave one the creeps. In
the evening we returned to the battery. At dawn we advanced
eastwards. The fierce trench mortaring was too much for our infantry.
It was compelled to retreat to the height where our post was located.
Now Russian tanks appeared on the battle scene. We abandoned our
apparatus and hopped it. We could not get away too soon or too fast
from those iron-clad monsters.

. . . Here I am sitting in a filthy hole, all tired and broken up. I
have no change of socks, nor soap and towel for a wash. Only the
howling of mortars – that is now our constant companion. What a
dog's life we lead!

**20 June**

Very eventful days have come and gone. Life here hangs by a thread. the war may be terrible and we may be cursing it, but it has its good side, too. It constantly enriches the experience of each one of us. We get new impressions of life and see its seamy side, but much that is of value and will never be repeated would be lost to us if we did not have to re-live it day after day.

**21 June**

I dig too much into my soul and in general do much too much thinking. I often catch myself trying to apprehend things that are not subject to reason. Rationalist! Perhaps it is Russia that weighs so heavily on my soul. I crave mental pabulum like a starving dog a bone. How I long to engage in some scientific work! All I have at hand to tide me over such moods is some *Münchener Lesebogen*, my constant silent companions. They exhilarate and comfort me. In their pages I discover myself and at times find answers to my abstruse questions. They are my true friends day in day out, especially in hours of solitary introspection.

Both men and officers are in a sullen mood. They all feel disconsolate and genuine enthusiasm is actually non-existent. They are all consumed with one ardent desire: to get out of this holocaust, to be relieved, to go home, at least on furlough. The offensive spirit has long since gone from our ranks.

**24 June**

A night of horrors! The last few hours that we had to spend in this shabby little village unexpectedly proved frightful in the extreme. At 1 a.m. we were awakened by explosions of unusual violence. We jumped out of our beds and stretched out on the floor. This was the first news we had that Stalin's heavy guns had arrived here. In an instant we were out of the house and sheltered, after a fashion, in the nearest basement. It was raining hard. The muddy puddles made it difficult to pass. The village was soon on fire. Sinister flames lit up the houses, streets and soldiers.

**6 July**

Last week brought no good news. Our present mode of existence does not meet with my approval. We are back once more to barrack life. We had hardly returned from the front when they started to drill us again. That's the Prussian system for you!

**9 July**

To-day was enough to drive you crazy. They goose-stepped us worse than rookies in an absolutely unbearable heat. But influential circles maintain that in this merciless drill lies the secret of our victories.

. . . Perhaps I shall be promoted this time. I've earned it long ago. Although I frequently know more than any of those N.C.O.'s, they trust me, a private first class with a substantial and comprehensive education, less than they do them. Such are the difficulties that have to be overcome.

### 19 July

Our immediate superiors embitter our lives with their petty tyranny in the exercise of their self-imposed authority. For instance, we are forbidden to unbutton our collars on the march. What martinets they are! They always overshoot the mark. There is no end to the reviews we have to pass and the duties we are assigned. The old Prussian drill sergeant regime in its pristine purity! And here it is even more strenuous than in the barracks.

### 25 July

I have cognized this whole mechanism and come to hate it. If I could only manage to escape from these dullards!

### 30 July

Sometimes I yield altogether to despair. For there is not a single person here to whom I can unbosom myself or who would really understand me. The people with whom I come in contact here are all so empty-headed, superficial and dull-witted. I have no choice but must needs remain alone with my thoughts. This is very difficult but I have become accustomed to it and shall get along somehow. I try to gain spiritual strength and comfort by solitary prayer. . . . I often picture to myself my return home. Great God, if that dream should ever come true! When that day arrives we shall return entirely different people, with entirely different conceptions of life, with a new appreciation of its blessings.

It sometimes seems to me that in many respects I am becoming a materialist. How often I catch myself engrossed in thought, not about philosophy, but some dainty morsel and other creature comforts. That of course does not mean that I am no longer the idealist I used to be. True, on witnessing some unjust, arbitrary act, I am often ready to fling my ideals to the winds, but then I would lose my sole support in the quiet hours of my solitude. It is in ideals alone that I found that perfection of which there is such dearth in a world full of envy and strife, injustice and tyranny, the innocent victims of which we so often are.

**6 August**

The Russians are attacking furiously. We return their fire measure for measure, not ceasing day or night. During short intervals we dig in. I am weary unto death. If this torture would only end soon.

**12 August**

My strength has been overtaxed and it literally takes my last ounce of energy to grind out these few lines. This terrible war cannot end too soon for me. I am nauseated with it all and wish I could get clear of the whole outfit, including those nice boys a bit higher up, those ordinary sergeants and sergeant-majors who do their utmost to make life sweeter for us. They fairly weigh us down with special jobs (foraging and the like) that really are a nuisance. They are enough to drive one to despair. I suffer acutely from all this. The life we are compelled to lead is without a ray of sunshine.

We are within a few miles of the Don and are told that we shall winter here.

**31 August**

. . . All our talk concerns two subjects: leave and women, yes women, even here in Russia. You often hear such talk from comrades as: "I consider myself married only in Germany . . ." One can readily imagine how these fellows spend their leisure time.

**13 September**

At last I can record the glad tidings that I was transferred back from my signaller's job in the trenches to my regular service at post V. Light of heart, I left on the tenth to enjoy this change from night to day. Shade and silence – what a treat!

**26 September**

We have again been relieved by Italians. Those wonderful, dream-like days at Post V. are a thing of the past. The order to prepare for immediate departure came to us like a bolt out of the blue . . .

To-day we are stationed at a small town about 10 miles from Kaprin and about the same distance from Rossosh. No one knows what is to become of us, and we least of all. We can give free rein to our fancy.

I'm afraid we may be disillusioned in our new assignment! Everybody says that winter will find us fighting, though nobody is sure of it. On the other hand, everyone in the innermost recesses of his heart cherishes the dream of returning to Germany or at least to the occupied regions. Anywhere to get away from Russia.

# MR CHURCHILL GOES TO MOSCOW, 12 AUGUST 1942

## *Henry C. Cassidy, journalist*

*The British prime minister went to Moscow to inform Marshal Stalin that there would be no "Second Front" – that is, an attack from the west – on the Nazi empire in 1942 or 1943.*

I was sitting in my living room at 4:30 P.M., August 12, talking with Robert Magidoff, when a roar penetrated the thin roof. We looked into the pale blue sky, where a light breeze was chasing white clouds illuminated by a bright sun, and saw three great, four-motored, fan-tailed American B-24 bombers pass overhead and coast to a landing at the central airport. Above them, so high they could hardly be seen, dipped an escort of Soviet fighters. It was Churchill, arriving with his party.

His coming had been kept generally secret. The correspondents, however, had known of it for days. Clark Kerr had locked himself in his embassy, declining to see anyone. Travelers from Teheran reported hectic preparations among the British there for an important reception. Others said a Soviet guard of honor had been sent out to the Kuibyshev airport, only to be told to return another day. In Moscow, special guards were detailed to the airport. The National Hotel was roped off and the sidewalk in front of it carpeted. The wall of the foreign office guest-house was given a fresh coat of black paint and supplies were carried into its yard. All that, for us, added up to a visit by Churchill.

Some of the correspondents saw the Prime Minister riding away from the airport. Even if they had not recognized him, his cigar, a rarity in Moscow, was enough to identify him. Others telephoned the British embassy and asked whether they could see Churchill's secretary. A slow-witted clerk said, "Just a moment, please, I'll ask him," and then returned, chastened, to say, "I don't know anything about him." We handed telegrams in to the press department, saying Churchill had arrived, and received the same answer: "Nothing is known about it." So the battle was on, and we could not describe it. Churchill, officially, was not in Moscow.

At the airport the visitors were met by a delegation of Soviet officials, with Molotov at their head. The flags of the Soviet Union, Great Britain, and the United States snapped from the flagpoles. A military band played the three national anthems. A guard of honor, composed of men chosen specially for their height, not to be outdone by the Buckingham Palace guards, stood at attention.

Churchill inspected the guard, and then spoke into a microphone for the newsreels. "We are determined that we will continue hand in hand, whatever our suffering, whatever our toils," he said. "We will continue hand in hand, like comrades and brothers, until every vestige of the Nazi regime has been beaten into the ground, until the memory only of it remains as an example and a warning for future times."

Averell Harriman, who came with Churchill as President Roosevelt's personal representative, also spoke briefly: "The President of the United States charged me to accompany the British Prime Minister on his eventful journey to Moscow at this crucial moment of the war. The President of the United States stands back of everything that Mr. Churchill has come to do here, and America will be fighting with the Russians hand in hand at the front."

Churchill gave his famous "V" for victory sign and turned away to his automobile. Behind him there was excited speculation over two subjects. One was Harriman's reference to America fighting with the Russians at the front. The other was Churchill's V sign. Most Russians who saw it thought the two fingers meant there would be two fronts. The word for victory, in Russian, is *pobeda*. He should have given the P sign in Moscow.

Churchill talked with Stalin for three hours and forty minutes at the Kremlin the evening of August 12. He conferred with Molotov the next afternoon and again with Stalin the next evening. What was said behind the closed doors, those on the inside would not say, those on the outside could not pretend to know.

It was natural to assume, however, that the principal subjects were those the whole world was then discussing: the German surge across the Don, east toward Stalingrad, south toward the Caucasus; and Russian anxiety over the second front. It was easy, also, to see the way the talks were going, from such indications as a conversation between two Englishmen which took place in my presence. "It's really too bad they brought the old gentleman out here," said one who was no youth himself. "It's not going so well, is it?" said the other. "The old boy's in a foul temper."

On the third evening, there was a Kremlin dinner, the most animated ever held in this series of traditional endings to official visits. Nearly one hundred guests, members of the British and United States missions in Moscow and highest Soviet leaders, trooped into the Catherine Hall of the Great Palace at 9 P.M. for the spectacle.

Stalin sat in the center of the long main table with Churchill on his right and Harriman on his left. Beside each of the guests of honor sat an interterpreter. Across the table was Molotov, with Clark Kerr on his right and Admiral Standley on his left.

There was a sensation at the very start when Churchill entered, wearing blue overalls with a zipper front, open at the neck and with no tie. It was the first time he had appeared in Moscow in this costume. It may have been the same costume which was admired in Washington, but not in Moscow; it was no success, particularly at a Kremlin dinner which the Russians, so informal on some occasions but so formal on others, consider as a great state occasion. No one asked the Prime Minister for an explanation of his attire, and he offered none. One Russian guest, who could not contain his curiosity, however, leaned over and asked a British general confidentially whether that was the kind of suit worn by British parachutists during commando raids on France.

Mixed with the meal were countless toasts. The first was by Stalin, the usual salutation to his guests. Molotov proposed a toast to President Roosevelt, to which Churchill responded with a booming "To the President," which could be heard all over the hall. Admiral Standley offered a libation to the union of Great Britain, the United States, and Russia. General Wavell made a brief speech in fluent, precise Russian. As the party warmed up, Stalin appeared to be growing higher, Churchill lower, in spirits.

There was a difficult moment when Clark Kerr proposed a toast to Stalin. Everyone rose to drink – except Churchill. Squatting heavily in his chair, he muttered across to his envoy, something to this effect: "Haven't you been in the diplomatic service long enough to know an ambassador addresses his words to the foreign minister of the country to which he is accredited?" An interpreter, meanwhile, was translating Clark Kerr's words. The ambassador's usually ruddy face flushed an even deeper red. When the translation was finished, he turned quickly to Molotov and spoke a few more polite words. Those were translated, and everyone – including Churchill, who then rose – drank the toast.

Stalin, by now, was in peak form. He stood, with a smile, and said something like this:

"I should like to propose a toast that no one can answer. It is to intelligence officers. They cannot answer, because no one knows who they are, but their work is important."

He went on to say he had been reading up on this subject, and recalled an incident which occurred during what he called the "Gibraltar" campaign of the last war. He evidently meant the "Gallipoli" campaign, a sore spot for Churchill, who then was first lord of the admiralty when the Allies failed to take the Dardanelles. Stalin pointed out the campaign was virtually won, but because of flaws in their intelligence work, the British did not realize or follow up their advantage, and so failed.

That was the most awkward moment of the meal. Stalin's toast could be taken to mean all sorts of things – that Allied intelligence officers were now working, unknown, virtually as spies, in the Soviet Union; that, as they had in the last war, they were again making mistakes. It was a direct gibe at Churchill.

Captain Jack Duncan, the United States naval attaché, a swashbuckling sailor from Springfield, Missouri, who was never fazed by any little thing like a toast, saved the situation. He rose and said:

"I can answer that toast to intelligence officers, because I'm one of them. If we make mistakes, it is because we know only what you tell us – and that's not much."

Stalin roared with laughter, and called down the table, "If there's anything you want to know, ask me. I'll be your intelligence officer."

Stalin left his seat, walked to Duncan's and drank a personal toast to him. And when the dinner broke up about 1 A.M., Stalin and Duncan walked out of the room together, arm in arm.

## HOLOCAUST: SS EXECUTION OF JEWS IN THE UKRAINE, 5 OCTOBER 1942

### Hermann Graebe

*Nazi ideology required the extermination of Europe's Jewry. In the occupied countries of east Europe the Nazis initially began their slaughter of the Jews with mass shootings by special duty groups ("Einsatzgruppen") of SS; when this proved too unsanitary and slow, the Jews of the East, like those of Western Europe, were transported to the death camps of Auschwitz, Belsen, Maidanek, Sobibor and Treblinka. Graebe was an engineer with a German construction firm in the Ukraine.*

. . . My foreman and I went directly to the pits. I heard rifle shots in quick succession from behind one of the earth mounds. The people who had got off the trucks – men, women and children of all ages – had to undress upon the order of an S.S. man, who carried a riding or dog whip. They had to put down their clothes in fixed places, sorted according to shoes, top clothing and under-clothing. I saw a heap of shoes of about 800 to 1,000 pairs, great piles of under-linen and clothing.

Without screaming or weeping these people undressed, stood around in family groups, kissed each other, said farewells and waited for a sign from another S.S. man, who stood near the pit, also with a whip in his hand. During the fifteen minutes that I stood near the pit I heard no complaint or plea for mercy . . .

An old woman with snow-white hair was holding a one-year-old child in her arms and singing to it and tickling it. The child was cooing with delight. The parents were looking on with tears in their eyes. The father was holding the hand of a boy about 10 years old and speaking to him softly; the boy was fighting his tears. The father pointed to the sky, stroked his head and seemed to explain something to him.

At that moment the S.S. man at the pit shouted something to his comrade. The latter counted off about twenty persons and instructed them to go behind the earth mound . . . I well remember a girl, slim and with black hair, who, as she passed close to me, pointed to herself and said "twenty-three years old."

I walked around the mound and found myself confronted by a tremendous grave. People were closely wedged together and lying on top of each other so that only their heads were visible. Nearly all had blood running over their shoulders from their heads. Some of the people were still moving. Some were lifting their arms and turning their heads to show that they were still alive. The pit was already two-thirds full. I estimated that it contained about a thousand people. I looked for the man who did the shooting. He was an S.S. man, who sat at the edge of the narrow end of the pit, his feet dangling into the pit. He had a tommy gun on his knees and was smoking a cigarette.

The people, completely naked, went down some steps and clambered over the heads of the people lying there to the place to which the S.S. man directed them. They lay down in front of the dead or wounded people; some caressed those who were still alive and spoke to them in a low voice. Then I heard a series of shots. I looked into the pit and saw that the bodies were twitching or the heads lying already motionless on top of the bodies that lay beneath them. Blood was running down their necks.

The next batch was approaching already. They went down into the pit, lined themselves up against the previous victims and were shot.

# RUSSIAN PRISONERS, JULY 1941

## *Benno Zieser*, Wehrmacht

*Hitler gave orders that Russian prisoners of war were not to be treated as other prisoners of war. About 2,600,000 Russian soldiers died in captivity, mostly from starvation and disease.*

Behind twelve-foot-high barbed-wire fences with watchtowers and machine guns and searchlight emplacements at intervals were thousands upon thousands of Russians, housed in primitive barracks. Each individual barrack was surrounded by barbed wire. The setup resembled a bear pit, and this impression was strengthened by the murderous big dogs which the guards held on short leads. The whole place exuded the same revolting, nauseating stink we'd smelled before when we saw our first transport of prisoners.

One of the camp guards opened the door to one of the barracks and shouted something. The prisoners came pouring out, falling all over one another. A sharp word of command lined them up three deep in front of us. A German-speaking prisoner, the barrack leader appointed by the guards, strove with incredible brutality to get some order into their ranks. The camp guard counted off fifty men, and sent the others back inside. Some of them tried to smuggle their way into the working party, but the Russkies who'd already been picked for the job fought back their rivals, yelling for the barrack leader. And he let the culprits have it, lashing out with a whip right and left, hollering and cursing, without a trace of pity for his own people.

All this was taking too long for the guard, so he slipped the leash of his quivering hound. With one leap the dog was in the thick of it and the next thing we knew he had the barrack leader's arm fast between his teeth. The camp guard watched all this with utter indifference; it never occurred to him to call off his dog. Meanwhile the barrack leader was trying desperately to shake the animal off. He looked pleadingly toward the camp guard. But when one of the beaten-up Russians tried to run back to the barracks, the dog dropped the barrack leader's arm. It was after the other man like lightning and got a good grip on his buttocks. The new victim started bawling like a baby, but with a final frantic effort he managed to reach the barracks door, leaving patches of trouser seat and underpants between the jaws of the hound. I never saw a more befuddled animal in my life. The camp guard roared with laughter. We could hear his coarse guffaw even after we'd set out with our fifty living skeletons.

When we left that place of misery behind we drew a deep breath. Our prisoners swayed like drunken men. Many didn't even have overcoats. Their uniforms were in tatters hanging loosely over their bones. They carried with them all they possessed – an empty meat can with a bit of wire around it for a handle, a twisted iron spoon. Only a few had a small bundle on their backs, containing perhaps some extra rags to wrap around their feet or a battered water canteen which they dared not carry openly for fear of the envy it might arouse in the others.

The supply distribution center was a level patch of ground, fenced off and housing a few drafty sheds. It was divided into three sections: an ammo dump, a fuel store and a food store. Trucks were continually coming and going, and the prisoners' job was to load and unload them.

We guards were supposed to help as little as possible, but it wasn't long before we, too, were hard at work. There was a lot to be done; besides, while working we didn't feel the cold quite so much.

The Russkies were completely debilitated. They could hardly keep on their feet, let alone perform the physical effort required of them. A team of four could scarcely lift a crate, a job that was child's play to Franzl and me. But they certainly did their utmost. Every one of them was out to curry favors. They vied with one another, they egged each other on. Then they'd peer over to see if we had noticed their zeal. That way, they hoped to earn better treatment, and perhaps a hunk of bread.

We felt sorry for those emaciated creatures. Among them were mere kids, not fully grown, as well as bearded old men who could have been our grandfathers. Without exception, they all begged for a scrap of food or a cigarette. They whined and groveled before us to wheedle something out of us, they were like whipped dogs. And if pity and disgust became too much for us and we did give them something, they'd kneel and kiss our hands and babble words of thanks which must have come from their rich religious vocabulary – and then we just stood there: we simply couldn't believe it.

These were human beings in whom there was no longer a trace of anything human; these were men who really had turned into animals. We found it nauseating, utterly repulsive. Yet – did we have any right to judge, since we'd never been forced to barter the last vestige of our pride for a crust of bread?

We gave them whatever we could spare. There were strict orders never to give any food to prisoners, but to hell with that! What we did give them was like a drop in the bucket. Nearly every day men died from exhaustion. The survivors, indifferent to all this dying, would cart their dead back to camp, to bury them there. There must have been more prisoners under the ground than there were alive.

One day, behind an ammo case, we found three dead Russians, their faces purple. Frozen to death. For some reason, they'd failed to join up for the march back to camp and had been put down as escapees. Yes, there were men who escaped – but only very, very few. It was tempting enough to slip away while on outside work, but only rarely did a man take advantage of the chance. Given the circumstances, any one of us would have clutched at the slightest opportunity to get away, but the Russian is a different sort of man.

Stray dogs were legion, among them the most extraordinary mongrels; the only thing they had in common was that they were indescribably scrawny. That made no difference to the prisoners. They were hungry – so why not eat roast dog? They were forever trying to catch the wary beasts. They'd also beg us with gestures and *bow-wows* and *bang-bangs* to kill a dog for them. There it was – shoot it! And we almost invariably did. It provided some sport for us, and also gave a modicum of pleasure to those human skeletons. Besides, those wild dogs were a regular plague.

When we brought one down, there followed a spectacle that could make a man puke. Yelling like mad, the Russkies would fall on the animal and tear it to pieces with their bare hands even before it was dead. The intestines they'd stuff in their pockets – a sort of iron ration. Then they'd light a fire, skewer bits of dog's meat on sticks and roast it. There were always fights over the bigger hunks. The burned flesh stank frightfully; there was almost no fat in it.

But they didn't have roast dog every day. Behind the barracks there was a big midden, a regular mountain of stinking waste, and if we didn't watch out they'd poke about in it and eat such things as decaying onions, the mere sight of which was enough to turn one's stomach.

One day, during the loading of provisions, a couple of bottles of vodka were broken and the liquor spilled out on the floor of the truck. The Russians clambered in and licked it up like cats. On the march back to camp three of them collapsed dead drunk.

## THE BATTLE FOR SEVASTAPOL, 7 JUNE–4 JULY 1942

### *General von Manstein, GOC 11th Army Ostheer*

*The major German offensive of 1942 was directed towards the south-east, the objective being the Don Basin and above all the Caucasian oilfields. To protect the right flank of the invasion, the Crimea was to be occupied, while the left flank would be secured by an advance on Stalingrad. The offensive failed, partly because, as at Sevastapol in the Crimea, Russian resistance was greater than expected.*

On the morning of 7 June, as dawn turned the eastern sky to gold and swept the shadows from the valleys, our artillery opened up in its full fury by way of a prelude to the infantry assault. Simultaneously the squadrons of the Luftwaffe hurtled down on to their allotted targets. The scene before us was indescribable, since it was unique in modern warfare for the leader of an army to command a view of his entire battlefield. To the north-west the eye could range from the woodlands that hid the fierce battles of LIV Corps' left wing from view right over to the heights south of the Belbek valley, for which we were to fight so bitterly. Looking due west, one could see the heights of Gaytany, and behind them, in the far distance, the shimmer of Severnaya Bay where it joined the Black Sea. Even the spurs of the Khersones peninsula, on which we were to find vestiges of Hellenic culture, were visible in clear weather. To the south-west there towered the menacing heights of

Zapun and the rugged cliffs of the coastal range. At night, within the wide circumference of the fortress, one saw the flashes of enemy gunfire, and by day the clouds of rock and dust cast up by the bursts of our heavy shells and the bombs dropped by German aircraft. It was indeed a fantastic setting for such a gigantic spectacle!

. . . The second phase of the offensive, lasting up to 17 June, was marked on both fronts by a bitter struggle for every foot of ground, every pill-box and every trench. Time and again the Russians tried to win back what they had lost by launching violent counter-attacks. In their big strong-points, and in the smaller pill-boxes too, they often fought till the last man and the last round. While the main burden of these battles was borne by the infantry and engineers, the advanced observation posts of our artillery still deserve special mention, since it was chiefly they who had to direct the fire which made it possible to take individual strong-points and pill-boxes. They, together with the assault guns, were the infantry's best helpmates.

On 13 June the valiant 16th Infantry Regiment of 22 Division, led by Colonel von Choltitz, succeeded in taking Fort Stalin, before which its attack had come to a standstill the previous winter. The spirit of our infantry was typified by one wounded man of this regiment who, pointing to his smashed arm and bandaged head, was heard to cry: "I can take this lot now we've got the Stalin!"

. . . 22 Division gained control along its whole front of the cliffs overlooking Severnaya Bay. There was extremely hard fighting for the railway tunnel on the boundary between 22 and 50 Divisions, out of which the enemy launched a strong counter-attack with a brigade that had recently arrived by cruiser. The tunnel was finally captured by shelling its entrance. Not only hundreds of troops came out but an even greater number of civilians, including women and children. Particular difficulty was experienced in winkling the enemy out of his last hideouts on the northern shore of the bay, where deep galleries for storing supplies and ammunition had been driven into the sheer wall of rock. These had been equipped for defence by the addition of steel doors. Since the occupants, under pressure from their commissars, showed no sign of surrendering, we had to try to blow the doors open. As our engineers approached the first of them, there was an explosion inside the casemate and a large slab of cliff came tumbling down, burying not only the enemy within but also our own squad of engineers. The commissar in command had blown the casemate and its occupants sky-high. In the end a second lieutenant from an assault battery, who had brought up his gun along the coastal road regardless of enemy shelling from the southern shore, managed to force the other casemates to open up after he had fired on their embrasures at point-blank range. Crowds of completely worn-out soldiers and civilians emerged, their commissars having committed suicide . . .

After our experience of Soviet methods to date we were bound to assume that the enemy would make a last stand behind Sevastopol's perimeter defences and finally in the city itself. An order from Stalin had been repeatedly wirelessed to the defenders to hold out to the last man and the last round, and we knew that every member of the civil population capable of bearing arms had been mustered.

And so 1 July began with a massed bombardment of the perimeter fortifications and the enemy's strong-points in the interior of the city. Before long our reconnaissance aircraft reported that no further serious resistance need be anticipated. The shelling was stopped and the divisions moved in. It seemed probable that the enemy had pulled the bulk of his forces out to the west the previous night.

But the struggle was still not over. Although the Soviet Coast Army had given up the city, it had only done so in order to offer further resistance from behind the defences which sealed off the Khersones peninsula – either in pursuance of Stalin's backs-to-the-wall order or else in the hope of still getting part of the army evacuated by Red Fleet vessels at night from the deep inlets west of Sevastopol. As it turned out, only very few of the top commanders and commissars were fetched away by motor-torpedo boat, one of them being the army commander, General Petrov. When his successor tried to escape in the same way he was intercepted by our Italian E-boat.

Thus the final battles on the Khersones peninsula lasted up till 4 July. While 72 Division captured the armour-plated fort of "Maxim Gorki II", which was defended by several thousand men, the other divisions gradually pushed the enemy back towards the extreme tip of the peninsula. The Russians made repeated attempts to break through to the east by night, presumably in the hope of joining up with the partisans in the Yaila Mountains. Whole masses of them rushed at our lines, their arms linked to prevent anyone from hanging back. At their head, urging them on, there were often women and girls of the Communist Youth, themselves bearing arms. Inevitably the losses which sallies of this kind entailed were extraordinarily high.

# STALINGRAD: "THE RAT WAR", OCTOBER 1942

## *Anonymous Officer, 24th Panzer Division*

*The battle for Stalingrad opened on 15 September 1942 and was fought street by street, house by house, in what the Germans called the* Rattenkrieg *("rat war")*

We have fought for fifteen days for a single house with mortars, grenades, machine-guns and bayonets. Already by the third day fifty-four German corpses are strewn in the cellars, on the landings, and the staircases. The front is a corridor between burnt-out rooms; it is the thin ceiling between two floors. Help comes from neighbouring houses by fire-escapes and chimneys. There is a ceaseless struggle from noon to night. From storey to storey, faces black with sweat, we bombed each other with grenades in the middle of explosions, clouds of dust and smoke. . . . Ask any soldier what hand-to-hand struggle means in such a fight. And imagine Stalingrad: eighty days and eighty nights of hand-to-hand struggle. . . . Stalingrad is no longer a town. By day it is an enormous cloud of burning, blinding smoke; it is a vast furnace lit by the reflection of the flames. And when night arrives, one of those scorching, howling, bleeding nights, the dogs plunge into the Volga and swim desperately to gain the other bank. The nights of Stalingrad are a terror for them. Animals flee this hell; the hardest storms cannot bear it for long; only men endure.

## STALINGRAD: A GERMAN SOLDIER'S VIEW, DECEMBER 1942

### *Benno Zieser*, Wehrmacht

*On 19 November the Russians launched a counter-attack which encircled the 270,000 German besiegers of Stalingrad. Hitler refused their commanding officer, Colonel-General von Paulus, permission to fight his way out. The* Luftwaffe *became increasingly unable to fly in supplies and by the year's end malnutrition, hypothermia and Red Army bullets were claiming thousands of* Wehrmacht *lives.*

One night the big freeze-up began and our second winter in that accursed country faced us grimly. A supply truck brought heavy overcoats, gloves and caps with earmuffs. But we froze miserably in our holes. Even the detonations of shells had a new, hard resonance, and the clods of earth they threw up were like slabs of granite.

It was an unwritten promise of the army that every man should get home after service abroad for more than a year, but we all knew they didn't dare send us back. Nevertheless, every day had a new crop of rumors – we were to be sent to France, to Greece, to Africa. But first, of course, a little time at home.

We in the ranks knew how spurious these rumours were – but how stubbornly we tried to believe them! Our one overmastering desire drove us to credulity – the desire to get somehow to the end of the dragged-out death we lived in.

There was always one way out, a practical way. This was for heaven in its mercy to send us a wound not severe enough to kill us but serious enough to take us home. A flesh wound – no good. They'd take care of that in a field hospital. The best thing was a bad fracture, if possible not one that made you a total cripple, nor too painful, but certainly one that meant a long period of recuperation. You needed luck, though – all the luck in the world – and there wasn't much to spread around.

Thinking such thoughts, we faced the Russkies' monster barrage that winter and the big-scale attack on our wedge between the Don and the Volga. They broke through.

A day came when we realized it was quite a while since a single truck had dared travel from our front to a rear base. Russian units had occupied every approach. At first they attacked vehicles only at night, then continuously both day and night. For a time our supply columns were linked up and moved in convoy, flanked by armor and motorcycle units. But even this the Russians became too strong for.

Reckless counterattacks, with huge losses, got nowhere. Slowly but surely the Soviet wedges in the sides of our wedge grew broader, and the German divisions were thrown back, on the one side far beyond the Don, the other eastward, back to that great mass of ruins, the city of Stalingrad.

In short, we were surrounded. Stalingrad became a great cauldron in which we were destined to simmer.

Now the tragedy began in earnest. A whole army was ground down to pulp. A battle with no prospect of success for the Germans went down a drain clogged with blood. The end approached fast – but it wasn't the one we'd all counted on less than two years before.

At first it seemed incredible that Germans could let themselves be caught like mice in such a giant trap. But in the Soviet Union the new word "cauldron battle" – *Kesselschlacht* – was soon a powerful slogan.

Among us the idea was presented – and momentarily prevailed – that it wasn't all a disaster, but another masterly stroke of the High Command. New tanks were mentioned, an offensive from the north, a pulverizing secret weapon.

We believed for awhile, but none of it was true, and slowly we began to realize the horror of the word a soldier fears most: *surrounded*.

The truth was borne in on us as remnants of division after division fell back defeated from all sides, away from the on-pressing enemy, crowding into the heart of Stalingrad's cauldron. Gradually the columns of converging transport blocked all roads. Guns were blown up, and weapons of all kinds, tanks included, that had stopped for want of fuel. Loaded trucks, bogged in the snow, burned up. Huge dumps of clothing and food were burned to escape enemy hands. Installations erected at enormous effort were destroyed.

Cut off, the men in field gray slouched on, filthy and louse-ridden, their weary shoulders sagging, from one untenable defense position to another. The icy winds of those great white wastes burned their skin to crumpled leather, lashed tears from sunken eyes that over-fatigue had almost sealed, penetrated through all uniforms and added rags to the very bone marrow. For those who could do no more there was always a kindly shroud of snow.

Less than 2,000 miles to the west was another world. There, people slept in soft warm beds; there, at midday, they sat down to eat as much as they liked from clean white table linen. Children laughed and even men were allowed to be happy.

But here, bereft of initiative, we let ourselves be driven, crawling ever onward or backward, obeying senseless orders to take up new positions and offer a resistance devoid of military meaning. It was a matter of indifference when the night sorties of the *Luftwaffe* to bring us in supplies became rarer, when the only warm food became a thin broth with infrequent cubes of horsemeat, or when we had to do with a couple of slices of bread all day.

We still couldn't help hearing the sound of enemy mortars, by old habit counting seconds before the bursts. We felt the earth shudder under HEs and watched the countless rockets of the Stalin organs.

Despite everything, it still seemed astonishing that we weren't the only ones left alive – that there were still red and violet flares splaying the heavens, warnings of infantry attack, warnings of tanks and urgent cries for help – from the other side. And then we fired into the yelling mass of Bolsheviks, fired as automatically as robots until at last their mammoth tanks, bearing down on us, forced yet another withdrawal back into the cauldron – which every day grew smaller and hotter.

My unit had shrunk pitiably. One man after another had dropped out, in his own blood or frozen in the unrelenting ocean of whiteness.

Franzl was a broken man, all hope abandoned that he might see his home again. But sometimes, when it was a little quiet and we crouched in our trench waiting for what would come next, he took the photographs from his wallet, the one of the unknown soldier and others of himself, his family and friends. Then I'd pull out a dog-eared picture of my home town and we'd get to talking of such things. These were the only times he seemed to waken.

But suddenly resumption of the barrage would jerk us back into reality and we'd realize with sharpened poignance the treasures that were lost.

Next to me in the trench, leaning on the rampart, he suddenly collapsed, knees giving way and his whole body settling like a spent balloon. "Franzl!" I shouted, unbelieving.

Even when, with horror, I saw one eye had been shot out, I couldn't believe the awful truth.

Then a scream shrilled inside my head – louder than any ·the military scientists had ever invented. The sky and snowy waste and everything else that had ruined our lives made an insane dance around me. And I grabbed my machine gun, scrambled out of the trench and ran toward whoever, whatever had fired that shot. In the morning mist I saw dark outlines of men, and the steel thing bucking madly at my hip mowed them down. I ran farther and farther, firing and firing, till like the blow of a cudgel something struck my arm.

*Zieser was among the lucky few of the German Sixth Army at Stalingrad; he was evacuated, wounded.*

## STALINGRAD: THE RUSSIAN ULTIMATUM, 8 JANUARY 1943

To the Commander-in-Chief of the German 6 Army, Colonel-General Paulus, or his representative, and to all the officers and men of the German units now besieged in Stalingrad.

6 German Army, formations of 4 Panzer Army, and those units sent to reinforce them have been completely encircled since 23 November 1942.

The soldiers of the Red Army have sealed this German Army Group within an unbreakable ring. All hopes of the rescue of your troops by a German offensive from the south or south-west have proved vain. The German units hastening to your assistance were defeated by the Red Army, and the remnants of that force are now withdrawing to Rostov.

The German air transport fleet, which brought you a starvation ration of food, munitions and fuel, has been compelled by the Red Army's successful and rapid advance repeatedly to withdraw to airfields more distant from the encircled troops.

. . . . The situation of your troops is desperate. They are suffering from hunger, sickness and cold. The cruel Russian winter has scarcely yet begun. Hard frosts, cold winds and blizzards still lie ahead. Your soldiers are unprovided with winter clothing and are living in appalling sanitary conditions.

You, as Commander-in-Chief, and all the officers of the encircled forces know well that there is for you no real possibility of breaking out. Your situation is hopeless, and any further resistance senseless.

In view of the desperate situation in which you are placed, and in order to save unnecessary bloodshed, we propose that you accept the following terms of surrender:

1. All the encircled German troops, headed by yourself and your staff, shall cease to resist.

2. You will hand over to such persons as shall be authorized by us, all members of your armed forces, all war materials and all army equipment in an undamaged condition.

3. We guarantee the safety of all officers and men who cease to resist, and their return at the end of the war to Germany or to any other country to which these prisoners of war may wish to go.

4. All personnel of units which surrender may retain their military uniforms, badges of rank, decorations, personal belongings and valuables and, in the case of high-ranking officers, their swords.

5. All officers, non-commissioned officers and men who surrender will immediately receive normal rations.

6. All those who are wounded, sick or frost-bitten will be given medical treatment.

Your reply is to be given in writing by ten o'clock, Moscow time, 9 January 1943. It must be delivered by your personal representative, who is to travel in a car bearing a white flag along the road that leads to the Konny siding at Kotlu-banj station. Your representative will be met by a fully-authorized Russian officer in District B, five hundred metres south-east of siding 564 at 10.00 hours on 9 January 1943.

Should you refuse our offer that you lay down your arms, we hereby give you notice that the forces of the Red Army and the Red Air Force will be compelled to proceed with the destruction of the encircled German troops. The responsibility for this will lie with you.

Representing Headquarters Red Army Supreme Command,
Colonel-General of the Artillery Voronov
The Commander-in-Chief of the Forces of the Don front,
Lieutenant-General Rokossovsky

*On Hitler's orders, von Paulus rejected the demand for surrender.*

# STALINGRAD: LAST LETTERS HOME, JANUARY 1943

## *Anonymous German soldiers*

*These letters are from the last post from Stalingrad, flown out shortly before the final German surrender. They never reached their destinations, being impounded – on Hitler's order – along with several hundred others and analyzed as to what they betrayed about, the state of Army morale. According to the subsequent* Wehrmacht *report, 2.1 per cent of the letters approved of the conduct of the war, 3.4 per cent were vengefully opposed to the war, 57.1 per cent were sceptical and negative, and 4.4 per cent were doubtful. Some 33.0 per cent were indifferent.*

. . . Once again I have held your picture in my hand. As I gaze at it my mind was filled with the memory of what we shared together on that glorious summer evening in the last year of peace, as we approached our house through the valley of flowers. The first time we found each other it was only the voice of our hearts that spoke; later came the voice of love and happiness. We talked of ourselves and the future that stretched out before us like a gaily coloured carpet.

That carpet is no more. The summer evening is no more; nor is the valley of flowers. And we are no longer together. Instead of the gaily coloured carpet there is an endless field of whiteness; there is no longer any summer, only winter, and there is no longer any future – not for me, at all events, and thus not for you either. All this time I have had a strange sensation which I could not explain, but today I know that it was fear for you. Over those many thousands of miles I was conscious that you felt the same about me. When you get this letter, listen very hard as you read it; perhaps you will hear my voice. We are told that we are fighting this battle for Germany, but only very few of us here believe that our senseless sacrifice can be of any avail to the homeland.

. . . So now you know that I am not coming back. Break it gently to Mother and Father. It has given me a terrible shock and the worst possible doubts about everything. Once I was strong and believed; now I am small and unbelieving. Much of what is going on here I shall never know about; but even the little bit I am in on is too much to stomach. Nobody can tell me that my comrades' died with words like "Germany" or "Heil Hitler!" on their lips. It cannot be denied that men are dying; but the last word a man speaks goes out to his mother or the person he loves most, or else it is merely a cry for help. I have already seen hundreds fall and die, and many, like myself, were in the Hitler Youth. But all those who could still do so shouted for help or called out the name of someone who could not really do anything for them.

The Führer has solemnly promised to get us out of here. This has been read out to us, and we all firmly believed it. I still believe it today, because I simply must believe in something. If it isn't true, what is there left for me to believe in? I would have no more use for the spring and the summer or any of the things that make life happy. Let me go on believing, dear Grete; all my life – or eight years of it, at least – I have believed in the Führer and taken him at his word. It's terrible the way people out here are

doubting, and so humiliating to hear things one cannot contra-
dict because the facts support them.

If what we were promised is not true, then Germany will be
lost, for no other promises can be kept after that. Oh, these
doubts, these terrible doubts. If only they were already dis-
pelled!

. . . I have now written you twenty-six letters from this accursed
city, and you have sent me seventeen replies. Now I shall write
just once again, and then no more. There, I have said it at last. I
have long wondered how to word this fateful sentence in such a
way as to tell you everything without its hurting too much.

I am bidding you farewell because the die has been cast since
this morning. I shall entirely disregard the military side of things
in this letter; that is purely a concern of the Russians. The only
question now is how long we shall hold out: it may be a few days
or a few hours. You and I have our life together to look back
upon. We have respected and loved one another and waited two
years. In a way it's a good thing this interval has elapsed, for
though it has intensified our desire to be together again it has
also greatly helped to estrange us. The passage of time is also
bound to heal the wounds caused by my not returning.

In January you will be twenty-eight, which is still very young
for such a pretty woman. I am glad I have been able to pay you
this compliment so often. You will miss me a lot, but that is no
reason why you should shut yourself off from other human
beings. Allow a few months to pass, but no more than that.
Gertrud and Claus need a father. Remember that you have to
live for the children, and don't make too much song and dance
about their father. Children forget quickly, particularly at that
age. Take a good look at the man of your choice and pay special
heed to his eyes and handshake, just as you did in our own case,
and you will not be disappointed. Most of all, bring the children
up to be upright men and women who can hold their heads high
and look everyone straight in the face. I am writing these lines
with a heavy heart – not that you would believe me if I said I
found it easy – but don't worry, I am not afraid of what is to
come. Always tell yourself – and the children, too, when they are
older – that their father was never a coward and that they must
never be cowards either.

. . . I was going to write you a long letter, but my thoughts keep
disintegrating like those houses under gunfire. I have still ten

hours left before this letter must be handed in. Ten hours are a long time when you are waiting; but they are short when you are in love. I am not at all nervous. In fact it has taken the East to make a really healthy man of me. I have long since stopped catching colds and chills; that's the one good thing the war has done. It has bestowed one other thing on me, though – the realization that I love you.

It's strange that one does not start to value things until one is about to lose them. There is a bridge from my heart to yours, spanning all the vastness of distance. Across that bridge I have been used to writing to you about our daily round and the world we live in out here. I wanted to tell you the truth when I came home, and then we would never have spoken of war again. Now you will learn the truth, the last truth, earlier than I intended. And now I can write no more.

There will always be bridges as long as there are shores; all we need is the courage to tread them. One of them now leads to you, the other into eternity – which for me is ultimately the same thing.

Tomorrow morning I shall set foot on the last bridge. That's a literary way of describing death, but you know I always liked to write things differently because of the pleasure words and their sounds gave me. Lend me your hand, so that the way is not too hard.

. . . What a calamity it is that the war had to come! All those beautiful villages laid waste and none of the fields tilled. And the most dreadful thing of all is how many people have died. Now they all lie buried in an enemy land. What a calamity, indeed! Be glad, all the same, that the war is being fought in a distant country and not in our beloved German homeland. That's a place it must never reach, or else the misery will be even worse. You must be really grateful for that and go down on your knees to thank your God. "On the banks of the Volga we stand on guard . . ." For all of you and for our homeland. If we were not here, the Russians would break through and wreck everything. They are very destructive and there are millions of them. They don't seem to care about the cold, but we feel it terribly.

I am lying in a hole in the snow and can only creep away to a cellar for a few hours at nightfall. You have no idea how much good that does me. We are at hand, so you have no need to be afraid. But our numbers get less and less, and if it goes on like this there will soon be no more of us. Germany has plenty of soldiers, though, and they are all fighting for the homeland. All of us want peace to come soon. The main thing is that we win. All keep your fingers crossed!

. . . I am finding this letter hard enough to write, but that is nothing like as hard as you are going to take it! The news it bears is not good news, I am afraid. Nor has it been improved by the ten days I waited. Our situation is now so bad that there is talk of our soon being entirely cut off from the outer world. A short while back we were assured that this post would go off quite safely, and if only I knew there would still be another opportunity to write I should wait a little longer. But that is just what I don't know, and for better or worse I must get this off my chest.

The war is over for me. I am in a field hospital in Gumrak waiting to be evacuated by air. Much as I long to get away, the deadline keeps being put off. My home-coming will be a great joy to us both, but the state in which I come will give you no cause for joy. It makes me quite desperate to think of lying before you as a cripple. But you must know sooner or later that both my legs have been shot off. I am going to be quite honest with you. My right leg is completely smashed and amputated below the knee; the left one has been taken off at the thigh. The medical officer thinks that with artificial limbs I should be able to run around like any normal person. The M.O. is a good man and means well. I hope he turns out to be right. Now you know it in advance. Dear Elise, if only I knew what you are thinking. I think of nothing else and have all day long to do it. And you are very much in my thoughts. Time and again I have wished I was dead, but that is a grave sin and does not bear mentioning.

. . . If there is a God, you told me in your last letter, He will bring me back to you safe and soon. And, you went on, God will always give His protection to a man like myself – a man who loves flowers and animals, has never done wrong to anybody, and is devoted to his wife and child.

I thank you for those words: I always carry the letter next to my heart. But, my dearest, if one weighs your words, and if you make God's existence dependent on them, you are faced with a terribly grave decision. I am a religious man, and you were always a believer. Now all that will have to change if we both draw the logical conclusions from our attitudes to date, for something has intervened which destroys everything we believed in. I am looking for the right words in which to say it. Or have you already guessed what I mean? There seemed to me to be such an odd tone about your last letter of 8th December. It's now the middle of January.

For a long time to come, perhaps for ever, this is to be my last letter. A comrade who has to go to the airfield is taking it along with him, as the last machine to leave the pocket is taking off tomorrow morning. The situation has become quite untenable. The Russians are only two miles from the last spot from which aircraft can operate, and when that's gone not even a mouse will get out, to say nothing of me. Admittedly several hundred thousand others won't escape either, but it's precious little consolation to share one's own destruction with other men . . .

## STALINGRAD: THE SUFFERING OF THE GERMAN TROOPS, LATE JANUARY 1943

### Joachim Wieder, Intelligence Officer, VIII Corps, German Sixth Army

The air lift had long ceased to function properly. An organised distribution of the supplies flown in was no longer possible. Since further landings had become impossible, in the end only canisters of food could be dropped at night on zones marked by flags and illuminated by spot-lights. But the approach was extremely difficult. After a long and dangerous flight of more than 300 kilometers, the aircraft had to daringly break through the ring of Russian anti-aircraft fire. In the choice of their drop zones they were dependent on the weather and the dispositions of the enemy. Seen overall, the help brought in so bravely by our tireless, courageous supply pilots was hardly noticeable any more. In addition, the canisters were increasingly being taken in on the spot by individual units. In the general dissolution and catastrophe it was every man for himself.

On all sides the Russians had pressed forward to the edge of the Stalingrad suburbs. The iron ring of destruction tightened ever closer around the place where the horrible fate of the doomed army was drawing to a close. The stage set of its downfall was eerie and ghostly. It was the gigantic pile of ruins and debris of Stalingrad that stretched for more than twenty kilometres along the high right bank of the Volga. A desolate city that had bled and died from a thousand wounds. For half a year destruction and death had celebrated orgies here and hardly left anything save the torn stumps of houses, naked rows of walls, chimneys sticking up from vast piles of rubble, gutted factories, formless hunks of concrete, torn up asphalt, twisted tram tracks lying on wrecked cars, piled up iron scrap, splintered tree trunks in the former parks with the remains of Soviet plaster statues, traces of fire and decay.

Under this uncanny waste of the skeletons of buildings stretched the subterranean ghostly expanse of cellar ruins, bunkers, fox-holes and communications trenches. These were places where life had crept away to hide, darkly overshadowed by ever present death. These were the places of terrible suffering and dying of many thousands of unhappy, abandoned, helpless human beings. Every hole, every bunker, every cellar, every space offering shelter was filled to overflowing.

Over the entire ruins of Stalingrad fell an almost unceasing barrage of artillery and mortar fire. This, together with the repeated air attacks, continued to cause new casualties among the human masses of the dying army which had flooded together in the city centre and were experiencing hell on earth during the last days of January.

The army of sick and wounded rapidly assumed horrifying dimensions. After the Russians had advanced to the region of Gumark and the general flight towards Stalingrad had reached its height, Army had rescinded its former order to the contrary and directed that the wounded were to be left behind, but without doctors or medical orderlies – which was a terrible cruelty. The collection points for wounded, the dressing-stations and hospitals in the city, had long been overcrowded anyway. Now they could no longer contain the masses of men needing help. Well-nigh more than half of the survivors, in other words, about 50,000 men, were sick or wounded. Thousands of them received no treatment or care at all, because there were no dressings, medicine, morphine – or room. Many men doomed to die vainly begged for medicine to kill their pain or end their suffering. The doctors, orderlies and grave-diggers could no longer cope with the tide of misery flooding over their heads.

And so they lay about in their thousands, crammed together in the cellars of the railway station, in those around the Square of the Fallen, in the corn silo, in the cellar of the theatre, in the former city Kommandantura, and in many other cellars, caves and holes in the ruins of Stalingrad, moaning, whimpering, freezing, wracked with fever, praying, but mostly apathetic and resigned to their suffering. The emaciated bodies were no longer able to resist even minor sicknesses, let alone spotted fever, dysentery, jaundice or other serious illnesses for which strain, hunger and frost had worked so tragically to prepare the ground. The many dead could no longer be buried in the stonily frozen ground. The bodies were simply covered with snow or stacked in some corner. They were also no longer registered and no one was concerned about collecting their dog-tags any longer.

Innumerable helplessly suffering and immobilised wounded found a horrible end in the cellars and ruins that caught fire or collapsed under the rain of shells and bombs. The multi-storey building of the Stalingrad Centre *Kommandantura*, which had become a hospital crammed to overflowing, went up in flames caused by artillery fire. After scenes of indescribable panic and despair, a sea of flames soon consumed the whole heap of stacked-up misery.

More and more, order and discipline broke down. Here and there in the cellars, the still able-bodied and combat-worthy hid among the sick and wounded. Cases of uncomradely conduct, theft of provisions, refusal to obey orders, and open mutiny mounted. Wandering about through the labyrinth of the ruins roamed soldiers who had left their posts without permission, stragglers from the various divisions, looters and foragers who, acting on their own behalf, searched for food or hid out of fear of being sent back to the lines.

These men knew that the canisters of food were not only being dropped on the marked zones. In other spots in the ruined city, in the rubble of buildings and dark courtyards, on the paths leading through the ruins and in the trenches, one could sometimes find something worth taking. Occasionally, instead of shells, whole packages of smoked sausage, hard-tack wrapped in cellophane and Schoka-Kola packs that had simply been thrown out of the aircraft rained down. The elementary drive of self-preservation no longer allowed the question of right or wrong to be raised. And in the same way that the differences between front line and rear echelon were being erased, so also were the differences in rank and position.

In the final days, summary law was imposed in Stalingrad with drastic punishments for any crime. Looters were to be shot within twenty-four hours. Patrols of officers were set up and the patrolling military police with their blinking tin badges on their chests had orders to take drastic action without compunction. Hundreds of German soldiers who had become weak in their misery thus became the victims of German bullets. In spite of this, one could not claim that the troops had become totally demoralised. The general suffering was too great and with it, the total apathy.

For the same reasons one could no longer generally speak of courageous fighting and heroic resistance. Certainly here and there individual deeds of courage, personal initiative and noble self-sacrifice were still being performed. But by and large only a mute submission to the inescapable fate remained to the bitter end. It was rather the silent heroism of acceptance, of suffering and submitting. There was hardly any longer a true soldier's death to be sought, but only a final desperate resistance out of self-preservation or the slow dying of long since exhausted, fought out, tortured human beings.

## STALINGRAD: THE END

### Sixth Army to High Command, 24 January 1943

. . . Troops without ammunition or food. Contact maintained with elements only of six divisions. Evidence of disintegration on southern, northern and western fronts. Effective command no longer possible. Little change on eastern front: eighteen thousand wounded without any supplies of dressings or drugs; 44, 76, 100, 305 and 384 Infantry Divisions destroyed. Front torn open as a result of strong break-throughs on three sides. Strong-points and shelter only available in the town itself; further defence senseless. Collapse inevitable. Army requests immediate permission to surrender in order to save lives of remaining troops.

Paulus

### Adolf Hitler to Sixth Army, 24 January 1943

Surrender is forbidden. 6 Army will hold their positions to the last man and the last round and by their heroic endurance will make an unforgettable contribution towards the establishment of a defensive front and the salvation of the Western world.

Adolf Hitler

### Sixth Army HQ to High Command, 05.45 hours, 31 January 1943

The Russians stand at the door of our bunker. We are destroying our equipment.

This station will no longer transmit.

*Von Paulus, against Hitler's orders, surrendered on 31 January. By 2 February the last German resistance at Stalingrad was over. Nearly 130,000 German soldiers died during the battle.*

## STALINGRAD: TAKEN PRISONER, 2 FEBRUARY 1943

### Joachim Wieder, Intelligence Officer, VIII Corps, German Sixth Army

*Wieder was among the 90,000 Germans taken prisoner in the final capitulation at Stalingrad. Very few survived to see their homeland. Wieder was returned to Germany in May 1950.*

On the morning of 2 February the news spread that the Russians were approaching with tanks and that people were surrendering everywhere without offering resistance. In our district the word was that there was to be no firing, but the troops were no longer resisting anyway. Just as one wipes away exhausted, half-dead flies in the autumn, the masses of tired human beings, worn out by their suffering and apathetically resigned to their fate, were being gathered in by the Russians and herded away. As far as they could still stand on their feet, they welled up out of the ruins, shelters and cellars and formed long lines of misery and helplessness in the streets. Our small surviving group had soon also become a speck somewhere within this formless mass.

In the early minutes of captivity I felt an easing of tension and relief. In the end, the insecurity of our situation between life and death had weighted down on all of us like lead. Was the road we were now going down not the way out of horror and fear? And did not the light and sweetness of a life in freedom possibly beckon at its end, admittedly in a far distant, veiled future? However, the transformation that suddenly took place within and around us was in some ways numbing and confusing.

The original deadening effect was gradually pushed aside by the approach of a world that was unknown to us. What first attracted my attention was the fresh, healthy appearance of the victors, their simple, enviable winter clothing and good weapons. Submachine-guns everywhere and the uniform picture of sheepskins, padded jackets, felt boots and fur caps with broad ear muffs swinging up and down.

The warmly bundled-up, well-nourished and splendidly equipped men of the Red Army, with their chunky, mostly red-cheeked faces, formed a stark contrast to our deathly pale, filthy, bearded and freezing figures of misery who hung exhausted and sick in their makeshift winter clothing, consisting of all kinds of furs, blankets, scarves, field-grey headgear, woollens and inadequate foot wear. This sudden meeting and comparison at once showed me how low we had sunk and how little we had been prepared for this murderous battle.

As if in a trance, I experienced the events and all the new impressions and feelings flooding down on me. I saw the muzzle of the cocked submachine-gun a Red Army soldier was aiming at my chest, who, searching impatiently, first grabbed my watch and then my pistol. I heard the calming words of a captain of the guard, who promised us life, safety and our personal property and then proudly accompanied the tired mass of his prisoners to the rear.

But such protection was not enough to spare us the initial bitter humiliations by the hate-filled victors. Malicious calls of "Fascist!", "Fritzi!", "Hitler kaputt!" alternated with threats, obviously dreadful curses and contemptuous spit. Like raging wolves, vengeful soldiers from the rear echelons fell on the helpless victims time and again to steal personal baggage and to vent their spleen. First my fur coat, an old family heirloom that had stood me in inestimable good stead in the east, was torn from my body. However, far more painful for me was the loss later on of all the things I had packed before going into captivity or carefully hidden on my person; a few small books and letters from home. With them and my wedding ring, the last tie that still visibly bound me to all I held dear and precious was torn from me. Nothing was left to me that outwardly reminded me of my former life. And my heart could only surrender them in bloody torment.

During the first sleepless night of my captivity this new misery remorselessly flooded over me in all its magnitude. I had been pulled out from among my comrades and fellow prisoners sitting crammed together in a farm house and initially taken to a guard house for interrogation. There I sat alone and deeply depressed among a group of joyfully noisy Red Army soldiers who first watched me with a mixture of curiosity and suspicion and soon left me to my own devices in the farthest corner of the room. While an endless fireworks display of captured German tracer ammunition was being explosively fired into the air outside in the triumph of victory, inside our guardroom gramophone music sounded for most of the night.

Wild dance rhythms rang out and time and again they were accompanied by the dank stamping of a row of felt boots that moved over the wooden floorboards with astonishing speed. The guards, who included slant-eyed Mongolians, looked strange enough. Some had decorated themselves in the most remarkable manner with captured German rings, watches, weapons and other objects. On their Red Army uniforms they wore German officers' daggers they had found and they had hung their pistols on the long chains of the German rifle-cleaning equipment.

Besides the dances, gramophone records of folk songs, Soviet choirs and marches were played incessantly. The same music was played over and over again, sometimes sad, sometimes filled with restrained emotions, sometimes with wild outbursts of feeling, all in a minor key and often of a strangeness of character that frightened me. Under a different set of circumstances this strange music could have intrigued me strongly. Now it only depressed and tormented me.

# STALINGRAD: AFTER THE FALL, 4 FEBRUARY 1943

## *Alexander Werth, war correspondent*

We set out at 3 p.m. on our fifty-mile trek from General Malinin's headquarters to Stalingrad. Our army driver said we would make it in four to five hours; it took us nearer thirteen.

There were half-a-dozen of us in a wretched van, without any seats or benches, sitting or half lying on bags or pieces of luggage. Every hour it became colder and colder. To add to our misery the back door of the van had no glass in it; it was almost as cold as driving in an open car.

It was a pity not to travel through this battle area during the day, but it couldn't be helped. Even so, I remember that night as one of my strangest experiences during the whole war. For one thing, I had never known such cold in all my life.

In the morning it had been only minus 20°, and then it was minus 30°, then minus 35°, then minus 40° and finally minus 44°. One has to experience 44° of frost to know what it means. Your breath catches. If you breathe on your glove, a thin film of ice immediately forms on it. We couldn't eat anything, because all our food – bread, sausage and eggs – had turned into stone. Even wearing *valenki* and two pairs of woollen socks, you had to move your toes all the time to keep the circulation going. Without *valenki* frostbite would have been certain, and the Germans had no *valenki*. To keep your hands in good condition, you had to clap them half the time or play imaginary scales. Once I took out a pencil to write down a few words: the first word was all right, the second was written by a drunk, the last two were the scrawl of a paralytic; quickly I blew on my purple fingers and put them back in the fur-lined glove.

And as you sit there in the van all huddled up and feeling fairly comfortable, you cannot bear to move, except your fingers and toes, and give your nose an occasional rub; a kind of mental and physical inertia comes over you; you feel almost doped. And yet you have to be on the alert all the time. For instance, I suddenly found the frost nibbling at my knees: it had got the right idea of attacking the tiny area between the end of my additional underwear and the beginning of the *valenki*! . . . Your only real ally, apart from clothes, on such occasions is the vodka bottle. And, bless it, it didn't freeze, and even a frequent small sip made a big difference. One could see what it must be like to fight in such conditions. For the last stage of the Battle of Stalingrad had been fought in weather only a little milder than it was on that February night.

The nearer we got to Stalingrad, the more bewildering was the traffic on the snow-bound road. This area, in which the battle had raged only so very recently, was now hundreds of miles from the front, and all the forces in Stalingrad were now being moved – towards Rostov and the Donets. About midnight we got stuck in a traffic jam. And what a spectacle that road presented – if one could still call it a road! For what was the original road and what was part of the adjoining steppe that had been taken in by this traffic – most of it moving west, but also some moving east – was not easy to determine. Between the two streams of traffic, there was now an irregular wall of snow that had been thrown up there by wheels and hoofs. Weird-looking figures were regulating the traffic – soldiers in long white camouflage cloaks and pointed white hoods; horses, horses and still more horses, blowing steam and with ice round their nostrils, were wading through the deep snow, pulling guns and gun-carriages and large covered wagons; and hundreds of lorries with their headlights full on. To the side of the road an enormous bonfire was burning, filling the air with clouds of black smoke that ate into your eyes; and shadow-like figures danced round the bonfire warming themselves; then others would light a plank at the bonfire, and start a little bonfire of their own, till the whole edge of the road was a series of small bonfires. Fire! How happy it made people on a night like this! Soldiers jumped off their lorries to get a few seconds of warmth, and have the dirty black smoke blow in their faces; then they would run after their lorry and jump on again.

Such was the endless procession coming out of Stalingrad: lorries, and horse sleighs and guns, and covered wagons, and even camels pulling sleighs – several of them stepping sedately through the deep snow as though it were sand. Every conceivable means of transport was being used. Thousands of soldiers were marching, or rather walking in large irregular crowds, to the west, through this cold deadly night. But they were cheerful and strangely happy, and they kept shouting about Stalingrad and the job they had done. Westward, westward!

# Part Five

---

## *Banzai*

### *The War in the Pacific, December 1941–June 1942*

# INTRODUCTION

The principal cause of war in the Far East was Japan's decision to acquire a Pacific empire. She had invaded China in the 1930s but the jewels she truly coveted were the colonial possessions of the British, the French and the Dutch. This imperial desire also led directly to hostilities with the USA, which was zealously protective of her influence in the region (and controlled the Philippines as a protectorate). By 7 December 1941 the Pacific was aflame as Japanese units attacked Pearl Harbor, Hong Kong, Wake Island, Guam and Midway. Malaya, Burma, the Dutch East Indies and the Philippines did not have long to wait until their turn came. When Corregidor fell on 6 May 1942, the Japanese controlled much of south-east Asia up to India and a Pacific empire which stretched from (part) of the Aleutians in the north to New Guinea in the south. They had proved themselves masters of amphibious landings and jungle fighting. In Malaya and Burma, in particular, the Japanese had used the jungle as a medium of war, whereas the British – whose colonies these were – tended to regard it as a no-go zone. It was only when the British and Americans learned that the jungle was neutral did they start to win in the Pacific on land. Yet, ultimately, the conflict in the Pacific was a sea-war, for the Japanese empire was oceanic – lands and islands separated by thousands of square miles of water. After destroying much of the American fleet at Pearl Harbor and sinking the Royal Navy's *Prince of Wales* and *Repulse*, the Imperial Japanese Navy seemed to rule the waves. Yet in just five minutes, between 10.25 and 10.30 on 7 May 1942, the whole course of the war in the Pacific changed. Those five minutes came in the carrier battle of Midway.

# PEARL HARBOR: THE VIEW FROM THE JAPANESE COCKPIT, 7 DECEMBER 1941

## Taisa Mitsuo Fuchida, Imperial Japanese Naval Air Service

*Fuchida led the strike force of 353 Japanese fighters and bombers that struck at Pearl Harbor at 7.49 a.m. on the sleepy Sunday morning of 7 December. The attack was launched from carriers 200 miles north of Oahu.*

On the flight deck a green lamp was waved in a circle to signal "Take off!" The engine of the foremost fighter plane began to roar. With the ship still pitching and rolling, the plane started its run, slowly at first but with steadily increasing speed. Men lining the flight deck held their breath as the first plane took off successfully just before the ship took a downward pitch. The next plane was already moving forward. There were loud cheers as each plane rose into the air.

Thus did the first wave of 183 fighters, bombers, and torpedo planes take off from the six carriers. Within fifteen minutes they had all been launched and were forming up in the still-dark sky, guided only by signal lights of the lead planes. After one great circling over the fleet formation, the planes set course due south for Oahu Island and Pearl Harbor. It was 0615.

Under my direct command were 49 level bombers. About 500 meters to my right and slightly below me were 40 torpedo planes. The same distance to my left, but about 200 meters above me, were 51 dive bombers, and flying cover for the formation there were 43 fighters. These other three groups were led by Lieutenant Commanders Murata, Takahashi, and Itaya, respectively.

We flew through and over the thick clouds which were at 2000 meters, up to where day was ready to dawn. And the clouds began gradually to brighten below us after the brilliant sun burst into the eastern sky. I opened the cockpit canopy and looked back at the large formation of planes. The wings glittered in the bright morning sunlight.

The speedometer indicated 125 knots and we were favored by a tail wind. At 0700 I figured that we should reach Oahu in less than an hour. But flying over the clouds we could not see the surface of the water, and, consequently, had no check on our drift. I switched on the radio-direction finder to tune in the Honolulu radio station and soon picked up some light music. By turning the antenna I found the exact direction from which the broadcast was coming and corrected our course, which had been five degrees off.

Continuing to listen to the program, I was wondering how to get below the clouds after reaching Oahu. If the island was covered by thick clouds like those below us, the level bombing would be difficult; and we had not yet had reports from the reconnaissance planes.

In tuning the radio a little finer I heard, along with the music, what seemed to be a weather report. Holding my breath, I adjusted the dial and listened intently. Then I heard it come through a second time, slowly and distinctly: "Averaging partly cloudy, with clouds mostly over the mountains. Cloud base at 3500 feet. Visibility good. Wind north, 10 knots."

What a windfall for us! No matter how careful the planning, a more favorable situation could not have been imagined. Weather conditions over Pearl Harbor had been worrying me greatly, but now with this information I could turn my attention to other problems. Since Honolulu was only partly cloudy, there must be breaks in the clouds over the island. But since the clouds over the mountains were at 1000 meters altitude, it would not be wise to attack from the northeast, flying over the eastern mountains, as previously planned. The wind was north and visibility good. It would be better to pass to the west of the island and make our approach from the south.

'. . .' we had been in the air for about an hour and a half. It was time that we were seeing land, but there was only a solid layer of clouds below. All of a sudden the clouds broke, and a long white line of coast appeared. We were over Kahuku Point, the northern tip of the island, and now it was time for our deployment.

There were alternate plans for the attack: If we had surprise, the torpedo planes were to strike first, followed by the level bombers and then the dive bombers, which were to attack the air bases including Hickam and Ford Island near the anchorage. If these bases were first hit by the dive bombers, it was feared that the resultant smoke might hinder torpedo and level-bombing attacks on the ships.

On the other hand, if enemy resistance was expected, the dive bombers would attack first to cause confusion and attract enemy fire. Level bombers, coming next, were to bomb and destroy enemy anti-aircraft guns, followed by the torpedo planes which would attack the ships.

The selection of attack method was for my decision, to be indicated by signal pistol: one "black dragon" for a surprise attack, two "black dragons" if it appeared that surprise was lost. Upon either order the fighters were immediately to dash in as cover.

There was still no news from the reconnaissance planes, but I had made up my mind that we could make a surprise attack, and thereupon ordered the deployment by raising my signal pistol outside the canopy and firing one "black dragon." The time was 0740.

With this order dive bombers rose to 4000 meters, torpedo bombers went down almost to sea level, and level bombers came down just under the clouds. The only group that failed to deploy was the fighters. Flying above the rest of the formation, they seemed to have missed the signal because of the clouds. Realizing this I fired another shot toward the fighter group. This time they noticed the signal immediately and sped toward Oahu.

This second shot, however, was taken by the commander of the dive bomber group as the second of two "black dragons," signifying a non-surprise attack which would mean that his group should attack first, and this error served to confuse some of the pilots who had understood the original signal.

Meanwhile a reconnaissance report came in from *Chikuma*'s plane giving the locations of ten battleships, one heavy cruiser, and ten light cruisers in the harbor. It also reported a 14-meter wind from bearing 080, and clouds over the U.S. Fleet at 1700 meters with a scale 7 density. The *Tone* plane also reported that "the enemy fleet is not in Lahaina Anchorage." Now I knew for sure that there were no carriers in the harbor. The sky cleared as we moved in on the target and Pearl Harbor was plainly visible from the northwest valley of the island. I studied our objective through binoculars. They were there all right, all eight of them. "Notify all planes to launch attacks," I ordered my radio man who immediately began tapping the key. The order went in plain code: "*To, to, to, to. . . .*" The time was 0749.

When Lieutenant Commander Takahashi and his dive-bombing group mistook my signal, and thought we were making a non-surprise attack, his 53 planes lost no time in dashing forward. His command was divided into two groups: one led by himself which headed for Ford Island and Hickam Field, the other, led by Lieutenant Sakamoto, headed for Wheeler Field.

The dive bombers over Hickam Field saw heavy bombers lined up on the apron. Takahashi rolled his plane sharply and went into a dive, followed immediately by the rest of his planes, and the first bombs fell at Hickam. The next places hit were Ford Island and Wheeler Field. In a very short time huge billows of black smoke were rising from these bases. The lead torpedo planes were to have started their run to the Navy Yard from over Hickam, coming from south of the bay entrance. But the sudden burst of bombs at Hickam surprised Lieutenant Commander Murata who had understood that his torpedo planes were to have attacked first. Hence he took a short cut lest the smoke from those bases cover up his targets. Thus the first torpedo was actually launched some five minutes ahead of the scheduled 0800. The time of each attack was as follows:

> 0755 Dive bombers at Hickam and Wheeler
> 0757 Torpedo planes at battleships
> 0800 Fighters strafing air bases
> 0805 Level bombers at battleships

After issuance of the attack order, my level bomber group kept east of Oahu going past the southern tip of the island. On our left was the Barbers Point airfield, but, as we had been informed, there were no planes. Our information indicated that a powerful anti-aircraft battery was stationed there, but we saw no evidence of it.

I continued to watch the sky over the harbor and activities on the ground. None but Japanese planes were in the air, and there were no indications of air combat. Ships in the harbor still appeared to be asleep, and the Honolulu radio broadcast continued normally. I felt that surprise was now assured, and that my men would succeed in their missions.

Knowing that Admirals Nagumo, Yamamoto, and the General Staff were anxious about the attack, I decided that they should be informed. I ordered the following message sent to the fleet: "We have succeeded in making a surprise attack. Request you relay this report to Tokyo." The radio man reported shortly that the message had been received by *Akagi*.

The code for a successful surprise attack was "*Tora, tora, tora.* . . ." Before *Akagi*'s relay of this message reached Japan, it was received by *Nagato* in Hiroshima Bay and the General Staff in Tokyo, directly from my plane! This was surely a long-distance record for such a low-powered transmission from an airplane, and might be attributed to the use of the word. "*Tora*" as our code. There is a Japanese saying, "A tiger (*tora*) goes out 1000 *ri* (2000 miles) and returns without fail."

I saw clouds of black smoke rising from Hickam and soon thereafter from Ford Island. This bothered me and I wondered what had happened. It was not long before I saw waterspouts rising alongside the battleships, followed by more and more waterspouts. It was time to launch our level bombing attacks so I ordered my pilot to bank sharply, which was the attack signal for the planes following us. All ten of my squadrons then formed into a single column with intervals of 200 meters. It was indeed a gorgeous formation.

The lead plane in each squadron was manned by a specially trained pilot and bombardier. The pilot and bombardier of my squadron had won numerous fleet contests and were considered the best in the

Japanese Navy. I approved when Lieutenant Matsuzaki asked if the lead plane should trade positions with us, and he lifted our plane a little as a signal. The new leader came forward quickly, and I could see the smiling round face of the bombardier when he saluted. In returning the salute I entrusted the command to them for the bombing mission.

As my group made its bomb run, enemy anti-aircraft suddenly came to life. Dark gray bursts blossomed here and there until the sky was clouded with shattering near misses which made our plane tremble. Shipboard guns seemed to open fire before the shore batteries. I was startled by the rapidity of the counter-attack which came less than five minutes after the first bomb had fallen. Were it the Japanese Fleet, the reaction would not have been so quick, because although the Japanese character is suitable for offensives, it does not readily adjust to the defensive.

Suddenly the plane bounced as if struck by a huge club. "The fuselage is holed to port," reported the radio man behind me, "and a steering-control wire is damaged." I asked hurriedly if the plane was under control, and the pilot assured me that it was.

No sooner were we feeling relieved than another burst shook the plane. My squadron was headed for *Nevada*'s mooring at the northern end of battleship row on the east side of Ford Island. We were just passing over the bay entrance and it was almost time to release our bombs. It was not easy to pass through the concentrated anti-aircraft fire. Flying at only 3000 meters, it seemed that this might well be a date with eternity.

I further saw that it was not wise to have deployed in this long single-column formation. The whole level bomber group could be destroyed like ducks in a shooting gallery. It would also have been better if we had approached the targets from the direction of Diamond Head. But here we were at our targets and there was a job to be done.

It was now a matter of utmost importance to stay on course, and the lead plane kept to its line of flight like a homing pigeon. Ignoring the barrage of shells bursting around us, I concentrated on the bomb loaded under the lead plane, pulled the safety bolt from the bomb release lever and grasped the handle. It seemed as if time was standing still.

Again we were shaken terrifically and our planes were buffeted about. When I looked out the third plane of my group was abeam of us and I saw its bomb fall! That pilot had a reputation for being careless. In training his bomb releases were poorly timed, and he had often been cautioned.

I thought, "That damn fellow has done it again!" and shook my fist in his direction. But I soon realized that there was something wrong with his plane and he was losing gasoline. I wrote on a small blackboard, "What happened?" and held it toward his plane. He explained, "Underside of fuselage hit."

Now I saw his bomb cinch lines fluttering wildly, and sorry for having scolded him, I ordered that he return to the carrier. He answered, "Fuel tank destroyed, will follow you," asking permission to stay with the group. Knowing the feelings of the pilot and crew, I gave the permission, although I knew it was useless to try taking that crippled and bombless plane through the enemy fire. It was nearly time for bomb release when we ran into clouds which obscured the target, and I made out the round face of the lead bombardier who was waving his hands back and forth to indicate that we had passed the release point. Banking slightly we turned right toward Honolulu, and I studied the anti-aircraft fire, knowing that we would have to run through it again. It was now concentrated on the second squadron.

While circling for another try, I looked toward the area in which the bomb from the third plane had fallen. Just outside the bay entrance I saw a large water ring close by what looked like a destroyer. The ship seemed to be standing in a floating dock, attached to both sides of the entrance like a gate boat. I was suddenly reminded of the midget submarines which were to have entered the bay for a special attack.

At the time of our sortie I was aware of these midget submarines, but knew nothing of their characteristics, operational objectives, force organization, or the reason for their participation in the attack. In *Akagi*, Commander Shibuya, a staff officer in charge of submarine operations, had explained that they were to penetrate the harbor the night before our attack; but, no matter how good an opportunity might arise, they were not to strike until after the planes had done so.

Even now the submarines were probably concealed in the bay, awaiting the air attack. Had the entrance been left open, there would have been some opportunity for them to get out of the harbor. But in light of what I had just seen there seemed little chance of that, and, feeling now the bitterness of war, I vowed to do my best in the assigned mission.

While my group was circling over Honolulu for another bombing attempt, other groups made their runs, some making three tries before succeeding. Suddenly a colossal explosion occurred in battleship row. A huge column of dark red smoke rose to 1000 feet and a stiff shock wave reached our plane. I called the pilot's attention to the spectacle, and he observed, "Yes, Commander, the powder magazine must have exploded. Terrible indeed!" The attack was in full swing, and smoke from fires and explosions filled most of the sky over Pearl Harbor.

My group now entered on a bombing course again. Studying battle-ship row through binoculars, I saw that the big explosion had been on *Arizona*. She was still flaming fiercely and her smoke was covering *Nevada*, the target of my group. Since the heavy smoke would hinder our bomber accuracy, I looked for some other ship to attack. *Tennessee*, third in the left row, was already on fire; but next in row was *Maryland*, which had not yet been attacked. I gave an order changing our target to this ship, and once again we headed into the anti-aircraft fire. Then came the "ready" signal and I took a firm grip on the bomb release handle, holding my breath and staring at the bomb of the lead plane.

Pilots, observers, and radio men all shouted, "Release!" on seeing the bomb drop from the lead plane, and all the others let go their bombs. I immediately lay flat on the floor to watch the fall of bombs through a peephole. Four bombs in perfect pattern plummeted like devils of doom. The target was so far away that I wondered for a moment if they would reach it. The bombs grew smaller and smaller until I was holding my breath for fear of losing them. I forgot everything in the thrill of watching the fall toward the target. They become small as poppy seeds and finally disappeared just as tiny white flashes of smoke appeared on and near the ship.

# PEARL HARBOR: THE VIEW FROM THE GROUND, 7 DECEMBER 1941

## *John Garcia*, **harbour worker**

I was sixteen years old, employed as a pipe fitter apprentice at Pearl Harbor Navy Yard. On 7 December 1941, oh, around 8.00 a.m., my grandmother woke me. She informed me that the Japanese were bombing Pearl Harbor. I said, "They're just practising." She said, no, it was real and the announcer is requesting that all Pearl Harbor workers report to work. I went out on the porch and I could see the anti-aircraft fire up in the sky. I just said, "Oh boy."

I was four miles away. I got out on my motor-cycle and it took me five, ten minutes to get there. It was a mess.

I was working on the USS *Shaw*. It was on a floating dry dock. It was in flames. I started to go down into the pipe fitter's shop to get my toolbox when another wave of Japanese came in. I got under a set of concrete steps at the dry dock where the battleship *Pennsylvania* was. An officer came by and asked me to go into the *Pennsylvania* and try to get the fires out. A bomb had penetrated the marine deck, and that was three decks below. Under that was the magazines: ammunition, powder, shells. I said, "There ain't no way I'm gonna go down there."

It could blow up any minute. I was young and sixteen, not stupid, not at sixty-two cents an hour. (Laughs.)

A week later, they brought me before a navy court. It was determined that I was not service personnel and could not be ordered. There was no martial law at the time. Because I was sixteen and had gone into the water, the whole thing was dropped.

I was asked by some other officer to go into the water and get sailors out that had been blown off the ships. Some were unconscious, some were dead. So I spent the rest of the day swimming inside the harbour, along with some other Hawaiians. I brought out I don't know how many bodies and how many were alive and how many dead. Another man would put them into ambulances and they'd be gone. We worked all day at that . . .

The following morning, I went with my tools to the *West Virginia*. It had turned turtle, totally upside down. We found a number of men inside. The *Arizona* was a total washout. Also the *Utah*. There were men in there, too. We spent about a month cutting the superstructure of the *West Virginia*, tilting it back on its hull. About 300 men we cut out of there were still alive by the eighteenth day. It took two weeks to get all the fires out. We worked around the clock for three days. There was so much excitement and confusion. Some of our sailors were shooting five-inch guns at the Japanese planes. You just cannot down a plane with a five-inch shell. They were landing in Honolulu, the unexploded naval shells. They have a ten-mile range. They hurt and killed a lot of people in the city.

When I came back after the third day, they told me that a shell had hit the house of my girl. We had been going together for, oh, about three years. Her house was a few blocks from my place. At the time, they said it was a Japanese bomb. Later we learned it was an American shell. She was killed. She was preparing for church at the time.

*Nearly 3,700 American soldiers, sailors, marines and civilians were lost at Pearl Harbor. Eighteen warships were sunk or damaged.*


## CABLE: PRESIDENT FRANKLIN D. ROOSEVELT TO PRIME MINISTER WINSTON CHURCHILL, 8 DECEMBER 1941

December 8, 1941

To the Former Naval Person*
London
The Senate passed the all-out declaration of war eighty-two to
nothing, and the House has passed it three hundred eighty-eight

---

* Churchill was a former First Lord of the Admiralty.

to one. Today all of us are in the same boat with you and the people of the Empire and it is a ship which will not and cannot be sunk.

F.D.R.

# THE JAPANESE BOMB MANILA, 8 DECEMBER 1941

## *Carlos P. Romulo, USMC*

*In the immediate aftermath of Pearl Harbor, the Japanese launched a southern offensive attacking Hong Kong, Malaysia, three American-held islands in the Pacific (Midway, Guam, Wake), Thailand, and the American air force bases in the Philippines.*

We hadn't long to wait after Pearl Harbor.

The next day I stood on the balcony of the *Herald* building and saw the first enemy planes cut down through the skies like great aerial bolos.

Fifty-four Japanese sky monsters, flashing silver in the bright noonday, were flying in two magnificently formed Vs.

Above the scream of the sirens the church bells solemnly announced the noon hour.

Unprotected and unprepared, Manila lay under the enemy planes – a city of ancient nunneries and chromium-fronted night clubs, of skyscrapers towering over nipa shacks, of antiquity and modernity, of East and West.

I heard the *Herald* staff clattering out of the building into Muralla Calle, where citizens in the customary spotless white were being herded by the police under the moss-covered old Spanish wall. Women clustered under the acacia trees in the park. I found myself grinning – a few of them had opened their umbrellas for additional protection!

Half-a-dozen bearded Fathers came out of the College of San Juan de Letran next door, looked up and saw the planes, and, gathering up their white robes, rushed back into the building.

The capital had stopped moving. Trams were frozen in their tracks. Cars and carromatas, drawn by skinny ponies, were pulled obediently against the kerbs. There were no signs of panic – everyone was watching the planes.

We had been expecting the raiders since yesterday's news of Pearl Harbor. Within a few hours of that attack other Japanese planes had vomited destruction over Davao, in the south, Aparri, in the north, Camp John Hay in Baguio, Clark Field, and the Iba landing field. They were certain to bomb Manila, the capital of the Philippines.

Something pressed between my feet. It was Cola, the office cat, her feline instincts alarmed by the sirens. Their screaming stopped, and in their place we heard the throbbing of the planes.

# THE LOSS OF THE *REPULSE* AND *PRINCE OF WALES*, OFF THE COAST OF MALAYA, 10 DECEMBER 1941

## *O.D. Gallagher, war correspondent*

*To protect its Far East naval base of Singapore, the British dispatched a surface fleet to intercept approaching Japanese invasion forces. In the event, the British were spotted first and were attacked by swarms of Japanese fighter-bombers. The British fleet had no air protection. The brand new battleship* Prince of Wales *and the battlecruiser* Repulse *were sunk in two hours. "In all the war," wrote Churchill, "I never received a more direct shock."*

The sky was luminous as pearl. We saw from the flag deck a string of black objects on the port bow. They turned out to be a line of landing barges, "like railway trucks", as a young signaller said. At 6.30 a.m. the loud-speaker voice announced: "Just received message saying enemy is making landing north of Singapore. We're going in."

We all rushed off to breakfast, which consisted of coffee, cold ham, bread, and marmalade. Back at action stations all the ship's company kept a look-out. We cruised in line-ahead formation, *Prince of Wales* leading, the *Repulse* second, and with our destroyer screen out.

Down the Malayan coast, examining with the help of terrier-like destroyers all coves for enemy landing parties.

At 7.55 a.m. *Prince of Wales* catapulted one of her planes on reconnaissance, with instructions not to return to the ship, but to land ashore after making a report to us on what she found.

We watched her become midget-size and drop out of sight behind two hummock-back islands, behind which was a beach invisible to us. We all thought that was where the enemy lay. But it reappeared and went on, still searching.

Meanwhile all the ship's company on deck had put on anti-flash helmets, elbow-length asbestos gloves, goggles and tin hats.

*Prince of Wales* looked magnificent. White-tipped waves rippled over her plunging bows. The waves shrouded them with watery lace, then they rose high again and once again dipped. She rose and fell so methodically that the effect of staring at her was hypnotic. The fresh breeze blew her White Ensign out stiff as a board.

I felt a surge of excited anticipation rise within me at the prospect of her and the rest of the force sailing into enemy landing parties and their escorting warships.

A young Royal Marines lieutenant who was my escort when first I went aboard the *Repulse* told me: "We've not had any action but we're a perfect team – the whole twelve hundred and sixty of us. We've been working together so long. We claim to have the Navy's best gunners."

My anticipatory reverie was broken by the voice from the loud-speakers again: "Hello, there. Well, we've sighted nothing yet, but we'll go down the coast having a look for them."

More exclamations of disappointment. The yeoman of signals said: "Don't say this one's off, too."

As we sped down Malaya's changing coastline the wag of the flag-deck said travel-talkwise: "On the starboard beam, dear listeners, you see the beauty spots of Malaya, land of the orang-outang."

Again the loud-speaker announces: "Nothing sighted."

The *Repulse* sends off one of her aircraft. The pilot is not the ginger-bearded New Zealander, as he tossed a coin with another pilot and lost the toss, which means that he stays behind.

We drift to the wardroom again until 10.20 a.m. We are spotted again by a twin-engined snooper of the same type as attacked Singapore the first night of this new war.

We can do nothing about it, as she keeps well beyond range while her crew presumably studies our outlines and compares them with silhouettes in the Jap equivalent of *Jane's Fighting Ships*.

At 11 a.m. a twin-masted single funnel ship is sighted on the starboard bow. The force goes to investigate her. She carries no flag.

I was looking at her through my telescope when the shock of an explosion made me jump so that I nearly poked my right eye out. It was 11.15 a.m. The explosion came from the *Prince of Wales*'s portside secondary armament. She was firing at a single aircraft.

We open fire. There are about six aircraft.

A three-quarter-inch screw falls on my tin hat from the bridge deck above from the shock of explosion of the guns. "The old tub's falling to bits," observes the yeoman of signals.

· That was the beginning of a superb air attack by the Japanese, whose air force was an unknown quantity.

Officers in the *Prince of Wales* whom I met in their wardroom when she arrived here last week said they expected some unorthodox flying from the Japs. "The great danger will be the possibility of these chaps flying their whole aircraft into a ship and committing hara-kiri."

It was nothing like that. It was most orthodox. They even came at us in formation, flying low and close.

Aboard the *Repulse*, I found observers as qualified as anyone to estimate Jap flying abilities. They know from first-hand experience what the RAF and the Luftwaffe are like. Their verdict was: "The

Germans have never done anything like this in the North Sea, Atlantic or anywhere else we have been."

They concentrated on the two capital ships, taking the *Prince of Wales* first and the *Repulse* second. The destroyer screen they left completely alone except for damaged planes forced to fly low over them when they dropped bombs defensively.

At 11.18 the *Prince of Wales* opened a shattering barrage with all her multiple pom-poms, or Chicago Pianos as they call them. Red and blue flames poured from the eight-gun muzzles of each battery. I saw glowing tracer shells describe shallow curves as they went soaring skyward surrounding the enemy planes. Our Chicago Pianos opened fire; also our triple-gun four-inch high-angle turrets. The uproar was so tremendous I seemed to feel it.

From the starboard side of the flag-deck I could see two torpedo planes. No, they were bombers. Flying straight at us.

All our guns pour high-explosives at them, including shells so delicately fused that they explode if they merely graze cloth fabric.

But they swing away, carrying out a high-powered evasive action without dropping anything at all. I realize now what the purpose of the action was. It was a diversion to occupy all our guns and observers on the air defence platform at the summit of the main-mast.

There is a heavy explosion and the *Repulse* rocks. Great patches of paint fall from the funnel on to the flag-deck. We all gaze above our heads to see planes which during the action against the low fliers were unnoticed.

They are high-level bombers. Seventeen thousand feet. The first bomb, the one that rocked us a moment ago, scored a direct hit on the catapult deck through the one hangar on the port side.

I am standing behind a multiple Vickers gun, one which fires 2,000 half-inch bullets per minute. It is at the after end of the flag-deck.

I see a cloud of smoke rising from the place where the final bomb hit. Another comes down bang again from 17,000 feet. It explodes in the sea, making a creamy blue and green patch ten feet across. The *Repulse* rocks again. It was three fathoms from the port side. It was a miss, so no one bothers.

Cooling fluid is spouting from one of the barrels of a Chicago Piano. I can see black paint on the funnel-shaped covers at the muzzles of the eight barrels actually rising in blisters big as fists.

The boys manning them – there are ten to each – are sweating, saturating their asbestos anti-flash helmets. The whole gun swings this way and that as spotters pick planes to be fired at.

Two planes can be seen coming at us. A spotter sees another at a different angle, but much closer.

He leans forward, his face tight with excitement, urgently pounding the back of the gun swiveller in front of him. He hits that back with his right hand and points with the left a stabbing forefinger at a single sneaker plane. Still blazing two-pounders the whole gun platform turns in a hail of death at the single plane. It is some 1,000 yards away.

I saw tracers rip into its fuselage dead in the centre. Its fabric opened up like a rapidly spreading sore with red edges. Fire . . .

It swept to the tail, and in a moment stabilizer and rudder became a framework skeleton. Her nose dipped down and she went waterward.

We cheered like madmen. I felt my larynx tearing in the effort to make myself heard above the hellish uproar of guns.

A plane smacked the sea on its belly and was immediately transformed into a gigantic shapeless mass of fire which shot over the waves fast as a snake's tongue. The *Repulse* had got the first raider.

For the first time since the action began we can hear a sound from the loud-speakers, which are on every deck at every action station. It is the sound of a bugle.

Its first notes are somewhat tortured. The young bugler's lips and throat are obviously dry with excitement. It is that most sinister alarm of all for seamen: "Fire!"

Smoke from our catapult deck is thick now. Men in overalls, their faces hidden by a coat of soot, man-handle hoses along decks. Water fountains delicately from a rough patch made in one section by binding it with a white shirt.

It sprays on the Vickers gunners, who, in a momentary lull, lift faces, open mouths and put out tongues to catch the cooling jets. They quickly avert faces to spit – the water is salt and it is warm. It is sea water.

The Chicago Piano opens up again with a suddenness that I am unable to refrain from flinching at, though once they get going with their erratic shell-pumping it is most reassuring.

All aboard have said the safest place in any battleship or cruiser or destroyer is behind a Chicago Piano. I believe them.

Empty brass cordite cases are tumbling out of the gun's scuttle-like exit so fast and so excitedly it reminds me of the forbidden fruit machine in Gibraltar on which I once played. It went amok on one occasion and ejected £8 in shillings in a frantic rush.

The cases bounce off the steel C deck, roll and dance down the sloping base into a channel for easy picking up later.

At 11.25 we see an enormous splash on the very edge of the horizon. The splash vanishes and a whitish cloud takes its place.

A damaged enemy plane jettisoning its bombs or another enemy destroyed? A rapid Gallup poll on the flag deck says: "Another duck down." Duck is a word they have rapidly taken from the Aussie Navy. It means enemy plane.

Hopping about the flag-deck from port to starboard, whichever side is being attacked, is the plump figure of the naval photographer named Tubby Abrahams.

He was a Fleet Street agency pictureman now in the Navy. But all his pictures are lost. He had to throw them into the sea with his camera. He was saved. So was United States broadcaster Cecil Brown, of Columbia System.

Fire parties are still fighting the hangar outbreak, oblivious of any air attack used so far. Bomb splinters have torn three holes in the starboard side of the funnel on our flag-deck.

Gazing impotently with no more than fountain pen and notebook in my hands while gunners, signallers, surgeons and range-finders worked, I found emotional release in shouting rather stupidly, I suppose, at the Japanese.

I discovered depths of obscenity previously unknown, even to me.

One young signaller keeps passing me pieces of information in between running up flats. He has just said: "A couple of blokes are caught in the lift from galley to servery. They're trying to get them out."

The yeoman of signals interjected: "How the bloody hell they got there, God knows."

There is a short lull. The boys dig inside their overalls and pull out cigarettes. Then the loud-speaker voice: "Enemy aircraft ahead." Lighted ends are nipped off cigarettes. The ship's company goes into action again. "Twelve of them." The flag-deck boys whistle. Someone counts them aloud: "One, two, three, four, five, six, seven, eight, nine – yes, nine." The flag-deck wag, as he levels a signalling lamp at the *Prince of Wales*: "Any advance on nine? Anybody? No? Well, here they come."

It is 12.10 p.m. They are all concentrating on the *Prince of Wales*. They are after the big ships all right. A mass of water and smoke rises in a tree-like column from the *Prince of Wales*'s stern. They've got her with a torpedo.

A ragged-edged mass of flame from her Chicago Piano does not stop them, nor the heavy instant flashes from her high-angle secondary armament.

She is listing to port – a bad list. We are about six cables from her.

A snottie, or midshipman, runs past, calls as he goes: "*Prince of Wales*'s steering gear gone." It doesn't seem possible that those slight-looking planes could do that to her.

The planes leave us, having apparently dropped all their bombs and torpedoes. I don't believe it is over, though. "Look, look!" shouts someone, "there's a line in the water right under our bows, growing longer on the starboard side. A torpedo that missed us. Wonder where it'll stop."

The *Prince of Wales* signals us again asking if we've been torpedoed. Our Captain Tennant replies: "Not yet. We've dodged nineteen."

Six stokers arrive on the flag-deck. They are black with smoke and oil and are in need of first aid. They are ushered down to the armoured citadel at the base of the mainmast.

The *Prince of Wales*'s list is increasing. There is a great rattle of empty two-pounder cordite cases as Chicago Piano boys gather up the empties and stow them away and clear for further action.

12.20 p.m. . . . The end is near, although I didn't know it.

A new wave of planes appears, flying around us in formation and gradually coming nearer. The *Prince of Wales* lies about ten cables astern of our port side. She is helpless.

They are making for her. I don't know how many. They are splitting up our guns as they realize they are after her, knowing she can't dodge their torpedoes. So we fire at them to defend the *Prince of Wales* rather than attend to our own safety.

The only analogy I can think of to give an impression of the *Prince of Wales* in those last moments is of a mortally wounded tiger trying to beat off the *coup de grâce*.

Her outline is hardly distinguishable in smoke and flame from all her guns except the fourteen-inchers. I can see one plane release a torpedo. It drops nose heavy into the sea and churns up a small wake as it drives straight at the *Prince of Wales*. It explodes against her bows.

A couple of seconds later another explodes amidships and another astern. Gazing at her turning over on the port side with her stern going under and with dots of men leaping from her, I was thrown against the bulkhead by a tremendous shock as the *Repulse* takes a torpedo on her portside stern.

With all others on the flag-deck I am wondering where it came from, when the *Repulse* shudders gigantically. Another torpedo.

Now men cheering with more abandon than at a Cup Final. What the heck is this? I wonder. Then see it is another plane down. It hits the sea in flames also. There have been six so far as I know.

My notebook, which I have got before me, is stained with oil and is ink-blurred. It says: "Third torp."

The *Repulse* now listing badly to starboard. The loud-speakers speak for the last time: "Everybody on main deck."

We all troop down ladders, most orderly except for one lad who climbs the rail and is about to jump when an officer says: "Now then –

come back – we are all going your way." The boy came back and joined the line.

It seemed slow going. Like all the others I suppose I was tempted to leap to the lower deck, but the calmness was catching. When we got to the main deck the list was so bad our shoes and feet could not grip the steel deck. I kicked off mine, and my damp stockinged feet made for sure movement.

Nervously opening my cigarette case I found I hadn't a match. I offered a cigarette to a man beside me. He said: "Ta. Want a match?" We both lit up and puffed once or twice. He said: "I'll be seeing you, mate." To which I replied: "Hope so, cheerio."

We were all able to walk down the ship's starboard side, she lay so much over to port.

We all formed a line along a big protruding anti-torpedo blister, from where we had to jump some twelve feet into a sea which was black – I discovered it was oil.

I remember jamming my cap on my head, drawing a breath and leaping.

Oh, I forgot – the last entry in my notebook was: "Sank about 12.20 p.m." I made it before leaving the flag-deck. In the water I glimpsed the *Prince of Wales*'s bows disappearing.

Kicking with all my strength, I with hundreds of others tried to get away from the *Repulse* before she went under, being afraid of getting drawn under in the whirlpool.

I went in the wrong direction, straight into the still spreading oil patch, which felt almost as thick as velvet. A wave hit me and swung me round so that I saw the last of the *Repulse*.

Her underwater plates were painted a bright, light red. Her bows rose high as the air trapped inside tried to escape from underwater forward regions, and there she hung for a second or two and easily slid out of sight.

## FLYING TIGER: AMERICAN VOLUNTEER GROUP PILOT IN ACTION AGAINST THE JAPANESE, 19 DECEMBER 1941

### *Claire L Chennault, AVG*

*A former USAAF pilot, Claire Chennault, recruited American volunteers to help the Chinese resist the Japanese invasion (begun in 1937). The first missions of the American Volunteer Group of the Chinese Nationalist Air Force began in December 1941. Eventually the "Flying Tigers" were reorganized as the 23rd Fighter Group of the USAAF.*

By dawn on the nineteenth we had thirty-four P-40s ready to fight at Kunming with a fighter-control headquarters hooked into the Yunnan warning net and the Chinese code rooms that were monitoring Japanese operational radio frequencies and decoding enemy messages. For the first time since mid-October I breathed easier.

It was this kind of lightning mobility that was necessary to realize the full potential of airpower. To achieve it meant that I would always have to operate on a skeletonized basis with airmen doubling in ground duties and a few key men doing the work of an entire staff. It meant that I could never afford the excess staff personnel required by more orthodox military organizations.

It was this ability to shift my combat operations six hundred and fifty miles in an afternoon and a thousand miles in twenty-four hours that kept the Japanese off balance for four bloody years and prevented them from landing a counterpunch with their numerically superior strength that might easily have put my always meager forces out of business.

We had little strain on our patience for the first pay-off on these tactics. December 19 passed quietly with three P-40 reconnaissance patrols over southern Yunnan but no sign of life from the enemy. At 9:45 A.M. on the twentieth my special phone from the Chinese code room rang. It was Colonel Wong Shu Ming, commander of the Chinese Fifth Air Force and Chinese chief of staff for the A.V.G. His message said, "Ten Japanese bombers crossed the Yunnan border at Laokay heading northwest."

From then on the battle unfolded over Yunnan as it had done a hundred times before in my head. Reports filtered in from the Yunnan net as the enemy bombers penetrated deeper into China.

"Heavy engine noise at station X-10."

"Unknowns overhead at station P-8."

"Noise of many above clouds at station C-23."

Position reports recorded on our fighter-control board added up to a course designed to bring the enemy bombers to about fifty miles east of Kunming, from which point they would probably begin the circling and feinting tactics designed to confuse the warning net before their final dash to the target.

I ordered the Second Squadron to make the interception. Jack Newkirk, of Scarsdale, New York, led one four-plane element in search of the bombers while Jim Howard, of St. Louis, son of former medical missionaries in China, led another four-plane formation on defensive patrol above Kunming. Sixteen planes of the First Squadron commanded by Robert Sandell, of San Antonio, Texas, were held in reserve in the stand-by area west of Kunming, ready to join the fray at the decisive moment.

I fired a red flare sending the Second and First Squadrons into the air and drove with my executive officer, Harvey Greenlaw, and interpreter, Colonel Hsu, to the great timbered clay pyramid looming above the grassy mounds of a Chinese graveyard on a gentle slope overlooking the field. This was our combat-operations shelter with a duplicate set of radio and phone communications. Inside the dark, dank interior we studied the plotting board by the light of matches held by Greenlaw while Hsu took phone reports from the Chinese net. Outside, the winter air of the Kunming plateau was crisp and clear. Scattered puffball clouds floated lazily above the city at 10,000 feet. Weather reports to the south indicated a solid overcast brushing the mountain peaks.

This was the decisive moment I had been awaiting for more than four years – American pilots in American fighter planes aided by a Chinese ground warning net about to tackle a formation of the Imperial Japanese Air Force, which was then sweeping the Pacific skies victorious everywhere. I felt that the fate of China was riding in the P-40 cockpits through the wintery sky over Yunnan. I yearned heartily to be ten years younger and crouched in a cockpit instead of a dugout, tasting the stale rubber of an oxygen mask and peering ahead into limitless space through the cherry-red rings of a gunsight.

Suddenly voices broke through the crackling radio static.

"There they are."

"No, no, they can't be Japs."

"Look at those red balls."

"Let's get 'em."

Then maddening silence. I ordered Sandell's reserve squadron to dive to Iliang about thirty miles southeast of Kunming along the Japs' line of probable approach. There was nothing more on the radio. The Chinese net reported the bombers had reversed course and were heading back toward Indo-China. Sounds of gunfire were heard, and the heavy fall of Japanese bombs in the mountains near Iliang was reported. There was nothing to do but return to the field and wait.

Chinese were already streaming back to the city from their refuge among the grave mounds, incredulous that no bombs had fallen. Howard's patrol over Kunming came down. They had seen nothing. Newkirk's flight returned, sheepish and chagrined over a bad case of buck fever on their first contact with the enemy. They had sighted the Jap formation of ten gray twin-engined bombers about thirty miles southeast of Kunming, but for a few incredulous seconds could hardly believe the bombers were really Japs. The bombers jettisoned their bombs, put their noses down for speed, and wheeled back toward Indo-China. By the time Newkirk's flight recovered and opened fire, the bombers had too big a lead – too big that is for everybody except Ed Rector. The last the other pilots saw of Rector he was still chasing the Japs at full throttle.

Finally Sandell's squadron came straggling in. From the whistling of the wind in their open gun barrels and the slow rolls as they buzzed the field, we knew they had been in a fight. They had sighted the Jap formation in full retreat over Iliang about thirty miles southeast of Kunming, scuttling along on top of a solid overcast with Rector still in pursuit.

As the P-40s dived to attack, everybody went a little crazy with excitement. All the lessons of Toungoo were forgotten. There was no teamwork – only a wild melee in which all pilots agreed that only sheer luck kept P-40s from shooting each other. Pilots tried wild 90-degree deflection shots and other crazy tactics in the 130-mile running fight that followed. Fritz Wolf of Shawano, Wisconsin, shot down two bombers and then cursed his armorer because his guns jammed.

When he landed and inspected the guns, he found they were merely empty. When the P-40s broke off three Jap bombers had gone down in flames and the remainder were smoking in varying degrees. Ed Rector was the only A.V.G. casualty. His long chase left him short of gas, forcing him to crash-land his P-40 in a rice paddy east of Kumming with minor injuries.

Back at the field most of the pilots were too excited to speak coherently.

"Well, boys," I told the excited pilots, "it was a good job but not good enough. Next time get them all."

I herded them into the operations shack for an hour before I let them eat lunch. We went over the fight in minute detail pointing out their mistakes and advising them on how to get all the bombers next time. Not until the spring of 1945 did I learn how close Sandell's flight had come to getting all the Japs in that first fight of the A.V.G.

Lewis Bishop of De Kalb Junction, New York, an A.V.G. pilot shot down five months after the Iliang battle and taken prisoner in Indo-China, met the Japanese pilot who led the raid. The Jap said his crew had been the sole survivors of the mission. Nine of the ten bombers had failed to return.

Bishop was a prisoner of the enemy for three years. He finally escaped by jumping from a moving train in North China while being transferred from Shanghai to Manchuria. He reached me in Kunming early in 1945 to write the final footnote to the A.V.G.'s first fight.

# THE FALL OF SINGAPORE: A CIVILIAN DIARY, 9–15 FEBRUARY 1942

## Dr OE Fisher, medical officer

*After inflicting a humiliating defeat on the British in the jungles of Malaya, the Japanese proceeded to Singapore – Britain's supposedly impregnable island naval base. Unfortunately, most of Singapore's 15 inch guns pointed seawards and the Japanese inconsiderately attacked from the landwards side. On 15 February the demoralized and ill-led British and Commonwealth forces on Singapore surrendered to the numerically inferior Imperial Japanese Army of General Yamashita. Well over a hundred thousand troops and civilians passed into captivity, many of them to die. Churchill called the surrender of Singapore "the worst disaster and largest capitulation in British history".*

### Wednesday February 4th
My birthday! Air raid 9 a.m. – went for docks again. Second air raid 11 a.m. – several sticks dropped fairly close to here. Few casualties admitted here. Caught out with one air raid casualty – house collapsed on him – no marks of external injury but abdomen swollen and tender – diagnosed intrapertoneal bleeding – cut open. Cirrhosis of liver with ascites.

Pahit party at Sister's Quarters in evening. After dinner Rupert Shelley got going with bawdy songs à la Residents' dinner.
    Cable from Father. Short alert during night.

### Thursday February 5th
Artillery fire throughout night and this morning. Went to town 10 a.m. First alert not till 10.30 a.m. Lasted 1¾ hours. Went for docks again.
    Met Black and Sola in town. Sola told me everyone in Brunei captured save Coghill and Cliffords who got away up Limbang river. Others interned in Belait Rest House. Sultan asked for Graham M. O. Brunei to remain but request refused. Our fighters very active in afternoon. Large fire out at sea. Did a few air raid casualties in evening. Governor visited hospital.
    3 alerts in early hours Friday morning.

### Friday February 6th
Two alerts in morning. One in afternoon.
    Terrific smoke pall from burning oil dump at Naval base. Artillery fire all day.
    Letter to Kitty. No alert during night.

### Saturday February 7th
Japs shell town. I hear whistle of shells for first time. Went down town

to collect pay. Met Joe Anderson and Kennedy. Hear that 300,000 cases whisky destroyed – deny our troops.

### Sunday February 8th
Two air alerts in morning. Went to Seaview hotel in morning with Rupert Shelley, Sisters Jones and Bullock. Operating in afternoon from 3.30 p.m. to 8 p.m. Terrific artillery fire all through night. Can see gun flashes all along north coast- both sides firing. Went up on roof to see it – saw coastal search light sweeping Johore Straits.

### Monday February 9th
Learnt that Japs had landed on north coast of island last night – fierce fighting taking place. Two air alerts in morning.

Received about 40 casualties – civilian and military – latter chiefly mortar wounds.

Went to Alexandra Military Hospital in evening to see Bingham.

### Tuesday February 10th
Japs effect further landings on north coast and occupy Tengah aerodrome. One alert in morning.

Go to town in afternoon with Rupert Shelley – town deserted. Shell fire and machine gun fire all night.

### Wednesday February 11th
Go to town in morning. Air of impending dissolution about the place. Numerous fires. Stick of bombs drop a waterspout in front of Cable & Wireless office whilst sending off cable to Kitty. Shells whistling past on way home to K. K. Innumerable air raids throughout day. Tanglin machine gunned. Farrar Park in front of hospital full of gun positions and troops digging in. All hospitals full save K. K.. Admit 60 casualties.

No sleep at night because of heavy guns close at hand.

### Thursday February 12th
### Friday February 13th
Working in theatre till midnight. Went to bed in flat as usual but awakened by the most terrific artillery barrage imaginable – 30 large guns in Farrar Park opposite. Later machine gun fire and rifle fire. Japs opened with field mortars. Got up 4 a.m. and visited Sisters Quarters to see everyone O. K.

### Saturday February 14th
Direct hits on Sisters Quarters and on end of front block of hospital by shells.

An orderly was cleaning an enamel plate when a piece of shrapnel went clean thro' plate making a circular hole in middle of plate – nobody hurt. Heavy fighting round reservoir.

**Sunday February 15th**
Hospital shelled and dive bombed from 2 p.m. till dusk – ghastly experience. 97 6 inch shells sent over. About 16 direct hits on hospital, 3 on nurses quarters and 2 on our flat. Had a hectic time putting patients under their beds with shells whizzing by. 12 people killed in hospital including Dr. Norris and Dr. Sinha. 60 cars burnt out in compound, fires burning furiously all round including huge fire at Singapore Traction Company's sheds opposite.

Singapore capitulated 7 p.m.. Slept the night in X ray dark room.

# BATAAN: DEATH IN A FOX-HOLE, MARCH 1942

## *William Camp, USMC*

*The main Japanese invasion of the Philippines – an American outpost in what Nippon sought to make its own corner of the Pacific – began on 22 December 1941. A fortnight later, American troops had been pushed back to the Bataan Peninsula on the west side of Manila Bay. Dogged resistance at Bataan continued until 8 April 1942 when the American garrison, starved, exhausted and diseased, capitulated.*

I lay there for about half an hour when Oakley grabbed his stomach and began groaning.

"Try what I did," I told him. "It'll make you feel better."

He crawled to the end of the hole and squatted there, grunting and groaning with pain. There are two kinds of dysentery in the Orient, one a mild form, which we called the "Yangtse rapids", and another which is more serious and requires a doctor's treatment.

"I've had the 'rapids' for a week," Oakley groaned. "Now this . . ."

He rolled over, writhing in pain.

"We gotta get him out of here," Witherspoon said to me. "He's got to go to hospital. He'll die if we don't get him out of here."

It was about ten o'clock in the morning, and the sun was high. We had been there since about ten o'clock the night before. Somewhere ahead of us were the Jap snipers. I was trying to decide which was worse, having him killed by the snipers or die of the awful cramps which were causing him to roll his eyes and froth at the mouth.

At last I decided it was worth a try. I stood up and started to climb out of the hole, so Witherspoon could help him up to me, and we could both drag him back. If we could cross that narrow strip of open space which lay between our fox-hole and the trees behind we would be safe.

From there on we could carry him back in a stretcher made of our shirts and a couple of saplings.

I had no sooner raised my head above the earth than a sudden burst of machine-gun fire splashed in the dust around me. I dropped back down, and Witherspoon shook his head.

"No use," he said. "We can't make it."

Oakley was clawing the earth now, and his finger-tips were bleeding. If I hadn't known what it was, I might have thought it was sunstroke or epilepsy. He was chewing his tongue, and the saliva which ran down his chin was pink with blood. His eyeballs were turned back in his head with only a little bit of the pupils showing.

"God! We've got to do something!" Witherspoon cried, his face ashen with fright. "We can't let him die like this!"

I dropped down and crawled over to where he lay. I took his head in my hands and tried to prise his jaws apart to release his tongue.

"Gimme something. Quick!" I said.

Witherspoon looked around, but there was nothing we could use to put in his mouth to prevent him eating his tongue.

"Here!" Witherspoon said, handing me a bayonet. "Try this."

"No! He'll kill himself with that. What if he falls on it or rolls over! It'll kill him."

But there was nothing else to do, so I pulled his jaws apart and Witherspoon placed the tip of the bayonet between his teeth. I released his jaws gently until his teeth touched the cold steel, and they began grinding against it. He was twitching convulsively, and with each breath his cries were becoming weaker and weaker until they were no more than a whisper. I held his head in my lap, while Witherspoon stroked his stomach, pressing down hard with downward strokes. Whatever it was inside him, it had to come out.

We did this for about an hour. The pain seemed to go away, and he stopped gritting his teeth against the tip of the bayonet.

"He's coming along all right now," I said. "He'll be over it in a minute."

"God! What is this?" Witherspoon exclaimed, looking at the back of his trousers. "It's blood!"

I put his head down and crawled towards his feet. His trousers were soaked with blood, and it was running down, seeping into the ground. I ripped off his trousers to his knees. They were soaked with it. There was an odour like rotted flesh, the same odour which hovered over Bataan day and night from the thousands of dead which lay in the sun.

"Haemorrhages," I said. "He's bleeding from behind."

"He'll bleed to death."

We rolled him over on his stomach and parted his legs. I placed my hand over him to try to stop the blood, but it came through my fingers. I tried stopping him up with the slimy dirt, but it was useless. The blood forced the mud poultice away.

He died a few minutes later without opening his eyes again. Since we couldn't move out of the hole we dug the sides in until his body was covered with the fresh earth.

## DEATH MARCH ON BATAAN: THE FIRST DAY, 10 APRIL 1942

### Lieutenant Colonel William Dyess, 21st Pursuit Squadron, USAAF

*Despite the condition of the surrendered US troops at Bataan, their captors – led by General Homma – made them march 65 miles north to Camp O'Donnell. About 40,000 Americans and Filipinos died in the infamous "Death March on Bataan" and in the first two months of imprisonment at O'Donnell. It was one of the worst Japanese atrocities of World War II.*

Ordinarily, the trip from Mariveles to Cabcaben field is a beautiful one with the grandeur of high greenclad mountains on the north and a view of the sea on the right. The white of the road contrasts pleasantly with the deep green of the tropical growth on either side.

But on this day there was no beauty. Coming toward us were seemingly interminable columns of Jap infantry, truck trains, and horse-drawn artillery, all moving into Bataan for a concentrated assault on Corregidor. They stirred up clouds of blinding dust in which all shape and form were lost.

Every few yards Jap noncoms materialized like gargoyles from the grayish white pall and snatched Americans out of line to be searched and beaten. Before we had gone two miles we had been stripped of practically all our personal possessions.

The Japs made no move to feed us. Few of us had had anything to eat since the morning of April 9. Many had tasted no food in four days. We had a little tepid water in our canteens, but nothing else.

The ditches on either side of the road were filled with overturned and wrecked American army trucks, fire-gutted tanks, and artillery our forces had rendered unusable. At intervals we saw mounds of captured food, bearing familiar trademarks. These had fallen almost undamaged into Jap hands.

As we marched along I rounded up the 110 officers and men of the 21st Pursuit. I didn't know yet what the score was, but I felt we would be in a better position to help one another and keep up morale if we were together.

We hadn't walked far when the rumor factory opened up. In a few minutes it was in mass production. There were all kinds of reports: We were going to Manila and Old Bilibid prison. We were going to San Fernando and entrain for a distant concentration camp. Trucks were waiting just ahead to pick us up. We doubted the last rumor, but hoped it was true.

The sun was nearing the zenith now. The penetrating heat seemed to search out and dissipate the small stores of strength remaining within us. The road, which until this moment had been fairly level, rose sharply in a zigzag grade. We were nearing Little Baguio.

I was marching with head down and eyes squinted for the dual purpose of protecting myself as much as possible from the dust and glare and keeping watch on the Jap guards who walked beside and among us. Halfway up the hill we reached a level stretch where a Japanese senior officer and his staff were seated at a camp table upon which were spread maps and dispatches.

As I came abreast he saw me and shouted something that sounded like, "Yoy!" He extended his hand, palm downward, and opened and closed the fingers rapidly. This meant I was to approach him. I pretended I didn't see him. He shouted again as I kept on walking. His third "Yoy!" vibrated with anger. The next I knew a soldier snatched me out of line and shoved me toward the table.

"Name!" shouted the officer. He was staring at the wings and my uniform. "You fly?"

I told him my name without mentioning my rank and said I had been a pilot.

"Where you planes?"

"All shot down." I made a downward, spinning motion with my hand.

"No at Cebu? No at Mindanao?"

"No Cebu. No Mindanao."

"Yaah. Lie! We know you got planes. We see. Sometimes one . . . two . . . sometimes three, four, five. Where you airfields?"

I shook my head again and made the spinning motion with my hand. But I located the airfields for him on his map. I pointed to Cabcaben, Bataan, and Mariveles. He knew about these, of course. He made an impatient gesture.

"One more. Secret field!"

"Nope. No secret field."

"True?"

"Yes. True."

"Where are tunnel? Where are underwater tunnel from Mariveles to Corregidor? Where are tunnels on Corregidor Rock?" He held the map toward me.

"I don't know of any tunnels. No tunnels; no place. I never was on Corregidor. I was only at Nichols field and Bataan."

"You flying officer and you never at Corregidor Rock!" His eyes were slits. His staff officers were angry, too. "LIE!" he shrieked and jumped up.

He was powerfully built, as are most Jap officers. He seized my shoulder and whirled me around with a quick twist that almost dislocated my arm. Then came a violent shove that sent me staggering toward the line. I expected a bullet to follow the push, but I didn't dare look back. This would have been inviting them to shoot. As I reached the marching line, the officer shouted something else. The guards shoved me and motioned that I should catch up with my group.

I wanted to be with them, but the double quick up the hill in the scalding heat and dust almost finished me. I had the thought, too, that the guards I passed might get the idea I was trying to escape. My bullet expectancy was so high it made my backside tingle from scalp to heels. I caught up as we were passing through Little Baguio. In a short time we were abreast the blackened ruins of Hospital No. 1, which had been bombed heavily a couple of days before.

Among the charred debris, sick and wounded American soldiers were walking dazedly about. There was no place for them to go.

Their only clothes were hospital pajama suits and kimonos. Here and there a man was stumping about on one leg and a crutch. Some had lost one or both arms. All were in need of fresh dressings. And all obviously were suffering from the shock of the bombing.

They looked wonderingly at the column of prisoners. When the Jap officers saw them, these shattered Americans were rounded up and shoved into the marching line. All of them tried to walk, but only a few were able to keep it up. Those who fell were kicked aside by the Japs.

The Japs forbade us to help these men. Those who tried it were kicked, slugged, or jabbed with bayonet points by the guards who stalked with us in twos and threes.

For more than a mile these bomb-shocked cripples stumbled along with us. Their shoulders were bent and the sweat streamed from their faces. I can never forget the hopelessness in their eyes.

Eventually their strength ebbed and they began falling back through the marching ranks. I don't know what became of them.

About a mile east of the hospital we encountered a major traffic jam. On either side of the congested road hundreds of Jap soldiers were unloading ammunition and equipment.

Our contingent of more than 600 American and Filipino prisoners filtered through, giving the Japs as wide a berth as the limited space permitted. This was to avoid being searched, slugged, or pressed into duty as cargadores [burden carriers].

Through the swirling dust we could see a long line of trucks, standing bumper to bumper. There were hundreds of them. And every last one was an American make. I saw Fords–which predominated–Chevrolets, GMCs, and others.

These were not captured trucks. They bore Jap army insignia and had been landed from the ships of the invasion fleet. It is hard to describe what we felt at seeing these familiar American machines, filled with jeering, snarling Japs. It was a sort of super-sinking feeling. We had become accustomed to having American iron thrown at us by the Japs, but this was a little too much.

Eventually the road became so crowded we were marched into a clearing. Here, for two hours, we had our first taste of the oriental sun treatment, which drains the stamina and weakens the spirit.

The Japs seated us on the scorching ground, exposed to the full glare of the sun. Many of the Americans and Filipinos had no covering to protect their heads. I was beside a small bush, but it cast no shade because the sun was almost directly above us. Many of the men around me were ill.

When I thought I could stand the penetrating heat no longer, I was determined to have a sip of the tepid water in my canteen. I had no more than unscrewed the top when the aluminum flask was snatched from my hands. The Jap who had crept up behind me poured the water into a horse's nosebag, then threw down the canteen. He walked on among the prisoners, taking away their water and pouring it into the bag. When he had enough he gave it to his horse.

Whether by accident or design we had been put just across the road from a pile of canned and boxed food. We were famished, but it seemed worse than useless to ask the Japs for anything. An elderly American colonel did, however. He crossed the road and after pointing to the food and to the drooping prisoners, he went through the motions of eating.

A squat Jap officer grinned at him and picked up a can of salmon. Then he smashed it against the colonel's head, opening the American's cheek from eye to jawbone. The officer staggered and turned back toward us, wiping the blood off.

It seemed as though the Japs had been waiting for just such a brutal display to end the scene. They ordered us to our feet and herded us back into the road.

We knew now the Japs would respect neither age nor rank. Their ferocity grew as we marched on into the afternoon. They no longer were content with mauling stragglers or pricking them with bayonet points. The thrusts were intended to kill.

We had marched about a mile after the sun treatment when I stumbled over a man writhing in the hot dust of the road. He was a Filipino soldier who had been bayoneted through the stomach. Within a quarter of a mile I walked past another. This soldier prisoner had been rolled into the path of the trucks and crushed beneath the heavy wheels.

The huddled and smashed figures beside the road eventually became commonplace to us. The human mind has an amazing faculty of adjusting itself to shock. In this case it may have been that heat and misery had numbed our senses. We remained keenly aware, however, that these murders might well be precursors of our own, if we should falter or lag.

As we straggled past Hospital No. 2 the Japs were setting up artillery and training it on Corregidor. The thick jungle hid the hospital itself, but we could see that guns were all around it. The Japs regarded this as master strategy; the Rock would not dare return their fire. I wondered what the concussion of the heavy guns would do to the stricken men in the hospital wards. The cannonade began after we had passed by.

A few minutes later a violent blow on the head almost sent me to my knees. I thought one of the Jap guns had made a direct hit on me. My steel helmet jammed down over my eyes with a clang that made my ears ring. I pulled it clear and staggered around to see a non-commissioned Jap brandishing a club the size of a child's baseball bat. He was squealing and pointing to the dented helmet. He lifted the club again. I threw the helmet into the ditch and he motioned me to march on. Like many of my comrades, I now was without protection against the merciless sun.

Jap artillery was opening up all along the southern tip of Bataan. The area behind us re-echoed to the thud and crash of heavy gunfire. Grayish smoke puffs speckled Corregidor's sides. The Rock was blasting back at the Japs, but most of its shells were falling in the Mariveles region whence we had come.

At sundown we crossed Cabcaben airfield, from which our planes had taken off not thirty-nine hours before. Here again Jap artillery was going into action. We were marched across the field and halted inside a rice paddy beyond. We had had no food or water, and none was offered, but we were grateful of the opportunity to lie down on the earth and rest. The guards kept to the edges of the paddy, leaving us plenty of room.

I was just dropping off when there came an outburst of yelling and screeching. The Japs had charged in among us and were kicking us to our feet. They herded us back to the road and started marching us eastward again. During the brief respite leg muscles had stiffened. Walking was torture.

It was dark when we marched across Bataan field, which with Cabcaben field I had commanded two days before. It was difficult walking in the darkness. Now and again we passed the huddled forms of men who had collapsed from fatigue or had been bayoneted. I didn't kid myself that I was safe simply because I was keeping up the pace. I would not have been surprised at any time to feel a Jap blade slide between my ribs. The bloodthirsty devils now were killing us for diversion.

The march continued until about 10 p.m. When we were halted some naïve individual started a rumor that we were to be given water. Instead we were about-faced and marched back to the westward. For two more hours we stumbled over the ground we had just covered.

It was midnight when we recrossed Bataan field and kept going. We were within a short distance of Cabcaben field when the Japs diverted the line into a tiny rice paddy. There was no room to lie down. Some of us tried to rest in a half squat. Others drew up their knees and laid their heads on the legs of the men next to them. Jap guards stood around the edges of the little field, their feet almost touching the outer fringe of men.

I heard a cry, followed by thudding blows at one side of the paddy. An American soldier so tortured by the thirst that he could not sleep had asked a Jap guard for water. The Jap fell on him with his fists, then slugged him into insensibility with a rifle butt.

The thirst of all had become almost unbearable, but remembering what had happened to the colonel earlier in the day we asked for nothing. A Jap officer walked along just after the thirsty soldier had been beaten. He appeared surprised that we wanted water. However, he permitted several Americans to collect canteens from their comrades and fill them at a stagnant carabao wallow which had been additionally befouled by seeping sea water. We held our noses to shut out the nauseating reek, but we drank all the water we could get.

## BURMA: THE BATTLE OF THE OILFIELDS, 18 APRIL 1942

### General W. J. Slim, 1st Burma Division

*After the Japanese captured Rangoon in early March 1942, the British in Burma (aided by Chinese troops under the command of the American general, "Vinegar Joe" Stilwell) beat a 900 mile retreat into India. A series of rearguard actions, such as the battle of the oilfields, at least allowed the extrication of the majority of Allied soldiery.*

The temperature that day was 114 degrees; the battlefield was the arid hideous, blackened shale of the oilfield; littered with wrecked derricks, flames roaring from the tanks, and shattered machinery and burning buildings everywhere. Over it all hung that huge pall of smoke. And there was no water.

At 6.30 in the morning, the Burma Division attacked. Progress was made, under cover of artillery, but the guns were running short of shells. Then some Burman troops faltered. In spite of this a by-pass road was cleared and a good deal of transport got down almost to the Pin Chaung itself, only to be held up by Japanese on the south bank. The British and Indian troops of the division fought doggedly over low ridge after ridge, the Japanese defending each one to the last man. A detachment of the Inniskillings struggled through to the Pin Chaung and enthusiastically greeted the troops it found there, believing them to be Chinese. They were Japanese who lured the Irishmen into an ambush. The tanks made a last attack on the road-block, but it was defended by several anti-tank guns, and the tanks bogged in the soft sand, became sitting targets. The attack, like that of the Chinese from the other side, petered to a standstill.

More Japanese were coming in from the east and were reported on the river. The situation was grave. At half-past four in the afternoon, Scott reported on the radio that his men were exhausted from want of water and continuous marching and fighting. He could hold that night, he thought, but if he waited until morning his men, still without water, would be so weakened they would have little or no offensive power to renew the attack. He asked permission to destroy his guns and transport and fight his way out that night. Scott was the last man to paint an unduly dark picture. I knew his men were almost at the end of their strength and in a desperate position. I could not help wishing that he had not been so close a friend. I thought of his wife and of his boys. There were lots of other wives, too, in England, India, and Burma whose hearts would be under that black cloud a couple of miles away. Stupid to remember that now! Better get it out of my head.

I thought for a moment, sitting there with the headphones on, in the van with the operator crouching beside me, his eyes anxiously on my face. Then I told Scott he must hand on. I had ordered a Chinese attack again with all available tanks and artillery for the next morning. If Burma Division attacked then we ought to break through and save our precious guns and transport. I was afraid too, that if our men came out in driblets as they would in the dark, mixed up with Japanese, the Chinese and indeed our own soldiers would fail to recognize them and their losses would be heavy. Scott took it as I knew he would. He said, "All right, we'll hang on and we'll do our best in the morning, but, for God's sake, Bill, make those Chinese attack."

I stepped out of the van feeling about as depressed as a man could. There, standing in a little half-circle waiting for me, were a couple of my own staff, an officer or two from the Tank Brigade, Sun, and the Chinese liaison officers. They stood there silent and looked at me. All commanders know that look. They see it in the eyes of their staffs and their men when things are really bad, when even the most confident staff officer and the toughest soldier want holding up, and they turn where they *should* turn for support – to their commander. And sometimes he does not know what to say. He feels very much alone.

"Well, gentlemen," I said, putting on what I hoped was a confident, cheerful expression, "it might be worse!"

One of the group, in a sepulchral voice, replied with a single word: "How?"

I could cheerfully have murdered him, but instead I had to keep my temper.

"Oh," I said, grinning, "it might be raining!"

Two hours later, it was – hard. As I crept under a truck for shelter I thought of that fellow and wished I *had* murdered him.

Throughout the might, as we sat inside a circle of laagered tanks just above the Pin Chaung we could hear and see the crump and flash of Japanese shells and mortar bombs flailing Scott's wretched men. His guns did not reply. They were down to about twenty rounds per gun now, and he was keeping those for the morning. Time and again the Japanese put in infantry attacks, attempting to infiltrate under cover of darkness and shelling. These attacks, one after the other, were beaten off, but certain of the Burma troops panicked and abandoned their positions, throwing extra strain on the British and Indians.

The day began for me before dawn with a severe blow. The Chinese attack across the Pin Chaung to take Twingon, a village about a mile south of the ford, which I had hoped would start soon after daylight could not be got ready in time. After a good deal of talk it was promised for twelve-thirty as the earliest possible hour. I was then faced with the problem of either telling Scott to hold his attack, which was due to go in at seven o'clock, or to let it go as arranged. I decided to let it go, rather than keep his men and transport sitting cramped and waterless under artillery, mortar, and air attack.

At seven o'clock the Burma Division resumed the attack, but a reinforced Japanese defence held it after it had made some progress. Meanwhile, on the north bank, while still urging the Chinese to hurry their preparations, we had managed to scrape up a small British force which attacked and, during the morning, actually got a squadron of tanks and some of the West Yorkshire Regiment across the Chaung.

This small success might have been expanded had not one of those infuriating mishaps so common in battle occurred. An officer some distance in rear, received a report that strong enemy forces were advancing to cut off the transport assembled about Gwegyo. Without realizing the situation forward, and still less that the threatening forces advancing on him were not Japanese but Chinese, he ordered back the tanks and accompanying infantry to deal with this new but imaginary danger.

Burma Division was once more halted in a tight perimeter and was being heavily shelled. The heat was intense, there was still no water, the troops were exhausted and they had suffered heavy casualties, their wounded of course, being still with them. At this stage the Burma battalions, in spite of the efforts of their officers, really disintegrated. 1 Burma Brigade reported that the bulk of their troops were no longer reliable; even 13 Brigade said that some of theirs were shaky. It was hardly to be wondered at; their ordeal had been terribly severe.

The Chinese attack, promised for 1230 hours, had now been postponed to 1400 hours. Just before that time it was again put back to 1600 hours. We managed, however, to get it off at 1500 hours instead. These delays were of course maddening, but I had not then learned that time means little to the average Chinaman. Actually, with their lack of signal equipment, of means of evacuating wounded and of replenishing ammunition, and their paucity of trained junior leaders, it was not surprising that to sort themselves out, reform, and start a fresh attack took time. The trouble was not with Sun, who was all energy and desire to attack, but with so many of his subordinates, who promised but did not perform, and in the delays and errors that occurred in getting his orders to them. One of their troubles, and a real one, was water. They could not attack until water had been replenished, and they had no means of fetching it up except a few petrol tins slung in pairs on a bamboo and carried, willow pattern plate fashion, across a man's shoulder. We got one of our few remaining water lorries and ran it up nearly to their front line, with orders to make continuous trips backwards and forwards. It went the first time and did not return. Eventually the British driver appeared on foot. He said, with soldierly embellishments, that having emptied the tank of water, the Chinese, in spite of his protests, emptied the radiator also, and, when he left to get help, were trying to empty the petrol tank as well! Sun dealt with that incident; we got the water lorry back and it ran regularly. Even so, when I was at one of the forward Chinese headquarters, a large and very fat Chinese officer protested volubly that it was impossible to attack as none of his men had water. He was deeply moved about it. I noticed that all the time he was so passionately describing the sufferings of his men he had a very large water bottle hanging from his belt, and that even at his most gesticulatory moments it lay snug against his ample posterior. I walked quietly up to him, lifted it, and shook it. It was full to the cork. There was a pause in his flow of language, and a moment's hush among the spectators. Then all shouted with laughter – in which the fat officer joined! Without more ado he agreed they could attack by 1500 hours, and they did.

Unhappily, before that time communication with Scott had ceased and his last desperate effort to break out could not be co-ordinated with the Chinese attack. His squadron of tanks had found and cleared a rough track, leading east, down to the Pin Chaung, over which it was hoped vehicles could move. Scott himself formed up the column, guns in front, wounded in ambulances and trucks next, followed by such vehicles as had survived the bombardment. With a spearhead of tanks and infantry the column lurched down the narrow, uneven path, through the low hillocks. But the trail turned to sand; the leading ambulances were bogged and the column stopped. As many wounded as possible were piled on the tanks, and Scott gave the order to abandon vehicles and fight a way out on foot across the Pin Chaung. This his men did, some in formed bodies, some in small groups, and on the other side they met the Chinese. At the sight of the water in the Chaung the mules which had come out with them went mad, and the men flung themselves face downwards into it. The haggard, red-eyed British, Indian, and Burmese soldiers who staggered up the bank were a terrible sight, but every man I saw, was still carrying his rifle. The two brigades of the division had reached Yenangyaung at a strength of not more than one; there they had lost in killed and wounded twenty per cent of that small number, with a considerable portion of their guns, mortars, and vehicles. None of these losses, either in men or equipment could be replaced. After its ordeal the division would be of no fighting value until it had rested, and, as best it could, reorganized. We collected it that night about Gwegyo.

When the Chinese did attack they went in splendidly. They were thrilled at the tank and artillery support they were getting and showed real dash. They took Twingon, rescuing some two hundred of our prisoners and wounded. Next day, the 20th April, the 38th Division attacked again and with tanks penetrated into Yenangyaung itself, repulsing a Japanese counter-attack. The fighting was severe and the Chinese acquitted themselves well, inflicting heavy losses, vouched for by our own officers. Sun now expected a really heavy Japanese attack at dawn on the 21st. I discussed this with him and agreed that he should come out of the town, back to the Pin Chaung. His division had done well and I did not want it frittered away in a house-to-house dog fight for the shell of Yenangyaung. In spite of the stories I had heard from American sources of Chinese unwillingness to fight. I had remembered how enthusiastic officers, who had served with our own Chinese Hongkong regiment, had been about their men, and I had expected the Chinese soldier to be tough and brave. I was, I confess, surprised at how he had responded to the stimulus of proper tank and artillery support, and at the aggressive spirit he had shown. I had never expected, either, to get a Chinese general of the calibre of Sun.

As I talked this over with Davies, my Chief of Staff and my mainstay, in these difficult times, we thought we saw a chance of striking back at the 33rd Japanese division. True, our 1st Burma Division, never really a division in either establishment or equipment, was at the moment incapable of action, but it was definitely recovering in the peace of Mount Popa, where we had sent it. In a week or two we might hope to have it back in the field at a strength, of say, a brigade. If we could get the 17th Division, still in Taungdwingyi, we might, with the Chinese 38th Division and anything else we could scrape up, try a counter-stroke. We were always building up our house of cards. Davies and I, and seeing it fall down – but we went on. So we renewed our attempts to persuade Burma Army to let us take the 17th Division from Taungdwingyi. Meanwhile the 38th Division and, as usual, 7 Armoured Brigade covered the 1st Burma Division as it lay gasping but not dying.

A number of our badly wounded had of necessity been left in the ambulances when the Burma Division had finally broken out. A young gunner officer volunteered to go back to discover their fate. Under cover of darkness he did so. The ambulances were still standing on the track, but every man in them had had his throat cut or been bayoneted to death.

## RAID ON TOKYO, 18 APRIL 1942

### *Colonel James Doolittle, USAAF*

*The bombing of Tokyo was an act of American defiance in the face of relentless Japanese advance in the Pacific. It was also a feat of airmanship, since it involved flying B-25 bombers off an aircraft carrier (the USS* Hornet*), something widely considered to be impossible, The raid was led by Colonel Doolittle, whose personal report is below.*

Took off at 8:18 AM ship time.

Take-off was easy. Night take-off would have been possible and practicable.

Circled carrier to get exact heading and check compass. Wind was from 300° plus-minus.

About a half hour later joined by AC 40–2292, Lt. Hoover, pilot, the second plane to take off.

About an hour out passed a Japanese camouflaged naval surface vessel of about 6,000 tons. Took it to be a light cruiser.

About two hours out passed a multi-motored land plane headed directly for our flotilla and flying at about 3,000 ft.–2 miles away – multi-motored bomber-gunner.

Passed and endeavored to avoid various civil and naval craft until land fall was made north of Grubo Shama(?).

Was somewhat north of desired course but decided to take advantage of error and approach from a northerly direction, thus avoiding anticipated strong opposition to the west.

Many flying fields and the air full of planes north of Tokyo. Mostly small biplanes apparently primary or basic trainers.

Encountered nine fighters in three flights of three. This was about ten miles north of the outskirts of Tokyo proper.

All this time had been flying as low as the terrain would permit.

Continued low flying due south over the outskirts of and toward the east center of Tokyo.

Pulled up to 1,200 ft., changed course to the southwest and incendiary-bombed highly inflammable section. Dropped first bomb at 1:30.

Anti-aircraft very active but only one near hit.

Lowered away to housetops and slid over western outskirts into low haze and smoke.

Turned south and out to sea.

Fewer airports on west side but many army posts.

Passed over small aircraft factory with a dozen or more newly completed planes on the line. No bombs left. Decided not to machine gun for reasons of personal security.

Had seen five barrage balloons over east central Tokyo and more in distance.

Passed on out to sea flying low.

Was soon joined again by Hoover who followed us to the Chinese coast.

Navigator plotted perfect course to pass north of Yoki Shima.

Saw three large naval vessels just before passing west end of Japan. One was flatter than the others and may have been a converted carrier.

Passed innumerable fishing and small patrol boats.

Made land fall somewhat north of course on China coast.

Tried to reach Chuchow on 4495 but couldn't raise.

It had been clear over Tokyo but became overcast before reaching Yoki Shima.

Ceiling lowered on coast until low islands and hills were in it. Just getting dark and couldn't live under overcast so pulled up to 6,000 and then 8,000 ft. in it. On instruments from then on though occasionally saw dim lights on ground through almost solid overcast. These lights seemed more often on our right and pulled us still farther off course.

Directed rear gunner to go aft and secure films from camera (unfortunately they were jerked out of his shirt front where he had put them, when his chute opened).

Decided to abandon ship. Sgt. Braemer, Lt. Potter, Sgt. Leonard and Lt. Cole in order. Left ship on A.F.C.E., shut off both gas cocks and I left. *Should have put flaps down.* This would have slowed down landing speed, reduced impact and shortened glide.

All hands collected and ship located by late afternoon of 19th.

Requested General Ho Yang Ling, Director of the Branch Government of Western Chekiang Province to have a lookout kept along the seacoast from Hang Chow bay to Wen Chow bay and also have all sampans and junks along the coast keep a lookout for planes that went down at sea, or just reached shore.

Early morning of 20th four planes and crews, in addition to ours, had been located and I wired General Arnold, through the Embassy at Chungking, "Tokyo successfully bombed. Due bad weather on China Coast believe all airplanes wrecked. Five crews found safe in China so far."

Wired again on the 27th giving more details.

Discussed possibility of purchasing three prisoners on the sea-coast from Puppet Government and endeavoring to take out the three in the lake area by force. Believe this desire was made clear to General Ku Cho-tung (who spoke little English) and know it was made clear to English-speaking members of his staff. This was at Shangjao. They agreed to try purchase of three but recommended against force due to large Japanese concentration.

Left airplane about 9:20 (ship time) after about 13 hours in the air. Still had enough gas for half hour flight but right front tank was showing empty. Had transferred once as right engine used more fuel. Had covered about 2,250 miles. Mostly at low speed, cruising but about an hour at moderate high speed which more than doubled the consumption for this time.

Bad luck:

(1) Early take-off due to naval contact with surface and air craft.

(2) Clear over Tokyo.
(3) Foul over China.
Good luck:
(1) A 25 m/h tail wind over most of the last 1,200 miles.

Take-off should have been made three hours before daylight, but we didn't know how easy it would be and the Navy didn't want to light up.

Dawn take-off, closer in, would have been better as things turned out. However, due to the bad weather it is questionable if even daylight landing could have been made at Chuchow without radio aid.

Still feel that original plan of having one plane take off three hours before dusk and others just at dusk was best all-round plan for average conditions.

Other ideas and impressions were discussed personally with Col. Cooper.

Should have kept accurate chronological record.

Should have all crew members instructed in *exact* method of leaving ship under various conditions.

JAMES H. DOOLITTLE
Airplane AC 40–2344–B-25-B

# BOOT CAMP: THE MAKING OF A MARINE, VIRGINIA, USA, 1942

*William Manchester, USMC*

Astonishingly, I adored Parris Island. Boot camp is a profound shock to most recruits because the Corps begins its job of building men by destroying the identity they brought with them. Their heads are shaved. They are assigned numbers. The DI is their god. He treats them with utter contempt. I am told that corporal punishment has since been banned on the island, but in my day it was quite common to see a DI bloody a man's nose, and some boots were gravely injured, though I know of none who actually died. I recall being baffled later when Patton was reprimanded for slapping a GI. All of us had endured much more than that. The gentlest punishments were those for dropping a rifle (sleeping on eight of them) and for eating candy (carrying an oozing mass of chocolate for two days). If the boot called it "candy" he would have been punished further, the proper expression being *pogey bait*. The Corps had its own language, and boots were required to learn it, just as the inhabitants of an occupied country must learn the conqueror's tongue. A bar was a *slopchute*, a latrine a *head*; swamps were *boondocks*, and field boots, *boondockers*. A rumor was *scuttlebutt*, because that was the name for water fountains, where rumors were spread; a deception was a *snow job*, gossiping was *shooting the breeze*, information was *dope*, news was *the scoop*, confirmed information was *the word*. You said "Aye, aye, sir," not "Yes, sir." The nape of the neck was the *stacking swivel*, after a rifle part. An officer promoted from the ranks was a *mustang*. Your company commander was *the skipper*. You never went on leave; you were *granted liberty*, usually in the form of a *forty-eight* or a *seventy-two*, depending on the number of hours you could be absent. If you didn't return by then, you were *over the hill*. Coffee was *Joe*; a coffeepot, *a Joe-pot*. Battle dress was *dungarees*. A cleanup of barracks, no matter how long it lasted, was a *field day*; a necktie was a *field scarf*, drummers and trumpeters were *field musics*. Duffle bags, though indistinguishable from those used by GIs, were *seabags*. To be *under hack* meant to be under arrest. To straighten up was to *square away*; a tough fighter was a *hard-charger*; underwear was *skivvies*; manipulating people was called *working one's bolt*. *Lad* was a generic term of address for any subordinate, regardless of age. One of my people, a twenty-eight-year-old Vermont school principal, was known, because of his advanced age, as "Pop." An officer five years his junior would summon him by snapping, "Over here, lad."

Some of these terms have crept into the language since World War II, but no one outside the service knew them then. Boots had to pick them up fast. They were courting trouble if they described their combat hardware as anything but 782 *gear*, that being the number of the form you had to sign as a receipt. It was equally unwise to call a deck a "floor," a bulkhead a "wall," an overhead a "ceiling," a hatch a "door," or a ladder "stairs." Every Marine was "Mac" to every other Marine; every U.S. soldier was a "doggie" and was barked at. The Corps' patois was astonishingly varied. To "sight in" or "zero" was to determine, by trial and error, the sight setting necessary to hit a bull's-eye with a given weapon. "Snap in" could mean sighting and aiming an unloaded rifle; it could also mean breaking into, or trying out for, a new job, somewhat like the army's "bucking for." As a noun, "secure" described an outdated movement in the manual of arms; as a verb, it signified anchoring something in place or ending an activity – thus, when the Battle of Tarawa was won, the island was "secure." "Survey" was even more flexible. It could mean, not only a medical discharge from the Corps (anyone feigning combat fatigue was "snapping in for a survey"), but also retirement from the Corps, disposing of worn-out clothing or equipment, or taking a second helping of chow. There was even a word for anything which defied description. It was "gizmo."

On Parris Island these and all other customs of the boot's new way of life were flouted at great risk. You were told that there were three ways of doing things: the right way, the wrong way, and the Marine Corps way. The Corps way was uncompromising. Failure to salute your superiors – including private first class – brought swift retribution. The worst discipline I saw came during floodlit midnight calisthentics. In one common exercise we paired off; each boot hoisted his rifle as you would hoist a battering ram and placed the butt against his buddy's forehead. The buddy would touch the butt and duck. The man with the rifle was supposed to try to strike his forehead before the other man could drop, but since you knew you were going to reverse roles, the sensible course was to let him get out of the way. Enter the vengeful noncom. *He* put a rifle butt against the offender's forehead and slugged him before there was time to dodge. The boot who merely suffered a concussion was lucky.

How could I enjoy this? Parts of it, of course, I loathed. But the basic concept fascinated me. I wanted to surrender my individuality, curbing my neck beneath the yoke of petty tyranny. Since my father's death I had yearned for stern discipline, and Parris Island, where he himself had learned discipline a quarter-century earlier, gave it to me in spades. Physically I was delicate, even fragile, but I had limitless reservoirs of energy, and I could feel myself toughening almost hourly. Everything I saw seemed exquisitely defined – every leaf, every pebble looked as sharp as a drawing in a book. I knew I was merely becoming a tiny cog in the vast machine which would confront fascism, but that was precisely why I had volunteered. Even today, despite the horrors which inevitably followed, I am haunted by memories of my weeks as a recruit. It is almost like recalling a broken marriage which, for one divorced partner, can never really end.

## TALES OF THE SOUTH PACIFIC: A GI WRITES HOME, MARCH 1942–JANUARY 1943

### Sergeant B. J. Kazazkow, US Army

*March 21, 1942*

Dear Mom:

We just enjoyed a very mild hurricane – the only damage done being the countryside made ideal for the growth of hordes of mosquitoes. I hate them so that when I manage to get one alive. I torture and maim him – then bury him alive. The war has made me hard and cruel!

Now for the local news – the sun beats down – as usual – and when it gets hot enough – a nice cool shower comes along. Between the incessant combination everything I own, either rusts, or turns greenmoldy. Constant cleaning of equipment is, therefore, in order.

*Sept. 22, 1942*

Dear Mom:

Today a big vicious sea bass, mouth agape, sped like a bullet upon his prey, a small mallett. As he sped into range, I held my breath, squeezed, and then let fly. Stunned, he turned to go – and crash! I let him have another charge – and lo and behold we had fish steak – baked, garnished, and savory, for dinner. I tell you, this place is a fisherman's paradise. So what? It isn't the first fish dinner we blasted out of the sea, but never before a sea bass, the size and taste of that one.

Some days ago I spent a solid day up in the nearby hills, trying to chase a deer or two – being anxious for a taste of venison again. All day, mind you, and got not a scent. Yesterday morning, with breakfast on the fire, two of the elusive creatures popped up in a nearby pasture – grazing to their hearts content – so-o we sneaked up on them, and fell upon them, blazing away, and got not a hit – they led us a merry chase, finally we lost them, and went back to our French toast, cereal and coffee. No vension. Deah, Deah!

Sounds more like a rich man's holiday than a war – no? Feeling top-hole, hope you are too.

Love and kisses,
Benny

*Jan. 8, 1943*

Dear Mom:

So its come – 1943, imagine being overseas for nearly a whole year – or at least it will be on January 23rd. On that day last winter we left New York – for parts unknown. We could have ended up in a much worse place, believe me. And time has flown, more rapidly than I ever thought possible, it seems like several weeks, instead of twelve months, since we landed.

And we landed looking for trouble, and we're still looking – and I don't think we'll ever find any here.

The past few nights I haven't been sleeping well, and I keep having dreams about you and home, and it's no good for my morale. I get very homesick, poor boy that I am.

. . . I suppose I'll visit you again, in my dreams tonight, and you

might leave some milk and cake on the table for me
   Goodnight . . .

Your loving son,
Benny

## HOME FRONT: "JIM CROW" IN THE ARMY

### *Private Milton Adams, 240 Quarter Master's Battalion*

*Adams writes to Warren Hastie, the US Government's adviser on "Colored Affairs".*

*Pvt. Milton Adams*
*Post Stockade*
*Camp Livingston, La.*
*May 13, 1942*

Dear Mr. W. H. Hastie:

I am private Milton Adams of Co. B. 240th Q. M. Bn of
Camp Livingston, La. I inlisted in the army Oct 17, 1942, in
Chicago, Ill. And since I been in the Army, I never had any
Trouble in the Army in or out of it in my life, until I came to
Camp Livingston. I am asking for the help of the N.A.A.C.P.
And the Crisis. I am not writing anything against the United
States Army. But I am going to tell you what the White officers
are doing to us races Soldiers down her in camp Livingston, La.
Since they can't very well hang us, they take the next steps,
which is court martial, and that is better know as rail-roading.
Now you don't stand a chance, before them. They are just like a
lynch mob with a neggro to hang. Well they do not want you
down hear in the Army, and I did not ask to come down hear I
was sent down hear. Well my trouble starter when they found
out that I was from Chicago, and I have had a bad deal every
since I been hear, I have tried to get away from hear, But it was
the same old story. When we finde some places for you to go, we
will let you go. Well my Commanding Officer did not like me
because, I ask him not to use the word niggers, and he saide I
was one of those smart nigger from up north. I was tried once for
a offince, and given 30 days and a $12.00 fine. Now after I had
finish my sentences, they saide they are going to try me over
again. I wish you would look into my case. I thought they could
not try any person a second time for the same offince. I really
taken all the punishment I can take I could not get a three day
pass or a furlo since I been in the army, until my mother pass
away in April. They have just about rob me out of very pay day,
for things I have never had. There are so many more case like

this, a unfair chance. I don't know what to do now. I don't want
do the wrong thing, so I am asking for help. But I am not going
to take any more of these unfair trials, because I did three
months in the stockade once for something I did not have any
thing to do with. It was because I was from Chicago, and thats
way every trial I ever had is base on the fact that I come from
Chicago. So I whish you look into this case, because I can prove
everything I am telling you. I will look forward to a answer from
you in few days.

> Respectfully yours,
> Pvt. Milton Adams
> Post Stockade
> Camp Livingston, La.

## BATTLE OF MIDWAY: ONE MAN'S DIARY, 4 JUNE 1942

### Robert J Casey, war correspondent

*The naval struggle between Japan and the USA for the Pacific waves culminated at
Midway in the Hawaiian archipelago. It was the first sea battle in which the opposing
fleets never saw each other: the fighting was done by carrier-based aircraft.*

JUNE 4, *Thursday*. North of Midway Islands.

*1:00.* Just learned that the Army planes from Midway located
another part of the Jap invasion force late Wednesday afternoon.

*6:00.* I got up for reveille and looked out at a clotted sky, a black sea
and odd gray moonlight.

*8:45.* I'm beginning to have a great deal of respect for Admiral
Spruance who is conducting this expedition. It is getting more and
more apparent as we steam toward the west that we haven't been
detected . . . It's a miracle but that seems to be the way of it.

We have an inferior force. It's probably one of the largest the United
States ever sent anywhere in a gesture of anger but what of it. About
half the Jap navy – and not the worst end of it – is out there ahead.

*9:10.* We make a right-angle turn. The wind stiffens, if that were
possible, and the SBD's and STB's go off.

It's much too windy for me to hear what's being said in sky control
so I don't know whether or not any contact has been made with the
Japs. Anyway the haul isn't too far for these planes if they have to go
all the way to Midway. It's comforting to see them up and something
of a relief, too. It won't be long now one way or the other and if
anything's coming to us we'll soon know it. If we don't get the Jap he'll
certainly get us.

From the signal yards the flags come down and the flags go up – red, yellow, blue, white, crossed, striped, checkered. Lads are running up and down the ladders of the foremast with dispatch blanks in their hands. It's all spectacular and beginning to be thrilling.

*10:30*. We go into a terrific lateral-pass maneuver and the ships start running across each other's bows. Donald Duck raises his voice: "Antiaircraft stations stand by to repel attack."

I go back to my place on the foremast. Then comes the usual wait and study of the sky. You can't help but think that this fine day which you were finding so useful to our bombers is going to be just as helpful to Hirohito's bombers.

*10:35*. Usual reports of approaching aircraft . . . "Unidentified plane, bearing three-three-eight – forty-eight thousand." "Unidentified plane bearing two-seven-oh – fifty-two thousand . . ." Everybody is tense of course because sometimes these hysterical shouts turn out to make sense.

We are now leading the procession abreast of the cans. A cruiser – a floating arsenal of ack-ack – has come over alongside our old carrier.

*10:45*. Ten planes show up off the starboard bow. They may be the *Yorktown*'s SBD's. As we glower at them we get the answer – the step pyramid of the *Yorktown*'s bridge structure comes up over the horizon. More planes are reported but the *Yorktown* claims them for her own and we withdraw from the contest.

We are still plowing along at top speed. On the lower decks the roar of the engines is so great that you have to shout to be heard a few feet. The cans, if we keep on at this rate, will have to refuel tonight. One lone gooney is sailing along with us easily and hopefully.

At the moment the carrier nearest us has sent out fighters, dive bombers, and torpedo planes. If the *Yorktown* has contributed as many as our old carrier, there ought to be about 180 planes on the way to the attack, 105 of them bombers or torpedo carriers.

*11:15*. A report has come in that one of our fortresses has attacked and damaged a carrier, presumably in the reserve group. The attack on Midway has been driven off – eight planes shot down over the island, the Marines claiming a bag of thirty off shore.

It's odd how the battle is shaping up to fit the specifications of the story the medical colonel told me when we went into Honolulu after the Coral Sea. The colonel said that the fight had already occurred. I said it hadn't. Nature as usual is imitating art.

*11:35*. We head now into the wind and it's very chilly. Some fighter planes are coming in, presumably part of our protective patrol. Against the sky they tumble along like a cloud of May flies. We're making crochet patterns all over the sea again.

*11:40*. There is some contact off the starboard quarter. Maybe that's why the fighters came in. They shoot over the rim of the sea and we continue our cotillion.

I'm getting sleepy. A gray half-moon hanging belatedly in the thin blue sky reminds me so much of myself.

*11:45*. Fighters come back to land on our carrier. Apparently a false alarm.

*12:00*. Mickey Reeves signaled me to come down to the bridge for a sandwich. So I was right at headquarters when first reports began to come in from our planes. The first message was brief. The Jap carriers had been located, a little belatedly, and they were virtually without air cover . . . Apparently all their planes had been sent out to make the conquest of Midway quick and easy. However, the squadron commander of the TBD unit reporting, said that his planes were virtually out of fuel.

"Request permission," he called, "to withdraw from action and refuel." The admiral's answer was terse.

"Attack at once."

So as I sat down in the chartroom to bite into a ham sandwich, the planes had begun to move in on the carriers. Whatever might be the result, we'd never be able to criticize the quality of our opportunity . . .

I sat there thinking. The Jap air admiral undoubtedly had figured us as permanent fixtures in the southwest Pacific where last he had had word of us. So just about now he'd be looking up at the sky suddenly clouded with SBD's and asking himself the Japanese equivalent of "Where the hell did those things come from?"

*12:45*. Enemy planes reported off port at twelve miles. New alert sounds. The kids drop their food and sidle off to their guns. The Grummans once more leap off our carrier.

*1:00*. Still no sign of the visitors. I guess the contact was another of those phonies that breed so rapidly in times like this.

*1:15*. Fifteen of the —————'s bombers come over. The squadron is intact and in tight formation, its work, whatever it was, finished.

*1:20*. The carriers swing around, apparently getting ready to take on returning planes which are now showing up in two's and three's. Everything is set to repel an attack, and with good reason. If these planes have failed in their mission or fought a draw or left the Jap carriers usable we may expect a quick and vicious attack in return. If by some remote juju we have put all four carriers out of commission we have just about gained mastery of the Pacific including the Japanese side of the international date line, or so the more educated of my spies tell me.

I went back to the wardroom and contemplated this phenomenon. Presently the word filtered back to us that the attack had been a complete success. All the carriers had been hit and severely damaged. At least three of them were burning. One, apparently, had been súnk in the first two or three minutes of the engagement.

One battleship of the north group of the force that we had attacked was afire. A second battleship had been hit. Reports from the Army told of hits on two more battleships and another carrier. Discounting these messages to the fullest extent and recognizing how easy it is for one observer to duplicate the report of another, it was still obvious that we had had something of a field day, still obvious that the bulk of Japan's attacking planes must presently be going into the drink for want of any other place to land.

*June 6, Saturday.* At sea west of Midway. Sunny. Calm. Warmer.

It is estimated on the basis of today's reports that between 18,000 and 20,000 men were killed in this brief battle. While we aren't wasting too much sympathy on our enemy at the moment, we are awed by the catastrophe that overtook him. There is chill in the thought that there, but for the Grace of God, go we. Had we been seen . . . Had the Japs attacked us before making the try for Midway . . .

# MIDWAY: THE DECISIVE FIVE MINUTES, 4 JUNE 1942

## *Taisa Mitsuo Fuchida, Imperial Japanese Naval Air Service*

As our fighters ran out of ammunition during the fierce battle they returned to the carriers for replenishment, but few ran low on fuel. Service crews cheered the returning pilots, patted them on the shoulder, and shouted words of encouragement. As soon as a plane was ready again the pilot nodded, pushed forward the throttle, and roared back into the sky. This scene was repeated time and again as the desperate air struggle continued.

Preparations for a counter-strike against the enemy had continued on board our four carriers throughout the enemy torpedo attacks. One after another, planes were hoisted from the hangar and quickly arranged on the flight deck. There was no time to lose. At 10.20 Admiral Nagumo gave the order to launch when ready. On *Akagi's* flight deck all planes were in position with engines warming up. The big ship began turning into the wind. Within five minutes all her planes would be launched.

Five minutes! Who would have dreamed that the tide of battle would shift completely in that brief interval of time?

Visibility was good. Clouds were gathering at about 3,000 metres, however, and though there were occasional breaks, they afforded good concealment for approaching enemy planes. At 10.24 the order to start launching came from the bridge by voice-tube. The Air Officer flapped a white flag, and the first Zero fighter gathered speed and whizzed off the deck. At that instant a look-out screamed: "Hell-Divers!" I looked up to see three black enemy planes plummeting towards our ship. Some of our machine-guns managed to fire a few frantic bursts at them, but it was too late. The plump silhouettes of the American Dauntless dive-bombers quickly grew larger, and then a number of black objects suddenly floated eerily from their wings. Bombs! Down they came straight towards me! I fell intuitively to the deck and crawled behind a command post mantelet.

The terrifying scream of the dive-bombers reached me first, followed by the crashing explosion of a direct hit. There was a blinding flash and then a second explosion, much louder than the first. I was shaken by a weird blast of warm air. There was still another shock, but less severe, apparently a near-miss. Then followed a startling quiet as the barking of guns suddenly ceased. I got up and looked at the sky. The enemy planes were already gone from sight.

The attackers had got in unimpeded because our fighters, which had engaged the preceding wave of torpedo planes only a few moments earlier, had not yet had time to regain altitude. Consequently, it may be said that the American dive-bombers' success was made possible by the earlier martyrdom of their torpedo planes. Also, our carriers had no time to evade because clouds hid the enemy's approach until he dived down to the attack. We had been caught flat-footed in the most vulnerable condition possible – decks loaded with planes armed and fuelled for an attack.

Looking about, I was horrified at the destruction that had been wrought in a matter of seconds. There was a huge hole in the flight deck just behind the amidship elevator. The elevator itself, twisted like molten glass, was dropping into the hangar. Deck plates reeled upwards in grotesque configurations, planes stood tail up, belching livid flame and jet-black smoke. Reluctant tears streamed down my cheeks as I watched the fires spread, and I was terrified at the prospect of induced explosions which would surely doom the ship. I heard Masuda yelling, "Inside! Get inside! Everybody who isn't working! Get inside!"

Unable to help, I staggered down a ladder and into the ready room. It was already jammed with badly burned victims from the hangar deck. A new explosion was followed quickly by several more, each causing the bridge structure to tremble. Smoke from the burning hangar gushed through passageways and into the bridge and ready room, forcing us to seek other refuge. Climbing back to the bridge, I could see that *Kaga* and *Soryu* had also been hit and were giving off heavy columns of black smoke. The scene was horrible to behold.

*Akagi* had taken two direct hits, one on the after rim of the amidship elevator, the other on the rear guard on the port side of the flight deck. Normally, neither would have been fatal to the giant carrier, but induced explosions of fuel and munitions devastated whole sections of the ship, shaking the bridge and filling the air with deadly splinters. As fire spread among the planes lined up wing to wing on the after flight deck, their torpedoes began to explode, making it impossible to bring the fires under control. The entire hangar area was a blazing inferno, and the flames moved swiftly towards the bridge.

*Midway cost the Americans the carrier* Yorktown *and 147 planes; the Japanese lost four carriers and a similar number of aircraft. The tide of war in the Pacific was now against the Japanese.*

# Part Six

Resistance & Reconquest

The War in Western and Southern Europe, November 1940–May 1945

# SWORDFISH ATTACK THE ITALIAN FLEET, TARANTO, 11 NOVEMBER 1940

## Lieutenant M.R. Maund RN, 824 Squadron

*The attack by Fleet Air Arm Swordfish on the Italian fleet at Taranto changed the balance of ship power in the Mediterranean, and consequently increased the difficulties for the Axis powers in supplying their armies in North Africa.*

The klaxon has gone and the starters are whirring as, stubbing out our cigarettes, we bundle outside into the chill evening air. It is not so dark now, with the moon well up in the sky, so that one can see rather than feel one's way past the aircraft which, with their wings folded for close packing, look more like four-poster bedsteads than front-line aeroplanes.

Parachute secured and Sutton harness pinned, the fitter bends over me, shouts "Good luck, sir" into my speaking-tube, and is gone. I call up Bull in the back to check intercom – he tells me the rear cockpit lighting has fused – then look around the orange-lighted cockpit; gas and oil pressures O.K., full tank, selector-switches on, camber-gear set, and other such precautions; run up and test switches, tail incidence set, and I jerk my thumb up to a shadow near the port wheel. Now comes the longest wait of all. 4F rocks in the slip-stream of aircraft ahead of her as other engines run up, and a feeling of desolation is upon me, unrelieved by the company of ten other aircraft crews, who, though no doubt entertaining similar thoughts, seem merged each into their own aircraft to become part of a machine without personality; only the quiet figures on the chocks seem human, and they are miles away.

The funnel smoke, a jet-black plume against the bright-starred sky, bespeaks of an increase in speed for the take-off; the fairy lights flick on, and with a gentle shudder the ship turns into wind, whirling the plan of stars about the foretop.

A green light waves away our chocks, orders us to taxi forward; the wings are spread with a slam, and as I test the aileron controls, green waves again. We are off, gently climbing away on the port bow where the first flame-float already burns, where the letter "K" is being flashed in black space. Here – in this black space – I discover Kemp, and close into formation; here also Kemp eventually gains squadron formation on Wilkinson, and the first wave is upon its way, climbing towards the north-west. At first the course is by no means certain, in fact Wilkinson is weaving, and station-keeping is a succession of bursts of speed and horrible air clawings, but in five minutes we have settled down a little.

At 4,000 feet we pass through a hole in scattered cloud – dark smudges above us at one moment, and the next stray fleece beneath airwheels filled with the light of a full moon.

Six thousand feet. God, how cold it is here! The sort of cold that fills you until all else is drowned save perhaps fear and loneliness. Suspended between heaven and earth in a sort of no-man's-land – to be sure, no man was ever meant to be here – in the abyss which men of old feared to meet if they ventured to the ends of the earth. Is it surprising that my knees are knocking together? We have now passed under a sheet of alto-stratus cloud which blankets the moon, allowing only a few pools of silver where small gaps appear. And, begob, Williamson is going to climb through it! As the rusty edge is reached I feel a tugging at my port wing, and find that Kemp has edged me over into the slipstream of the leading sub-flight. I fight with hard right stick to keep the wing up, but the sub-flight has run into one of its clawing moments, and quite suddenly the wing and nose drop and we are falling out of the sky. I let her have her head, and see the shape of another aircraft flash by close overhead. Turning, I see formation lights ahead and climb up after them, following them through one of the rare holes in this cloud mass. There are two aircraft sure enough, yet when I range up alongside, the moonglow shows up the figures 5A – that is Olly. The others must be ahead. After an anxious few minutes some dim lights appear among the upper billows of the cloud, and opening the throttle we lumber away from Olly after them. Poor old engine – she will get a tanning this trip.

The sub-flight is reassembled now at 8,000 feet. We have to come to the edge of the cloud. The regular flashing of a light away down to starboard claims my attention. "There's a flashing light to starboard, Bull, can you place it?" "Oh, yes," and that is all – the poor devil must be all but petrified with the cold by now.

Then the coast appears. Just a band of dull wrinkled greyness. Bull arouses himself from his icicles enough to be able to tell me that we have roughly forty minutes to go, and I enough to remind him to close the overload tank-cock before we go in. But we make no turn to get out to seaward again; instead we shape our course parallel to the coastline, not more than five miles away, giving away in one act any chance of surprise we might have hoped for.

Years later. Some quaint-coloured twinkling flashes like liverspots have appeared in the sky to starboard. It is some time before I realise their significance; we are approaching the harbour; and the flashes are HE shells bursting in a barrage on the target area. We turn towards the coast and drop away into line astern, engines throttled back. For ages we seem to hover without any apparent alteration; then red, white, and green flaming onions come streaming in our direction, the HE bursts get closer, and looking down to starboard I see the vague smudge of a shape I now know as well as my own hand. We are in attacking position. The next ahead disappears as I am looking for my line of approach, so down we go in a gentle pause, glide towards the north-western corner of the harbour. The master-switch is made, a notch or two back on the incidence wheel, and my fear is gone, leaving a mind as clear and unfettered as it has ever been in my life. The hail of tracer at 6,000 feet is behind now, and there is nothing here to dodge; then I see that I am wrong, it is not behind any more. They have shifted target; for now, away below to starboard, a hail of red, white, and green balls cover the harbour to a height of 2,000 feet. This thing is beyond a joke.

A burst of brilliance on the north-eastern shore, then another and another as the flare-dropper releases his load, until the harbour shows clear in the light he has made. Not too bright to dull the arc of raining colour over the harbour where tracer flies, allowing, it seems, no room to escape unscathed.

We are now at 1,000 feet over a neat residential quarter of the town where gardens in darkened squares show at the back of houses marshalled by the neat plan of streets that serve them. Here is the main road that connects the district with the main town. We follow its line and as I open the throttle to elongate the glide a Breda swings round from the shore, turning its stream of red balls in our direction. This is the beginning. Then another two guns farther north get our scent – white balls this time – so we throttle back again and make for a black mass on the shore that looks like a factory, where no balloons are likely to grow. A tall factory chimney shows ahead against the water's sheen. We must be at a hundred feet now and soon we must make our dash across that bloody water. As we come abreast the chimney I open the throttle wide and head for the mouth of the Mare Piccolo, whose position, though not visible, can be judged by the lie of the land. Then it is as though all hell comes tumbling in on top of us – it must have been the fire of the cruisers and Mare Piccolo canal batteries – leaving only two things in my mind, the line of approach to the dropping position and a wild desire to escape the effects of this deathly hailstorm.

And so we jink and swerve, an instinct of living guiding my legs and right arm; two large clear shapes on our starboard side are monstrous in the background of flares. We turn until the right-hand battleship is between the bars of the torpedo-sight, dropping down as we do so. The water is close beneath our wheels, so close I'm wondering which is to happen first – the torpedo going or our hitting the sea – then we level out, and almost without thought the button is pressed and a jerk tells me the "fish" is gone.

We are back close to the shore we started from, darting in and out of a rank of merchant ships for protection's sake. But our troubles are by no means over; for in our dartings hither and thither we run slap into an Artigliere-class destroyer. We are on top of her fo'c's'le before I realise that she hasn't opened fire on us, and though I am ready for his starboard pompom, he was a sitting shot at something between fifty and a hundred yards. The white balls come scorching across our quarter as we turn and twist over the harbour; the cruisers have turned their fire on us again, making so close a pattern that I can smell the acrid smoke of their tracer. This is the end – we cannot get away with this maelstrom around us. Yet as a trapped animal will fight like a fury for its life, so do we redouble our efforts at evasion. I am thinking, "Either I can kill myself or they can kill me," and flying the machine close down on the water wing-tips all but scraping it at every turn, throttle full open and wide back.

With a shock I realise that we are clear of the worst of it, anyway. Ahead is the island that lies between the horns of the outer harbour, a low black mass that, at our speed of 120 knots, is suddenly upon us. We blithely sail by its western foot, oblivious of what it may contain, when comes the tearing sound of shell as red balls spurt from a position no more than a hundred yards away, passing close ahead of us. Away we turn to starboard, then, as the stream grows, round to port again, and so we zigzag out into the open sea.

# LUNCH WITH DE GAULLE, LONDON, 20 JANUARY 1941

## Harold Nicolson, MP

*Harold Nicolson records a meeting with General Charles de Gaulle, the leader of the Free French movement.*

### 20 January 1941

I lunch with General de Gaulle at the Savoy. Attlee and Dalton are there. De Gaulle looks less unattractive with his hat off, since it shows his young hair and the tired and not wholly benevolent look in his eyes. He has the taut manner of a man who is becoming stout and is conscious that only the exercise of continuous muscle-power can keep his figure in shape. I do not like him. He accuses my Ministry of being "Pétainiste." [follower of Marshal Pétain, the leader of the puppet government set up in southern France by the Germans, which had its capital at Vichy] "*Mais non*," I say, "*Monsieur la Général.*" "*Enfin, Pétainisant.*" "*Nous travaillons*," I said, "*pour la France entière.*" "*La France entière*," he shouted, "*c'est la France Libre. C'est moi!*" Well, well. I admit he has made a great Boulangiste gesture. But the spectre of General Boulanger passes across my mind. He begins to abuse Pétain, saying that once again he has sold himself to Laval, saying that Weygand showed cowardice when bombed at the front. Osusky says that French opinion imagines that de Gaulle and Pétain are at heart as one. "*C'est une erreur*," he says sharply. I am not encouraged.

To change the subject I say that I have received a letter from occupied France which I was surprised had passed the censor. De Gaulle says that he had received a long letter of the most Gaulliste nature, the writer of which had written on the top, "I am sure the censor will stop this." Underneath in violet ink was written, "*La censure approve totalement*." We discuss Darlan [Admiral of the Vichy French Fleet]. He says that Darlan loves his ships as a race-horse owner loves his horses. It does not matter to him whether he races at Longchamps or on Epsom Downs. What matters is that it should be a great race and that he should win it. "*Mais il manque d'estomac*." Had he been a strong man, he would either have fought his fleet with us against the Italians or fought with the Germans against us. As it was, he was preserving his race-horses and they would become old, old, old . . .

## ONE MAN'S WAR: THE DIARY OF A TRAINEE BOMBER PILOT, 26 JANUARY–18 MAY 1941

### *Flying Officer Michael Scott, RAF Bomber Command*

*Diary: 26 January 1941.* I have got my wings, and am expecting my commission through at any time now. I had a filthy journey yesterday, with a temperature and incipient 'flu, which has luckily died away today. I passed out 13th at Grantham, Arthur being 14th! He and I tied for our Navigation Test, which was very satisfactory.

*24 February.* The Course has started at last. Two hours' cockpit drill on the Blenheim. Everything is so inaccessible that it is very hard to place one's hand on the right knob at the right time. I seem to have lost none of my old skill on the Link, in spite of being so out of practice.

*25 February.* More cockpit drill and Link. Also Snooker, which I enjoyed for three minutes, and then loathed more and more for the rest of the game.

*27 February.* Twenty-five! But I don't feel any older than I did yesterday. Thank God we have finished lectures and start flying tomorrow, though the thought of flying a Blenheim terrifies me.

*3 March.* Over four hours in the air. Solo after $2\frac{1}{4}$ hours, which is satisfactory. Blenheims are very nice to fly, though I find the landings very tricky, holding off too high, I think, and getting the stick back too far. I went over Newbury yesterday and bust up a game of football. The boys were much impressed – by nothing, I'm afraid.

*15 March.* More flying at last. $1\frac{1}{2}$ hours instrument finishing up by trying to land wheels up! I felt as if I had never flown a Blenheim and was completely ham-handed. Dirty-Dog Houlston put up the Hydraulic Selector Lever, which foxed me completely, BF that I was. Blast!

Yesterday Fl/Lt Hill wrote himself off shooting up the 'drome. He hit a tree on the boundary, probably not seeing it until too late. A sad end to a DFC. I expect I shall do plenty of low flying myself, but not with a crew on board.

*18 March.* Over three hours in the air. A cloudy day with wisps of mist below 3,000'. I went up to 11,000' to look at the sea over Cromer way and then descended in spirals over Blocking Lake. A grand life.

*21 March.* $^{3}/_{4}$ hour IF (Blind take-offs). Quite successful. I seem to have no trouble with the instruments now. 100 mins. solo, a deplorable effort. I tried a one engine circuit without success, and made a very shaky landing. Then I went up above the clouds and lost myself. What an aviator! I am hoping that one day I shall not frighten myself too much, especially for the sake of the crew.

I hope to get back to Bicester soon, possibly before the end of term at Cheam. I want very much to see the boys again before the end of term.

*25 March.* The long nose is a delight to fly – much easier than the short, and freer in the controls. It is steadier and easier to keep at a constant A/S.

*30 March.* A trip with a staff-pilot to bomb. Julian did very well; average error 77 yards, much the best of the day. We had a trip together in the afternoon, with no success, as the bombsight was WS. A snappy landing at 45' to the landing T finished a satisfactory day. We shall go to the OT [Officer Training] flight soon.

*8 April.* A bit too much flying. A $4\frac{1}{2}$ hour trip in the morning, Kettering – Doncaster – York – Lincoln – Royston – Kettering – Bicester – Upwood – Henswell – York – Henswell – Melton – Mowbray – Bicester. Then no lunch and an hour's map-reading in the afternoon which resolved itself into a trip to Aylesbury, and then to Newbury, where I shot up WJM and family, who were waving in his garden. We returned via Henley, and I was too tired to land properly, and had to go round again twice. Poor Julian. Photos of Lincoln Cathedral and Shefford Junction.

*20 April.* Low bombing level 250′. Not a bad effort. Average error 65–55 yards. Red landings in a cross wind.

*21 April.* More low level bombing. Much better. 35–30–34–18 yards average error. The last was the pilot's best so far (11 yards!). Landings good.

*26 April.* Operations loom on the horizon, but I have hardly realized their imminence yet. I would [prefer] cloud-cover to low level at present, so I am praying for cloudy weather.

*1 May.* Wattisham. 1 van-load take-off with + 9 boost. They are very heavy to land with such a weight, and I had to go round again once.

*17 May.* Got up at 2.30 to do a night cross country. Unfortunately we fouled the landing T on the way out to take-off, and so our early rising came to nought. Formation in the afternoon. This was quite good for a first effort, though I got rather close once or twice! On the battle order for tomorrow.

*18 May (Sunday).* A very heavy day, all formation flying. I found this very hard work at first, but it came a bit easier toward the end. We went over to Watton to join up with 21 and 89. Apparently we are to do a show on Tuesday morning with fighter escort. May the gods be with us! Formation flying is the most companionable of pursuits. Twelve dots in the sky linked by a spirit of fellowship and each dependent upon the rest. What more could a man ask! Today is the first day of Summer.

*Scott took off for his first operational flight on 24 January 1942. He was killed in action that night. His sister, Flora, added a footnote to his diary in her handwriting: "First Operation Flight. Missing over North Sea. Never heard of again". Among Michael Scott's effects was found a last letter, to be opened only in the event of his death.*

*Torquay, 21 June 1940*

Dear Daddy,

As this letter will only be read after my death it may seem a somewhat macabre document, but I do not want you to look on it in that way. I have always had a feeling that our stay on earth, that thing which we call "Life", is but a transitory stage in our development and that the dreaded monosyllable "Death" ought not to indicate anything to be feared. I have had my fling and must now pass onto the next stage, the consummation of all earthly experience. So don't worry about me: I shall be alright.

I would like to pay tribute to the courage which you and mother have shown, and will continue to show in these trying times. It is easy to meet an enemy face to face . . . but the unseen enemies Hardship, Anxiety and Despair are a very different problem. You have held the family together as few could have done, and I take my hat off to you.

Now a bit about myself. You know I hated the idea of war, and that hate will remain with me for ever. What has kept me going is the spiritual force to be derived from music, its reflection in my own feelings, and the power it has to uplift a soul above earthly things. Mark has the same experience as I have, though his medium of encouragement is poetry. Now I am off to the source of music and can fulfill the vague longing of my soul in becoming part of the fountain whence all good comes. I have no belief in an omnipresent God, but I *do* believe most strongly in a spiritual force which was the source of our being, and which will be our ultimate good. If there is anything worth fighting for, it is the right to follow on our own paths to this good, and to prevent our children from having their souls sterilized by Nazi doctrines. The most terrible aspect of Nazism is its system of education, of driving in instead of leading out, and putting the state above all things spiritual. And so I have been fighting.

A few last words about the disposal of my scant possessions. I would like Mark to have my wireless and records in the belief that he will get out of them as much as I have done. I have nothing else of instrinsic value except my golf clubs, which you can distribute as you think fit. If I have any balance at the bank, which is extremely unlikely, could you arrange that Flora use it as she thinks fit, as she has been an ideal pair in our relation to each other.

All I can do now is to voice my faith that this war will end in victory and that you will have many years before you in which to resume a normal civil life. Good luck to you!

# THE GERMAN AIRBORNE ASSAULT ON CRETE, 20 MAY 1941

## *Baron von der Heydte, 1st Battalion, 3rd German Parachute Regiment*

*Greece was invaded in October 1940 by Mussolini but, as in North Africa, his troops did not match his imperial dreams. Again Hitler came to Mussolini's rescue and accordingly dispatched the Wehrmacht into Greece on 6 April 1941. The Greek government, correctly deducing Hitler's intentions, had already requested British help, which arrived as a mixed British and Commonwealth force some 60,000 strong. It was unable to halt the field grey invader and by May 11 all Greece was in Axis hands – with the exception of the island of Crete, held by 14,000 Greeks, Britons, Australians and New Zealanders under General Freyburg. On 20 May the Germans came to Crete in the largest airborne assault in history.*

Slowly, infinitely slowly, like the last drops wrung from a drying well, the minutes passed. Again and again I glanced stealthily at my wrist-watch. There is nothing so awful, so exhausting, as this waiting for the moment of a jump. In vain I tried to compel myself to be calm and patient. A strange unrest had also gripped most of those who were flying with me . . . Scarcely able to bear it any longer, I stepped once again to the open door. We were just flying over the beaches. The thin strip of surf, which looked from above like a glinting white ribbon, separated the blue waters from the yellow-green of the shore. The mountains reared up before us, and the 'planes approaching them looked like giant birds trying to reach their eyries in the rocks.

We were still flying inland as if to run against a dark mountainside. It seemed almost as though we could touch the steep slopes upon which trees and solitary buildings appeared like toys. Then our left wing dipped and we swung away from the mountains out again, and at that moment there came the pilot's order, "Prepare to jump!"

Everyone rose and started to fasten his hook to the static line which ran down the centre of the body of the 'plane. And while we stood there, securing our hooks, we noticed that we were losing height, and the pressure of air became hard, almost painful, to the ear.

Next came the order, "Ready to Jump!"

In two strides I was at the door, my men pressing close behind me, and grasped the supports on either side of it. The slipstream clutched at my cheeks, and I felt as though they were fluttering like small flags in the wind.

Suddenly, a lot of little white clouds appeared from nowhere and stood poised in the air about us. They looked harmless enough, like puffs of cottonwool, for the roar of the 'plane's engines had drowned the sound of the ack-ack shells' detonation.

Below me was the village of Alikianon. I could see people in the streets staring up at us, others running away and disappearing into doorways. The shadows of our 'planes swept like ghostly hands over the sun drenched white houses, while behind the village there gleamed a large mirror – the reservoir – with single coloured parachutes, like autumn leaves, drifting down towards it.

Our 'plane slowed down. The moment had come.

"Go!"

I pushed with hands and feet, throwing my arms forward as if trying to clutch the black cross on the wing. And then the slipstream caught me, and I was swirling through space with the air roaring in my ears. A sudden jerk upon the webbing, a pressure on the chest which knocked the breath out of my lungs – and then – I looked up and saw, spread over me, the wide-open, motley hood of my parachute . . .

It was remarkably quiet, almost peaceful, in the olive grove where I was standing. Apart from the drone of homing aeroplanes, there was no sound – no human voice, nor even a rifle-shot. It is a strange feeling to be dropped suddenly into an alien land with orders to conquer it. Every tree, every bush, every blade of grass holds its secret. Mechanically I glanced at my wrist-watch. It showed exactly 7.15 – 7.15 a.m. on May 20th, 1941.

## CRETE: PYRRHIC VICTORY, 28 MAY 1941

### Baron von der Heydte, 3rd German Parachute Regiment

*By 28 May the battle for Crete was clearly won by the invading Germans and the British were forced into a humiliating evacuation. Yet, Crete cost Nazi Germany dear: 4,000 of the Wehrmacht's elite troops were killed in the campaign (the 3rd Battalion of the 1st Assault Regiment lost 400 of its 600 men on the the first day alone), a loss not easily recovered. Hitler was reputedly put off airborne invasions forever as a result of the Teutonic blood spilled into the soil of Crete.*

The garden suburb of Chaleppas on the coast was reported by our scouts to have escaped the bombardment, so my adjutant sensibly suggested that we should transfer our headquarters there.

"The battle for Canea is over, sir," he said. "The fight for comfortable billets has now begun."

I agreed to his proposal, and selected as my headquarters a small villa on the coast near the building which, until now, had housed the British Consulate. The villa, like most of the other houses in the district, had been evacuated. It had a pleasant terrace and a well in the garden from which we were able to draw delicious cold water. Since we had nothing better to do for the moment I suggested to my staff that we should take advantage of the lull to have a bathe. We undressed and started splashing each other like fifteen-year-olds, and it was while we were thus disporting ourselves that a British soldier suddenly appeared at the garden gate. The villa had apparently been used as a British headquarters, and I suppose the soldier, in his ignorance, had arrived with a message for the staff. I do not know who was the more astonished, he or ourselves, but in any event he realized his mistake more quickly than we and hastily beat a retreat.

He was the last British soldier I saw in the battle for Canea.

General Student visited us almost immediately after the fall of Canea. Had fourteen days really elapsed since I had last seen him issuing orders in Athens? He had visibly altered. He seemed much graver, more reserved, and older. There was no evidence in his features that he was joyful over the victory – his victory – and proud at the success of his daring scheme. The cost of victory had evidently proved too much for him. Some of the battalions had lost all their officers, and in several companies there were only a few men left alive.

. . . The battle for Crete was to prove the overture to the great tragedy which reached its climax at El Alamein and Stalingrad. For the first time there had stood against us a brave and relentless opponent on a battleground which favoured him. On this occasion things had gone well with us, but it seemed almost a miracle that our great and hazardous enterprise had succeeded. How it did, I cannot say to this day. Success had suddenly come to us at a moment when, as so often happens in war, we had ceased to believe in the possibility of success.

My interview with General Student was brief and to the point. In answer to his questions I concisely reported our experiences in the attack and told him of our losses. When I had finished he grasped me firmly by the hand and held it for a long time.

"I thank you," was all he said; but the grasp of his hand and those three short words were quite sufficient for me.

Once the action was over, one of our primary tasks was to collect and bury our dead. I ordered that a common cemetery should be made on the road from Alikianou to Canea, near the spot where my first company had been held up, for the dead of both my own battalion and the British and Greek troops who had opposed us. At the entrance to the cemetery we erected a large cross. On one side of its pedestal was the following inscription:

> In these olive groves and on the heights of Perivolia these men of
> the 1st Battalion of the 3rd Parachute Regiment fought, and
> won and died.

On tablets to the left and right of this inscription the names of our
dead were engraved, while the reverse side of the pedestal carried an
inscription as follows:

> In valiant combat against the Battalion one hundred and fifty-
> six members of the following British regiments died for their
> King and Country.

Beneath were inscribed the names of the units to which the British
troops who had fought against us had belonged.

Once the bodies of the dead had been retrieved and the cemetery
been completed, I invited the British officers who had fought in our
sector and been taken prisoner to attend the consecration of the
memorial.

The survivors of my battalion paraded at the cemetery. I spoke first
to them in German, then added a few words in English. The senior
British officer replied. And at that moment we did not consider
ourselves enemies, but friends who had been defeated by the same
harsh fate.

. . . During that very same evening the sentry at my headquarters
reported that a young Greek lady had arrived and wished to speak to
me. Automatically I thought of Ariadne; but this young woman did
not bear a sword. She had brought a large bunch of white flowers
which she asked me to lay on the graves of the German, British and
Greek soldiers who had been buried in the cemetery.

## HOLOCAUST: MEDICAL EXPERIMENTS AT DACHAU, 1941–45

### Franz Blaha

*Dachau in Germany was one of the principal Nazi concentration camps for "undesir-*
*ables": Jews, Slavs, political opponents and gypsies.*

I, Franz Blaha, being duly sworn, depose and state as follows:

I was sent as a prisoner to the Dachau Concentration Camp in
April 1941, and remained there until the liberation of the camp in
April 1945. Until July 1941 I worked in a Punishment Company.
After that I was sent to the hospital and subjected to the experiments
in typhoid being conducted by Dr Mürmelstadt. After that I was to be

made the subject of an experimental operation, and only succeeded in avoiding this by admitting that I was a physician. If this had been known before I would have suffered, because intellectuals were treated very harshly in the Punishment Company. In October 1941 I was sent to work in the herb plantation, and later in the laboratory for processing herbs. In June 1942, I was taken into the hospital as a surgeon. Shortly afterwards I was directed to conduct a stomach operation on twenty healthy prisoners. Because I would not do this I was put in the autopsy room, where I stayed until April 1945. While there I performed approximately 7,000 autopsies. In all, 12,000 autopsies were performed under my direction.

From mid-1941 to the end of 1942 some 500 operations on healthy prisoners were performed. These were for the instruction of the SS medical students and doctors and included operations on the stomach, gall bladder, spleen and throat. These were performed by students and doctors of only two years' training, although they were very dangerous and difficult. Ordinarily they would not have been done except by surgeons with at least four years' surgical practice. Many prisoners died on the operating table and many others from later complications. I performed autopsies on all these bodies. The doctors who supervised these operations were Lang, Mürmelstadt, Wolter, Ramsauer and Kahr. *Standartenführer* Dr Lolling frequently witnessed these operations.

During my time at Dachau I was familiar with many kinds of medical experiments carried on there with human victims. These persons were never volunteers but were forced to submit to such acts. Malaria experiments on about 1,200 people were conducted by Dr Klaus Schilling between 1941 and 1945. Schilling was personally asked by Himmler to conduct these experiments. The victims were either bitten by mosquitoes or given injections of malaria sporozoites taken from mosquitoes. Different kinds of treatment were applied, including quinine, pyrifer, neosalvarsan, antipyrin, pyramidon and a drug called 2516 Behring. I performed autopsies on bodies of people who died from these malaria experiments. Thirty to forty died from the malaria itself. Three to four hundred died later from diseases which proved fatal because of the physical condition resulting from the malaria attacks. In addition there were deaths resulting from poisoning due to overdoses of neosalvarsan and pyramidon. Dr Schilling was present at the time of my autopsies on the bodies of his patients.

In 1942 and 1943 experiments on human beings were conducted by Dr Sigismund Rascher to determine the effects of changing air pressure. As many as twenty-five persons were put at one time into a specially constructed van in which pressure could be increased or decreased as required. The purpose was to find out the effects of high altitude and of rapid parachute descents on human beings. Through a window in the van I have seen the people lying on the floor of the van. Most of the prisoners who were made use of died as a result of these experiments, from internal haemorrhages of the lungs or brain. The rest coughed blood when taken out. It was my job to take the bodies out and to send the internal organs to Munich for study as soon as they were found to be dead. About 400 to 500 prisoners were experimented on. Those not dead were sent to invalid blocks and liquidated shortly afterwards. Only a few escaped.

Rascher also conducted experiments on the effect of cold water on human beings. This was done to find a way for reviving aviators who had fallen into the ocean. The subject was placed in ice-cold water and kept there until he was unconscious. Blood was taken from his neck and tested each time his body temperature dropped one degree. This drop was determined by a rectal thermometer. Urine was also periodically tested. Some men lasted as long as twenty-four to thirty-six hours. The lowest body temperature reached was nineteen degrees C., but most men died at twenty-five degrees C., or twenty-six degrees C. When the men were removed from the ice water attempts were made to revive them by artificial warmth from the sun, from hot water, from electro-therapy or by animal warmth. For this last experiment prostitutes were used and the body of the unconscious man was placed between the bodies of two women. Himmler was present at one such experiment. I could see him from one of the windows in the street between the blocks. I have personally been present at some of the cold-water experiments when Rascher was absent, and I have seen notes and diagrams on them in Rascher's laboratory. About 300 persons were used in these experiments. The majority died. Of those who lived many became mentally deranged. Those not killed were sent to invalid blocks and were killed, just as were the victims of the air-pressure experiments. I only know two who survived – a Jugoslav and a Pole, both of whom have become mental cases.

Liver-puncture experiments were performed by Dr Brachtl on healthy people, and on people who had diseases of the stomach and gall bladder. For this purpose a needle was jabbed into the liver of a person and a small piece of liver was extracted. No anaesthetic was used. The experiment is very painful and often had serious results, as the stomach or large blood vessels were often punctured and haemorrhage resulted. Many persons died of these tests, for which Polish, Russian, Czech and German prisoners were employed. Altogether these experiments were conducted on about 175 people.

Phlegmone experiments were conducted by Dr Schütz, Dr Babor, Dr Kieselwetter and Professor Lauer. Forty healthy men were used at a time, of whom twenty were given intra-muscular, and twenty intravenous, injections of pus from diseased persons. All treatment was forbidden for three days, by which time serious inflammation and in many cases general blood poisoning had occurred. Then each group was divided again into groups of ten. Half were given chemical treatment with liquid and special pills every ten minutes for twenty-four hours. The rest were treated with sulphanamide and surgery. In some cases all of the limbs were amputated. My autopsy also showed that the chemical treatment had been harmful and had even caused perforations of the stomach wall. For these experiments Polish, Czech and Dutch priests were ordinarily used. Pain was intense in such experiments. Most of the 600 to 800 persons who were used finally died. Most of the others became permanent invalids and were later killed.

In the autumn of 1944 there were sixty to eighty persons who were subjected to salt-water experiments. They were locked in a room and for five days were given nothing to swallow but salt water. During this time their urine, blood and excrement were tested. None of these prisoners died, possibly because they received smuggled food from other prisoners. Hungarians and gypsies were used for these experiments.

It was common practice to remove the skin from dead prisoners. I was commanded to do this on many occasions. Dr Rascher and Dr Wolter in particular asked for this human skin from human backs and chests. It was chemically treated and placed in the sun to dry. After that it was cut into various sizes for use as saddles, riding breeches, gloves, house slippers and ladies' handbags. Tattooed skin was especially valued by SS men. Russians, Poles and other inmates were used in this way, but it was forbidden to cut out the skin of a German. This skin had to be from healthy prisoners and free from defects. Sometimes we did not have enough bodies with good skin and Rascher would say, "All right, you will get the bodies." The next day we would receive twenty or thirty bodies of young people. They would have been shot in the neck or struck on the head so that the skin would be uninjured. Also we frequently got requests for the skulls or skeletons of prisoners. In those cases we boiled the skull or the body. Then the soft parts were removed and the bones were bleached and dried and reassembled. In the case of skulls it was important to have a good set of teeth. When we got an order for skulls from Oranienburg the SS men would say, "We will try to get you some with good teeth." So it was dangerous to have a good skin or good teeth.

## A "CIRCUS" OVER FRANCE, AUGUST 1941
### Flight Lieutenant "Johnnie" Johnson, 616 Squadron RAF

*The Battle of Britain won, RAF Fighter Command increasingly provided escort duty ("circuses") to bombers making sallies over occupied France. Johnson ended WWII as the highest scoring RAF pilot.*

High summer, and the air is heavy with the scent of white clover as we lounge in our deck-chairs watching a small tractor cut down the long clover and grass on our airfield. In some places it is almost a foot high, but it is not dangerous and we know that if we are skilful enough to stall our Spitfires just when the tips of the grasses caress the wheels then we shall pull off a perfect landing.

It is Sunday, and although it is not yet time for lunch we have already escorted some Stirlings to bomb an inland target. For some obscure reason the Luftwaffe seem to oppose our week-end penetrations with more than their usual ferocity, and now we are waiting for the second call which will surely come on this perfect day.

For once our chatter is not confined to Messerschmitts and guns and tactics. Yesterday afternoon Nip and I borrowed the Padre's car, a small family saloon, and drove to Brighton for dinner. Before the return journey we collected two pilots from 145 Squadron, and in the small hours, wedged together, began the journey back to Tangmere. Nip was driving, the rest of us asleep, and along the front at Hove he had a vague recollection of some confusion and shouting and a half-hearted barrier stretched across part of the road. He pressed on and thought little of the incident, but soon after the engine ran unevenly and became very hot. Somehow we coaxed the car home. Next morning a close inspection revealed a sinister hole just below the rear window. Shocked, we traced the path of the bullet, for it turned out that a sentry at Hove had challenged us and, not receiving a suitable reply, had opened fire. The bullet had passed between the two pilots on the back seat, had continued between Nip and me at shoulder height, drilled a neat hole through the dashboard, grazed the cylinder head and ploughed out through the radiator. Small wonder that the little car had barely struggled back to Tangmere! The Padre is more concerned with our lucky escape than the damage to his car, but Billy Burton is incensed that his pilots should have to run a gauntlet of fire at Hove. He is busy penning a letter to the military, but we keep out of his way, for we think that he is opening his attack from a very insecure base.

There is a fine haze and the soft bulk of the South Downs is barely discernible. We can just see the spire of Chichester cathedral, but above the haze the visibility is excellent and you can see Lille from fifty miles.

Lille! It lies seventy miles inland from Le Touquet and marks the absolute limit of our daylight penetrations over France. We often escort bombers to Lille, for it is a vital communications centre and contains important heavy industries. Not unnaturally the Luftwaffe are very sensitive about it. Their ground-control organization has time to assess our intentions and bring up fighter reinforcements, and the run-up to the target is always strongly contested. We can be sure of a stiff fight when Lille is the target for the bombers.

The ops. phone rings and the airman who answers it calls out to the C.O.; Billy Burton listens and replaces the receiver.

"That was the wing commander. Take-off at 1325 with 610 and 145. We shall be target-support wing to the bombers. It's Lille again."

Suddenly the dispersal hut is full of chatter and activity. We shall be the last Spitfires in the target area, for our job is to see that the beehive leaves the area without interference. The sun will be almost directly overhead, and the Messershmitts will be there, lurking and waiting in its strong glare. We shall fight today.

Highly coloured ribbons are pinned across the large map on the wall to represent the tracks of the beehive and the six supporting fighter wings, so that the map looks like one of those bold diagrams of London's Underground system. The two flight sergeants talk with their respective flight commanders about the serviceability of our Spitfires, and our names and the letters of our aircraft are chalked up on a blackboard which shows three sections of finger-fours.

It is fascinating to watch the reactions of the various pilots. They fall into two broad categories; those who are going out to shoot and those who secretly and desperately know they will be shot at, the hunters and the hunted. The majority of the pilots, once they have seen their names on the board, walk out to their Spitfires for a pre-flight check and for a word or two with their ground crews. They tie on their mae-wests, check their maps, study the weather forecast and have a last-minute chat with their leaders or wingmen. These are the hunters.

The hunted, that very small minority (although every squadron usually possessed at least one), turned to their escape kits and made quite sure that they were wearing the tunic with the silk maps sewn into a secret hiding-place; that they had at least one oilskin-covered packet of French francs, and two if possible; that they had a compass and a revolver and sometimes specially made clothes to assist their activities once they were shot down. When they went through these agonized preparations they reminded me of aged countrywomen meticulously checking their shopping-lists before catching the bus for the market town.

A car pulls up outside and our leader* stumps into the dispersal hut, breezy and full of confidence. "They'll be about today, Billy. We'll run into them over the target, if not before. Our job is to see the Stirlings get clear and cover any stragglers. Stick together. Who's flying in my section?"

"Smith, Cocky and Johnnie, sir," answers Billy Burton.

"Good," Bader grins at us. "Hang on and get back into the abreast formation when I straighten out. O.K.?"

"O.K. sir," we chorus together.

The wing commander makes phone calls to Stan Turner and Ken Holden. Brief orders followed by a time check. Ten minutes before we start engines, and we slip unobtrusively to our Spitfires, busy with our own private thoughts. I think of other Sunday afternoons not so very long ago when I was at school and walked the gentle slopes of Charnwood Forest clad in a stiff black suit. Our housemaster's greatest ambition was to catch us seniors red-handed smoking an illicit cigarette. And I think of my own father's deep-rooted objections to any form of strenuous activity on the Sabbath during the holidays at Melton Mowbray.

My ground crew have been with the squadron since it was formed and have seen its changing fortunes and many pilots come and go. They know that for me these last few moments on the ground are full of tension, and as they strap me in the cockpit they maintain an even pressure of chatter. Vaguely I hear that the engine is perfect, the guns oiled and checked and the faulty radio set changed and tested since the last flight. The usual cockpit smell, that strange mixture of dope, fine mineral oil, and high-grade fuel, assails the nostrils and is some-how vaguely comforting. I tighten my helmet strap, swing the rudder with my feet on the pedals, watch the movement of the ailerons when I waggle the stick and look at the instruments without seeing them, for my mind is racing on to Lille and the 109s.

Ken starts his engine on the other side of the field and the twelve Spitfires from 610 trundle awkwardly over the grass. Bader's propeller begins to turn, I nod to the ground crew and the engine coughs once or twice and I catch her with a flick of the throttle and she booms into

---

* The legendary, legless Douglas Bader, call-sign "Dogsbody".

a powerful bass until I cut her back to a fast tick-over. We taxi out to the take-off position, always swinging our high noses so that we can see the aircraft ahead. The solid rubber tail-wheels bump and jolt on the unyielding ground and we bounce up and down with our own backbones acting as shock absorbers.

We line our twelve Spitfires diagonally across one corner of the meadow. We wait until Ken's squadron is more than half-way across the airfield and then Bader nods his head and we open out throttles together and the deep-throated roar of the engines thunders through the leather helmets and slams against our ear-drums. Airborne, and the usual automatic drill. We take up a tight formation and I drop my seat a couple of notches and trim the Spitfire so that it flies with the least pressure from hands and feet.

One slow, easy turn on to the course which sends us climbing parallel to the coast. Ken drops his squadron neatly into position about half a mile away and Stan flanks us on the other side. Woodhall calls from the ops. room to his wing leader to check radio contact:

"Dogsbody?"

"O.K., O.K."

And that's all.

We slant into the clean sky. No movement in the cockpit except the slight trembling of the stick as though it is alive and not merely the focal point of a superb mechanical machine. Gone are the ugly tremors of apprehension which plagued us just before the take-off. Although we are sealed in our tiny cockpits and separated from each other, the static from our radios pours through the earphones of our tightly fitting helmets and fills our ears with reassuring crackles. When the leader speaks, his voice is warm and vital, and we know full well that once in the air like this we are bound together by a deeper intimacy than we can ever feel on the ground. Invisible threads of trust and comradeship hold us together and the mantle of Bader's leadership will sustain and protect us throughout the fight ahead. The Tangmere Wing is together.

We climb across Beachy Head, and over Pevensey Bay we swing to the starboard to cross the Channel and head towards the French coast. Some pilot has accidentally knocked on his radio transmitter and croons quietly to himself. He sounds happy and must be a Canadian, for he sings of "The Chandler's Wife" and the "North Atlantic Squadron". He realizes his error and we hear the sudden click of his transmitter, and again the only sound is the muted song of the engine.

Now Bader rocks his wings and we level out from the climb and slide out of our tight formation. We take up our finger-four positions with ourselves at 25,000 feet and Ken and Stan stacked up behind us. It is time to switch the gun button from "safe" to "fire" and to turn on the reflector sight, for we might want them both in a hurry.

"O.K. Ken?" from Bader.

"O.K., Dogsbody."

"Stan?" from Bader again.

"You bet."

The yellow sands of the coast are now plainly visible, and behind is a barren waste of sandhills and scrub. Well hidden in these sandhills are the highly trained gunners who serve the 88 mm. batteries. We breast the flak over Le Touquet. The black, evil flowers foul the sky and more than the usual amount of ironmongery is hurled up at us. Here and there are red marker bursts intended to reveal our position to the Messerschmitts. We twist and pirouette to climb above the bed of flak, and from his relatively safe position, high above, Stan sees our plight and utters a rude comment in the high-pitched voice he reserves for such occasions. The tension eases.

On across the Pas de Calais and over the battlefields of a half-forgotten war against the same foe. From the Tangmere ops. Room Woodhall breaks the silence:

"Dogsbody, from Beetle. The beehive is on time and is engaged."

"O.K."

"Fifty-plus about twenty miles ahead of you," from Woodhall.

"Understood," replies Bader.

"Thirty-plus climbing up from the south and another bunch behind them. Keep a sharp look-out," advises the group captain.

"O.K. Woodie. That's enough," answers the wing leader, and we twist our necks to search the boundless horizons.

"Looks like a pincer movement to me," comments some wag. I suspect it is Roy Marple's voice, and again the tension slackens as we grin behind our oxygen masks. Woodhall speaks into his microphone with his last item of information.

"Dogsbody. The rear support wing is just leaving the English coast." (This means we can count on some help should we have to fight our way out.) "Course for Dover – 310 degrees." (This was a last-minute reminder of the course to steer for home.) Woodhall fades out, for he has done his utmost to paint a broad picture of the air situation. Now it is up to our leader.

"Dogsbody from blue one. Beehive at twelve o'clock below. About seven miles."

"O.K. I see them," and the wing leader eases his force to starboard and a better up-sun position.

The high-flying Messerschmitts have seen our wing and stab at Stan's top-cover squadron with savage attacks from either flank.

"Break port, Ken." (From a pilot of 610.)

"Keep turning."

"Tell me when to stop turning."

"Keep turning. There's four behind!"

"Get in, red section."

"We're stuck into some 109s behind you, Douglas." (This quietly from Stan.)

"O.K. Stan."

"Baling out."

"Try and make it, Mac. Not far to the coast." (This urgently from a squadron commander.)

"No use. Temperatures off the clock. She'll burn any time. Look after my dog."

"Keep turning, yellow section."

So far the fight has remained well above us. We catch fleeting glimpses of high vapour trials and ducking, twisting fighters. Two-thirds of the wing are behind us holding off the 109s and we force on to the target area to carry out our assigned task. We can never reform into a wing again, and the pilots of 145 and 610 will make their way home in twos and fours. We head towards the distant beehive, well aware that there is now no covering force of Spitfires above us.

The Stirlings have dropped their heavy load of bombs and begin their return journey. We curve slowly over the outskirts of Lille to make sure the beehive is not harried from the rear. I look down at a pall of debris and black smoke rising from the target five miles below, and absurdly my memory flashes back to contrast the scene with those other schoolboy Sunday afternoons.

"Dogsbody from Smith. 109s above. Six o'clock. About twenty-five or thirty."

"Well done. Watch 'em and tell me when to break."

I can see them. High in the sun, and their presence only betrayed by the reflected sparkle from highly polished windscreens and cockpit covers.

"They're coming down, Dogsbody. Break left." And round to port we go, with Smith sliding below Bader and Cocky and me above so that we cover each other in this steep turn. We curve round and catch a glimpse of four baffled 109s climbing back to join their companions, for they can't stay with us in a turn. The keen eyes of Smith saved us from a nasty smack that time.

"Keep turning, Dogsbody. More coming down," from Cocky.

"O.K. We might get a squirt this time," rejoins Bader. What a man, I think, what a man!

The turn tightens and in my extreme position on the starboard side

I'm driving my Spitfire through a greater radius of curve than the others and falling behind. I kick on hard bottom rudder and skid inwards, down and behind the leader. More 109s hurtle down from above and a section of four angle in from the starboard flank. I look round for other Spitfires but there are none in sight. The four of us are alone over Lille.

"Keep turning. Keep turning." (From Bader.) "They can't stay with us." And we keep turning, hot and frightened and a long way from home. We can't keep turning all bloody day, I think bitterly.

Cocky has not re-formed after one of our violent breaks. I take his place next to Bader and the three of us watch the Messerschmitts, time their dives and call the break into their attacks. The odds are heavily against us.

We turn across the sun and I am on the inside. The blinding light seems only two feet above Bader's cockpit and if I drop further below or he gains a little more height, I shall lose him. Already his Spitfire has lost its colour and is only a sharp, black silhouette and now it has disappeared completely, swallowed up by the sun's fierce light. I come out of the turn and am stunned to find myself alone in the Lille sky.

The Messerschmitts come in close for the kill. At this range their camouflage looks dirty and oil-stained, and one brute has a startling black-and-white spinner. In a hot sweat of fear I keep turning and turning, and the fear is mingled with an abject humiliation that these bastards should single me out and chop me at their leisure. The radio is silent, or probably I don't hear it in the stress of trying to stay alive. I can't turn all day. Le Touquet is seventy hostile miles away; far better to fight back and take one with me.

Four Messerschmitts roar down from six o'clock. I see them in time and curve the shuddering, protesting Spitfire to meet them, for she is on the brink of a high-speed stall. They are so certain of my destruction that they are flying badly and I fasten on to tail-end Charlie and give him a long burst of fire. He is at the maximum range, and although my shooting has no apparent effect some of my despair and fear on this fateful afternoon seems to evaporate at the faint sound of the chattering machine guns. But perhaps my attack has its just reward, for Smith's voice comes loud and clear over the radio.

"One Spit behind, Dogsbody. A thousand yards. Looks like he's in trouble."

Then I see them. Two aircraft with the lovely curving wings that can only belong to Spitfires. I take a long breath and in a deliberately calm voice:

"It's me Dogsbody – Johnnie."

"O.K. Johnnie. We'll orbit here for you. Drop in on my starboard. We'll get a couple of these————"

There is no longer any question of not getting home now that I am with Bader again. He will bring us safely back to. Tangmere and I know he is enjoying this, for he sounds full of confidence over the radio. A dozen Messerschmitts still shadow our small formation. They are well up-sun and waiting to strike. Smith and I fly with our necks twisted right round, like the resting mallard ducks one sees in the London parks, and all our concentration focussed on the glinting shoal of 109s.

"Two coming down from five o'clock, Dogsbody. Break right," from me. And this time mine is the smallest turn so that I am the first to meet the attack. A 109 is very close and climbing away to port. Here is a chance. Time for a quick shot and no danger of losing the other two Spitfires if I don't get involved in a long tail chase. I line up my Spitfire behind the 109, clench the spade-grip handle of the stick with both hands and send short bursts into his belly at less than a hundred yards. The 109 bursts apart and the explosion looks exactly the same as a near burst of heavy flak, a vicious flower with a poisonous glowing centre and black swirling edges.

I re-form and the Messerschmitts come in again, and this time Bader calls the break. It is well judged and the wing leader fastens on to the last 109 and I cover his Spitfire as it appears to stand on its tail with wisps of smoke plummeting from the gun ports. The enemy aircraft starts to pour white smoke from its belly and thick black smoke from the engine. They merge together and look like a long, dirty banner against the faded blue of some high cirrus cloud.

"Bloody good shooting, sir."

"We'll get some more."

Woodhall – it seems an eternity since we last heard him – calls up to say that the rear support wing is over Abbeville. Unbelievably the Messerschmitts which have tailed us so long vanish and we are alone in the high spaces.

We pick up the English coast near Dover and turn to port for Sussex and Tangmere. We circle our airfield and land without any fuss or aerobatics, for we never know until we are on the ground whether or not a stray bullet has partially severed a control cable.

Woodhall meets us and listens to his wing leader's account of the fight. Bader has a tremendous ability to remember all the details and gives a graphic résumé of the show. The group captain listens carefully and says that he knew we were having a hard time because of the numerous plots of enemy formations on his operations table and our continuous radio chatter. So he had asked 11 Group to get the rear support wing over France earlier than planned, to lend a hand. Perhaps the shadowing Messerschmitts which sheered off so suddenly had seen the approach of this Spitfire wing.

Bader phones Ken and Stan while the solemn Gibbs pleads with us to sit down and write out our combat reports.

"Please do it now. It will only take two minutes."

"Not likely Gibbs. We want some tea and a shower and . . ."

"You write them and we'll sign them," suggests a pilot.

Cocky walks in. He came back on the deck after losing us over Lille and landed at Hawkinge short of petrol.

"Dinner and a bottle at Bosham tonight, Johnnie?"

"Right," I answer at once.

"Count me in too," says Nip.

The group captain is trying to make himself heard above the din.

"You chaps must watch your language. It's frightful. And the Waafs seem to be getting quite used to it. They don't bat an eyelid any more. But I'm sure you don't know how bad it sounds. I had it logged this afternoon." And he waves a piece of paper in his hand.

Someone begins to read out from the record. We roar with laughter, slap each other on the back and collapse weakly into chairs, but this reaction is not all due to the slip of paper. Woodhall watches us and walks to the door hoping that we don't see the grin which is creasing his leathery countenance.

We clamber into our meagre transports, one small van per flight, and drive to Shopwhyke. We sit on the lawn and drink tea served by Waafs. These young girls wear overalls of flowered print and look far more attractive and feminine than in their usual masculine garb of collar and tie. One of our officers is a well-known concert pianist and he plays a movement from a Beethoven concerto, and the lovely melody fills the stately house and overflows into the garden. The sweat from the combats of but an hour ago is barely dry on our young bodies.

## THE HOME FRONT: THE GREAT MAN CHASE, ENGLAND, DECEMBER 1941

### *Anonymous member of the British Women's Auxiliary Air Force*

The main consequence of a lot of women living together seems to be that since everyone realizes that everyone else's emotions, aims and actions are similar to their own conventional barriers and restraints are torn down and conversation gets down to bedrock.

The presence of both sexes always imposes restraint in conversation. The soldier's fumbling excuse for hard swearing is always "Oh, well, when a lot of us lads get together [. . .]" Similarly when women are together in our circumstances, we use words we wouldn't think of bringing out in public.

Not only in choice of words, but also in choice of topic and depth of discussion is this new candour created. Even at women's tea parties . . . women are on their guard against each other and don't admit their basic feelings . . . But here we've got to know each other well: we're all in the same boat and we're all after the same thing. So why kid each other?

And what is this thing we're all after? Obviously, a man. Preferably an officer or a sergeant pilot. I should say that 85 per cent of our conversation is about men, dances (where we meet men), 15 per cent about domestic and shop matters and a negligible proportion on other matters.

But to get a man is not sufficient. It's easy to get a man. In fact it's difficult not to. Competitive factors in the Great Man-Chase are under the following headings:

1. Quality: The desirable qualities are rank, wings, looks, money, youth in that order. Rank is unbelievably important. There's a Wing-Commander here whose only redeeming feature is that he's young. He isn't good-looking, he's owned to be a great bore and he's extremely "fast" (which is *not* a recommendation) yet he could go out with any woman on the station he cared to ask. No one would refuse . . . The height of sex-rank is commission and wings. Higher commission, the better. Sergeant pilots and ground commissions tie for second place. This includes army officers. Ground stripes come a poor third. For the rest as far as most Ops girls are concerned, there is little hunting-value. In the term "looks" I include charm, personality, etc. This counts only as a narrow comparison viz P/O [Pilot Officer] A is better than P/O B because he is more charming, but we'd rather go out with P/O B who is *not* charming, than with Sergeant C who *is* (and he's good-looking too). Members of the Army without commissions don't get a look in at all . . .

2. Quantity: Naturally the more men one can fasten to one's train the more prestige one gains in the Chase.

3. Intensity – a deliberately vague term embodying length of affair, extent of ardour and its manifestations.

Of course the longer you can keep your man, the higher up you are in the competition. It's better if he's madly in love with you. He shouldn't be seen in public with other women. And telegrams, chocolates, cigarettes and really "classy" evenings out all put you one step higher on the ladder. As far as physical manifestations are concerned, the average Ops girl admittedly likes a man who can kiss well, eyes "wandering" with suspicion and definitely abstains from actual immorality. Technique in kissing is of first importance . . . Further than kissing is not eyed favourably. "I *like* Bill and he *is* a Squadron Leader and all that but I simply can't face the coping I have to do every evening." ("Coping" having become the accepted term for dealing with unwanted passion.) So the eligible men are those who kiss well but "know when to stop" . . .

It seems to me that practically the entire object of the Chase is a matter of vanity and prestige . . .

Becoming of necessity subjective: I allowed myself to drift into this chase for the past few months and have discovered:

*a.* That I am happiest when I am conducting two or three successful affairs with eligibles as above.

*b.* That I am second happiest when I am *pretending to other girls* that they are successful affairs as above . . .

A girl in our Control had been trying very hard to get a date with a new officer. She was sitting next to him in the Ops room one day full of concentration in her conversation when suddenly she smiled, looked across at me, and mouthed the words "Got him!"

# ESCAPE FROM COLDITZ, 5 JANUARY 1942

## Airey Neave

*Schloss Colditz was a POW camp to which the Germans sent the most troublesome of Allied officer prisoners. It was intended to be escape proof.*

On the morning of 5 January 1942 Luteyn and I were ready to escape. We held a conference with Pat Reid and "Hank" Wardle and decided to try immediately after the nine o'clock *Appell* that evening. Our compasses, maps and a small bundle of notes were ready for hiding inside our bodies. The uniforms were now intact beneath the stage and our civilian clothes had so far escaped detection in their "hide". In a moment of supreme confidence, I collected the addresses of relatives of my companions. Then flushed and excited, I lay down to sleep throughout the afternoon and early evening.

A few minutes before nine I went down to the courtyard, when the snow was falling lightly. The turrets cast long shadows in the light of the moon and the steep walls enfolded me for what I believed to be the last time. There was once more the eternal sound of hundreds of men taking their meagre exercise in clogs. I stood waiting for the *Appell*, eyeing the Dutch contingent where Luteyn was waiting ready to join me. We wore cardboard leggings painted with black polish. I wore my usual combination of battledress and sweater, and my Army boots, being brown, were also darkened with black polish. Underneath I had my "civilian clothes" with a pair of R.A.F. trousers. I had an over-powering sense that this was my last evening in the castle. The certainty grew with every minute, making me composed and determined.

There was a sharp order of dismissal and, mingling with the dispersing prisoners, Pat Reid, "Hank' Wardle, Luteyn and I hurried quickly into the senior officers'' quarters. In the darkness of the theatre we felt our way beneath the stage, then carefully prised up the loose floor-boards. Pat Reid lifted the trap called "Shovewood", which on its underside was whitewashed, disguising the hole in the ceiling of the passage below. I could see the strong, determined lines on his face as he worked in the glow of a cigarette-lighter. The trap removed, the mattress-cover rope was let down through the hole in the ceiling. Cautiously we climbed down, holding the boxes of uniforms, and landed with soft bumps on the floor of the passage.

The bright lights from the courtyard shone through the cobwebbed windows in the outer wall of the passage. Treading softly in our socks, we reached the door of the gate-bridge. Pat Reid, shining his lighter on the lock, swiftly picked it. It opened without a sound, for he had oiled the hinges earlier in the week. We were in the half-light of a narrow corridor. We walked quietly across it and stopped at the door that led to the guard-house.

The German uniform overcoats were unpacked in silence and we put them over our workmen's clothes, leaving our battledress in the boxes. As we pulled on our boots there was no sound except the grating of Pat Reid's wire searching in the lock. A minute passed, and suddenly came fear and exasperation. The door would not open. Beneath our feet we could hear the creaking of the gates and the voices of sentries changing guard. We stood motionless, fully dressed as German officers, and waited with pounding hearts. Pat Reid spoke in a hoarse whisper:

"I'm afraid I can't get it open!"

He continued turning the wire in the lock. I could hear the wire rasping against the rusty metal as he tried again and again to open it. Ten minutes passed in terrible suspense. Through the cobwebbed window I could see the snow falling. I folded my arms and waited. Suddenly there was the noise of old hinges creaking. A quick snap and the door swung open, showing us the dim interior of the attic.

"Good luck," said Pat Reid, and shook hands.

We waited till the door was locked behind us and we could no longer hear his muffled steps. Then we crept carefully to the top of stone spiral stairs at an open door on the other side of the attic. A wireless in the guard-room on the ground floor was playing organ music. It was the moment to go down, for the music was loud. We walked quickly down the first flight of stairs, past the door of the officers' mess on the first floor where a light showed beneath. We waited, then stepped confidently down through darkness, into the passage beside the guard-room. The guard-room door was half open, and I caught a glimpse of German uniforms inside, as we marched smartly into the blinding whiteness of the snow under the arc-lights.

The testing time had come. I strode through the snow trying to look like a Prussian. There stood the sentry, the fallen snow covering his cap and shoulders, stamping his feet, just as I had pictured him. He saluted promptly, but he stared at us, and as our backs were turned I felt him watching. We walked on beneath the first archway and passed the second sentry without incident. Then, between the first and second archways, two under-officers talking loudly came from the *Kommandantur*. They began to march behind us. I felt Luteyn grow tense beside me. I clasped my hands behind my back with an air of unconcern. I might have been casually pacing an English parade ground. In a moment of excitement I had forgotten my part. "March with your hands at your sides, you fool," came a fierce sharp whisper from my companion.

Again I saw the bicycles near the clock tower. Could they be ridden fast in this thick snow? We passed beneath the tower, saluted by the sentry, and came to the fateful wicket-gate. As Luteyn opened it I watched the under-officers, their heads bowed to the driving snow, march on across the moat bridge. Down we went into the moat, stumbling and slipping, until we reached its bed. A soldier came towards us from the married quarters. He reached us, stopped and stared deliberately. I hesitated for a moment ready to run, but Luteyn turned on him quickly and in faultless German said crossly, "Why do you not salute?"

The soldier gaped. He saluted, still looking doubtful, and began to walk up the side of the moat towards the wicket-gate. We did not look back but hastened up to the path on the far side, and, passing the married quarters, came to the high oak paling which bordered the pathway above the park. We were still within the faint glare of searchlights. Every moment that we stayed on the pathway was dangerous. Lifting ourselves quickly over the paling, we landed in thick snow among the tangle of trees. My cardboard belt was torn and broken and with it into the darkness vanished the holster.

Groping among the trees we struggled through frozen leaves down the steep bank and made for the outer stone wall. It was five minutes before we were at the bottom of the slope. Helped by Luteyn, I found a foothold in the stones of the wall and sat astride the coping. The wall, descending steeply with the tree-covered slope, was shrouded in snow and ice. Each time that I tried to pull Luteyn on top, I lost my foothold and slid backwards through the steep angle of the wall. Then, with numbed hands, I caught him beneath the armpits and, after great efforts, hoisted him up beside me. For a minute we sat breathless in the cold air clinging to the coping, and then jumped a distance of twelve feet. We fell heavily on the hard ground in the woods outside the castle grounds. I was bruised and shaken and frightened. I stood leaning against a tree looking at Luteyn. Another minute passed in the falling snow.

"Let's go," I said, and we began to climb towards the east, seeking the direction of Leisnig, a small town six miles away.

*Luteyn and Neave reached neutral Switzerland four days later.*

## NOTIFICATION OF THE DEATH OF ACTING SQUADRON LEADER ERNEST MASON, RAF, FEBRUARY 1942

Telegram                                              25.2.1942

FROM AIR MINISTRY KINGSWAY DEEPLY REGRET TO INFORM YOU THAT YOUR SON ACTING SQUADRON LEADER ERNEST MITCHELSON MASON DFC IS NOW REPORTED TO HAVE LOST HIS LIFE AS RESULT OF AIR OPERATIONS ON 15TH FEBRUARY 1942 STOP LETTER CONFIRM-ING THIS TELEGRAM FOLLOWS STOP THE AIR COUNCIL EXPRESS THEIR PROFOUND SYMPATHY STOP
UNDER SECRETARY OF STATE AIR MINISTRY

Air Ministry, London.
27th February 1942

Madam,

I am commanded by the Air Council to inform you that they have with great regret to confirm the telegram in which you were notified of the further news that your son, Acting Squadron Leader Ernest Mitchelson Mason, DFC, Royal Air Force, lost his life as the result of air operations on 15th February, 1942.

His body was recovered and buried by Army personnel.

The Air Council desire me to express their profound sym-pathy with you in your bereavement.

I am, Madam,
Your obedient Servant,
for Air Ministry.

# RAID ON DIEPPE, 19 AUGUST 1942

## Ross Munro, Canadian war correspondent

*The raid on Dieppe was designed to test the strength of German coastal defences in occupied France with a view to opening a second front (the first being the Russian) against Hitler. Five thousand Canadians were launched in a seaborne raid against the heavily fortified town of Dieppe.*

Even before we put to sea some had an ominous feeling about what was ahead of them on the other side of the Channel. Nobody said anything but many were wondering how the security had been in the time since 7 July. Did the Germans know the Canadians were going to France and were they waiting? This was the question being asked in many minds.

They were puzzled, too, why the raid had been decided upon so suddenly. They would have liked more time to adjust themselves.

I shared most of their mental discomfort. For the first hour or so I ran over the plan and studied my maps and photographs and was surprised I had forgotten so much of the detail. I found misgivings growing in my mind. This seemed somewhat haphazard, compared with the serene way in which the cancelled raid was mounted.

The final Dieppe plan was altered only slightly from the one prepared for July. British Commandos were assigned to tasks on the flanks previously allotted to paratroopers.

. . . It was one of the finest evenings of the summer. The sea was smooth, the sky was clear and there was the slightest of breezes. The ships cleared and the Royals went to dinner before making their final preparations. In the wardroom, the officers sat around the tables and dined in Navy style, as the last sunshine poured through the open portholes. We had a good meal and everyone ate hungrily, for on the way to the boats all we had had was haversack fare – a few bully-beef sandwiches.

The Royals officers were in good spirits at dinner. Looking around the table you would never have thought that they were facing the biggest test of their lives. They joked and bantered across the tables and renewed old friendships with the naval officers whom they had known in "practice Dieppe" training days.

. . . We were about ten miles from the French coast and until now there hadn't been a hitch in the plan. The minefield was behind us. The boats filled with infantrymen were lowered as the *Emma* stopped and anchored. Nobody spoke. Silence was the strict order but as our boat, which was the largest of the landing craft and was jammed with about eighty soldiers, pushed off from the *Emma*, a veteran sailor leaned over and in a stage whisper said, "Cheerio, lads, all the best; give the bastards a walloping." Then we were drifting off into the darkness and our coxswain peered through the night to link up with the rest of our assault flotilla.

. . . Eyes were accustomed to the darkness now and we could discern practically all our little craft; the sea was glossy with starlight.

The boats plunged along, curling up white foam at their bows and leaving a phosphorescent wake that stood out like diamonds on black velvet.

We were about seven or eight miles from Dieppe when the first alarm shook us. To our left there was a streak of tracer bullets – light blue and white dots in the night – and the angry clatter of automatic guns. This wasn't according to plan and everyone in that boat of ours tightened up like a drum. We kept our heads down behind the steel bulwark of our little craft, but it was so crowded there that even to crouch was crowding someone beside you. I sat on a cartful of 3-inch mortar bombs. More tracer bullets swept across ahead of us and some pinged off our steel sides. A big sailor by my side rigged his Lewis gun through a slit at the stern of our boat and answered with a few short bursts. A blob in the night that was an enemy ship – an armed trawler or more likely an E-boat – was less than two hundred yards away. It was firing at half a dozen craft including ours, which was in the lead at that time. From other directions came more German tracer. There might have been four ships intercepting us.

There wasn't much we could do. There isn't any armament on these assault craft to engage in a naval action against E-boats or trawlers. Our support craft didn't seem to be about at that particular time. It looked as if we were going to be cut up piecemeal by this interception; our flotilla already had been broken up from the close pattern of two columns we had held before the attack.

I blew up my lifebelt a little more. A few more blasts of tracer whistled past and then there was a great flash and a bang of gun-fire behind us. In the flash we could see one of our destroyers speeding up wide-open to our assistance. It fired a dozen rounds at the enemy ships and they turned and disappeared towards the French coast. They probably went right into Dieppe harbour and spread the word that British landing craft were heading in.

. . . Our coxswain tried to take us in to one section of the beach and it proved the wrong spot. Before he grounded he swung the craft out again and we fumbled through the smoke to the small strip of sand which was the Puits beach. The smoke was spotty and the last thirty yards was in the clear. Geysers from artillery shells or mortar bombs shot up in our path. Miraculously we weren't hit by any of them. The din of the German ack-ack guns and machine-guns on the cliff was so deafening you could not hear the man next to you shout.

The men in our boat crouched low, their faces tense and grim. They were awed by this unexpected blast of German fire, and it was their initiation to frightful battle noises. They gripped their weapons more tightly and waited for the ramp of our craft to go down.

We bumped on the beach and down went the ramp and out poured the first infantrymen. They plunged into about two feet of water and machine-gun bullets laced into them. Bodies piled up on the ramp. Some staggered to the beach and fell. Bullets were splattering into the boat itself, wounding and killing our men.

I was near the stern and to one side. Looking out the open bow over the bodies on the ramp, I saw the slope leading a short way up to a stone wall littered with Royals casualties. There must have been sixty or seventy of them, lying sprawled on the green grass and the brown earth. They had been cut down before they had a chance to fire a shot.

A dozen Canadians were running along the edge of the cliff towards the stone wall. They carried their weapons and some were firing as they ran. But some had no helmets, some were already wounded, their uniforms torn and bloody. One by one they were cut down and rolled down the slope to the sea.

I don't know how long we were nosed down on that beach. It may have been five minutes. It may have been twenty. On no other front have I witnessed such a carnage. It was brutal and terrible and shocked you almost to insensibility to see the piles of dead and feel the hopelessness of the attack at this point.

There was one young lad crouching six feet away from me. He had made several vain attempts to rush down the ramp to the beach but each time a hail of fire had driven him back. He had been wounded in the arm but was determined to try again. He lunged forward and a streak of red-white tracer slashed through his stomach.

I'll never forget his anguished cry as he collapsed on the blood-soaked deck: "Christ, we gotta beat them; we gotta beat them!" He was dead in a few minutes.

. . . For the rest of that morning one lost all sense of time and developments in the frantic events of the battle. Although the Puits landing had obviously failed and the headland to the east of Dieppe would still be held by the Germans, I felt that the main attack by three infantry battalions and the tanks had possibly fared better on the beach in front of the town.

Landing craft were moving along the coast in relays and the destroyers were going in perilously close to hit the headlands with shell-fire. I clambered from one landing craft to another to try to learn what was going on. Several times we were bombed too closely by long, black German planes that sailed right through our flak and our fighter cover.

Smoke was laid by destroyers and our planes along the sea and on the beach. Finally the landing craft in which I was at the time, with some naval ratings, touched down on the sloping pebble main beach which ran about sixty yards at that point to a high sea wall and the Esplanade, with the town beyond.

Smoke was everywhere and under its cover several of our ratings ran on to the beach and picked up two casualties by the barbed wire on the beach, lugging them back to the boat. I floundered through the loose shale to the sea-wall. There was heavy machine-gun fire down the beach towards the Casino. A group of men crouched twenty yards away under the shelter of the sea-wall.

The tobacco factory was blazing fiercely. For a moment there was no firing. It was one of those brief lulls you get in any battle. I thought our infantry were thick in the town but the Esplanade looked far too bare and empty.

There was no beach organization as there should have been. Some dead lay by the wall and on the shale. The attack here had not gone as planned either. A string of mortar bombs whanged on the Esplanade. The naval ratings waved and I lunged back to the boat as the beach battle opened up again. In choking smoke we pulled back to the boat pool.

. . . Then the German air force struck with its most furious attack of the day. All morning long, British and Canadian fighters kept a constant patrol over the ships and the beaches, whole squadrons twisting and curling in the blue, cloud-flecked sky. Hundreds of other planes swept far over northern France, intercepting enemy fighters and bombers long before they reached Dieppe. Reconnaissance planes kept a constant lookout on the roads from Amiens and Abbeville and Rouen where reinforcements could be expected. There were air combats going on practically all morning long. It was the greatest air show since the Battle of Britain in the fall of 1940, and the R.A.F. and R.C.A.F. had overwhelming superiority. The High Command had hoped the German air force would be lured into the sky and most of the enemy strength in western Europe came up.

. . . Bullets screeched in every direction. The whole sky and sea had gone mad with the confusion of that sudden air attack, and a dozen times I clung to the bottom of the boat expecting that this moment was the last as we were cannoned or another stick of bombs churned the sea.

Several landing craft near us blew up, hit by bombs and cannon shells. There was nothing left. They just disintegrated. These craft had been trying to make the main beach again, as we had been, to take off troops on the withdrawal.

*Dieppe was an unmitigated disaster. More than 3,000 Canadians were killed, wounded or taken prisoner in the raid.*

# THE TWATS IN THE OPS ROOM, 1942

## *Anon*

*RAF aircrew song. To the tune of "John Brown's Body".*

We had been flying all day long at one hundred fucking feet,
The weather fucking awful, fucking rain and fucking sleet,
The compass it was swinging fucking south and fucking north,
But we made a fucking landfall in the Firth of Fucking Forth.

*Ain't the Air Force fucking awful?*
*Ain't the Air Force fucking awful?*
*Ain't the Air Force fucking awful?*
*We made a fucking landing in the Firth of Fucking Forth.*

We joined the Air Force 'cos we thought it fucking right,
But don't care if we fucking fly or fucking fight,
But what we do object to are those fucking Ops Room twats,
Who sit there sewing stripes on at the rate of fucking knots.

# HOLOCAUST; THE JEWS ARE ROUNDED UP, AMSTERDAM, 19 NOVEMBER 1942

## *Anne Frank*

*The Nazis deported some 500,000 Jews from occupied western Europe to the SS death camps. These included 104,000 Jews from the Netherlands.*

### Thursday, 19 November 1942

Dussel has told us a lot about the outside world, which we have missed for so long now. He had very sad news. Countless friends and acquaintances have gone to a terrible fate. Evening after evening the green and grey army lorries trundle past. The Germans ring at every front door to enquire if there are any Jews living in the house. If there are, then the whole family has to go at once. If they don't find any, they go on to the next house. No one has a chance of evading them unless one goes into hiding. Often they go round with lists, and only ring when they know they can get a good haul. Sometimes they let them off for cash – so much per head. It seems like the slave hunts of olden times. But it's certainly no joke; it's much too tragic for that. In the evenings, when it's dark, I often see rows of good, innocent people accompanied by crying children, walking on and on, in charge of a couple of these chaps, bullied and knocked about until they almost drop. No one is spared – old people, babies, expectant mothers, the sick – each and all join in the march of death.

How fortunate we are here, so well cared for and undisturbed. We wouldn't have to worry about all this misery were it not that we are so anxious about all those dear to us whom we can no longer help.

I feel wicked sleeping in a warm bed, while my dearest friends have been knocked down or have fallen into a gutter somewhere out in the cold night. I get frightened when I think of close friends who have now been delivered into the hands of the cruellest brutes that walk the earth. And all because they are Jews!

*Anne Frank was later taken to Belsen herself, where she died in 1945.*

## OFFICER SELECTION, BRITAIN, 1943

### *Rifeman Alex Bowlby, Rifle Brigade*

I had volunteered for the Army – I hadn't fancied being called up – and this, plus the fact of my having been to one of the public schools which the regiment preferred its officers from, automatically ear-marked me as a potential officer. This upset my platoon sergeant even more than my arms-drill. One bleak November morning he could stand it no longer. The squad was practising gas-drill. I had hidden myself in the back rank but the Sergeant had turned the squad round. When everyone else had replaced their respirators I was still wrestling with the head-piece. The eye of the Sergeant was upon me. Desperately I rammed home the head-piece. When I buttoned up the respirator it bulged like a pregnant serpent. The Sergeant moved in for the kill. Unbuttoning the respirator he replaced it correctly. Then he thrust his face into mine.

"If you ever get a commission my prick's a bloater!"

A week later I was sent to a War Office Selection Board. Its highlight was an interview with a psychiatrist. I thought this would be fun. When I entered his room I had to stop myself giggling. He motioned me to sit down, and continued to correct papers (we had all answered a word-association test). After five minutes' silence I no longer found anything funny about the interview. After ten minutes I felt like screaming.

The psychiatrist suddenly looked up from the papers. He stared at me until I had to look down.

"You were unhappy at school, are extremely self-conscious, and find it difficult to concentrate. Correct?"

I nodded dumbly, wondering how on earth he did it.

"Both your parents are neurotic, aren't they?"

"I – I don't know."

"H'm. Have you ever had a woman?"

"No."

"Do you want to?"

"Of course!"

The psychiatrist gave me another long stare. I ended up looking at the floor.

"What do you like most in life?"

"Poetry, I suppose."

"Why?"

"Because it's part of my ideals."

"What ideals?"

"I don't quite know how to explain. I suppose my ideals are what I believe in."

"What do you believe in?"

"Helping other people. Doing what I feel is right."

The psychiatrist leant across the table.

"What would your feelings be if you bayoneted a German?"

This was much better.

"I'd feel sorry for him. I don't think he would have caused the war any more than I did."

The psychiatrist frowned.

"Well, what would you feel if *you* were bayoneted by a German?"

"A great deal of pain."

"Yes, but *what else?*"

I couldn't think of anything else.

"Nothing."

The psychiatrist glared at me. I stared back. We looked at each other until I felt dizzy.

"You should avoid going out alone at nights," he said finally.

I nearly burst out laughing. But he hadn't quite finished.

"And if you don't give up these so-called ideals of yours you'll go mad within eighteen months."

I was so shaken I couldn't speak. Finally I said: "But what shall I do?"

"That's up to you."

When I got out of the room I fainted.

For some weeks afterwards my nerves were all to bits. I lived for letters from a friend who slowly convinced me that the psychiatrist was talking through his hat.

## ONE MAN'S WAR: AN AMERICAN AIRMAN'S LETTER, 1943

### Sergeant Carl Goldman, USAAF

*Goldman was an aerial gunner on a B-17 Flying Fortress with the Eighth Air Force in England. The letter below was to his family, "To be opened in case of casualty only". He was lost in action over western Europe.*

*Feb. 16, 1943*

Dear Mom, Pop, Frances, Edith, Marion, Leon and Aaron:
    Am going on a raid this afternoon or early in the morning. There is a possibility I won't return.
    In any event, please do not worry too much about me as everyone has to leave this earth one way or another and this is the way. I have selected.
    I was not forced to go to gunnery school and even after I arrived overseas I could have gotten off combat had I chosen to do so.
    If after this terrible war is over, the world emerges a saner place to live; if all nationalities are treated equal; pogroms and persecutions halted, then, I'm glad I gave my efforts with thousands of others for such a cause.
    Wish I had time to write more, but sometimes the less said the better, so goodbye – and good luck – always.

Carl

## THE DAMBUSTERS RAID, RUHR VALLEY, 16 MAY 1943

### Guy Gibson, RAF

*The famous "bouncing bomb" attack on the Ruhr Valley dams by RAF 617 Squadron was intended to disrupt production in Germany's industrial heartland. Nineteen Lancaster bombers led by Wing Commander Guy Gibson took part in the raid, eight of which were lost. Two dams, the Möhne and Eder, were destroyed, bringing widespread flooding; a third dam, the Sorpe, survived the bomb that hit it. Here Guy Gibson describes the attack on the Möhne dam. He was killed in action a year later.*

The minutes passed slowly as we all sweated on this summer's night, sweated at working the controls and sweated with fear as we flew on.

Every railway train, every hamlet and every bridge we passed was a potential danger, for our Lancasters were sitting targets at that height and speed. We fought our way past Dortmund, past Hamm – the well-known Hamm which has been bombed so many times; we could see it quite clearly now, its tall chimneys, factories and balloons capped by its umbrella of flak like a Christmas tree about five miles to our right; then we began turning to the right in between Hamm and the little town of Soest, where I nearly got shot down in 1940. Soest was sleepy now and did not open up, and out of the haze ahead appeared the Ruhr hills.

"We're there," said Spam.

"Thank God," said I, feelingly.

As we came over the hill, we saw the Möhne Lake. Then we saw the dam itself. In that light it looked squat and heavy and unconquerable; it looked grey and solid in the moonlight, as though it were part of the countryside itself and just as immovable. A structure like a battleship was showering out flak all along its length, but some came from the powerhouse below it and nearby. There were no searchlights. It was light flak, mostly green, yellow and red, and the colours of the tracer reflected upon the face of the water in the lake. The reflections on the dead calm of the black water made it seem there was twice as much as there really was.

"Did you say these gunners were out of practice?" asked Spam, sarcastically.

"They certainly seem awake now," said Terry.

They were awake all right. No matter what people say, the Germans certainly have a good warning system. I scowled to myself as I remembered telling the boys an hour or so ago that they would probably only be the German equivalent of the Home Guard and in bed by the time we arrived.

It was hard to say exactly how many guns there were, but tracers seemed to be coming from about five positions, probably making twelve guns in all. It was hard at first to tell the calibre of the shells, but after one of the boys had been hit, we were informed over the RT that they were either 20-mm type or 37-mm, which, as everyone knows, are nasty little things.

We circled around stealthily, picking up the various landmarks upon which we had planned our method of attack, making use of some and avoiding others; every time we came within range of those bloody-minded flak-gunners they let us have it.

"Bit aggressive, aren't they?" said Trevor.

"Too right they are."

I said to Terry, "God, this light flak gives me the creeps."

"Me, too," someone answered.

For a time there was a general blind on the subject of light flak, and the only man who didn't say anything was Hutch, because he could not see it and because he never said anything about flak, anyway. But this was not the time for talking. I called up each member of our formation and found, to my relief, that they had all arrived, except, of course, Bill Astell. Away to the south, Joe McCarthy had just begun his diversionary attack on the Sorpe. But not all of them had been able to get there; both Byers and Barlow had been shot down by light flak after crossing the coast; these had been replaced by other aircraft of the rear formation. Bad luck, this being shot down after crossing the coast, because it could have happened to anybody; they must have been a mile or so off track and had got the hammer. This is the way things are in flying; you are either lucky or you aren't. We, too, had crossed the coast at the wrong place and had got away with it. We were lucky.

Down below, the Möhne Lake was silent and black and deep, and I spoke to my crew.

"Well boys, I suppose we had better start the ball rolling." This with no enthusiasm whatsoever. "Hello, all Cooler aircraft. I am going to attack. Stand by to come in to attack in your order when I tell you."

Then to Hoppy: "Hello, 'M Mother'. Stand by to take over if anything happens."

Hoppy's clear and casual voice came back. "OK, Leader. Good luck."

Then the boys dispersed to the pre-arranged hiding-spots in the hills, so that they should not be seen either from the ground or from the air, and we began to get into position for our approach. We circled wide and came around down moon, over the high hills at the eastern end of the lake. On straightening up we began to dive towards the flat, ominous water two miles away. Over the front turret was the dam silhouetted against the haze of the Ruhr Valley. We could see the towers. We could see the sluices. We could see everything. Spam, the bomb-aimer, said, "Good show. This is wizard." He had been a bit worried, as all bomb-aimers are, in case they cannot see their aiming points, but as we came in over the tall fir trees his voice came up again rather quickly. "You're going to hit them. You're going to hit those trees."

"That's all right, Spam. I'm just getting my height."

To Terry: "Check height, Terry."

To Pulford: "Speed control, Flight-Engineer."

To Trevor: "All guns ready, gunners."

To Spam: "Coming up, Spam."

Terry turned on the spotlights and began giving directions – "Down – down – down. Steady – steady." We were then exactly sixty feet.

Pulford began working the speed; first he put on a little flap to slow us down, then he opened the throttles to get the air-speed indicator exactly against the red mark. Spam began lining up his sights against the towers. He had turned the fusing switch to the "ON" position. I began flying.

The gunners had seen us coming. They could see us coming with our spotlights on for over two miles away. Now they opened up and the tracers began swirling towards us; some were even bouncing off the smooth surface of the lake. This was a horrible moment: we were being dragged along at four miles a minute, almost against our will, towards the things we were going to destroy. I think at that moment the boys did not want to go. I know I did not want to go. I thought to myself, "In another minute we shall all be dead – so what?" I thought again, "This is terrible – this feeling of fear – if it is fear." By now we were a few hundred yards away, and I said quickly to Pulford, under my breath, "Better leave the throttles open now and stand by to pull me out of the seat if I get hit." As I glanced at him I thought he looked a little glum on hearing this.

The Lancaster was really moving and I began looking through the special sight on my windscreen. Spam had his eyes glued to the bombsight in front, his hand on his button; a special mechanism on board had already begun to work so that the mine would drop (we hoped) in the right spot. Terry was still checking the height. Joe and Trev began to raise their guns. The flak could see us quite clearly now. It was not exactly inferno. I have been through far worse flak fire than that; but we were very low. There was something sinister and slightly unnerving about the whole operation. My aircraft was so small and the dam was so large; it was thick and solid, and now it was angry. My aircraft was very small. We skimmed along the surface of the lake, and as we went my gunner was firing into the defences, and the defences were firing back with vigour, their shells whistling past us. For some reason, we were not being hit.

Spam said, "Left – little more left – steady – steady – steady – coming up." Of the next few seconds I remember only a series of kaleidoscopic incidents.

The chatter from Joe's front guns pushing out tracers which bounced off the left-hand flak tower.

Pulford crouching beside me.

The smell of burnt cordite.

The cold sweat underneath my oxygen mask.

The tracers flashing past the windows – they all seemed the same colour now – and the inaccuracy of the gun positions near the power-station; they were firing in the wrong direction.

The closeness of the dam wall.

Spam's exultant, "Mine gone."

Hutch's red Very lights to blind the flak-gunners.

The speed of the whole thing.

Someone was saying over the RT, "Good show, leader. Nice work."

Then it was all over, and at last we were out of range, and there came over us all, I think, an immense feeling of relief and confidence.

Trevor said, "I will get those bastards," and he began to spray the dam with bullets until at last he, too, was out of range. As we circled round we could see a great 1000-feet column of whiteness still hanging in the air where our mine had exploded. We could see with satisfaction that Spam had been good, and it had gone off in the right position. Then, as we came close, we could see that the explosion of the mine had caused a great disturbance upon the surface of the lake and the water had become broken and furious, as though it were being lashed by a gale. At first we thought that the dam itself had broken, because great sheets of water were slopping over the top of the wall like a gigantic basin. This caused some delay, because our mines could only be dropped in calm water, and we would have to wait until all became still again.

We waited.

We waited about ten minutes, but it seemed hours to us. It must have seemed even longer to Hoppy, who was the next to attack. Meanwhile, all the fighters had now collected over our target. They knew our game by now, but we were flying too low for them; they could not see us and there were no attacks.

At last – "Hello, "M Mother". You may attack now. Good luck."

"OK. Attacking."

Hoppy, the Englishman, casual, but very efficient, keen now on only one thing, which was war. He began his attack.

He began going down over the trees where I had come from a few moments before. We could see his spotlights quite clearly, slowly closing together as he ran across the water. We saw him approach. The flak, by now, had got an idea from which direction the attack was coming, and they let him have it. When he was about 100 yards away someone said, hoarsely, over the RT: "Hell! He has been hit."

"M Mother" was on fire; an unlucky shot had got him in one of the inboard petrol tanks and a long jet of flame was beginning to stream out. I saw him drop his mine, but his bomb-aimer must have been wounded, because it fell straight on to the power-house on the other side of the dam. But Hoppy staggered on, trying to gain altitude so that his crew could bale out. When he had got to about 500 feet there was a vivid flash in the sky and one wing fell off; his aircraft disintegrated and fell to the ground in cascading, flaming fragments. There it began to burn quite gently and rather sinisterly in a field some three miles beyond the dam.

Someone said, "Poor old Hoppy!"

Another said, "We'll get those bastards for this."

A furious rage surged up inside my own crew, and Trevor said, "Let's go in and murder those gunners." As he spoke, Hoppy's mine went up. It went up behind the power-house with a tremendous yellow explosion and left in the air a great ball of black smoke; again there was a long wait while we watched for this to clear. There was so little wind that it took a long time.

Many minutes later I told Mickey to attack; he seemed quite confident, and we ran in beside him and a little in front; as we turned, Trevor did his best to get those gunners as he had promised.

Bob Hay, Mickey's bomb-aimer, did a good job, and his mine dropped in exactly the right place. There was again a gigantic explosion as the whole surface of the lake shook, then spewed forth its cascade of white water. Mickey was all right; he got through. But he had been hit several times and one wing-tank lost all its petrol. I could see the vicious tracer from his rear-gunner giving one gun position a hail of bullets as he swept over. Then he called up, "Okay. Attack completed." It was then that I thought that the dam wall had moved. Of course we could not see anything, but if Jeff's theory had been correct, it should have cracked by now. If only we could go on pushing it by dropping more successful mines, it would surely move back on its axis and collapse.

Once again we watched for the water to calm down. Then in came Melvyn Young in "D Dog". I yelled to him, "Be careful of the flak. It's pretty hot."

He said, "Okay."

I yelled again, "Trevor's going to beat them up on the other side. He'll take most of it off you."

Melvyn's voice again. "Okay. Thanks." And so as "D Dog" ran in we stayed at a fairly safe distance on the other side, firing with all guns at the defences, and the defences, like the stooges they were, firing back at us. We were both out of range of each other, but the ruse seemed to work, and we flicked on our identification lights to let them see us even more clearly. Melvyn's mine went in, again in exactly the right spot, and this time a colossal wall of water swept right over the dam and kept on going. Melvyn said, "I think I've done it. I've broken it." But we were in a better position to see than he, and it had not rolled down yet. We were all getting pretty excited by now, and I screamed like a schoolboy over the RT: "Wizard show, Melvyn. I think it'll go on the next one."

Now we had been over the Möhne for quite a long time, and all the while I had been in contact with Scampton Base. We were in close contact with the Air Officer Commanding and the Commander-in-Chief of Bomber Command, and with the scientist, observing his own greatest scientific experiment in Damology. He was sitting in the operations room, his head in his hands, listening to the reports as one after another the aircraft attacked. On the other side of the room the Commander-in-Chief paced up and down. In a way their job of waiting was worse than mine. The only difference was that they did not know that the structure was shifting as I knew, even though I could not see anything clearly.

When at last the water had all subsided I called up No. 5 – David Maltby – and told him to attack. He came in fast, and I saw his mine fall within feet of the right spot; once again the flak, the explosion and wall of water. But this time we were on the wrong side of the wall and could see what had happened. We watched for about five minutes, and it was rather hard to see anything, for by now the air was full of spray from these explosions, which had settled like mist on our windscreens. Time was getting short, so I called up Dave Shannon and told him to come in.

As he turned I got close to the dam wall and then saw what had happened. It had rolled over, but I could not believe my eyes. I heard someone shout, "I think she has gone!" Other voices took up the cry and quickly I said, "Stand by until I make a recce." I remembered that Dave was going in to attack and told him to turn away and not to approach the target. We had a closer look. Now there was no doubt about it; there was a great breach 100 yards across, and the water, looking like stirred porridge in the moonlight, was gushing out and rolling into the Ruhr Valley towards the industrial centres of Germany's Third Reich.

Nearly all the flak had now stopped, and the other boys came down from the hills to have a closer look to see what had been done. There was no doubt about it at all – the Möhne Dam had been breached and the gunners on top of the dam, except for one man, had all run for their lives towards the safety of solid ground; this remaining gunner was a brave man, but one of the boys quickly extinguished his flak with a burst of well-aimed tracer. Now it was all quiet, except for the roar of the water which steamed and hissed its way from its 150-foot head. Then we began to shout and scream and act like madmen over the RT, for this was a tremendous sight, a sight which probably no man will ever see again.

Quickly I told Hutch to tap out the message, "Nigger", to my station, and when this was handed to the Air Officer Commanding there was (I heard afterwards) great excitement in the operations room. The scientist jumped up and danced round the room.

Then I looked again at the dam and at the water, while all around me the boys were doing the same. It was the most amazing sight. The whole valley was beginning to fill with fog from the steam of the gushing water, and down in the foggy valley we saw cars speeding along the roads in front of this great wave of water, which was chasing them and going faster than they could ever hope to go. I saw their headlights burning and I saw water overtake them, wave by wave, and then the colour of the headlights underneath the water changing from light blue to green from green to dark purple, until there was no longer anything except the water bouncing down in great waves. The floods raced on, carrying with them as they went – viaducts, railways, bridges and everything that stood in their path. Three miles beyond the dam the remains of Hoppy's aircraft were still burning gently, a dull red glow on the ground. Hoppy had been avenged.

Then I felt a little remote and unreal sitting up there in the warm cockpit of my Lancaster, watching this mighty power which we had unleashed; then glad, because I knew that this was the heart of Germany, and the heart of her industries, the place which itself had unleashed so much misery upon the whole world.

We knew, as we watched, that this flood-water would not win the war; it would not do anything like that, but it was a catastrophe for Germany.

I circled round for about three minutes, then called up all aircraft and told Mickey and David Maltby to go home and the rest to follow me to Eder, where we would try to repeat the performance.

# SICILY: THE SEABORNE LANDINGS, 9–10 JULY 1943

## *Captain Douglas Grant, Royal Marines*

*The principal reason for the Allied invasion of Sicily in July 1943 was that it gave the victorious British and American forces in North Africa something to do. The Dieppe raid had proved that the Allies were not yet ready for an invasion of occupied France. The Italian island of Sicily was a natural substitute; if an invasion went well, the Allies could move up into Italy and perhaps bring about the fall of the Duce; if it flunked, there was no great loss. As is the nature of war, the invasion of Sicily – codenamed "Husky" – was something in between. Ten Allied divisions (2 of them airborne) descended on Sicily, defended by 12 divisions (10 of them second-rate Italian, 2 of them first-rate German). The initial landings went well and by 11 July the British Eighth Army had captured*

*Syracuse; by the 15th the American Seventh Army had reached Porto Empedocle. Thereafter, Axis resistance stiffened and not until 17 August did the Allies make a triumphal march into Messina. By then, the Germans had evacuated, along with much of their equipment. The invasion of Sicily did indeed precipitate the fall of Mussolini, at which Hitler set in train his secret plan for occupation of Italy by the* Wehrmacht. *Hitler was temperamentally incapable of giving up territory (and astonishingly loyal to Mussolini), while for the Allies to go on and invade Italy was a matter of prestige. The vague strategic reasons for the Italian campaign notwithstanding, every yard of its soil was contested.*

"Lower away!" the incisive command was given and we went down smoothly and horizontally to meet the water. . . .

I was soon cold and stiff with standing in the bows and crept into the little space that had been saved for me under the gunwales; but the stench of vomit and the retching made it impossible to stay there for long and I preferred to shiver in the spray than to be sick. I climbed up again into the fresh air and succeeded in dulling my thoughts by watching, until I was almost hypnotized, the fluctuating wakes of the craft ahead. The time insensibly passed until a singular star trembled and fell like a liquid drop from the sky on my right. I was following its quavering descent when another, bright crimson like a prick of blood, suddenly hung above it, poised momentarily, and began to fall after the first. This was the signal for spurts of light, like fiery morse code to lace the darkness and intersect each other's staccato lines in a geometrical pattern. The paratroops had been dropped. I saw now that we were sailing parallel to a long hump of land and warned the men to stand by.

Before I was fully aware of our position, the craft deployed and the cliff's dark bulk rose immediately before us. The landing ramp fell forward and shouting, "Follow me!" I clambered down into the water that was disturbed into white spume by the men of the first wave struggling ashore. I lurched and stumbled forward, up to the waist in water that bellied against me, and furiously strove for the sheltering lee of the cliff to escape from the diabolic racket of machine-gun fire that whipped overhead. The smallest man in my troop fell in a pot-hole beside me and, surfacing with difficulty, unleashed an incantation of curses but still retained a firm grasp on his mortar's bipod. I made a last violent effort and found myself freed from the water and at the base of the low cliff. The cliff was not a vertical but a retreating face, up which it was easy to crawl if little weight was put on its crumbling clay jags. I climbed until it flattened out into a slope, and took cover in a sand dune as the machine-gun lashed a foot above my head along the rank of men on the skyline immediately to my front.

My sergeant-major and batman joined me and together we hurriedly ran over the rough ground along the cliff to the right, unravelling as we went the telephone cable that would be connected to the mortars on the strip of beach. We fixed the telephone and, calling up the mortars, found that they were ready to fire . . .

I began to get back my wind, and my senses which had been dulled by the strenuous action and became aware again of danger. We had not examined the house in our flurry to set up the telephone, but we suddenly imagined we heard the quiet movements of someone inside. It was not the solid building which it had appeared on the aerial photograph, but a crazy hut of wattle and rushes with one door and no windows. My batman manned the telephone while the sergeant-major and I crept round to the front and flung the door open so violently that it fell off its upper hinge, at the same time covering with our revolvers the square room that our torches lit up. It was entirely empty and only the black ashes of a charcoal fire in the centre of the earth floor showed that it must have been occupied. While we were examining it, we heard the batman order the mortars into action; two green Verey lights had been sent up by the attacking troop and their signal called for supporting fire against a pre-arranged target. A dozen rounds were fired before they signalled us by a red Verey light to cease fire.

# SICILY: AMERICAN COUNTER-ATTACK AT BIAZZA RIDGE, 9 JULY 1942

## *General James M. Gavin, 505 Parachute Regimental Combat Team, US 82nd Airborne Division*

By then it was broad daylight, about 8:30 A.M. In less than a mile we reached a point where a small railroad crossed the road. On the right was a house where the gatekeeper lived. There was a striped pole that could be lowered to signal the automotive and donkey-cart traffic when a train approached. Just ahead was a ridge, about a half a mile away and perhaps a hundred feet high. The slope to the top was gradual. On both sides of the road were olive trees and beneath them tall brown and yellow grass, burnt by the summer sun. I had no idea where we were at the time, but I later learned the place was called Biazza Ridge.

The firing from the ridge increased. I told Lieutenant Wechsler to deploy his platoon on the right and to move on to seize the ridge. Then I sent word to Cannonball to bring his battalion up as promptly as he could.

We moved forward. I was with Wechsler, and in a few hundred yards the fire became intense. As we neared the top of the ridge, there was a rain of leaves and branches as bullets tore through the trees, and there was a buzzing like the sound of swarms of bees. A few moments later, Wechsler was hit and fell. Some troopers were hit; others continued to crawl forward. Soon we were pinned down by heavy small-arms fire, but so far nothing else.

I made my way back to the railroad crossing, and in about twenty minutes Major William Hagen joined me. He was the battalion executive for the 3rd Battalion. He said the battalion was coming up. I asked where Cannonball was, and he said that he had gone back to the 45th Division to tell them what was going on. I ordered Hagen to have the troops drop their packs and get ready to attack the Germans on the ridge as soon as they came up. By that time we had picked up a platoon of the 45th Division that happened to be there, part of a company from the 180th Infantry. There was also a sailor or two who had come ashore in the amphibious landings. We grabbed them also.

The attack went off as planned, and the infantry reached the top of the ridge and continued to attack down the far side. As they went over the top of the ridge, the fire became intense. We were going to have a very serious situation on our hands. This was not a patrol or a platoon action. Mortar and artillery fire began to fall on the ridge, and there was considerable machine-gun fire. I was worried about being enveloped on the right; some of the 45th Infantry Division should have been down on the left toward the beaches, but the right was wide open, and so far I had no one I could send out to protect that flank. If the German column was coming from Biscari, the tactical logic would have suggested that they bypass me on the right and attack me from the rear. At that time I had a few engineers I kept in reserve, and two 81-mm. mortars. They were commanded by a young officer, Lieutenant Robert May, who had been my first sergeant almost a year earlier when I had commanded C Company of the 503rd Parachute Infantry. He sent two or three troopers off to the right as a security patrol. Later, men with Mountain Pack 75-mm. artillery pieces from the 456th Parachute Artillery joined me. These were artillery pieces that could be broken down into several parts and carried by paratroopers or mules. Occasionally, troopers, having heard where we were, would come in from the direction of Vittoria. I began to try to dig in on the back of the crest of the ridge. The ground was hard shale, and I made little headway. The entrenching shovel was too frail, so I used my helmet to dig; it wasn't much better. But we needed protection from the mortar fire that was becoming quite heavy, and I kept digging.

The first wounded began to crawl back over the ridge. They all told the same story. They fired their bazookas at the front plate of German tanks, and then the tanks swiveled their huge 88-mm. guns at them and fired at the individual infantrymen. By this time the tanks could be heard, although I could not see any because of the smoke and dust and the cover of vegetation. Hagen came in, walking and holding his thigh, which had been torn badly by fire. Cannonball had gone forward to command the attack. It did not seem to be getting anywhere, however, as the German fire increased in intensity and our wounded were coming back in greater numbers.

The first German prisoners also came back. They said they were from the Hermann Goering Parachute Panzer Division. I remember one of them asking if we had fought the Japanese in the Pacific; he said he asked because the paratroopers had fought so hard. Ahead of us, mixed with the olive trees, were low grapevines that covered men on the ground quite completely. I went back a few hundred yards to check the 81-mm. mortars and to see how many other troopers had joined us. A few had. Lieutenant May had been hit by mortar fragments. I talked to the crews of the two Pack 75-mm. artillery pieces and told them we were going to stay on the ridge no matter what happened. We agreed that they should stay concealed and engage the less heavily armored underbellies of the tanks when they first appeared at the top of the rise. It was a dangerous tactic, but the only thing we could do, and tanks are vulnerable in that position. I was determined that if the tanks overran us, we would stay and fight the infantry.

I went back to try to dig my foxhole. By then it had become evident that I would never get deep enough, so I decided to dig the front end about eighteen inches deep, and the back end about a foot deep; then if I sat down in it and put my head between my knees, a tank could roll over me without doing too much damage. So I continued from time to time, when circumstances permitted, to try and get farther into the ground.

At the height of the fighting the first German Messerschmitts appeared overhead. To my surprise, they ignored us and attacked the small railroad gatekeeper's house repeatedly. They must have thought that that was the command post; it was indeed a logical place for it to be. They did not attack any of us near the top of the ridge. A few more troopers were still coming in. Now added to the enemy small-arms fire was the tank fire.

Captain Al Ireland, who was still with me, suggested that he go back to the 45th Division and get help. It was the best idea I had heard all day. I had been so busy handling the tactical crisis that the possibility had never entered my mind. The mortar fire continued in intensity, and moving along the back of the ridge to check the security on the right and the position of a 75-mm. gun the troopers were dragging up, I found myself lying on the ground bouncing from the concussion. The best way to protect yourself was to place your palms flat on the ground as though you were about to start doing push-ups, and thus absorb the shock of the ground jolts.

In front of us, beyond the vineyard and about four hundred yards to the right, was a small group of buildings. Slowly, very slowly, a German tank became visible. We first saw the right track of the tank come around the corner of the stone house. Then we saw the muzzle of the gun. A Tiger tank is an awesome thing to encounter in combat. Weighing more than sixty tons, and armed with an 88-mm. gun and machine guns, it was far more formidable that anything we had ever seen, and we had nothing in our own armored forces to compare with it.

The artillery paratroopers decided that they would take a chance and engage it directly with a 75-mm. gun. The 75 was the only artillery piece the parachutists could get in 1943. No one had ever intended that the 75 would be an antitank gun, certainly not against the front of a Tiger. Nevertheless, the paratroopers snaked their gun up the ridge until they were plainly visible and could get a direct line of sight on the tank. Field artillery in the front lines, shades of gallant Pelham at Fredericksburg! The tank inched forward, the driver probably hoping that we did not see him. It was obvious that his problem was to get far enough out so he could swing the gun at us and then fire directly, but in order to do this he had to get at least half of the tank exposed. It continued to move out slowly, very slowly. The crew of our 75 mm. were on their knees and lying down, with the gun loaded and ready to fire.

Suddenly there was a tremendous explosion. The tank had fired and hit the ground just in front of the gun, knocking the troopers like tenpins in all directions. I was standing just at the left rear, watching the action, and I was knocked down too. Probably I hit the ground instinctively. The troopers got up and ran off like startled quail. A second later they realized, to their embarrassment, what they were doing, and they ran back to the gun. They fired one round that hit the tank or the corner of the building. In the smoke and dust the tank backed out of sight.

That was the last we saw of it. To my amazement, none of the gun crew were hurt. Tanks began to work their way forward off to our left, coming directly up through the vineyard. Although the tank we fired at had backed up, I got the impression that the tank activity was increasing and that we were facing a pretty heavy attack that would come over the ridge at any moment. Back to digging, with little progress.

Two troopers came from my left rear in an Italian tracked personnel carrier. They were equipped with rifles and wanted to go over the top of the ridge to engage the Germans. I suggested that they not do it, warning them that they would be knocked out, but they insisted they could take care of themselves. They added that they wanted to "scare the Krauts" into thinking that we too had armor.

They had hardly gotten over the top of the ridge when a direct hit exploded the vehicle into flames. All the next day it was still there, smoking, with two skeletons in the front seat. An ambulance that must have been from the 45th Division showed up, and a doctor from the 505th took it over. He drove it over the ridge – he was on the running board. It was engaged in fire, and he was knocked to the ground.

I had established an aid station with medics who were off to the left, a couple of hundred yards away. They were bandaging casualties and giving them morphine and sulfa. The fire continued in considerable volume into midafternoon. About this time Cannonball came over the ridge and said that all the men in his battalion were killed, wounded, or pinned down and ineffective. I told him we were going to stay at the top of the ridge with what we had and fight the German infantry that came with the tanks. He said that we didn't have a chance, that we'd be finished if we tried to stay there. He went to the rear. I could have relieved him of his command, but I knew how he felt and I let him go.

About four o'clock a young ensign, who had parachuted with me the first night, came up with a radio and said he could call for naval gunfire. I was a bit nervous about it, because we didn't know precisely where we were, and to have the Navy shoot at us would only add to the danger and excitement of what was turning out to be quite a day. We tried to fix our position in terms of the railroad crossing over the road, and he called for a trial round. It came down precisely where the tank had disappeared. He then called for a concentration, and from then on the battle seemed to change. I kept thinking of Shiloh, bloody Shiloh. General Grant, sheltered under the riverbank, his command overrun, refused to leave the field, counterattacked, and the battle was won.

In about an hour I heard that more troopers were coming, and at six o'clock I heard that Lieutenant Harold H. Swingler and quite a few troopers from Regimental Headquarters Company were on the road. Swingler had been a former intercollegiate boxing champion; he was a tough combat soldier. He arrived about seven o'clock. In his wake appeared half a dozen of our own Sherman tanks. All the troopers cheered loud and long; it was a very dramatic moment. The Germans must have heard the cheering, too, although they did not know then what it was about. They soon found out.

By now no more wounded were coming back. A heavy pall of dust and acrid smoke covered the battlefield. I decided it was time to counterattack. I wanted to destroy the German force in front of us and to recover our dead and wounded. I felt that if I could do this and at the same time secure the ridge, I would be in good shape for whatever came next – probably a German attack against our defenses at daylight, with us having the advantage of holding the ridge. Our attack jumped off on schedule: regimental clerks, cooks, truck drivers, everyone who could carry a rifle or a carbine was in the attack. The Germans reacted, and their fire increased in intensity. Just about two hundred yards from the top of the ridge Swingler crawled up on a cut through which the paved road ran and saw a German Tiger tank with the crew standing outside looking at it. He dropped a grenade among them and killed them, and thus we captured our first Tiger. There were several bazooka hits on the front plate with holes about the size of one's little finger, but they went in only about an inch or so. The sloped armor on the Tiger was about four and a half inches thick. Soon we overran German machine guns, a couple of trucks, and finally we captured twelve 120-mm. Russian mortars, all in position with their ammunition nearby and aiming stakes out. They were obviously all ready to fire. Apparently our men had either killed, captured, or driven off the German crews. The attack continued, and all German resistance disappeared, the Germans having fled from the battlefield.

That same night, learning that the Germans had completely withdrawn from the action at Biazza Ridge, I moved my command post from the top of the ridge back about a half mile under the olive trees. I deployed the troopers for the night, expecting an attack from the direction of Biscari to come into our right flank, probably at daylight.

## HOME FRONT: FIRESTORM IN HAMBURG, 27 JULY 1943

### Else Wendel, housewife

*From early 1942, RAF Bomber Command – soon to be joined by the United States Army's Eighth Air Force – began a strategic bombing offensive against Germany. The targets for this offensive were military, industrial – and civil. A four-day bombing raid on Hamburg in July 1943 caused a "firestorm" which burnt down 80 per cent of buildings and killed 40,000 people, a fifth of them children.*

On the Tuesday night, 27 July, the bombers came back. In that raid over 45,000 [An overestimation: see above] people in Hamburg died. Mama and her friends went down into their cellar. The air warden stored sand and water and piled up tools ready for any digging that might be necessary.

It was the worst raid Mama had ever known. For hours they huddled there, with bombs crashing nearer, and the ceaseless rumblings of falling masonry. Then there was the loudest crash of all. The air warden ran out. He came back, his face grey. "Leave the cellar at once!" he called. "A phosphorus bomb has fallen at the entrance door. Quick, all of you . . ."

An indescribable panic started. Mothers grabbed children and rushed madly away. People fell over each other and Mama was separated from her friends. She didn't see them again. Out in the street people just rushed blindly away from the bomb, thinking of nothing else. An old man came near Mama, who was now standing dazed and alone. "Come with me," he said. She picked up her suitcase and followed him. It was unbearably hot in the street.

"I can't go through this. There's a cellar there not burning, I shall go down there," she told him.

"Don't be a fool," he said. "All the houses here will catch fire soon, it's only a matter of time."

A woman with two children joined them. "Come on," said the old man. "This looks the clearest way."

There were walls of flame round them now. Suddenly into the square came a fire engine drawn by two startled horses. They swerved aside, and one of the terrified children rushed down a side street. The mother followed, leaving her boy behind. As the first child reached a burning house, some blazing wood fell near her, setting her clothes alight. The mother threw herself on top of the child to try and smother the flames, but as she did so the whole top floor of the house opposite crashed down on the two of them.

The old man grabbed the boy's hand firmly. "You come with us," he ordered.

"I'll wait for my mummy," said the boy.

"No," said the old man, trying to make his voice sound harsh. "It's getting too hot here. We will wait for your mummy farther away from the fire."

Mama intervened quickly. "We will find the best way out, and then come back and fetch your mummy."

"All right," said the little boy.

They went the same way as the horses, thinking the animals'

instinct might have led them to safety. The boy fell down but got up, then fell down again.

"We can't go on like this," said the man, pulling them towards a cellar. "There's water here, pour it over your coats, and we'll put them over our heads and try that way."

Up in the square again, the man took a hasty glance round and then grabbed the boy's hand. "Now – come this way," he told them. Mama grabbed her suitcase. "Put it down," shouted the old man. "Save yourself, you can't bring that as well."

But Mama would not let go. She took the boy's hand in her left hand and the case in her right. Out in the square it was like a furnace. Sweat poured down her body as they began to run. The smoke seeped through the wet coats and began to choke them. Only for a few yards could she carry the suitcase, then she dropped it and left it without another thought. The little boy ran between them, taking steps twice as fast as their own. He fell again and again, but was hauled to his feet. Were they still on the track of the horses? They didn't know, for every moment or two they had to turn to avoid burning wood and pylons which hurtled down from the houses around. Bodies were still burning in the road. Sometimes they stumbled against them. But on they went, with the little boy's feet running tap, tap, tap between them. A dog was howling madly somewhere. It sounded more pathetic and lost than they themselves. At last they came to a small green place, and ran to the centre of it and fell on their faces, the little boy between them. They fell asleep like exhausted animals, but only for a few minutes. The old man woke first.

"Wake up," he said, shaking them both. "The fire is catching up with us."

Mama opened her eyes. They were lying in a small field, and the houses on one side were now alight; worse than alight; some kind of explosive material was there as well, it seemed. A great flame was shooting straight out towards them. A flame as high as the houses and nearly as wide as the whole street. As she stared in fascination the giant flame jerked back and then shot forward towards them again.

"My God, what is it?" she said.

"It's a fire-storm," the old man answered.

"The beginning of one. Quick, come along, there's no time to lose. In a minute there will be dozens of flames like that and they'll reach us; quick, come on, we must run. I think there's a small stream on the other side of this field."

Mama got up and bent over the boy. "Poor little thing, what a shame to wake him." She shook him gently. "Get up! We must run again."

The child did not stir. The man bent down and pulled him to his feet. "Come on, boy," he said. The child swayed and fell again. The man sank to his knees beside the child and took his hands.

"Oh, no!" he said in a shocked voice. "No, it can't be. My God, he's dead!" The tears began to pour down his blackened face. He bent down lower over the little figure and began to whisper to it.

"You were a good little boy, a very brave little boy," he said, stroking the child's face with a woman's tenderness. "As long as Hamburg has boys as brave as you she won't die." He kissed the child's face very gently. "Sleep well, little boy," he whispered. "Sleep well; you got a kinder death than your mummy and sister. They were burnt alive like rats."

Mama became nervous; another tongue of flame shot out from the side street. The roaring of the flames became stronger. The old man seemed quite oblivious now of their danger.

"Come on," she called out. "The boy is dead. We can't help him any more. Come on, we must go on."

The old man did not look up. "No," he said. "You go on by yourself. I shall die with this little boy."

Mama yelled through the roaring wind. "You're crazy! Come on!" The old man did not answer. He kissed the child's forehead again.

In despair Mama grabbed the man in her arms and tried to pull him away. Sparks were now beginning to reach their coats. Suddenly a hot gust of wind blew their coats off their backs, sending them blazing through the air. This brought the man to life again. He jumped up and started to run. As they raced across the field, the flames crept behind them. Once they fell and then got up and ran on. The field seemed wider and wider as they raced towards the stream, but at last they reached it. Unable to say another word, they both fell on the banks and slept, or perhaps they fainted first and slept afterwards.

## US BOMBERS RAID THE OIL REFINERIES AT PLOESTI, RUMANIA, 1 AUGUST 1943

### Captain John S. Young, USAAF

*The bombing of the Ploesti refineries, one of the main sources of fuel for the Nazi war effort, was carried out by 177 B-24s flying from bases in North Africa.*

On previous missions, we had bombed whatever we could find. We had gone out with general instructions to find Rommel and give him hell. When we hit the European mainland, we had made a lot of saturation raids. But for the Ploesti mission, every plane in every element was given a pinpoint – and we had to find it. There were no secondary targets. Col. John R. "Killer" Kane, our group CO, was not being dramatic when he said, "Either we hit Ploesti or we'll die trying."

We examined hundreds of still photographs. We saw motion pictures taken from the air before the war, showing us exactly what the area would look like from our bombers. We attended lectures given by a former manager of one of the Ploesti plants. And we had a detailed relief map of the surrounding territory, complete with roads and even trees. Finally, a miniature model of the targets, drawn and constructed to an exact scale, was laid out on the desert, and we practice bombed it for weeks.

We ran approximately twelve missions over that replica of the oil fields, approaching, attacking, and departing exactly as we intended doing on the actual raid. Each element was given a specific dummy target which had been erected to resemble the real thing, and we practiced until we could bomb it in our sleep. When we finally did get over the real Ploesti, our movements were almost automatic. In a low-altitude raid, you have to know precisely where you are going because you don't see your target until you are on top of it. And we knew we could only make one pass.

Our *Liberators* were modified considerably for the mission. An extra releasable fuel tank was added in the bomb bay. The top-turret guns in the lead planes were arranged so that they would fire forward, so the first ships could strafe the entire area, with the following planes protecting their rear. Extra .50s were mounted in the noses of the lead planes.

Five bomb groups made the raid. Colonel Kane and I were piloting the lead ship of the first element. The second group was on our right wing, a third on the left, another further to the left, and the fifth on the extreme left. We flew a flat V, wingtip to wingtip – no plane in the entire formation was more than twenty-five feet away from another plane.

We had forty-eight planes in our element, flying in sections of five. The first four sections had ten planes each, with an eight-plane section bringing up the rear. Each of the first twenty ships carried 1,000-pound bombs with sixty-minute delayed-action fuzes. The sixty-minute fuzes were a precaution against premature explosions damaging the last planes over the target. In practice bombings, we got the entire flight across the target within a minute and fifteen seconds, but we were prepared for the possibility that some ships might get lost on the way and reach the target late. Each plane in the last three elements carried 500-pounders with forty-five second delayed-action fuzes.

Weather conditions were perfect when we took off at 0710. We crossed the Mediterranean at 2,000 feet. At our initial point we ran into thick cumulus clouds at 10,000 feet and lowering. Over Yugoslavia, the clouds started settling in, and we had only about 1,000 feet of visibility over the 9,500-foot mountains. As we came into the Danube Valley, we dropped down to 2,500 feet and followed the Danube River to our target.

All the way across the Mediterranean and over part of Occupied Europe, we didn't even see an enemy plane. It was like a practice mission but, naturally, we maintained radio silence. In that long ride, I don't think anybody said a word.

About thirty-five minutes from our target, we lowered to twenty feet off the ground. And I mean twenty feet. We were coming in so low our plane actually had to pull up to avoid hitting a man on a horse. That horse probably is still running.

The fun started when we spotted a freight train sided at a railroad junction. There must have been fifty cars full of oil just inviting our personal attention. T/Sgt. Fred Leard, our right-waist gunner, and Sergeant Weckessler, top-turret gunner, were mighty eager boys. They called Colonel Kane on the interphone and asked if they could "test" their guns. They had gone through a routine test just after we left the field, and everything was in proper working order. But they wanted to make sure, and if a German oil train was sitting beneath them – well, that was just coincidental. The colonel, never a man to object to a "routine" check, gave his approval and the "test" began.

All the other gunners decided that their guns needed a check, too. It probably marked the first time in history that a routine gun inspection resulted in a Nazi train being blown right off its tracks.

About two miles from the target, the flak guns bellowed out a reception comparable to none I had seen in 330 combat hours against some heavily defended targets. Most of it was 20-mm stuff, with some 40-mm and a lot of machine guns. The fire was plenty accurate.

A mile and a half from the refineries, we opened up with our .50s aiming at the oil tanks which held about 55,000 gallons of oil. They started to explode, throwing smoke and flames about 500 feet into the air. There we were, buzzing in at twenty feet, doing 200 miles per hour, flying through intensive flak and bouncing around between oil fires. Play that on your harmonica sometime.

Our particular targets were the Orion and Astra Romana refineries. They had smokestacks about 210 feet high, so we had to climb to about 250 feet to drop our bombs. Flames were biting in through the bomb-bay doors, the heavy smoke fires made visibility difficult, and the flak fire was beating a hellish tattoo all over our ship, but with all the practice under our belt we had no difficulty picking out our targets. We laid our bombs down the middle.

Forty of the forty-eight planes in our element got over the target. One cracked up on the takeoff, and seven others turned back with mechanical troubles. The rest of us didn't miss.

After the bombs were away, we dropped back to twenty feet, and about fifty ME-109s and '110s jumped on us from the right. We were flying so low they couldn't dive on us, but they did lazy eights all over our formation and caused us plenty of trouble.

The housing around the propeller and three cylinders of our number-four engine were shot out. Two feet of the prop on the number-one engine was smashed, tearing a foot-and-a-half hole in the left aileron. The motor was vibrating like a bucking bronco. And we had a wing-cell leak in number three. We (I say "we" because Colonel Kane and I were both flying that airplane) put on ten degrees of flaps – no more. Ten degrees gives you the best lift without creating too much drag. We kept our wings straight by using the rudder, not the ailerons. Use of ailerons under those conditions is liable to drag a wing down.

We were still at twenty feet – maybe less. As a matter of fact, Lt. R. B. Hubbard, our radio operator, called Colonel Kane and suggested that we get some altitude because we were collecting a mess of branches, leaves, and cornstalks. The colonel investigated, and I'll be damned if Hubbard didn't hand him a cornstalk!

The fighters kept coming in, and we accounted for three. They attacked for about twenty minutes, and we just put the ship on the ground and ran like hell.

We muddled through the fighter attack and staggered away from the target on two and a half engines. About 200 miles south of the refineries, we realized that we couldn't return over the Mediterranean with our battered ship. We decided to hug a land route going back. The chief topic of conversation was picking a good place to set her down. Everybody was pestering our navigator, Lt. Norman Whalen. For my money he's the best in the business. He finally had to tell the colonel, "Look, if you guys will just leave me alone for a while, maybe I'll find a field." We left him alone. Whalen was navigating for two other damaged planes which were following, and the three of us were being covered by Lt. Royden LeBrecht. Nothing had happened to his ship.

We crossed an enemy airfield at 1,500 feet, and the flak batteries opened up. I don't know who was more surprised. But we got away without trouble.

In order to gain altitude to cross a mountain range, we threw out everything that was movable. We released the extra gasoline tank and tossed out oxygen bottles, gas masks, ammunition, radio equipment, and anything that a screwdriver could dismantle. I haven't yet seen the humor in LeBrecht's remark but he called and inquired: "What the hell are you doing? Redecorating?"

We finally got up to 6,600 feet, but we needed 7,000 feet to cross the mountains. By picking our way through canyons and ravines, and with some lucky updrafts, we managed to get over.

The plane was hobbling along now at 130 miles per hour, and we knew that it might stall at around 125 mph. It was still flying, however, and we kept plugging along. We had a choice of putting her down on land or flying across open water to the nearest Allied landing field. The colonel and I realized that there was a good chance the ship would flop into the water, but we had come too far to worry about that. As we crossed the coast, Whalen gave us an ETA of 2150 for the selected airfield.

Whalen was on the nose to within a minute. Exactly fourteen hours and forty minutes after we left Africa, we let her down.

We had to crash-land the plane, but nobody was hurt and the first thing I did after we got away from the ship was to kiss the navigator. Yes, I really kissed him.

# THE RESCUE OF MUSSOLINI FROM GRAN SASSO, 12 SEPTEMBER 1943

## Captain Otto Skorzeny, Waffen SS

*Obliged to resign as Duce by a coup d'etat, Mussolini was imprisoned in mountains north of Rome by Italians intent on surrender to the Allies. It was from this fastness that Hitler determined that Mussolini should be rescued, a task he entrusted to Otto Skorzeny, Chief of Waffen SS Special Troops. To achieve the element of surprise, Skorzeny opted for a glider landing on the rocky slope of Gran Sasso.*

"Helmets on!" I shouted as the hotel, our destination, came in sight, and then: "Slip the tow-ropes!" My words were followed by a sudden silence, broken only by the sound of the wind rushing past. The pilot turned in a wide circle, searching the ground – as I was doing – for the flat meadow appointed as our landing-ground. But a further, and ghastly, surprise was in store for us. It was triangular all right, but so far from being flat it was a steep, a very steep hillside! It could even have been a ski-jump . . .

It was easy to see that a landing on this "meadow" was out of the question. My pilot, Lieutenant Meyer, must also have realized that the situation was critical, as I caught him looking all round. I was faced with a ticklish decision. If I obeyed the express orders of my General I should abandon the operation and try to glide down to the valley. If I was not prepared to do so, the forbidden crash-landing was the only alternative.

It did not take me long to decide. I called out: "Crash landing! As near to the hotel as you can get!" The pilot, not hesitating for a second, tilted the starboard wing and down we came with a rush. I wondered for a moment whether the glider could take the strain in the thin air, but there was little time for speculation. With the wind shrieking in our ears we approached our target. I saw Lieutenant Meyer release the parachute brake, and then followed a crash and the noise of shattering wood. I closed my eyes and stopped thinking. One last mighty heave, and we came to rest.

The bolt of the exit hatch had been wrenched away, the first man was out like a shot and I let myself fall sideways out of the glider, clutching my weapons. We were within fifteen metres of the hotel! We were surrounded by jagged rocks of all sizes, which may have nearly smashed us up but had also acted as a brake so that we had taxied barely twenty metres. The parachute brake now folded up immediately behind the glider.

The first Italian sentry was standing on the edge of a slight rise at one corner of the hotel. He seemed lost in amazement. I had no time to bother about our Italian passenger, though I had noticed him falling out of the glider at my side, but rushed straight into the hotel. I was glad that I had given the order that no one must fire a shot before I did. It was essential that the surprise should be complete. I could hear my men panting behind me. I knew that they were the pick of the bunch and would stick to me like glue and ask no explanations.

We reached the hotel. All the surprised and shocked sentry required was a shout of "*mani in alto*" (hands up). Passing through an open door, we spotted an Italian soldier engaged in using a wireless set. A hasty kick sent his chair flying from under him and a few hearty blows from my machine-pistol wrecked his apparatus. On finding that the room had no exit into the interior of the hotel we hastily retraced our steps and went outside again.

We raced along the façade of the building and round the corner to find ourselves faced with a terrace two and a half metres high. Corporal Himmel offered me his back and I was up and over in a trice. The others followed in a bunch.

My eyes swept the façade and lit on a well-known face at one of the windows of the first storey. It was the Duce! Now I knew that our effort had not been in vain! I yelled at him: "Away from the window!" and we rushed into the entrance hall, colliding with a lot of Italian soldiers pouring out. Two machine-guns were set up on the floor of the terrace. We jumped over them and put them out of action. The Carabinieri continued to stream out and it took a few far from gentle blows from my weapon to force a way through them. My men yelled out *"mani in alto"*. So far no one had fired a shot.

I was now well inside the hall. I could not look round or bother about what was happening behind me. On the right was a staircase. I leaped up it, three steps at a time, turned left along a corridor and flung open a door on the right. It was a happy choice. Mussolini and two Italian officers were standing in the middle of the room. I thrust them aside and made them stand with their backs to the door. In a moment my Untersturmführer Schwerdt appeared. He took the situation in at a glance and hustled the mightily surprised Italian officers out of the room and into the corridor. The door closed behind us.

We had succeeded in the first part of our venture. The Duce was safely in our hands. Not more than three or four minutes had passed since we arrived!

At that moment the heads of Holzer and Benz, two of my subordinates, appeared at the window. They had not been able to force their way through the crowd in the hall and so had been compelled to join me via the lightning-conductor. There was no question of my men leaving me in the lurch. I sent them to guard the corridor.

I went to the window and saw Radl and his SS men running towards the hotel. Behind them crawled Obersturmführer Merzel, the company commander of our Friedenthal special unit and in charge of glider No. 4 behind me. His glider had grounded about 100 metres from the hotel and he had broken his ankle on landing. The third group in glider No. 5 also arrived while I was watching.

I shouted out: "Everything's all right! Mount guard everywhere!"

I stayed a little while longer to watch gliders 6 and 7 crash-land with Lieutenant Berlepsch and his parachute company. Then before my very eyes followed a tragedy. Glider 8 must have been caught in a gust; it wobbled and then fell like a stone, landed on a rocky slope and was smashed to smithereens.

Sounds of firing could now be heard in the distance and I put my head into the corridor and shouted for the officer-in-command at the hotel. A colonel appeared from nearby and I summoned him to surrender forthwith, assuring him that any further resistance was useless. He asked me for time to consider the matter. I gave him one minute, during which Radl turned up. He had had to fight his way through and I assumed that the Italians were still holding the entrance, as no one had joined me.

The Italian colonel returned, carrying a goblet of red wine which he proffered to me with a slight bow and the words: "To the victor!"

A white bedspread, hung from the window, performed the functions of a white flag.

After giving a few orders to my men outside the hotel I was able to devote attention to Mussolini, who was standing in a corner with Untersturmführer Schwerdt in front of him. I introduced myself: "Duce, the Führer has sent me! You are free!"

Mussolini embraced me: "I knew my friend Adolf Hitler would not leave me in the lurch," he said.

## THE LANDINGS AT SALERNO, 9 SEPTEMBER 1943

### John Steinbeck, war correspondent

*On 3 September Montgomery's Eighth Army crossed from Sicily to attack Reggio Calabaria. The main attack on the Italian mainland came six days later at Salerno, thirty miles south of Naples. Being one of the few possible places for an invasion in mountainous southern Italy, the Allies were expected by Germans who had ringed the hills with artillery. John Steinbeck – more famous as the writer of the novel* The Grapes of Wrath – *reported the landings for the New York* Herald Tribune.

There is a good beach at Salerno, and a very good landing at Red Beach No. 2. The ducks were coming loaded ashore and running up out of the water and joining the lines of trucks, and the pontoon piers were out in the water with large landing cars up against them. Along the beach the bulldozers were at work pushing up sand ramps for the trucks to land on and just back of the beach were the white tapes that mean land mines have not been cleared out.

There are little bushes on the sand dunes at Red Beach south of the Sele River, and in a hole in the sand buttressed by sand bags a soldier sat with a leather covered steel telephone beside him. His shirt was off and his back was dark with sunburn. His helmet lay in the bottom of the hole and his rifle was on a little pile of brush to keep the sand out of it. He had staked a shelter half on a pole to shade him from the sun, and he had spread bushes on top of that to camouflage it. Beside him was a water can and an empty "C" ration can to drink out of.

The soldier said, "Sure you can have a drink. Here, I'll pour it for you." He tilted the water can over the tin cup. "I hate to tell you what it tastes like," he said. I took a drink. "Well, doesn't it?" he said. "It sure does," I said. Up in the hills the 88's were popping and the little bursts threw sand about where they hit, and off to the seaward our cruisers were popping away at the 88's in the hills.

The soldier slapped at a sand fly on his shoulder and then scratched the place where it had bitten him. His face was dirty and streaked where the sweat had run down through the dirt, and his hair and his eyebrows were sunburned almost white. But there was a kind of gayety about him. His telephone buzzed and he answered it, and said, "Hasn't come through yet, sir, no sir. I'll tell him." He clicked off the phone.

"When'd you come ashore?" he asked. And then without waiting for an answer he went on. "I came in just before dawn yesterday. I wasn't with the very first, but right in the second." He seemed to be very glad about it. "It was hell," he said, "it was bloody hell." He seemed to be gratified at the hell it was, and that was right. The great question had been solved for him. He had been under fire. He knew now what he would do under fire. He would never have to go through that uncertainty again. "I got pretty near up to there," he said, and pointed to two beautiful Greek temples about a mile away. "And then I got sent back here for beach communications. When did you say you got ashore?" and again he didn't wait for an answer.

"It was dark as hell," he said, "and we were just waiting out there." He pointed to the sea where the mass of the invasion fleet rested. "If we thought we were going to sneak ashore we were nuts," he said. "They were waiting for us all fixed up. Why, I heard they had been here two weeks waiting for us. They knew just where we were going to land. They had machine guns in the sand dunes and 88's on the hills.

"We were out there all packed in an L. C. I. and then the hell broke loose. The sky was full of it and the star shells lighted it up and the tracers crisscrossed and the noise – we saw the assault go in, and then one of them hit a surf mine and went up, and in the light you could see them go flying about. I could see the boats land and the guys go wiggling and running, and then maybe there'd be a lot of white lines and some of them would waddle about and collapse and some would hit the beach.

"It didn't seem like men getting killed, more like a picture, like a moving picture. We were pretty crowded up in there though, and then all of a sudden it came on me that this wasn't a moving picture. Those were guys getting the hell shot out of them, and then I got kind of scared, but what I wanted to do mostly was move around. I didn't like being cooped up there where you couldn't get away or get down close to the ground.

"Well the firing would stop and then it would get pitch black even then, and it was just beginning to get light too but the 88's sort of winked on the hills like messages, and the shells were bursting all around us. They had lots of 88's and they shot at everything. I was just getting real scared when we got the order to move in, and I swear that is the longest trip I ever took, that mile to the beach. I thought we'd never get there. I figured that if I was only on the beach I could dig down and get out of the way. There was too damn many of us there in that L. C. I. I wanted to spread out. That one that hit the mine was still burning when we went on by it. Then we bumped the beach and the ramps went down and I hit the water up to my waist.

"The minute I was on the beach I felt better. It didn't seem like everybody was shooting at me, and I got up to that line of brush and flopped down and some other guys flopped down beside me and then we got feeling a little foolish. We stood up and moved on. Didn't say anything to each other, we just moved on. It was coming daylight then and the flashes of the guns weren't so bright. I felt a little like I was drunk. The ground heaved around under my feet and I was dull. I guess that was because of the firing. My ears aren't so good yet. I guess we moved up too far because I got sent back here.' He laughed openly. 'I might have gone on right into Rome if some one hadn't sent me back. I guess I might have walked right up that hill there."

The cruisers began firing on the hill and the 88's fired back. From over near the hill came the heavy thudding of 50-caliber machine guns. The soldier felt pretty good. He knew what he could do now. He said, "When did you say you came ashore?"

## HOME FRONT: RACHEL THE RIVETER, SAN DIEGO, 1943

### Rachel Wray, hand riveter, Consolidated Aircraft

I grew up on a farm in northeastern Oklahoma, knowing nothing but the Depression. My father lost the farm, and we moved to town just when I was starting junior high school. I lived there until the eleventh grade, when I was forced to quit school to go to work.

When I was nineteen I fell in love with a boy from Oklahoma. George was also from a depressed area and joined the Navy to get ahead. He was stationed in California, and I decided to come and join him. I felt there would be more opportunity in California, and I was determined that I was going to have a different life.

I had twenty-five dollars when I left Oklahoma. I answered an ad in the paper looking for riders to California and paid twelve dollars for the trip. I arrived here with twelve dollars to my name and lived with friends until I could get work.

I got a job as a pastry cook at a restaurant in Whittier, a very exclusive place. I was making fifteen dollars (and board) a week and was very proud of myself. George and I were planning to marry. Then

Pearl Harbor was attacked, and his ship was sent out to fight in the Pacific.

After he left I knew I had to make it on my own. I saw an ad in the paper announcing the opening of a school for vocational training in aircraft. I was looking for the opportunity to learn something else, and I wanted to earn more money. I worked during the day cooking and went to school at night studying bench mechanics and riveting, how to read blueprints and use different aircraft tools.

After about three months the instructor said, "There's no use in you spending any more time here. You can go out and get a job." He gave me my graduation slip, and I went down to San Diego to look around, because George's mother lived there. I went to Convair, which was Consolidated Aircraft then, and they hired me.

I was one of the first women hired at Convair and. I was determined that I wasn't going to lose the job and be sent back to working as a pastry cook. Convair had a motto on their plant which said that anything short of right is wrong, and that stuck with me. I went to work in the riveting group in metal-bench assembly. The mechanics would bring us the job they had put together, and we would take the blueprints and rivet what they brought us.

They would always put the new people with another person, a "leadman." The man I went to work for was really great. He saw my determination and would give me hard jobs to do. The other girls would say, "Joplin, don't give her that, I'll do it." But he would say, "I'm going to break her in right, I'm going to do it the hard way." He told me later that he had made a mistake and been too easy with the other girls.

I tackled everything. I had a daring mother who was afraid of nothing: horses, farm implements, anything, so maybe I inherited a little bit of that from her. I remember my brother, who was in the Air Corps at the time, and his friends laughed at me one day thinking I couldn't learn this mechanical stuff. I can still see them, but it only made me more determined. I think it probably hurt their pride a little bit that I was capable of doing this.

Pretty soon I was promoted to bench-mechanic work, which was detailed hand-riveting. Then I was given a bench with nothing to do but repair what other people had ruined. I visited a man recently who's seventy-four years old, and he said to my daughter, "All we had to do was foul up a job and take it to her and she'd fix it."

I loved working at Convair. I loved the challenge of getting dirty and getting into the work. I did one special riveting job, hand riveting that could not be done by machine. I worked on that job for three months, ten hours a day, six days a week, and slapped three-eighth- or three-quarter-inch rivets by hand that no one else would do. I didn't have that kind of confidence as a kid growing up, because I didn't have that opportunity. Convair was the first time in my life that I had the chance to prove that I could do something, and I did. They finally made me a group leader, although they didn't pay me the wage that went with the job, because I was a woman.

Our department was a majority of women. Many of the women had no training at all, particularly the older women. We had women in our department who were ex-schoolteachers, -artists, housewives, so when we could give them a job from the production line, the job would have to be set up for them. I'd sit them down and show them how to use the drill press, the size drill to use, the size of screws, the kind of rivets, whether it was an Army rivet or a Navy rivet – a Navy rivet was an icebox rivet, the Army rivet was not – and so on. Then I would go back and check to see if the riveting was okay, and if there were any bad rivets, they had to take them out. Most of the time I had to take them out myself. As a group leader that's what I did, and I did it at the same time I was doing my job as a bench mechanic. There were four male group leaders and myself. Theoretically we should have been classified as group leaders and paid for that type of work, but we were not. I felt that was discrimination and that we were being used by the company and fought against it.

Shortly after I went to work at Convair I was chosen by the people in our work group to sit on the wage-review board. The company had automatic wage reviews, and when I first started, those were the only raises that we received. The women were lucky, though, if we got a five-cent-an-hour increase on a review. Some of the women got three cents, some of the women even got two cents, and some of the women were passed over. To us it seemed that the men's pay automatically went up, and ours didn't. I was fortunate enough to get raises later, even a ten-cent raise, and I actually had an assistant foreman come up to me and say, "Don't say anything to the other girls about getting a raise." I told him, "I don't discuss my personal wages, but how about the other women who are deserving too?" So on the wage board I fought for the other women as much as I fought for myself. The highest-paid women at that time were making around $.80 an hour, but the men were probably making $1.15 to $1.50 an hour for identically the same work. In fact, there was a lot of feeling that the women were producing more work than the men on final assembly and on the bench because of their agility with their hands.

Some of the things we did change. For example, they were forced to classify you because of your work. And somewhere in the back of their minds they had the idea that they were not going to make a woman anything but a B-mechanic. As a B-mechanic you could only go to $1.00 an hour, and they were determined that no woman would ever become an A-mechanic or an A-riveter. But we really fought that and we proved to them by bringing them on the job that we were doing A-mechanic work and producing more than the men. So I got my A-mechanic classification and a raise to $1.15 an hour.

I also sat on the safety board the whole time I was at Convair, for the safety requirements they demanded of women were more un-reasonable than what they demanded of men. In the beginning we had caps and uniforms we were supposed to wear, but the women rebelled at that. We felt that we could be safe and wear the clothes we wanted. Eventually the company did become a little more relaxed about dress, so we won some victories there too.

## "WAITING, WAITING, WAITING": THE LIFE OF A POW, GERMANY, 1944

### *Sergeant Nell, Green Howards*

*Nell was captured at Marsa Matruh in June 1942 and imprisoned in a succession of Italian and German POW camps. He was finally liberated in April 1945.*

*New Year's Day 1944*. They can't win. Hitler is losing lives for nothing. We heard yesterday that the Russians have launched an offensive of 300,000 men. The Russian steam-roller. May it roll everything before it. An educational scheme is afoot. At first I enrolled for English, Electricity and Psychology, but have since changed to the London Matriculation Course. I wonder, can I do it? How much longer is the war going to last? I could put up with fighting but this endless turning over of days in a POW camp, waiting – waiting – waiting. When is it going to end?

*5 February*. I went to the theatre this evening and saw the play *Boy Meets Girl*. When a man is dressed as a woman he looks astoundingly like the authentic article. None of us have been on speaking terms with a woman for some time; perhaps that has something to do with it. It is almost two years since I even spoke to a woman. Letters!!! Three of them, two from Eve and one from Father. At long last I have got letters from my darling Eve. Oh, Evie, my sweet.

*20 February*. My thirtieth birthday. But I kept it a secret. I am worried about Gerry. He has fallen to pieces because he has failed (in his own estimation) as a writer. Since last June he has been working on a novel and now he finds that he can't carry on. He is distressed and eating next to nothing. Eve wonders if I have changed much. I wonder how much she has changed and in what ways? I take for granted that she will be much prettier. I wonder if she can cook yet? Oh, Evie, my darling, if you knew this terrible longing I have for you. A little boy may cry for what he wants. Poor Eve, she doesn't know it, but for some time I am going to be her baby. What a delightful mother I am going to have. Eve, my darling – or shall I say "Mummy"?

Later. I think the Germans are worrying about the war. They have issued three blankets to every Russian prisoner and have given them coal. It is rather late in the day to be humane. Thousands of Russians have died of TB as a result of malnutrition by the Germans. They actually hope that their treatment of hapless POWs will be forgotten. British and French prisoners are treated well but the other nationalities get no more consideration than animals. As I lay listening to the drone of hundreds of planes and the explosion of their bombs, I thought of the children and old people, terrified and being maimed and killed and rendered homeless. And then I thought of Eve.

*26 April.* At the bath-house today I saw some Russians who had just bathed. They were naked, waiting for their bodies to dry in the air (they have no towels). What a ghastly sight they were, nothing but skin and bone. Their skin was stretched tightly over their ribs, their stomachs were distended like bladders, there was no flesh where their buttocks should have been. It would be inconceivable that human beings could treat their fellow man as the Germans are treating the Russians were we not here to see it. And I was in the same condition once. May-day is a National holiday to celebrate their National Socialist Party's coming into power. It will be their last celebration.

. . . I am thirty years of age and going bald, what will Eve think when she sees me? There is nothing but a spiritual link between us and the war would seem to be slowly but surely breaking it. And I am sure my heart will break with it . . . The *Camp* – that propaganda paper for POW's – has shown us the type of temporary house to be supplied to people in Britain after the war. It is made of steel and has four rooms. Not very big but it will do until proper houses are provided. I wonder if Eve and I shall get one? Oh, how I long for the day when we can live together!

*21 June.* A man has just been shot and killed. He was reaching through the fence to pick some wild strawberries when a German soldier drew his pistol and shot him . . . Writing! Mine is getting worse. We write, they say, as we live. I am nervous so I must write nervously . . . If I weren't a prisoner I could be with my Eve. It makes me wild when I think of it. Eve is very sweet in her last letter. She asks me to marry her as soon as I get home. Gosh! I never knew that the time would come when a girl would ask *me* to marry her! Letters are so few and far between. They are next important to food – they *are* spiritual food for us prisoners. I want Evie all day . . . I have agreed with her regarding our not having children until we have our own home. Our children must not be left to chance as I was. My childhood was a mild form of Hell. Roll on peace and the scaffold for the Nazis.

## A RESISTANCE GROUP BLOWS UP A TRAIN, FRANCE, 1944

### George Millar, SOE

*Millar was an agent of the British Special Operations Executive working with the French Resistance.*

One day after lunch Philippe asked if he might take some of the others out and do a job on the Vesoul railway. We had just heard a train pass below us in the valley, and this was such an unusual sound that it roused us to action. Boulaya refused permission, but I persuaded him to let Philippe take out the Pointu and two new lads, Communists whom Maurice and Philippe together had rescued from imprisonment in the German hospital in Besançon, where they had been convalescing from German-inflicted wounds. The four of them departed happily on foot, carrying an arsenal of miscellaneous weapons and the heavy tools we used for unscrewing the railway lines. They promised to work as far afield as Miserey. Things appeared to go badly. That afternoon we heard the sound of firing, and the story came back to us that while they were derailing a train near Miserey a German truck full of soldiers passed on the road and opened fire. The Maquisards replied and then withdrew.

One by one that evening the young men dribbled back into the camp, bringing with them all their weapons and the tools. The story of the Germans was true, but Philippe had turned their arrival to our profit, for while the little battle was going on he had walked into Miserey station, found another train there and obliged the railwaymen to start it at full speed. This, crashing into the derailed train in the cutting, broke up the battle and allowed the other three Maquisards to withdraw in good order. On the way home Philippe and the Pointu seized a third train near Devecey, made all the occupants descend, and hurled this train on to the wreckage near Miserey. This was a wonderful day's work. I cycled out to see it, and I knew that if the enemy still had a crane he would need it for this, and it would be a long job. The cutting was deep, and the wreckage was well wedged in.

But our Philippe was irresistible. Boulaya gave him a holiday in Besançon to celebrate this important victory. He spruced himself up and left on a new bicycle. (We had just taken eight new ones from the police in Besançon, and Boulaya and I each bought one on the black market, so we were now astoundingly well off for bicycles.) Bronzed and bleached by the sun now, Philippe looked more cherubic than ever.

Unable to avoid the scene of his crime, he cycled past the still smoking remains where the Gestapo were examining tracks and questioning civilians and railwaymen. He saw another locomotive in Miserey station. Unarmed as he was, he cursed and swore at the railwaymen until they sent their engine rushing down the track. It hit the wreckage while the Gestapo were still there, and jumping, said onlookers, thirty feet into the air it landed upside down on the other side of the heap of twisted metal. Its wheels continued to revolve for some time. Already crowds were gathering for this fantastic sight. Cycling excursions were setting out from all the villages. Many of them were to have their money's worth. Philippe, tranquilly continuing on his way to Besançon, found another train and again, with only his gruff and determined voice to help him, succeeded in getting it launched at full speed on the right rails. In front of a large audience this train added itself to the heap in the cutting.

Sightseers were still visiting the place six weeks later. And it was known locally as "the mountain of Miserey"; This closed the Vesoul line until (and, alas, after) the Allied armies arrived.


# FLYING FOR THE FATHERLAND: A GERMAN FIGHTER PILOT INTERCEPTS HEAVY BOMBERS, 10–21 FEBRUARY 1944

## *Heinz Knoke*, Luftwaffe

*10th February*, 1944.

"Enemy concentrating in sector Dora-Dora," reports the operations room.

At 1038 hours we take off.

"Climb to 25,000 feet over Rheine," run my orders. Specht is ill, and I am temporarily in command of the formation.

25,000 feet over Lake Dümmersee we sight the enemy.

It is a truly awe-inspiring spectacle which confronts us. There are approximately 1,000 of the heavy bombers flying eastwards along a wide frontage with a strong fighter escort. I have never before seen such a mighty air armada: the target obviously is Berlin. Including the fighter escort the total American strength I estimate at 1,200.

Against them we are forty aircraft. Yet even if we were only two, we should still have to engage the enemy.

I pick a group of Fortresses flying on the left flank of the main body and close in for a frontal attack. The Americans apparently guess my intention. At the critical moment they alter course slightly, and thus my attack is in vain.

Swinging off to the right and round in a wide arc, I wait until we are again flying ahead of the enemy, and then come round for a second frontal attack. With my forty Messerschmitts in a tight Vic-formation I want to cut a swath through the ranks of the enemy.

By radio I urge my pilots to keep calm and make every shot count. We keep close together. I notice Thunderbolts behind. They cannot intercept us before we dive into the enemy bombers.

Raddatz holds his plane flying almost wing-tip to wing-tip alongside mine. He waves across to me just before we open fire on our targets. Just as I am seeking out my opponent and adjusting the sights on him, there, is a bright flash from the aircraft next to mine. Raddatz immediately plummets down vertically. I cannot follow him down, because I am too busy firing now.

I continue closing upon my Fortress, firing at the control cabin in the nose, until I have to pull up sharply in order to avoid a head-on collision.

My salvo has registered. The Fortress rears up on its tail. In alarm the heavy bombers following swerve out of the way. Then the left wing drops, and the huge plane goes down out of control in its final death-dive, to disintegrate some 5,000 or 10,000 feet below.

More than ten other Fortresses are shot down.

Flying alone, I am suddenly set upon by eight Mustangs. The pilots are evidently inexperienced. After a few sharp turns and loops I get away, and soon I am round on the tail of one of them. Just when I am about to open fire, however, I find myself again surrounded by a pack of Thunderbolts. I have to break away and zoom up in a corkscrew climb. This manœuvre has been my salvation frequently before. No opponent has ever succeeded in following me up. For nearly half an hour I keep trying to get into a position to fire on the tail of a Mustang or Lightning, but without success.

Eventually I dive into a group of Fortresses from the rear and fire at one of them. Before I have a chance to observe the result of my salvo, I am again set upon by a pair of Thunderbolts. Both have distinctive checkerboard black-and-white markings on the engine cowling. I peel off in a steep dive into a cloud.

At 1141 I again land at Wunsdorf. There I learn that Raddatz is dead. That is a heavy blow for the Flight. Raddatz had been with the Flight ever since its formation. I never met a more brilliant pilot. He was the finest of comrades. I cannot believe that he is in fact no more.

*11th February*, 1944.

Today over Mainz we had a wild dog-fight with American fighters, who were escorting their Fortresses. We landed at Wiesbaden between engagements.

*20th February*, 1944.

The Squadron had two long engagements today with formations of Fortresses over North Germany and the North Sea.

Specht was forced down and had to make an emergency landing on the Danish island of Aroe.

Bad shooting on my part caused me to miss a good opportunity of adding to my score.

*21st February*, 1944.

Today I flew two more missions. We had orders to draw off the escorting fighters at any cost and keep them engaged in combat with us. Other Squadrons meanwhile attacked the heavy bombers. That cost my Squadron two more dead.

# A LETTER FOR TITO, JUGOSLAVIA, SPRING 1944

## *Fitzroy Maclean*

*Maclean was the British military aide to Tito (aka Josip Broz), the communist resistance leader in Jugoslavia. The British regarded Tito as a more stalwart opponent of the Axis occupiers than the Serbian Chetniks of Draza Mihailovic, and supported his war effort accordingly. This tied down twenty Axis divisions before they were booted out of the country. Jugoslavia was the only occupied country to free itself from Nazi occupation.*

I was right: we had been dropped from very low indeed; no sooner had my parachute opened, than I hit the ground with considerably more force than was comfortable. Looking up, I saw Randolph Churchill coming down almost on top of me. The expression of satisfaction which dawned on his face as he realised that his parachute had opened rapidly gave way to one of disgust as he glanced down to see the ground rushing up to meet him. Then, narrowly missing a telegraph pole, he came to rest with a sudden bump in a patch of melting snow and mud. A little farther away Slim Farish and the rest of the "stick" were landing at intervals of a few yards from one another – a neat bit of grouping on the part of the pilot, though personally I should not have minded if we had had a little more height to spare.

But we were not left long to reflect on such technicalities. Already John Selby, in the rôle of master of ceremonies, was upon us. Six weeks with the Partisans, which had included several forced marches, had, I noticed, made him a good deal less portly, and changed him in appearance from an immaculate Wing-Commander to something between a brigand and a dispatch rider. But his salute was as spectacular and his manner as urbane and soothing as ever. With him came Slavko Rodic, tall, pale and elegant with a neat dark moustache. His troops had provided the reception party for my first drop at Mrkonicgrad and were now performing the same service again.

They had not greatly changed. Weather-beaten and battle stained, they wore the usual medley of captured enemy equipment and uniforms, only now there was here and there a suit of British battle-dress, a pair of boots, a Mills grenade or a Sten gun as a token of our aid. No sooner had my feet touched the ground, than a guard of honour was formed, ready for me to inspect. From the violence of their ceremonial drill it was clear that they more than made up in keenness for anything they might lack in orthodoxy of appearance.

Then horses were brought and Rodic and I, having played our part in the ceremony, sprang into the saddle and set off at a gallop up the road to the village, followed by the rest of the party, while the guard of honour turned to the task of collecting the containers of supplies which had been dropped at the same time as we had.

Bosanski Petrovac lies on the verge of one of the rare stretches of flat grassland in the highlands of Bosnia. On the far side, perhaps two or three miles away, was a range of dark hills, and in front of us, as we rode, the ground rose again, sloping gently up towards the village, which itself was built on the side of a hill, a typical Bosnian hamlet with its wood and plaster cottages.

In the upper room of one of these a meal had been prepared. It was a good meal, though not so good, our hosts explained with engaging frankness, as the one they had prepared the day before and then eaten themselves when they found we were not coming. At any rate we were hungry and did justice both to the stew which they gave us and to the local *slivovica*.

As we ate, I discussed plans with Slavko Rodic. The military situation was still fluid, and Tito and his staff were living in the woods until they could find somewhere to re-establish their headquarters. I wanted to see Tito as soon as possible, and Rodic said that he would take me to him himself. After Slim Farish, Randolph and the others had been installed in a peasant's house with instructions to stay where they were until further notice, we set out. It was getting dark as we rode down the village street and lights were beginning to twinkle in some of the windows.

Slavko had always prided himself on having good horses, and the two which we rode were admirable. The escort, which accompanied us, were also well mounted and we pushed along at a brisk pace. It was getting dark when we left, and as we reached higher ground it grew colder and the snow lay deep on the track we were following through the forest. The snow deadened the sound of our horses' hooves, and, in the darkness, you could only dimly discern the form of the horse and rider in front of you. As I rode, muffled in the warm privacy of my great-coat, I turned over in my mind the various points which I had to discuss with Tito. Then Slavko, who had been riding with the rear-guard caught up with me, and we fell to talking of our lives before the war and of what we hoped to make of them when the war was over. In peace-time he had been some kind of engineer or surveyor; now, still in his twenties, he was a Partisan leader; when the war was over, if he survived, there would be work of some kind for him to do in the new Jugoslavia. That this new Jugoslavia would emerge triumphant, whatever the obstacles to be overcome, was for him, as for them all, a certainty, and had so been from the first.

We had a long way to go, and, even though we rode fast, it was after midnight when, in the thickest part of the forest, we were suddenly challenged by an unseen sentry. We gave the password and our names and, having done so, were allowed to proceed. It was still snowing and, as we rode on, we could make out lights dimmed by the falling snow, shining among the trees, and, going towards these, came on a group of wooden huts. A Partisan took our horses, and another, recognising me, came forward and said that Tito was waiting up and wanted to see me as soon as I arrived. If I would come he would take me to him.

Picking our way through the trees, we came to a small, roughly built hut of freshly sawn planks. Inside, a light was burning. A sentry, on guard at the door, made way for me, and I went in.

As he came forward to meet me, I saw that Tito no longer had on the plain dark tunic and breeches which he used to favour, but was wearing instead a kind of uniform with, on his sleeve, a roughly embroidered laurel leaf encircling a star. Since our last meeting, the Anti-Fascist Council meeting at Jajce had bestowed on him the specially created rank of Marshal of Jugoslavia, at the same time setting up a "provisional Government" in which he occupied the dominant position. When I congratulated him on this honour he seemed slightly embarrassed. "They would do it," he said, and smiled deprecatingly. For a moment it occurred to me that, while character-istically enjoying the magnificence of his new title, he perhaps at the same time rather regretted the days when, holding no other office save that of Military Commander of the Partisan forces, he had been known to all by an unadorned nickname. Then we sat down; food and drink were brought, and we started to talk.

We had much to tell each other. As a start, I handed Tito the letter which I had brought him from the Prime Minister. He had had no warning of it, and I watched his face closely to see how he liked it, as one watches a child with a new toy.

There could be no doubt of the effect. As he broke open the seal, and, unfolding the crisp sheet of heavy paper within, saw the address of 10 Downing Street at the top and the Prime Minister's signature at the foot, a broad smile of unaffected delight spread slowly over his face, which became broader still when he found a large signed photograph of Mr. Churchill in a separate envelope. I offered to translate the letter for him, but he insisted on trying to make it out on his own, turning to me for help over the more complicated passages, and giving way to fresh demonstrations of pleasure as he came to complimentary references to the prowess of the Partisans and promises of Allied assistance. He was clearly very much pleased.

He had reason to be. Tito's career up to now had taken him underground, behind the scenes. He had been perpetually in conflict with the established order. Despite this, perhaps because of this, he attached great importance to outward appearances. Already the revolutionary process which he had set in motion was carrying him, the revolutionary, upwards and onwards towards a new established order which, ultimately, would take the place of that which was being overthrown. The high-sounding title of Marshal of Jugoslavia which had been bestowed on him by his own people was an outward and visible sign of this, even though its recipient might still be hiding in the mountains and forests. But, hitherto, he had received but little recognition from the outside world. The Germans, it is true, had put a price, and a very high one, on his head, but the Great Powers, whose ally he was, had been slow to discern in him and his Movement a force to be taken into account; even the Russians showed little active interest in him. Now, at last, with the arrival of Mr. Churchill's letter, he was beginning to come into his own internationally. He was in direct and formal communication with one of the Big Three, with the Prime Minister of a Great Power. Mr. Churchill made it clear that he regarded him as an ally and as such promised him all possible help. Moreover he invited him to correspond with him through me on all matters of importance. This was no longer so very far removed from official recognition. It was at any rate a very big step forward.

Next I gave Tito some account of the greatly increased assistance which he was now to receive. I told him in detail of the steps which were being taken to improve the existing system of air supplies and air support; of the scheme for training his men as pilots and tank-crews.

He was delighted and said that he would immediately set about collecting good men from all over the country to be trained. These he would then have smuggled down to the coast and shipped across the Adriatic by schooner.

Then I asked what progress the German offensive was making. He replied that the first fury of the German attack had spent itself without the enemy being able to win a decisive success. Now the Partisans, having once again successfully denied the enemy a target, were beginning to hit back all over the country, and the Germans were getting as good as they gave. The trouble was that his men lacked everything: food, clothing, boots, ammunition. He could only hope that the promised supplies would come before it was too late. Meanwhile the situation had to some extent been stabilised locally, and he expected to be able to move his headquarters before long to the neighbourhood of Drvar, a part of Bosnia which had long been outstandingly faithful to the Partisan cause.

Finally we talked of the islands and of the prospects of converting Vis into a firm base from which we could harass the enemy and smuggle across supplies to the mainland. The other islands had by now all been occupied by the Germans, and we agreed that we should need to act quickly if we were to be in time to save Vis from their fate.

We talked till the early hours of the morning. Then, bidding Tito good night, I followed one of the guards through the snow to the hut which had been allotted me. Gordon Alston and Hilary King, my new signals officer, were lying asleep in some straw which was spread on a kind of shelf stretching the whole length of the hut. Waking, they told me of their adventures since their hurried departure from Jajce. A Partisan with immense moustaches was sitting by an improvised stove, stoking it from time to time, and in the intervals inspecting by its light the recesses of his shirt, which he had taken off and was examining with meticulous care. "*Usi*," he said resignedly. "Lice." I took the canvas Foreign Office bag in which I had brought the Prime Minister's letter, filled it with straw to make a pillow, wrapped myself in my greatcoat and was soon asleep.

Next morning we were wakened with a mug of captured ersatz coffee and a mess tin of yellow maize porridge by the bewhiskered Partisan, who, in addition to being my bodyguard, also fulfilled the rôles of cook and batman. Having eaten my breakfast, I cleaned out my mess tin and used it for boiling some snow-water on the stove, to shave in. It was an agreeably compact mode of life, with no time, space or energy wasted on unnecessary frills.

# COWARDICE, CASSINO, SPRING 1944
## *Howard L. Bond, US 36th Infantry Division*

*The German campaign in Italy was led by the doughty Field Marshal Kesselring, who established a series of defensive lines the width of the peninsula. It was, as Kesselring appreciated, ideal defensive terrain, mountainous and crossed by fast-moving rivers. As one line fell, he retreated to another further north. Amongst the most formidable of these lines was the Gustav Line, with Monte Cassino at its centre, dominating the Liri Valley and thus the route to Rome. The first battle for Monte Cassino began on 17 January 1944; the fourth and last opened on 11 May 1944.*

Toward the end of the morning a young second lieutenant named F————came into our room. He was wet, dirty, and he looked very tired, even sick. He sat near the stove, quietly soaking up as much heat as he could and drying his wet clothing. The colonel told him to wait there until the jeep came to take him to the rear. The lieutenant said simply, "Yes, sir," and went on warming himself. The sergeant and I stepped outside for a moment, and from him I learned that F———— was under arrest. He had come back from across the river and left his men on the other side. His excuse was that he had returned to get help. I later found out that F————was not averse to talking about his experience; in fact, after he had warmed himself, he seemed eager to explain. It had been terrible over there, he said. The men were pinned down by machine-gun fire and could not move forward at all. Big shells came in on their positions. He thought that at least half of his company had been killed or wounded. He was a good swimmer, and so he had set out to get help. He could have sent one of his men back, he realized, but it was too dangerous for the others to make the trip. When reaching his battalion commander, he was charged with deserting his troops and sent back to division headquarters, technically under arrest, to await the army's justice. He was too tired really to care very much then, and still too frightened by the terrible night down in the fog and cold of the riverbank, with huge shells crashing nearby and with machine-gun fire everywhere, the sharp angry crack of bullets passing close, and the shattering explosion of field mines. "But I'm a good swimmer, I was the one to go," he protested again and again, "a good swimmer." He was a big man physically and rather good-looking, one could tell, under the dirt and three days' growth of beard on his face. He had had a college education and was commissioned through R.O.T.C. His family was respected back home. Yet he had left his men and come back across the river. I did not say anything, for there was nothing I could say; but he broke out again, as if he were still speaking to his battalion commander.

"You don't know what it was like over there. Germans everywhere, mortar shells crunching down in front of us and behind us, the screams of the wounded men . . ." The only way to get help was to go back, he had thought. He should have been the one to risk it, get out in the open, swim the icy river, crawl up the far bank, and bring aid to his men. Wasn't this an officer's job? His men were in a bad – a terribly bad – spot, and he would try to save them. Why didn't his battalion commander see that? He was doing his duty. But all his battalion commander could see was that he had deserted, left his troops across the river when he should have stayed with them. And now he sat by the warm stove, the heat working its way slowly into his aching, shivering body, and he listened to the sound of small-arms fire in the distance, a morally broken man.

He tried to escape the truth, this I know, for some years later I met him back in the United States. I ran into him by chance in a hotel lobby. He wanted very much to have a drink with me so that he could explain yet again, to himself as much as to me, why he had come back. "My men were in a bad way. They needed help. . . ." Army justice had been merciful with him, and he had been reassigned to some quartermaster unit, far behind the lines and the fighting. As I watched him that morning in the staff officer's headquarters, I wondered if I, too, someday would come back across a river, and I began to understand for the first time that in war it is most often the strong and the brave who are killed, while the weaklings live on.

## CASSINO: THE END, 16–18 MAY 1944

### *Major Fred Majdalany, Lancashire Fusiliers*

07.10 hours. Time to get ready. The shouts of the sergeant-majors. Jokes and curses. The infantry heaving on to their backs and shoulders their complicated equipment, their weapons and the picks and shovels they have to carry, too, so that they can quickly dig in on their objective. The individuals resolving themselves into sections and platoons and companies. Jokes and curses.

"Able ready to move, sir."

"Baker ready to move, sir."

"Charlie ready to move, sir."

"Dog ready to move, sir."

The column moved off along the track we'd taken the previous night. It was Tuesday morning. It was the fifth day of the offensive. In England the headlines were announcing that the Gustav Line was smashed except for Cassino and Monastery Hill. "Except" was the operative word. That was our job now. To break through and cut off Cassino and the Monastery.

On the stroke of nine there was an earth-shaking roar behind us as four hundred guns opened fire almost as one. With a hoarse, exultant scream four hundred shells sped low over our heads to tear into the ground less than five hundred yards in front, bursting with a mighty antiphonal crash that echoed the challenge of the guns. It was Wagnerian.

From then on the din was continuous and simultaneous: the thunder of the guns, the hugely amplified staccato of the shell-bursts close in front, and the vicious overhead scream that linked them with a frenzied counterpoint. And sometimes the scream became a whinny, and sometimes a kind of red-hot sighing, but most of the time it was just a scream – a great, angry baleful scream. The fury of it was elemental, yet precise. It was a controlled cyclone. It was splendid to hear, as the moment of actual combat approached.

The makers of films like to represent this scene with shots of soldiers crouching dramatically in readiness, and close-ups of tense, grim faces. Whereas the striking thing about such moments is the matter-of-factness and casualness of the average soldier. It is true that hearts are apt to be thumping fairly hard, and everyone is thinking, "Oh, Christ!" But you don't in fact look grim and intense. For one thing you would look slightly foolish if you did. For another you have too many things to do.

The two leading companies were due to advance exactly eight minutes after the barrage opened. So those eight minutes were spent doing such ordinary things as tying up boot laces, helping each other with their equipment, urinating, giving weapons a final check, testing wireless sets to make certain they were still netted, eating a bar of chocolate. The officers were giving last-minute instructions, marshalling their men into battle formations, or having a final check-up with the tank commanders with whom they were going to work.

Those who were not in the leading companies were digging like fiends, for they knew that the temporary calm would be quickly shattered as soon as the tanks and the leading infantry were seen emerging from it.

Meanwhile the barrage thundered on, and to its noise was added the roar of the Shermans' engines. A great bank of dust and smoke welled slowly up from the area the shells were pounding, so that you couldn't see the bursts any more. The sputtering of the 25-pounders rippled up and down the breadth of the gun-lines faster than bullets from a machine-gun, so numerous were they.

At eight minutes past nine they moved. Geoff led his company round the right end, Mark led his round the left end of the bank which concealed us from the enemy in front. Then the Shermans clattered forward, with a crescendo of engine-roar that made even shouted conversation impossible. The battle was on.

Geoff and Mark were to reach the start-line in ten minutes, at which time the barrage was due to move forward two hundred yards. Geoff and Mark would edge us as close to it as possible – perhaps within a hundred and fifty yards, and they'd wait until it moved on again, and then, following quickly in its wake, their bayonets and Brens would swiftly mop up any stunned remnants that survived. And while they were doing this the protective Shermans would blast with shells and machine-guns any more distant enemy post that sought to interfere.

Then the barrage would move forward another two hundred yards. The process would be repeated until the first objective had been secured – farm areas in each case. Then Kevin, who would soon be setting off, would pass his company through Geoff's and assault the final objective, the code word for which was "Snowdrop". When Kevin wirelessed "Snowdrop" the day's work would be largely done. Highway Six would be only two thousand yards away.

To-day was crucial. To-day would decide whether it was to be a break-through or a stabilized slogging-match here in the flat entrance to the Liri Valley, with our great concentrations of men and material at the mercy of the Monastery O.P.

The Boche reacted quickly. Within a few minutes of our barrage opening up the shells started coming back. The scream of their shells vied with the scream of ours. Salvo after salvo began to rain down on the farms and the groves to our rear, where our supporting echelons were massed ready to follow in the wake of the assault. The sun's rays, growing warmer every minute, cleared the last of the morning mist. The Monastery seemed to shed the haze as a boxer sheds his dressing-gown before stepping into the ring for the last round. Towering in stark majesty above the plain, where the whole of our force was stretched out for it to behold. This was the supreme moment – the final reckoning with the Monastery.

Mortar-bombs began to land on the crest immediately in front. The bits sizzled down on our positions. Ahead the machine-guns were joining in. The long low bursts of the Spandaus: and the Schmeissers, the German tommyguns that have an hysterical screech like a Hitler peroration. There were long answering rattles from the Besas of the Shermans. Then the *Nebelwerfers*, the six-barrelled rocket-mortars, as horrific as their name . . . The barrels discharge their huge rockets one at a time with a sound that is hard to put into words. It is like someone sitting violently on the bass notes of a piano, accompanied by the grating squeak of a diamond on glass. Then the clusters of canisters sail through the air with a fluttering chromatic whine, like jet-propelled Valkyries . . . There were several regiments of them facing us, and the existing cacophony was soon made infinitely more hideous by scores of Valkyries. They were landing well behind. For the time being the Boche were concentrating everything on the farms and the woods, that were crammed with concentrations of trucks and tanks and supplies of all kinds.

"You may as well push off now, Stuart," John said. A minute later the fourth company moved round the right end of the bank and went the way of the others. The first of the prisoners came in. Six para-troops. Able Company's. Four large blond ones and two little dark ones. They were sent straight back.

Smoke-shells were being poured on to Monastery Hill now in a frantic effort to restore the mist. They had some effect, but they couldn't blot it out. The barrage seemed to get a second wind and the guns seemed to be firing faster than ever. The German shells were taking their toll of the rear areas. Four farms were on fire. We could see three ammunition-trucks blazing. Three more prisoners: one wounded, the other two helping him along. A grinning fusilier in charge. Some wounded in from Baker Company. All walking cases. Running commentary from tank liaison officer – "Rear Link". He sits in a Honey tank at our H.Q. and acts as wireless link between the squadron fighting with us in front and the tanks' regimental head-quarters. "Both companies moving well. Machine-gun has opened up on Baker Company. Freddie Troop moving round to cope." The sharp crack of the Shermans' seventy-fives, and a burst of Besa that seems to go on for ever. That must be Freddie Troop "coping".

"Okay now," says Rear Link. "On the move again."

The *Nebelwerfers* have quietened down. They're easy to spot. Perhaps the counter-battery boys have got on to them. Our turn now. They're shelling our ridge as well as mortaring it. Some close ones. Rear Link has news. How Troop reports that five men have just come out of a building it has been blasting for five minutes and surrendered. Able Company report all's well. Baker report all's well. Charlie Company, following up, report all seems to be well in front, some wounded on the way back from Able. Three shells just above us. A signaller is hit.

The barrage ends. The effect is like the end of a movement in a symphony when you want to applaud and don't. From now on the guns will confine themselves to steady visitations on the enemy's rear. Unless the infantry want something hit. In which case the whole lot will switch in a very few minutes on to the place the infantry want hit.

The infantry want something hit now. The voice on the wireless says, "Two machine-guns bothering me from two hundred yards north of Victor Eighty-two. Can you put something down?" John tells Harry, who is eating a sandwich. Harry gets on the wireless and says, "Mike target – Victor Eighty-two – north two hundred – five rounds gunfire." The shells scream over. Harry says, "We may as well make sure." He orders a repeat. The voice on the wireless says, "Thanks. That seems to have done the trick. They're not firing any more." Harry finishes his sandwich.

Rear Link has been deep in conversation with the left-hand troop commander. Rear Link thinks the companies have reached the first objective. No, not quite. It is all right on the left. But the right company seems to have run into something. Trouble from a farm. Tanks moving round to help. A lot of firing, ours and theirs. Rear Link says the tanks are pouring everything they've got into the farm. Twelve more prisoners – they look more shaken than the others. They had a bad spot in the barrage. Rear Link asks the troop commander how the battle is going on the right. The troop commander says it is a bit confused. A platoon is moving round to a flank. The farm seems to be strongly held. A reserve troop has joined in. A tank has been hit and has "brewed up". Baker on the left report that they are on their first objective. Charlie report they are moving up to pass through Baker. The *Nebelwerfers* again. Not as many as before. Some of them, at any rate, have been discouraged by the counter-battery fire. They seem to be going for the Bailey a mile back on the main track. Our anti-tank guns are in that area waiting to be called forward. Hope they are all right. Get Charles on the wireless and ask him. Charles says two trucks hit. One man killed and ten wounded. It has been all right since the first shelling. Able Company report that they are now firmly on first objective. Some casualties getting the farm. But they've killed a lot of Germans, and got eleven prisoners. They're digging in. The tanks are protecting their right, which seems horribly open. The tanks are in great form. They won't stop firing. They are spraying everything that could possibly conceal a German.

It has become very unhealthy behind our ridge. They are still mainly hitting the top of it. So long as they stay up there it won't be too bad. But there is always a nasty uncertainty about it. If they add a few yards to the range they'll be landing right among us. One or two have already come half-way down the slope.

Rear Link getting excited again. He's been talking to one of the troop commanders. Rear Link says Charlie appear to be on their objective. Can he signal "Snowdrop" to his R.H.Q.? John says, "No, not yet." Rear Link gets another message from the tanks. Rear Link says Charlie have started to dig in. Can he signal "Snowdrop"? John says, "No. They haven't consolidated yet." Kevin reports that he has arrived and is digging in. He says he has sent back more prisoners. More wounded, more prisoners, more *Nebelwerfers*, more shells, and the Monastery horribly clear. Rear Link has another conversation with the tanks. "How about "Snowdrop", sir?" Rear Link almost pleads. "Not yet," John says. "Not until they have consolidated."

They're shelling us hard now. Not on the crest any more, but just over our heads and to our right. It is a different battery. They seem like 105s. They are coming over in eights. About every thirty seconds. The hard digging earlier in the morning is paying a good dividend. The last three salvoes landed right on our mortars, but they are well dug in and they get away without a single casualty. None of the shells has landed more than thirty yards from the command post. It is very frightening. Kevin on the wireless. Charlie Company are being counter-attacked with tanks. More shells on us. Twelve this time. Two of them within twenty yards. Behind, fortunately. Harry has taken a bearing on the guns and passed it back to the counter-battery people. Kevin on the wireless again. The leading Boche tank has got into a hull-down position fifty yards from his leading platoon. He has had some casualties. Our tanks trying to deal with it but hampered by very close-wooded country and a sunken lane that is an obstacle. Boche infantry are edging forward under cover of the fire from their tanks. More shells on the command post. The same place still. If they switch thirty yards to their left we've had it. That is the frightening thing. Wondering if they'll make a switch before they fire again. The accuracy of the guns is their downfall. John tries to get Kevin on the wireless. The signaller cannot get through. His toneless signaller-voice goes on saying, "Hello Three, hello Three, hello Three, hello Three." But he cannot get an answer. A closer shell blasted me against the bank. It is a queer feeling when you are brought to earth by blast. There is an instant of black-out, then sudden consciousness of what has happened: then an agonized wait for a spasm of pain somewhere on your person. Finally, a dull reactionary shock as you slowly discover you are intact. The signaller's voice again, "Cannot – hear – you – clearly – say – again – say again – that's – better – hear – you – okay." Kevin on the wireless. There is a tank deadlock. The rival tanks are now very close, on opposite sides of the same shallow crest. If either moves the other will get it the second the turret appears above the crest. The German cannot be outflanked. He has chosen his position cunningly. The sunken lane protects him. Kevin has had more casualties. More shells on the command post. Intense machine-gun fire from the direction of Kevin's company. Not a vestige of haze round the Monastery. This is the climax. No word from Kevin. John saying, "Are you through to Charlie Company yet?" The signaller-voice tonelessly persevering: "Hear my signals, hear my signals, hello Three . . . hear you very faintly . . ." Then, after an eternity, "Through now, sir. Message for you, sir." It is Kevin on the wireless. A fusilier has knocked out the tank with a Piat. It has killed the crew. The tank is on fire. The others are withdrawing. The infantry are withdrawing. Charlie Company are getting some of them as they withdraw. The counter-attack is finished. Consolidation may proceed. The tension is broken.

It went from mouth to mouth. "Bloke called Jefferson knocked out the tank with a Piat. Bloody good show! Bloke called Jefferson knocked out the tank with a Piat. Bloody good show! Bloody good show – bloke called Jefferson . . ." It passed from one to another till all the signallers knew, the stretcher-bearers, and the mortar crews, and the pioneers: and the anti-tank gunners waiting some way behind, and some sappers who were searching for mines along the track verges. Till the whole world knew. "A chap called Jefferson . . ."

Kevin on the wireless. "No further attacks. Consolidation completed."

"Get on to Brigade," John said, "and report 'Snowdrop'."

"Snowdrop," the Adjutant told Brigade.

"Snowdrop," Brigade told Division.

"Snowdrop," Division told Corps.

"Snowdrop," Corps told Army.

In all the headquarters all the way back they rubbed out the mark on their operations maps showing our position in the morning and put it in again twelve hundred yards farther forward, on the chalk-line called "Snowdrop". It was ten past two. The battle had been going for six hours.

"Command post prepare to move," John said.

We advanced in extended order through the long corn, as the ground was completely flat and without cover. The smell of the barrage still lingered, and the lacerated ground testified to its thoroughness. Wondering how many of the farms away to the right were still occupied by Boche; wondering how many machine-guns were concealed in the woods and the olive groves which stretched across the front a thousand yards ahead. Wondering if anyone had spotted our wireless aerials, which are impossible to conceal, and which always give away a headquarters.

There wasn't a vestige of cover in the half-mile stretch to where the reserve company had dug in. There was still a lot of firing in front, mainly from the tanks. They were taking no chances with the open right flank. They were dosing all the farms in turn. With nine tell-tale wireless aerials swaying loftily above the heads of the sweating signallers who carried the sets on their backs, we pushed on quickly through the long corn, wishing it was a good deal longer. And the Monastery watched us all the way.

As soon as the command post was established in the area of the reserve company, John went forward to where Kevin's company were, and he took me with him. They had turned the area into a compact little strong-point. It had to be compact, because there were fewer than fifty of them left out of ninety who had set off in the morning. Besides which, the country was so thick with trees that you couldn't see more than fifty yards ahead. They had adapted some of the excellent German trenches to face the other way. Some were reading the highly-coloured magazines left behind by the Boche. These were filled with lurid artists' impressions of the Cassino fighting bearing such captions as "Our paratroop supermen defying the Anglo-American hordes in living Hell of Cassino". They were all on that level. There was one copy of a sumptuous fashion magazine, which seemed slightly incongruous, and suggested that the Rhine-maidens weren't all the drab blue-stockings the Nazis made them out to be. There was one of the famous new steel pill-boxes: an underground three-roomed flatlet, which included a well-stocked larder. Only its small, rounded, steel turret protruded above the ground, and this was skilfully camouflaged.

A few yards away Jefferson's tank was still burning. They were all talking about Jefferson. They were all saying he saved the company. The tank had wiped out a section at sixty yards' range, and was systematically picking off the rest of the company in ones and twos until fewer than fifty were left. Then Jefferson, on an impulse, and without orders, snatched up a Piat and scrambled round to a position only a few yards from the tank. Unable to get in a shot from behind cover, he had stood up in full view of the enemy and fired his weapon standing up, so that the back-blast of the exploding bomb knocked him flat on his back. Then he had struggled to his feet and aimed a shot at the second tank – but the tank was hurriedly pulling back, and with it the Boche infantry. It was one of those things that aren't in the book. Jefferson was typical of the best Lancashire soldiers – quiet and solid and rather shy, yet able in an emergency to act quickly without seeming to hurry. Such men are nice to have around in battles. It was one of those deeds the full implications of which don't really strike you till some time later, then leave you stunned and humble.

. . . During the night we received orders to continue the advance at 6 a.m. and secure the next objective-line, "Bluebell". This was to synchronize with the Poles, who were to make a final attempt to work round from our old position north-east of Cassino and cut the highway from their side.

It was well after three by the time everyone had been fed, ammunition had been replenished, and orders for the new attack had been given out. Before he went to sleep John said, "I'm going to put Jefferson in for the V.C."

At a quarter to six the earth trembled, and once again the shells started pouring overhead so thickly that at times you fancied you could see them. At the same time another lot of guns began to pound Monastery Hill in support of the Polish attack. In next to no time dust and smoke and yellow flame enveloped the Monastery itself, so that when our Dog and Baker Companies passed through Charlie Company on the stroke of six it was hidden from view. This was the kill. We were going in for the kill. The Poles were sweeping round from the right: we, two and a half miles away in the valley, were on our way to seal it off from the left. It shouldn't be long now. And once we had cut the Highway the very qualities that had made the Monastery an impregnable bastion for so long would turn it into an equally formidable death-trap. For so long the guardian and protector of its garrison, it would round on them in its death-throes and destroy them.

Compared with the previous day, we had a fairly easy advance. There were some snipers and one or two isolated machine-guns, but they didn't seem disposed to resist very strongly, and by ten Baker and Dog, assisted by fresh tanks, were nicely settled on Bluebell, another thousand yards on. We were ordered to push on as fast as possible. So Baker and Dog advanced again, to the final objective line, "Tulip", twelve hundred yards farther on. And Able, Charlie and Command Post pushed on to the area just cleared by Dog and Baker. By four o'clock in the afternoon Dog and Baker both signalled that they were established on "Tulip" – both had O.P.s directly overlooking Highway Six. Both asked permission to carry on and cut the road and search beyond it. We were ordered to stay where we were, however, as the exact position of the Poles was not known and mistakes might occur if we both started milling around by the road. We dominated it from where we were. We had done what was required of us. We were to stay where we were until we had further orders. The job was nearly done.

During the night Dog and Baker were told to patrol as far as the road. Not till the following morning were we allowed to send anyone beyond it. By that time it had ceased to be a military feat. It was a formal ceremony. So John sent a special patrol of three corporals, all holders of the M.M. They crossed the Highway and carried out a careful search of the gullies and ruined buildings on the far side of it, but the only Germans they could find were dead ones. Their time was not wasted, however. Each returned with a Schmeisser gun, a camera, a watch and a pair of binoculars of impeccable German manufacture. An hour later the Poles entered the Monastery. As so often happens when great events are awaited with prolonged and excessive anxiety, the announcement of the fall of Monte Cassino was rather an anti-climax. It was Thursday, 18 May. The battle had lasted a week. The job was done.

## HOME FRONT: PURE HELL FOR A GUY NOT IN UNIFORM, CANADA, 1943

*Anonymous*

Don't let anyone ever tell you it was all blue sky and sunshine for a guy not in uniform in those years. Sometimes it was pure hell.

Fellows who had tried to enlist and had been turned down, they got this little pin they could wear, and if people knew what it meant, then they were okay. I was a deferment, vital to the war effort. A classification like that meant I had no pin, and to a lot it looked like I was just running away from the whole thing.

Well, like hell I was. I was a master mechanic and stationary engineer and I worked in this little factory just outside Hamilton, and the family who owned it had wangled a job making parts for bearings for Liberty ships. If the government had given the contract to some-body bigger they'd have been better off, but as it was, we were vital to the war effort.

I was 29 and just ripe for a uniform, but there I was, keeping that damned plant going, running back and forth between the machine shop and the boiler room like an Olympic champion. Eighteen hours in a day and ten on Sunday was nothing, keeping that plant going. Every time I'd tell the boss to shove it – he was a canny old Scots bugger – he'd give me a raise and run off to the procurement board and get my deferment renewed. I couldn't have joined the army even if I'd wanted to.

That didn't help me, though. Look at me now. Well, back in 1943 I was still six-foot-one, and I was a good 195 pounds and none of it fat, but because I could make an engine part on a lathe out of scrap iron I'd find in the back of the shop, I was essential. And I took shit for it. Ask my wife.

We couldn't go to a dance. We'd be bumped on the floor by army and navy types. The air force wasn't too bad. But you'd hear all sorts of cracks like, "Maybe he's got a wooden leg," or, "Is that silver plate in his head where they pour the sawdust in?" and, "I guess his old man's got money," and on and on. Christ, if there were a thousand insults, I heard them all. We finally stopped going to dances. The wife just couldn't take it any more. She used to cry about it.

You got it on the streets, remarks you heard as you walked by, and I remember once on a streetcar I was sitting at the back and I felt something tapping the bottom of my foot and there was a paratrooper kicking me, and when I looked at him he gave me the up-yours sign. Sure, I could have got up and whaled him one, but he had two buddies with him and if you don't think that's what they were waiting for me to do, then you're wrong. You had to watch yourself.

There were thousands of us, I guess. Maybe we should have formed our own organization. A Mafia thing or something. For me, I just developed a hard shell. It got so I was immune, or I'm telling you now I was. I wasn't really. You kind of got the feeling of what it must be like to be a Negro in Georgia.

My father-in-law, who knew what I was doing at the foundry, he would hear these insults and he'd get madder than anyone. Once we were fishing near Guelph in that little river and some soldiers were down the bank with some girls drinking beer and playing around, and soon we heard a few remarks come up our way. Harry, my father-in-law, that scored him out and he went down and told them a thing or two, what I was doing, and I can still remember one of the girls laughing and saying, "Ah, fuck off, willya. We know exactly what he is."

It all ended pretty well when the war ended. A few of my friends when they got back from overseas would make the odd remark, joking, in a nonjoking kind of way, but that ended pretty soon too. But I can tell you now, right now, that I know I was more valuable in that plant patching up that equipment than if I'd killed five Germans a day.

# D-DAY: EMBARKATION, 4 JUNE 1944

## *Alan Moorehead, war correspondent*

*The Allied invasion of Normandy, 6 June 1944, was the greatest seaborne invasion in history. Some 160,000 troops – British, American, French, Polish and Canadian – embarked in 5,000 craft from southern England to make the journey to Hitler's "Fortress Europe".*

At three o'clock we were standing in a line on the path leading up to the gate. The young naval officer came by festooned with his explosives and rather surprisingly took up a position behind me. As each new group of troops turned up they exchanged wisecracks with the others already arrived. "Blimey, 'ere's the Arsenal" . . . "'Ome for the 'olidays" . . . "Wot's that, Arthur?" "Them's me water-wings, dearie." Even after waiting another hour there was still optimism in the ranks. Then we marched out through the gate and got on to the vehicles. An officer was running down the line making sure everyone was on board. He blew a whistle and we started off. Five miles an hour. Down Acacia Avenue. Round the park into High Street; a mile-long column of ducks and three-ton lorries; of Jeeps and tanks and bulldozers. On the sidewalk one or two people waved vaguely. An old man stopped and mumbled, "Good luck." But for the most part the people stared silently and made no sign. They knew we were going. There had been rehearsals before but they were not deceived. There was something in the way the soldiers carried themselves that said all too clearly "This is it. This is the invasion." And yet they were cheerful still. It was a relief to be out of the camp and moving freely in the streets again. Every now and again the column halted. Then we crept on slowly again towards the hards.

Two hours went by and the soldiers began to grow bored. They seized on anything for amusement. When a girl came by on a bicycle she was cheered with salacious enthusiasm from one end of the column to the other. An athlete dressed in a pink suit began to pace round the cricket field. The soldiers watched him with relish for a minute. Then, "Hyah, Pinkie." "Careful, dearie." Derisive shouting followed him round the ground. Towards the end of the column a soldier who was trained as a sniper took down his rifle with its telescopic sights and fixed them upon two lovers who were embracing at the farther end of the park. His friends gathered round him while he gave them a lewd commentary on what he saw. The soldiers were becoming very bored. It grew dark and the cricket match ended. Every hour or so a tea-waggon came round and the men ran towards it with their enamel mugs. One after another the lights in the houses were blacked out and the soldiers, left alone in the empty street, lapsed into complete listlessness and tiredness. Rumours kept passing back and forth from vehicle to vehicle. "Our ship has fouled its anchor." "There has been a collision in the harbour." Or more spectacularly, "We have already made a landing on the Channel Islands."

Towards ten o'clock the officers began running down the column shouting for the drivers to start. We began to edge forward slowly and presently came out on the dark promenade along the sea. There were many ships, both those moving in the sound and those which had brought their bows up on to the hard and had opened their gates to receive the vehicles. We were marked down for the Landing Ship Tank 816. A clamour of light and noise was coming out of its open bows. One after another the vehicles crept down the ramp and on to the great lift that took them to the upper deck. The sailors kept shouting to one another as they lashed down the trucks on the upper deck. All night the thump of army boots against the metal deck went on.

## IKE'S DAY BEFORE D-DAY, SHAEF ADVANCE (NEAR PORTSMOUTH), 5 JUNE 1944

### Captain Harry C. Butcher

*Butcher was the naval aide to Eisenhower, the Supreme Allied Commander of the Allied Expeditionary Force in Europe.*

D-Day is now almost irrevocably set for to-morrow morning, about 6.40, the time varying with tides at different beaches, the idea being to strike before high tide submerges obstacles which have to be cleared away.

"Irrevocable" becomes practically absolute around dusk, Ike said this afternoon while talking to the press and radio men, who heard him explain for more than an hour the "greatest operation we have ever attempted".

This morning Ike went to South Parade Pier in Portsmouth to see the loading of some British soldiers aboard LCILs 600, 601, and 602. He always gets a lift from talking with soldiers. He got one this morning, which partially offset the impatience with which he viewed the cloudy weather which had been predicted clear. While talking to the press he noticed through the tent door a quick flash of sunshine and said: "By George, there *is* some sun."

This evening Ike and a party, including press, are driving to the Newbury area to see the paratroopers of the American 101st Division load for the great flight – one which Leigh-Mallory said would cost so heavily in lives and planes.

About midnight he will have returned and will stop at the Naval Headquarters for a last-minute check on news, and then return to the camp and bed. He expects to return to the Naval Headquarters around 6.30 to get actual news.

The actual decision was confirmed and made final this morning at 4.15 after all the weather dope had been assembled. During yesterday the weather looked as if we might have to postpone for at least two days, until Thursday, with possibility of two weeks. Pockets of "lows" existed all the way from western Canada across the United States and the Atlantic, and were coming our way. What was needed was a benevolent "high" to counteract or divert at least one of the parading lows. During the night, that actually occurred. During the day, Force U, the U.S. task force which started from Falmouth at the western end of the Channel at 6 a.m. Sunday, had become scattered, owing to the gale-like wind sweeping southern England and the Channel. But Admiral Kirk had heard some encouraging news that the scattering was not as bad as feared. It was enough better by the early-morning session to warrant the gamble, which only Ike could take, and he did, but with the chance of decent weather in his favour for possibly only two days. After that we hope to be ashore, and while weather will still be vitally important, we will have gotten over the historic hump.

Air Chief Marshal Tedder told me that at the Sunday-night meeting when the decision was made to launch OVERLORD, subject to final review at the 4 a.m. meeting, Monday morning, the weatherman who had spoken for all the weather services, after having given a rather doleful report, was asked, "What will the weather be on D-Day in the Channel and over the French coast?" He hesitated, Tedder said, for two dramatic minutes and finally said, conscientiously and soberly, "To answer that question would make me a guesser, not a meteorologist."

Despite the refusal of the weather man to be a "guesser", Ike had to take the responsibility of making the decision without satisfactory assurance from the meteorologist – responsibility which Tedder said Ike took without hesitation.

What does the Supreme Commander do just now? Before lunch he played this aide "Hounds and Fox", he being the hounds, and he won consistently, there being a trick in being a hound. We played a game of crackerbox checkers, and just as I had him cornered with my two kings and his one remaining king, damned if he didn't jump one of my kings and get a draw.

At lunch we talked of old political yarns, he having known my old friend Pat Harrison when he was coming up as a young Congressman. I told the story of the Harrison–Bilbo campaign in which the latter supported Governor Conner for Senator against Pat. One of Pat's supporters told a rally the trouble with Pat was that he was too damned honourable and should use Bilbo's tactics. These he illustrated by the famous yarn of Mamma and Papa Skunk and their nine children, which ends with Papa alluding to a new and terrible odour wafting into their nostrils, and adding, "I don't know what it is, Mamma Skunk and children dear, but whatever it is, we must get some of it."

So we talked, during the lunch, on Senators and skunks and civet cats.

After lunch I shepherded the press and radio men to our little camp, introducing them all round, especially to Mickey, Hunt, Williams, and the rest. Ike took over in his tent, and as usual held them on the edge of their chairs. The nonchalance with which he announced that we were attacking in the morning and the feigned nonchalance with which the reporters absorbed it was a study in suppressed emotion which would interest any psychologist.

The names, as I recall them, are: Robert Barr, for BBC; Stanley Burch, for Reuter's; Ned Roberts, of UP, and Red Mueller, of NBC, who had been with us before. In the order named, they are covering colour and personalities of the high command for British radio, British press agencies, American associations, and American networks. In a word, world-wide coverage for the public. Also two lads from the Army Pictorial Service.

Ike has just had a phone call from Beetle at SHAEF Main that de Gaulle, whose visit here yesterday is a story in itself, now says he will not broadcast to-morrow, D-Day, as agreed yesterday. Objects to one paragraph of Ike's broadcast already recorded. De Gaulle's objection has to do with his recognition as the exclusive French authority with which we are to deal in France. Ike said that if he doesn't come through, we'll deal with someone else, another of those last-minute things that worry the devil out of the SC. General "Red" Bull said yesterday that no one in the world could carry the political and military problems as well as Ike. Got to run to dinner.

## D-DAY: A PARATROOPER LISTS HIS KIT, WELFORD AERODROME, 5 JUNE 1944

### Donald Burgett, US 101st Airborne Division

*The seaborne invasion of Normandy was preceded by an airborne assault by the US 101st, US 82nd and the British 6th Airborne divisions. This airborne assault was intended to protect the flanks of the five Normandy beaches where the infantry would land. In the darkness of the evening of 5 June these airborne divisions emplaned on airfields all over the south of England. The paratroopers had to carry fantastic quantities of kit into battle.*

My personal equipment consisted of: one suit of ODs, worn under my jump suit – this was an order for everyone – helmet, boots, gloves, main chute, reserve chute, Mae West, rifle, .45 automatic pistol, trench knife, jump knife, hunting knife, machete, one cartridge belt, two bandoliers, two cans of machine-gun ammo totalling 676 rounds of .30 ammo, 66 rounds of .45 ammo, one Hawkins mine capable of blowing the track off a tank, four blocks of TNT, one entrenching tool with two blasting caps taped on the outside of the steel part, three first-aid kits, two morphine needles, one gas mask, a canteen of water, three days' supply of K rations, two days' supply of D rations (hard tropical chocolate bars), six fragmentation grenades, one Gammon grenade, one orange smoke and one red smoke grenade, one orange panel, one blanket, one raincoat, one change of socks and underwear, two cartons of cigarettes and a few other odds and ends.

*Unsurprisingly, Burgett could hardly walk and had to be helped into the plane by Air Corps personnel. On the flight over, Burgett and his comrades knelt on the floor and rested the weight of the gear and parachutes on the seat behind. The British paratroopers were only slightly less encumbered.*

# D-DAY: COMBAT JUMP OVER NORMANDY, 6 JUNE 1944

## *General Matthew B. Ridgway, Commander US 82nd Airborne Division*

We flew in a V of V's, like a gigantic spearhead without a shaft. England was on double daylight saving time, and it was still full light, but eastward, over the Channel, the skies were darkening. Two hours later night had fallen, and below us we could see the glints of yellow flame from the German anti-aircraft guns on the Channel Islands. We watched them curiously and without fear, as a high-flying duck may watch a hunter, knowing that we were too high and far away for their fire to reach us. In the plane the men sat quietly, deep in their own thoughts. They joked a little and broke, now and then, into ribald laughter. Nervousness and tension, and the cold that blasted through the open door, had its effects upon us all.

Wing to wing, the big planes snuggled close in their tight formation, we crossed to the coast of France. I was sitting straight across the aisle from the doorless exit. Even at fifteen hundred feet I could tell the Channel was rough, for we passed over a small patrol craft – one of the check points for our navigators – and the light it displayed for us was bobbing like a cork in a millrace. No lights showed on the land, but in the pale glow of a rising moon, I could clearly see farm and field below. And I remember thinking how peaceful the land looked, each house and hedgerow, path and little stream bathed in the silver of the moonlight. And I felt that if it were not for the noise of the engines we could hear the farm dogs baying, and the sound of the barnyard roosters crowing for midnight.

A few minutes later we suddenly went into cloud, thick and turbulent. I had been looking out of the doorway, watching with a profound sense of satisfaction the close-ordered flight of that great sky caravan that stretched as far as the eye could see. All at once they were blotted out. Not a wing light showed. The plane began to yaw and plunge, and in my mind's eye I could see the other pilots, fighting to hold course, knowing how great was the danger of a collision in the air.

You could read concern on the grim, set faces of the men in my plane as they turned to peer out of the windows, looking for the wink of the little lavender lights on the wing tips of the adjoining planes. Not even our own wing lights showed in that thick murk. It was all up to the pilots now. There was nothing I could do, and I did it. I pulled my seat belt tighter and sat back and closed my eyes, taking comfort from the words of Hal Clark, Commanding General of the Troop Carrier Wing, whose planes transported us.

"Matt," he had told me before the take-off, "come hell or high wind, my boys will put you there, right on the button."

The cloud and rough air lasted only a few minutes, though it seemed far longer. As suddenly as we had entered the storm, we broke free. All at once there was the moon again, and clear skies, and the sharp outlines of the land below, the little fields and hedgerows. But nowhere in the sky, in my field of vision, could I see another plane.

It was too late now to worry about that. Beside the door a red light glowed. Four minutes left. Down the line of bucket seats, the No. 4 man in the stick stood up. It was Captain Schouvaloff, brother-in-law of Fëdor Chaliapin, the opera singer. He was a get-rich-quick paratrooper, as I was, a man who had had no formal jump training. I was taking him along as a language officer, for he spoke both German and Russian, and we knew that in the Cotentin Peninsula, which we were to seize, the Germans were using captured Russians as combat troops.

A brilliant linguist, he was also something of a clown. Standing up, wearing a look of mock bewilderment on his face, he held up the hook on his static line – the life line of the parachutist which jerks his canopy from its pack as he dives clear of the plane.

"Pray tell me," said Schouvaloff, in his thick accent, "what does one do with this strange device?"

That broke the tension. A great roar of laughter rose from the silent men who were standing now, hooked up and ready to go.

"Are we downhearted", somebody yelled.

"HELL NO!" came back the answer.

A bell rang loudly, a green light glowed. The jumpmaster, crouched in the door, went out with a yell – "Let's go!" With a paratrooper still laughing, breathing hard on my neck, I leaped out after him . . .

# D-DAY: THE AIRBORNE LANDINGS, 6 JUNE 1944

*Major Friedrich Hayn,* **Wehrmacht** *Staff Officer*

At 01.11 hours – an unforgettable moment – the field telephone rang. Something important was coming through: while listening to it the General stood up stiffly, his hand gripping the edge of the table. With a nod he beckoned his chief of staff to listen in. "Enemy parachute troops dropped east of the Orne estuary. Main area Bréville-Ranville and the north edge of the Bavent forest. Counter-measures are in progress." This message from 716 Intelligence Service struck like lightning.

Was this, at last, the invasion, the storming of "*Festung Europa*"? Someone said haltingly, "Perhaps they are only supply troops for the French Resistance?" . . . The day before, in the St Malo area, many pieces of paper had been passing from hand to hand or had been dropped into the letterboxes; they all bore a mysterious announcement: *La carotte rouge est quittée.* Furthermore, our wireless operators had noticed an unusually large volume of coded traffic. Up till now, however, the Resistance groups had anxiously avoided all open action; they were put off by the danger of premature discovery and consequent extermination.

Whilst the pros and cons were still being discussed, 709 Infantry Division from Valognes announced: "Enemy parachute troops south of St Germain-de-Varreville and near Ste Marie-du-Mont. A second drop west of the main Carentan-Valognes road on both sides of the Merderet river and along the Ste Mère-Eglise-Pont-l'Abbé road. Fighting for the river crossing in progress." It was now about 01.45 hours.

Three dropping zones near the front! Two were clearly at important traffic junctions. The third was designed to hold the marshy meadows at the mouth of the Dives and the bridge across the canalized Orne near Ranville. It coincided with the corps boundary, with the natural feature which formed our northern flank but would serve the same purpose for an enemy driving south. It is the task of parachute troops, as advance detachments from the air, to occupy tactically important areas and to hold them until ground troops, in this case landing forces, fight their way through to them and incorporate them into the general front. Furthermore in Normandy they could, by attacking the strongpoints immediately west of the beach, paralyse the coastal defences. If it really was the task of the reported enemy forces to keep open the crossings, it meant that a landing would soon take place and they were really in earnest!

# D-DAY: THE LANDINGS, 6 JUNE 1944

*Throughout the night of 5 June the Allied armada made its way across the Channel, arriving off the Normandy coast in the steely dawn of the 6th, when the troops were ordered into the assault craft in which they would make the final approach.*

## Lieutenant H.T. Bone, East Yorkshire Regiment

In the Mess decks we blacked our faces with black Palm Olive cream and listened to the naval orders over the loudhailer. Most of us had taken communion on the Sunday, but the padre had a few words to say to us. Then the actual loading into craft – swinging on davits – the boat lowering and finally "Away boats". While this was going on, all around could be seen the rest of the convoy, with battleships and cruisers firing their big guns every few minutes and destroyers rushing round. One had been hit by something and only the up-ended part of its bows remained in view. As our flotilla swung into line behind its leader we raised our flag, a black silk square with the white rose of Yorkshire in the centre . . . It was some distance to the beaches, and it was a wet trip. All of us had a spare gas-cape to keep us dry and we chewed our gum stolidly. Mine was in my mouth twelve or fourteen hours later and I usually hate the stuff and never touch it. Shielding ourselves from the spray and watching the fire going down from all the supporting arms and the Spits [Spitfires] overhead, the time soon passed . . . Suddenly there was a jarring bump on the left, and looking up from our boards we saw one of the beach obstacles about two feet above our left gunwale with a large mine on top of it, just as photographs had shown us. Again a bump, on the right, but still we had not grounded. The Colonel and the flotilla leader were piloting us in, and for a few brief minutes nothing happened except the music of the guns and the whang of occasional bullets overhead, with the sporadic explosions of mortar bombs and the background of our own heavy machine-gun fire. The doors opened as we grounded and the Colonel was out. The sea was choppy and the boat swung a good bit as one by one we followed him. Several fell in and got soaked through. I was lucky. I stopped for a few seconds to help my men with their wireless sets and to ensure they kept them dry. As we staggered ashore we dispersed and lay down above the water's edge.

*The bloodiest fighting of the day came at Omaha beach, where the US 1st and 29th Infantry divisions had the ill luck to encounter a crack* Wehrmacht *division, the 352nd, on a training manoeuvre. Omaha was also the most topographically difficult of the beaches, dominated as it is by a high cliff.*

## Captain Joseph T. Dawson, US 1st Infantry Division

We landed at H + 30 minutes [7.00 am] and found . . . both the assault units rendered ineffective because of the enormous casualties they suffered. Fortunately, when we landed there was some let-up in the defensive fire from the Germans. Even so the boat containing assault unit Company G, which I commanded, took a direct hit from the artillery of the Germans, and I suffered major casualties. I lost about twenty men out of a total complement of 250 from that hit on my boat, and this included my naval officer who was communications link with the Navy, who were to support us with their fire from the battleships and cruisers some 8,000 yards out in the water.

As soon as we were able to assemble we proceeded off the beach through a minefield which had been identified by some of the soldiers who had landed earlier. We knew this because two of them were lying there in the path I selected. Both men had been destroyed by the mines. From their position, however, we were able to identify the path and get through the minefield without casualties and proceed up to the crest of the ridge which overlooked the beach. We got about halfway up when we met the remnants of a platoon of E Company, commanded by Lieutenant Spalding. This was the only group – somewhere less than twenty men – we encountered who had gotten off the beach. They had secured some German prisoners, and these were sent to the beach under escort. Above me, right on top of the ridge, the Germans had a line of defences with an excellent field of fire. I kept the men behind and, along with my communications sergeant and his assistant, worked our way slowly up to the crest of the ridge. Just before the crest was a sharp perpendicular drop, and we were able to get up to the crest without being seen by the enemy. I could now hear the Germans talking in the machine-gun nest immediately above me. I then threw two grenades, which were successful in eliminating the enemy and silencing the machine-gun which had been holding up our approach. Fortunately for me this action was done without them having any awareness of my being there, so it was no hero . . . it was an act of God, I guess.

# ONE MAN'S WAR: A NORMANDY DIARY, 6 JUNE 1944–24 JUNE 1944

## Corporal G.E. Hughes, 1st Battalion, Royal Hampshire Regiment

*Diary, 6 June 1944*
06.00 Get in LCA. Sea very rough. Hit the beach at 7.20 hours.

Murderous fire, losses high. I was lucky T[hank] God. Cleared three villages. Terrible fighting and ghastly sights.

*June 7*. Still going. Dug in at 02:00 hrs. Away again at 05.30. NO FOOD. Writing few notes before we go into another village. CO out of action, adjutant killed. P Sgt lost. I do P Sgt['s job]. More later.

*June 8*. 07.30, fire coming from village. Village cleared. Prisoners taken. Night quite good but German snipers lurking in wood. Had 2 hrs' sleep. Second rest since the 6th.

*June 9*. 06.30 hrs went on wood clearing. Germans had flown. Only one killed for our morning's work. We are now about 8 to 10 miles inland. Promoted to Sgt.

*June 10*. Joan darling, I have not had you out of my thoughts. T[hank] God I have come so far. We have lost some good men. Our brigade was only one to gain objectives on D-Day.

The French people give us a good welcome. Had wine.

*June 11*. Contact with enemy. Lost three of my platoon. Very lucky T[hank] God. Only had 5 hours sleep in 3 days.

*June 12*. This day undescrible [sic] mortar fire and wood fighting. Many casualties. T[hank] God I survived another day.

*June 13*. Just had my first meal since Monday morning. Up all night. Everyone in a terrible state. I keep thinking of u.

*June 14*. Counter-attack by Jerry from woods. Mortar fire. 13 of my platoon killed or missing. After heavy fighting yesterday CSM also wounded, also Joe. O[fficer] C[ommanding] killed. I am one mass of scratches. Advanced under creeping barrage for 3 miles. Drove Jerry back. It is hell. 3 Tiger tanks came here, up to lines during night.

*June 16*. [resting] Received letter from home. Wrote to Joan and Mum.

*June 17*. [resting]

*June 18*. Day of Hell. Counter-attack.

*June 19*. Day of Hell. Counter-attack.

*June 20*. Day of Hell. Advanced. Counter-attacked.

*June 21*. Quiet day. We have been fighting near Tilley [Tilly]. Bayonet charge. Shelled all day. Letters from home.

*June 22*. Out on patrol. Got within 35 yards of Tiger before spotting it. Got back safely T[hank] God. Shelled to blazes. Feeling tired out.

*June 23*. No sleep last night. Exchanged fire, out on patrols all day, went on OP for 4 hours. Stand-to all night. Casualties.
    Just about had enough.

*June 24*. Had to go back to CCS [Casualty Clearing Station]. Malaria.

*Sergeant Hughes was hospitalized with malaria for most of the rest of the Normandy campaign.*

# SNIPING, NORMANDY, 26 JUNE 1944

## *Ernie Pyle, war correspondent*

Sniping, as far as I know, is recognized as a legitimate means of warfare. And yet there is something sneaking about it that outrages the American sense of fairness.

I had never sensed this before we landed in France and began pushing the Germans back. We have had snipers before – in Bizerte and Cassino and lots of other places. But always on a small scale.

Here in Normandy the Germans have gone in for sniping in a wholesale manner. There are snipers everywhere. There are snipers in trees, in buildings, in piles of wreckage, in the grass. But mainly they are in the high, bushy hedgerows that form the fences of all the Norman fields and line every roadside and lane.

It is perfect sniping country. A man can hide himself in the thick fence-row shrubbery with several days' rations, and it's like hunting a needle in a haystack to find him.

Every mile we advance there are dozens of snipers left behind us. They pick off our soldiers one by one as they walk down the roads or across the fields.

It isn't safe to move into a new bivouac area until the snipers have been cleaned out. The first bivouac I moved into had shots ringing through it for a full day before all the hidden gunmen were rounded up. It gives you the same spooky feeling that you get on moving into a place you suspect of being sown with mines.

In past campaigns our soldiers would talk about the occasional snipers with contempt and disgust. But here sniping has become more important, and taking precautions against it is something we have had to learn and learn fast.

One officer friend of mine said: "Individual soldiers have become sniper-wise before, but now we're sniper-conscious as whole units."

Snipers kill as many Americans as they can, and then when their food and ammunition run out they surrender. To an American, that isn't quite ethical. The average American soldier has little feeling against the average German soldier who has fought an open fight and lost. But his feelings about the sneaking snipers can't very well be put into print. He is learning how to kill the snipers before the time comes for them to surrender.

As a matter of fact this part of France is very difficult for anything but fighting between small groups. It is a country of little fields, every one bordered by a thick hedge and a high fence of trees. There is hardly anyplace where you can see beyond the field ahead of you. Most of the time a soldier doesn't see more than a hundred yards in any direction.

In other places the ground is flooded and swampy with a growth of high, junglelike grass. In this kind of stuff it is almost man-to-man warfare. One officer who had served a long time in the Pacific says this fighting is the nearest thing to Guadalcanal that he has seen since.

## BUZZ BOMBS ON KENT, JUNE 1944

### Lionel King, eight-year-old schoolboy

*The first German FZG-76 flying bomb (the V-1 to the British) landed on Britain on 12 June 1944. Another 9,000 followed until September, when their launch positions in northern France were overrun. There was no escape for London and the south-east; the Germans then launched their A-4 (the V-2 to the Allies) rockets, which killed 2,500 between 8 September 1944 and 29 March 1945.*

On the night of 12 June the first of Hitler's V1s fell on London and the South East. News spread in from the Kent and Sussex coasts of aircraft with "jet nozzles", "fire exhausts" and odd engine sounds. Over Kent some of these craft had suddenly stopped and fallen with a devastating explosion to follow. Bombing of course was familiar to our family. We had moved from West Ham earlier in the war. I'd spent endless nights in the dugout in the garden unable to sleep because of Nanny's snoring. Now it was happening in the daytime too.

The first came over one afternoon. Our windows and doors were open in those fine June days and the drone of the approaching flying bomb was quite unmistakable. It gave us little warning. Ten seconds and the engine cut out directly overhead. There was an oddly resounding explosion about half a mile away.

The Boy Foot, as my mother called him, cycled up there and reported back: "King Edward Road – there's debris everywhere. Fire brigade and wardens are there, still digging 'em out. I saw it coming. I was up on the roof." I was envious of his roof. You could have seen anything from there.

"Where's King Edward Road, Mum?" asked Doug.

"By the County Ground. It's where Mr Gibbons lives – you know, he's in the Home Guard with Dad'.'

Next day we took to the shelter when we heard the drone. Again the engine cut out, again seemingly over the house. Then it spluttered into life again. Doug and I laughed out loud. It was all rather a joke. Mum told us to duck. The droning engine had stopped. Eight second wait. A disappointing, unspectacular bang.

"I'll find out where it dropped when I go up the shops in a minute," said Mum. "Don't open the door to any knocks." Later she told us it had fallen on a railway siding behind the dust destructor. Three old railway trucks were destroyed, a railwayman had told her.

Soon so many V1s were coming over the authorities gave up air-raid warnings. They would have been sounding the siren all the time. When a bomb announced its approach, Doug and I dived for the shelter, not forgetting to grab our cat Jimmy if he was in sight. Sometimes Mum was out shopping and we went to the shelter alone. We were never worried or afraid. It was all over in ten seconds anyway.

One such afternoon a V1 fell further up the road. We jumped out of the shelter and saw a huge mushroom of dust and rubble rising above the rooftops. You could see individual bricks and planks of wood sailing up into the clear sky. It looked after a few seconds like a ragged umbrella. The traffic picked up again in the road. We ran through the house to the front door. Droves of people were rushing up the road, some on bicycles, many in great distress, towards the scene. Many we knew by sight.

"There goes that man from the oil shop," exclaimed Doug. We'd never seen him this side of the counter before. The dust cloud had settled now. The first ambulances were pulling up at the Rest Centre at the church opposite. Scruffy-looking people, some shaking, were being helped in. Mum appeared. "Back into the house!" she barked. "Nanny will be home from work soon. She'll tell you all about it."

Nanny came in later. The buzz bomb had fallen by her factory. "Mrs Lea has copped it. It fell on her house in Lea Hall Road. It's in a state round there. When it exploded the foreman told her she could go round and see if her place was all right. I went with her. We went through it two or three minutes after it happened . . ." The incident was not without humour for Doug and me. "A spotter on Jenkins's roof saw it coming. He just threw himself over the edge. It's eighty feet off the ground."

## THE ATTEMPTED ASSASSINATION OF ADOLF HITLER, EASTERN GERMANY, 20 JULY 1944

### Heinrich Bucholz

*Dismayed by Hitler's conduct of the war, a group of senior officers decided to assassinate him during a conference at his Eastern Front HQ, the "Wolf's Lair". A briefcase containing a bomb with a time fuse was placed under the map table by Colonel Count von Stauffenberg. Bucholz was a stenographer at the Wolf's Lair.*

I remember it as a clap of thunder coupled with a bright yellow flash and clouds of thick smoke. Glass and wood splintered through the air. The large table on which all the situation maps had been spread out and around which the participants were standing – only we stenographers were sitting – collapsed. After a few seconds of silence I heard a voice, probably Field Marshal Keitel, shouting: "Where is the Führer?" Then further shouts and screams of pain arose.

*The Führer survived the bomb attempt. His injuries and subsequent medical treatment were noted by Theo Morell, his private physician.*

Right forearm badly swollen, prescribed acid aluminum acetate compresses. Effusion of blood on right shinbone has subsided. On back of third or fourth finger of left hand there is a large burn blister. Bandage. Occiput partly and hair completely burned, a palm-size second degree skin burn on the middle of the calf and a number of contusions and open flesh wounds. Left forearm has effusion of blood on interior aspect and is badly swollen, can move it only with difficulty – he is to take two Optalidons at once, and two tablespoons of Brom-Nervacit before going to sleep.

## AMERICAN BLITZKRIEG: THE BREAK-OUT IN NORMANDY, 24–25 JULY 1944

### General Fritz Bayerlain, Panzer Lehr

*After establishing a continuous bridgehead in Normandy, the Allied campaign had ground to a halt against strong German encirclement. The perimeter was dramatically broken by*

*General "Lightning Joe" Collin's VII Corps in late July. Fritz Bayerlain was in VII Corp's path.*

By about 23 July, US troops had gained suitable jump-off positions for their offensive and had taken Saint-Lô. Panzer Lehr Division held a 6000-yard sector west of the town and, by allocating only weak reserves, had formed a defence zone of 4000 yards in depth. The fifty or sixty tanks and self-propelled anti-tank guns still remaining to the division were deployed in static positions as armoured anti-tank guns and the Panzer Grenadiers were well dug in on their field positions.

On 24 July, 400 American bombers attacked our sector, but without doing much damage. My AA battalion even managed to shoot down ten of their aircraft. The expected ground attack did not come.

But on the next day, there followed one of the heaviest blows delivered by the Allied air forces in a tactical role during the whole of the war. I learnt later from American sources that on 25 July a force consisting of 1600 Flying Fortresses and other bombers had bombed the Panzer Lehr's sector from nine in the morning until around midday. Units holding the front were almost completely wiped out, despite, in many cases, the best possible equipment of tanks, anti-tank guns and self-propelled guns. Back and forth the bomb carpets were laid, artillery positions were wiped out, tanks overturned and buried, infantry positions flattened and all roads and tracks destroyed. By midday the entire area resembled a moon landscape, with the bomb craters touching rim to rim, and there was no longer any hope of getting out any of our weapons. All signal communications had been cut and no command was possible. The shock effect on the troops was indescribable. Several of the men went mad and rushed dementedly round in the open until they were cut down by splinters. Simultaneous with the storm from the air, innumerable guns of the US artillery poured drum-fire into our field positions.

# GUERILLA AMBUSH IN CRETE, AUGUST 1944

## W. Stanley Moss

*Moss was a British officer charged with organising a partisan band against the German occupiers of Crete.*

The stage was patently set for action; and we found little difficulty in deciding what form that action should take. The Germans, bent on razing Anoyia to the ground, would in all likelihood arrive upon the scene in the early morning. They would certainly travel to the village along the Heraklion–Retimo road; and thus, if they could be waylaid before leaving their transport and deploying, Anoyia might be saved. With George and Deerslayer, I chose six of Mihale Xilouris's men to accompany us and the Russians.* We would have liked to have taken more, but our supply of automatics was now exhausted, so we were obliged to limit the total number of our force to fifteen men. In addition, we asked for a couple of Anoyians to act as guides for us, at which a score immediately volunteered, and we compromised by taking four.

In the late afternoon we set off northwards, walking fast and feeling that now, at last, our luck must change. All the way to Anoyia we kept meeting more refugees, some of them leading mules piled high with impedimenta, others travelling with only their *sakulis* slung across their backs. They greeted us in passing, waving and calling and wishing us well.

It was dark when we reached the village. The streets were deserted, nor did any light burn in the windows. There was a vast stillness in the air, which our imaginations charged with an electric expectancy. We hurried onwards until, at midnight, we stopped at a deserted garden to feed ourselves on a dinner of grapes and water-melons. After a short rest, we continued on our way; and at three o'clock in the morning we arrived at the main road. It did not take us long to discover the sort of position ideally suited for an ambush; a sharp curve in the road, bounded on three sides by high ground, with a little bridge in the centre of it.

Straightway we busied ourselves with laying twin rows of Hawkins grenades across the bridge. Fortunately the tarmac was in an ill state of repair, so the task of concealing the mines proved no great problem; and by dawn, at five o'clock, we were all lying in readiness at our posts.

It was an hour later that, for the first time, we heard a warning whistle from our scout on the high ground above us. Every man fingered his trigger, intently watching the bend in the road; but it was no German transport that we were soon to see approaching us: it was a flock of sheep, a shepherd, two small boys, and a dog. Hurriedly we scrambled down to the road and waylaid the man telling him that he would have to spend the next few hours in our care. We did not dare risk allowing him to proceed on his journey, lest he should speak of having seen us, so we placed him and his entourage under the charge of one of our Anoyian guides, who led them, protesting only slightly, to a small valley which was situated about a quarter of a mile behind our position.

* escaped Russian POWs.

But this was only a beginning. During the next hour over eighty civilians, several flocks of sheep, donkeys, goats, and mules came stumbling in all innocence upon our emplacement. It transpired that there was a market day being held at a nearby village; but, by the time we had finished hustling each successive batch of arrivals off the road, it was rather we who appeared to be holding most of the market, for the little valley behind us, crammed to the full with bleating, braying livestock, looked like a corral after the most successful of round-ups.

By seven o'clock, however, the stream of market-bound peasants had thinned to a minimum, and the atmosphere reverted from that of the farmyard to one of waiting and expectancy. The sky was of the palest blue; and the young sun, with no warmth to cheer us, fumbled about the rocks where we lay concealed. Nobody spoke.

Then suddenly the look-out's whistle blew again; and in a moment we heard the rumble of a lorry engine, growing louder and louder until, swinging into view around the bend, a three-ton utility van bore down towards us. We could see two Germans sitting in the front seat, and half a dozen labourers perched upon the open sides of the back.

Just before the truck ran on to the mines, some of the Cretans, unable to contain their eagerness any further, opened fire. Then the truck blew up. Momentarily the whole scene vanished in a cloud, while falling pieces of metal clattered on to the rocks about us; but, when the smoke cleared, we were able to see the buckled frame of the truck, and a dead German huddled behind the shattered wind-screen, and his companion lying with his skull smashed to pulp on the roadway. The six labourers had been thrown clear by the explosion, and now they were scrambling down the embankment to shelter under the bridge. Straightway Deerslayer was after them, leaping like a cat from his vantage point at the roadside; but just as he was about to overtake them, one of them turned and hurled a rock into his face.

Spitting blood from his mouth, Deerslayer rushed at the man, smiting him on the jaw with the butt of his automatic and sending him tumbling among the boulders.

The remainder straightway put up their hands, and cowered in the shadow of the bridge like cornered rabbits. The man who had thrown the rock tried to scramble to his feet, only to receive a kick in the teeth which again sent him sprawling. Then Deerslayer called to one of the Anoyians and told him to escort the six captives back to the valley.

Once they had gone, we resumed our ambush positions – and scarcely had we got back to our posts than we heard a cry from the look-out.

The echo of his voice was still alive among the reverberate rocks when another three-tonner, pulling a large trailer, hove into sight around the bend; but the driver, on seeing the battered bulk of the first truck on the bridge, immediately jammed on his brakes, and the vehicle stopped dead. It was well out of range of our Sten guns, but this did not deter the Cretans, who each emptied a magazine of bullets vaguely in its direction. The driver, meanwhile, put the vehicle into reverse and tried to turn round, but he succeeded only in ditching the trailer.

We left our positions and started to make our way from rock to rock towards the truck; then, as the range narrowed, we paused at every few paces to fire at it. We could see a German N.C.O. in the front seat, and several Italians in the back. After a moment's hesitation, they all jumped clear of the truck and started running for their lives back down the road, with George, Deerslayer, and myself in hot pursuit. Then the German, pulling a Luger out of his holster, started firing at us over his shoulder; but his shots were wildly inaccurate, and we could hear the bullets fizzling overhead and whining away into the mountainside.

The Italians, like sheep, were running in a close bunch; so, when we stopped for a moment to take proper aim and fire into their midst, we were not surprised to see three of them stagger and collapse on the roadway.

By the time we had overtaken the prostrate bodies and dragged them into the ditch, the distance between us and the remainder of the quarry had increased to about two hundred yards. Nevertheless, the German continued firing at us. He fired two shots over our heads, and a third smacked into the rocks at the roadside. We watched him as he turned again to fire a fourth shot; but no shot came, and in disgust he hurled his empty pistol into the ditch.

For nearly a mile we chased them, sometimes losing sight of them around a bend in the road, and at others finding them running, as it were, in the opposite direction to ourselves as they followed a hairpin curve. Then, abruptly, we lost them altogether.

We raced for the spot where we had last seen them, and there we came upon a mule-track which branched at right-angles to the road; so up the track we went, until, some five minutes later, we reached a tiny village. A small boy was standing in the cobbled lane, and he waved gleefully to us as we approached.

"Where are they?" George shouted.

Without hesitation, the boy pointed to an empty-looking house at the end of the lane.

I sent Deerslayer round the back of the house, then with George slowly approached its front entrance. When we were within ten yards of it, we shouted for the men to come out; but there was no reply, so I fired a burst through one of the windows, and scarcely had the sound of the last shot died away than the four men, hands high above their heads, came tumbling out of the doorway, closely followed by Deer-slayer. He treated the German to a brisk kick in the pants, and cuffed the Italians over the ears. Then I told them to get moving. They did not appear to understand what was wanted of them, and turned towards us, their eyes brimful of terror and bewilderment; so George fired a couple of shots at their heels – and this they understood.

The small boy applauded us delightedly as we passed, while other villagers, attracted by the sound of the shooting, stood gaping in their doorways to watch our departure. Back to the road we went, our prisoners running before us with their hands clasped across the back of their necks; and thus, with sporadic shots to remind them that we were at their heels, we brought them back at a brisk trot to the scene of the ambush.

In our absence, we discovered a *Volkswagen* had driven into the trap, and its two German occupants had been swiftly despatched. Unfor-tunately, however, the vehicle had been ditched on a corner in such a way as to give ample warning of danger to any further traffic, so we were obliged to relinquish our positions in favour of an adjacent curve in the road which did not so admirably suit our purpose.

Ten minutes must have passed before we again heard the look-out's warning, this time heralding the advent of a large utility truck which contained an Italian labour gang. At the first shot the vehicle pulled up, and the Italians, excitedly waving white handkerchiefs, jumped to the road and surrendered themselves with only verbal protest; but I believe their animated chatter betokened rather a fear of their lives than indignation at their capture. As they were hurried away, I drove the truck round the curve in the road and left it in the ditch.

We resumed our ambush positions. George, I noticed, was chalking up the number of our morning's catch on a rock, and he grinned happily at me, as though to convey his satisfaction at the way things were going for us. In actual fact, however, I was growing a trifle anxious at the non-appearance of any German fighting troops. The time was already half-past eight, and we all knew that whenever the enemy descended on a village they preferred to go into action at dawn; but there was nothing we could do but wait and hope for the best, so we settled ourselves among the rocks and listened impatiently for the look-out's whistle. One of the Russians, squatting behind a boulder just below me, started humming a harvesting song, and his voice found an incongruous accompaniment in the razor-strop croaking of a host of cicadas. The war seemed somehow to have deserted us for a while; and the feeling of tension which we all held in our hearts was unobtrusively absorbed by the sun-warmed peacefulness of the scene about us.

For nearly an hour we waited.

Then, like a knife, the shrill scream of the whistle shattered the placid mirror of the morning, and I saw the look-out, standing on a high rock, frantically waving his arms.

We heard the dull throb of a powerful engine growing louder and louder, insinuating itself into the gentle exhalations of the landscape. There was little doubting the identity of the vehicle now approaching us; and when, a moment later, it lumbered into view, I do not think a man among us was surprised at recognising the familiar, ungainly shape of a troop transport. Its thirty-five, steel-helmeted occupants were seated in the back like twin rows of tailor's dummies, and altogether one felt as though one were witnessing the clattering advent of some squat, multi-ringed armadillo. The sun flashed across the wind-screen, and the steel of barrels and helmets glinted like revolving mirrors in the white heat.

All unsuspecting, the driver brought the vehicle slowly round the bend until it was directly below us. Then, with our fifteen Sten guns, we opened fire.

Most of the Germans died in their seats before they knew what was happening, but some, trying desperately to disentangle their weapons, managed to rise to their feet, and four of them survived to jump to the road. We saw them go scrambling down the slope on the other side and take refuge behind the low stone wall of a vineyard.

Then, quite suddenly, everything became strangely quiet. There came an occasional groan from a dying man in the lorry, and we could hear the water boiling over in the radiator; but, apart from these sounds and a few despairing shots from the Germans in the vineyard, there was scarcely anything to disturb the peace of that very lovely morning. We could see the dead men sitting in stuffed positions on the benches, and there was blood and oil dripping on to the tarmac. And we could smell the nauseating stench of burned rubber and cordite and petrol. And somewhere a nightingale was singing, because nightingales in Crete seem mostly to sing in the daytime. Nobody moved or spoke. It was like that moment at the end of a great play, when the curtain has descended and the audience is still too enthralled to applaud. But the moment is short – and short indeed it was for us that morning. A cannon shell, smashing into the rocks in our midst, brought us violently to our senses.

In the excitement of the moment, nobody had noticed the arrival of an armoured car. And now it came towards us, very slowly, firing into the rocks where we were hidden, with an officer standing in the turret to direct its fire. He must have been a very brave man, because everybody started to shoot at him and still he would not put his head down, but pulled out a Luger instead and returned our fire, very calmly and with great accuracy. And all the time the armoured car kept on coming, nearer and nearer. The Cretans, in their ignorance, started hurling Mills bombs at it; but their missiles, far from making any impression upon the armour, served only to shower the rocks about us with ricocheting fragments of stone and metal.

It was at this moment that one of our Anoyian followers – an elderly man, dressed in ancient clothes and grasping a firing-piece which looked as though it must have remained concealed in a chimney-stack since the Turkish invasion – elected to perform an act of temerarial bravado. With a shout, he jumped to the road, placing himself directly in the path of the oncoming vehicle, and started firing at it. The age of his rifle was such that after each shot he had to reload; and, in this fashion, he had just time to fire three shots before a cannon shell struck him in the stomach and sent him spinning into the ditch. Indeed, I was amazed that he had survived as long as he had.

This incident, however, rather than allaying the bellicose instincts of my fellows, gave rise to a further act of reckless daring, the protagonist on this occasion being none other than Deerslayer. Upon seeing his wounded countryman lying in the ditch, he leaped out from behind the rock where he had sought shelter, scrambled down to the road, hoisted the unconscious man on to his shoulders, and started slowly to clamber back up the slope, attended the while by a hail of bullets, not only from the armoured car, but also from the group of Germans in the vineyard opposite.

By this time the remainder of the Cretans, with the exception of George, showed themselves more than ready to take their leave; nor did I make any move to restrain them. It seemed that only one thing remained to be done before raising the ambush and that was to put the armoured car out of action. The vehicle was now so close upon us that the chance to attack it from the rear became a distinct possibility; so, calling for a volunteer from the Russian party, I told him of my intention. He was a pleasant-looking youth, with fair hair and blue eyes that gave him an almost Nordic appearance, and he was quick to understand what was wanted of him. Via rocks and boulders, we would make our way to the rear of the armoured car, while the remainder of the party gave us covering fire from the flank! Then, once we had reached the vehicle's blind spot, we would descend to the ditch, crawl along it until we came level with the car's rear wheels, and finally jump aboard and throw hand grenades down the turret. The Russian conveyed this information to his colleagues, while I explained the situation to George. As we spoke, cannon shells continued to burst among the rocks around us, treating our urgent speech to the rudest of punctuation.

Now, all was in readiness, and with Vanya – for that was the Russian's name – I wriggled towards our starting point. Our greatest danger, we realised, lay in our initial effort to reach the rear of the car without drawing fire, and in doing this we would have to make a dash across a ten yard gap of completely open ground before being able to find concealment behind a massively substantial rock formation. So off we went, one after the other, in a breakneck rush for our immediate objective.

Once there, grateful for the brief asylum with which the huge boulders provided me, I paused to review the position from this new standpoint; and happily I found that there would now be little difficulty in crawling down to the ditch and approaching the target from behind.

"Vanya," I said in a whisper, and thrust out my arm behind me as if to grasp him.

"Vanya."

There was no reply; only a shot from the car-commander's Luger.

Slowly I turned, suddenly apprehensive and frightened at what I might see. Nor did my presentiment deceive me. Face downwards, his limbs spreadeagled as if in a primitive crucifixion, the Russian's body lay as it had fallen, midway between the two boulders that had been our havens. The blonde hair was bright with blood – brighter because of the blondness – and the fingers, as if petrified, clutched at the parched grass in a way that no live fingers could.

I turned away, not horrified, but bewildered. One's thoughts race at moments such as these; and now, quite suddenly, I realised why the German had shot Vanya rather than me. The Russian had been wearing British battle-dress, while I was dressed from top to toe in Cretan black; and so, with a split-second choice of targets, the German had picked upon that man whom he had considered the more worthwhile victim. Could Fate ever have been more unjust . . . or more kind?

From now on, the task was simple. Maintaining a steady volume of fire from the rocks above, the covering party persisted in occupying the attentions of the enemy, while I, completely sheltered from sight and bullet, was able to clamber into the ditch without obstruction. Only twenty yards separated me from the target. I could see the car-commander, oblivious of my approach, continuing his courageous, almost foolhardy, retaliation; and thus he continued, firing from time to time, until I had drawn level with him. I had now only to watch for

the moment when, as before, he would have to change the magazine of
his pistol.

There was not long to wait. A shot was fired, the steel helmet
bobbed down. To jump on to the back of the car and drop a grenade
into the turret took a matter of seconds. The cannon did not fire again.

# FALAISE: THE KILLING FIELD, 19 AUGUST 1944

## *Johnnie Johnson, RAF*

*The break-out by the Americans in Normandy allowed them to hook around the Germans,
who were then caught in the so-called "Falaise Pocket", where they were subjected to
constant air attacks.*

A gleam of reflected sunshine on metal here, a swirl or eddy of dust
there, or fresh tracks leading across the fields were sufficient evidence
to bring down the fighter-bombers with their assorted armoury of
weapons. When darkness fell and brought some relief to the battered
Germans there was time to take stock of the situation and to add up
the score. My own pilots had amassed a total of slightly more than 200
destroyed or damaged vehicles, plus a few tanks attacked with doubtful results. For once the weather was in our favour, and the forecast for
the morrow was fine and sunny. The pilots turned in immediately
after dinner, for they would require all their energy for the new day.
As they settled down to sleep, they heard the continuous drone of our
light bombers making their flight across the beach-head to harry the
enemy columns throughout the short night.

The Canadians were up well before the dawn, and the first pair of
Spitfires retracted their wheels as the first hint of a lighter sky
flushed the eastern horizon. The Germans were making strenuous
efforts to salvage what equipment they could from the débâcle and
get it across the Seine. Such enemy action had been anticipated:
some of the Typhoon effort was diverted to attacking barges and
small craft as they ferried to and fro across the river. Once more the
Spitfire pilots turned their attention to the killing-ground and
attacked all manner of enemy transports wherever they were to
be found. They were located on the highways and lanes, in the
woods and copses, in small villages and hamlets, beneath the long
shadows of tall hedges, in farmyards and even camouflaged with
newly mown grass to resemble haystacks. During the previous night
many of the enemy had decided to abandon a great proportion of
their transports: they could be seen continuing the retreat on foot
and in hastily commandeered farm-carts. Sometimes the despairing
enemy waved white sheets at the Spitfires as they hurtled down to

attack; but these signs were ignored; our own ground troops were still some distance away and there was no organisation available to round up large numbers of prisoners.

On this day, 19th August, my Canadians claimed a total of almost 500 enemy transports destroyed or damaged, of which many were left burning. Even so, this score was not outstanding since Dal Russel's wing easily outstripped us with a score of more than 700. Afterwards our efforts in the Falaise gap gradually petered out, for the transports and personnel of the German Seventh Army had either been eliminated or had withdrawn across the Seine. The Falaise gap ranks as one of the greatest killing-grounds of the war, and is a classic example of the devastating effects of tactical air power when applied in concentrated form against targets of this nature. During these few days, pilots of the Second Tactical Air Force flew more than 12,000 missions and practically wiped out no less than eight infantry divisions and two armoured Panzer divisions. The Second Tactical Air Force had in fact turned an enemy retreat into a complete rout.

After the fighting had ebbed away from Falaise, we decided to drive there and see the results of our attacks at first hand. We thought that we were prepared for the dreadful scenes, which Eisenhower later said could only be described by Dante. On the last flights the stench from the decaying bodies below had even penetrated through the cockpit canopies of the Spitfires. Another, and perhaps the most important, object of our visit was to bring back a suitable German staff car, since it was obvious that we should soon be on the move across France, and a comfortable Mercedes would provide a welcome change from our hard-riding jeeps. After we left Falaise behind, all the roads were so choked with burnt-out German equipment that it was quite impossible to continue the journey. The bloated corpses of unfortunate domestic animals also lay in our path, so we took to the fields and tried to make some progress across country. Each spinny and copse contained its dreadful quota of dead Germans lying beside their wrecked vehicles, and once we came across the body of what had been a beautiful woman lying sprawled across the back seat of a staff car. We found our limousines, which consisted of Renaults, Citroëns, Mercedes and strangely enough a smooth Chevrolet. We had brought ropes, jacks and a few jerrycans of petrol, but it was impossible to extricate any of the cars. Soon we abandoned our search and left the fields and lanes, heavy with their rotting burden in the warm sunshine.

# ARNHEM: AT THE BRIDGE, 18–29 SEPTEMBER 1944

## *Lieutenant E.M. Mackay, 1st Airborne Division*

*The debacle of Falaise behind it, the German Army recognised the impossibility of holding a new line in France and fought a retreat until it reached defensible positions: the great waterways of northern Europe, the Rhine, the Meuse and the Schelde. Thus by mid September most of France, the whole of Belgium and Luxembourg, and part of Holland was in Allied hands. The task remained of breaching the new German line. To this end, the Allies launched Market Garden, a massive airborne assault to capture the bridges along the Eindhoven–Arnhem road, thus allowing armour to drive to the Rhine at Arnhem, where it would cross into Germany. After that, the Ruhr – Germany's industrial heartland – was there for the plucking. The seizure of the bridges at Eindhoven and Nijmegen by the American 101st and 82nd Airborne Division was successful, but the seizure of the bridge at Arnhem by the British 1st Airborne Division was not. Although most paratroopers got to earth safely on the far side of the Rhine on 17 September, they found themselves in the neighbourhood of the 9th and 10th SS Panzer Divisions which were refitting after their mauling in Normandy.*

*Monday*

We still had six hours to go till dawn. I made a hurried reconnaissance of the school. It had a basement, two floors and an attic, and I decided to fight the battle from the first-floor, merely holding the basement and ground-floor, and to observe from the attic. I had fifty men (seven wounded), one other lieutenant, six Bren guns, plenty of ammunition and grenades, and a certain amount of explosive; no anti-tank weapons, very little food, and only the water in our water-bottles; no medical supplies except morphia and field dressings.

There was a breathing-space of an hour before the next attacks were made: two were driven off before dawn. During lulls we went out and collected one or two wounded paratroops from the area.

Dawn was heralded by a hail of fire from the house we had been driven out of a few hours previously. As it was only 20 yards away, our positions on the northern face of the school became untenable for anything but observation. As soon as it was fully light, we could see the exact positions held by the enemy next door. They very foolishly remained in them, and it was easy to form a plan to eliminate them. One machine-gun was fired by remote control from one end of our northern face. It drew all the fire, while from the other end we opened up with two Bren guns, and killed all the machine-gun crews. More of the enemy attempted to recover the guns, and were immediately eliminated. The time was now 8 am.

Meanwhile a battle seemed to be developing round our southern face. The Germans were putting in a strong attack on the house 60 yards south of us, and against a small force holding the other corner of the cross-roads on the opposite side of the street. A great deal of firing was going on and tracers were flashing all around. Someone was firing a light ack-ack gun straight down the street. It was all very confusing. No one seemed to know who was who. We joined in with our southern machine-guns as best we could. The battle seemed to be reaching a climax about 9.30 when a cry came from one of the west rooms to say an armoured car had just gone past the window.

I rushed over and was in time to see a second go by. The ramp was on a level with our first-floor, with its edge about 12 yards away. We could do nothing against these armoured cars, having no antitank weapons. However, after five had gone by, some armoured half-tracks tried to sneak through. These have no roof on them and so were dead meat. The first went by with a rush, but we managed to land a grenade in it. The second came on with its machine-guns blazing, and a man beside me was killed before we could stop it by killing the driver and co-driver. The crew of six tried to get out and were shot one by one, lying round the half-track as it stood there in the middle of the road.

This caused the remaining half-tracks to stop just out of view, and gave me a breathing-space to organise a system for their elimination. Ten minutes later two came on together, firing everything they had, in an attempt to force the passage. As they passed the one that was already knocked out, we shot the driver and co-driver of the leading half-track. The driver must have been only wounded, as he promptly put it in reverse, and collided with the one behind. They got inextricably entangled, and we poured a hail of fire into the milling mass, whereupon one went on fire.

As the crew tried to get out of both, they were promptly killed. The score was beginning to mount. Another tried to take advantage of the billowing smoke to get through. It was similarly dealt with and there were no survivors. There appeared to be a lull, when suddenly I heard a clanking just below me. It was about 5 feet away and I looked straight into its commander's face. I don't know who was the more surprised. It must have climbed down the side of the ramp and was moving down a little path, 9 feet wide, between it and the school.

His reaction was quicker than mine; for with a dirty big grin he loosed off three shots with his luger. The only shot that hit me smashed my binoculars, which were hanging round my neck. The boys immediately rallied round, and he and his men were all dead meat in a few seconds. The half-track crashed into the northern wing of the school.

There was a further lull of about half an hour, when another half-track came down the ramp at full speed. The driver was promptly killed. The vehicle swung right, rushed down the side of the ramp, crashed head-on into the southern wing, just below us, where the rest of the crew were dispatched. While this was going on, another nosed out from behind the burning trio on the road. The same system was employed, and another eight Germans joined the growing pile. We were doing well, and our casualties were comparatively light.

It was nearing mid-day, and although there was a certain amount of clanking in the distance, no further attempt was made to force a crossing from the south. In any case the bridge was now blocked by burning vehicles. This lull was too good to last. Ten minutes later, with a sighing sound, fifteen mortar bombs landed on and around us. I could hear fire orders being given in English from the other side of the ramp, and realised we were being mortared by our own side. Leaning out of the nearest window, I gave vent to some fruity language at the top of my voice, the authenticity of which could not be doubted. The mortaring stopped.

To clinch matters, we let loose our old African war-cry of "Whoa Mahomet". This had an immediate effect, and was taken up by all the scattered points and houses round the bridge. The firing died down, and soon the air was ringing with the sound. Morale leapt up. Throughout the succeeding days this was the only means of telling which buildings were being held. It was one thing the Germans, with all their cleverness, could not imitate . . .

*Tuesday*
. . . Suddenly there was an appalling explosion in the south-west corner room. I rushed over with my batman. It seemed to be full of debris and someone was groaning in a corner. There was a blinding flash, and the next thing I remember was someone shaking me and slapping my face. I had been blown across the room, and was half buried under a pile of fallen brickwork. The whole south-west corner of the school, plus part of the roof, had been blown away. Everyone had become a casualty, and, by the time I was brought round, had been carried below, including my batman, who was blinded.

I found out later that the weapon that wrought this havoc was an anti-tank projector, which threw a twenty-pound bomb. The enemy failed to follow up his advantage, many of the boys being dazed by the explosions. We were given a breathing-space, but not for long.

Twenty minutes later, on looking out of a window, I was amazed to see a dozen Germans below me, calmly setting up a machine-gun and a mortar. They were talking and were evidently under the impression that all resistance in the house had ceased. A hurried reconnaissance revealed that we were entirely surrounded by about sixty Germans, at the range of some 10 feet, who were unaware of our existence.

It seemed too good to be true. All the boys were tee'd up at their windows, grenades ready with the pins out. On a signal, grenades were dropped on the heads below. This was followed up instantly by all our machine-guns and sub-machine-guns (six Brens and fourteen Stens) firing at maximum rate. The boys, disdaining cover, stood up on the windowsills, firing machine-guns from the hip. The night dissolved in sound, the din was hideous, the heavy crash of the Brens mixed with the high-pitched rattle of the Stens, the cries of wounded men, punctuated by the sharp explosions of grenades, and swelling above it all the triumphant war-cry, "Whoa Mahomet".

It was all over in a matter of minutes, leaving a carpet of field-grey round the house, together with a few machine-guns and mortars. . . .

*Wednesday*
By morning I had to issue more Bensedrine to face the dawn attack. No one had now had any sleep for seventy-two hours. The water had given out twelve hours ago and the food twenty-four hours ago. As expected, with dawn the tanks came rolling up from the waterfront, with infantry supporting. We were now alone on the east of the bridge. Every house was burnt down, with the exception of the one on the opposite corner of the cross-roads, which was in German hands.

We drove off three attacks in two hours. The school was now like a sieve. Wherever you looked you could see daylight. The walls were no longer bullet-proof, rubble was piled high on the floors, laths hung down from the ceilings, a fine white dust of plaster covered everything. Splattered everywhere was blood: it lay in pools in the rooms, it covered the smocks of the defenders, and ran in small rivulets down the stairs. The men themselves were the grimmest sight of all: eyes red-rimmed for want of sleep, their faces, blackened by fire-fighting, wore three days' growth of beard. Many of them had minor wounds, and their clothes were cut away to expose a roughly fixed, blood-soaked field-dressing. They were huddled in twos and threes, each little group manning positions that required twice their number. The only clean things in the school were the weapons. These shone brightly in the morning sun, with their gleaming clips of ammunition beside them. Looking at these men I realised I should never have to give the order "These positions will be held to the last round and the last man." They were conscious of their superiority. Around them lay four times their number of enemy dead.

By ten o'clock the enemy gave up their attempts to take the school by storm. They concentrated on the force now under the arches of the bridge, about eighty men, nearly all that remained of the original four hundred. These were eliminated by about two o'clock, when our last cry of "Whoa Mahomet" was answered by silence. We were now the last organised position holding out near the bridge. It was a matter of time before we succumbed . . .

*Montgomery ordered the remnants of the British 1st Airborne Division to withdraw across the river on the night of the 25th–26th. Only 2,400 men out of 9,000 got away.*

# PROSTITUTION, NAPLES, 4 OCTOBER 1944

## *Sergeant Norman Lewis, Field Security Service*

Somewhere a few miles short of Naples proper, the road widened into something like a square, dominated by a vast semi-derelict public building, plastered with notices and with every window blown in. Here several trucks had drawn up and our driver pulled in to the kerb and stopped too. One of the trucks was carrying American Army supplies, and soldiers, immediately joined by several from our truck, were crowding round this and helping themselves to whatever they could lay hands on. Thereafter, crunching through the broken glass that littered the pavement, each of them carrying a tin of rations, they were streaming into the municipal building.

I followed them and found myself in a vast room crowded with jostling soldiery, with much pushing forward and ribald encouragement on the part of those in the rear, but a calmer and more thoughtful atmosphere by the time one reached the front of the crowd. Here a row of ladies sat at intervals of about a yard with their backs to the wall. These women were dressed in their street clothes, and had the ordinary well-washed respectable shopping and gossiping faces of working-class housewives. By the side of each woman stood a small pile of tins, and it soon became clear that it was possible to make love to any one of them in this very public place by adding another tin to the pile. The women kept absolutely still, they said nothing, and their faces were as empty of expression as graven images. They might have been selling fish, except that this place lacked the excitement of a fish market. There was no soliciting, no suggestion, no enticement, not even the discreetest and most accidental display of flesh. The boldest of the soldiers had pushed themselves, tins in hand, to the front, but now, faced with these matter-of-fact family-providers driven here by empty larders, they seemed to flag. Once again reality had betrayed the dream, and the air fell limp. There was some sheepish laughter, jokes that fell flat, and a visible tendency to slip quietly away. One soldier, a little tipsy, and egged on constantly by his friends, finally put down his tin of rations at a woman's side, unbuttoned and lowered himself on her. A perfunctory jogging of the haunches began and came quickly to an end. A moment later he was on his feet and buttoning up again. It had been something to get over as soon as possible. He might have been submitting to field punishment rather than the act of love.

Five minutes later we were on our way again. The tins collected by my fellow travellers were thrown to passers-by who scrambled wildly after them. None of the soldiers travelling on my truck had felt inclined to join actively in the fun.

## THE SUICIDE OF FIELD MARSHAL ERWIN ROMMEL, GERMANY, 14 OCTOBER 1944

### Manfred Rommel

*The field marshal was implicated in the outer edges of the plot to assassinate Hitler. In October the Führer decided on revenge. Manfred Rommel, a young artillery officer at the time, is the field marshal's son.*

At about twelve o'clock a dark-green car with a Berlin number stopped in front of our garden gate. The only men in the house apart from my father, were Captain Aldinger, a badly wounded war-veteran corporal and myself. Two generals – Burgdorf, a powerful florid man, and Maisel, small and slender – alighted from the car and entered the house. They were respectful and courteous and asked my father's permission to speak to him alone. Aldinger and I left the room. "So they are not going to arrest him," I thought with relief, as I went upstairs to find myself a book.

A few minutes later I heard my father come upstairs and go into my mother's room. Anxious to know what was afoot, I got up and followed him. He was standing in the middle of the room, his face pale. "Come outside with me," he said in a tight voice. We went into my room. "I have just had to tell your mother," he began slowly, "that I shall be dead in a quarter of an hour." He was calm as he continued: "To die by the hand of one's own people is hard. But the house is surrounded and Hitler is charging me with high treason. 'In view of my services in Africa,'" he quoted sarcastically, "I am to have the chance of dying by poison. The two generals have brought it with them. It's fatal in three seconds. If I accept, none of the usual steps will be taken against my family, that is against you. They will also leave my staff alone."

"Do you believe it?" I interrupted.

"Yes," he replied. "I believe it. It is very much in their interest to see that the affair does not come out into the open. By the way, I have been charged to put you under a promise of the strictest silence. If a single word of this comes out, they will no longer feel themselves bound by the agreement."

I tried again. "Can't we defend ourselves . . ." He cut me off short.

"There's no point," he said. "It's better for one to die than for all of us to be killed in a shooting affray. Anyway, we've practically no ammunition." We briefly took leave of each other. "Call Aldinger, please," he said.

Aldinger had meanwhile been engaged in conversation by the generals' escort to keep him away from my father. At my call, he came running upstairs. He, too, was struck cold when he heard what was happening. My father now spoke more quickly. He again said how useless it was to attempt to defend ourselves. "It's all been prepared to the last detail. I'm to be given a state funeral. I have asked that it should take place in Ulm. In a quarter of an hour, you, Aldinger, will receive a telephone call from the Wagnerschule reserve hospital in Ulm to say that I've had a brain seizure on the way to a conference." He looked at his watch. "I must go, they've only given me ten minutes." He quickly took leave of us again. Then we went downstairs together.

We helped my father into his leather coat. Suddenly he pulled out his wallet. "There's still 150 marks in there," he said. "Shall I take the money with me?"

"That doesn't matter now, Herr Field Marshal," said Aldinger.

My father put his wallet carefully back in his pocket. As he went into the hall, his little dachshund which he had been given as a puppy a few months before in France, jumped up at him with a whine of joy. "Shut the dog in the study, Manfred," he said, and waited in the hall with Aldinger while I removed the excited dog and pushed it through the study door. Then we walked out of the house together. The two generals were standing at the garden gate. We walked slowly down the path, the crunch of the gravel sounding unusually loud.

As we approached the generals they raised their right hands in salute. "Herr Field Marshal," Burgdorf said shortly and stood aside for my father to pass through the gate. A knot of villagers stood outside the drive. Maisel turned to me, and asked: "What battery are you with?"

"36/7, Herr General," I answered.

The car stood ready. The SS driver swung the door open and stood to attention. My father pushed his Marshal's baton under his left arm and with his face calm, gave Aldinger and me his hand once more before getting in the car.

The two generals climbed quickly into their seats and the doors were slammed. My father did not turn again as the car drove quickly off up the hill and disappeared round a bend in the road. When it had gone Aldinger and I turned and walked silently back into the house. "I'd better go up and see your mother," Aldinger said. I went upstairs again to await the promised telephone call. An agonizing depression excluded all thought.

I lit a cigarette and tried to read again, but the words no longer made sense. Twenty minutes later the telephone rang. Aldinger lifted the receiver and my father's death was duly reported. That evening we drove into Ulm to the hospital where he lay. The doctors who received us were obviously ill at ease, no doubt suspecting the true cause of my father's death. One of them opened the door of a small room. My father lay on a camp-bed in his brown Africa uniform, a look of contempt on his face.

It was not then entirely clear what had happened to him after he left us. Later we learned that the car had halted a few hundred yards up the hill from our house in an open space at the edge of the wood. Gestapo men, who had appeared in force from Berlin that morning, were watching the area with instructions to shoot my father down and storm the house if he offered resistance. Maisel and the driver got out of the car, leaving my father and Burgdorf inside. When the driver was permitted to return ten minutes or so later, he saw my father sunk forward with his cap off and the marshal's baton fallen from his hand. Then they drove off at top speed to Ulm, where the body was unloaded at the hospital; afterwards. General Burgdorf drove on to Ulm *Wehrmacht* Headquarters where he first telephoned to Hitler to report my father's death and then to the family of one of his escort officers to compose the menu for that night's dinner. General Burgdorf, who was hated for his brutality by ninety-nine per cent of the Officer Corps, ended his own life in Berlin in April 1945, after staggering round drunk with Bormann for several days in the Führer's bunker.

Perhaps the most despicable part of the whole story was the expressions of sympathy we received from members of the German Government, men who could not fail to have known the true cause of my father's death and in some cases had no doubt themselves contributed to it, both by word and deed. I quote a few examples:

*In the Field*
*16 October 1944*

Accept my sincerest sympathy for the heavy loss you have suffered with the death of your husband. The name of Field

Marshal Rommel will be for ever linked with the heroic battles in North Africa.

ADOLF HITLER

*Führer's Headquarters*
*26 October 1944*

The fact that your husband, Field Marshal Rommel, has died a hero's death as the result of his wounds, after we had all hoped that he would remain to the German people, has deeply touched me. I send you, my dear Frau Rommel, the heartfelt sympathy of myself and the German *Luftwaffe*.

In silent compassion, Yours,

GÖRING, *Reichsmarschall des Grossdeutschen Reiches*

# HOLOCAUST: SURVIVAL IN AUSCHWITZ, OCTOBER 1944

## *Primo Levi, prisoner*

*Levi was a member of the Italian anti-fascist resistance. He was deported to the SS death camp at Auschwitz in 1944. He survived to become a Nobel prize-winner.*

We fought with all our strength to prevent the arrival of winter. We clung to all the warm hours, at every dusk we tried to keep the sun in the sky for a little longer, but it was all in vain. Yesterday evening the sun went down irrevocably behind a confusion of dirty clouds, chimney stacks and wires, and today it is winter.

We know what it means because we were here last winter; and the others will soon learn. It means that in the course of these months, from October till April, seven out of ten of us will die. Whoever does not die will suffer minute by minute, all day, every day: from the morning before dawn until the distribution of the evening soup we will have to keep our muscles continually tensed, dance from foot to foot, beat our arms under our shoulders against the cold. We will have to spend bread to acquire gloves, and lose hours of sleep to repair them when they become unstitched. As it will no longer be possible to eat in the open, we will have to eat our meals in the hut, on our feet, everyone will be assigned an area of floor as large as a hand, as it is forbidden to rest against the bunks. Wounds will open on everyone's hands, and to be given a bandage will mean waiting every evening for hours on one's feet in the snow and wind.

Just as our hunger is not that feeling of missing a meal, so our way of being cold has need of a new word. We say "hunger," we say "tiredness," "fear," "pain," we say "winter" and they are different things. They are free words, created and used by free men who lived in comfort and suffering in their homes. If the Lagers had lasted longer a new, harsh language would have been born; and only this language could express what it means to toil the whole day in the wind, with the temperature below freezing, wearing only a shirt, underpants, cloth jacket and trousers, and in one's body nothing but weakness, hunger and knowledge of the end drawing nearer.

In the same way in which one sees a hope end, winter arrived this morning. We realized it when we left the hut to go and wash: there were no stars, the dark cold air had the smell of snow. In roll-call square, in the gray of dawn, when we assembled for work, no one spoke. When we saw the first flakes of snow, we thought that if at the same time last year they had told us that we would have seen another winter in Lager, we would have gone and touched the electric wire-fence; and that even now we would go if we were logical, were it not for this last senseless crazy residue of unavoidable hope.

Because "winter" means yet another thing.

Last spring the Germans had constructed huge tents in an open space in the Lager. For the whole of the good season each of them had catered for over a thousand men: now the tents had been taken down, and an excess two thousand guests crowded our huts. We old prisoners knew that the Germans did not like these irregularities and that something would soon happen to reduce our number.

One feels the selections arriving. "*Selekcja*": the hybrid Latin and Polish word is heard once, twice, many times, interpolated in foreign conversations; at first we cannot distinguish it, then it forces itself on our attention, and in the end it persecutes us.

This morning the Poles had said "*Selekcja*." The Poles are the first to find out the news, and they generally try not to let it spread around, because to know something which the others still do not know can always be useful. By the time that everyone realizes that a selection is imminent, the few possibilities of evading it (corrupting some doctor or some prominent with bread or tobacco; leaving the hut for Ka-Be or vice-versa at the right moment so as to cross with the commission) are already their monopoly.

In the days which follow, the atmosphere of the Lager and the yard is filled with "*Selekcja*": nobody knows anything definite, but all speak about it, even the Polish, Italian, French civilian workers whom we secretly see in the yard. Yet the result is hardly a wave of despondency: our collective morale is too inarticulate and flat to be unstable. The fight against hunger, cold and work leaves little margin for thought, even for this thought. Everybody reacts in his own way, but hardly anyone with those attitudes which would seem the most plausible as the most realistic, that is with resignation or despair.

All those able to find a way out, try to take it; but they are the minority because it is very difficult to escape from a selection. The Germans apply themselves to these things with great skill and diligence.

Whoever is unable to prepare for it materially, seeks defense elsewhere. In the latrines, in the washroom, we show each other our chests, our buttocks, our thighs, and our comrades reassure us: "You are all right, it will certainly not be your turn this time, . . . *du bist kein Muselmann* . . . more probably mine . . ." and they undo their braces in turn and pull up their shirts.

Nobody refuses this charity to another: nobody is so sure of his own lot to be able to condemn others. I brazenly lied to old Wertheimer; I told him that if they questioned him, he should reply that he was forty-five, and he should not forget to have a shave the evening before, even if it cost him a quarter-ration of bread; apart from that he need have no fears, and in any case it was by no means certain that it was a selection for the gas chamber; had he not heard the *Blockältester* say that those chosen would go to Jaworszno to a convalescent camp?

It is absurd of Wertheimer to hope: he looks sixty, he has enormous vericose veins, he hardly even notices the hunger any more. But he lies down on his bed, serene and quiet, and replies to someone who asks him with my own words; they are the command-words in the camp these days: I myself repeated them just as – apart from details – Chajim told them to me, Chajim, who has been in Lager for three years, and being strong and robust is wonderfully sure of himself; and I believed them.

On this slender basis I also lived through the great selection of October 1944 with inconceivable tranquility. I was tranquil because I managed to lie to myself sufficiently. The fact that I was not selected depended above all on chance and does not prove that my faith was well-founded.

Monsieur Pinkert is also, a priori, condemned: it is enough to look at his eyes. He calls me over with a sign, and with a confidential air tells me that he has been informed – he cannot tell me the source of information – that this time there is really something new: the Holy See, by means of the International Red Cross . . . in short, he personally guarantees both for himself and for me, in the most absolute manner, that every danger is ruled out; as a civilian he was, as is well known, attaché to the Belgian embassy at Warsaw.

Thus in various ways, even those days of vigil, which in the telling seem as if they ought to have passed every limit of human torment, went by not very differently from other days.

The discipline in both the Lager and Buna is in no way relaxed: the work, cold and hunger are sufficient to fill up every thinking moment.

Today is working Sunday, *Arbeitssonntag*: we work until 1 p.m., then we return to camp for the shower, shave and general control for skin diseases and lice. And in the yards, everyone knew mysteriously that the selection would be today.

The news arrived, as always, surrounded by a halo of contradictory or suspect details: the selection in the infirmary took place this morning; the percentage was seven per cent of the whole camp, thirty, fifty per cent of the patients. At Birkenau, the crematorium chimney has been smoking for ten days. Room has to be made for an enormous convoy arriving from the Poznan ghetto. The young tell the young that all the old ones will be chosen. The healthy tell the healthy that only the ill will be chosen. Specialists will be excluded. German Jews will be excluded. Low Numbers will be excluded. You will be chosen. I will be excluded.

At 1 p.m. exactly the yard empties in orderly fashion and for two hours the gray unending army files past the two control stations where, as on every day, we are counted and recounted, and past the military band which for two hours without interruption plays, as on every day, those marches to which we must synchronize our steps at our entrance and our exit.

It seems like every day, the kitchen chimney smokes as usual, the distribution of the soup is already beginning. But then the bell is heard, and at that moment we realize that we have arrived.

Because this bell always sounds at dawn, when it means the reveille; but if it sounds during the day, it means "*Blocksperre*," enclosure in huts, and this happens when there is a selection to prevent anyone avoiding it, or when those selected leave for the gas, to prevent anyone seeing them leave.

Our *Blockältester* knows his business. He has made sure that we have all entered, he has the door locked, he has given everyone his card with his number, name, profession, age and nationality and he has ordered everyone to undress completely, except for shoes. We wait like this, naked, with the card in our hands, for the commission to reach our hut. We are hut 48, but one can never tell if they are going to begin at hut 1 or hut 60. At any rate, we can rest quietly at least for an hour, and there is no reason why we should not get under the blankets on the bunk and keep warm.

Many are already drowsing when a barrage of orders, oaths and blows proclaims the imminent arrival of the commission. The *Blockältester* and his helpers, starting at the end of the dormitory, drive the crowd of frightened, naked people in front of them and cram them in the *Tagesraum* which is the Quartermaster's office. The *Tagesraum* is a room seven yards by four: when the drive is over, a warm and compact human mass is jammed into the *Tagesraum*, perfectly filling all the corners, exercising such a pressure on the wooden walls as to make them creak.

Now we are all in the *Tagesraum*, and besides there being no time, there is not even any room in which to be afraid. The feeling of the warm flesh pressing all around is unusual and not unpleasant. One has to take care to hold up one's nose so as to breathe, and not to crumple or lose the card in one's hand.

The *Blockältester* has closed the connecting-door and has opened the other two which lead from the dormitory and the *Tagesraum* outside. Here, in front of the two doors, stands the arbiter of our fate, an SS subaltern. On his right is the *Blockältester*, on his left, the quartermaster of the hut. Each one of us, as he comes naked out of the *Tagesraum* into the cold October air, has to run the few steps between the two doors, give the card to the SS man and enter the dormitory door. The SS man, in the fraction of a second between two successive crossings, with a glance at one's back and front, judges everyone's fate, and in turn gives the card to the man on his right or his left, and this is the life or death of each of us. In three or four minutes a hut of two hundred men is "done," as is the whole camp of twelve thousand men in the course of the afternoon.

Jammed in the charnel-house of the *Tagesraum*, I gradually felt the human pressure around me slacken, and in a short time it was my turn. Like everyone, I passed by with a brisk and elastic step, trying to hold my head high, my chest forward and my muscles contracted and conspicuous. With the corner of my eye I tried to look behind my shoulders, and my card seemed to end on the right.

As we gradually come back into the dormitory we are allowed to dress ourselves. Nobody yet knows with certainty his own fate, it has first of all to be established whether the condemned cards were those on the right or the left. By now there is no longer any point in sparing each other's feelings with superstitious scruples. Everybody crowds around the oldest, the most wasted-away, and most "muselmann"; if their cards went to the left, the left is certainly the side of the condemned.

Even before the selection is over, everybody knows that the left was effectively the "*schlechte Seite*," the bad side. There have naturally been some irregularities: René, for example, so young and robust, ended on the left; perhaps it was because he has glasses, perhaps because he walks a little stooped like a myope, but more probably because of a simple mistake: René passed the commission immediately in front of me and there could have been a mistake with our cards. I think about it, discuss it with Alberto, and we agree that the hypothesis is probable; I do not know what I will think tomorrow and later; today I feel no distinct emotion.

It must equally have been a mistake about Sattler, a huge Transylvanian peasant who was still at home only twenty days ago; Sattler does not understand German, he has understood nothing of what has taken place, and stands in a corner mending his shirt. Must I go and tell him that his shirt will be of no more use?

There is nothing surprising about these mistakes: the examination is too quick and summary, and in any case, the important thing for the Lager is not that the most useless prisoners be eliminated, but that free posts be quickly created, according to a certain percentage previously fixed.

The selection is now over in our hut, but it continues in the others, so that we are still locked in. But as the soup-pots have arrived in the meantime, the *Blockältester* decides to proceed with the distribution at once. A double ration will be given to those selected. I have never discovered if this was a ridiculously charitable initiative of the *Blockältester*, or an explicit disposition of the SS, but in fact, in the interval of two or three days (sometimes even much longer) between the selection and the departure, the victims at Monowitz-Auschwitz enjoyed this privilege.

Ziegler holds out his bowl, collects his normal ration and then waits there expectantly. "What do you want?" asks the *Blockältester*: according to him, Ziegler is entitled to no supplement, and he drives him away, but Ziegler returns and humbly persists. He was on the left, everybody saw it, let the *Blockältester* check the cards; he has the right to a double ration. When he is given it, he goes quietly to his bunk to eat.

Now everyone is busy scraping the bottom of his bowl with his spoon so as not to waste the last drops of the soup; a confused, metallic clatter, signifying the end of the day. Silence slowly prevails and then, from my bunk on the top row, I see and hear old Kuhn praying aloud, with his beret on his head, swaying backward and forward violently. Kuhn is thanking God because he has not been chosen.

Kuhn is out of his senses. Does he not see Beppo the Greek in the bunk next to him, Beppo who is twenty years old and is going to the gas chamber the day after tomorrow and knows it and lies there looking fixedly at the light without saying anything and without even thinking any more? Can Kuhn fail to realize that next time it will be his turn? Does Kuhn not understand that what has happened today is an abomination, which no propitiatory prayer, no pardon, no expiation by the guilty, which nothing at all in the power of man can ever clean again?

If I were God, I would spit at Kuhn's prayer.

# THE FALL OF AACHEN, 17 SEPTEMBER 1944

## George Mucha, war correspondent

*Aachen was the first major German town to fall to the Allies, in this case, the American First Army.*

I have just returned to Brussels after four days of street fighting in Aachen. I have seen the city of German Emperors being wiped out after it had refused the offer of honourable surrender, and I found its people crushed to desperation by a double misery, by our onslaught and by the cruelties of their Nazi masters. When I first approached Aachen, the town was burning. From an American observation post just above the city I could see immense columns of smoke rising to the sky where some sixty Allied dive-bombers were freely forming up for attack and diving unmolested on their objective. As the bombs came down, red jets of flame spouted up among the houses which stood there silent without a sign of life. It was an eerie sight, no enemy guns, no movements in the streets, only the incessant rumbling of explosions. And then we went in. On both sides of the deserted streets stood empty carcasses of burnt-out houses; glass, debris and tree branches were strewn on the pavements, and almost in every street a building was burning like a huge torch.

We arrived at a huge concrete surface shelter. These shelters are ugly, gloomy constructions with many floors above and below the ground, where hundreds of civilians were hiding for the last five weeks in darkness and stench. Army officers and the police had the entrance blocked, and no one was allowed to leave the place. In the meantime, Gestapo and soldiers were looting the town, grabbing in mad lust the property of their own people, although they had no hope to carry it away. The Army refused to open the shelter. For several hours it was besieged by American soldiers, then a German officer offered to surrender, if he was allowed to take away all his things, plus his batman.

Lieutenant Walker, a young Company Commander, made no

effort to accept such a ridiculous offer and threatened to use flame-throwers. That helped. The doors opened and out came the drabbest, filthiest inhabitants of the underworld I have ever seen, as people came stumbling out into the light, dazed, then catching a breath of fresh air, and finally starting to jabber, push, scream and curse. Some precipitated themselves to me, brandishing their fists. "Where have you been so long?" they shouted. "Why didn't you deliver us sooner from those devils?" It was a stunning sight. These were the people of the first German town occupied by the Allies. And they were weeping with hysterical joy amidst the smouldering ruins of their homes. "We have been praying every day for you to come," said a woman with a pale, thin face. "You can't imagine what we have had to suffer from them." And then came the insults. Bloodhound, bandit, gangster. All this was the beloved Führer. There is no one who can hate and curse so thoroughly as the Germans, and these people were all green with hate of the Nazis. It was no trick. I certainly would not be cheated.

It was the breakdown of a nation after having played for five years on the wrong cards. Maybe it was the rage of a gangster, let down by his gang-leader, but it was a hatred you find only in civil wars.

# THE US ARMY SLOGS UP ITALY, WINTER 1944

## Ernie Pyle, war correspondent

*The war the GIs fought in the Appenine mountains.*

The war in Italy was tough. The land and the weather were both against us. It rained and it rained. Vehicles bogged down and temporary bridges washed out. The country was shockingly beautiful, and just as shockingly hard to capture from the enemy. The hills rose to high ridges of almost solid rock. We couldn't go around them through the flat peaceful valleys, because the Germans were up there looking down upon us, and they would have let us have it. So we had to go up and over. A mere platoon of Germans, well dug in on a high, rock-spined hill, could hold out for a long time against tremendous onslaughts.

I know the folks back home were disappointed and puzzled by the slow progress in Italy. They wondered why we moved northward so imperceptibly. They were impatient for us to get to Rome. Well, I can say this – our troops were just as impatient for Rome. But on all sides I heard: "It never was this bad in Tunisia." "We ran into a new brand of Krauts over here." "If it would only stop raining." "Every day we don't advance is one day longer before we get home."

Our troops were living in almost inconceivable misery. The fertile black valleys were knee-deep in mud. Thousands of the men had not been dry for weeks. Other thousands lay at night in the high mountains with the temperature below freezing and the thin snow sifting over them. They dug into the stones and slept in little chasms and behind rocks and in half-caves. They lived like men of prehistoric times, and a club would have become them more than a machine-gun. How they survived the dreadful winter at all was beyond us who had the opportunity of drier beds in the warmer valleys.

That the northward path was a tedious one was not the fault of our troops, nor of their direction either. It was the weather and the terrain and the weather again. If there had been no German fighting troops in Italy, if there had been merely German engineers to blow the bridges in the passes, if never a shot had been fired at all, our northward march would still have been slow. The country was so difficult that we formed a great deal of cavalry for use in the mountains. Each division had hundreds of horses and mules to carry supplies beyond the point where vehicles could go no farther. On beyond the mules' ability, mere men – American men – took it on their backs.

On my way to Italy, I flew across the Mediterranean in a cargo plane weighted down with more than a thousand pounds beyond the normal load. The cabin was filled with big pasteboard boxes which had been given priority above all other freight. In the boxes were packboards, hundreds of them, with which husky men would pack 100, even 150, pounds of food and ammunition, on their backs, to comrades high in those miserable mountains.

But we could take consolation from many things. The air was almost wholly ours. All day long Spitfires patrolled above our fighting troops like a half-dozen policemen running up and down the street watching for bandits.

What's more, our artillery prevailed – and how! We were prodigal with ammunition against those rocky crags, and well we might be, for a $50 shell could often save ten lives in country like that. Little by little, the fiendish rain of explosives upon the hillsides softened the Germans. They always were impressed by and afraid of our artillery, and we had concentrations of it there that were demoralizing.

And lastly, no matter how cold the mountains, or how wet the snow, or how sticky the mud, it was just as miserable for the German soldier as for the American.

Our men were going to get to Rome all right. There was no question about that. But the way was cruel. No one who had not seen that mud, those dark skies, those forbidding ridges and ghostlike clouds that unveiled and then quickly hid the enemy, had the right to be impatient with the progress along the road to Rome.

The mountain fighting went on week after dreary week. For a while I hung around with one of the mule-pack outfits. There was an average of one mule-packing outfit for every infantry battalion in the mountains. Some were run by Americans, some by Italian soldiers.

The pack outfit I was with supplied a battalion that was fighting on a bald, rocky ridge nearly 4,000 feet high. That battalion fought constantly for ten days and nights, and when the men finally came down less than a third of them were left.

All through those terrible days every ounce of their supplies had to go up to them on the backs of mules and men. Mules took it the first third of the way. Men took it the last bitter two-thirds, because the trail was too steep even for mules.

The mule skinners of my outfit were Italian soldiers. The human packers were mostly American soldiers. The Italian mule skinners were from Sardinia. They belonged to a mountain artillery regiment, and thus were experienced in climbing and in handling mules. They were bivouacked in an olive grove alongside a highway at the foot of the mountain. They made no trips in the daytime, except in emergencies, because most of the trail was exposed to artillery fire. Supplies were brought into the olive grove by truck during the day, and stacked under trees. Just before dusk they would start loading the stuff on to mules. The Americans who actually managed the supply chain liked to get the mules loaded by dark, because if there was any shelling the Italians instantly disappeared and could never be found.

There were 155 skinners in this outfit and usually about eighty mules were used each night. Every mule had a man to lead it. About ten extra men went along to help get mules up if they fell, to repack any loads that came loose, and to unpack at the top. They could be up and back in less than three hours. Usually a skinner made just one trip a night, but sometimes in an emergency he made two.

On an average night the supplies would run something like this – 85 cans of water, 100 cases of K ration, 10 cases of D ration, 10 miles of telephone wire, 25 cases of grenades and rifle and machine-gun ammunition, about 100 rounds of heavy mortar shells, 1 radio, 2 telephones, and 4 cases of first-aid packets and sulfa drugs. In addition, the packers would cram their pockets with cigarettes for the boys on top; also cans of Sterno, so they could heat some coffee once in a while.

Also, during that period, they took up more than 500 of the heavy combat suits we were issuing to the troops to help keep them warm. They carried up cellophane gas capes for some of the men to use as sleeping bags, and they took extra socks for them too.

Mail was their most tragic cargo. Every night they would take up sacks of mail, and every night they'd bring a large portion of it back down – the recipients would have been killed or wounded the day their letters came.

On the long man-killing climb above the end of the mule trail they used anywhere from 20 to 300 men a night. They rang in cooks, truck drivers, clerks, and anybody else they could lay their hands on. A lot of stuff was packed up by the fighting soldiers themselves. On a big night, when they were building up supplies for an attack, another battalion which was in reserve sent 300 first-line combat troops to do the packing. The mule packs would leave the olive grove in bunches of twenty, starting just after dark. American soldiers were posted within shouting distance of each other all along the trail, to keep the Italians from getting lost in the dark.

Those guides – everybody who thought he was having a tough time in this war should know about them. They were men who had fought all through a long and bitter battle at the top of the mountain. For more than a week they had been far up there, perched behind rocks in the rain and cold, eating cold K rations, sleeping without blankets, scourged constantly with artillery and mortar shells, fighting and ducking and growing more and more weary, seeing their comrades wounded one by one and taken down the mountain.

Finally sickness and exhaustion overtook many of those who were left, so they were sent back down the mountain under their own power to report to the medics there and then go to a rest camp. It took most of them the better part of a day to get two-thirds of the way down, so sore were their feet and so weary their muscles.

And then – when actually in sight of their haven of rest and peace – they were stopped and pressed into guide service, because there just wasn't anybody else to do it. So there they stayed on the mountain-side, for at least three additional days and nights that I know of, just lying miserably alongside the trail, shouting in the darkness to guide the mules.

They had no blankets to keep them warm, no beds but the rocks. And they did it without complaining. The human spirit is an astounding thing.

# THE BATTLE OF THE BULGE: THE AFTERMATH, JANUARY 1945

### *Martha Gellhorn, war correspondent*

*With defeat staring him in the face, Hitler tried one last gamble on the western front: an offensive by two Panzer armies in the Ardennes, intended to sweep through to Antwerp, thus encircling a large part of the Allied forces. Operation Autumn Mist duly began on 16 December 1944. Yet the participatory Panzer armies were not the Panzer armies of old. As Sepp Dietrich, commanding officer of the Sixth SS Panzer Army, testily put it: "All Hitler wants me to do is to cross a river, capture Brussels, and then go on and take Antwerp. And all this in the worst time of the year through the Ardennes when the snow is waist deep and there isn't room to deploy four tanks abreast let alone armoured divisions. When it doesn't get light until eight and it's dark again at four and with re-formed divisions made up chiefly of kids and sick old men – and at Christmas." By 31 January the Germans were back at their start line.*

They all said it was wonderful Kraut-killing country. What it looked like was scenery for a Christmas card: smooth white snow hills and bands of dark forest and villages that actually nestled. The snow made everything serene, from a distance. At sunrise and sunset the snow was pink and the forests grew smoky and soft. During the day the sky was covered with ski tracks, the vapor trails of planes, and the roads were dangerous iced strips, crowded with all the usual vehicles of war, and the artillery made a great deal of noise, as did the bombs from the Thunderbolts. The nestling villages, upon closer view, were mainly rubble and there were indeed plenty of dead Krauts. This was during the German counteroffensive which drove through Luxembourg and Belgium and is now driven back. At this time the Germans were being "contained", as the communiqué said. The situation was "fluid" – again the communiqué. For the sake of the record, here is a little of what containing a fluid situation in Kraut-killing country looks like.

The road to Bastogne had been worked over by the Ninth Air Force Thunderbolts before the Third Army tanks finally cleared the way. A narrow alley was free now, and two or three secondary roads leading from Bastogne back to our lines. "Lines" is a most inaccurate word and one should really say "leading back through where the Germans weren't to where the Americans were scattered about the snowscape." The Germans remained on both sides of this alley and from time to time attempted to push inward and again cut off Bastogne.

A colleague and I drove up to Bastogne on a secondary road through breath-taking scenery. The Thunderbolts had created this scenery. You can say the words "death and destruction" and they don't mean anything. But they are awful words when you are looking at what they mean. There were some German staff cars along the side of the road; they had not merely been hit by machine-gun bullets, they had been mashed into the ground. There were half-tracks and tanks literally wrenched apart, and a gun position directly hit by bombs. All around these lacerated or flattened objects of steel there was the usual riffraff: papers, tin cans, cartridge belts, helmets, an odd shoe, clothing. There were also, ignored and completely inhuman, the hard-frozen corpses of Germans. Then there was a clump of houses, burned and gutted, with only a few walls standing, and around them the enormous bloated bodies of cattle.

The road passed through a curtain of pine forest and came out on a flat, rolling snow field. In this field the sprawled or bunched bodies of Germans lay thick, like some dark shapeless vegetable.

We had watched the Thunderbolts working for several days. They flew in small packs and streaked in to the attack in single file. They passed quickly through the sky and when they dived you held your breath and waited; it seemed impossible that the plane would be able to pull itself up to safety. They were diving to within sixty feet of the ground. The snub-nosed Thunderbolt is more feared by the German troops than any other plane.

You have seen Bastogne and a thousand other Bastognes in the newsreels. These dead towns and villages spread over Europe and one forgets the human misery and fear and despair that the cracked and caved-in buildings represent. Bastogne was a German job of death and destruction and it was beautifully thorough. The 101st Airborne Division, which held Bastogne, was still there, though the day before the wounded had been taken out as soon as the first road was open. The survivors of the 101st Airborne Division, after being entirely surrounded, uninterruptedly shelled and bombed, after having fought off four times their strength in Germans, look – for some unknown reason – cheerful and lively. A young lieutenant remarked, "The tactical situation was always good." He was very surprised when we shouted with laughter. The front, north of Bastogne, was just up the road and the peril was far from past.

At Warnach, on the other side of the main Bastogne road, some soldiers who had taken, lost and retaken this miserable village were now sightseeing the battlefield. They were also inspecting the blown-out equipment of two German tanks and a German self-propelled gun which had been destroyed here. Warnach smelled of the dead; in subzero weather the smell of death has an acrid burning odor. The soldiers poked through the German equipment to see if there was anything useful or desirable. They unearthed a pair of good bedroom slippers alongside the tank, but as no one in the infantry has any chance to wear bedroom slippers these were left. There was a German Bible but no one could read German. Someone had found a German machine pistol in working order and rapidly salted it away; they hoped to find other equally valuable loot.

The American dead had been moved inside the smashed houses and covered over; the dead horses and cows lay where they were, as did a few dead Germans. An old civilian was hopelessly shovelling grain from some burned and burst sacks into a wheelbarrow; and farther down the ruined street a woman was talking French in a high angry voice to the chaplain, who was trying to pacify her. We moved down this way to watch the goings-on. Her house was in fairly good shape; that is to say, it had no windows or door and there was a shell hole through the second-floor wall, but it was standing and the roof looked rain proof. Outside her parlor window were some German mines, marked with a white tape. She stood in her front hall and said bitterly that it was a terrible thing, she had left her house for a few moments that morning, and upon returning she found her sheets had been stolen.

"What's she saying?" asked an enormous soldier with red-rimmed blue eyes and a stubble of red beard. Everyone seems about the same age, as if weariness and strain and the unceasing cold leveled all life. I translated the woman's complaint.

Another soldier said, "What does a sheet look like?"

The huge red-bearded man drawled out, "My goodness," a delicious expression coming from that face in that street. "If she'd of been here when the fighting was going on, she'd act different."

Farther down the street a command car dragged a trailer; the bodies of Germans were piled on the trailer like so much ghastly firewood.

We had come up this main road two days before. First there had been a quick tempestuous scene in a battalion headquarters when two planes strafed us, roaring in to attack three times and putting machine-gun bullets neatly through the second-storey windows of the house. The official attitude has always been that no Germans were flying reclaimed Thunderbolts, so that is that. No one was wounded or killed during this brief muck-up. One of the battalion machine-gunners, who had been firing at the Thunderbolts; said, "For God's sake, which side are those guys fighting on?" We jumped into our jeep and drove up nearer the front, feeling that the front was probably safer.

A solitary tank was parked close to a bombed house near the main road. The crew sat on top of the tank, watching a village just over the hill which was being shelled, as well as bombed by the Thunderbolts. The village was burning and the smoke made a close package of fog around it, but the flames shot up and reddened the snow in the foreground. The armed forces on this piece of front consisted, at the moment, of this tank, and out ahead a few more tanks, and somewhere invisibly to the left a squadron of tanks. We did not know where our infantry was. (This is what a fluid situation means.) The attacked village would soon be entered by the tanks, including the solitary watchdog now guarding this road.

We inquired of the tank crew how everything went. "The war's over," said one of the soldiers, sitting on the turret. "Don't you know that? I heard it on the radio, a week ago. The Germans haven't any gasoline. They haven't any planes. Their tanks are no good. They haven't any shells for their guns. Hell, it's all over. I ask myself what I'm doing here," the tankist went on. "I say to myself, boy, you're crazy; sitting out here in the snow. Those ain't Germans, I say to myself, didn't they tell you on the radio the Germans are finished?"

As for the situation, someone else on the tank said that they would gratefully appreciate it if we could tell them what was going on.

"The wood's full of dead Krauts," said another, pointing across the road. "We came up here and sprayed it just in case there was any around and seems the place was full of them, so it's a good thing we sprayed it all right. But where they are right now, I wouldn't know."

"How's your hen?" asked the Captain, who had come from Battalion HQ to show us the way. "He's got a hen," the Captain explained. "He's been sweating that hen out for three days, running around after it with his helmet."

"My hen's worthless," said a soldier. "Finished, no good, got no fight in her."

"Just like the Germans," said the one who listened to the radio.

Now two days later the road was open much farther and there was even a rumor that it was open all the way to Bastogne. That would mean avoiding the secondary roads, a quicker journey, but it seemed a good idea to inquire at a blasted German gun position. At this spot there were ten Americans, two sergeants and eight enlisted men; also two smashed German bodies, two dead cows and a gutted house.

"I wouldn't go up that road if I was you," one of the sergeants said. "It's cut with small-arms fire about a quarter of a mile farther on. We took about seventeen Heinies out of there just a while back, but some others must of got in."

That seemed to settle the road.

"Anyhow," the sergeant went on, "They're making a counter-attack. They got about thirty tanks, we heard, coming this way."

The situation was getting very fluid again.

"What are you going to do?" I said.

"Stay here," said one of the soldiers.

"We got a gun," said another.

War is lonely and individual work; it is hard to realize how small it can get. Finally it can boil down to ten unshaven gaunt-looking young men, from anywhere in America, stationed on a vital road with German tanks coming in.

"You better take that side road if you're going to Bastogne," the second sergeant said.

It seemed shameful to leave them. "Good luck," I said, not knowing what to say.

"Sure, sure," they said soothingly. And later on they got a tank and the road was never cut and now if they are still alive they are somewhere in Germany doing the same work, as undramatically and casually – just any ten young men from anywhere in America.

About a mile from this place, and therefore about a mile and a half from the oncoming German tanks, the General in command of this tank outfit had his headquarters in a farmhouse. You could not easily enter his office through the front door, because a dead horse with spattered entrails blocked the way. A shell had landed in the farmyard a few minutes before and killed one cow and wounded a second, which was making sad sounds in a passageway between the house and the barn.

The air-ground-support officer was here with his van, checking up on the Thunderbolts who were attacking the oncoming German tanks. "Argue Leader," he said, calling on the radio-phone to the flight leader. "Beagle here. Did you do any good on that one?"

"Can't say yet," answered the voice from the air.

Then over the loud-speaker a new voice came from the air, talking clearly and loudly and calmly. "Three Tigers down there with people around them."

Also from the air the voice of Argue Leader replied rather peevishly, "Go in and get them. Don't stand there talking about it." They were both moving at an approximate speed of three hundred miles an hour.

From the radio in another van came the voice of the Colonel commanding the forward tank unit, which was stopping this counter-attack on the ground. "We got ten and two more coming," said the Colonel's voice. "Just wanted to keep you posted on the German tanks burning up here. It's a beautiful sight, a beautiful sight, over."

"What a lovely headquarters," said a soldier who was making himself a toasted cheese sandwich over a small fire that served everyone for warmth and cookstove. He had opened the cheese can in his K ration and was doing an excellent job, using a German bayonet as a kitchen utensil.

"Furthermore," said a lieutenant, "they're attacking on the other side. They got about thirty tanks coming in from the west too."

"See if I care," remarked the soldier, turning his bread carefully so as to toast it both ways. A shell landed, but it was farther up the road.

There had been a vaguely sketched general ducking, a quick reflex action, but no one of course remarked it.

Then Argue Leader's voice came exultantly from the air. "Got those three. Going home now. Over."

"Good boys," said the ground officer. "Best there is. My squadron."

"Listen to him," said an artillery officer who had come over to report. "You'd think the Thunderbolts did everything. Well, I got to get back to work."

The cow went on moaning softly in the passageway. Our driver, who had made no previous comment during the day, said bitterly, "What I hate to see is a bunch of livestock all beat up this way. Goddammit, what they got to do with it? It's not their fault."

Christmas had passed almost unnoticed. All those who could, and that would mean no farther forward than Battalion Headquarters, had shaved and eaten turkey. The others did not shave and ate cold K rations. That was Christmas. There was little celebration on New Year's Eve, because everyone was occupied, and there was nothing to drink. Now on New Year's Day we were going up to visit the front, east of Luxembourg City. The front was quiet in the early afternoon, except for artillery, and a beautiful fat-flaked snowstorm had started. We decided, like millions of other people, that we were most heartily sick of war; what we really wanted to do was borrow a sled and go coasting. We borrowed a homemade wooden sled from an obliging little boy and found a steep slick hill near an abandoned stone quarry. It was evidently a well-known hill, because a dozen Luxembourg children were already there, with unsteerable sleds like ours. The sky had cleared and the ever present Thunderbolts returned and were working over the front less than four kilometers away. They made a lot of noise, and the artillery was pounding away too. The children paid no attention to this; they did not watch the Thunderbolts, or listen to the artillery. Screaming with joy, fear, and good spirits, they continued to slide down the hill.

Our soldier driver stood with me at the top of the hill and watched the children. "Children aren't so dumb," he said. I said nothing. "Children are pretty smart',' he said. I said nothing again. "What I mean is, children got the right idea. What people ought to do is go coasting."

When he dropped us that night he said, "I sure got to thank you folks. I haven't had so much fun since I left home."

On the night of New Year's Day, I thought of a wonderful New Year's resolution for the men who run the world: get to know the people who only live in it.

There were many dead and many wounded, but the survivors

contained the fluid situation and slowly turned it into a retreat, and finally, as the communiqué said, the bulge was ironed out. This was not done fast or easily; and it was not done by those anonymous things, armies, divisions, regiments. It was done by men, one by one – your men.

## THE BATTLE OF THE REICHSWALD: 8 FEBRUARY 1945

### John Foley, British Tank Officer

*Five months after Arnhem, the Allies were back in the northern Rhineland, this time by land. To break into Germany, the British 21st Army Group had the uneviable task of negotiating the supposedly impenetrable, ten-miles-deep Reichswald Forest, whose western edge formed the Dutch-German border.*

I was nearly blasted from my blankets by a deafening barrage of noise. The ground shook with the fury of the cannonade and the walls of the sixty-pound tent whipped in and out like sparrows' wings.

It was the softening-up bombardment, and it lasted until nearly ten-thirty.

We sat up in our blankets, and by means of a mixture of shouting and sign language we agreed that we'd never heard such a noise. Sleep was quite out of the question, so we dressed and went outside the tent. Overhead a solid curtain of Bofors tracers indicated that even the 40 mm. anti-aircraft guns were being used to thicken-up the barrage, and the sky behind us was alight with the continual flicker of gunfire.

From the front of our wood it seemed that the edge of the Reichswald was a solid mass of explosions and it appeared impossible that anything could live in that inferno.

"It should be a walk-over by half-past ten!" shouted Bob Webster; but we both knew that the Germans had a peculiar aptitude for emerging unscathed from the fiercest bombardment. Still, it was an encouraging thought.

Dead on the dot of ten-thirty we emerged from our wood and headed for the Reichswald. In front of us the Black Watch moved purposefully forward; little groups of men hurrying over the ground, while others spreadeagled themselves behind what cover they could and fired their rifles and Bren guns calmly and methodically.

We had expected the start to be slow for us, because we were scheduled to wait around quite a bit while the funnies cleared lanes through the minefield. But bit by bit reports came back over the radio indicating that it wasn't the mines which were causing the delay, but the mud.

The smooth green turf quickly churned up into black, track-clinging mud. One by one the Churchills sank on their bellies, their tracks spinning uselessly around in the bog. There was one road across the battlefield, but this had quite rightly been earmarked for essential wheeled vehicles only. To have put tanks on it would soon have made it as impassable as the rest of the ground.

. . . Then the enemy began to recover from the six-hour bombardment. Eruptions of dirt indicated mortar and artillery fire coming down on our infantry and one or two of them started coming back, stolidly plodding along while holding a bloodstained arm or shoulder. Stretcher-bearers dealt swiftly and efficiently with those who couldn't walk, and still the Black Watch went forward until they reached a group of farm buildings where they were scheduled for a short halt.

We pulled into the buildings with them and I looked around for the Company Commander. He was walking along a bit of a road, quietly smoking his pipe. With his little cane and his red hackle on the side of his cap, he might well have been taking a Sunday morning stroll down Aldershot High Street, except that vicious little spurts of dust were cracking about his heels.

He raised his stick in greeting when he saw Five Troop, and completely indifferent to the bullets kicking up the dirt around him he strolled across to *Avenger* and swung up to the turret.

"Going very well so far," he said pleasantly. "How're your funny-boys getting on with breaching that minefield?"

"They're all bogged," I said gloomily. "Look here, aren't you being shot at?"

"Oh, never mind that," he said. "It's only got nuisance value. Well, it's a pity you can't get across that minefield. Looks like we'll have to go on without you."

. . . Slowly we fought our way through the interminable Reichswald Forest. And each day the great trees steadily dripped rain on to us, and succeeded in blotting out most of the grey daylight.

The fringes of the forest were shell-torn and shattered, with untidy heaps of dead Germans flung about in grotesque attitudes.

## CROSSING THE GERMAN BORDER, 28 FEBRUARY 1945

### *John Foley, British Tank Officer*

I stared curiously at my first German civilian. He was an old man, dressed in shabby serge and an engine-driver's sort of cap. His grizzled face regarded us from above a bushy white moustache as we clattered

over the broken frontier barrier. And then I heard *Angler*'s driver's
hatch being thrown open, and when I looked over my shoulder I saw
Smith 161 leaning out and staring questioningly at the old German.

"We on the right road for Berlin, mate?" asked Smith 161, with a
perfectly straight face.

I swear the old blue eyes winked, as the man tugged at his grizzled
moustache and said: "*Berlin? Ja, ja! Gerade aus!*"

"I thought the Germans had no sense of humour," said Pickford,
when we got moving again.

"I know," I said. "But he can remember Germany before Hitler,
and probably before the Kaiser, too."

*By 3 March 1945, the Allies were emplaced along the Rhine from Dusseldorf to the Dutch
frontier. The entire German hinterland lay before them. Moreover, thanks to the foolishness
of the Germans the centre of the front had one bridge (at Remagen) over the Rhine left intact.
The American First Army poured across it. Disregarding Berlin as a prize – the Russians
were already closing on the German capital from the East – Eisenhower drove through central
Germany. After heavy fighting at the Remagen bridgehead, the American First Army then
swung north to meet the Ninth Army and the British (who had forced the Rhine at Wesel),
surrounding the Ruhr. On 21 April the German commander in the Ruhr Pocket, Field
Marshal Model, shot himself. Elsewhere in western Germany the Allies were proceeding up
to 30 miles a day. German resistance had collapsed. On 25 April the Americans and the
Russians shook hands at Torgau to the east of Leipzig.*

# A BOMB HITS THE PROPAGANDA MINISTRY, BERLIN, 13 MARCH 1945

## *Joseph Goebbels*

*Joseph Goebbels was one of the principal ring-leaders of Nazism and head of the Nazi's
Ministry of Public Enlightenment and Propaganda.*

This evening's Mosquito raid was particularly disastrous for me
because our Ministry was hit. The whole lovely building on the
Wilhelmstrasse was totally destroyed by a bomb. The throne-room,
the Blue Gallery and my newly rebuilt theatre hall are nothing but a
heap of ruins. I drove straight to the Ministry to see the devastation
for myself. One's heart aches to see so unique a product of the
architect's art, such as this building was, totally flattened in a
second. What trouble we have taken to reconstruct the theatre hall,
the throne-room and the Blue Gallery in the old style! With what
care have we chosen every fresco on the walls and every piece of
furniture! And now it has all been given over to destruction. In
addition fire has now broken out in the ruins, bringing with it an

even greater risk since 500 bazooka missiles are stored underneath the burning wreckage. I do my utmost to get the fire brigade to the scene as quickly and in as great strength as possible, so as at least to prevent the bazooka missiles exploding.

As I do all this I am overcome with sadness. It is twelve years to the day – 13 March – since I entered this Ministry as Minister. It is the worst conceivable omen for the next twelve years.

## IN DYING WE LIVE: LAST TESTAMENT OF A DANISH ANTI-NAZI, 4 APRIL 1945

### Seaman Kim Malthe-Bruun

*Malthe-Bruun was executed by the SS for running arms to a Danish resistance group.*

*Western Prison, German Section, Cell* 411
*April* 4, 1945

Dear Mother: To-day, together with Jörgen, Nils, and Ludwig, I was arraigned before a military tribunal. We were condemned to death. I know that you are a courageous woman, and that you will bear this, but, hear me, it is not enough to bear it, you must also understand it. I am an insignificant thing, and my person will soon be forgotten, but the thought, the life, the inspiration that filled me will live on. You will meet them everywhere – in the trees at springtime, in people who cross your path, in a loving little smile. You will encounter that something which perhaps had value in me, you will cherish it, and you will not forget me. And so I shall have a chance to grow, to become large and mature. I shall be living with all of you whose hearts I once filled. And you will all live on, knowing that I have preceded you, and not, as perhaps you thought at first, dropped out behind you. You know what my dearest wish has always been, and what I hoped to become. Follow me, my dear mother, on my path, and do not stop before the end, but linger with some of the matters belonging to the last space of time allotted to me, and you will find something that may be of value both to my sweetheart and to you, my mother.

I travelled a road that I have never regretted. I have never evaded the dictate of my heart, and now things seem to fall into place. I am not old, I should not be dying, yet it seems so natural to me, so simple. It is only the abrupt manner of it that frightens us at first. The time is short, I cannot properly explain it, but my soul is perfectly at rest . . .

When I come right down to it, how strange it is to be sitting here and writing this testament. Every word must stand, it can never be amended, erased, or changed. I have so many thoughts. Jörgen is sitting here before me writing his two-year-old daughter a letter for her confirmation. A document for life. He and I have lived together, and now we die together, two comrades . . .

I see the course that things are taking in our country, and I know that grandfather will prove to have been right, but remember – and all of you must remember this – that your dream must not be to return to the time before the war, but that all of you, young and old, should create conditions that are not arbitrary but that will bring to realisation a genuinely human ideal, something that every person will see and feel to be an ideal for all of us. That is the great gift for which our country thirsts – something for which every humble peasant boy can yearn, and which he can joyously feel himself to have a part in and to be working for.

Finally, there is a girl whom I call mine. Make her realise that the stars still shine and that I have been only a milestone on her road. Help her on: she can still become very happy.

In haste – your eldest child and only son,

Kim

## ITALIAN PARTISANS TAKE THEIR REVENGE, TRIESTE, 13 APRIL 1945

### Geoffrey Cox, British Eighth Army

The Germans were beaten; that was as clear as any fact in the world. The battle all over the world was won. The Russians were up to Berlin, the British and Americans were rounding up whole armies. To be killed now was like being killed after the end of the war. It seemed wasteful as well as evil. Hate came back into my mind then, as into many other minds in the Division as this final offensive wore on in battles which, against any other foe, would have been unnecessary, and which claimed casualties in hundreds and thousands.

At the new area a group of partisans with red scarves were waiting. They had been stopped by our own troops down by the river bank as suspicious characters. Enthusiastically (they were not yet disillusioned) they explained that they wanted to help. They had been told that there were several Germans hiding in this area. One, they said, was patently an officer. Gold braid had been seen on his shoulders. Could they not carry on with the search?

It took only five minutes to get their papers checked and to set them loose. At the same time we put part of the Headquarters Defence Platoon out on the same quest. "Any prisoners you can get will be valuable," I told the bearded partisan leader. He grinned. "Si, si. Prigionieri", he said.

Half an hour later there were shots down by the river bank. An hour later the partisans were back. They had found the Germans, three of them. One was certainly an officer. Where was he? Ah, he tried to escape. A very foolish fellow. "*Molto stupido, molto stupido.*" But here were his documents. And they handed over a blood-stained bundle.

I opened the top pay-book. Hauptmann. So he was an officer all right. An anti-tank gunner. Two passport photographs fell out of the book. The face on them might well have come from a stock propaganda shot of the stern S.S. man. Here were those deep-set eyes, that hard thin mouth, that cheek crossed with duelling scars, that sleek yellow hair, that square German head of the ideal Nazi type. Every detail in the book bore out the picture. . . . The medal of the Iron Cross, its ribbon stained crimson brown above its red, black and white, lay among the papers.

The Hauptmann's book was full of photographs of Storm Troops and of soldiers, of sisters in white blouses and dark shirts, of a heavy-built father with close-cropped hair, of other young officers with the same relentless faces. This was the type Hitler had loosed on Europe, brave, desperate, efficient. And now he had come to his end in an Italian field, shot down by an Italian farmer's boy with a Sten gun, shot in the back, I learned later, as he crouched in hiding. There he would lie, in some nameless, unmarked grave. There, I felt that evening, as the light faded from the sky, he deserved to lie. It was fitting that he should have been shot down by a man who, however unaware of his role, represented the ordinary people in arms. For that was the force this man had most mocked, the force he and his type had set out to smash and drag behind the wheels of their imperial staff cars. Here, in a remote corner of Italy, were symbolised the two great forces really locked in this struggle – Fascism and the people. If there was brutality in the way the people had killed this Fascist, I for one was unmoved. A tribunal greater than any we could erect, that of history itself, had carried out this verdict.

*The German Army in Italy surrendered unconditionally on 2 May.*

# HOLOCAUST: A REPORTER VISITS BELSEN, 19 APRIL 1945

## *Richard Dimbleby, BBC*

*A radio dispatch, broadcast 1945. As the Allies advanced, they stumbled upon Nazi Germany's darkest horrors.*

I picked my way over corpse after corpse in the gloom, until I heard one voice raised above the gentle undulating moaning. I found a girl, she was a living skeleton, impossible to gauge her age for she had practically no hair left, and her face was only a yellow parchment sheet with two holes in it for eyes. She was stretching out her stick of an arm and gasping something, it was "English, English, medicine, medicine", and she was trying to cry but she hadn't enough strength. And beyond her down the passage and in the hut there were the convulsive movements of dying people too weak to raise themselves from the floor.

In the shade of some trees lay a great collection of bodies. I walked about them trying to count, there were perhaps 150 of them flung down on each other, all naked, all so thin that their yellow skin glistened like stretched rubber on their bones. Some of the poor starved creatures whose bodies were there looked so utterly unreal and inhuman that I could have imagined that they had never lived at all. They were like polished skeletons, the skeletons that medical students like to play practical jokes with.

At one end of the pile a cluster of men and women were gathered round a fire; they were using rags and old shoes taken from the bodies to keep it alight, and they were heating soup over it. And close by was the enclosure where 500 children between the ages of five and twelve had been kept. They were not so hungry as the rest, for the women had sacrificed themselves to keep them alive. Babies were born at Belsen, some of them shrunken, wizened little things that could not live, because their mothers could not feed them.

One woman, distraught to the point of madness, flung herself at a British soldier who was on guard at the camp on the night that it was reached by the 11th Armoured Division; she begged him to give her some milk for the tiny baby she held in her arms. She laid the mite on the ground and threw herself at the sentry's feet and kissed his boots. And when, in his distress, he asked her to get up, she put the baby in his arms and ran off crying that she would find milk for it because there was no milk in her breast. And when the soldier opened the bundle of rags to look at the child, he found that it had been dead for days.

There was no privacy of any kind. Women stood naked at the side of the track, washing in cupfuls of water taken from British Army trucks. Others squatted while they searched themselves for lice, and examined each other's hair. Sufferers from dysentery leaned against the huts, straining helplessly, and all around and about them was this awful drifting tide of exhausted people, neither caring nor watching. Just a few held out their withered hands to us as we passed by, and blessed the doctor, whom they knew had become the camp commander in place of the brutal Kramer.

I have never seen British soldiers so moved to cold fury as the men who opened the Belsen camp this week.

# THE FUNERAL OF PRESIDENT ROOSEVELT, GEORGIA, 20 APRIL 1945

## Douglas B. Cornell

*Franklin Delano Roosevelt, US President, had died on the morning of 12 April. He was buried at his family home in Georgia. He was succeeded as US President by Harry S. Truman, the Vice-President.*

As President Truman looked on with a face frozen in grief, Franklin D. Roosevelt was committed today to the warm brown earth of his native soil.

Under a cloudless, spring sky, the body of the late Chief Executive was lowered solemnly into a grave in the flower garden of his family estate.

Watching with strained faces were members of the family, dignitaries of government and little sad-faced groups of plain people – the employees on the place and neighbours from the countryside.

A detail of grey-clad cadets from the US Military Academy at West Point fired a volley of three farewell salutes. A bugler played "Taps", its sweet but still sad notes echoing through the wooded estate.

Soldiers, sailors and marines, who had held an American flag over the casket, folded it and handed it to Mrs Roosevelt.

The garden where Mr Roosevelt rests lies between the family home where he was born sixty-three years ago and the library which houses his state papers and the gifts of a world which recognized him as one of its pre-eminent leaders.

It was exactly ten a.m. when the first gun of a presidential salute was fired from a battery in the library grounds to the east of the quarter-acre garden. They boomed at solemnly spaced intervals.

An honour guard lining the hemlock hedge around the garden stood at attention.

A few moments later, the distant melody of a bugle came to those within the garden. A flight of bombers and another of training planes droned overhead.

The beat of muffled drums in slow cadence rolled through the wooded hills above the Hudson. In the distance, gradually drawing nearer, a band played a funeral dirge.

Promptly at ten-thirty a.m., the National Anthem sounded and, as the wheels of the caisson noisily ground the gravel of the roadway, the notes of "Nearer, My God, to Thee", were played softly. Through a passageway at one corner, the elderly, grey-bearded rector of the President's Episcopal Church at Hyde Park walked across the newly clipped grass toward the grave.

The Rev. George W. Anthony was wearing the black and white surplice and stole of the clergy. He removed a black velvet skull-cap and took his position at the head of the grave, toward the west.

"All that the father giveth me shall come to me," the Rev. Mr Anthony said.

A lone plane circling above almost drowned his words as he declared that unto Almighty God "we commit his body to the ground; earth to earth, ashes to ashes, dust to dust."

There was a stirring in the crowd.

"Blessed are the dead who die in the Lord," the rector intoned. "Lord, have mercy upon us. Christ, have mercy upon us. Lord, have mercy upon us."

The pastor repeated the words of the Lord's Prayer. Elliott's lips moved with him.

The services followed the ordinary Episcopal burial rites for the dead. There were no words of eulogy, only the word of God.

Near its conclusion the Rev. Mr Anthony recited the poem written by John Ellerton in 1870: "Now the labourer's task is o'er; now the battle-day is past."

"Father, in Thy gracious keeping we now leave Thy servant sleeping," the rector continued.

The services were brief. They were over by ten-forty-five. The flag which Mrs Roosevelt clutched tightly was handed to Elliott, and the family filed out.

## THE GERMANY ARMY SURRENDERS, LÜNEBERG HEATH, 3 MAY 1945

### Field Marshal Montgomery

On 3 May Field Marshal Keitel sent a delegation to my headquarters on Lüneburg Heath, with the consent of Admiral Dönitz, to open negotiations for surrender. This party arrived at eleven-thirty hours and consisted of:

General-Admiral von Friedeburg, C.-in-C. of the German Navy.

General Kinzel, Chief of Staff to Field Marshal Busch, who was commanding the German land forces on my northern and western flanks.

Rear-Admiral Wagner.

Major Freidel, a staff officer.

This party of four was later joined by Colonel Pollek, another staff officer.

They were brought to my caravan site and were drawn up under the Union Jack, which was flying proudly in the breeze. I kept them waiting for a few minutes and then came out of my caravan and walked towards them. They all saluted, under the Union Jack. It was a great moment; I knew the Germans had come to surrender and that the war was over. Few of those in the signals and operations caravans at my Tac Headquarters will forget the thrill experienced when they heard the faint "tapping" of the Germans trying to pick us up on the wireless command link – to receive the surrender instructions from their delegation.

I said to my interpreter, "Who are these men?" He told me.

I then said, "What do they want?"

Admiral Friedeburg then read me a letter from Field Marshal Keitel offering to surrender to me the three German armies withdrawing in front of the Russians between Berlin and Rostock. I refused to consider this, saying that these armies should surrender to the Russians. I added that, of course, if any German soldiers came towards my front with their hands up they would automatically be taken prisoner. Von Friedeburg said it was unthinkable to surrender to the Russians as they were savages, and the German soldiers would be sent straight off to work in Russia.

I said the Germans should have thought of all these things before they began the war, and particularly before they attacked the Russians in June 1941.

Von Friedeburg next said that they were anxious about the civilian population in Mecklenburg, who were being overrun by the Russians, and they would like to discuss how these could be saved. I replied that Mecklenburg was not in my area and that any problems connected with it must be discussed with the Russians. I said they must understand that I refused to discuss any matter connected with the situation on my eastern flank between Wismar and Domitz; they must approach the Russians on such matters. I then asked if they wanted to discuss the surrender of their forces on my western flank. They said they did not. But they were anxious about the civilian population in those areas, and would like to arrange with me some scheme by which their troops could withdraw slowly as my forces advanced. I refused.

I then decided to spring something on them quickly. I said to von Friedeburg:

"Will you surrender to me all German forces on my western and northern flanks, including all forces in Holland, Friesland with the Frisian Islands and Heligoland, Schleswig-Holstein, and Denmark? If you will do this, I will accept it as a tactical battlefield surrender of the enemy forces immediately opposing me, and those in support of Denmark."

He said he could not agree to do this. But he was anxious to come to some agreement about the civilian population in those areas; I refused to discuss this. I then said that if the Germans refused to surrender unconditionally the forces in the areas I had named, I would order the fighting to continue; many more German soldiers would then be killed, and possibly some civilians also from artillery fire and air attack. I next showed them on a map the actual battle situation on the whole western front; they had no idea what this situation was and were very upset. By this time I reckoned that I would not have much more difficulty in getting them to accept my demands. But I thought that an interval for lunch might be desirable so that they could reflect on what I had said. I sent them away to have lunch in a tent by themselves, with nobody else present except one of my officers. Von Friedeburg wept during lunch and the others did not say much.

After lunch I sent for them again, and this time the meeting was in my conference tent with the map of the battle situation on the table. I began this meeting by delivering an ultimatum. They must surrender unconditionally all their forces in the areas I had named; once they had done this I would discuss with them the best way of occupying the areas and looking after the civilians; if they refused, I would go on with the battle. They saw at once that I meant what I said. They were convinced of the hopelessness of their cause but they said they had no power to agree to my demands. They were, however, now prepared to recommend to Field Marshal Keitel the unconditional surrender of all the forces on the western and northern flanks of 21 Army Group. Two of them would go back to OKW, see Keitel, and bring back his agreement.

I then drew up a document which summarized the decisions reached at our meeting, which I said must be signed by myself and von Friedeburg, and could then be taken to Flensburg, and given to Keitel and Dönitz.

*The instrument of surrender was signed on 7 May 1945. The war in Europe was over. Eisenhower sent the following laconic dispatch to the Allied Chiefs of Staff:*

The mission of this Allied Force was fulfilled at three a.m., local time, 7 May 1945. Eisenhower.

# VICTORY IN EUROPE CELEBRATIONS, 8 MAY 1945

## *Mollie Panter-Downes, London*

The big day started off here with a coincidence. In the last hours of peace, in September, 1939, a violent thunderstorm broke over the city, making a lot of people think for a moment that the first air raid had begun. Early Tuesday morning, VE Day, nature tidily brought the war to an end with an imitation of a blitz so realistic that many Londoners started awake and reached blurrily for the bedside torch. Then they remembered, and, sighing with relief, fell asleep again as the thunder rolled over the capital, already waiting with its flags. The decorations had blossomed on the streets Monday afternoon. By six that night, Piccadilly Circus and all the city's other focal points were jammed with a cheerful, expectant crowd waiting for an official statement from Downing Street. Movie cameramen crouched patiently on the rooftops. When a brewer's van rattled by and the driver leaned out and yelled "It's all over", the crowd cheered, then went on waiting. Presently word spread that the announcement would be delayed, and the day, which had started off like a rocket, began to fizzle slowly and damply out. Later in the evening, however, thousands of Londoners suddenly decided that even if it was not yet VE Day, it was victory, all right, and something to celebrate. Thousands of others just went home quietly to wait some more.

When the day finally came, it was like no other day that anyone can remember. It had a flavour of its own, an extemporaneousness which gave it something of the quality of a vast, happy village fete as people wandered about, sat, sang, and slept against a summer background of trees, grass, flowers, and water. It was not, people said, like the 1918 Armistice Day, for at no time was the reaction hysterical. It was not like the Coronation, for the crowds were larger and their gaiety, which held up all through the night, was obviously not picked up in a pub. The day also surprised the prophets who had said that only the young would be resilient enough to celebrate in a big way. Apparently the desire to assist in London's celebration combusted spontaneously in the bosom of every member of every family, from the smallest babies, with their hair done up in red-white-and-blue ribbons, to beaming elderly couples who, utterly without self-consciousness, strolled up and down the streets arm in arm in red-white-and-blue paper hats. Even the dogs wore immense tricoloured bows. Rosettes sprouted from the slabs of pork in the butcher shops, which, like other food stores, were open for a couple of hours in the morning. With their customary practicality, housewives put bread before circuses. They waited in the long bakery queues, the string bags of the common round in one hand and the Union Jack of the glad occasion in the other. Even queues seemed tolerable that morning. The bells had begun to peal and, after the night's storm, London was having that perfect, hot, English summer's day which, one sometimes feels, is to be found only in the imaginations of the lyric poets.

The girls in their thin, bright dresses heightened the impression that the city had been taken over by an enormous family picnic. The number of extraordinarily pretty young girls, who presumably are hidden on working days inside the factories and government offices, was astonishing. They streamed out into the parks and streets like flocks of twittering, gaily plumaged cockney birds. In their freshly curled hair were cornflowers and poppies, and they wore red-white-and-blue ribbons around their narrow waists. Some of them even tied ribbons around their bare ankles. Strolling with their uniformed boys, arms candidly about each other, they provided a constant, gay, simple marginal decoration to the big, solemn moments of the day. The crowds milled back and forth between the Palace, Westminster, Trafalgar Square, and Piccadilly Circus, and when they got tired they simply sat down wherever they happened to be – on the grass, on doorsteps, or on the kerb – and watched the other people or spread handkerchiefs over their faces and took a nap. Everybody appeared determined to see the King and Queen and Mr Churchill at least once, and few could have been disappointed. One small boy, holding on to his father's hand, wanted to see the trench shelters in Green Park too. "You don't want to see shelters today," his father said. "You'll never have to use them again, son." "Never?" the child asked doubtfully. "Never!" the man cried, almost angrily. "*Never!* Understand?" In the open space before the Palace, one of the places where the Prime Minister's speech was to be relayed by loudspeaker at three o'clock, the crowds seemed a little intimidated by the nearness of that symbolic block of grey stone. The people who chose to open their lunch baskets and munch sandwiches there among the flower beds of tulips were rather subdued. Piccadilly Circus attracted the more demonstrative spirits.

By lunchtime, in the Circus, the buses had to slow to a crawl in order to get through the tightly packed, laughing people. A lad in the black beret of the Tank Corps was the first to climb the little pyramidal Angkor Vat of scaffolding and sandbags which was erected early in the war to protect the pedestal of the Eros statue after the figure had been removed to safekeeping. The boy shinnied up to the top and took a tiptoe Eros pose, aiming an imaginary bow, while the crowd roared. He was followed by a paratrooper in a maroon beret, who, after getting up to the top, reached down and hauled up a blonde young woman in a very tight pair of green slacks. When she got to the top, the Tank Corps soldier promptly grabbed her in his arms and, encouraged by ecstatic cheers from the whole Circus, seemed about to enact the classic role of Eros right on the top of the monument. Nothing came of it, because a moment later a couple of GIs joined them and before long the pyramid was covered with boys and girls. They sat jammed together in an affectionate mass, swinging their legs over the sides, wearing each other's uniform caps, and calling down wisecracks to the crowd. "My God," someone said, "think of a flying bomb coming down on this!" When a firecracker went off, a hawker with a tray of tin brooches of Monty's head happily yelled that comforting, sometimes fallacious phrase of the blitz nights, "All right, mates, it's one of ours!"

All day long, the deadly past was for most people only just under the surface of the beautiful, safe present, so much so that the Government decided against sounding the sirens in a triumphant "all clear" for fear that the noise would revive too many painful memories. For the same reason, there were no salutes of guns – only the pealing of the bells, and the whistles of tugs on the Thames sounding the doot, doot, doot, dooooot of the "V", and the roar of the planes, which swooped back and forth over the city, dropping red and green signals toward the blur of smiling, upturned faces.

It was without any doubt Churchill's day. Thousands of King George's subjects wedged themselves in front of the Palace throughout the day, chanting ceaselessly "We want the King" and cheering themselves hoarse when he and the Queen and their daughters appeared, but when the crowd saw Churchill there was a deep, full-throated, almost reverent roar. He was at the head of a procession of Members of Parliament, walking back to the House of Commons from the traditional St Margaret's Thanksgiving Service. Instantly, he was surrounded by people – people running, standing on tiptoe, holding up babies so that they could be told later they had seen him, and shouting affectionately the absurd little nurserymaid name, "Winnie, Winnie!" One of two happily sozzled, very old, and in- credibly dirty cockneys who had been engaged in a slow, shuffling dance, like a couple of Shakespearean clowns, bellowed, "That's 'im, that's 'is little old lovely bald 'ead!" The crowds saw Churchill again later, when he emerged from the Commons and was driven off in the back of a small open car, rosy, smiling, and looking immensely happy. Ernest Bevin, following in another car, got a cheer too. One of the throng, an excited East Ender, in a dress with a bodice concocted of a Union Jack, shouted, "Gawd, fancy me cheering Bevin, the chap who makes us work!" Herbert Morrison, sitting unobtrusively in a corner of a third car, was hardly recognized, and the other Cabinet Ministers did no better. The crowd had ears, eyes, and throats for no one but Churchill, and for him everyone in it seemed to have the hearing, sight, and lungs of fifty men. His slightly formal official broadcast, which was followed by buglers sounding the "cease firing" call, did not strike the emotional note that had been expected, but he hit it perfectly in his subsequent informal speech ("My dear friends, this is your victory . . .") from a Whitehall balcony.

All day long, little extra celebrations started up. In the Mall, a model of a Gallic cock waltzed on a pole over the heads of the singing people. "It's the Free French," said someone. The Belgians in the crowd tagged along after a Belgian flag that marched by, its bearer invisible. A procession of students raced through Green Park, among exploding squibs, clashing dustbin lids like cymbals and waving an immense Jeyes Disinfectant poster as a banner. American sailors and laughing girls formed a conga line down the middle of Piccadilly and cockneys linked arms in the Lambeth Walk. It was a day and night of no fixed plan and no organized merriment. Each group, danced its own dance, sang its own song, and went its own way as the spirit moved it. The most tolerant, self-effacing people in London on V E Day were the police, who simply stood by, smiling benignly, while soldiers swung by one arm from lamp standards and laughing groups tore down hoardings to build the evening's bonfires. Actually, the police were not unduly strained. The extraordinary thing about the crowds was that they were almost all sober. The number of drunks one saw in that whole day and night could have been counted on two hands – possibly because the pubs were sold out so early. The young service men and women who swung arm in arm down the middle of every street, singing and swarming over the few cars rash enough to come out, were simply happy with an immense holiday happiness. They were the liberated people who, like their counterparts in every celebrating capital that night, were young enough to outlive the past and to look forward to an unspoilt future. Their gaiety was very moving.

Just before the King's speech, at nine Tuesday night, the big lamps outside the Palace came on and there were cheers and ohs from children who had never seen anything of that kind in their short, blacked-out lives. As the evening wore on, most of the public buildings were floodlighted. The night was as warm as midsummer, and London, its shabbiness now hidden and its domes and remaining Wren spires warmed by lights and bonfires, was suddenly magnificent. The handsomest building of all was the National Gallery, standing out honey-coloured near a ghostly, blue-shadowed St Martin's and the Charles I bit of Whitehall. The illuminated and floodlighted face of Big Ben loomed like a kind moon. Red and blue lights strung in the bushes around the lake in St James's Park glimmered on the sleepy, bewildered pelicans that live there.

By midnight the crowds had thinned out some, but those who remained were as merry as ever. They went on calling for the King outside the Palace and watching the searchlights, which for once could be observed with pleasure . . .

### James Byrom, soldier, Germany

On VE night the victorious armies got drunk according to a long-cherished plan. I think I must have been on duty, for I was as sober as a judge and I remember standing at a dormer window in the great *Luftwaffe* hospital at Wismar, looking at the magnificent sunset and thinking that I had now come almost full circle, back to the sea that washed the shores of Sweden.

On a ward balcony below me wounded Germans were talking quietly. Presently, as the glow of their cigarettes confirmed that it was dark, the victory celebrations began. Up from the British lines came brilliant flares, singly and in clusters, but without pattern or prodigality, as if one soldier in each platoon had been given an official coloured hat and told to fling it in the air. But farther away, in the Russian lines, the glow of bonfires steadily lit up the sky. Distance subdued the flickering, making static cones that were slightly blurred by smoke or mist; and I could fancy that they were ghost fires, the fires of other historic triumphs, so strongly did I feel them as a symbol of the unreality of victory in relation to the recurring failure to keep the peace.

### "A Correspondent", The *Hereford Times*

Passing through the village of Stoke Lacy early on Tuesday afternoon one was startled to see an effigy of Hitler in the car park at the Plough. That evening a crowd began to gather, and word went round that Hitler was to be consumed in flames at 11 p.m. At that hour excitement was intense, when Mr W. R. Symonds called upon Mr

S. J. Parker, the Commander of No. 12 Platoon of the Home Guard, to set the effigy alight. In a few minutes the body of Hitler disintegrated as his 1,000-year empire had done. First his arm, poised in the Hitler salute, dropped as smartly as it was ever raised in real life . . . then a leg fell off, and the flames burnt fiercely to the strains of "Rule Britannia", "There'll Always be an England", and "Roll Out the Barrel". The crowd spontaneously linked hands and in a circle 300-strong sang the National Anthem.

# Part Seven

*The Road to Berlin*

*The Eastern Front,
February 1943–May 1945*

# INTRODUCTION

Stalingrad was not the only German disaster on the Russian front in 1943. Taking advantage of German disorder, a generalized Russian offensive created a salient around Kursk. This proved a temptation beyond resistance for the Germans, who sought to cut the salient's "neck" and thus encircle and destroy the Russian armies within. Kursk was to be a "beacon" to the world, Hitler informed his generals, proof that Germany was still invincible and, less prosaically, victory at Kursk would prevent any major Russian offensives in the summer of 1943. At 4.30 a.m. on 5 July, the German attack at Kursk opened, and over the next week there followed the greatest tank battle in history, with 7,000 tanks thrown into the inferno. The Germans lost, partly because their attack was anticipated, partly because the new generation of Russian tanks was superior to their own. The margin of victory was small but it was enough. Thereafter, even Hitler seemed to have lost faith in his – and the German army's – ability to win on the Eastern Front, where the few scant reserves were soon to be bled to halt the new Allied front in Sicily. By the autumn, the Germans had been pushed back to the Dnieper. On 3 November the Red Army captured Kiev. Everywhere, the Red Army was unstoppable. For good reason. By autumn/winter 1943 the Russians outnumbered the Germans on the Eastern Front 2–1 (5,512,000 to 2,468,000), and possessed 8,400 tanks compared to the German's 2,300. No amount of Hitlerite rhetoric, fanatical fighting by elite SS units and clever military tactics by the supremely able Manstein and Heinrici could halt the Russians because they were too numerous and were producing much more military hardware (as well as enjoying substantial aid from their allies Britain and America). And thus it was that the Nazis' ultimate nightmare came to pass. Not only did they lose their

possessions in Russia and Poland, but by January 1945 the "unter-
mensch" hordes of Russia had broken into Germany itself. Five
months later they took Berlin itself. With the Red Army at the door,
Hitler committed suicide.

The Reich which was to last "A Thousand Years" lasted just twelve.

## "CONCENTRATED SLAUGHTER": A RUSSIAN CAVALRY AND TANK ATTACK, KORSUN, UKRAINE, 17 FEBRUARY 1943

### Major Kampov, Red Army Officer

All that evening the Germans had been in a kind of hysterical
condition. The few remaining cows in the village were slaughtered
and eaten with a sort of cannibal frenzy. When a barrel of pickled
cabbage was discovered in one hut, it led to wild scrambles. Altogether they had been very short of food ever since the encirclement;
with the German army in constant retreat, they didn't have large
stores anywhere near the front line. So these troops at Korsun had
been living mostly by looting the local population; they had done so
even before the encirclement.

They had also had a lot to drink that night, but the fires started by the
U-2s and then the bombing and the shelling sobered them up. Driven
out of their warm huts they had to abandon Shanderovka. They flocked
into the ravines near the village, and then took the desperate decision to
break through early in the morning. They had almost no tanks left –
they had all been lost and abandoned during the previous days' fighting, and what few tanks they still had now had no petrol. In the last few
days the area where they were concentrated was so small that transport
planes could no longer bring them anything. Even before, few of the
transport planes reached them, and sometimes the cargoes of food and
petrol and munitions were dropped on our lines.

So that morning they formed themselves into two marching columns of about 14,000 each, and they marched in this way to Lysianka
where the two ravines met. Lysianka was beyond our front line, inside
the "corridor". The German divisions on the other side were trying to
batter their way eastward, but now the "corridor" was so wide that
they hadn't much chance.

They were a strange sight, these two German columns that tried to
break out of the encirclement. Each of them was like an enormous
mob. The spearhead and the flanks were formed by the SS men of the
Wallonia Brigade and the Viking Division in their pearl-grey uniforms. They were in a relatively good state of physique. Then, inside

the triangle, marched the rabble of the ordinary German infantry, very much more down at heel. Right in the middle of this, a small select nucleus was formed by the officers. These also looked relatively well fed. So they moved westward along two parallel ravines. They had started out soon after 4 a.m., while it was still completely dark. We knew the direction from which they were coming. We had prepared five lines – two lines of infantry, then a line of artillery, and then two more lines where the tanks and cavalry lay in wait . . . We let them pass through the first three lines without firing a shot. The Germans, believing that they had dodged us and had now broken through all our defences, burst into frantic jubilant screaming, firing their pistols and tommy-guns into the air as they marched on. They had now emerged from the ravines and reached open country.

Then it happened. It was about six o'clock in the morning. Our tanks and our cavalry suddenly appeared and rushed straight into the thick of the two columns. What happened then is hard to describe. The Germans ran in all directions. And for the next four hours our tanks raced up and down the plain crushing them by the hundred. Our cavalry, competing with the tanks, chased them through the ravines where it was hard for tanks to pursue them. Most of the time the tanks were not using their guns lest they hit their own cavalry. Hundreds and hundreds of cavalry were hacking at them with their sabres, and massacred the Fritzes as no one had ever been massacred by cavalry before. There was no time to take prisoners. It was a kind of carnage that nothing could stop till it was all over. In a small area over 20,000 Germans were killed. I had been in Stalingrad; but never had I seen such concentrated slaughter as in the fields and ravines of that small bit of country. By 9 a.m. it was all over. Eight thousand prisoners surrendered that day. Nearly all of them had run a long distance away from the main scene of the slaughter; they had been hiding in woods and ravines.

# CITADEL: TANK BATTLE AT KURSK, 4 JULY 1943
## *General von Mellenthin*, Wehrmacht

*Even before the surrender of Stalingrad, the Red Army launched an offensive to seize back territories lost in 1942. One result of the offensive was the creation of a salient, centered on Kursk, a hundred miles deep into the German line. On 15 April, Hitler issued a secret directive ordering the elimination of the Kursk salient. "Victory," Hitler declared, would "shine like a beacon to the world".*

*Unfortunately for Hitler, the attack was anticipated. Moreover, the new Russian tanks, SU-122 and SU-152, outclassed the German Panthers and Ferdinands.*

The Battle of Kursk began at 15.00 hours on 4 July with an attack on the forward Russian lines, preceded by a short but sharp artillery preparation and air bombardment. On the front of XLVIII Panzer Corps, these lines ran some three miles south of the villages of Luchanino, Alexejewka and Sawidowka. Grenadiers and riflemen supported by assault guns and engineers penetrated the Russian forward line that evening. During the night the tanks were moved up and P.G.D. *"Gross Deutschland"* was ordered to advance next morning between Ssyrzew and Luchanino. 3 and 11 Panzer Divisions were to attack on the flanks of *"Gross Deutschland"*. But as bad luck would have it, a violent cloudburst that night transformed the ground along the banks of the stream between Ssyrzew and Sawidowka into a morass. This proved of the greatest advantage to the Russian second line to the north of the stream and immensely increased its already considerable defensive strength.

On the second day of the attack we met our first setback, and in spite of every effort the troops were unable to penetrate the Russian line. *"Gross Deutschland"*, assembling in dense formation and with the swamp on its immediate front, was heavily shelled by Russian artillery. The engineers were unable to make suitable crossings, and many tanks fell victims to the Red Air Force – during this battle Russian aircraft operated with remarkable dash in spite of German air superiority. Even in the area taken by the German troops on the first day Russians appeared from nowhere, and the reconnaissance units of *"Gross Deutschland"* had to deal with them. Nor was it possible to cross the stream and swamp on the night 5/6 July. On the left flank the attacks of 3 Panzer Division against Sawidowka were as unsuccessful as those of *"Gross Deutschland"* against Alexejewka and Luchanino. The entire area had been infested with mines; and the Russian defence along the whole line was supported by tanks operating with all the advantages of high ground. Our assault troops suffered considerable casualties, and 3 Panzer Division had to beat off counter-attacks. In spite of several massive bombing attacks by the Luftwaffe against battery positions, the Russian defensive fire did not decrease to any extent.

On 7 July, the fourth day of "Citadel", we at last achieved some success. *"Gross Deutschland"* was able to break through on both sides of Ssyrzew, and the Russians withdrew to Gremutshy and Ssyrzewo. The fleeing masses were caught by German artillery fire and suffered very heavy casualties; our tanks gained momentum and wheeled to the north-west. But at Ssyrzew that afternoon they were halted by strong defensive fire, and Russian armour counter-attacked. However, on the right wing we seemed within reach of a big victory; the grenadier regiment of *"Gross Deutschland"* was reported to have reached Werchopenje. On the right flank of "*Gross Deutschland*" a battle-group was formed to exploit this success; it consisted of the reconnaissance detachment and the assault-gun detachment and was told to advance as far as Height 260.8 to the south of Nowosselowka. When this battle-group reached Gremutshy they found elements of the grenadier regiment in the village. The grenadiers were under the illusion that they were in Nowosselowka and could not believe that they were only in Gremutshy. Thus the report of the so-called success of the grenadiers was proved wrong; things like that happen in every war and particularly in Russia.

On 8 July the battle-group, consisting of the reconnaissance detachment and assault-gun detachment of "*Gross Deutschland*", advanced up the main road, and reached Height 260.8; it then wheeled to the west to ease the advance of the divisional Panzer regiment and the Panzer Grenadiers who by-passed Werchopenje on the east. This village was still held by considerable enemy forces and the rifle regiment attacked it from the south. Height 243.0, immediately to the north of Werchopenje, was held by Russian tanks, which had a magnificent field of fire. The attack of the Panzers and grenadiers broke down in front of this hill; the Russian tanks seemed to be everywhere and singled out the spearhead of "*Gross Deutschland*", allowing it no rest.

That afternoon the battle-group on the right of "*Gross Deutschland*" repulsed seven attacks by Russian armour and knocked out twenty-one T.34s. XLVIII Panzer Corps ordered the *Schwerpunkt* of "*Gross Deutschland*" to wheel westward and bring some help to 3 Panzer Division where the threat to the left flank remained as grave as ever. Neither Height 243.0 nor the western outskirts of Werchopenje were taken on that day – it could no longer be doubted that the back of the German attack had been broken and its momentum had gone.

The slow progress of the southern pincer was disappointing, but we had in fact done much better than our comrades on the northern flank of the salient . . .

After a week of hard and almost uninterrupted fighting "*Gross Deutschland*" was showing signs of exhaustion and its ranks had been thinned out considerably. On 10 July this division was ordered to wheel to the south and south-west and clean up the enemy on the left flank. The Panzer regiment, the reconnaissance detachment and the grenadier regiment were to advance towards Height 243.0 and to the north thereof; they were then to seize 247.0 to the south of Kruglik and move southwards from there to the small forest north of Beresowka where the Russians were holding up 3 Panzer Division; strong formations of the Luftwaffe were to support this attack.

The air bombardment was extraordinarily effective and the War Diary of the reconnaissance detachment describes it as follows:

"With admiration we watch the Stukas attacking the Russian tanks uninterruptedly and with wonderful precision. Squadron after squadron of Stukas come over to drop their deadly eggs on the Russian armour. Dazzling white flames indicate that another enemy tank has "brewed up". This happens again and again."

Supported by the splendid efforts of the Luftwaffe, *"Gross Deutschland"* made a highly successful advance; heights 243.0 and 247.0 were taken, and Russian infantry and armour fled before the Panzers and sought refuge in the wood north of Beresowka. Trapped between *"Gross Deutschland"* and 3 Panzer, it seemed as if the enemy on the left flank had at last been liquidated, and the advance to the north could now be resumed. On 11 July XLVIII Panzer Corps issued orders for the units of *"Gross Deutschland"* to be relieved by 3 Panzer Division during the night; *"Gross Deutschland"* was to assemble astride the road south of Height 260.8, and to stand by for an advance to the north. In view of the breakdown of Model's attack, a successful advance in this quarter offered the only hope of victory.

On the night 11/12 July the units of *"Gross Deutschland"* were relieved by 3 Panzer Division according to plan, but the Panzer Grenadiers moved off with a sense of uneasiness. The last stages of the relief were carried out under heavy enemy shelling, and the men of *"Gross Deutschland"* left their trenches to the accompaniment of the battle noises of a Russian counter-attack. Their fears – alas – came true, for that very night 3 Panzer Division was thrown out of its forward positions.

On the morning of 12 July *"Gross Deutschland"* was assembled and concentrated astride the road south of Nowosselowka, waiting to launch the decisive advance to the north at first light on the 13th. 12 July was their first day without fighting; this breathing space was used to replenish ammunition and fuel and to carry out such repairs as could be effected in the forward area. Reconnaissance to the north reported that Nowosselowka only seemed to be occupied by insignificant forces. Heavy firing was heard to the west, and the news from 3 Panzer Division was not encouraging.

On 13 July patrolling to the north was intensified, but the expected order to advance did not come through – instead unpleasant reports were received from neighbouring formations. Strong Russian counter-attacks had been launched against the S.S. Panzer Corps and 11 Panzer Division; it was true that the number of Russian tanks knocked out on the whole front was enormous, but new tanks took the place of the casualties; faithful to their principle the Russians kept on throwing in fresh troops, and their reserves seemed inexhaustible. On the afternoon of 13 July, the Corps Commander, General von Knobelsdorff, appeared at the Battle Headquarters of "*Gross Deutschland*" and gave orders which left no hope for any advance to the north: in fact the division was again to attack westwards.

By the evening of 14 July it was obvious that the timetable of the German attack had been completely upset. At the very beginning of the offensive, the piercing of the forward Russian lines, deeply and heavily mined as they were, had proved much more difficult than we anticipated. The terrific Russian counter-attacks, with masses of men and material ruthlessly thrown in, were also an unpleasant surprise. German casualties had not been light, while our tank losses were staggering. The Panthers did not come up to expectations; they were easily set ablaze, the oil and petrol feeding systems were inadequately protected, and the crews were insufficiently trained. Of the eighty Panthers available when battle was joined only a few were left on 14 July. The S.S. Panzer Corps was no better off, while on the northern flank 9 Army had never penetrated more than seven miles into the Russian lines and was now at a complete standstill. 4 Panzer Army had indeed reached a depth of twelve miles, but there were another sixty miles to cover before we could join hands with Model.

On 13 July, Field-Marshals von Manstein and Kluge were summoned to East Prussia, and Hitler informed them that "Citadel" must be called off immediately as the Allies had landed in Sicily; troops must be transferred from the Eastern Front to deal with the invasion. Manstein had not committed all his forces and was in favour of continuing the offensive as a battle of attrition; by smashing up Russian armoured reserves in the Kursk salient we might forestall major offensives in other sectors. This situation should have been foreseen before "Citadel" was launched; we were now in the position of a man who has seized a wolf by the ears and dare not let him go. However, Hitler declared that the attack must stop forthwith.

The Russian High Command had conducted the Battle of Kursk with great skill, yielding ground adroitly and taking the sting out of our offensive with an intricate system of minefields and anti-tank defences. Not satisfied with counter-attacking in the salient, the Russians delivered heavy blows between Orel and Bryansk and made a serious penetration. With Hitler's decision to go on to the defensive, the situation on the Eastern Front became very critical. 4 Panzer Army was informed that the S.S. Panzer Corps would be withdrawn immediately for operations in Italy, while XLVIII Panzer Corps was told to release "*Gross Deutschland*" and send it to the assistance of Field-Marshal von Kluge's Army Group Centre. In the circumstances it was impossible to hold our gains in the Kursk salient, and by 23 July 4 Panzer Army had been pushed back to its start line.

"Citadel" had been a complete and most regrettable failure. It is true that Russian losses were much heavier than German; indeed, tactically the fighting had been indecisive. 4 Panzer Army took thirty-two thousand prisoners, and captured or destroyed more than two thousand tanks and nearly two thousand guns. But our Panzer divisions – in such splendid shape at the beginning of the battle – had been bled white, and with Anglo-American assistance the Russians could afford losses on this colossal scale.

*In the two months after Kursk, the German army in the East was pushed back 150 miles along a 650-mile front.*

# HOME FRONT: A RUSSIAN AVIATION FACTORY, MOSCOW, 1943

## *Wendell Wilkie*

*By 1943 the USSR was producing 34,900 aircraft a year for the war effort.*

I spent one entire day looking at a Soviet aviation plant. I saw other factories in Russia, candy factories, munition factories, foundries, canneries, and power plants. But this aviation plant, now located outside of Moscow, remains most vivid in my memory.

It was a big place. My guess would be that some 30,000 workers were running three shifts and that they were making a very presentable number of airplanes every day . . .

American aviation experts were with me on this inspection, and they confirmed my impression that the planes we saw wheeled from the end of the assembly line and tested on an airfield next to the factory were good planes. And, peculiarly enough, they pronounced the armored protection for the pilots the best of any they knew on any plane anywhere in the world. I am no aviation expert, but I have inspected a good many factories in my life. I kept my eyes open, and I think my report is fair.

Parts of the manufacturing process were crudely organized. The wings of the Stormovik are made of plywood, compressed under steam pressure, and then covered with canvas. The woodworking shops seemed to me to rely too much on hand labor, and their product showed it. Also, some of the electrical and plating shops were on the primitive side.

With these exceptions, the plant would compare favorably in output and efficiency with any I have ever seen. I walked through shop after shop of lathes and punching presses. I saw machine tools assembled from all over the world, their trade-names showing they came from Chemnitz, from Skoda, from Sheffield, from Cincinnati, from Sverdlovsk, from Antwerp. They were being efficiently used.

More than thirty-five per cent of the labor in the plant was done by women. Among the workers we saw boys not more than ten years old, all dressed in blue blouses and looking like apprentice students, even though the officials of the factory pulled no punches in admitting that the children work, in many of the shops, the full sixty-six-hour week worked by the adults. Many of the boys were doing skilled jobs on lathes, and seemed to be doing them extremely well.

On the whole, the plant seemed to us Americans to be overstaffed. There were more workers than would be found in a comparable American factory. But hanging over every third or fourth machine was a special sign, indicating that its worker was a "Stakhanovite," pledged to overfulfill his or her norm of production . . . The walls of the factory carried fresh and obviously honored lists of those workers and those shops which were leading in what was apparently a ceaseless competition for more and better output. A fair conclusion would be that this extra incentive, which was apparent in the conversation of any worker we stopped to talk to at random, made up for a large part, but not all, of the handicap of relative lack of skill.

The productivity of each individual worker was lower than in the United States. Russian officials admitted this to me freely. Until they can change this by education and training, they explained, they must offset it by putting great emphasis on patriotic drives for output and by recruiting all the labor power, even that of children and old women, that they can find. Meanwhile, and there was nothing done with mirrors here, we could see the planes leaving the cavernous doors of the final assembly unit, testing their machine guns and cannon on a target range, and then taking to the air over our heads.

## "STALIN'S ORGANS": THE SOUND OF DEATH, EASTERN FRONT, 1943

### *Gert Ledig*, **Wehrmacht**

*The Red Army's fearsome Katyusha rocket launchers were nicknamed "Stalin's Organs" by German troops on the Eastern Front.*

It started with a roar of an infuriated beast in the distance, a dull groaning noise unlike anything else in the world. It echoed over a few *versts* like a hunting cry. Twice or three times it roared. Then came the creaking of a badly tuned organ. Paralysis descended upon the front line. The rattle of machine-guns fell silent. The snipers drew their rifles back behind the parapet. The mortar crews huddled close together and the words of command froze on the lips of the gunner officers. The runner slowed down his pace. Then hell was let loose. Countless flashes of fire slashed the wood. Nearly a hundred shells burst in the trees or on the ground. A deafening thunder . . . Flames, gunpowder, pieces of copper as big as a fist, earth and mud . . . A battery with four guns, ammunition boxes, cartridges, tools and horses was hurled into the mud. An hour later it burst on a field kitchen. The driver and his mate, the cook, the provisions for sixty men and twenty-five gallons of watery soup were strewn to the four winds. A few minutes later it wailed down on a company marching up to the lines to relieve – eighty men carefully smartened up with polished boots and oiled rifles from the rear lines on their way to the front. The forty men who reached the trenches were filthy dirty, blood-stained and demoralized. Two hours, two days, two weeks . . . Somewhere a tank detachment was on the move preparatory to action. In the shelter of a hollow the commander assembled his troops to give them their final orders. A swish on the horizon. Five or six seconds of oppressive silence and then the shots burst out of the blue. Screams . . . Shrapnel rained down on the empty tanks. The junior officer had great difficulty in finding enough drivers to bring back the twelve tanks with their dead crews inside. And everyone who had felt the earth shudder and had seen the smoke of the explosions in the sky thanked – each in his own fashion – destiny or God that someone else had caught it and that he had been spared once more.

## WOUNDED SS TROOPS, CHERKASSY, FEBRUARY 1944

### Leon Degrelle, Legian Wallonie

*Degrelle was the commander of the Belgian Walloon volunteers fighting with the SS-Division Wiking. Hitler is reputed to have said that he wished that the diehard Degrelle was his son.*

From our makeshift position in Nowo-Buda we had been expecting the breakthrough to come on Monday. By Tuesday it had still not come. When would it happen? What were we to live on in the meantime – that is if we managed to escape the bullets?

Wherever we found ourselves, we soon came under enemy fire. Sanderowka was under fire day and night from "Stalin's organs". Wherever we went we came upon dead horses, smashed-up vehicles and corpses which we no longer had time to bury. We had turned the kolkhoz (Russian collective farm) into a field hospital, which was open on all sides, but at least provided a roof for our wounded soldiers. We had completely run out of medicaments, and there was no more material for bandages to be found in the whole of the pocket. To get hold of bandaging our medical orderlies had to wrestle the peasant girls to the floor and pull down their long military underpants – presents from German Don Juans. They screamed and ran off, holding on tight to their skirts. We just let them scream.

The Stalin's organs bombarded the *kolkhoz*. The roof caved in. Dozens of wounded men were killed in the bloody confusion. Others went crazy, letting out terrifying screams. The barracks had to be evacuated. Even our wounded men now had to stay out in the open. For several days and nights more than 1,200 wounded men from other units lay out in the open on hundreds of farm carts on a bed of straw. The rain had soaked them to the skin and now they were at the mercy of the biting frost.

Since Tuesday morning it had been 20 degrees below freezing, and lying outside in their hundreds were wounded men whose faces were nothing more than a hideous violet mass, men with amputated arms and legs, dying men, their eyes rolling convulsively.

Snow fell endlessly in the evening. It was soon a foot high. Twenty or thirty thousand people waited in our village for some kind of military end to the drama, with no sort of accommodation. Oblivious to the danger, the people stood out in the open in groups around fires they had lit in the snow. Sleep was impossible. Lying out in this biting cold would have meant certain death. The flames from burning the *isbas* could be seen from far away. In the valley hundreds of little fires burned, around which disconsolate shadows huddled, soldiers with reddened eyes and ten-day-old beards, warming their yellow fingers. They waited. Nothing happened.

They were still there in the morning – they didn't even bother trying to get some food. Their eyes looked to the south-west. Wild rumours were flying around. Hardly anyone listened to them any more. The silence was suddenly broken by the Stalin's organs. Everyone threw themselves down into the snow and then got to their feet again wearily. Wounded men screamed out. The doctors saw to them, to salve their consciences . . .

Twelve hundred wounded men still lay on the carts. Many of them had given up asking for help. They lay crushed together under a miserable cover, all their efforts geared to the task of staying alive. Hundreds of vehicles stood in a confused huddle. Horses reduced to skeletons chewed on the wooden slats of the carts in front of them. Here and there you could hear isolated groans and cries of wounded men. Crazed men raised themselves up, bleeding and with snow in their hair. What was the point of driving yourself crazy thinking of how you might feed these unfortunate men? They hid their heads under the covers. Every now and then the drivers would brush off the snow from these lifeless bodies with their hands. Many had been lying on these carts for ten days. They could feel themselves rotting alive. No injection could ease their most unbearable pains. There was nothing to be had. Nothing! Nothing! All they could do was wait – wait for death or a miracle. The number of yellowing bodies beside the carts kept increasing. Nothing could surprise us any more, nothing could stir our feelings. When you've witnessed such horrors, your senses are dumb.

## WARSAW UPRISING: A PARTISAN GROUP IS TRAPPED IN THE SEWERS, 26 SEPTEMBER 1944

### Anonymous fighter, "Polish Home Army"

*Twenty thousand resistance fighters of the Polish Home Army rose in revolt against the German garrison in Warsaw, capturing half the city before they were crushed. Although the advancing Russians were only thirty miles away they could not or would not (Stalin had no wish to see an independent Poland) help. Ten thousand Polish Home Army fighters were killed in the eight weeks of the uprising.*

It was 26 September. For the last fortnight I and my radio group had been in Mokotow, where the situation was critical, not to say hopeless, just as it had been in the Old Town a month earlier. We were on a narrow strip of territory like an island, with the Germans all round.

We carried her in turns, stumbling over corpses, knapsacks and arms. It was horrible. Ewa's demented howling mingled with other unearthly screams. She was not the only one.

I felt my strength ebbing away. At one point I lost my footing and fell heavily. My companions, Oko and Geniek, helped to put me on my feet again.

We set Ewa down and covered her with overcoats; we had to rest. She sat, propped against the side wall of the sewer, no longer screaming, and with glassy eyes. A procession of ghastly phantoms kept filing past us, some of them howling as Ewa did only a short time ago. Those screams, multiplied by echoes, were about as much as one could stand.

Then a new party approached. I wanted to warn them that we were resting, but before I could do so one of them had fallen, and the others, no longer aware of what they were doing, went over him, trampling him down into the bottom of the sewer – automatically, quite unconscious of the fact that he was still alive. In the same way they would have walked over us.

When they had passed we got up. Ewa no longer gave any sign of life, nor did the man who had been trampled on. We walked on.

We passed a barricade put across the sewer by the Germans. After some time we caught up with the group which had passed us. Then we came to another barricade. This one was well built and was a real obstacle. There was no way through here. I turned back with my group, and some of the others followed. When we came to the first barricade, the one we had just passed, we met a party of people who told us feverishly that the sewer beyond the barricade in the direction of Mokotow was flooded. So we should never get to the top!

A despairing argument took place between the two groups, the one that had brought the news of the flooding and the one that had come up against the impenetrable barricade. By then people had lost their senses; they were shouting in their fury and anguish.

Some remnant of judgment indicated a return to Mokotow. It was not very likely to succeed, but it was the only way of keeping alive – no matter for how long; the only thing that mattered was not to die in the sewer.

The gas was affecting our eyes more and more the whole time. I felt just as if I had sand under my eyelids; my head, too, was rolling to one side in a queer way. The mass of people all round were still arguing how to save themselves. From time to time a hideous bubbling was heard, as one more person whose strength had gone slipped into the foul liquid. But even more unbearable would be the voice of some woman pulling him out: "Look, he's alive, he's smiling! My darling, you'll soon be on top again!" Oh God, not to see it, not to hear it!

I realized during my increasingly rarer spells of clarity that I was beginning to lose consciousness. I held on to one thought: to get back to the surface. I did not want someone else to hear the splash and the bubbling which my ears would not hear.

I shouted then, at the top of my voice:

"Make way, I'll lead you out!"

But the angry yells which met me on all sides were the worst thing yet.

"Who said that? Fifth columnist! Shoot him!"

This shouting, like a sharp lash, spurred me to an extra effort. I escaped. I had enough sense left to realize that at such a moment what they threatened could well happen. Edging sideways close to the wall, my group and I crossed the barricade unnoticed by the rest.

We were over on the other side. We were going back, come what might.

At once we were deep in it. After a few steps we could no longer feel the bottom, but with the help of planks, knapsacks and abandoned bundles, we managed to keep our heads above the surface. After a short time we again felt the ground under our feet. The cold water and the absence of the blasted gas helped to clear our heads, and, holding each other's hands, we crawled slowly forward. Forward, that was what mattered. I knew that by following that sewer we were bound to come out in Dworkowa Street. We had to make it.

At 4 p.m., seventeen hours after we first went down into the sewers, we were pulled out of them by S.S. men in Dworkowa Street.

## GERMANS FLEE THE RUSSIAN ADVANCE, DANZIG, 9 MARCH 1945

### Hans Gliewe, schoolboy

*Danzig in the so-called "Polish Corridor" had been the pretext for the German invasion of Poland in 1939.*

I don't think I'll ever forget that 9 March in Danzig as long as I live. . . . We had found a place to stay with a woman whose name was Schranck. Then, at seven o'clock in the evening, the sirens started to howl. The crashing started right away, the floor shook and the windows rattled. We rushed down the stairs and ran for the nearest air-raid shelter.

The shelter was so crowded we barely squeezed inside. Several hundred refugees had been living in it for days. When we finally dared to come out the sky was red, and over the houses were piles of black smoke. Then we saw that our house was burning, too. We had lost even our baggage.

The fires hissed and crackled. Some horses had torn loose and were galloping down the pavement. Children got under their hooves. Rafters fell down from burning houses. We finally fled back into the air-raid shelter. Next morning we went out again into the ruined streets, and looked for another place to stay. We found someone we knew, and they took us in. We slept on the floor. Mother was out almost all day trying to find something for us to eat.

That night, more refugees came and wanted to crawl under. Very late in the night came still another woman with a little baby on her arm. The baby was white in the face, its skin looked transparent and all wrinkled. The baby's right thigh had been torn off, and the little stump was wrapped in bloody rags.

The woman must have been young, but she wore old, torn clothes and looked fifty. She was very shy. She made me think of a scared animal. She had nothing with her, only the child. For a long time she said nothing, only sat there on her chair.

Then she said, "God Almighty, I never thought I'd get as far as this. We were between the Russians all the time. We're from Marienburg. The first wave of Russians came. They shot Father. They took our watches, and with us they did, oh, what they do . . ."

She went on: "The first lot moved on. Many of them knew a little German, and they told us we should get out because those who came after were even worse. So I took my child and left. I went after them. I thought these are through now, and the next wave will take a little while. I just wanted to stay between the two waves. I walked and I walked. Tanks kept coming, and the Mongols on them, and then it started again. My Joachim lay beside me, crying all the time. When it was over we went on walking. In the evening a couple of trucks caught up with us. I wanted to hide in the snow in the ditch but then I saw they were Germans. I ran out on the road and begged them to take me along. I told them about the tanks, and they cursed and swore.

"On the truck there were other women with their children. We got near a clump of woods. Someone shot at us. The soldiers drove on into another wood, and got off. They did not want to go on, they said, they wanted to surrender to the Russians. We were terribly frightened and cried and wept and begged. But they just said, Do you think we want to get away from Ivan just to be strung up by the chain dogs*? Then a corporal pulled an automatic pistol on them and said, "You yellow bastards, if you don't get moving with those women right away I'll shoot you down." But they just grinned at him, and one of them said, "Go ahead and shoot, you couldn't get that truck moving, could you? You're stuck, too."

"But at last some of them drove on with us. All of a sudden there was a crash. The truck stopped and we were thrown all over each other. Some women were lying on the floor of the truck and bleeding. Then another crash. Joachim had disappeared. So I grabbed this child and ran away. Later I met a soldier and he bandaged it. I don't know its name. But I'm calling him Joachim. All night I walked, then a truck took me for a while, then I walked again.' She was silent. After a while she suddenly started to sob, and then she said, 'I'm so tired."

An S.S. patrol came next morning and confiscated the house. By noon we were out in the street. We were not allowed to go back into the air-raid shelter. The people who had come on their carts could at least crawl into the straw. We went from door to door looking for a place. Many people slammed the door in our faces when they heard

* Soldiers' slang for military police and S.S. commandos rounding up "shirkers". (*Translator's note.*)

we were from old German territory. They called us Nazis, and blamed us for everything that had happened to Danzig. One man shouted at us: "Why did you have to take us into your Germany! We were better off before! Without the likes of you we'd still be at peace! If only the Poles would come back quickly!"

So we were out on the street. There were Russian fighter planes. There were so many, the city had given up sounding the alarm. When it got dark we went into a hallway, put our blankets on the floor, and huddled together for the night. The cold from the stone floor got through the blanket and through our clothes. My teeth rattled and I had shivers. Later in the night a soldier came by and gave us his blanket. He said, "Don't stay here, by to-morrow their artillery will have got the range. I bet they'll be here in a week. Get out into a suburb, or to the coast. There are still some ships with East Prussians sailing from Pillau, and some of them stop in here . . ."

Next day we spent in the broken trolley cars that were lined up in one place. There were many refugees there. Most of us had not eaten properly for days. Some woman pulled out a cold boiled potato, and everybody envied her. The farmers on the wagons were better off. And the people of Danzig had food, too. But we came from a different section and the shops didn't want to sell to us on our ration tickets. Two little boys fought over a piece of bread.

In the evening we got into the railway station and somehow found a place on a train going north to Oliva. In Oliva we found a house that was deserted. But we were awakened before morning. Russian artillery was shooting away, and from the road we heard the tramping of soldiers and of the many people who were fleeing south into Danzig. When it got light and I saw such a lot of soldiers, I thought the Russians simply couldn't get through. But the soldiers with whom I spoke just sneered and asked me how I expected them to stop the Russian tanks – they had beautiful field guns, to be sure, but no ammunition, they couldn't shoot their buttons, and the tanks wouldn't stop out of respect for the orders of the stronghold commander. They said the Russians were only a mile and a half away. We were so frightened!

We stood in our cellar door, not knowing what to do. Other refugees came along, dragging their feet.

Then a soldier came by with a truck; he said he was driving to Neufahrwasser and would take us along. So we went. It was getting warmer and the streets were mud. Trucks blocked the road all the way. In one place, soldiers were digging trenches right next to the road. We saw many of the search commandos of the military police and the S.S. leading away soldiers they had arrested. And this constant flow of ragged people rushing past. I'll never forget it – sometimes one of those faces comes back to me in a dream.

We drove across the airport; there was nothing there but a few shot-up machines. Russian planes came over several times but they did not shoot. Then we got to the port. There were no ships. People said that all the Navy evacuation ships were now sailing from Gdynia. The sea looked grey. There was just a few small private cutters that had got out of the Navy confiscation order somehow or other. In front of the port commander's place people stood in long lines. He looked at us sadly and said, "I have no more ships for you. Over there, in the barracks, there are thousands already, waiting." Then he smiled grimly and said, "A few cutters are still sailing. But I'm afraid you can't afford them. They charge a thousand marks a head."

Mother still had eight hundred marks for the three of us.

"All I can tell you," said the port commander, "is to wait here in camp. Perhaps you'll be lucky . . . perhaps . . ."

So we went into the camp. We opened the door of one of the wooden barracks. A cloud of stench came to meet us. Hundreds of people sat in there, crowded together on filthy straw piles. The washing hung from strings across the room. Women were changing their children. Others were rubbing their bare legs with some smelly frost ointment. My brother pulled Mother's coat and said, "Please, Mummy, let's go away from here." But we were grateful to find room on a pile of straw next to an old, one-armed East Prussian who had come down along the Frische Nehrung.

Near me lay a very young woman whose head was shorn almost to the skin and whose face was all covered with ugly sores. She looked terrible. Once when she got up I saw that she walked with a cane. The East Prussian told us that she had been a woman auxiliary; the Russians had caught her in Roumania in the autumn of 1944 and had taken her to a labour camp. She had escaped somehow and trekked up here. He said she was only eighteen or nineteen. I tried not to, but I couldn't help looking at her.

A few hours later we couldn't stand the barracks any more and ran away. We preferred the cold. We went to the port. Mother tried to make a deal with one of the skippers. But he would not take anyone aboard for less than eight hundred marks a head. He'd rather go back empty. Mother was ready to kill him with her bare hands.

By the time it got dark we were so cold that we went back to the barracks in spite of everything. We found just enough room to sit back to back. Next to us sat a woman whose child had just gone down with dysentery. Next morning it lay there, so little and pale.

An Italian prisoner of war who worked on the piers told us that a small ship from Koenigsberg had arrived and was docking a little farther up the coast. The woman next to us went to take the ferry and go over there. She left the child behind with us and promised to come back and fetch us. She kept her word, too. When she came back she told us that she had met an acquaintance from Koenigsberg who for five hundred marks and her ring had promised to smuggle her and her child on the ship. He could do nothing for us, but she would not forget us. And she did not forget us. We ran away from the barracks for the second time and paid an Italian to row us over to the dock where the ship was. He looked at us sadly, and said in his poor German he would like to go home, too. On the dock we waited near the ship, and finally our "neighbour" from the barracks – she made out we were her real neighbours – persuaded her acquaintance to smuggle us aboard, too.

Most of those on the ship were from Koenigsberg. Some of them had gone ashore and were now coming back. We walked along with them as if we belonged. Then we hid in the cold, draughty hold of the ship. We huddled close together, but still we were terribly cold. But we did not dare to move, let alone go up, for fear they would recognize us as stowaways.

The night went by. The rumble of artillery over Danzig grew very loud. A man who had been up on deck said the sky was all red with the fires. We were so happy and grateful that we could lie in the draughty hold of the ship. But we were shaking with fear that we would be found out and put ashore.

Then the ship pulled out, and we breathed again.

## GOTTERDAMMERUNG: HITLER PLANS THE DESTRUCTION OF GERMANY, 18 MARCH 1945

### Colonel-General Heinz Guderian, Chief of the General Staff

At this time Speer, whose attitude towards the course of events was becoming one of increasing scepticism, came to see me. He brought me the information that Hitler intended to arrange for the destruction of all factories, water and electrical installations, railways and bridges before they should fall into enemy hands. Speer rightly pointed out that such a crazy deed must result in mass misery and death to the population of Germany on a scale never before seen in history. He asked for my help in ensuring that no such order be carried out. I readily agreed to give it him and I immediately set to work drafting an order in which I laid down the defensive lines that were to be held throughout Germany and specifically ordered that only immediately in front of these few lines might demolitions be carried out. Nothing else whatever in Germany was to be destroyed. All installations that served to feed the populace and to provide it with work were to remain untouched. On the next day I took my draft to Jodl, who had to be informed of its contents since it dealt with a matter which concerned all parts of the Armed Forces. Jodl submitted my draft to Hitler, but unfortunately not when I was present. When I saw him again on the following day, and asked him what Hitler's reaction had been, he gave me an order of Hitler's to read which was the exact contrary of Speer's and my intentions.

In order to give an example of Speer's forthright manner of speech, I should like to quote an extract from a memorandum which he submitted to Hitler on March 18th, 1945, when he and I were trying to prevent the destruction of bridges and factories:

It must be established that, in the event of the battles moving further into German territory, nobody is entitled to destroy industrial installations, mining installations, electrical and other utility works, communication facilities, or inland waterways. A destruction of bridges on the scale at present envisaged would do more damage to our communications network than all the air raids of the past years. Their destruction implies the elimination of all chance of survival for the German people. . . .

We have no right, at this stage of the war, to order demolitions which would affect the future existence of the German people. If the enemy has decided to destroy this nation, which has fought with unparalleled bravery, then the enemy must bear the guilt before history for such a deed. It is our duty to leave the German nation all possible facilities which will enable that nation to re-arise at some time in the distant future.

Hitler's reaction to this memorandum of Speer's, with the conclusions of which I too had identified myself, culminated in these words:

If the war should be lost, then the nation, too, will be lost. That would be the nation's unalterable fate. There is no need to consider the basic requirements that a people needs in order to continue to live a primitive life. On the contrary, it is better ourselves to destroy such things, for this nation will have proved itself the weaker and the future will belong exclusively to the stronger Eastern nation. Those who remain alive after the battles are over are in any case only inferior persons, since the best have fallen.

He frequently produced shocking remarks of this sort. I have myself heard him talk in this way, and I replied to him that the German nation would live on: that, according to the laws of nature, it would live on even if the contemplated destructions were carried out: and that such destruction would simply burden that nation with new and avoidable miseries if his intentions were carried out.

Despite all this the order for destruction was issued on March 19th and this was followed, on March 23rd, by instructions from Bormann for its implementation. The demolitions were to be the responsibility of the Gauleiters in their capacity as commissars for the defence of the Reich. The armed forces had refused to undertake this duty. Bormann had ordered that the populace of the threatened territories be transported to the interior of Germany or, if this proved impossible, be made to march there on foot. The carrying out of this order would have resulted in a catastrophe on a gigantic scale, since no measures to ensure a food supply were taken.

The military authorities therefore combined with Speer to frustrate the implementation of this insane order. Buhle prevented the issue of explosives so that the demolitions could not be carried out. Speer visited one command post after another explaining what the consequences must be if the order were obeyed. We could not prevent all destruction, but we succeeded in considerably reducing the amount that was carried out.

# A MEETING WITH HITLER, APRIL 1945

## *Gerhardt Boldt*, Wehrmacht

*Hitler descended to his purpose-built bunker under Berlin's Chancellery on 16 January and it was from there that he directed the last gasps of Nazi resistance to the flood of Anglo-American and Russian armies which now engulfed Germany itself. Boldt was a junior Wehrmacht officer seconded to the bunker HQ to prepare war maps.*

It was now four p.m. and most of those who are to take part in the conference have assembled in the ante-room. They stand or sit together in groups, talk and eat sandwiches while drinking real coffee or brandy. The Chief beckons me forward to introduce me. He is surrounded by Field-Marshal Keitel, General Jodl, Grand-Admiral Dönitz, and Bormann. Next to them are grouped their ADCs. In one corner, near a small table holding a telephone, Himmler is talking to the General of the SS Fegelein, the permanent representative of Himmler with Hitler. Fegelein is married to a sister of Eva Braun, the future wife of Hitler. His whole attitude now already displays the brazen assurance of a brother-in-law of the head of the German Reich.

Kaltenbrunner, the dreaded head of the Supreme Reich Security Office, stands apart, alone and reading a document. The permanent Deputy of the Reich Press Chief with Hitler, Lorenz, makes conversation with the Standard Leader Zander, Bormann's deputy. Reich Marshal Göring is sitting at a round table in the centre of the ante-room, together with the officers of his staff, the Generals Koller and Christians. Hitler's chief ADC, General Burgdorf, now crosses the ante-room and disappears into the studio. Shortly afterwards he reappears in the open doorway:

"The Führer requests your presence!" Göring leads and all the others follow behind him in their order of rank.

Hitler stands alone in the centre of the huge room, turned towards the ante-room. They approach in their order of entry, and he greets nearly everyone by a handshake, silently, without a word of welcome. Only once in a while he asks a question, which is answered by "Yes, Führer" or "No, Führer." I remain standing near the door and wait for the things that are bound to come. It is certainly one of the most remarkable moments of my life. General Guderian speaks with Hitler apparently concerning myself, for he looks in my direction. Guderian beckons, and I approach Hitler. Slowly, heavily stooping, he takes a few shuffling steps in my direction. He extends his right hand and looks at me with a queerly penetrating look. His handshake is weak and soft without any strength. His head is slightly wobbling. (This struck me later on even more, when I had the leisure to observe him.) His left arm hangs slackly and his hand trembles a good deal. There is an indescribable flickering glow in his eyes, creating a fearsome and totally unnatural effect. His face and the parts round his eyes give the impression of total exhaustion. All his movements are those of a senile man.

## THE BATTLE OF BERLIN: SOVIET GUNS OPEN FIRE, 20 APRIL 1945

### Colonel-General Chuikov, Eighth Guards Army

A battery of heavy howitzers was stationed on an open grassy space beside a wood. Dark, ragged clouds were sailing across the sky. The earth seemed to doze, shivering a little from time to time from shellfire in the distance. The gun crews had already run out the howitzers, and were awaiting the command to fire. The muzzles were trained on Berlin . . . on the fortifications of Fascist Berlin – "Fire!" The heavy shells flew up, cleaving the air with a whistling sound. The path had been opened. In the morning I went up to my observation post. It was in a large five-storeyed building near the Johannisthal aerodrome. From a corner room here, where there was a jagged hole in the wall, on got a view of the southern and south-eastern parts of Berlin. Roofs, roofs without end, with here and there a break in them – the work of landmines. In the distance factory chimneys and church spires stood out. The parks and squares, in which the young leaves were already out seemed like little outbreaks of green flame. Mist lay along the streets, mingled with dust raised by the previous night's artillery fire. In places the mist was overlaid by fat trails of black smoke, like mourning streamers. And somewhere in the center of the city ragged yellow plumes rose skywards as bombs exploded. The heavy bombers had already started their preliminary "working-over" of the targets for the forthcoming attack . . . Suddenly the earth shuddered and rocked under my feet. Thousands of guns announced the beginning of the storming operation.

## BERLIN: SS FANATICS HOLD OUT AT THE REICHSTAG, 28 APRIL–1 MAY 1945

### Anonymous German soldier

*Nearly half a million Russian troops encircled inner Berlin on 26 April. Resistance by rag-tag elements of the* Wehrmacht, *the SS and* Volksturm *(Home Guard) was fanatical, and it was with heavy cost that the Russians reached the centre of the city. Early on the 29th they closed to a quarter of a mile of Hitler's bunker. The next day the Führer of the "Thousand Year Reich" committed suicide.*

The close combat boys went into action. Their leader was SS-*Obersturmführer* [First Lieutenant] Babick, battle commandant of the *Reichstag*. Babick now waged the kind of war he had always dreamed of. Our two battery commanders, Radloff and Richter, were reduced to taking orders from him. Babick's command post was not in the *Reichstag* itself but in the cellar of the house on the corner of Dorotheenstrasse and the Hermann Goring Strasse, on the side nearer the Spree. There he ruled from an air-raid shelter measuring some 250 sq ft. Against the wall stood an old sofa and in front of it a dining table on which a map of the center of Berlin was spread out. Sitting on the sofa was an elderly marine commander and next to him two petty officers. There were also a few SS men and, of course, SS-*Obersturmführer* Babick bending over his map. He played the great general and treated everyone present in the dim candle-lit room to great pearls of military wisdom. He kept talking of final victory, cursed all cowards and traitors and left no one in any doubt that he would summarily shoot anyone who abandoned the Führer.

Babick was tremendously proud of his successes. He was hoping for reinforcements. From somewhere or another, marines had come to Berlin on the night of 28 April, led by the very Lieutenant-Commander who was now hanging about the cellar with nothing to say for himself. Babick never moved from his map, plotting the areas from which he expected reinforcements and even the arrival of "Royal Tigers" [heavy tanks]. Babick was still bubbling over with confidence. For one thing, he thought himself perfectly safe in his shelter. SS sentries were posted outside, others barred the corridor to the *Reichstag*, and Royal Tigers, our finest weapons, were apparently just around the corner. He had divided his men into groups of five to ten. One group was commanded by SS-*Untersturmführer* [Second Lieutenant] Undermann; he was posted south of the Moltke Bridge in the Ministry of the Interior (the building the Russians called "Himmler's House") and the bridge itself lay in his line of fire.

Then an SS ensign, aged about 19, came to Babick with the report that Undermann and his men had come across some alcohol and that they had got roaring drunk. As a precaution he had brought Undermann along; he was waiting outside. Babick roared out the order: "Have him shot on the spot!" The ensign clicked his heels and ran out. Seconds later we heard a burst of fire from a submachine-gun. The boy reappeared and reported: "Orders carried out." Babick put him in charge of Undermann's unit. Our ranks in the *Reichstag* got thinner and thinner. Part of our battery gradually dispersed, and by the night of 30 April, no more than 40 to 50 people, soldiers and civilians, were left in the cellar. This remnant was now busy looking for the safest possible hiding-places. There we intended to sit tight until the Russians came. But they kept us waiting for another 24 hours. At dawn on 1 May, we heard over our portable radio that the Führer had "fallen in the battle for the *Reich* Capital," his wife at his side. Goebbels and his family had gone the same way. We were our own masters, at long last.

## THE FALL OF BERLIN: A CITIZEN'S VIEW, 26 APRIL–1 MAY 1945

### *Claus Fuhrman, Berliner*

Panic had reached its peak in the city. Hordes of soldiers stationed in Berlin deserted and were shot on the spot or hanged on the nearest tree. A few clad only in underclothes were dangling on a tree quite near our house. On their chests they had placards reading: "We betrayed the Führer." The Werewolf pasted leaflets on the houses: "Dirty cowards and defeatists/We've got them all on our lists!"

The SS went into underground stations, picked out among the sheltering crowds a few men whose faces they did not like, and shot them then and there.

The scourge of our district was a small one-legged Hauptscharführer of the SS, who stumped through the street on crutches, a machine pistol at the ready, followed by his men. Anyone he didn't like the look of he instantly shot. The gang went down cellars at random and dragged all the men outside, giving them rifles and ordering them straight to the front. Anyone who hesitated was shot.

The front was a few streets away. At the street corner diagonally opposite our house Walloon Waffen SS had taken up position; wild, desperate men who had nothing to lose and who fought to their last round of ammunition. Armed Hitler Youth were lying next to men of the Vlassov White Russian Army.

The continual air attacks of the last months had worn down our morale; but now, as the first shells whistled over our heads, the terrible pressure began to give way. It could not take much longer now, whatever the Walloon and French Waffen SS or the fanatic Hitler Youth with their 2-cm. anti-aircraft guns could do. The end was coming and all we had to do was to try to survive this final stage.

But that was by no means simple. Everything had run out. The only water was in the cellar of a house several streets away. To get bread one had to join a queue of hundreds, grotesquely adorned with steel helmets, outside the baker's shop at 3 a.m. At 5 a.m. the Russians started and continued uninterruptedly until 9 or 10. The crowded mass outside the baker's shop pressed closely against the walls, but no one moved from his place. Often the hours of queuing had been spent in vain; bread was sold out before one reached the shop. Later one could buy bread only if one brought half a bucket of water.

Russian low-flying wooden biplanes machine-gunned people as they stood apathetically in their queues and took a terrible toll of the waiting crowds. In every street dead bodies were left lying where they had fallen.

At the last moment the shopkeepers, who had been jealously hoarding their stocks, not knowing how much longer they would be allowed to, now began to sell them. Too late! For a small packet of coffee, half a pound of sausages, thousands laid down their lives. A salvo of the heavy calibre shells tore to pieces hundreds of women who were waiting in the market hall. Dead and wounded alike were flung on wheelbarrows and carted away; the surviving women continued to wait, patient, resigned, sullen, until they had finished their miserable shopping.

The pincers began to narrow on the capital. Air raids ceased; the front lines were too loose now for aircraft to distinguish between friend and foe. Slowly but surely the T.52 tanks moved forward through Prenzlauer Allee, through Schonhauser Allee, through Kaiserstrasse. The artillery bombardment poured on the city from three sides in unbroken intensity. Above it, one could hear sharply close and distinct, the rattling of machine-guns and the whine of bullets.

Now it was impossible to leave the cellar. And now the bickering and quarrelling stopped and we were suddenly all of one accord. Almost all the men had revolvers; we squatted in the farthest corner of the cellar in order to avoid being seen by patrolling SS, and were firmly determined to make short shrift of any Volkssturm men who might try to defend our house.

Under the direction of a master mason who had been a soldier in Russia for two years we "organized" our supplies. We made a roster for parties of two or three to go out and get water and bread. We procured steel helmets; under artillery fire we heaped up mountains of rubble outside the cellar walls in order to safeguard against shells from tanks.

The Nazis became very quiet. No one took the Wehrmacht communiqué seriously now, although Radio Berlin went on broadcasting it until 24 April. A tiny sheet of paper, the last newspaper of the Goebbels press, *Der Panzerbär* [the tank bear] announced Goering's deposition and the removal of the "government" seat to Flensburg.

We left the cellar at longer and longer intervals and often we could not tell whether it was night or day. The Russians drew nearer; they advanced through the underground railway tunnels, armed with flame-throwers; their advance snipers had taken up positions quite near us; and their shots ricocheted off the houses opposite. Exhausted German soldiers would stumble in and beg for water – they were practically children; I remember one with a pale, quivering face who said, "We shall do it all right; we'll make our way to the north west yet." But his eyes belied his words and he looked at me despairingly. What he wanted to say was, "Hide me, give me shelter. I've had enough of it." I should have liked to help him; but neither of us dared to speak. Each might have shot the other as a "defeatist".

An old man who had lived in our house had been hit by a shell splinter a few days ago and had bled to death. His corpse lay near the entrance and had already began to smell. We threw him on a cart and took him to a burnt-out school building where there was a notice: "Collection point for Weinmeisterstrasse corpses." We left him there;

one of us took the opportunity of helping himself to a dead policeman's boots.

The first women were fleeing from the northern parts of the city and some of them sought shelter in our cellar, sobbing that the Russians were looting all the houses, abducting the men and raping all the women and girls. I got angry, shouted I had had enough of Goebbels' silly propaganda, the time for that was past. If that was all they had to do, let them go elsewhere.

Whilst the city lay under savage artillery and rifle fire the citizens now took to looting the shops. The last soldiers withdrew farther and farther away. Somewhere in the ruins of the burning city SS-men and Hitler Youth were holding out fanatically. The crowds burst into cellars and storehouses. While bullets were whistling through the air they scrambled for a tin of fish or a pouch of tobacco.

On the morning of 1 May our flat was hit by a 21-cm. shell and almost entirely destroyed. On the same day water carriers reported that they had seen Russian soldiers. They could not be located exactly; they were engaged in house-to-house fighting which was moving very slowly. The artillery had been silent for some time when at noon on 2 May rifle fire too ceased in our district. We climbed out of our cellar.

From the street corner Russian infantry were slowly coming forward, wearing steel helmets with hand grenades in their belts and boots. The SS had vanished. The Hitler Youth had surrendered.

Bunny rushed and threw her arms round a short slit-eyed Siberian soldier who seemed more than a little surprised. I at once went off with two buckets to fetch water, but I did not get beyond the first street corner. All men were stopped there, formed into a column and marched off towards the east.

A short distance behind Alexanderplatz everything was in a state of utter turmoil and confusion. Russian nurses armed with machine-pistols were handing out loaves of bread to the German population. I took advantage of this turmoil to disappear and got back home safely. God knows where the others went.

After the first wave of combatant troops there followed reserves and supply troops who "liberated" us in the true Russian manner. At our street corner I saw two Russian soldiers assaulting a crying elderly woman and then raping her in full view of the stunned crowd. I ran home as fast as I could. Bunny was all right so far. We had barricaded the one remaining room of our flat with rubble and charred beams in such a manner that no one outside could suspect that anyone lived there.

Every shop in the district was looted. As I hurried to the market I was met by groups of people who were laden with sacks and boxes.

Vast food reserves belonging to the armed forces had been stored there. The Russians had forced the doors open and let the Germans in.

The cellars, which were completely blacked out, now became the scene of an incredible spectacle. The starving people flung themselves like beasts over one another, shouting, pushing and struggling to lay their hands on whatever they could. I caught hold of two buckets of sugar, a few boxes of preserves, sixty packages of tobacco and a small sack of coffee which I quickly took back home before returning for more.

The second raid was also successful. I found noodles, tins of butter and a large tin of sardines. But now things were getting out of hand. In order not to be trampled down themselves the Russians fired at random into the crowds with machine-pistols, killing several.

I cannot remember how I extricated myself from this screaming, shouting chaos; all I remember is that even here in this utter confusion, Russian soldiers were raping women in one of the corners.

Bunny had meanwhile made me promise not to try to interfere if anything were to happen to her. There were stories in our district of men being shot trying to protect their wives. In the afternoon two Russians entered our flat, while Bunny was sitting on the bed with the child. They looked her over for some time; evidently they were not very impressed with her. We had not washed for a fortnight, and I had expressly warned Bunny not to make herself tidy, for I thought the dirtier and more neglected she looked the safer.

But the two gentlemen did not seem to have a very high standard as far as cleanliness was concerned. With the usual words, "Frau komm!" spoken in a menacing voice, one of them went towards her. I was about to interfere; but the other shouted "Stoi" and jammed his machine-pistol in my chest. In my despair I shouted "Run away, quick"; but that was, of course, impossible. I saw her quietly lay the baby aside, then she said, "Please don't look, darling." I turned to the wall.

When the first Russian had had enough they changed places. The second was chattering in Russian all the time. At last it was over. The man patted me on the shoulder: "Nix Angst! Russki Soldat gut!"

## ORDER OF THE DAY NO. 369, 9 MAY 1945

### *Stalin, Marshal of the Soviet Union*

ORDER OF THE DAY NO. 369

On May 8, 1945, in Berlin, representatives of the German High Command signed the Instrument of unconditional surrender of the German armed forces.

The Great Patriotic War which the Soviet people waged against the German-Fascist invaders is victoriously concluded. Germany is utterly routed.

Comrades Red Army men, Red Navy men, Sergeants, Petty Officers, Officers of the Army and Navy, Generals, Admirals and Marshals, I congratulate you upon the victorious termination of the Great Patriotic War.

To mark complete victory over Germany, to-day, May 9, the day of victory, at 22.00 hours (Moscow time), the capital of our Motherland, Moscow, on behalf of the Motherland, shall salute the gallant troops of the Red Army, the ships and units of the Navy, which have won this brilliant victory, by firing thirty artillery salvos from one thousand guns.

Eternal glory to the heroes who fell in the fighting for the freedom and independence of our Motherland!

Long live the victorious Red Army and Navy!

STALIN, Marshal of the Soviet Union,

Supreme Commander-in-Chief

# Part Eight

*Setting Sun*

*The War in the Pacific,
July 1942–September 1945*

# THE DEFENCE OF HENDERSON FIELD, GUADALCANAL, 24 OCTOBER 1942

## *Sergeant Mitchell Paige, USMC*

*On 7 August 1942 the Americans landed a division of Marines on Guadalcanal in the Eastern Solomons and seized the jungle-strip airfield the Japanese were building there. The Japanese counter-attacked vigorously, and both sides poured men and matériel into Guadalcanal. The island was ringed by a series of massive naval confrontations, while the battle on land centred on the struggle for the airbase, now renamed Henderson Field. The peak of the fighting came in October.*

Before we could get set up darkness came and it started raining like hell. It was too black to see anything, so I crawled along the ridge-front until it seemed I had come to the nose. To make sure I felt around with my hands and the ridge seemed to drop away on all sides. There we set up.

With the guns set up and the watches arranged, it was time for chow. I passed the word along for the one can of "Spam" and the one can of "borrowed peaches" that we had with us. Then we found out some jerk had dropped the can of peaches and it had rolled down the ridge into the jungle. He had been too scared to tell us what he had done. I shared out the "Spam" by feeling for a hand in the darkness and dropping into it. The next morning I sent out a couple of scouts to "look over the terrain". So we got our peaches back.

That night Smitty and I crawled out towards the edge of the nose and lay on our backs with the rain driving into our faces. Every so often I would lift up and call some of the boys by name to see if they were still awake and to reassure myself as well as them.

I must have been two o'clock in the morning when I heard a low mumbling. At once I got Smitty up. A few minutes later we heard the same noise again. I crawled over to the men and told them to stand by. I started figuring. The Japs might not know we were on the nose and might be preparing to charge us, or at any moment they might discover our positions. I decided to get it over with. As soon as the men heard the click of my pin coming out of the grenade, they let loose their grenades too.

Smitty was pulling out pins as I threw the grenades. The Japs screamed, so we knew we had hit them. We threw a few more grenades and then there was silence.

All that second day we dug in. We had no entrenching tools so we used bayonets. As night came I told the men we would have a hundred per cent watch and they were not to fire until they saw a Jap.

About the same time as the night before we heard the Japs talking again. They were about a hundred yards from the nose. It was so damned quiet, you could hear anything. I crawled around to the men and told them to keep quiet, look forward and glue their ears to the ground. As the Japs advanced we could hear the bushes rustle. Suddenly all hell broke loose.

All of us must have seen the Japs at the same time. Grenades exploded everywhere on the ridge-nose, followed by shrieks and yells. It would have been death to fire the guns because muzzle flashes would have given away our positions and we could have been smothered and blasted by a hail of grenades. Stansbury, who was lying in the foxhole next to mine, was pulling out grenade-pins with his teeth and rolling the grenades down the side of the nose. Leipart, the smallest guy in the platoon, and my particular boy, was in his foxhole delivering grenades like a star pitcher.

Then I gave the word to fire. Machine-guns and rifles let go and the whole line seemed to light up. Pettyjohn yelled to me that his gun was out of action. In the light from the firing I could see several Japs a few feet away from Leipart. Apparently he had been hit because he was down on one knee. I knocked off two Japs with a rifle but a third drove his bayonet into Leipart. Leipart was dead; seconds later, so was the Jap. After a few minutes, I wouldn't swear to how long it was, the blitz became a hand-to-hand battle. Gaston was having trouble with a Jap officer, I remember that much. Although his leg was nearly hacked off and his rifle all cut up, Gaston finally connected his boot with the Jap's chin. The result was one slopehead with one broken neck.

Firing died down a little, so evidently the first wave was a flop. I crawled over to Pettyjohn, and while he and Faust covered me I worked to remove a ruptured cartridge and change the belt-feed pawl. Just as I was getting ready to feed in a belt of ammo, I felt something hot on my hand and a sharp vibration. Some damned slopehead with a light machine-gun had fired a full burst into the feeding mechanism and wrecked the gun.

Things got pretty bad on the second wave. The Japs penetrated our left flank, carried away all opposition and were possibly in a position to attack our ridge-nose from the rear. On the left, however, Grant, Payne and Hinson stood by. In the centre, Lock, Swanek and McNabb got it and were carried away to the rear by corpsmen. The Navy boys did a wonderful job and patched up all the casualties, but they were still bleeding like hell and you couldn't tell what was wrong with them, so I sent them back. That meant that all my men were casualties and I was on my own. It was lonely up there with nothing but dead slopeheads for company, but I couldn't tell you what I was thinking about. I guess I was really worrying about the guns, shooting as fast as I could, and getting a bead on the next and nearest Jap.

One of the guns I couldn't find because it wasn't firing. I figured the guys had been hit and had put the gun out of action before leaving. I was always very insistent that it for any reason they had to leave a gun they would put it out of action so that the Japs wouldn't be able to use it. Being without a gun myself, I dodged over to the unit on my right to get another gun and give them the word on what was going on. Kelly and Totman helped me bring the gun back towards the nose of the ridge and we zig-zagged under an enemy fire that never seemed to stop. While I was on the right flank I borrowed some riflemen to form a skirmish line. I told them to fix bayonets and follow me. Kelly and Totman fed ammo as I sprayed every inch of terrain free of Japs. Dawn was beginning to break and in the half-light I saw my own machine-gun still near the centre of the nose. It was still in working order and some Japs were crawling towards it.

We got there just in time. I left Kelly and Totman and ran over to it.

For too many moments it seemed as though the whole Japanese Army was firing at me. Nevertheless three men on the right flank thought I might be low on ammunition and volunteered to run it up to me. Stat brought one belt and he went down with a bullet in the stomach. Reilly came up with another belt. Just as he reached the gun, he was hit in the groin. His feet flew out and nearly knocked me off the gun. Then Jonjeck arrived with a belt and stopped a bullet in the shoulder. As I turned I saw a piece of flesh disappear from his neck. I told him to go back for medical aid, but he refused. He wanted to stay up there with me. There was not time to argue; so I tapped him on the chin, hard enough so that he went down. That convinced him that I wanted my order obeyed.

My ears rang when a Jap sighted in on me with his light machine-gun but luckily he went away to my left. Anyway, I decided it was too unhealthy to stay in any one place for too long, so I would fire a burst and then move. Each time I shifted, grenades fell just where I had been. Over the nose of the ridge in the tall grass, which was later burned for security, I thought I saw some movement. Right off the nose, in the grass, thirty Japs stood up. One of them was looking at me through field-glasses. I let them have it with a full burst and they peeled off like grass under a mowing machine.

After that, I guess I was so wound up that I couldn't stop. I rounded up the skirmish line, told them I was going to charge off the nose and I wanted them to be right behind me. I picked up the machine-gun, and without noticing the burning hot water jacket, cradled it in my arms. Two belts of ammo I threw around my shoulders. The total weight was about 150 pounds, but the way I felt I could have carried three more without noticing it. I fed one of the belts off my shoulders into the gun, and then started forward. A colonel dropped about four feet in front of me with his yellow belly full of good American lead. In the meantime the skirmish line came over the nose, whooping like a bunch of wild Indians. We reached the edge of the clearing where the jungle began and there was nothing left either to holler at or shoot at. The battle was over with that strange sort of quietness that always follows.

The first thing I did was to sit down. I was soaked in perspiration and steam was rising in a cloud from my gun. My hand felt funny. I looked down and saw through my tattered shirt a blister which ran from my fingertips to my forearm. Captain Ditta came running up, slapped me on the back and gave me a drink, from his canteen.

For three days after the battle, we camped around the nose. They estimated that there were 110 Japs dead in front of my sector. I don't know about that, but they started to smell so horribly that we had to bury them by blasting part of the ridge over on top of them. On the third day we marched twelve miles back to the airport. I never knew what day it was, and what's more I didn't care.

## THE KOKODA TRAIL, NEW GUINEA, SEPTEMBER– NOVEMBER 1942

### George H. Johnston, war correspondent

*Despite the setback of Midway, the Japanese persisted in summer 1942 in advancing southwards across New Guinea towards Allied-held Port Moresby. The intervening Owen Stanley mountains made for the worst terrain of the war in the Pacific.*

I may be wrong, for I am no soothsayer, but I have an idea that the name of the "Kokoda Trail" is going to live in the minds of Australians for generations, just as another name, Gallipoli, lives on as freshly today, twenty-seven years after it first gained significance in Australian minds. For thousands of Australians who have walked the weary, sodden miles of this dreadful footpath – and these Australians are the fathers of the next generation – it will be the one memory more unforgettable than any other that life will give them.

Five days ago the Japanese began their resistance again – on the wide shallow plateau of the Gap, the pass through the forbidding spurs of the main range. The weather is bad, the terrain unbelievably terrible, and the enemy is resisting with a stubborn fury that is costing us many men and much time. Against the machine gun nests and mortar pits established on the ragged spurs and steep limestone ridges our advance each day now is measured in yards. Our troops are fighting in the cold mists of an altitude of 6700 feet, fighting viciously because they have only a mile or two to go before they reach the peak of the pass and will be able to attack downhill – down the *north* flank of the Owen Stanley's. That means a lot to troops who have climbed every inch of that agonizing track, who have buried so many of their cobbers and who have seen so many more going back, weak with sickness or mauled by the mortar bombs and bullets and grenades of the enemy, men gone from their ranks simply to win back a few more hundred yards of this wild, unfriendly, and utterly untamed mountain. Tiny villages which were under Japanese domination a few weeks ago are back in our hands – Ioribaiwa, Nauro Creek, Menari, Efogi, Kagi, Myola – and we are fighting now for Templeton's Crossing.

Fresh troops are going up the track, behind on the slimy trail from which the tide of war has ebbed and in ebbing has scattered the debris of death and destruction all the way along the green walls that flank the snaking ribbon of rotten mud. The men are bearded to the eyes. Their uniforms are hotch-potches of anything that fits or is warm or affords some protection from the insects. I remember years ago how we used to laugh at newsreels showing the motley troops of China when they were fighting the Japanese in the days when the men of Tokyo could do no wrong in the eyes of the western world. These men on the Kokoda track look more unkempt, more ragged, than any of the Chinese of those old film shots. . . .

There are many Japanese graves, some crude, some elaborate, all marked with the piece of sapling bearing Japanese ideographs. There are many crudely penciled signs stuck in the bushes or nailed to the trees: "Bodies two Australians – 'th Battalion, 25 yards into Bush." "Twelve Jap Bodies 50 yards northwest." "Unknown Australian Body, 150 yards down slope." In the green half-light, amid the stink of rotten mud and rotting corpses, with the long lines of green-clad Australians climbing wearily along the tunnel of the track, you have a noisome, unforgetable picture of the awful horror of this jungle war.

There are the bodies, too, of native carriers, tossed aside by the Japs to die, discarded callously and left unburied in the jungle. These natives were recruited in Rabaul, sent to Buna, roped together in the stinking holds of Japanese freighters, and then thrown into the enemy's carrier lines. They received little food, no medical attention and payment with worthless, newly printed Japanese one shilling notes of their invasion currency. They died in their hundreds of overwork, malnutrition and sickness.

Since then the Japs have made their stand in the toughest area of the pass through the Owen Stanley's – a terrible terrain of thick mountain timber, great rocks drenched in rain, terrifying precipices and chasms. Often the troops have to make painfully slow progress by clawing with hands and feet at slippery rock faces overlooking sheer drops into the jungle. The almost constant rain or mist adds to the perils of sharp limestone ridges, narrow ledges flanked by chasms, slimy rocks, and masses of slow moving mud.

In this territory the Japanese are fighting, with a stubborn tenacity that is almost unbelievable, from an elaborate system of prepared positions along every ridge and spur. Churned up by the troops of both armies, the track itself is now knee deep in thick, black mud. For the last ten days no man's clothing has been dry and they have slept – when sleep was possible – in pouring rain under sodden blankets. Each man carries all his personal equipment, firearms, ammunition supply and five days' rations. Every hour is a nightmare.

General Allen, who had fought in the last war and who has been leading these Australians in the attack on the Kokoda Trail, says without hesitation: "This is the toughest campaign of the A.I.F. in this or any other war." . . .

The Australians have re-conquered the Owen Stanley Range. Today, on November 2, they marched into Kokoda unopposed, through lines of excited natives who brought them great baskets of fruit and decked them with flowers. They marched back to the little plateau where Colonel Owen had died so many weary weeks before. They marched downhill through Isurava and Deniki, where many of them had fought the bloody rearguard action of August. The Japs had fled. Patrols cautiously went ahead to scout, squirmed their way through the rubber trees to test out Kokoda's defenses. But Kokoda was empty. There was no sound but the droning of insects and the noise of the rain pattering through the trees. Kokoda, "key to the Owen Stanley's," had been abandoned by the Japanese without a fight. Their defense of Kokoda had been the pass through the range, and they had failed to hold that defense line.

# BEHIND ENEMY LINES: CHINDITS ATTACK JAPANESE-HELD VILLAGE, BURMA, 28 MARCH 1943

## Bernard Fergusson, Commander no. 5 Column "Chindits"

*In February 1943, General Orde Wingate led a long-range patrol a thousand miles behind Japanese lines in Burma. The patrollers subsequently became dubbed "Chindits" after the Burmese mystical creature the "chinthe". Of the 318 men who set out with No. 5 column, only 95 returned.*

The moon was still low, and where the track was flanked with trees it had been very dark: but here, where it was open, one could get a good view of the sleeping houses, moonlit on the east but with deep shadows on the west side of each. It all seemed still and peaceful; no sentries were guarding the approach; and I began to think that we had been playing our bivouac drama to an empty house. I was worried at the column being jammed together on the track behind me, with no means of getting off it should the village prove to be held. The men were very silent, fully realising how much depended on the next few minutes; the only noise came from the mules, as they shifted their feet and creaked their saddlery. I told Duncan to organise a resumed search for a way into the jungle from the track, while I went forward with Philippe Stibbé's platoon to investigate; I passed the word also for a couple of Karens to act as interpreters.

Without waiting for Philippe to complete his orders, I moved cautiously forward with Po Po Tou and Jameson. As we went, we saw over the *bizat* the reflection of a fire against one of the houses on the left. Seventy yards or so from the fork in the track, we came to a T-junction, flanked by houses, and with a small track only, between two large houses, continuing the line of that on which we were: we had obviously come on to the main east and west track.

The fire was about forty yards along to the left, in the compound of the second house. With a grenade in my right hand I walked quietly towards it. Round it, symmetrically, one on each side, sat four men. They looked so peaceful and innocent that I immediately concluded that they were Burmese; and in that tongue (of which my knowledge was limited to a few sentences) I asked, "What is the name of this village?"

The men on the far side looked up, and those on this side looked round: I was only three yards from them. They were Japs. Resisting a curious instinct which was prompting me to apologise for interrupting them, I pulled the pin out of my grenade, which had suddenly become sticky with sweat, and lobbed it – oh, so neatly – into the fire. I just caught the expression of absolute terror on their faces; they were making no attempt to move; and ran. It was a four-second grenade, and went off almost at once. I looked round when I heard it go, and they were all sprawling on the ground.

Back at the T-junction, Philippe had just arrived and was looking eager. I told him to get in at once with the bayonet and capture that end of the village. As I spoke, a man ran past me from the direction of the fire: I shot him in the side with my pistol, and he sprawled on the ground for a moment, but was up and away again in a flash.

Philippe lost no time, but as he reached the point on the track opposite the fire, light machine-guns opened up; he and his men had to go to ground, though not before they had spitted several men running out of the house beyond the fire. I called to Philippe to ask if he could get on, but he shouted back in a singularly calm voice:

"I don't think we can – it's pretty hot. I'm afraid I've been hit myself."

I told him to hand over to his platoon serjeant and to try the right flank, and they nipped into some houses on that side of the track; but by now another light machine-gun had opened up, and there were a good many bullets flying about. Duncan had come up by now, and as he arrived we heard movement from the house immediately to our left, a matter of ten yards. This was followed by two or three shots by our ears; Duncan hove a couple of grenades into it, and there were loud groans, which went on, diminuendo, to the end of the action, but no more shooting.

I was worried about the man who had run past me early on; it was obvious that he had gone to rouse other Japs at that end of the village. So I sent Peter Dorans down there with some men of column head-quarters who suddenly appeared, to block that approach. Most of them came back almost immediately, and when I asked them what the hell they were playing at, they replied that Corporal Dorans had told them they were in the way; and, confiscating their grenades, had sent all of them back except two.

I went back down to the fork tracks, and got hold of Jim Harman. I told him that Philippe's platoon would keep the Japs in play from where they were, and that he was to take his platoon up the little track and catch the Japs in flank. There was still no news from the rear about any signs of a route into the jungle. I went back to Philippe and warned him what was going to happen, shouting across the same information to Serjeant Thornborrow over the way. Somewhere in the darkness we heard a motor-cyclist trying to start up his machine.

Philippe was hit in the shoulder; not badly, but he had lost a good deal of blood. I was talking to him and Corporal Litherland, who had also been hit: the two of them were at the foot of a tree on the right of the track up which we had come, just at the junction. Suddenly there was a rush of Japs up the track from the right, where Peter Dorans was and two or three grenades came flaming through the air: the Japs have a glowing fuse on their grenades, very useful in a night action to those at whom they are thrown. One rolled to within a few yards of me, and I flung myself down behind a dark shadow which I took to be a fold in the ground; I realised only too clearly as soon as I was down that it was nothing more substantial than the shadow of a tree in the moonlight. The thing went off, and I felt a hot, sharp pain in the bone of my hip. At that moment there was a series of loud explosions: Peter, from the ditch where he was lying, had rolled half a dozen grenades among the Japs. Where I had seen them dimly in the moonlight and shadows, there was now a heap of writhing bodies, into which Peter was emptying his rifle. There was no further attack from that side.

I hopped to my feet and was overjoyed to find I was all right and able to walk. But poor Philippe had been hit again, this time in the small of the back; so had Corporal Litherland, and a third man who had been groaning and was now dead.

Philippe could still walk, and I told him to go back out of the way down the column. He walked a couple of yards, said "Blast, I've forgotten my pack," picked it up and went off. This was the last time I saw him. Litherland also, with some help, was able to walk down the track.

There came a burst of shooting and some grenades from the little track where Jim and the commandos had gone. Thornborrow and his men were firing occasional rounds when they thought they saw a target, but another effort to get forward brought more casualties. I went back to the fork to see how Jim had got on, and I found him already back.

"There was an l.m.g. there," he said, "but we've knocked it out. I've been right up to the main track, and I believe we could get the animals through that way."

Alec Macdonald was beside me, and immediately said:

"I'll have a look. Come on," and disappeared up the track. I had a feeling that, having failed on Peter Dorans' flank, the Japs would try and come in on the right, somewhere down the column; so I passed the word back to try and work a small flank guard into the jungle on that side if possible. Then I went back to the T-junction, and made arrangements to attract all the attention we could, so as to give Alec a free run. (I seemed to spend the whole action trotting up and down that seventy yards of track.)

There came another burst of fire from the little track, a mixture of l.m.g., tommy-guns and grenades. The commando platoon alone in the column had tommy-guns, which was one of the reasons I had selected them for the role. Their cheerful rattle, however, meant that the little track was no longer clear. I hurried back to the fork, and there found Denny Sharp.

"This is going to be no good," I said. "Denny, take all the animals you can find, go back to the *chaung* and see if you can get down it. We'll go on playing about here to keep their attention fixed; I'll try and join you farther down the *chaung*, but if I don't then you know the rendezvous. Keep away from Chaungmido, as we don't want to get brigade muddled up in this."

Back to the T-junction I went, and found on the right of the track the Burrif platoon. They had two or three casualties from "overs"; Jameson had one in the shoulder, and so did another splendid N.C.O., Nay Dun, whose name always made me think of a trout fly. I told John to take them back, but he must have sent them under Pam Heald, because he himself still remained with me at the end of the action.

Another casualty was Abdul the Damned. Somehow he had wandered up into the battle leading Duncan's horse: armouring being at a discount, Duncan had made him into his syce, and jolly good he had become. Abdul had a nasty wound in the shoulder and was weeping bitterly, howling like a child: the horse had also been hit in the shoulder, and could barely walk: Duncan shot it there and then.

The sound of shooting opened up where I had expected it; away back down the column, the flank attack was coming in. It was audibly beaten off, and I sent another message down the column warning them to look out for a repeat performance still farther down the line. Then a messenger arrived, and said:

"Captain Macdonald's killed, sir."

"Nonsense," I said. "How do you know?"

"Mr. Harman's back, sir. And he's badly wounded."

I went back to the fork. Jim was there, with blood streaming from a wound in his head, and his left arm held in his right hand. Alec had led the way down the track, with Jim following; then Serjeant Pester and then Pte. Fuller. They had met two l.m.g.s, new ones, which had opened up. Alec had fallen instantly, calling out, "Go on in, Jim!" Jim had been hit in the head and shoulder, Pester was unhurt, Fuller killed. Jim and Pester between them had knocked out both guns, and the track was again clear. They had had a look at Alec on the way back, and he was dead.

I reckoned we had killed a good many Japs, one way and another, but it was nearly six o'clock and would soon be light; and what I dreaded more than anything else was the possibility of being caught in daylight on the track, with little, lithe Japs, unencumbered by packs or weariness, able to crawl under the bushes at ground level and snipe the guts out of us. There was no sign of any animals; Denny seemed to have got them back all right, but what, if any, luck he was having at the *chaung* I didn't know. At that moment somebody (I think John Fraser) came up with the news that a place had been found a couple of hundred yards back where you could squeeze through the bamboo into a stretch of disused paddy, beyond which there was open teak jungle. This decided me. At this moment came the noise of the "repeat performance" on the tail of the column which we had been expecting. There was a couple of minutes of shooting, then it too stopped.

"Well, what do we do now?" I said vaguely to John and Duncan.

"Well, you'd better make your mind up, and bloody quick too!" said Duncan affably.

# AN ALLIED INTELLIGENCE OFFICER IS EXECUTED BY THE JAPANESE, NEW GUINEA, 29 MARCH 1943

## *Anonymous Japanese soldier*

All four of us – Kurokawa, Nishiguchi, Yawate and myself – assembled in front of Headquarters at 1500 hrs . . . The "Tai" commander Komai, who came to the observation post today, told us personally that in accordance with the compassionate sentiments of Japanese *Bushido*, he was going to kill the prisoner himself, with his favourite sword. So we gathered to observe this. After we had waited a little more than ten minutes, the truck came along.

The prisoner who is at the side of the guard house is given his last drink of water. The surgeon, Major Komai, and Headquarters Platoon Commander come out of the Officers' Mess, wearing their military swords. The time has come. The prisoner with his arms bound and his long hair now cropped short totters forward. He probably suspects what is afoot but he is more composed than I thought he would be. Without more ado, he is put on the truck and we set out for our destination.

I have a seat next to the surgeon. About ten guards ride with us. To the pleasant rumble of the engine, we run swiftly along the road in the growing twilight. The glowing sun has set behind the western hills. Gigantic clouds rise before us and dusk is falling all around. It will not be long now. As I picture the scene we are about to witness, my heart beats faster.

I glance at the prisoner. He has probably resigned himself to his fate. As though saying farewell to the world, he looks about as he sits in the truck, at the hills, the sea, and seems in deep thought. I feel a surge of pity and turn my eyes away. The truck runs along the seashore now. We have left the Navy guard sector behind us and now come into the Army sector. Here and there we see sentries in the grassy fields and I thank them in my heart for their toil, as we drive on; they must have "got it" in the bombing the night before last; there were great gaping holes by the side of the road, full of water from the rain. In a little over twenty minutes, we arrive at our destination and all get off.

Major Komai stands up and says to the prisoner, "We are going to kill you." When he tells the prisoner that in accordance with Japanese *Bushido* he would be killed with a Japanese sword and that he would have two or three minutes' grace, he listens with bowed head. He says a few words in a low voice. He is an officer, probably a flight lieutenant. Apparently, he wants to be killed with one stroke of the sword. I hear him say the word "one"; the Major's face becomes tense as he replies, "Yes."

Now the time has come and the prisoner is made to kneel on the bank of a bomb crater, filled with water. He is apparently resigned. The precaution is taken of surrounding him with guards with fixed bayonets, but he remains calm. He even stretches his neck out. He is a very brave man indeed. When I put myself in the prisoner's place and think that in one minute it will be goodbye to this world, although the daily bombings have filled me with hate, ordinary human feelings make me pity him.

The Major has drawn his favourite sword. It is the famous *masamune* sword which he has shown us at the observation station. It glitters in the light and sends a cold shiver down my spine. He taps the prisoner's neck lightly with the back of the blade, then raises it above his head with both arms and brings it down with a powerful sweep. I had been standing with muscles tensed but in that moment I closed my eyes.

A hissing sound – it must be the sound of spurting blood, spurting from the arteries: the body falls forward. It is amazing – he has killed him with one stroke.

The onlookers crowd forward. The head, detached from the trunk, rolls forward in front of it. The dark blood gushes out. It is all over. The head is dead white, like a doll. The savageness which I felt only a little while ago is gone, and now I feel nothing but the true compassion of Japanese *Bushido*.

A corporal laughs: "Well – he will be entering Nirvana now." A seaman of the medical unit takes the surgeon's sword and, intent on paying off old scores, turns the headless body over on its back and cuts the abdomen open with one clean stroke. They are thick-skinned, these *keto* [hairy foreigner – term of opprobrium for a white man]; even the skin of their bellies is thick. Not a drop of blood comes out of the body. It is pushed into the crater at once and buried.

Now the wind blows mournfully and I see the scene again in my mind's eye. We get on the truck again and start back. It is dark now. We get off in front of Headquarters. I say goodbye to the Major and climb up the hill with Technician Kurokawa. This will be something to remember all my life. If I ever get back alive, it will make a good story to tell; so I have written it down.

# HOME FRONT: INTERNMENT OF JAPANESE AMERICANS, 1943

*Iwao Matsushita*

Fort Missoula, Montana
Jan. 2, 1943

The Honorable Francis Biddle,
Attorney General,
Washington, D.C.
Dear Mr Biddle,

I, Iwao Matsushita, an alien Japanese, have been detained in Fort Missoula, since Dec. 28, 1941, and I was recently notified about my internment order, despite the fact the Hearing Board made a recommendation for my release.

Since I read your article in a magazine last spring, regarding your policy of treating "alien enemies" – the words, you mentioned, you even didn't like to use – you have been occupying the innermost shrine of my heart as my only refuge and savior. So when I received your internment order, I was naturally greatly disappointed, because according to your interpretation in the magazine, you intern only those aliens whom you consider to be potentially dangerous to the public safety.

Now, my conscience urges me to make a personal heart-to-heart appeal to you. Kindly allow me to make a brief statement about myself.

I was born a Christian in a Methodist minister's family, educated in an American Mission School, came to this country in 1919 from sheer admiration of the American way of life. I have always been living, almost half and best part of my life, in Seattle, Wash . . . and never went to Japan for the last twenty-four years, despite the fact there were many such opportunities, simply because I liked this country, and the principles on which it stands.

I have never broken any Federal, State, Municipal, or even traffic laws, and paid taxes regularly. I believe myself one of the most upright persons. I have never been, am not, and will never be potentially dangerous to the safety of the United States. There isn't an iota of dangerous elements in me, nor should there be any such evidence against me.

On the contrary I have done much good to the American public. For instance, several years ago, I taught Japanese

Language in the University of Washington, Seattle, without any compensation to help out the institution, which couldn't get appropriation for that purpose from the State. I might prove to be of some service in this capacity.

I am quite sure that my life history and my statement regarding loyalty in the hearing record will certainly convince you that I am a bona fide loyal resident.

My wife, with whom I have never been separated even for a short time during the last twenty-five years, and who has the same loyalty and admiration for this country, is living helplessly and sorrowfully in Idaho Relocation Center. You are the only person who can make us join in happiness and let us continue to enjoy the American life.

Therefore, please give my case your special reconsideration and let me anticipate your favorable answer.

Yours respectfully,<br>Iwao Matsushita

## "ONE FOR EVERY SLEEPER": FORCED LABOUR ON THE BURMA–SIAM RAILWAY, MAY 1943

### *Jeffrey English, British POW*

*English was put to work by the Japanese on the Burma–Siam railway, where conditions caused the death of two out of three POWs.*

The work here was again on a rock cutting, about a mile from the camp and reached through the usual little track of churned-up mud. The shifts changed over down at the cutting, not back at camp, and so the men were paraded at 7 a.m. to be counted, and then had to march down to commence work at 8 a.m. The party coming off duty had to march back to the camp, and did not arrive until some time after 8.30 a.m. But that did not mean ten and a half hours for food and sleep. On five days a week rations had to be collected from the river, which involved going out at 1.30 p.m. and getting back between 5 p.m. and 6 p.m.

At our previous camp the ration parties had been drawn from the semi-sick, but here *all* men not bedded down had to go on the working parties to the cutting, and so the afternoon ration parties had to be found from the now off-duty night shift. A man would work or be going to and from work for the best part of fourteen hours, do a four-hour ration fatigue, and have only six hours out of twenty-four for feeding, cleaning himself up, and sleeping.

For the first week or so, when we still had over 300 "fit" in the combined Anglo-Australian camp, each individual only got two ration fatigues a week. It would have been even less, but of course one half of our 300 were on the day shift, and only the other half were on the unhappy night shift.

On three pints of rice a day, all this, of course, was impossible and flesh and blood could not stand the strain; and in addition to the overwork we had dysentery and other diseases spreading at a frightening pace. As the numbers of "fit" men dwindled, the burden carried by the remainder consequently grew, until after only a few weeks the fitter men were doing all five ration fatigues a week as well as working the night shift in the cutting, and only having two days a week of real rest. As they gradually cracked up, more unfortunates, just past the crisis of their exhaustion or illnesses but in no way fully recovered, would be forced out in their place, lasting in their turn perhaps three or four days before they themselves had to be replaced by yet others not quite so ill.

Just as this gruelling programme put that at our previous camp in the shade, so did the new Nip Engineers make the last lot look like gentlemen. There, they had generally beaten only those whom they caught flagging or had somehow provoked their precariously balanced ill-humour; but here they beat up indiscriminately, beating every man in a gang if they wanted it to go faster, and two of them in particular were simply blood-thirsty sadists.

They were known to us as "Musso" and "The Bull", and they seemed to compete amongst themselves as to who could cause the most hurt. They were both on the night shift, and both would come on duty with a rope's end strapped to the wrist. These they plied liberally, and they also carried a split-ended bamboo apiece, whilst Musso in particular would lash out with anything which came handy, such as a shovel. Every morning two or three men would come back to camp with blood clotted on their faces and shoulders or matted in their hair, whilst others would return with puffy scarlet faces but no eye lashes or eye brows, these having been burnt off where they'd had a naked acetylene flare waved slowly across the eyes – a favourite trick of another Nip known to us as "Snowdrop".

They drove the men on, not just to make them work, but as a cruel master drives a beast of burden to force it on to further efforts greater than it can manage; and one would see half a dozen men staggering along with an 18-foot tree trunk, or rolling an outsize boulder to the edge of the cutting, with the Nip running alongside lashing out at them or kicking their knees and shin and ankles to keep them going.

Frequently men fainted, and to make sure that they weren't

shamming, the Nip would kick them in the stomach, ribs or groin. If the man still didn't move, the favourite trick was to roll him over face downwards, and then jump up and down on the backs of his knees, so as to grind the kneecaps themselves into the loose gravel. If he fell on his side, a variation was to stand on the side of his face and then wriggle about, grinding and tearing his undercheek in the gravel: and as a way of telling a faked faint from a real one, both of these methods are, believe me, highly efficacious.

On one occasion a man was beaten up so badly by the Nips that they thought he wouldn't live, and so they got four prisoners and told them to bury him under a heap of rocks. The prisoners observed that he wasn't yet dead, but the Nips indicated that that didn't matter – they could bury him alive. It was only after a great deal of persuasion by a spunky Australian officer (who naturally took a personal bashing for his trouble, but didn't let that deter him) that the Nips eventually changed their minds and let the man be carried back to camp. He was carried on a stretcher, and came round later; but the beating had sent him almost off his head; he disappeared into the jungle and we couldn't find him for two days. On the third day he crept in for food; but he was now quite mental and became a gibbering idiot at the mere sight of a Nip. Had we bedded him down in a hospital tent, he could very well have simply popped off again; and so we found him a job in the cook-house where he would be working with others, and he worked there for a shaky fortnight before he packed it in and died.

At the next camp up the road, at Hintok, whence we sometimes drew our rations, they literally beat one man to death. He was discovered resting in the bushes down at their cutting when he ought to have been working, and the Nips took him down to the cutting in front of all the other prisoners and gave him a terrific beating up. He fainted once or twice, and was brought round by the usual Nip methods; and they continued in this way until they could bring him round no more. He wasn't quite dead yet, and was carried back to camp: but although he regained consciousness he avoided going out again on the next shift by the simple device of dying.

The Hintok Nips were on much of a par with our own Musso and The Bull: and another pretty case arose from the familiar story of the Nips demanding a working party of 120 men when the most that Hintok could muster was 105. The Nips went into the hospital tent and brought out the first fifteen of those bedded down, all of whom were dysentery cases, some of them in a very bad way indeed. They were forced to join the parade, and they set off for the cutting. One man in particular was very, very bad, but no one was allowed to lag behind and help him get along, and after several collapses he at last could go no further.

He arrived back at the camp dragging himself through the mud on his hands and knees, and was put back into the hospital: but when the Nips returned that night they knew that they'd been one short all day. They dug him out from the hospital, supported by a man on either side as he could no longer stand by himself, and then with all the typical gallantry of the Japanese, they started in and beat him up. He lay writhing on the ground whilst they beat and kicked him senseless, and although they left him breathing he was dead within two hours.

In a similar case at our own camp, three men, all very sick, passed out on the way to work, and Musso sent the squad officer back to bring them down. They were rounded up and shepherded in, and Musso, as they approached, rushed forward and started beating them with a stout bamboo. He broke the first bamboo on one of them, seized another one and broke that one too, and then got a pick handle and used it as a two-handed club. He bashed them unmercifully, and then ordered them to pick up a length of rail from the light railway, and carry it over to the rock face. It being the night shift, there was no overhead scorching sun to add to their woes; but he ordered them to hold the length of rail above their heads.

No matter how he beat them, they couldn't get it above their heads, but at last they got it to chest level, and there he kept them holding it for the best part of twenty minutes. Every time they sagged he laid in with the pick-handle, and as they couldn't even ward off the blows with their hands they were in a horrible state by the time he let them go.

That same night Musso further distinguished himself. A fellow called "B———" (I'll just call him that lest his widow might read this) had been holding a chisel and his mate missed with his sledge-hammer and crushed B———'s hand. Musso blamed B——— for not holding the chisel upright, and instead of knocking him off work and letting him have his broken fingers set, he put him onto the job of turning the big crank which worked one of the generators floodlighting the cutting. The handle was far too heavy for him to turn with his one good hand, so that he had to use the bleeding pulp of his crushed hand as well. Musso stood over him, and every time he flagged and the lights dimmed, he was beaten with a bamboo. He was kept at it for nearly an hour, during which time he twice fainted; but when he fainted for the third time he didn't come round. He was helped back to camp at the end of the shift, and he died a week later from cholera, from which he had probably already been sickening when Musso did his stuff on him.

Musso, mark you, was merely a private soldier – a private soldier under no restraint or the exercise of any control by his superiors. His

was one of the few names which we managed to find out and retain –
he was Superior Private Kanaga – and I must confess to having shed
not a single tear when I learnt, after the war, that both he and The
Bull were hanged after trial by the War Crimes Commission. What
happened to Snowdrop I never learnt.

By the end of only three weeks at this new camp we were at the end
of our tether. In our part of the camp alone we had fifty dead, 150
bedded down in hospital, and only fifty working; and the Australians
had comparable figures but over double the size of ours.

Even the Nips realized that something had got to be done, for the
men they still had were dropping of exhaustion: although they had
tried to keep them going by sheer brutality alone, there comes a time
when any amount of flogging seems preferable to more work.

The Nips had a bright idea. They explained that the fit working
men needed more food than did those bedded down in hospital, which
seemed eminently logical. The shine went off the ball, however, when
they further explained that the way in which they would introduce the
differential would be to keep the rations for the fit men exactly as they
were – but would reduce the hospital to two meals a day.

# A POSTCARD FROM A POW, 1943

## Thomas Smithson, British Army

*The sender was imprisoned by the Japanese in Taiwan. He writes to his wife on a
postcard issued by the Imperial Japanese Army.*

MY DEAREST EILEEN

RECEIVED CARDS AND LETTER'S. HAPPY TO KNOW YOU WELL AND
EVERYONE AT HOME. DEAREST I MISS YOU MORE EACH DAY. NEVER
AGAIN SHALL WE SEPARATE. ALL I ASK OF THIS WORLD IS MY OWN
LITTLE COTTAGE AND REMAINDER OF MY LIFE IN YOUR SWEET COM-
PANIONSHIP. GOD BLESS YOU, DEAR.

LOVE, EVER, YOURS TOM

# A MARINE CORPS PILOT IS SHOT DOWN, BOUGAINVILLE, 3 JANUARY 1944

## Gregory Boyington, VMF-214 Squadron, USMC

*"Pappy" Boyington was the leader of the "Black Sheep" squadron.*

It was before dawn on January 3, 1944, on Bougainville. I was
having baked beans for breakfast at the edge of the airstrip the
Seabees had built, after the Marines had taken a small chunk of land

on the beach. As I ate the beans, I glanced over at row after row of white crosses, too far away and too dark to read the names. But I didn't have to. I knew that each cross marked the final resting place of some Marine who had gone as far as he was able in this mortal world of ours.

Before taking off everything seemed to be wrong that morning. My plane wasn't ready and I had to switch to another. At the last minute the ground crew got my original plane in order and I scampered back into that. I was to lead a fighter sweep over Rabaul, meaning two hundred miles over enemy waters and territory again.

We coasted over at about twenty thousand feet to Rabaul. A few hazy clouds and cloud banks were hanging around – not much different from a lot of other days.

The fellow flying my wing was Captain George Ashmun, New York City. He had told me before the mission: "You go ahead and shoot all you want, Gramps. All I'll do is keep them off your tail."

This boy was another who wanted me to beat that record, and was offering to stick his neck way out in the bargain.

I spotted a few planes coming up through the loosely scattered clouds and signaled to the pilots in back of me: "Go down and get to work."

George and I dove first. I poured a long burst into the first enemy plane that approached, and a fraction of a second later saw the Nip pilot catapult out and the plane itself break out into fire.

George screamed over the radio: "Gramps, you got a flamer!"

Then he and I went down lower into the fight after the rest of the enemy planes. We figured that the whole pack of our planes was going to follow us down, but the clouds must have obscured us from their view. Anyway, George and I were not paying too much attention, just figuring that the rest of the boys would be with us in a few seconds, as usually was the case.

Finding approximately ten enemy planes, George and I commenced firing. What we saw coming from above we thought were our own planes – but they were not. We were being jumped by about twenty planes.

George and I scissored in the conventional Thatch-weave way, protecting each other's blank spots, the rear ends of our fighters. In doing this I saw George shoot a burst into a plane and it turned away from us, plunging downward, all on fire. A second later I did the same to another plane. But it was then that I saw George's plane start to throw smoke, and down he went in a half glide. I sensed something was horribly wrong with him. I screamed at him: "For God's sake, George, dive!"

Our planes could dive away from practically anything the Nips had out there at the time, except perhaps a Tony. But apparently George never heard me or could do nothing about it if he had. He just kept going down in a half glide.

Time and time again I screamed at him: "For God's sake, George, dive straight down!" But he didn't even flutter an aileron in answer to me.

I climbed in behind the Nip planes that were plugging at him on the way down to the water. There were so many of them I wasn't even bothering to use my electric gun sight consciously, but continued to seesaw back and forth on my rudder pedals, trying to spray them all in general, trying to get them off George to give him a chance to bail out or dive – or do something at least.

But the same thing that was happening to him was now happening to me. I could feel the impact of the enemy fire against my armor plate, behind my back, like hail on a tin roof. I could see enemy shots progressing along my wing tips, making patterns.

George's plane burst into flames and a moment later crashed into the water. At that point there was nothing left for me to do. I had done everything I could. I decided to get the hell away from the Nips. I threw everything in the cockpit all the way forward – this means full speed ahead – and nosed my plane over to pick up extra speed until I was forced by the water to level off. I had gone practically a half mile at a speed of about four hundred knots, when all of a sudden my main gas tank went up in flames in front of my very eyes. The sensation was much the same as opening the door of a furnace and sticking one's head into the thing.

Though I was about a hundred feet off the water, I didn't have a chance of trying to gain altitude. I was fully aware that if I tried to gain altitude for a bail-out I would be fried in a few more seconds.

At first, being kind of stunned, I thought: "Well, you finally got it, didn't you, wise guy?" and then I thought: "Oh, no you didn't!" There was only one thing left to do. I reached for the rip cord with my right hand and released the safety belt with my left, putting both feet on the stick and kicking it all the way forward with all my strength. My body was given centrifugal force when I kicked the stick in this manner. My body for an instant weighed well over a ton, I imagine. If I had had a third hand I could have opened the canopy. But all I could do was to give myself this propulsion. It either jettisoned me right up through the canopy or tore the canopy off. I don't know which.

There was a jerk that snapped my head and I knew my chute had caught – what a relief. Then I felt an awful slam on my side – no time to pendulum – just boom-boom and I was in the water.

# ONE MAN'S WAR: THE ARAKAN FRONT, BURMA, JANUARY–FEBRUARY 1944

## Troop-Sergeant Clive Branson, Royal Armoured Corps

*Branson writes to his wife. He had seen action before the Burma campaign; a Communist, he'd fought for the International Brigade in the Spanish Civil War. Branson was killed during fighting for the Ngankedank Pass at the end of February, 1944.*

16 January 1944

From now on my letters will consist of scraps of paper written at odd moments during the coming campaign. We are only a few miles from the front line, and yet see very little sign of war – an occasional distant barrage, a few aeroplanes and, yesterday, AA puffs chasing a Jap machine. As to my own feelings, very rarely I feel a tinge of fear, plus regret. In the main I worry whether I shall command my tank as a Communist ought. I only hope I shall do the job efficiently. I am keeping very fit; in spite of being many years older than most of the fellows, I can still do everything they do, except run – there I am beat.

My gunner, Monte, has just got back from a trip to the forward area. What most impressed him is that while the British and Japs shell, mortar and bomb each other, cattle continue to graze on the battlefield, and peasants with children work on the road and farmsteads. He came across five graves of British soldiers, with the only mark a beer bottle – no cross, etc. The fellows, on hearing this, said it was a fine sign of good spirits, and just as good as any other tombstone.

26 January 1944

We are now only a few hundred yards away from glory. "There are those who would like to philosophize on the question of sacrificing space to gain time." You will remember the reference. But even so, it is still like a mad hatter's picnic. We make our beds down, we sit around and chat, we sunbathe (not so openly as before) and we sleep. While overhead scream mortars, etc. To this, and all other incidents of war, such as AA, Jap planes, or our own barrage, the lads react with "Ignore it" or "Quiet!", and just carry on sleeping or reading. But I must say one thought runs through my head continually – Spain. This morning a party is going to watch some strategic bombing. I am sending two others of my crew on the principle that the more each man knows of the landscape, the better in every way. The bombers are just coming over. We climbed up on our tanks to have a grandstand view of twelve Liberators and dozens of Vengeance dive-bombers exterminating the Jap positions at Razabil cross-roads. Now that the bombers have gone there is a real barrage of small stuff. This may be the solution of the Burma problem. Now I am ever so excited to hear the reports of what was the effect. It may seem strange to you that in a sort of way I cannot help gloating over the affair. It is the reverse of Spain a hundredfold.

4 February 1944

This morning we cleaned up the tank, made ourselves more comfortable and prepared for rain, and did some washing. One fellow caught a snake about eighteen inches long, green on top and, just behind the head, a salmon pink. I have just seen what may be the smallest moth I have ever seen, white, with blue-black markings on wings, and light brown head. I must get ready for a tank commander's lecture.

Today a VIP is turning up, so we have to be in overalls, boots and berets, instead of our usual shorts and stripped to the waist. "How long have you been in the army? Always in this regiment? How long troop sergeant? Find things all right in this country?" And in everyone's mind is one thought, how to get on with the war, instead of being asked useless questions.

## THE SKIRMISH AT ADMIN BOX, BURMA, 8 FEBRUARY 1944

### Brigadier Geoffrey C. Evans, 9th Brigade, 5th Division

*Britain's steady advance into the Arakan was met on 4 February by a counter-attack by the Japanese 55th Division, which enveloped the British administrative centre at Sinzweye, a flat clearing surrounded by jungle. All the advantages lay with the attacking Japanese. Brigadier Evans was ordered to "Stay put and keep the Japanese out".*

Bursts of rifle and automatic fire broke out about three hundred yards from Box Headquarters. These were accompanied by more shouting and then screams and cries for help. I heard a voice say in the darkness: "Good God, they've got into the hospital."

This was a dreadful thought, as there was very little that could be done until daylight. The defenders were a section of West Yorkshires and twenty walking wounded armed with rifles. It would be sheer folly to send in an infantry attack to drive out the enemy. Only the West Yorkshires were available and they did not know the geography of the hospital, nor would they be able to distinguish between friend and foe in the dark. To call on artillery and mortars was out of the question as our own men would be killed.

I got on the telephone to Munshi to send in a patrol to try and find out what was happening, but the carrier that was sent was driven off by grenades. Clearly the enemy were in greater strength than I had expected. We could only wait for the day to come and take what comfort we might from the fact that the wards, theatres and resuscitation installations were dug down. In the darkness the Japanese might miss them; otherwise, when they discovered that they had entered a hospital, they might take what prisoners they could and leave the remainder. . . .

The full details of what had happened we learned later from the pitifully small number of survivors of the thirty-six-hour ordeal, which was only ended when A Company of the West Yorkshires drove the enemy out. The Orderly Medical Officer, Lieutenant Basu of the Indian Army Medical Corps, was lying on a stretcher in the medical inspection room resting, when a group of men rushed in from the dispensary at about 9 pm. One man seized his arm, while another threatened him with a bayonet. "*Aiyo*", they ordered, "Come on."

Basu was taken to the Japanese commander, who was in the darkened officers' ward busily scribbling notes. Through an interpreter, the questioning began. "What is your name? What is the name of this place?"

The next question made it clear that the Japanese knew they were in a hospital, and therefore what followed was done quite deliberately and in cold blood. "How many patients are in this hospital?" they asked. "How many of them are British officers? What other personnel are there?"

Basu stalled as best he could. "I am here for three days only," he said. "I don't know much about the organisation here."

"What army units are posted here? How many of them are British and how many Indian?"

"I am a doctor," said Basu. "I am interested in medicine, not military tactics."

At this, one angry Japanese soldier brought the point of his bayonet against the doctor's head as though to finish him off unless he answered the questions more satisfactorily. But the Japanese commander cut in brusquely: "Show us to the telephone."

Basu thought quickly. "It would be dangerous to go near it," he said. "There is a machine-gun post just beside it."

"Then show my men to the operating theatre and the laboratory," ordered the Japanese officer.

Basu could not get out of this. But he took them to the small theatre which was used only for minor operations. As bad luck would have it, while the Japanese hunted round the theatre for anything they could lay their hands on in the way of bandages and cotton wool, they came on three of the hospital officers asleep. They were awakened and made prisoners. With Basu, they were taken back to the commander for further questioning. It was quite clear that the one piece of information the enemy were particularly anxious to discover was where the supply depot was situated. Basu kept up his presence at ignorance: "I don't know; I tell you I'm only here for a few days. I've been too busy looking after patients to find time to visit the supply depot."

All the officers had their hands tied tightly behind their backs and they were taken to join the British and Indian other ranks, who had been trussed in a similar painful fashion.

The Japanese officer pulled out his sword, waved it over their heads threateningly, sheathed it and withdrew.

The purpose of this melodramatic gesture became clear almost at once. It was intended to cause the maximum alarm to the Indians as an inducement to make them desert to the Japanese to save their lives. The offer came almost immediately.

A man whose appearance suggested he was Indian was brought in.

"There is no need to worry," he assured the Indians. "No need at all to worry. You will be taken to Rangoon to join the Indian Independence League."

"What is your native country?" Basu asked him.

"I come from Maungdaw, in Burma," he answered.

Later that night, the five Indian medical officers were taken to the dispensary and ordered to pack up drugs for the Japanese. They were particularly interested in quinine, morphine, anti-tetanus and anti-gas-gangrene serum. They wanted to know what was in every phial. Those they did not want they threw to one side. Sally, in 9 Brigade Headquarters, could hear the bottles breaking.

When the Japanese had taken all they wanted, they drove the medical officers back to the watercourse where the rest of the captives were seated in acute discomfort because the bindings on their wrists were cutting into the flesh. Those who asked for water were jabbed with a heavy stick by a Japanese sentry.

The following morning a carrier pushed through the bushes towards the medical inspection room and one Japanese soldier dragged the trussed British other ranks out in front so that they should receive the first burst of fire. When the automatic gun of the carrier opened up, the prisoners desperately tried to find shelter, but they were handicapped because their hands were lashed behind their backs. Some of them were killed and others were wounded. The Japanese looked on grinning. They, too, had suffered casualties. They selected six of the Indian soldiers and ordered them to help to carry seven wounded Japanese.

The stretcher-bearers struggled southwards through the jungle the whole of that day. When night came, the Japanese cooked food for themselves but gave none to the Indians. Next morning, still having had nothing to eat, the Indians were given packs to carry and it was not until the early hours of the following morning that they reached their destination. This was the Buthidaung Tunnel, where there were about a thousand Japanese living. The tunnel was used as a store for arms, ammunition, guns and transport. During the day, six Indians came to see them. "You need not worry," they told them. "You will have trouble for a few days, but then you will be sent to Rangoon to work. Our major will fix things and you will not be tortured by the Japanese." One of their visitors, a Madrassi, said: "There are now 400,000 followers of Subhas Bhose. In two months we shall reach Chittagong."

Seven days later, the six Indian soldiers were taken out of the tunnel, ordered to strip off their clothes beside a sixty-foot-deep gorge, and then were shot by a Japanese officer and five men. Four were killed and their bodies were kicked down the gorge where already more than twenty bodies lay decomposing. One of the Indian soldiers, a RIASC ambulance driver, was shot through the right arm, left shoulder and right hand by the Japanese officer and managed to fall down the gorge without being kicked. At the bottom he discovered that the sixth member of his party, a labourer, although badly wounded, was still conscious. When the Japanese had gone, he helped the other man to move across the gorge, but after a hundred yards the labourer lost consciousness and he had to leave him. Five days later, after living on water and leaves, the ambulance driver staggered into the regimental aid post of 3/14 Punjab Regiment, one of 9 Brigade's units.

Meanwhile, back at the hospital in the Box, the Japanese raiding party had completed their crime. Wounded prisoners received no attention. Those who cried out were shot or bayoneted. Men lying helplessly in bed were killed. In one shelter were a British lieutenant, a major of the Gurkhas and a Signals sergeant. They were being tended by a captain of the RAMC. Four West Yorkshires, whose defence post was overrun in the attack, joined them. When day came, they lay still so that the Japanese might not notice them. During the morning they heard a shout outside and the RAMC Captain asked: "What do you want?"

The shout – it sounded like "You go" – was repeated. The Captain shook his head and lay down again. "Who is it?" asked the Lieutenant.

"It's a Jap," said the Captain. At that moment one of the Japanese soldiers appeared and shot him through the right thigh. The Captain shouted: "I am a doctor – Red Cross – I am a medical officer."

The Japanese shot dead the Captain, the Gurkha Major, two British soldiers and a mess servant. The Lieutenant and the three surviving British soldiers lay still. They stayed like that all day, and when darkness came they managed to leave the hospital and find the safety of the nearest West Yorkshire post.

A British private of the RAMC – one of a party of twenty – survived to describe his experience. He was tied by his neck to another man – as they all were – kicked, cuffed and cracked over the head by rifle butts, and used as a shield on top of a trench by the Japanese when the carrier attacked. Just before dark on February 8 a Japanese officer told the twenty men: "Come and get treatment."

They were taken along a dried-up watercourse to a clearing with a running stream. Through the whole hot day they had been allowed only two bottles of water between them. And now they stood by the stream. But they were not allowed to drink. The Japanese opened up at them with rifles. Seventeen of them were killed. That night Lieutenant Basu and nine men who had been wounded when a mortar exploded near them lay in a watercourse, some dying, some crying for water. The Japanese shot one man and bayoneted another who cried too loudly. Just before they left, the Japanese stood in front of them, their rifles ready.

"We are Red Cross people," said Basu – he and another doctor both had their stethoscopes slung round their necks. "We are doctors and hospital workers. We have nothing to do with actual warfare."

Most of them wore Red Cross badges on their arms. It made no difference. The Japanese shot them all.

Lieutenant Basu was shot at twice. He was left stunned. At first he was not sure whether he was alive or dead. He felt at his ear, but there was no blood on his fingers. He could still see and his thoughts became clear once more. He realised how vulnerable he was lying there still alive. So he reached out to the body of one of his dead friends and put his hand on the wounds until it was covered with blood, and then he smeared the blood over his face and head and down his shirt front, so that the Japanese would think he, too, was mortally wounded. He slipped groaning into a trench, and there he spent the night.

On the morning of February 9 the West Yorkshires cleared the Japanese out of the hospital. Their task was made all the more difficult because the enemy had camouflaged their machine-gun posts cunningly with stretchers in the wards and theatre. Fortunately, before the attacks began, most of the wounded had been removed from the hospital to a dried-up watercourse lying to the north. As it was, we found in the hospital area the bodies of thirty-one patients and four doctors – doctors whose services were to be desperately needed in the days to come.

# CLOSE-QUARTER FIGHTING, BURMA, MARCH 1944
## *John Masters, Long Range Penetration Unit (Chindits)*

*On 5 March 1944, Wingate's Chindits began landing 100 miles behind enemy lines to cut off the Japanese divisions "Marching on Delhi". The Japanese reacted furiously to this incursion.*

The second crisis came when the close-quarter fighting at the Deep reached the limit of human tolerance. I decided I must force the Japanese farther away, at any cost. First, we removed the secondary charges from the three-inch mortars and fired them with primaries only. The bombs, fired from the middle of the block, arched high and fell five or ten yards from our forward positions. Next, I called for a heavy air strike, and told the air force to use 250-pound bombs. I expected to kill twenty of my own men if they bombed accurately, forty if they didn't.

Six fighter-bombers came. Chesty, standing with a radio in a trench above the Deep, brought them down on successive east-west runs across the foot of the sector, their target being the outer limit of our wire. They raced down from the sky, one behind the other, the great bombs slipped loose and whistled, shining, down. All my mortars opened rapid fire, all the machine-guns opened rapid fire. The hill quaked and heaved, the noise beat in huge waves against my ear-drums, steel splinters whined and droned over the hill and far out across the valley, trees crashed and fell, raw white wounds gaping, all the leaves vanished and hung in the boiling smoke and dust. The aircraft dived lower, firing their multiple .50-calibre machine-guns. For long moments one monstrous tearing roar filled earth and sky and being.

When they flew away, no one moved for a long time, and no one fired. We went down to remove and replace our casualties. There were none.

One enemy sniper lived, and fired a few shots during the rest of the day, and the usual attack followed that night, but the following day no Japanese were within two hundred yards of our wire. I bombed them again, this time with B-25s.

The enemy began to use his heavy mortar. Its shell weighed sixty pounds (the shell of our heaviest, the three-inch, weighed ten pounds), and when it landed on a weapon pit it saved the need for burying parties. Every day Tommy and his padre moved about across the Deep sector, under sniping, speaking to the men in the trenches, pausing here and there to pick up a handful of yellow-stained earth and sprinkle it over the torn "grave", and say a short prayer.

The rain now fell steadily. The Deep sector looked like Passchendaele – blasted trees, feet and twisted hands sticking up out of the earth, bloody shirts, ammunition clips, holes half full of water, each containing two pale, huge-eyed men, trying to keep their rifles out of the mud, and over all the heavy, sweet stench of death, from our own bodies and entrails lying unknown in the shattered ground, from Japanese corpses on the wire, or fastened, dead and rotting, in the trees. At night the rain hissed down in total darkness, the trees ran with water and, beyond the devastation, the jungle dripped and crackled.

A Japanese light machine-gun chatters hysterically, and bullets clack and clap overhead. Two Very lights float up, burst in brilliant whiteness. Click, click, click – boom, crash, boom, three mortar bombs burst in red-yellow flashes on the wire.

The third crisis came on May 17. On that day our Lightnings (P-38s) patrolled the valley for several hours, searching for the guns which had done us so much damage. They did not find them. Towards evening the P-38s left and I went down to the water point, as I usually did, to wash, shave, and brush up for the night's battle. While I was shaving, the enemy began to shell the block with 105s and 155s. Twelve guns or more were firing. Soap all over my face, I looked across at the ridge to the west, where the enemy had once put a mortar, and saw movement there. Mortar bombs from the ridge whistled into the block. The shelling grew more urgent and I walked quickly up to my command post – I tried never to run.

The shelling concentrated on the Deep and became a violent, continuous drumfire. My stomach felt empty and I was ready to vomit. I should have relieved the King's Own. This was more than human flesh could stand. Nothing to do now though. The attack would come in immediately after the bombardment.

The shelling increased again. For ten minutes an absolute fury fell on the Deep.

Major Heap, the second-in-command of the King's Own, tumbled in, his face streaked and bloody and working with extreme strain. "We've had it, sir," he said. "They're destroying all the posts, direct hits all the time . . . all machine-guns knocked out, crews killed . . . I don't think we can hold them if . . . the men are . . ."

I didn't wait to hear what the men were. I knew. They were dead, wounded, or stunned.

I took the telephone and called Tim Brennan, commanding 26 Column of the Cameronians, and told him to bring his whole column to the ridge crest at once, with all weapons and ammunition, man-handled, ready to take over the Deep. "Yes, sir," he said pleasantly. I had time to call Henning and order him to spread out to occupy Brennan's positions as well as his own, before going quickly, my breath short, to the hill crest.

The shelling stopped as I reached it. Tim arrived. Johnny Boden, the mortar officer, arrived. Now, now, the Japanese must come. I told Boden to stand by with smoke and HE to cover the Cameronians; 26 Column arrived, at the double. Still no assault. Tim ran down the forward slope, his men behind him. I waited crouched on the ridge top. Ordered Boden to open up with his mortars. The enemy must have this blasted slope covered by machine-guns. I knew they had. They didn't fire. It was twilight, but down the slope in the smoke I could clearly see Cameronians jumping into the waterlogged trenches, King's Own struggling out and up towards me. The Cameronian machine-guns arrived, men bent double under the ninety-pound loads of barrel and tripod. Bombs burst, smoke rose in dense white clouds. I told the officer to move the machine-guns again, after full dark, if he could. "Of course, sir," he said impatiently.

The men of the King's Own passed by, very slowly, to be gathered by Heap into reserve. They staggered, many were wounded, others carried wounded men, their eyes wandered, their mouths drooped open. I wanted to cry, but dared not, could only mutter, "Well done, well done," as they passed.

The minutes crawled, each one a gift more precious than the first rain. I sent wire down, and ammunition, and took two machine-guns from Henning's 90 Column, and put them in trenches on the crest, ready to sweep the whole slope. Full darkness came, with rain. An hour had passed, a whole hour since the enemy bombardment ended. In our own attacks we reckoned a thirty-second delay as fatal.

With a crash of machine-guns and mortars the battle began. All night the Cameronians and the Japanese 53rd Division fought it out. Our machine-guns ripped them from the new positions. Twice the Japanese forced into the barbed wire with Bangalore torpedoes, and the blasting rain of the mortars wiped them out. At four am, when they launched their final assault to recover their bodies, we had defeated them.

# AN ENGLISH OFFICER ESCAPES THE JAPANESE, MALAYA, MAY 1944

## *Colonel F. Spencer Chapman, 5th Seaforth Highlanders*

*Chapman entered the jungle of Malaya in 1942 to organise stay-behind parties; he did not leave it for three years.*

Although my hosts did not attempt to tie me up, they took no other chances. There were three sentries who seemed to be particularly interested in my welfare. An N.C.O. who carried a pistol – I saw him take it out of its holster, cock it, and push it into the belt of his raincoat. A sentry with fixed bayonet who strolled up and down beyond the fire in front of the tent. Another with a tommy-gun hovered on the edge of the firelight and seemed to be watching the jungle as if they expected my friends might attempt a rescue. Alas! how little fear there was of that!

My tent-fellows slept in all their clothes, including boots, and were thus able to dispense with blankets. I lay between my English-speaking friend and another officer in the centre of the tent and therefore directly in front of the fire, which was only a few yards from my feet. It was quite light enough to read, and the encircling jungle night looked inky black by contrast, though I knew there would soon be a moon. My neighbours seemed to fall asleep instantly, but were restless and noisy sleepers. We were so crowded that one or the other often rolled against me or put a knee affectionately over mine and I had to push them back, observing with satisfaction that no amount of manhandling seemed to disturb them – though my guard showed signs of disapproval.

In the days when I was a fieldcraft instructor I had read every book on escaping and used to lecture on the subject. But none of the methods I had advocated seemed to be of much practical use now . . .

At about one o'clock I woke up. The N.C.O. on duty had been changed and the new one did not seem so vigilant. I watched him closely, and while pretending restlessly to stretch my arms, I was able little by little to ease up the canvas behind my head. Before I could continue operations I had to do something about the fire which, in the chill early morning, had been made larger and more brilliant than ever. I now had an inspiration which traded, most ungenerously, on the natural good manners of my hosts. After a few preliminary hiccoughs, I got up, retching horribly, and pretended to be violently sick. I had saved up spittle for a time and the results, especially the noise, were most realistic. The N.C.O. was quite sympathetic and I explained that the heat of the fire was so great that I was unable to sleep and was indeed – as he had seen – very ill. He immediately called up the sentries and together they damped down the fire and raked it further from the tent.

From there the firelight still shone on my blanket sleeping-bag, but I was able to put on my rubber shoes (which I should have to wear until daylight) and then to collect some of the miscellaneous gear belonging to my bed-fellows – a haversack, a tin hat, some spare boots, and a despatch case (which, unfortunately, I could not open and it was too heavy to take away), and pushed them down into my sleeping-bag, tastefully arranging the boots to resemble my own feet thrust into the corners of the bag. Meanwhile, with legs doubled up, and watching the guard through half-closed eyes, I worked myself further and further back into the angle of the tent. A Japanese rifle caused much discomfort to my backbone; I thought how careless of them to have left it there, and wished I could have taken it with me, but it would have been too much of an encumbrance.

I waited till one sentry was out of sight, the other at the far end of his beat, and the N.C.O. not actually looking at me. Then, in one movement I thrust myself violently through the opening at the bottom of the canvas. I heard a "ping", as a peg gave or a rope broke, and a sudden guttural gasp from the N.C.O. – and I was out in the jungle.

# LIFE IN A JAPANESE POW CAMP, JUNE 1944–AUGUST 1945

### Anton Bilek, mechanic USAAF

*Bilek was captured at Bataan in 1942.*

In June of '44, they asked for another detail to go to Japan. I volunteered for it. I talked to a buddy, Bob, who I knew from Chicago. I said, "Let's get the hell out of here." We'd been hearing some rumors where our troops are movin' up, gettin' some foothold into the islands here. Down south, Guadalcanal and this stuff. When they come in, they're not gonna come in like a ballet dancer. They're gonna come in with both guns firin' from the hip. They can't afford to be very fussy. We could be bombed by 'em or shot by 'em.

We went to Japan and were fortunate we chose that detail. The ship that left right after us with another sixteen hundred men aboard was torpedoed by one of our submarines. All sixteen hundred drowned. We lost close to five thousand men killed by our U.S. Navy, on freighters being transported to Japan. None of the ships were marked, so our navy people didn't know this.

It was a mean old freighter, rusty goddamn thing, full of bedbugs. It stunk to high heaven. It took us sixty days from Manila to Moji, Japan. We stopped at Formosa for two weeks, loadin' up with salt. It's the only ballast we had.

We worked in a coal mine in Omuta, about twenty-five miles east of Nagasaki, across the bay. We were surprised at the nice quarters we had. The food was tremendous. In other words, we got some vegetables in our soup. One time we got a bun. For sixty days on the boat, we had nothin' but wormy rice. You swallowed all the worms. We called that our protein. They quarantined us, because we were in such poor shape after sixty days of two dabs of rice a day. They decided we needed some rest and a little bit more food, so we could do some work in the mines.

The mines were the property of Count Mitsui, the industrialist. We were really workin' for him. Plus they had Korean prisoners. The Japanese who supervised us were, you might say, 4-Fs, either too old for the army or somethin' wrong with 'em. We'd work, maybe six or eight of us, with one Jap supervisor.

You did find some good Japs there. Some of the old men were nice to us. But the majority could not see looking up at an American who was much taller than him. This they hated with a passion. I got the devil whaled out of me quite a few times because I couldn't understand. The school they took us to, the Jap would hold up a shovel or a pick and say the Japanese word. You gotta remember all this. My first day in the mine, he talks to me and I couldn't understand. So he decked me. It made him feel good, I guess.

Once in a while you'd find a good Jap. Right away you learned his name. If you could get Fiji-san or Okamoto-san, he's a good one. Some of them guys would take you on the side and you'd sit down and rest. One time, at the end of the day, while I was waitin' for the little train to take our shift out, I laid back against the rock wall, put my cap over my eyes, and tried to get some rest. The guy next to me says, "God damn, I wish I was back in Seattle." I paid no attention. Guys were always talking about being back home. He said, "I had a nice restaurant there and I lost it all." I turned around and looked and it's a Japanese. He was one of the overseers. I was flabbergasted.

He said, "Now just don't talk to me. I'll do all the talkin'." He's talkin' out of the side of his mouth. He says, "I was born and raised in Seattle, had a nice restaurant there. I brought my mother back to Japan. She's real old and knew she was gonna die and she wanted to come home. The war broke out and I couldn't get back to the States. They made me come down here and work in the coal mines." I didn't know what the hell to say to the guy. Finally the car come down and I says, "Well, see you in Seattle someday." And I left. I never saw him after that.

One of the Japanese officers in our camp was born and raised in Riverside, California. He pitched for his college team. He was the chief interpreter. He was no good. He'd sneak around and listen to us in the dark, and if he didn't like what we were sayin', he'd turn us in.

Our camp was one of the worst. Both camp commanders were executed by war-crimes trial, and two of the guards, because of the treatment to war prisoners.

I lost about fifty pounds in the war. Once I came down with double pneumonia. This was the big killer, and I beat it. The doctor was elated. They'd given me up. No sooner do I get rid of it than I come down with beriberi again. I swelled up. This was the worst I had. I was so big I was like a walrus. I couldn't move. If I had to defecate, they'd roll me over on the side and put the bedpan up against my butt and then they'd wash me. Your hand is so big around, you could stick your finger in it and make a big hole. They had to make a special bed for me.

# BAMBOO, DYSENTERY, LEECHES: A MARAUDER ON THE JUNGLE PATH, JULY 1944
## Charlton Ogburn, 5307th Composite Unit

*Known as "Merrill's Marauders" after its commanding officer, Brigadier-General Frank D. Merrill, the 5307th was an American long-range penentration unit operating in Burma.*

The country we had to cross in bypassing the Japanese was a conglomeration of hills resembling the patternless jumble of waves in a tide rip and often so steep your feet would go out from under you while you were climbing. ("The steeper the hill the less distance you got to fall before you hit it. So what the hell are you complaining about?") Sometimes the slopes were too much for the mules; the packs would have to be unloaded and broken up and the pieces carried up or passed up from hand to hand. The platoons took in rotation the task of hacking a passage through the towering, tangled, resistant vegetation that buried hillsides, valleys and ridges together and reduced us in scale to crawling animalcules in its somnolent depths. Within the platoons, officers shared with the men the labor of chopping. The young bamboo would slash out like saber blades when severed; the old, resisting like steel the blows of the dulled machetes, could hardly be cut at all. (The cuticle of bamboo has a high content of the material quartz consists of: silica.) Little of it would fall. You could cut a passage for hours, for days on end, and nothing would happen; the tops of the growth were too interwoven for any of it to break loose. So the bamboo had to be cut twice, at the ground and at a height above the peaks of the mules' loads. The head of the column sounded like a spike-driving crew on a railroad, but the jungle imprisoned the sound, as it did us, and within a small fraction of the column's length to the rear, nothing could be heard. The men in the van struck savagely at the unyielding stems, as if the vegetation were an enemy that had to be done to death, until, soaked with sweat, their arms heavy, and gasping for breath, they would fall back to the end of the platoon and be replaced. It was like a column of slaves clearing a path for the pampered and despotic ruler of an ancient Asian empire.

We fought and toiled to reach Shaduzup as if it were salvation. But, Christ, how I hated its uncouth syllables! Shadu'zup! On to Shadu'zup! I pictured it as a cowled and sheeted figure like one of those ghoulish Moslem women. The days of that tortuous march were to remain forever living in my mind, though merged with other days of other marches that preceded or followed – not that it mattered; they were all alike anyway.

We were twelve hours a day on the trail, as a rule – whether there was a trail or not. When there was not, it was mostly a matter of standing and waiting while they slashed away up front. Pack, weapon, ammunition, knife, canteen, all grew heavier; the straps they were slung on cut into the flesh. You could sit down and lean back on your pack to rest your shoulders, but holding your head at a 45-degree angle was hard on your neck, and anyhow you might have to struggle to your feet again immediately. So usually you just stood, leaning slightly forward like an old farm horse in his harness to bring your center of gravity over your feet. If a break were ordered it would pay you to take your pack off, but the mule-leaders had little respite. The mules lived only to get the spray of bamboo leaves that was just out of reach, and the palms of the leaders' hands were burned or their shoulders jerked half out of joint, depending upon whether they were holding the halter ropes loosely or firmly. One would hardly have thought it, but the continual yanking of the mules was a major trial to those who had to control them.

While we marched, men were continually falling out beside the trail, taking care to remain in plain sight lest they be shot in trying to rejoin the column. Dysentery was already the scourge of the organization; much of the command could have been carried in the morning report as walking dead.

On everyone's uniform there were dark, stiff patches. These were of dried blood, from leech bites. The country was infested with these repulsive little rubbery monsters, black worms with suction cups at both ends able to contract to pea-sized balls or elongate themselves to a couple of inches. They did give us the pleasure of going after them with the lighted ends of cigarettes. It required nice judgment to bring the heat close enough to persuade them to disengage without cooking them before they had a chance to. Unfortunately, Mother Nature – whose passion is for equalizing odds – had endowed the little pests with the capacity of clamping on and opening a lesion without your feeling anything, especially if you were asleep. Then after you had found one of them on you and got him off you were liable to have difficulty stanching the flow of blood, for their saliva contained an anticoagulant, a heparin-like agent, according to Doc Kolodny. Caifson Johnson oozed blood for days from some leech bites and one of the platoon leaders went around for an equal length of time with a ruby-red eyeball, the result of a leech's fastening onto it during the night. All of us were more or less bloody all the time, and the mules suffered worse than we; their fetlocks were generally dark red and slimy with blood. In addition, eggs deposited in their lesions by a kind of fly hatched out into screw worms.

Compared with the combat platoons, the communications platoon had nothing to complain about. It was a fact, though, that after their work was over, at the end of the day's march, ours began. We generally had help in clearing enough of the forest to make room for our antenna, but the responsibility rested on us. The problem was a different one from opening a trail. It was not enough to hack out a tunnel; the roof of the forest had to come down. So we would cut farther and farther out and tug at the bamboo and vines, then cut some more and pull some more until a section of the canopy finally sagged to the ground. When we had cleared enough for our wire and had got it erected – and bamboo at least provided the world's best poles – we could turn to the job of producing enough current to heave our signal out through the woods and over the intervening miles to Merrill's headquarters, wherever they might be, and to our base at Dinjan, in Assam. This was done with a hand-cranked generator, which might be likened to an upended bicycle without wheels or handlebars; you sat on the seat and pedaled by hand. The drag on the crank was proportionate to the power output of the set you were working, and the AN/PRC-1 was designed to reach a long way. To keep it going was like forcing a bicycle uphill just before you have to get off and walk. It took everyone in the platoon working by turns to keep the glutton satisfied.

# ASSAULT INTO HELL: A MARINE LANDS ON PELELIU, 15 SEPTEMBER 1944

## Eugene B. Sledge, 1st Marine Division, USMC

*Sledge was a mortarman. Peleliu is a small island in Pacific.*

H-hour, 0800. Long jets of red flame mixed with thick black smoke rushed out of the muzzles of the huge battleships' 16-inch guns with a noise like a thunderclap. The giant shells tore through the air toward the island, roaring like locomotives.

"Boy, it must cost a fortune to fire them 16-inch babies," said a buddy near me.

"Screw the expense," growled another.

Only less impressive were the cruisers firing 8-inch salvos and the host of smaller ships firing rapid fire. The usually clean salty air was strong with the odors of explosives and diesel fuel. While the assault waves formed up and my amphibious tractor lay still in the water with engines idling, the tempo of the bombardment increased to such intensity that I couldn't distinguish the reports of the various types of weapons through the thunderous noise. We had to shout at each other to be heard. The big ships increased their fire and moved off to the flanks of the amtrac formations when we started in so as not to fire over us at the risk of short rounds.

We waited a seeming eternity for the signal to start toward the beach. The suspense was almost more than I could bear. Waiting is a major part of war, but I never experienced any more supremely agonizing suspense than the excruciating torture of those moments before we received the signal to begin the assault on Peleliu. I broke out in a cold sweat as the tension mounted with the intensity of the bombardment. My stomach was tied in knots. I had a lump in my throat and swallowed only with great difficulty. My knees nearly buckled, so I clung weakly to the side of the tractor. I felt nauseated and feared that my bladder would surely empty itself and reveal me to be the coward I was. But the men around me looked just about the way I felt. Finally, with a sense of fatalistic relief mixed with a flash of anger at the navy officer who was our wave commander, I saw him wave his flag toward the beach. Our driver revved the engine. The treads churned up the water, and we started in – the second wave ashore.

We moved ahead, watching the frightful spectacle. Huge geysers of water rose around the amtracs ahead of us as they approached the reef. The beach was now marked along its length by a continuous sheet of flame backed by a thick wall of smoke. It seemed as though a huge volcano had erupted from the sea, and rather than heading for an island, we were being drawn into the vortex of a flaming abyss. For many it was to be oblivion.

The lieutenant braced himself and pulled out a half-pint whiskey bottle.

"This is it, boys," he yelled.

Just like they do in the movies! It seemed unreal.

He held the bottle out to me, but I refused. Just sniffing the cork under those conditions might have made me pass out. He took a long pull on the bottle, and a couple of the men did the same. Suddenly a large shell exploded with a terrific concussion, and a huge geyser rose up just to our right front. It barely missed us. The engine stalled. The front of the tractor lurched to the left and bumped hard against the rear of another amtrac that was either stalled or hit. I never knew which.

We sat stalled, floating in the water for some terrifying moments. We were sitting ducks for the enemy gunners. I looked forward through the hatch behind the driver. He was wrestling frantically with the control levers. Japanese shells were screaming into the area and exploding all around us. Sgt. Johnny Marmet leaned toward the driver and yelled something. Whatever it was, it seemed to calm the driver, because he got the engine started. We moved forward again amid the geysers of exploding shells.

Our bombardment began to lift off the beach and move inland. Our dive bombers also moved inland with their strafing and bombing. The Japanese increased the volume of their fire against the waves of amtracs. Above the din I could hear the ominous sound of shell fragments humming and growling through the air.

"Stand by," someone yelled.

I picked up my mortar ammo bag and slung it over my left shoulder, buckled my helmet chin strap, adjusted my carbine sling over my right shoulder, and tried to keep my balance. My heart pounded. Our amtrac came out of the water and moved a few yards up the gently sloping sand.

"Hit the beach!" yelled an NCO moments before the machine lurched to a stop.

The men piled over the sides as fast as they could. I followed Snafu, climbed up, and planted both feet firmly on the left side so as to leap as far away from it as possible. At that instant a burst of machine-gun fire with white-hot tracers snapped through the air at eye level, almost grazing my face. I pulled my head back like a turtle, lost my balance, and fell awkwardly forward down onto the sand in a tangle of ammo bag, pack, helmet, carbine, gas mask, cartridge belt, and flopping canteens. "Get off the beach! Get off the beach!" raced through my mind.

Once I felt land under my feet, I wasn't as scared as I had been coming across the reef. My legs dug up the sand as I tried to rise. A firm hand gripped my shoulder. "Oh god, I thought, it's a Nip who's come out of a pillbox!" I couldn't reach my kabar – fortunately, because as I got my face out of the sand and looked up, there was the worried face of a Marine bending over me. He thought the machine-gun burst had hit me, and he had crawled over to help. When he saw I was unhurt, he spun around and started crawling rapidly off the beach. I scuttled after him.

Shells crashed all around. Fragments tore and whirred, slapping on the sand and splashing into the water a few yards behind us. The Japanese were recovering from the shock of our prelanding bombard-ment. Their machine-gun and rifle fire got thicker, snapping viciously overhead in increasing volume.

Our amtrac spun around and headed back out as I reached the edge of the beach and flattened on the deck. The world was a nightmare of flashes, violent explosions, and snapping bullets. Most of what I saw blurred. My mind was benumbed by the shock of it.

I glanced back across the beach and saw a DUKW (rubber-tired amphibious truck) roll up on the sand at a point near where we had just landed. The instant the DUKW stopped, it was engulfed in thick, dirty black smoke as a shell scored a direct hit on it. Bits of debris flew into the air. I watched with that odd, detached fascination peculiar to men under fire, as a flat metal panel about two feet square spun high into the air then splashed into shallow water like a big pancake. I didn't see any men get out of the DUKW.

Up and down the beach and out on the reef, a number of amtracs and DUKWs were burning. Japanese machine-gun bursts made long splashes on the water as though flaying it with some giant whip. The geysers belched up relentlessly where the mortar and artillery shells hit. I caught a fleeting glimpse of a group of Marines leaving a smoking amtrac on the reef. Some fell as bullets and fragments splashed among them. Their buddies tried to help them as they struggled in the knee-deep water.

I shuddered and choked. A wild desperate feeling of anger, frus-tration, and pity gripped me. It was an emotion that always would torture my mind when I saw men trapped and was unable to do anything but watch as they were hit. My own plight forgotten momentarily, I felt sickened to the depths of my soul. I asked God, "Why, why, why?" I turned my face away and wished that I were imagining it all. I had tasted the bitterest essence of war, the sight of helpless comrades being slaughtered, and it filled me with disgust.

I got up. Crouching low, I raced up the sloping beach into a defilade. Reaching the inland edge of the sand just beyond the high-water mark, I glanced down and saw the nose of a huge black and yellow bomb protruding from the sand. A metal plate attached to the top served as a pressure trigger. My foot had missed it by only inches.

I hit the deck again just inside the defilade. On the sand immediately in front of me was a dead snake about eighteen inches long. It was colorful, somewhat like American species I had kept as pets when a boy. It was the only snake I saw on Peleliu.

Momentarily I was out of the heavy fire hitting on the beach. A strong smell of chemicals and exploding shells filled the air. Patches of coral and sand around me were yellowed from the powder from shell blasts. A large white post about four feet high stood at the edge of the defilade. Japanese writing was painted on the side facing the beach. To me, it appeared as though a chicken with muddy feet had walked up and down the post. I felt a sense of pride that this was enemy territory and that we were capturing it for our country to help win the war.

One of our NCOs signaled us to move to our right, out of the shallow defilade. I was glad, because the Japanese probably would pour mortar fire into it to prevent it being used for shelter. At the moment, however, the gunners seemed to be concentrating on the beach and the incoming waves of Marines.

I ran over to where one of our veterans stood looking to our front and flopped down at his feet. "You'd better get down," I yelled as bullets snapped and cracked all around.

"Them slugs are high, they're hittin' in the leaves, Sledgehammer," he said nonchalantly without looking at me.

"Leaves, hell! Where are the trees?" I yelled back at him.

Startled, he looked right and left. Down the beach, barely visible, was a shattered palm. Nothing near us stood over knee high. He hit the deck.

"I must be crackin' up, Sledgehammer. Them slugs sound just like they did in the jungle at Gloucester, and I figured they were hittin' leaves," he said with chagrin.

"Somebody gimme a cigarette," I yelled to my squad mates nearby.

Snafu was jubilant. "I toldja you'd start smokin', didn't I, Sledgehammer?"

# ONE MAN'S WAR: A MARINE WRITES HOME, 25 SEPTEMBER 1944

## *Lieutenant Richard Kennard, 5th Regiment, 1st Marine Division*

On the island of Peleliu

Dear Mother and Dad:

This is D-Day plus ten and my first opportunity to write and say that I am alive and well. You want the details, so here goes: On D-Day this island was blasted by the most terrific amount of naval gunfire and air bombardment that was ever given to any piece of enemy territory. It was a wonderful show as seen from the landing boat I was in a thousand yards off shore. The island is surrounded by a wide coral reef, over which the LTVs (amphibian tractors) transported us after we changed into them from the transport ship's Higgins boats.

I landed with the battalion executive officer at H plus 120, a half hour late. So many amphibs were knocked out on their first run into the beach that succeeding waves were late coming in. I saw no dead Japs on the beach – only dead and wounded Marines. The Nips had taken off to their caves and pillboxes in this island fortress. The smoke of battle was so thick I could hardly see ahead of me. I spent the morning and afternoon of that first day with the company commander of an assault company advancing south down the island. While in a mangrove swamp I received a radio message from my colonel to move across the island and get into position to register the artillery on a certain spot. This meant leaving the unit to which I was attached. Our team struggled along and suddenly got pinned down by sniper fire. We were exhausted, and as I felt that I had myself and FO team out in front of the lines of the adjacent attacking battalion, I decided to move back to where we first hit the beach. We got there at 6:00 pm and fell into a large crater utterly exhausted. All night long there was firing of small arms, and the beach was under constant shell-fire from the enemy's mortars. The Japs kept themselves and their weapons hidden in the coral caves in the hills, where no kind of gunfire can get them out. How I lived through that night is beyond me, when so many men were hit by shrapnel from the mortars.

D-Day plus one I got out of the crater where we had spent the night and started to go back to my unit when my radio man was hit by flying shrapnel. He was evacuated. The infantry had been forced back during the night, so I tried to get up the beach in the other direction to our CP. It took me two hours to go four hundred yards, the enemy mortar barrage up and down the beach was so terrific. I was always able to seek a deep trench in the sand, and fortunately no shells landed on us, though many were killed and wounded not more than ten feet away from where I was lying. At the battery position, which I finally reached at noon, we took off our packs and rested. I took my men down to the beach two hundred yards away from the battery to see my CO, and while there, the Japs laid down a heavy mortar barrage on H Battery. Two guns were knocked out, many boys wounded and killed (I can't mention figures). The 105 ammo blew up and everything was destroyed there. My pack burned up completely, with the New Testament Marilyn gave me and all the pictures of her that I was carrying.

Because G Battery lost two of its guns when the DUKWs sank on the way into the beach, it combined with the two remaining guns left from H Battery. D + 2 and D + 3 I spent in the southern part of the island with the men not needed on the guns as a reserve for the infantry outfit. We set up beach defenses and killed quite a few Japs who tried to counterattack our line at night.

On D + 4 I went to an OP with a new FO team up in the coral hills. There for two days and nights it was a perfect hell. The temperature was 134 degrees, no shade at all, and the Nips were continually shelling us on the top of the ridge I was on, or shooting their machine guns. I was under sniper fire continually, and let me tell you, it is an awful feeling to have those bullets whiz past your head. I still don't understand how I could have gone through all this without being hit, when I was deliberately shot at so often. Many boys near me were hit by sniper fire or shrapnel from the Jap mortars, which could never be located. During the night I had to observe and direct fire three different times, and once while doing so, a Jap sneaked up the ridge and was about to crawl into our CP. I woke up two men near me and we opened up on him. He sure looked good stone dead the next morning. I hate to think what would have happened had that Jap had a chance to throw some grenades in on us. Of course, I never slept while on OP, for it was too dangerous. After two days of hell on "Suicide Ridge" or "Bloody Nose", as the hills here are called, I came down to the southern part of the island and had a good night's sleep and a day of rest.

Then I was sent up to the hills again with another FO team four days ago. I forgot to say that while leaving the OP where I had spent two days, a Jap sniper shot one of my men in the knee.

While carrying him out on the stretcher and almost to safety, he fired again. The bullets went right through my legs and hit one of my other men in the ankle. I got them into a medical jeep safely and sent them off to the beach. All casualties are evacuated to the hospital ships off shore.

Today I came down from the awful coral hills after three days and dangerous nights up there as the FO. There were more wounded and killed when the Japs shelled the ridge this morning. None of us were hit this time, thank God. I have my fingers crossed every minute up there in the front lines, and pray each night that I won't get hit. For the present. I have been relieved by another officer and FO team. In a few days, I suppose, they'll send me up there again, but I hope most of the mopping-up process will be over with by then. I'm lucky to be alive and uninjured now, after going through what I have tried to describe to you. We have the airport and all south of the hills. It just seems impossible to get the Japs out of those coral caves, though, and I don't know how the problem is going to be solved . . .

War is terrible, just awful, awful. You have no idea how it hurts to see American boys all shot up, wounded, suffering from pain and exhaustion, and those that fall down, never to move again. After this is all over, I shall cherish and respect more than anything else all that which is sweet, tender, and gentle. This has been the toughest fight in Marine Corps history. We have won an excellent, important airfield, and I am proud that I have been able to do my part in taking the objective. The war on this island isn't over yet, however, so I still have my fingers crossed and keep very alert and careful. I am doing my best for you all at home who count upon my safe return, someday soon, I hope. You may take excerpts from this letter, Dad, but I don't want anything printed publicly at all.

> Much love to you all
> (Your son and Lynn's sweetheart)

Dick

## MARINES STORM A PILLBOX, NGESEBUS, 28 SEPTEMBER 1944

### *Eugene B. Sledge, 1st Marine Division, USMC*

*Ngesebus is a small island off Peleliu.*

After we moved farther inland, we received orders to set up the mortars on the inland side of a Japanese pillbox and prepare to fire on the enemy to our company's front. We asked Company K's gunnery sergeant, Gy. Sgt. W. R. Saunders, if he knew of any enemy troops in the bunker. It appeared undamaged. He said some of the men had thrown grenades through the ventilators, and he was sure there were no live enemy inside.

Snafu and I began to set up our mortar about five feet from the bunker. Number One mortar was about five yards to our left. Cpl. R. V. Burgin was getting the sound-powered phone hooked up to receive fire orders from Sgt. Johnny Marmet, who was observing.

I heard something behind me in the pillbox. Japanese were talking in low, excited voices. Metal rattled against an iron grating. I grabbed my carbine and yelled, "Burgin, there're Nips in that pillbox."

All the men readied their weapons as Burgin came over to have a look, kidding me with, "Shucks, Sledgehammer, you're crackin' up." He looked into the ventilator port directly behind me. It was rather small, approximately six inches by eight inches, and covered with iron bars about a half inch apart. What he saw brought forth a stream of curses in his best Texas style against all Nippon. He stuck his carbine muzzle through the bars, fired two quick shots, and yelled, "I got 'em right in the face."

The Japanese inside the pillbox began jabbering loudly. Burgin was gritting his teeth and calling the enemy SOBs while he fired more shots through the opening.

Every man in the mortar section was ready for trouble as soon as Burgin fired the first shot. It came in the form of a grenade tossed out of the end entrance to my left. It looked as big as a football to me. I yelled "Grenade!" and dove behind the sand breastwork protecting the entrance at the end of the pillbox. The sand bank was about four feet high and L-shaped to protect the entrance from fire from the front and flanks. The grenade exploded, but no one was hit.

The Japanese tossed out several more grenades without causing us injury, because we were hugging the deck. Most of the men crawled around to the front of the pillbox and crouched close to it between the firing ports, so the enemy inside couldn't fire at them. John Redifer and Vincent Santos jumped on top. Things got quiet.

I was nearest the door, and Burgin yelled to me, "Look in and see what's in there, Sledgehammer."

Being trained to take orders without question, I raised my head above the sand bank and peered into the door of the bunker. It nearly cost me my life. Not more than six feet from me crouched a Japanese machine gunner. His eyes were black dots in a tan, impassive face topped with the familiar mushroom helmet. The muzzle of his light machine gun stared at me like a gigantic third eye.

Fortunately for me, I reacted first. Not having time to get my carbine into firing position, I jerked my head down so fast my helmet almost flew off. A split second later he fired a burst of six or eight rounds. The bullets tore a furrow through the bank just above my head and showered sand on me. My ears rang from the muzzle blast and my heart seemed to be in my throat choking me. I knew damned well I had to be dead! He just couldn't have missed me at that range.

A million thoughts raced through my terrified mind: of how my folks had nearly lost their youngest, of what a stupid thing I had done to look directly into a pillbox full of Japanese without even having my carbine at the ready, and of just how much I hated the enemy anyway. Many a Marine veteran had already lost his life on Peleliu for making less of a mistake than I had just made.

Burgin yelled and asked if I were all right. A hoarse squawk was all the answer I could muster, but his voice brought me to my senses. I crawled around to the front, then up on top of the bunker before the enemy machine gunner could have another try at me.

Redifer yelled, "They've got an automatic weapon in there." Snafu disagreed, and a spirited argument ensued. Redifer pointed out that there surely was an automatic weapon in there and that I should know, because it came close to blowing off my head. But Snafu was adamant. Like much of what I experienced in combat, this exchange was unreal. Here we were: twelve Marines with a bull by the tail in the form of a well-built concrete pillbox containing an unknown number of Japanese with no friendly troops near us and Snafu and Redifer – veterans – in a violent argument.

Burgin shouted, "Knock it off," and they shut up.

Redifer and I lay prone on top of the bunker, just above the door. We knew we had to get the Japanese while they were bottled up, or they would come out at us with knives and bayonets, a thought none of us relished. Redifer and I were close enough to the door to place grenades down the opening and move back before they exploded. But the Japanese invariably tossed them back at us before the explosion. I had an irrepressible urge to do just that. Brief as our face-to-face meeting had been, I had quickly developed a feeling of strong personal hate for that machine gunner who had nearly blasted my head off my shoulders. My terror subsided into a cold, homicidal rage and a vengeful desire to get even.

Redifer and I gingerly peeped down over the door. The machine gunner wasn't visible, but we looked at three long Arisaka rifle barrels with bayonets fixed. Those bayonets seemed ten feet long to me. Their owners were jabbering excitedly, apparently planning to rush out. Redifer acted quickly. He held his carbine by the barrel and used the butt to knock down the rifles. The Japanese jerked their weapons back into the bunker with much chattering.

Behind us, Santos yelled that he had located a ventilator pipe without a cover. He began dropping grenades into it. Each one exploded in the pillbox beneath us with a muffled *bam*. When he had used all of his, Redifer and I handed him our grenades while we kept watch at the door.

After Santos had dropped in several, we stood up and began to discuss with Burgin and the others the possibility that anyone could still be alive inside. (We didn't know at the time that the inside was subdivided by concrete baffles for extra protection.) We got our answer when two grenades were tossed out. Luckily for the men with Burgin, the grenades were thrown out the back. Santos and I shouted a warning and hit the deck on the sand on top of the pillbox, but Redifer merely raised his arm over his face. He took several fragments in the forearm but wasn't wounded seriously.

Burgin yelled, "Let's get the hell outa here and get a tank to help us knock this damn thing out." He ordered us to pull back to some craters about forty yards from the pillbox. We sent a runner to the beach to bring up a flamethrower and an amtrac armed with a 75mm gun.

As we jumped into the crater, three Japanese soldiers ran out of the pillbox door past the sand bank and headed for a thicket. Each carried his bayoneted rifle in his right hand and held up his pants with his left hand. This action so amazed me that I stared in disbelief and didn't fire my carbine. I wasn't afraid, as I had been under shell fire, just filled with wild excitement. My buddies were more effective than I and cut down the enemy with a hail of bullets. They congratulated each other while I chided myself for being more curious about strange Japanese customs than with being combat effective.

The amtrac rattling toward us by this time was certainly a welcome sight. As it pulled into position, several more Japanese raced from the pillbox in a tight group. Some held their bayoneted rifles in both hands, but some of them carried their rifles in one hand and held up their pants with the other. I had overcome my initial surprise and joined the others and the amtrac machine gun in firing away at them. They tumbled onto the hot coral in a forlorn tangle of bare legs, falling rifles, and rolling helmets. We felt no pity for them but exulted over their fate. We had been shot at and shelled too much and had lost too many friends to have compassion for the enemy when we had him cornered.

The amtrac took up a position on a line even with us. Its commander, a sergeant, consulted Burgin. Then the turret gunner fired three armor-piercing 75mm shells at the side of the pillbox. Each time our ears rang with the familiar *wham–bam* as the report of the gun was followed quickly by the explosion of the shell on a target at close range. The third shell tore a hole entirely through the pillbox. Fragments kicked up dust around our abandoned packs and mortars on the other side. On the side nearest us, the hole was about four feet in diameter. Burgin yelled to the tankers to cease firing lest our equipment be damaged.

Someone remarked that if fragments hadn't killed those inside, the concussion surely had. But even before the dust settled, I saw a Japanese soldier appear at the blasted opening. He was grim determination personified as he drew back his arm to throw a grenade at us.

My carbine was already up. When he appeared, I lined up my sights on his chest and began squeezing off shots. As the first bullet hit him, his face contorted in agony. His knees buckled. The grenade slipped from his grasp. All the men near me, including the amtrac machine gunner, had seen him and began firing. The soldier collapsed in the fusilade, and the grenade went off at his feet.

Even in the midst of these fast-moving events, I looked down at my carbine with sober reflection. I had just killed a man at close range. That I had seen clearly the pain on his face when my bullets hit him came as a jolt. It suddenly made the war a very personal affair. The expression on that man's face filled me with shame and then disgust for the war and all the misery it was causing.

My combat experience thus far made me realize that such sentiments for an enemy soldier were the maudlin meditations of a fool. Look at me, a member of the 5th Marine Regiment – one of the oldest, finest, and toughest regiments in the Marine Corps – feeling ashamed because I had shot a damned foe before he could throw a grenade at me! I felt like a fool and was thankful my buddies couldn't read my thoughts.

Burgin's order to us to continue firing into the opening interrupted my musings. We kept up a steady fire into the pillbox to keep the Japanese pinned down while the flame-thrower came up, carried by Corporal Womack from Mississippi. He was a brave, good-natured guy and popular with the troops, but he was one of the fiercest looking Marines I ever saw. He was big and husky with a fiery red beard well powdered with white coral dust. He reminded me of some wild Viking. I was glad we were on the same side.

Stooped under the heavy tanks on his back, Womack approached the pillbox with his assistant just out of the line of our fire. When they got about fifteen yards from the target, we ceased firing. The assistant reached up and turned a valve on the flamethrower. Womack then aimed the nozzle at the opening made by the 75mm gun. He pressed the trigger. With a *whoooooooosh* the flame leaped at the opening. Some muffled screams, then all quiet.

## MACARTHUR RETURNS TO THE PHILIPPINES, 20 OCTOBER 1944

*Two and half years after he was forced to leave Bataan, General MacArthur returned.*

People of the Philippines: I have returned. By the grace of Almighty God our forces stand again on Philippine soil – soil consecrated in the blood of our two peoples. . . . Rally to me. Let the indomitable spirit of Bataan and Corregidor lead on.

## KAMIKAZE ATTACKS, LEYTE GULF, 27 NOVEMBER 1944

### Seaman First Class James J. Fahey, US Navy

*Fahey was a gunner on the light cruiser USS* Montpellier.

*Diary: 27 November 1944*
At 10.50 A.M. this morning General Quarters sounded, all hands went to their battle stations. At the same time a battleship and a destroyer were alongside the tanker getting fuel. Out of the clouds I saw a big Jap bomber come crashing down into the water. It was not smoking and looked in good condition. It felt like I was in it as it hit the water not too far from the tanker, and the 2 ships that were refueling. One of our P-38 fighters hit it. He must have got the pilot. At first I thought it was one of our bombers that had engine trouble. It was not long after that when a force of about 30 Jap planes attacked us. Dive bombers and torpedo planes. Our two ships were busy getting away from the tanker because one bomb-hit on the tanker and it would be all over for the 3 ships.

The 2 ships finally got away from the tanker and joined the circle. I think the destroyers were on the outside of the circle. It looked funny to see the tanker all by itself in the center of the ships as we circled it, with our guns blazing away as the planes tried to break through. It was quite a sight, better than the movies . . . Jap planes were coming at us from all directions. Before the attack started we did not know that they were suicide planes, with no intention of returning to their base. They had one thing in mind and that was to crash into our ships, bombs and all. You have to blow them up, to damage them doesn't mean much. Right off the bat a Jap plane made a suicide dive at the cruiser *St. Louis*, there was a big explosion and flames were seen shortly from the stern. Another one tried to do the same thing but he was shot down. A Jap plane came in on a battleship with its guns blazing away. Other Jap planes came in strafing one ship, dropping their bombs on another and crashing into another ship. The Jap planes were falling all around us, the air was full of Jap machine gun bullets. Jap planes and bombs were hitting all around us. Some of our ships were being hit by suicide planes, bombs and machine gun fire . . . While all this was taking place our ship had its hands full with Jap planes. We knocked our share of planes down but we also got hit by 3 suicide planes, but lucky for us they dropped their bombs before they crashed into us. In the meantime exploding planes overhead were showering us with their parts. It looked like it was raining plane parts. They were falling all over the ship. Quite a few of the men were hit by big pieces of Jap planes. We were supposed to have air coverage but all we had was 4 P-38 fighters, and when we opened up on the Jap planes they got out of the range of our exploding shells. They must have had a ring side seat of the show. The men on my mount were also showered with parts of Jap planes. One suicide dive bomber was heading right for us while we were firing at other attacking planes and if the 40 mm. mount behind us on the port side did not blow the Jap wing off it would have killed all of us. When the wing was blown off it, the plane turned some and bounced off into the water and the bombs blew part of the plane onto our ship. Another suicide plane crashed into one of the 5 inch mounts, pushing the side of the mount in and injuring some of the men inside. A lot of 5 inch shells were damaged. It was a miracle they did not explode. If that happened the powder and shells would have blown up the ship. Our 40 mm. mount is not too far away. The men threw the 5 inch shells over the side. They expected them to go off at any time. A Jap dive bomber crashed into one of the 40 mm. mounts but lucky for them it dropped its bombs on another ship before crashing. Parts of the plane flew everywhere when it crashed into the mount. Part of the motor hit Tomlinson, he had chunks of it all over him, his stomach, back, legs etc. The rest of the crew were wounded, most of them were sprayed with gasoline from the plane. Tomlinson was thrown a great distance and at first they thought he was knocked over the side. They finally found him in a corner in bad shape. One of the mt. Captains had the wires cut on his phones and kept talking into the phone, because he did not know they were cut by shrapnel until one of the fellows told him. The explosions were terrific as the suicide planes exploded in the water not too far away from our ship. The water was covered with black smoke that rose high into the air. The water looked like it was on fire. It would have been curtains for us if they had crashed into us.

Another suicide plane just overshot us. It grazed the 6 inch turret. It crashed into Leyte Gulf. There was a terrific explosion as the bombs exploded, about 20 ft. away. If we were going a little faster we would have been hit. The Jap planes that were not destroyed with our shells crashed into the water close by or hit our ships. It is a tough job to hold back this tidal wave of suicide planes. They come at you from all directions and also straight down at us at a very fast pace but some of the men have time for a few fast jokes, "This would be a great time to run out of ammunition." "This is mass suicide at its best." Another suicide plane came down at us in a very steep dive. It was a near miss, it just missed the 5 inch mount. The starboard side of the ship was showered with water and fragments . . . This was very close to my 40 mm. mount and we were showered with debris. If the suicide plane exploded on the 5 inch mount, the ammunition would have gone up, after that anything could happen.

Planes were falling all around us, bombs were coming too close for comfort. The Jap planes were cutting up the water with machine gun fire. All the guns on the ships were blazing away, talk about action, never a dull moment . . . Parts of destroyed suicide planes were scattered all over the ship . . . The deck near my mount was covered with blood, guts, brains, tongues, scalps, hearts, arms etc. from the Jap pilots. . . . They had to put the hose on to wash the blood off the deck. The deck ran red with blood . . .

. . . I have not heard how many planes our ship shot down but at one period of the attack our ship shot down 4 suicide planes within 2 minutes. I think most of the Jap planes that attacked us were destroyed. The attack lasted for 2 hours, we went to battle stations at 10:50 A.M. in the morning and secured at 2:10 P.M. in the afternoon. The action took place not too far from Leyte. Every ship had its hands full with the Jap planes during those 2 hours. The Japs started the attack with 30 planes but after that more planes kept joining them.

After we secured from General Quarters the men looked the ship over to see the damage. The ship was a mess, part of it was damaged, cables were down, steel life lines snapped and steel posts broken. Big pieces of Jap planes were scattered all over the ship, life rafts damaged. Our empty shell cases were everywhere. Some of the other ships were in worse condition than ours. The wounded were brought down to sick bay and some had to be operated on at once.

When it was all over the tanker was still in the middle of the circle and the Japs did not hit it . . .

# "A FRIGHTFUL FATE": JAPANESE SOLDIERS HOLD OUT IN THE MANGROVE SWAMPS OF RAMREE, BURMA, 17 JANUARY–22 FEBRUARY 1945

## *Captain Eric Bush RN, SNO Advanced Force "W"*

*Ramree is an island separated from the mainland of Burma by mangrove swamps.*

As soon as the bridge-head was secured, our troops advanced down the west coast road; but neither they, nor the *Queen Elizabeth*'s bombardment, could shift the Japs, so our troops were ordered to by-pass them and march on Ramree town. Destroyers were sent up the eastern shores to support them, while further landings were made. The Japanese position was thus turned, ending their effective resistance. Those who survived drifted into the swamps, seeking to escape to the mainland, but a frightful fate awaited them.

Three days after the initial assault, I had been landed to join General Lomax at his headquarters in Kyaulkpyu. Here, in a tumbledown house formerly occupied by the Japanese military staff, we planned Operation *Block*. It directed the Army to drive the Japanese into the swamps and the Navy to block their escape routes. The destroyers *Pathfinder* and *Paladin* were ordered as far up the *chaungs* as we dared send them. Mine-sweepers and M.L.s penetrated farther still, while minor landing-craft, with army machine-gun sections embarked, were hidden in the mangroves. A prey to flies, mosquitoes, scorpions, and, most horrible, the crocodiles, and without food or water, the Japanese died in hundreds. By night some tried to swim or raft across the *chaungs* on bamboos plugged at either end, and were shot by our patrols. Others, trying to escape in native boats, met a similar fate. It can hardly be possible that, in their decision to quit, the Japanese could have realized the appalling conditions.

Then suddenly we changed our plan. We lit up the *chaungs* at night with searchlights, motor car headlamps, flares, signal lamps, torches – anything we could find. That surprised the Japs and helped us slaughter more of them.

In the misty dawn of February 19th, after a night in which more than a hundred of the enemy had been ambushed, a Japanese officer, who could bear it no longer, came floating down the Mingaung Chaung sitting astride a log. He gave himself up to M.L. 437, where he was allowed to rest while I was being fetched with an interpreter.

"*Konnichi wa.*"

He struggled painfully to his feet and bowed politely at our greeting. He was short and dark, about forty years old, and wore a stubble of beard and thick, matted hair. Naked except for a *fundoshi* round his loins, he presented a pathetic sight with his body scratched and bruised and a mass of insect bites.

"Who are you?" we asked.

"I am Captain Asahina of the Medical Corps", he explained, giving details of his regiment and next of kin. Then, in answer to further questions, he explained that he had obeyed orders by staying on Ramree Island; he had also obeyed orders by suffering the terrible hardships of the mangrove swamp; but, as his Divisional Commander had not kept his promise to evacuate him, he saw no reason to be ashamed of being made a prisoner of war.

It was not the practice of the Japanese Army to tell their soldiers how to behave when captured, as no one was expected to give himself up. Asahina, therefore, had to decide for himself what he should do or say. He had been kindly treated (instead of being killed by his captors as he had probably been led to expect) and had been given food and drink, which he had accepted and enjoyed. It was now up to him as a Japanese gentleman to return this hospitality in some way. If he could do so by answering questions, his conscience would be clear. He adopted this attitude throughout the interrogation, ending with a promise to try and persuade his colleagues to come out of their hiding-places and follow his example.

So early next morning Asahina was put on the bridge of our M.L. and told to shout down a loud-hailer while we cruised up and down. A pair of landing-craft followed with guards embarked and cargo nets stretched across their holds to house the prisoners.

I can hear Asahina's raucous voice as I write. I can see him, in borrowed clothes, much too big for him, peering over the bridge screen. "*Atsumare*", he shouted all the time as he called on his men to surrender.

The sun rose and sank. But not a single Japanese appeared. At sunset I returned to base, telling the *chaung* blockers to get on with the killing.

That night the interpreter showed me some photographs taken off Japanese bodies found floating about in the *chaungs*. They were not just snapshots, but photograph albums pages thick. Although relations between man and wife in Japan are more a matter of duty than of love in the way we understand it, fathers adore their children as these photographs showed. Yet they chose to die rather than surrender.

On February 22nd the ships and craft were withdrawn. Next day a few survivors crawled out of the swamps in search of food and water and were dealt with by our soldiers. Of the 1,000 Japs who had held Ramree, no more than twenty surrendered.

# THE TUNNELS OF IWO JIMA, FEBRUARY–MARCH 1945

## *USMC Correspondents*

*Iwo Jima was sought by the US as a site for fighter planes to escort B29s on raids on Japan. The volcanic island, 800 miles from Tokyo was heavily fortified by the Japanese, who had mined it with tunnels. The invasion, launched on 19 February, was expected to take eight days; it took five weeks and cost 6,821 American lives and almost every one of the 21,000 Japanese garrison.*

No one knew how many Japs were in the ridge or where they had come from, or when. A supply captain, coming up from the rear, saw what was going on and radioed for tanks and demolitions men. More Marines from neighboring units gathered. They inspected the ridge from safety points behind some rocks.

When the tanks arrived, the Marines had started the step-by-step of again cleaning out the ridge. The dangerous and tedious work that had originally been done on D plus 16 by the front-line troops had to be repeated. The Marines threw smoke bombs and phosphorous grenades against the rocks and moved in with bazookas and automatic weapons. When the smoke drifted away, they had to shoot fast, or a Jap would catch them from one of the many holes. The tanks hurled their 75s at every position their gunners could locate. Engineers tried to fling dynamite charges into the caves.

Despite their preponderance of weapons, the Marines found that there were too many holes. They would attack one only to be shot at from another one half a dozen feet away. Moreover, the ridge was not a straight wall but, in many places, curved like an S. Entranceways protected each other, so that Marines would be hit in the back from holes guarding the one they were assaulting. The interconnecting tunnels inside the ridge also allowed the Japs to play deadly tag with the Marines. They would shoot out of one hole. But by the time Marines got close enough to that hole, the Japs had left it and were shooting from another one twenty yards away and higher up in the wall. The Marines had to post guards at every hole they could see in order to attack any of them. The tunnel also curved and twisted inside the ridge. The Japs could escape the straight trajectory weapons and grenades thrown into the cave entrances, merely by running back into the interior.

Finally flamethrowers were called. They threw long jets of flaming liquid into the holes and along the curving walls of the tunnels. The roaring flames did the trick. The Marines heard the Japs howling. A few rushed out of the caves on fire. The Marines shot them or knocked them down and beat out the flames and took them prisoners. When the Marines began to hear muffled explosions inside the caves, they guessed that some of the Japs were blowing themselves up with hand grenades.

The scene became wild and terrible. More Japs rushed screaming from the caves. They tumbled over the rocks, their clothes and bodies burning fiercely. Soon the flame-throwers paused. A Marine lifted himself cautiously into view. There were no shots from the caves. A Jap with his clothes in rags hunched himself out of one hole, his arms upraised. The Marines stood up behind the rocks and waved to him to come out. The Jap indicated that there were more who would like to surrender. The Marines motioned him to tell them to come out.

Almost forty scared and beaten men emerged from different holes. Some of them had round pudding faces. They grinned nervously and said they were Koreans. They had been forced by the Japs to stay in the caves. They said that everyone else in the caves had either been burned to death or had committed suicide.

The Marines sent them to the rear. Then they groped cautiously among the rocks from hole to hole, examining each entranceway. Dead bodies, some hit by bullets and grenade fragments, some burned into frightful black lumps, lay in the holes. The smell was overwhelming and men turned away in disgust.

The battle of the ridge seemed over. An officer made a note to bring up demolition crews as soon as they could be spared by the front-line companies. They would seal up the holes in this troublesome ridge. The Marines gathered their casualties and drifted away. The tanks shifted into reverse and backed out. Peacefulness settled once more over the area.

But it was not for long. The sudden death, which we had come on, was to strike again from the ridge, this time bitterly close.

That same day, several hours later, Sergeant Reid Chamberlain (El Cajon, Calif.) came up to the aid station. He was on his way to a front-line company. Chamberlain was a prominent figure in the Marine Corps. He had served with General MacArthur on Bataan and Corregidor early in the war. He had escaped from Corregidor to help organize Filipino guerrilla bands. He had stayed in the Philippines a year and a half and had been commissioned a lieutenant in the U.S. Army. Finally he had returned to America and been awarded the Distinguished Service Cross. Then he had resigned his Army commission, re-enlisted as a sergeant in the Marines, and had come overseas again. He was now a battalion runner with the 21st Regiment. He was short and handsome and wore a brown mustache.

Despite the publicity that had been given to his exploits as a guerrilla leader in the Philippines, he had stayed modest and unassuming and was one of the most popular men in the outfit.

A small group of us accompanied Chamberlain to the front-line company. We began to cross the clearing which we thought had been rid of Jap sniper fire. To escape occasional mortar shells that were dropping in the open, we clung perhaps too closely to the rocky walls of the ridge. We were picking our way among the stones and the burned Jap bodies when three shots rang out from the hillside. We scattered and tried to run behind some boulders. Chamberlain drew his pistol and looked frantically around. There was another shot. We heard a thud. We thought the bullet had struck the curving side of the ridge.

When we reached safe spots, we paused and looked back. Our hearts beat wildly. Chamberlain was nowhere in sight. An ambulance driver and an automatic rifleman were crouched behind nearby rocks, their teeth clenched, their hands gripping their weapons. They were trying to find the hole from which the shots had come. We called Chamberlain but received no answer. Slowly we tried to edge back. Rifle shots cracked at us from several holes, and we ducked again.

The long, rocky ridge was once more alive with enemy. Again Marines began to gather, coming up cautiously to help us. They dashed from rock to rock and slid among the boulders, trying to seek cover from the many caves that looked out at us. We told them about Chamberlain, lying somewhere among the rocks. We formed a team quickly and began crawling forward. When the Japs fired at us again, the men covering us saw where the shots were coming from. They sent a stream of automatic fire at the holes and "buttoned up" the Japs. One burly sergeant stood straight up without a helmet on and, gritting his teeth, fired his carbine from his hip, moving directly at a hole as he fired. The jeep ambulance driver finally reached Chamberlain's body and lifted his head. A trickle of blood flowed from behind his ear. His eyes were open, but he was dead.

There is nothing you can say or do when a good friend is suddenly killed in battle. You feel stunned, angry, sad and somewhat frustrated. We could have fired point-blank the rest of the day at those holes. The Japs would only have laughed at us. In an instant they had claimed one of our best men. Chamberlain's wonderful war record had ended abruptly. After so many heroic deeds, it seemed an added tragedy that he was killed while doing nothing but walking. There was nothing anybody could do about it.

# THE DAGGER DIVISION TAKES MANDALAY, 20 MARCH 1945

## *John Masters, 4th Prince of Wales' Own Gurkha Rifles*

*Field Marshal Slim's plan for the defeat of the Japanese Army in Burma was to make the Japanese fight in the open country around Mandalay, where his armour and aircraft could be used to best effect. Thus part of the Fourteenth Army moved down the Irrawaddy from the north and west, while another moved secretly to reach the Irrawaddy far below the confluence with the Chinwin. The "Dagger" Division was the 19th Indian Division, commanded by General "Pete" Rees.*

We stood, so to speak, on top of Mandalay. We also stood, at much closer range, on top of a good many Japanese. The temples, cellars and mysterious chambers covering Mandalay Hill were made of reinforced concrete. The 4th Gurkhas had taken the summit, and no Japanese was alive and visible; but scores of them were alive, invisible, in the subterranean chambers.

A gruesome campaign of extermination began, among the temples of one of the most sacred places of the Buddhist faith. Sikh machine-gunners sat all day on the flat roofs, their guns aimed down the hill on either side of the covered stairway. Every now and then a Japanese put out his head and fired a quick upward shot. A Sikh got a bullet through his brain five yards from me. Our engineers brought up beehive charges, blew holes through the concrete, poured in petrol, and fired a Very light down the holes. Sullen explosions rocked the buildings and the Japanese rolled out into the open, but firing. Our machine-gunners pressed their thumb-pieces. The Japanese fell, burning. We blew in huge steel doors with Piats, rolled in kegs of petrol or oil, and set them on fire with tracer bullets. Our infantry fought into the tunnels behind a hail of grenades, and licking sheets of fire from flame-throwers. Grimly, under the stench of burning bodies and the growing pall of decay, past the equally repellent Buddhist statuary (showing famine, pestilence, men eaten by vultures) the battalions fought their way down the ridge to the southern foot – to face the moat and the thirty-foot-thick walls of Fort Dufferin.

Pete brought up the medium artillery, and the 5.5s hurled their 60-pound shells at the wall, over open sights, from four hundred yards. The shells made no impression. He called in the air force. P-47s tried skip bombing, B-24s dropped some 1,000-pound bombs, some inside the fort and some outside – among our troops.

We found a municipal employee who knew where the sewers led out of the fort, and prepared an assault party. All the while the infantry fought in the brick and stone rubble of the burning city, among corpses of children and dead dogs and the universal sheets of corrugated-iron. The night the sewer assault was to go in the Japanese withdrew from Mandalay. Next morning coal-black Madrassi sappers blew in the main gate, and Pete walked in, surrounded by a cheering, yelling mob of a dozen races. Just as Pete – but not his superiors – had planned, the Dagger Division had taken Mandalay.

## OKINAWA: AN INFANTRYMAN'S NIGHTMARE, APRIL 1945

### John Garcia, 7th Division US Infantry

*Like Iwo Jima, Okinawa was sought as a fighter-base for P-51s. Like Iwo Jima it was honeycombed by the Japanese with defensive tunnels.*

Our next stop was Okinawa. We landed there on April 1, '45. No opposition. Several days later, we got word that President Roosevelt had died. We were all sort of down – boom! They said a man called Truman replaced him. I said, "Who is Truman?" We were there eighty-two days. I did what I had to do. When I saw a Japanese, I shot at him and ducked. Shot and ducked, that's all I did. I was always scared until we took Hill 87.

We buried General Ushijima and his men inside a cave. This was the worst part of the war, which I didn't like about Okinawa. They were hiding in caves all the time, women, children, soldiers. We'd get up on the cliff and lower down barrels of gasoline and then shoot at it. It would explode and just bury them to death.

I personally shot one Japanese woman because she was coming across a field at night. We kept dropping leaflets not to cross the field at night because we couldn't tell if they were soldiers. We set up a perimeter. Anything in front, we'd shoot at. This one night I shot and when it came daylight, it was a woman there and a baby tied to her back. The bullet had all gone through her and out the baby's back.

That still bothers me, that hounds me. I still feel I committed murder. You see a figure in the dark, it's stooped over. You don't know if it's a soldier or a civilian.

I was drinking about a fifth and a half of whiskey every day. Sometimes homemade, sometimes what I could buy. It was the only way I could kill. I had friends who were Japanese and I kept thinking every time I pulled a trigger on a man or pushed a flamethrower down into a hole: What is this person's family gonna say when he doesn't come back? He's got a wife, he's got children, somebody.

They would show us movies. Japanese women didn't cry. They

would accept the ashes stoically. I knew different. They went home and cried.

I'd get up each day and start drinking. How else could I fight the war? Sometimes we made the booze, sometimes we bought it from the navy. The sailors stole it from their officers. (Laughs.) Sometimes it cost us seventy-five dollars a bottle, sometimes it cost us a Japanese flag. You'd take a piece of parachute silk, make a circle on it, put a few bullet holes in it, give it to the navy, and they'd give you a bottle of whiskey . . .

Oh, I still lose nights of sleep because of that woman I shot. I still lose a lot of sleep. I still dream about her. I dreamed about it perhaps two weeks ago . . . (He lets out a deep breath; it's something more turbulent than a sigh.)

*John Garcia was speaking in 1984.*

## "I SHALL FALL LIKE A BLOSSOM FROM A RADIANT CHERRY TREE": A KAMIKAZE PILOT'S LAST LETTER, MAY 1945

### *Flying Petty Officer First Class Isao Matsuo, Special Attack Corps*

*The first suicide attacks by Japanese pilots came at Leyte Gulf on 25 October 1944. "Kamikaze" strikes increased thereafter as the military situation worsened for the Japanese. During the battle of Okinawa, no less than 1,900 kamikaze missions were flown against the US fleet standing off the island.*

Dear Parents:

Please congratulate me. I have been given a splendid opportunity to die. This is my last day. The destiny of our homeland hinges on the decisive battle in the seas to the south where I shall fall like a blossom from a radiant cherry tree.

I shall be a shield for His Majesty and die cleanly along with my squadron leader and other friends. I wish that I could be born seven times, each time to smite the enemy.

How I appreciate this chance to die like a man! I am grateful from the depths of my heart to the parents who have reared me with their constant prayers and tender love. And I am grateful as well to my squadron leader and superior officers who have looked after me as if I were their own son and given me such careful training.

Thank you, my parents, for the twenty-three years during which you have cared for me and inspired me. I hope that my present deed will in some small way repay what you have done for me. Think well of me and know that your Isao died for our country. This is my last wish, and there is nothing else that I desire.

I shall return in spirit and look forward to your visit at the Yasukuni Shrine. Please take good care of yourselves.

How glorious is the Special Attack Corps' Giretsu Unit whose Suisei bombers will attack the enemy. Movie cameramen have been here to take our pictures. It is possible that you may see us in newsreels at the theater.

We are sixteen warriors manning the bombers. May our death be as sudden and clean as the shattering of crystal.

Written at Manila on the eve of our sortie.

Isao

Soaring into the sky of the southern seas, it is our glorious mission to die as the shields of His Majesty. Cherry blossoms glisten as they open and fall.

# THE ALLIES DECIDE TO DROP THE ATOMIC BOMB ON JAPAN, POTSDAM, 25 JULY 1945

## *President Harry S. Truman*

*Diary: Potsdam 25 July 1945*

We met at eleven today. That is Stalin, Churchill, and the US President. But I had a most important session with Lord Mountbatten and General Marshall before that. We have discovered the most terrible bomb in the history of the world. It may be the fire destruction prophesied in the Euphrates Valley Era, after Noah and his fabulous Ark.

Anyway we "think" we have found the way to cause a disintegration of the atom. An experiment in the New Mexican desert was startling – to put it mildly. Thirteen pounds of the explosive caused the complete disintegration of a steel tower 60 feet high, created a crater 6 feet deep and 1,200 feet in diameter, knocked over a steel tower ½ mile away and knocked men down 10,000 yards away. The explosion was visible for more than 200 miles and audible for 40 miles and more.

This weapon is to be used against Japan between now and August 10th. I have told the Sec. of War, Mr Stimson, to use it so that military objectives and soldiers and sailors are the target and not women and children. Even if the Japs are savages, ruthless, merciless and fanatic, we as the leader of the world for the common welfare cannot drop this terrible bomb on the old capital or the new.

He and I are in accord. The target will be a purely military one and we will issue a warning statement asking the Japs to surrender and save lives. I'm sure they will not do that, but we will have given them the chance. It is certainly a good thing for the world that Hitler's crowd or Stalin's did not discover this atomic bomb. It seems to be the most terrible thing ever discovered, but it can be made the most useful.

*The following day, 26 July, the Allies called upon Japan to surrender. The alternative they said was "prompt and utter destruction". Japan did not surrender.*

## HIROSHIMA, 6 AUGUST 1945

### *Colonel Tibbets, USAAF*

*The destruction promised by the Allies came on 6 August, when three B29s of the US Air Force took off from Tinian and flew to Hiroshima, the eighth largest city in Japan. One of the planes, the Enola Gay, carried an atomic bomb. The commander of the mission was Colonel Tibbets.*

Up to this point it was common practice in any theatre of war to fly straight ahead, fly level, drop your bombs, and keep right on going, because you could bomb several thousands of feet in the air and you could cross the top of the place that you had bombed with no concern whatsoever. But it was determined by the scientists that, in order to escape and maintain the integrity of the aircraft and the crew, that this aeroplane could not fly forward after it had dropped the bomb. It had to turn around and get away from that bomb as fast as it could. If you placed this aeroplane in a very steep angle of bank to make this turn, if you turned 158 degrees from the direction that you were going, you would then begin to place distance between yourself and that point of explosion as quickly as possible. You had to get away from the shock wave that would be coming back from the ground in the form of an ever expanding circle as it came upwards. It's necessary to make this turn to get yourself as far as possible from an expanding ring and 158 degrees happened to be the turn for that particular circle. It was difficult. It was something that was not done with a big bomber aeroplane. You didn't make this kind of a steep turn – you might almost call it an acrobatic manoeuvre – and the big aircraft didn't do these things. However, we refined it, we learned how to do it. It had been decided earlier that there was a possibility that an accident could occur on take-off, and so therefore we would not arm this weapon until we had left the runway and were out to sea. This of course meant that had there been an accident there would have been an explosion from normal powder charges but there would not have been a nuclear explosion. As I said this worried more people than it worried me because I had plenty of faith in my aeroplane. I knew my engines were good. We started our take-off on time which was somewhere about two-forty-five I think, and the aeroplane went on down the runway. It was loaded quite heavily but it responded exactly like I had anticipated it would. I had flown this aeroplane the same way before and there was no problem and there was nothing different this night in the way we went. We arrived over the initial point and started in on the bomb run which had about eleven minutes to go, rather a long type of run for a bomb but on the other hand we felt we needed this extra time in straight and level flight to stabilize the air speed of the aeroplane, to get everything right down to the last-minute detail. As I indicated earlier the problem after the release of the bomb is not to proceed forward but to turn away. As soon as the weight had left the aeroplane I immediately went into this steep turn and we tried then to place distance between ourselves and the point of impact. In this particular case that bomb took fifty-three seconds from the time it left the aeroplane until it exploded and this gave us adequate time of course to make the turn. We had just made the turn and rolled out on level flight when it seemed like somebody had grabbed a hold of my aeroplane and gave it a real hard shaking because this was the shock wave that had come up. Now after we had been hit by a second shock wave not quite so strong as the first one I decided we'll turn around and go back and take a look. The day was clear when we dropped that bomb, it was a clear sunshiny day and the visibility was unrestricted. As we came back around again facing the direction of Hiroshima we saw this cloud coming up. The cloud by this time, now two minutes old, was up at our altitude. We were 33,000 feet at this time and the cloud was up there and continuing to go right on up in a boiling fashion, as if it was rolling and boiling. The surface was nothing but a black boiling, like a barrel of tar. Where before there had been a city with distinctive houses, buildings and everything that you could see from our altitude, now you couldn't see anything except a black boiling debris down below.

*The first atomic bomb to be dropped in warfare killed 80,000 inhabitants – a quarter of Hiroshima's inhabitants.*

## NAGASAKI, 9 AUGUST 1945

### *Tatsuichiro Akizuki*

*Three days after Hiroshima a second atomic bomb was dropped, this time on Nagasaki. Tatsuichiro Akizuki was working in Nagasaki as a doctor when the bomb landed.*

It was eleven o'clock. Father Ishikawa, who was Korean, aged about thirty-six and the hospital chaplain, was listening in the hospital chapel to the confessions of those Catholics who had gone to him to confess, one after the other, before the great festival, on 15 August, of the Ascension of the Virgin Mary, which was only a week away. Brother Joseph Iwanaga was toiling outside the hospital with some farm workers, digging another air-raid shelter in the shrubbery in the centre of the hospital yard. Mr Noguchi had just begun to repair the apparatus used to lift water from the well. Other members of staff were busy providing a late breakfast. Some were filling big bowls with miso soup; others were carrying them through the corridors or up the stairs. The hospital was a hive of activity after the all-clear.

"Well, we'll soon be getting our breakfast," I said to Miss Murai. "The patient must be hungry."

So was I, but before we had our breakfast we would have to finish treating all the out-patients.

I stuck the pneumo-thorax needle into the side of the chest of the patient lying on the bed. It was just after eleven a.m.

I heard a low droning sound, like that of distant aeroplane engines.

"What's that?" I said. "The all-clear has gone, hasn't it?"

At the same time the sound of the plane's engines, growing louder and louder, seemed to swoop down over the hospital.

I shouted: "It's an enemy plane! Look out – take cover!"

As I said so, I pulled the needle out of the patient and threw myself beside the bed.

There was a blinding white flash of light, and the next moment – *Bang! Crack!* A huge impact like a gigantic blow smote down upon our bodies, our heads and our hospital. I lay flat – I didn't know whether or not of my own volition. Then down came piles of debris, slamming into my back.

The hospital has been hit, I thought. I grew dizzy, and my ears sang.

Some minutes or so must have passed before I staggered to my feet and looked around. The air was heavy with yellow smoke; white flakes of powder drifted about; it was strangely dark.

Thank God, I thought – I'm not hurt! But what about the patients?

As it became brighter, little by little our situation grew clearer. Miss Murai, who had been assisting me with the pneumo-thorax, struggled to her feet beside me. She didn't seem to have been seriously injured, though she was completely covered with white dust. "Hey, cheer up!" I said. "We're not hurt, thank God!"

I helped her to her feet. Another nurse, who was also in the consulting room, and the patient, managed to stand up. The man, his face smeared white like a clown and streaked with blood, lurched towards the door, holding his bloody head with his hands and moaning.

I said to myself over and over again: Our hospital has suffered a direct hit – We've been bombed! Because the hospital stood on a hill and had walls of red brick, it must, I thought, have attracted the attention of enemy planes. I felt deeply and personally responsible for what had happened.

The pervading dingy yellow silence of the room now resounded with faint cries – "Help!" The surface of the walls and ceiling had peeled away. What I had thought to be clouds of dust or smoke was whirling brick-dust and plaster. Neither the pneumo-thorax apparatus nor the microscope on my desk were anywhere to be seen. I felt as if I were dreaming.

I encouraged Miss Murai, saying: "Come on, we haven't been hurt at all, by the grace of God. We must rescue the in-patients." But privately I thought it must be all over with them – the second and third floors must have disintegrated, I thought.

We went to the door of the consulting room which faced the main stairway, and there were the in-patients coming down the steps, crying: "Help me, doctor! Oh, help me, sir." The stairs and the corridor were heaped with timbers, plaster, debris from the ceiling. It made walking difficult. The patients staggered down towards us, crying: "I'm hurt! Help me!" Strangely, none seemed to have been seriously injured, only slightly wounded, with fresh blood dripping from their faces and hand.

If the bomb had actually hit the hospital, I thought, they would have been far more badly injured.

"What's happened to the second and third floors?" I cried. But all they answered was – "Help me! Help!"

One of them said: "Mr Yamaguchi has been buried under the debris. Help him."

No one knew what had happened. A huge force had been released above our heads. What it was, nobody knew. Had it been several tons of bombs, or the suicidal destruction of a plane carrying a heavy bomb-load?

Dazed, I retreated into the consulting room, in which the only upright object on the rubbish-strewn floor was my desk. I went and sat on it and looked out of the window at the yard and the outside world. There was not a single pane of glass in the window, not even a frame – all had been completely blown away. Out in the yard dun-coloured smoke or dust cleared little by little. I saw figures running. Then, looking to the south-west, I was stunned. The sky was as dark as pitch, covered with dense clouds of smoke; under that blackness, over the earth, hung a yellow-brown fog. Gradually the veiled ground became visible, and the view beyond rooted me to the spot with horror.

All the buildings I could see were on fire: large ones and small ones and those with straw-thatched roofs. Further off along the valley, Urakami Church, the largest Catholic church in the east, was ablaze. The technical school, a large two-storeyed wooden building, was on fire, as were many houses and the distant ordnance factory. Electricity poles were wrapped in flame like so many pieces of kindling. Trees on the nearby hills were smoking, as were the leaves of sweet potatoes in the fields. To say that everything burned is not enough. It seemed as if the earth itself emitted fire and smoke, flames that writhed up and erupted from underground. The sky was dark, the ground was scarlet, and in between hung clouds of yellowish smoke. Three kinds of colour – black, yellow and scarlet – loomed ominously over the people, who ran about like so many ants seeking to escape. What had happened? Urakami Hospital had not been bombed – I understood that much. But that ocean of fire, that sky of smoke! It seemed like the end of the world.

I ran out into the garden. Patients who were only slightly hurt came up to me, pleading for aid.

I shouted at them: "For heaven's sake! You're not seriously wounded!"

One patient said: "Kawaguchi and Matsuo are trapped in their rooms! They can't move. You must help them!"

I said to myself: Yes, we must first of all rescue those seriously ill tubercular patients who've been buried under the ruins.

I looked southwards again, and the sight of Nagasaki city in a sea of flames as far as the eye could reach made me think that such destruction could only have been caused by thousands of bombers, carpet-bombing. But not a plane was to be seen or heard, although even the leaves of potatoes and carrots at my feet were scorched and smouldering. The electricity cables must have exploded underground, I thought.

And then at last I identified the destroyer – "That's it!" I cried. "It was the new bomb – the one used on Hiroshima!"

# Epilogue

## The Execution of Nazi War Criminals at Nuremberg, 1946

# EXECUTION OF NAZI WAR CRIMINALS, NUREMBERG, 16 OCTOBER 1946

## *Kingsbury Smith, American Press Representative*

*The trials held by the International Military Tribunal at Nuremberg found twelve of the surviving members of Nazi Germany guilty of crimes against humanity. The twelve, who included Martin Bormann, tried in absentia, were sentenced to death by hanging.*

Hermann Wilhelm Göring cheated the gallows of Allied justice by committing suicide in his prison cell shortly before the ten other condemned Nazi leaders were hanged in Nuremberg gaol. He swallowed cyanide he had concealed in a copper cartridge shell, while lying on a cot in his cell.

The one-time Number Two man in the Nazi hierarchy was dead two hours before he was scheduled to have been dropped through the trapdoor of a gallows erected in a small, brightly lighted gymnasium in the gaol yard, thirty-five yards from the cell block where he spent his last days of ignominy.

Joachim von Ribbentrop, foreign minister in the ill-starred regime of Adolf Hitler, took Göring's place as first to the scaffold.

Last to depart this life in a total span of just about two hours was Arthur Seyss-Inquart, former *Gauleiter* of Holland and Austria.

In between these two once-powerful leaders, the gallows claimed, in the order named, Field Marshal Wilhelm Keitel; Ernst Kaltenbrunner, once head of the Nazis' security police; Alfred Rosenberg, arch-priest of Nazi culture in foreign lands; Hans Frank, *Gauleiter* of Poland; Wilhelm Frick, Nazi minister of the interior; Fritz Sauckel, boss of slave labour; Colonel General Alfred Jodl; and Julius Streicher, who bossed the anti-Semitism drive of the Hitler Reich.

As they went to the gallows, most of the ten endeavored to show bravery. Some were defiant and some were resigned and some begged the Almighty for mercy.

All except Rosenberg made brief, last-minute statements on the scaffold. But the only one to make any reference to Hitler or the Nazi ideology in his final moments was Julius Streicher.

Three black-painted wooden scaffolds stood inside the gymnasium, a room approximately thirty-three feet wide by eighty feet long with plaster walls in which cracks showed. The gymnasium had been used only three days before by the American security guards for a basketball game. Two gallows were used alternately. The third was a spare for use if needed. The men were hanged one at a time, but to get the executions over with quickly, the military police would bring in a man while the prisoner who preceded him still was dangling at the end of the rope.

The ten once great men in Hitler's Reich that was to have lasted for a thousand years walked up thirteen wooden steps to a platform eight feet high which also was eight feet square.

Ropes were suspended from a crossbeam supported on two posts. A new one was used for each man.

When the trap was sprung, the victim dropped from sight in the interior of the scaffolding. The bottom of it was boarded up with wood on three sides and shielded by a dark canvas curtain on the fourth, so that no one saw the death struggles of the men dangling with broken necks.

Von Ribbentrop entered the execution chamber at 1.11 a.m. Nuremberg time. He was stopped immediately inside the door by two Army sergeants who closed in on each side of him and held his arms, while another sergeant who had followed him in removed manacles from his hands and replaced them with a leather strap.

It was planned originally to permit the condemned men to walk from their cells to the execution chamber with their hands free, but all were manacled immediately following Göring's suicide.

Von Ribbentrop was able to maintain his apparent stoicism to the last. He walked steadily toward the scaffold between his two guards, but he did not answer at first when an officer standing at the foot of the gallows went through the formality of asking his name. When the query was repeated he almost shouted, "Joachim von Ribbentrop!" and then mounted the steps without any sign of hesitation.

When he was turned around on the platform to face the witnesses, he seemed to clench his teeth and raise his head with the old arrogance. When asked whether he had any final message he said, "God protect Germany," in German, and then added, "May I say something else?"

The interpreter nodded and the former diplomatic wizard of Nazidom spoke his last words in loud, firm tones: "My last wish is that Germany realize its entity and that an understanding be reached between the East and the West. I wish peace to the world."

As the black hood was placed in position on his head, von Ribbentrop looked straight ahead.

Then the hangman adjusted the rope, pulled the lever, and von Ribbentrop slipped away to his fate.

Field Marshal Keitel, who was immediately behind von Ribbentrop in the order of executions, was the first military leader to be executed under the new concept of international law – the principle that professional soldiers cannot escape punishment for waging aggressive wars and permitting crimes against humanity with the claim they were dutifully carrying out orders of superiors.

Keitel entered the chamber two minutes after the trap had dropped beneath von Ribbentrop, while the latter still was at the end of his rope. But von Ribbentrop's body was concealed inside the first scaffold; all that could be seen was the taut rope.

Keitel did not appear as tense as von Ribbentrop. He held his head high while his hands were being tied and walked erect toward the gallows with a military bearing. When asked his name he responded loudly and mounted the gallows as he might have mounted a reviewing stand to take a salute from German armies.

He certainly did not appear to need the help of guards who walked alongside, holding his arms. When he turned around atop the platform he looked over the crowd with the iron-jawed haughtiness of a proud Prussian officer. His last words, uttered in a full, clear voice, were translated as "I call on God Almighty to have mercy on the German people. More than 2 million German soldiers went to their death for the fatherland before me. I follow now my sons – all for Germany."

After his black-booted, uniformed body plunged through the trap, witnesses agreed Keitel had showed more courage on the scaffold than in the courtroom, where he had tried to shift his guilt upon the ghost of Hitler, claiming that all was the Führer's fault and that he merely carried out orders and had no responsibility.

With both von Ribbentrop and Keitel hanging at the end of their ropes there was a pause in the proceedings. The American colonel directing the executions asked the American general representing the United States on the Allied Control Commission if those present could smoke. An affirmative answer brought cigarettes into the hands of almost every one of the thirty-odd persons present. Officers and GIs walked around nervously or spoke a few words to one another in hushed voices while Allied correspondents scribbled furiously their notes on this historic though ghastly event.

In a few minutes an American Army doctor accompanied by a Russian Army doctor and both carrying stethoscopes walked to the first scaffold, lifted the curtain and disappeared within.

They emerged at 1.30 a.m. and spoke to an American colonel. The colonel swung around and facing official witnesses snapped to attention to say, "The man is dead."

Two GIs quickly appeared with a stretcher which was carried up and lifted into the interior of the scaffold. The hangman mounted the gallows steps, took a large commando-type knife out of a sheath strapped to his side and cut the rope.

Von Ribbentrop's limp body with the black hood still over his head was removed to the far end of the room and placed behind a black canvas curtain. This all had taken less than ten minutes.

The directing colonel turned to the witnesses and said, "Cigarettes out, please, gentlemen." Another colonel went out the door and over to the condemned block to fetch the next man. This was Ernst Kaltenbrunner. He entered the execution chamber at 1.36 a.m., wearing a sweater beneath his blue double-breasted coat. With his lean haggard face furrowed by old duelling scars, this terrible successor to Reinhard Heydrich had a frightening look as he glanced around the room.

He wet his lips apparently in nervousness as he turned to mount the gallows, but he walked steadily. He answered his name in a calm, low voice. When he turned around on the gallows platform he first faced a United States Army Roman Catholic chaplain wearing a Franciscan habit. When Kaltenbrunner was invited to make a last statement, he said, "I have loved my German people and my fatherland with a warm heart. I have done my duty by the laws of my people and I am sorry my people were led this time by men who were not soldiers and that crimes were committed of which I had no knowledge."

This was the man, one of whose agents – a man named Rudolf Hoess – confessed at a trial that under Kaltenbrunner's orders he gassed 3 million human beings at the Auschwitz concentration camp!

As the black hood was raised over his head Kaltenbrunner, still speaking in a low voice, used a German phrase which translated means, "Germany, good luck."

His trap was sprung at 1.39 a.m.

Field Marshal Keitel was pronounced dead at 1.44 a.m. and three minutes later guards had removed his body. The scaffold was made ready for Alfred Rosenberg.

Rosenberg was dull and sunken-cheeked as he looked around the court. His complexion was pasty-brown, but he did not appear nervous and walked with a steady step to and up the gallows.

Apart from giving his name and replying "no" to a question as to whether he had anything to say, he did not utter a word. Despite his avowed atheism he was accompanied by a Protestant chaplain who followed him to the gallows and stood beside him praying.

Rosenberg looked at the chaplain once, expressionless. Ninety seconds after he was swinging from the end of a hangman's rope. His was the swiftest execution of the ten.

There was a brief lull in the proceedings until Kaltenbrunner was pronounced dead at 1.52 a.m.

Hans Frank was next in the parade of death. He was the only one of the condemned to enter the chamber with a smile on his countenance.

Although nervous and swallowing frequently, this man, who was converted to Roman Catholicism after his arrest, gave the appearance of being relieved at the prospect of atoning for his evil deeds.

He answered to his name quietly and when asked for any last statement, he replied in a low voice that was almost a whisper, "I am thankful for the kind treatment during my captivity and I ask God to accept me with mercy."

Frank closed his eyes and swallowed as the black hood went over his head.

The sixth man to leave his prison cell and walk with handcuffed wrists to the death house was sixty-nine-year-old Wilhelm Frick. He entered the execution chamber at 2.05 a.m., six minutes after Rosenberg had been pronounced dead. He seemed the least steady of any so far and stumbled on the thirteenth step of the gallows. His only words were, "Long live eternal Germany," before he was hooded and dropped through the trap.

Julius Streicher made his melodramatic appearance at 2.12 a.m.

While his manacles were being removed and his hands bound, this ugly, dwarfish little man, wearing a threadbare suit and a well-worn bluish shirt buttoned to the neck but without a tie (he was notorious during his days of power for his flashy dress), glanced at the three wooden scaffolds rising up menacingly in front of him. Then he glared around the room, his eyes resting momentarily upon the small group of witnesses. By this time, his hands were tied securely behind his back. Two guards, one on each arm, directed him to Number One gallows on the left of the entrance. He walked steadily the six feet to the first wooden step but his face was twitching.

As the guards stopped him at the bottom of the steps for identification formality he uttered his piercing scream: "Heil Hitler!"

The shriek sent a shiver down my back.

As its echo died away an American colonel standing by the steps said sharply, "Ask the man his name." In response to the interpreter's query Streicher shouted, "You know my name well."

The interpreter repeated his request and the condemned man yelled, "Julius Streicher."

As he reached the platform, Streicher cried out, "Now it goes to God." He was pushed the last two steps to the mortal spot beneath the hangman's rope. The rope was being held back against a wooden rail by the hangman.

Streicher was swung around to face the witnesses and glared at them. Suddenly he screamed, "*Purim Fest 1946.*" (Purim is a Jewish holiday celebrated in the spring, commemorating the execution of Haman, ancient persecutor of the Jews described in the Old Testament.)

The American officer standing at the scaffold said, "Ask the man if he has any last words."

When the interpreter had translated, Streicher shouted, "The Bolsheviks will hang you one day."

When the black hood was raised over his head, Streicher said, "I am with God."

As it was being adjusted, Streicher's muffled voice could be heard to say, "Adele, my dear wife."

At that instant the trap opened with a loud bang. He went down kicking. When the rope snapped taut with the body swinging wildly, groans could be heard from within the concealed interior of the scaffold. Finally, the hangman, who had descended from the gallows platform, lifted the black canvas curtain and went inside. Something happened that put a stop to the groans and brought the rope to a standstill. After it was over I was not in a mood to ask what he did, but I assume that he grabbed the swinging body and pulled down on it. We were all of the opinion that Streicher had strangled.

Then, following removal of the corpse of Frick, who had been pronounced dead at 2.20 a.m., Fritz Sauckel was brought face to face with his doom.

Wearing a sweater with no coat and looking wild-eyed, Sauckel proved to be the most defiant of any except Streicher.

Here was the man who put millions into bondage on a scale unknown since the pre-Christian era. Gazing around the room from the gallows platform he suddenly screamed, "I am dying innocent. The sentence is wrong. God protect Germany and make Germany great again. Long live Germany! God protect my family."

The trap was sprung at 2.26 a.m. and, as in the case of Streicher, there was a loud groan from the gallows pit as the noose snapped tightly under the weight of his body.

Ninth in the procession of death was Alfred Jodl. With the black coat-collar of his *Wehrmacht* uniform half turned up at the back as though hurriedly put on, Jodl entered the dismal death house with obvious signs of nervousness. He wet his lips constantly and his features were drawn and haggard as he walked, not nearly so steady as Keitel, up the gallows steps. Yet his voice was calm when he uttered his last six words on earth: "My greetings to you, my Germany."

At 2.34 a.m. Jodl plunged into the black hole of the scaffold. He and Sauckel hung together until the latter was pronounced dead six minutes later and removed.

The Czechoslovak-born Seyss-Inquart, whom Hitler had made ruler of Holland and Austria, was the last actor to make his appearance in this unparalleled scene. He entered the chamber at 2.38 ½ a.m., wearing glasses which made his face an easily remembered caricature.

He looked around with noticeable signs of unsteadiness as he limped on his left clubfoot to the gallows. He mounted the steps slowly, with guards helping him.

When he spoke his last words his voice was low but intense. He said, "I hope that this execution is the last act of the tragedy of the Second World War and that the lesson taken from this world war will be that peace and understanding should exist between peoples. I believe in Germany."

He dropped to death at 2.45 a.m.

With the bodies of Jodl and Seyss-Inquart still hanging, awaiting formal pronouncement of death, the gymnasium doors opened again and guards entered carrying Göring's body on a stretcher.

He had succeeded in wrecking plans of the Allied Control Council to have him lead the parade of condemned Nazi chieftains to their death. But the council's representatives were determined that Göring at least would take his place as a dead man beneath the shadow of the scaffold.

The guards carrying the stretcher set it down between the first and second gallows. Göring's big bare feet stuck out from under the bottom end of a khaki-coloured United States Army blanket. One blue-silk-clad arm was hanging over the side.

The colonel in charge of the proceedings ordered the blanket removed so that witnesses and Allied correspondents could see for themselves that Göring was definitely dead. The Army did not want any legend to develop that Göring had managed to escape.

As the blanket came off it revealed Göring clad in black silk pyjamas with a blue jacket shirt over them, and this was soaking wet, apparently the result of efforts by prison doctors to revive him.

The face of this twentieth-century freebooting political racketeer was still contorted with the pain of his last agonizing moments and his final gesture of defiance.

They covered him up quickly and this Nazi warlord, who like a character out of the days of the Borgias, had wallowed in blood and beauty, passed behind a canvas curtain into the black pages of history.

# SOURCES AND ACKNOWLEDGMENTS

The editor has made every effort to locate all persons having rights in the selections appearing in this anthology and to secure permission for usage from the holders of such rights. Any queries regarding the use of material should be addressed to the editor c/o the publishers.

## Part I: Blitzkrieg

Anderson, Sir John, "The Protection of Your Home Against Air Raids", quoted in *Lilliput Goes to War*, ed Kaye Webb, Hutchinson, 1985

Austin, Richard ("Gun Buster"), "Dunkirk: The View from the Beaches" is an extract from *Return Via Dunkirk*, Hodder & Stoughton, 1940

Bess, Demaree, "Paris Falls" is an extract from *The Story of World War II*, ed Curt Riess, 1944

Chamberlain, Neville, "Britain Declares War on Germany", quoted in *Voices from Britain*, ed Henning Krabbe, Allen & Unwin, 1947

Churchill, Winston S., "Churchill Offers 'Blood, Toil, Tears and Sweat'", quoted in *The World's Great Speeches*, ed Lewis Copeland, Lawrence W. Lamm and Stephen J. McKenna, Dover, 1999

Churchill, Winston S., "The Battle of Britain: The View from the Operations Room, No. 11 Fighter Group" is an extract from *The Second World War*, Volume II, Cassell, 1949

Cowles, Virginia, "Finland: Guerilla War in the Snow" (originally published as "Killed in Finnish Snow"), *Sunday Times*, 4 February 1940

Flower, Desmond, "Battle of Britain: The Blitz", quoted in *The War 1939–1945*, ed Desmond Flower and James Reeves, Cassell & Company, 1960

Fuchs, Karl, "A German Tank Gunner Trains for War" is reprinted from *Sieg Heil!*, ed Horst Fuchs Richardson, Anchor, 1987

Grigg, Joseph W., "Poland: Inside Fallen Warsaw", United Press, 1939

Guderian, Heinz, "German Panzers Invade Poland" is an extract from *Panzer Leader*, Michael Joseph, 1952, trans Constantine Fitzgibbon

Hall, Roger, "Battle of Britain: Dogfight Over South-East England" is an extract from *Clouds of Fear*, Bailey Brothers & Swinfen Ltd, 1975. Copyright © 1975 RMD Hall

Heide, Dirk van de, "Operation Yellow: The German Attack on Rotterdam" is an extract from *My Sister and I*, Harcourt, Brace and World Inc, 1941. Copyright © Harcourt, Brace & World Inc

Hillary, Richard, "Battle of Britain: A Burn Victim" is an extract from *The Last Enemy*, Macmillan, 1943. Copyright © 1942 Richard Hillary. Reprinted by permission of Macmillan

Hitler, Adolf, "Hitler Orders War: Directive Number 1", quoted in *Panzer Leader*, Michael Joseph, 1952, trans Constantine Fitzgibbon

Karol, K.S. "A Polish Cadet in Inaction" is an extract from *Between Two Worlds*, Henry Holt, 1987

Macbeth, George, "The Home Front: A Child's View" is an extract from *A Child of War*, Jonathan Cape, 1987

Marchant, Hilde, "Evacuation of Children," quoted in *The Faber Book of Reportage*, ed John Carey, Faber & Faber, 1987

Murrow, Edward R., "The Blitz", broadcast 13 September 1940. Copyright © CBS Inc.

Panter-Downes, Mollie, "London at War", *The New Yorker*, September 1939. Copyright © 1939 Mollie Panter-Downes

Pexton, L.D. "The Battle of France: A British Soldier's Diary", unpublished diary, Imperial War Museum, London

Priestley, J.B., "The Blitz", BBC broadcast 15 September 1940, quoted in *The Long March of Everyman*, ed Theo Barker, Andre Deutsch/British Broadcasting Corporation, 1975

Rommel, Erwin, "Operation Yellow: Crossing the Meuse", "The Battle of France: 7th Panzer Division Break Out" are extracts from *The Rommel Papers*, ed B.H. Liddell Hart, Collins, 1953. Copyright © 1953 B.H. Liddell Hart, renewed 1981 Lady Liddell Hart, Fritz Bayerlain-Dittmar and Manfred Rommel.

Shirer, William, "France Surrenders" is an extract from *Berlin Diary: The Journal of a Foreign Correspondent, 1934–1941*, Alfred A. Knopf, 1941. Copyright © 1940, 1941 William Shirer. Renewed 1968 William Shirer

Stowe, Leland, "Norway: German Paratroopers March into Oslo" is an extract from *The Story of World War II*, ed Curt Riess, 1944

Toomey, Jack, "One Man's War: Private Jack Toomey in France", unpublished letter, Imperial War Museum, London

Vaux, P.A.I., "Battle of France: Counter-Attack at Arras", quoted in *Freedom's Battle Volume 3: The War on Land 1939–1945*, ed Ronald Lewin, Hutchinson, 1969

Wiart, Adrian Carton de, "Norway: The Rout of the BEF" is an extract from *Happy Odyssey*, Jonathan Cape, 1950

Wissler, D.H., "Battle of Britain: A British Fighter Pilot's Diary", unpublished diary, Imperial War Museum, London

Woolf, Virgina, "The Blitz" is an extract from *A Writer's Diary*, Harcourt Brace and Co. 1954. Copyright © 1954 Leonard Woolf. Copyright renewed 1982 by Quentin Bell and Angelica Garnett

## Part II: The Battle of the Atlantic

Carse, Robert, "Voyage to Murmansk" is an extract from *The Story of World War II*, ed Curt Riess, Garden City Publishing, 1944

Curry, Frank, "One Man's War: The Diary of an Asdic Operator" is reprinted from Veterans Affairs Canada website

Healiss, Ronald, "Survival" is extracted from "Arctic Rescue", *70 True Stories of the Second World War*, Odhams Press Ltd., nd

Kennedy, Ludovic, "The Pursuit of the *Bismarck*" is an extract from *On My Way to the Club*, Collins, 1989

Knight, Esmond, "HMS *Hood* is Sunk", quoted in *Freedom's Battle; Volume I: The War at Sea 1939–45*, ed John Winton, Hutchinson, 1967

Kretschmer, Otto, "U-99 Attacks a Convoy", quoted in *The Battle of the Atlantic*, Donald MacIntyre, TS Batsford Ltd. 1961. Copyright © 1961 Donald MacIntyre

Macintyre, Donald, "Hunting U-boats" is an extract from *U-boat Killer*, Weidenfeld & Nicolson, 1956

Prien, Gunther, "The *Royal Oak* is Torpedoed" is an extract from *Hitler and His Admirals*, Anthony Martienssen, Secker & Warburg, 1948

Schaefer, Heinz, "A U-boat is depth-charged" is an extract from *U-Boat 977*, William Kimber, 1952

Washbourn, R.E., "The Battle of the River Plate", quoted in *Freedom's Battle, Volume I: The War at Sea 1939–45*, ed John Winton, Hutchinson, 1967

Wemyss, D.E.G., "Fatal Six Weeks" is an extract from *Relentless Pursuit*, William Kimber, 1965


## Part III: The War in the Desert

Anon, "Heis Uber Afrikas Boden" is reproduced from *Panzer*! website

Anonymous British Gunner, "In the Cauldron", quoted in *The War 1939–1945*, ed Desmond Flower and James Reeves, Cassell & Company Ltd, 1960

Bayerlain, Fritz, "El Alamein: The Defeat of the Afrika Korps", quoted in *The War 1939–1945*, ed Desmond Flower and James Reeves, Cassell & Company Ltd, 1960

Berndt, Alfred, "Rommel's Ailing Health" is an extract from *The Rommel Papers*, ed B.H. Liddell Hart, Collins, 1953. Copyright © 1953 B.H. Liddell Hart, renewed 1981 Lady Liddell Hart, Fritz Bayerlain-Dittmar and Manfred Rommel

Crimp, R.L., "One man's war: Desert weariness" is an extract from "The Diary of a Desert Rat", unpublished M.S., Imperial war Museum

Crisp, Robert, "Operation Crusader: Tank Battle at Sidi Rezegh" is an extract from *Brazen Chariots*, Frederick Muller, 1959. Copyright © 1959 Robert Crisp

Douglas, Keith, "El Alamein: German prisoners", "El Alamein: After the Battle" are extracts from *Alamein to Zem Zem*, ed Desmond Graham, Oxford University Press, 1979

Green, John, "One Man's War: The Diary of a British Soldier at El Alamein" was first published in *The Mammoth Book of War Diaries & Letters*, ed Jon E. Lewis, Robinson 1998. Copyright © 1998 the heirs of John Green. Reproduced by permission

Joly, Cyril, "The Italians Surrender at Beda Fomm", "A Tank is 'Brewed-Up'" are extracts from *Take These Men*, Penguin Books, 1956

Maund, M.R., "Swordfish Attack the Italian Fleet" is quoted in *Freedom's Battle, Volume I: The War at Sea 1939–45*, ed John Winton, Hutchinson, 1967

Mellenthin, General von, "The Fall of Tobruk", is an extract from *Panzer Battles*, 1939–45, Cassell, 1955

Middleton, C., "F battery in Action at Thala", quoted in *The Royal Artillery Commemoration Book 1939–1945*, ed W.E. Duncan et al, G. Bell & Sons, 1950

Montgomery, Bernard, "Montgomery Takes Over as Commander Eighth Army", "El Alamein: The Plan" are extracts from *The Memoirs of Field-Marshal The Viscount Montgomery of Alamein*, William Collins, Sons & Co. Ltd, 1958. Copyright © 1958 Bernard Law, Viscount Montgomery of Alamein

Moorehead, Alan, "The Battleground", "Tunis Falls" are extracts from *African Trilogy*, Hamish Hamilton, 1944

Peniakoff, Vladimir, "Blowing Up Tanks Behind Enemy Lines", is an extract from *Popski's Private Army*, Jonathan Cape, 1950. Copyright © 1950 Vladimir Peniakoff

Pyle, Ernie, "Operation Torch: GI Meals" is an extract from *Here is Your War*, World Publishing Co., 1945

Rommel, Erwin, "Dearest Lu", "Tobruk: The Conqueror Enters", "El Alamein: The View from the Afrika Korps", "A Meeting with the Fuhrer" are extracts from *The Rommel Papers*, ed B.H. Liddell Hart, Collins, 1953. Copyright © 1953 B.H. Liddell Hart, renewed 1981 Lady Liddell Hart, Fritz Bayerlain-Dittmar and Manfred Rommel

Roosevelt Jnr, Theodore, "Fighting Like the Devil", quoted in *Lines of Battle*, ed Annette Tapert, Times Books, 1987. Original letter held in the Manuscript Division of the Library of Congress

Salisbury, Ray, "Envoi", quoted in *Letters Home*, ed. Mina Curtiss, Little Brown and Company, 1944

Schmidt, Heinz Werner, "Enter Rommel" is an extract from *With Rommel in the Desert*, Harrap, 1951

*Part IV: Barbarossa*

Adolf Hitler, "To Sixth Army", quoted in *Stalingrad*, Heinz Schroter, Michael Joseph, 1955

Anonymous German soldiers, "Stalingrad: Last Letters Home" are extracts from *Last Letters from Stalingrad*, Methuen, 1956

Anonymous Officer, 24th Panzer Division, "Stalingrad: 'The Rat War'", quoted in The *Second World War*, John Keegan, Arrow Books, 1990

Blumentritt, Gunther, "The Wehrmacht Advances into Russia" is an extract from *The Fatal Decisions*, ed W. Richardson and S. Freidin, Michael Joseph, 1956

Cassidy, Henry C., "Mr Churchill Goes to Moscow" is an extract from *The Story of World War II*, ed Curt Riess, Garden City Publishing, 1944

Fuchs, Karl, "We're going to Show . . ." is reprinted from *Sieg Heil!*, ed Horst Fuchs Richardson, Anchor, 1987

Graebe, Hermann, "Holocaust: SS Execution of Jews in the Ukraine" is an extract from *Nazi Conspiracy and Aggression*, US Government Printing Office, 1946

Guderian, Heinz, "Operation Barbarossa: Invasion of the Soviet Union" is an extract from *Panzer Leader*, Michael Joseph, 1952. Trans Constantine Fitzgibbon

Haape, Heinrich, "The Arrival of 'General Winter'", is an extract from *Moscow Tram Stop*, Collins, 1957

Knoblich, Wolfgang, "One Man's War: A Wehrmacht Soldier's Diary of the Russian Front" is an extract from *True to Type*, Hutchinson, 1946

Manstein, General Erich von, "The Battle for Sevastapol" is an extract from *Lost Victories*, Methuen, 1958

Rudel, Hans, "Stukas Dive Bomb the Soviet Fleet", is an extract from *Stuka Pilot*, Corgi, 1957. Trans Lynton Hudson

Sixth Army HQ, "To High command", quoted in *Stalingrad*, Heinz Schroter, Michael Jospeh, 1955

Werth, Alexander, "Leningrad during the Blockade" is an extract from *Moscow War Diary*, Alfred A. Knopf, 1942. Copyright © 1942 Alexander Werth

Werth, Alexander, "Stalingrad: After the Fall" is an extract from *Russia at War*, Barry & Rockcliff, 1964

Wieder, Joachim, "Stalingrad: The Suffering of the German Troops", "Stalingrad: Taken Prisoner" are extracts from *Stalingrad: Memories & Reassessments*, Joachim Wieder & H. Graf von Einsiedel, Arms & Armour Press, 1993. Copyright © 1993 Joachim Wieder

Zieser, Benno, "Russian Prisoners", "Stalingrad: A German Soldier's View" are extracts from *The Road to Stalingrad*, Ballantine Books, 1956. Copyright © 1956 Benno Zieser

## Part V: Banzai

Adams, Milton, "Home Front: 'Jim Crow' in the Army" is an extract from *Taps for a Jim Crow Army*, ed Philip McGuire, 1983

Camp, William, "Baatan: Death in a Fox-Hole" is an extract from *Retreat, Hell!*, Constable, 1944

Casey, Robert J., "Battle of Midway: One Man's Diary" is an extract from *The Story of World War II*, ed Curt Riess, Garden City Publishing Co., 1944

Chennault, Claire L., "Flying Tiger: An American Volunteer Group Pilot in Action Against the Japanese" is an extract from *Way of a Fighter*, G.P. Putnam's Sons, 1949. Copyright © 1949 Claire L. Chennault

Doolittle, James, "Raid on Tokyo" is an extract from *Bombs Away!*, ed Stanley M. Ulanoff, Doubleday & Company, Inc., 1971

Dyess, William, "Death March on Bataan" is an extract from *The Dyess Story*, G.P. Putnam's Sons, 1944. Copyright © 1944 Marajen Stevick Dyess

Fisher, O.E., "The Fall of Singapore: A Civilian Diary", reprinted from *Diary of the Invasion of Singapore*, http://freespace.virgin.net/sam. campbell/message.ht.

Fuchida, Mitsuo, "Pearl Harbor: The View from the Japanese Cockpit" (originally "I Led the Attack on Pearl Harbor" is extracted from *Bombs Away!*, ed Stanley M. Ulanoff, Doubleday & Company, Inc., 1971

Fuchida, Mitsuo, "Midway: The Decisive Five Minutes" is from *Midway: The Battle that Doomed Japan* (with Masataka Okumiya), Hutchinson, 1957

Gallagher, O.D., "The Loss of the *Repulse* and *Prince of Wales*", *Daily Express*, 12 December 1941

Garcia, John, "Pearl Harbor: The View from the Ground" is an extract from "*The Good War*": *An Oral History of World War II*, ed Studs Turkel, Hamish Hamilton, 1985. Copyright © 1984 Studs Terkel

Manchester, William, "Boot Camp: The Making of a Marine" is an extract from *Goodbye, Darkness*, Little Brown, 1980

Romulo, Carlos P., "The Japanese Bomb Manila" is an extract from *I Saw the Fall of the Philippines*, Harrap, 1943

Slim, W.J., "Burma: The Battle of the Oilfields" is an extract from *Defeat Into Victory*, Cassell & Co. Ltd. 1956

## Part VI: Resistance & Reconquest

Air Ministry, "Notification of the Death of Acting Squadron Leader Ernest Mason" is quoted in *Freedom's Battle II: The War in the Air*, ed Gavin Lyall, Hutchinson, 1968

Anonymous, "Home Front: Pure Hell for a Guy Not in Uniform" is an extract from *Six War Years, 1939–45: Memories of Canadians at Home and Abroad*, Doubleday, 1974. Copyright © 1974 Barry Broadfoot

Anonymous WAAF, "The Home Front: The Great Man Chase" is an extract from *Speak for Yourself*, ed Angus Calder & Dorothy Sheridan, Jonathan Cape Ltd., 1984. Copyright © 1984 the Tom Harrisson Mass-Observation Archive

Bayerlain, Fritz, "American Blitzkrieg" is an extract from *The Rommel Papers*, ed B.H. Liddell Hart, Collins, 1953. Copyright © 1953 B.H. Liddell Hart, renewed 1981 Lady Liddell Hart, Fritz Bayerlain-Dittmar and Manfred Rommel

Blaha, Franz, "Holocaust: Medical Experiments at Dachau" is an extract from *Trial of the Major German War Criminals*, Proceedings of the International Military Tribunal at Nuremberg, HMSO, 1946

Bond, Howard L., "Cowardice, Cassino" is an extract from *Return to Cassino*, Doubleday, 1964

Bone, H.T., "D-Day: The Landings", unpublished letter, Imperial War Museum, London

Bowlby, Alex, "Officer Selection" is an extract from *The Recollections of Rifleman Bowlby*, Leo Cooper Ltd, 1969. Copyright © 1969 Alex Bowlby

Burgett, Donald, "D-Day: A Paratrooper Lists His Kit" is an extract from *Curahee!*, Hutchinson, 1967

Butcher, Harry C., "Ike's Day Before D-Day" is an extract from *Three Years with Eisenhower*, William Heinemann Ltd, 1946

Byrom, James, "Victory in Europe Celebration" is an extract from *Unfinished Man*, Chatto & Windus, 1957

Cornell, Douglas B., "The Funeral of President Roosevelt", AP dispatch, April 1945. Copyright © 1945 Associated Press

Cox, Geoffrey, "Italian Partisans Take Their Revenge" is an extract from *The Road to Trieste*, Heinemann, 1947

Dimbleby, Richard, "Holocaust: A Reporter Visits Belsen" (originally "The Cess Pit Beneath" is an extract from *Richard Dimbleby: Broadcaster*, ed Leonard Miall, BBC, 1966. Copyright © 1966 BBC

Foley, John, "The Battle of the Reichswald", "Crossing the German Border" are extracts from *Mailed Fist*, Panther Books, 1956

Frank, Anne, "Holocaust: The Jews are Rounded Up" is an extract from *Anne Frank's Diary*, Vallentine Mitchell & Co., Ltd. Copyright © 1958 Vallentine, Mitchell & Co., Ltd

Gavin, James M., "Sicily: An American Counter-Attack at Biazza Ridge" is extracted from *Eyewitness to World War II*, ed Stephen W. Sears, Houghton Mifflin, 1991. Copyright © 1991 American Heritage, a division of Forbes Inc.

Gellhorn, Martha, "The Battle of the Bulge: The Aftermath" (originally "The Battle of the Bulge") is an extract from *The Face of War*, Granta Books, 1988. Copyright © 1945 Martha Gellhorn

Gibson, Guy, "The Dambusters Raid" is an extract from *Enemy Coast Ahead*, Michael Joseph, 1946. Copyright © 1956 the Estate of Guy Gibson

Goebbels, Joseph, "A Bomb Hits the Propaganda Ministry" is an extract from *The Goebbels Diaries*, ed Hugh Trevor-Roper, Secker & Warburg, 1978

Goldman, Carl, "One Man's War: An American Airman's Letter" is an extract from *Jewish Youth: Letters from American Soldiers*, J. Rontch, 1945

Grant, Douglas, "Sicily: The Seaborne Landings" is an extract from *The Fuel of the Fire*, Cresset Press, 1950

Heydte, Baron von der, "The German Airborne Assault on Crete", "Crete: Pyrrhic Victory" are extracts from *Daedalus Returned*, Hutchinson, 1958

Hughes, G.E., "One Man's War: A Normandy Diary", unpublished diary, Imperial War Museum, London

Johnson "Johnnie", "A 'Circus' Over France", "Falaise: the Killing Field" are extracts from *Wing Leader*, Goodall Publications, 1990. Copyright © 1956, 1974, 1990 J.E. Johnson

King, Lionel, "Buzz Bombs on Kent" is an extract from *People at War*, ed Michael Moynihan, David & Charles, 1974

Knoke, Heinz, "Flying for the Fatherland" is an extract from *I Flew for the Fuhrer*, Corgi, 1956. Trans John Ewing

Levi, Primo, "Holocaust: Survival in Auschwitz" is an extract from *Survival in Auschwitz*, Summit Books, 1986. Copyright © 1986 Summit Books

Lewis, Norman, "Prostitution" is an extract from *Naples '44*, Collins, 1978

Mackay, E.M., "Arnhem: At the Bridge" is an extract from *Royal Engineers' Journal*, Vol. LXVIII, No. 4

Maclean, Fitzroy, "A Letter for Tito" is an extract from *Eastern Approaches*, Jonathan Cape, 1949. Copyright © 1949 Fitzroy Maclean

Maidalany, Fred, "Cassino: The End" is an extract from *The Monastery*, The Bodley Head, 1945. Copyright © 1945 the estate of Fred Maidalany

Malthe-Bruun, Kim, "In Dying We Live" is an extract from *Heroic Heart*, Random House, 1955.

Maund, M.R., "Swordfish Attack the Italian Fleet" is quoted in *Freedom's Battle, Volume I: The War at Sea 1939–45*, ed John Winton, Hutchinson, 1967

Millar, George, "A Resistance Group Blows Up a Train" is an extract from *Maquis*, Heinemann, 1945

Montgomery, Bernard, "The German Army Surrenders" is an extract from *The Memoirs of Field-Marshal The Viscount Montgomery of Alamein*, William Collins, Sons & Co. Ltd, 1958. Copyright © 1958 Bernard Law, Viscount Montgomery of Alamein

Moorehead, Alan, "D-Day: Embarkation" is an extract from *Eclipse*, Hamish Hamilton, 1945. Copyright © 1945 Alan Moorehead

Moss, W. Stanley, "Guerilla ambush in Crete, August 1944" is an extract from *Ill Met by Moonlight*, Harrap, 1950

Mucha, George, "The Fall of Aachen" is an extract from *Voices from Britain: Broadcast History 1939–45*, ed Henning Krabbe, Allen & Unwin, 1947

Munro, Ross, "Raid on Dieppe" is an extract from *Gauntlet to Overlord*, Macmillan (Canada), 1945

Neave, Airey, "Escape from Colditz" is an extract from *They Have Their Exits*, Hodder & Stoughton, 1953

Nell, Sgt., "Waiting, Waiting, Waiting", quoted in *Private Words*, ed. Ronald Blythe, Viking 1991.

Nicolson, Harold, "Lunch with De Gaulle" is an extract from *Harold Nicolson, Diaries & Letters 1939–45*, ed Nigel Nicolson, Collins, 1971

Panter-Downes, Mollie, "Victory in Europe Celebration" (originally "Letter from London"), *The New Yorker*, 12 May 1945. Copyright © 1945 Mollie Panter-Downes

Pyle, Ernie, "The U.S. Army Slogs Up Italy", "Sniping, Normandy" are from the Washington *Daily News*. Copyright © 1944 and 1945 the Scripps Howard Foundation

Ridgway, Matthew B., "D-Day: Combat Jump" is an extract from *Soldier*, 1956, Harper & Bros., 1956

Rommel, Manfred, "The Suicide of Field Marshal Erwin Rommel" is an extract from *The Rommel Papers*, ed B.H. Liddell Hart, Collins, 1953. Copyright © 1953 B.H. Liddell Hart, renewed 1981 Lady Liddell Hart, Fritz Bayerlain-Dittmar and Manfred Rommel

Scott, Michael, "One Man's War: The Diary of a Trainee Bomber Pilot", unpublished diary, Imperial War Museum, London

Skorzeny, Otto, "The Rescue of Mussolini from Gran Sasso" is an extract from *Special Mission*, Robert Hale Ltd, 1957. Copyright © 1957 Otto Skorzeny

Steinbeck, John, "The Landings at Salerno" (originally published as "It Was as Dark as Hell"), New York *Herald Tribune*, 4 October 1943. Copyright © 1943 NY *Herald Tribune*

Wendel, Else, "Home Front: Firestorm in Hamburg" is an extract from *Hausfrau at War*, Odhams Press, 1947

Wray, Rachel, "Home Front: Rachel the Riveter" is an extract from *The Home Front: America During World War II*, Mark Harris, Putnam, 1984. Copyright © 1984 Mark J. Harris

Young, John S., "US Bombers Raid the Oil Refineries at Ploesti" is extracted from *Bombs Away!*, ed Stanley M. Ulanoff, Doubleday & Company, Inc., 1971

## Part VII: The Road to Berlin

Anonymous Fighter, "Warsaw Uprising" is an extract from *The Unseen and Silent*, Sheed & Ward, 1954

Boldt, Gerhard, "A Meeting with Hitler" is an extract from *In the Shelter with Hitler*, Citadel Press, 1948

Degrelle, Leon, "Wounded SS Troops" is an extract from *Eyewitness War*, The Publishing Corporation UK Ltd., 1995. Copyright © 1995 Marshall Cavendish

Fuhrman, Claus, "The Fall of Berlin" is an extract from *Follow My Leader*, Louis E. Hagen, Allan Wingate, 1951

Gliewe, Hans, "Germans Fleeing the Russian Advance" is an extract from *Flight in the Winter*, Juergen Thorwald, Hutchinson, 1953

Guderian, Heinz, "Gotterdammerung" is an extract from *Panzer Leader*, Michael Joseph, 1952, trans Constantine Fitzgibbon

Kampov, Major, "Concentrated Slaughter" is an extract from *Russia at War*, Alexander Werth, Barry & Rockcliff, 1964

Mellenthin, General von, "Citadel" is an extract from *Panzer Battles*, Cassell, 1955

Stalin, Marshal, "Order of the Day No. 369" is a quotation from *The Pocket History of the Second World War*, ed Henry Steele Commager, Pocket Books, 1945

Wilkie, Wendell, "Home Front: A Russian Aviation Factory" is an extract from *One World*, Simon & Schuster, 1943


## Part VIII: Setting Sun

Akizuki, Tatsuichiro, "Nagasaki" is an extract from *Nagasaki 1945*, Quartet, 1981. Copyright © Tatsuiro Akizuki and Keiichi Nagata

Anonymous Japanese Soldier, "An Allied Intelligence Officer is Executed" is an extract from *MacArthur, 1941–45: Victory in the Pacific*, Charles A. Willoughby and John Chamberlain, McGraw-Hill, 1956

Bilek, Anton, "Life in a Japanese P.O.W. Camp" is an extract from *"The Good War": An Oral History of World War II*, ed. Studs Terkel, Hamish Hamilton, 1985

Boyington, Gregory, "A Marine Corps Pilot is Shot Down" is an extract from *Baa Baa Black Sheep*, Putnam's, 1958

Branson, Clive, "One Man's War: The Arakan Front" is an extract from *British Soldier in India*, British Communist Party, 1994

Bush, Eric, "'A Frightful Fate'" is an extract from *Bless Our Ship*, Allen & Unwin, 1958

Chapman, F. Spencer, "An English Officer Escapes the Japanese", *The Jungle is Neutral*, Chatto & Windus, 1975

English, Jeffrey, "One for Every Sleeper" is an extract from *One for Every Sleeper*, Robert Hale Ltd., 1989. Copyright © 1989 Jeffrey English

Evans, Geoffrey C., "The Skirmish at Admin Box" is an extract from *The Desert and the Jungle*, William Kimber, 1959

Fahey, James J., "Kamikaze Attacks" is an extract from *Pacific War Diary*, Houghton Mifflin, 1963. Copyright © James J. Fahey

Fergusson, Bernard, "Behind Enemy Lines" is an extract from *Beyond the Chindwin*, Corgi, 1957

Garcia, John, "Okinawa: An Infantryman's Nightmare" is an extract from "*The Good War*": *An Oral History of World War II*, ed. Studs Terkel, Hamish Hamilton, 1985. Copyright © 1984 Studs Terkel

Johnston, G.H., "The Kokoda Trail", quoted in *The Pocket History of the Second World War*, ed. Henry Steele Commager, Pocket Books, 1945

Kennard, Richard, "One Man's War: A Marine Writes Home" is an extract from *Combat Letters Home*, Dorance & Company, 1958

Masters, John, "Close-Quarter Fighting", "The Dagger Division Takes Mandala" are extracts from *The Road Past Mandalay*, Michael Joseph, 1961

Matsuo, Isao, " 'I Shall Fall Like a Blossom from a Radiant Cherry Tree' " is an extract from *The Divine Wind*, ed Rikihei Inoguchi et al, Hutchinson, 1959

Matsushita, Iwao, "Home Front: Internment of Japanese Americans" is quoted in *Letters of a Nation*, ed. Andrew Carroll, Kodansha America Inc., 1997

Ogburn, Charlton, "Bamboo, Dysentery, Leeches" is an extract from *The Marauders*, William Morrow & Company, 1956. Copyright © Charlton Ogburn, 1956, 1959, 1982

Paige, Mitchell, "The Defence of Henderson Field" is an extract from *The Old Breed*, George McMillan, Infantry Journal Press, 1949. Copyright © 1949 Infantry Journal Inc.

Sledge, Eugene B., "Assault into Hell", "Marines Storm a Pill-Box" are extracts from *With the Old Breed*, Presidio Press, 1981. Copyright © 1981 E.B. Sledge

Tibbets, Colonel, "Hiroshima" is an extract from *The World at War*, Mark Arnold-Forster, Methuen-Mandarin, 1989. Copyright © 1973, 1981 Thames Television Ltd

Truman, Harry S., "The Allies decide to drop the Atomic Bomb" is an extract from *Off the Record: The Private Papers of Harry S. Truman*, Harper & Row, 1986

USMC Correspondents, "The Tunnels of Iwo Jima" is an extract from *US Marines on Iwo Jima*, The Dial Press, Inc., 1945. Copyright © 1945 The Dial Press Inc. and The Infantry Journal

*Epilogue: The Execution of Nazi War Criminals at Nuremberg*

Smith, Kingsbury, "Execution of Nazi War Criminals" is an extract from *It Happened in 1946*, 1947